The Globalization and Development Reader

The Globalization and Development Reader

Perspectives on Development and Global Change

Edited by

J. Timmons Roberts
and
Amy Bellone Hite

Blackwell
Publishing

BLACKWELL PUBLISHING
350 Main Street, Malden, MA 02148-5020, USA
9600 Garsington Road, Oxford OX4 2DQ, UK
550 Swanston Street, Carlton, Victoria 3053, Australia

First published 2007 by Blackwell Publishing Ltd

1   2007

Library of Congress Cataloging-in-Publication Data

The globalization and development reader : perspectives on development and global change /
edited by J. Timmons Roberts and Amy Bellone Hite.
    p. cm.
    Includes bibliographical references and index.
    ISBN-13: 978-1-4051-3236-7 (hardback : alk. paper)
    ISBN-10: 1-4051-3236-1 (hardback : alk. paper)
    ISBN-13: 978-1-4051-3237-4 (pbk. : alk. paper)
    ISBN-10: 1-4051-3237-X (pbk. : alk. paper)   1. Developing countries–Economic conditions.
2. Developing countries–Social conditions.   3. Globalization.   I. Roberts, J. Timmons.
II. Hite, Amy Bellone.
    HC59.7.G564 2006
    330.9172'4–dc22

                                                                      2006024576

A catalogue record for this title is available from the British Library.

Set in 10 on 12.5 pt Dante
by SNP Best-set Typesetter Ltd, Hong Kong
Printed and bound in Singapore
by Markono Print Media Pte Ltd

The publisher's policy is to use permanent paper from mills that operate a sustainable forestry policy, and
which has been manufactured from pulp processed using acid-free and elementary chlorine-free practices.
Furthermore, the publisher ensures that the text paper and cover board used have met acceptable
environmental accreditation standards.

For further information on
Blackwell Publishing, visit our website:
www.blackwellpublishing.com

Contents

About the Editors

Amy Bellone Hite is Assistant Professor and Chairperson of the Department of Sociology at Xavier University in New Orleans, Louisiana, where she teaches Social Theory, Social Policy, Social Problems, Urban Sociology, and Comparative Sociology. She is coeditor of *From Modernization to Globalization* (Blackwell, 2000) with J. Timmons Roberts. Her research on development in Latin America also appears in *Latin American Research Review* and *Studies in Comparative International Development*. She is currently researching inequalities associated with the rebuilding and repopulation of New Orleans following Hurricane Katrina.

J. Timmons Roberts completed his PhD in the Sociology of Comparative International Development at the Johns Hopkins University. After serving in Latin American Studies and Sociology at Tulane University, he is now Professor of Sociology and Director of the Environmental Science and Policy Program at the College of William and Mary in Virginia, USA. He is currently a James Martin 21st Century Professor at Oxford University in the Environmental Change Institute. He is co-author of over forty articles and four other books: *From Modernization to Globalization* (coedited with Amy Bellone Hite, Blackwell, 2000), *Chronicles from the Environmental Justice Frontline* (2001), *Trouble in Paradise: Globalization and Environmental Crises in Latin America* (2003), *A Climate of Injustice: Global Inequality, North-South Politics, and Climate Policy* (2007). His current collaborative research examines the role of foreign aid in addressing environmental issues in developing nations.

Preface and Acknowledgments

You may wonder, "Why do we need yet *another* book about globalization?" Globalization can be a daunting subject, and the term "development" is loaded enough to turn off thoughtful people of many ideological stripes. "Globalization" – the spread of economies, cultures, and power across national borders – has become a buzzword which is usually evoked unquestioningly. It is used so sloppily that it often produces little illumination. Because it is widely seen as inevitable and nearly inalterable, globalization is often presented as a force that must be embraced without reserve, but doing so benefits some people while putting others at grave risk. For its part, Leonard Frank once called development "a whore of a word," since it hid within its rosy and altruistic-sounding exterior the selfish interests of imperialistic governments, expansionist firms, careerist professionals, and international "humanitarian" agencies that benefit from the neediness of poor nations. So do we simply throw these terms in the rubbish bin?

Policy wonks, corporate visionaries, academic types, or empire-builders are not the only ones trying to understand the dazzling global changes going on: everyone concerned about their future is. Our goal in compiling the selections for this book and its previous edition has been to demystify the social impacts of large-scale global economic change. We seek to offer nonspecialist audiences carefully selected and manageable excerpts of the best parts of path-breaking texts. We hope these provide readers with tools to understand globalization and development better, to question them, and to rethink their inevitability and direction.

Readers familiar with our previous volume (titled *From Modernization to Globalization*) will note that sixteen of the twenty-seven are new selections, supported by six revised editorial introductions. The new selections are concentrated in the latter three sections on globalization. Our increased focus on globalization reflects the explosion of work on the subject since we put that edition together in the late 1990s. Selections in Parts I and II provide something of a conceptual genealogy of some contemporary perspectives on globalization and development. They supply classic efforts to understand how societies have changed with industrialization and modernization. The latter three sections present current debates on globalization and development. Readers wanting to grasp the meaning of the much bandied-about concept might want to flip straight to Part III, "What is

Globalization?" Those wanting to review debates about globalization could flip ahead to Part IV. Part V examines major social movements opposing globalization and where they seem to be going: labor unions, environmentalists, and women's movements. The "Editors' Introduction" at the start is designed to help new readers by introducing the early thinking on these topics, by Adam Smith, the Modernizationists, and the Dependency thinkers. In other words, this book needn't be read front to back, but there would be value in doing so.

Global climate change, trade and currency imbalances, and the foundations of Middle Eastern petro-states are only a few of the threats to the stability of the whole global economic and political system. The arrival of terrorist extremism in the wealthiest nations supports Mark Duffield's argument in his piece here that everyone's security requires attention to basic social development in the most forgotten corners of the world. Wise decisions in the face of change require understanding the way things are currently going, but also awareness of alternative ways in which governments, firms, international organizations and individuals might respond. Fortunately there is new space opening for policy-makers to rethink their positions toward globalization: we are pleased that since our first edition of this book some devout pro-globalization authors and policy-makers have begun to question what was called the "Washington Consensus," and consider ways of reshaping globalization. What seemed like inevitable progress on major free-trade treaties like the WTO are far more uncertain than they were when we put the last touches to the first edition in early 1999.

In addition to the authors of the selections we present here, many individuals contributed to this volume. At Blackwell, we owe special thanks to Justin Vaughan, Ken Provencher, and Juanita Bullough. Their patience and support for the project were invaluable. Bradley Parks lent extensive early assistance. We also thank our many reviewers of the previous edition and our proposed changes, who alerted us to important omissions and possible additions. We were unable to include all the important work suggested, and we had to shorten some pieces more than might have been ideal: we hope readers will take up these authors' work more fully. Finally, we owe many, many thanks to the love and support our families have offered as we pored over this manuscript during hours that were rightly theirs: Holly, John, Quinn, Phoebe, Will, and Owen.

J. T. R. and A. B. H.
September 2006

Acknowledgments to Sources

The editors and publisher gratefully acknowledge the permission granted to reproduce the copyright material in this book:

Appelbaum, Richard and Edna Bonacich, from Gay Seidman and Robert Ross (eds.), "Would Including a Social Clause in Trade Treaties Help or Hinder?" in Paul S. Ciccantell (ed.), *Newsletter of the Section on the Political Economy of the World System* (PEWS News, Fall 2003). Reprinted by permission of Paul Ciccantell, PEWS News.

Armbruster, Ralph, "Globalization and Cross-Border Labor Organizing", pp. 3–5 in "Forum: Problems and Prospects for a Global Labor Movement," from *Journal of World Systems Research* 4:1 (Winter 1998). http://jwsr.ucr.edu/. Copyright © 1998. Reprinted by permission of Bradley Nash, Jr., and Ralph Armbruster-Sandoval.

Arrighi, Giovanni, Beverly J. Silver, and Benjamin Brewer, "Industrial Convergence, Globalization, and the Persistence of the North–South Divide," pp. 3–4, 6–8, 16–27 from *Studies in Comparative International Development* 38:1 (Spring, 2003). © 2003 by The City University of New York. Reprinted by permission of Transaction Publishers.

Cardoso, Fernando Henrique, "Dependency and Development in Latin America," from *New Left Review* 74 (July/August), 1972. Reprinted by permission of New Left Review.

Castells, Manuel, pp. 260–84 from "The Informational Mode of Development and the Restructuring of Capitalism," in Ida Susser (ed.), *The Castells Reader on Cities and Social Theory* (Oxford: Blackwell, 2002). Copyright © 2002 by Manuel Castells; editorial matter and organization copyright © Ida Susser. Reprinted by permission of the author.

Desai, Manisha, "Transnational Solidarity: Women's Agency, Structural Adjustment, and Globalization," Nancy A. Naples and Manisha Desai (eds.), from *Women's Activism and Globalization: Linking Local Struggles and Transnational Politics* (New York: Routledge, 2002). Copyright © 2002 by Routledge. Reprinted by permission of Routledge/Taylor & Francis Group, LLC.

Duffield, Mark, "The New Development–Security Terrain," pp. 1–17 and notes from *Global Governance and the New Wars* (London: Zed Books, 2001). Copyright © 2001 by Mark Duffield. Reprinted by permission of Zed Books Ltd.

Evans, Peter, "Counterhegemonic Globalization: Transnational Social Movements in the Contemporary Political Economy," from Thomas Janoski, Alexander M. Hicks, and Mildred Schwartz (eds.), *Handbook of Political Sociology* (Cambridge: Cambridge University Press, 2005). Copyright © 2005 by Cambridge University Press. Reprinted by permission of the author and publisher.

Frank, Andre Gunder, "The Development of Underdevelopment," from *Monthly Review* 18 (4), 1969. Copyright © 1969 by Monthly Review Press. Reprinted by permission of Monthly Review Foundation.

Friedman, Thomas L., "It's a Flat World, After All," from *The World Is Flat: A Brief History of the Twenty-first Century* (New York: Farrar, Straus, and Giroux, 2005). Reprinted by permission of Farrar, Straus, and Giroux.

Fröbel, Folker, Jürgen Heinrichs, and Otto Kreye, "The New International Division of Labor in the World Economy," from *The New International Division of Labour* (Cambridge University Press, 1980). Copyright © 1980 by Cambridge University Press. Reprinted by permission of the publisher.

Gereffi, Gary, "Rethinking Development Theory: Insights from East Asia and Latin America," from A. Douglas Kincaid and Alejandro Portes (eds.), *Comparative National Development: Society and Economy in the New Global Order* (University of North Carolina Press, 1994). Copyright © 1994 by the University of North Carolina Press. Reprinted by permission of the publisher.

Held, David and Anthony McGrew, "Reconstructing World Order: Towards Cosmopolitan Social Democracy," pp. 118–36 from *Globalization/Anti-Globalization* (Cambridge: Polity, 2002). Reprinted by permission of the publisher.

Huntington, Samuel, "The Change to Change: Modernization, Development, and Politics," from *Comparative Politics*, 3 (April 1971). © 1992 by The City University of New York. Reprinted by permission of the author and *Comparative Politics*.

Huntington, Samuel, *Political Order in Changing Societies* (New Haven, CT: Yale University Press, 1968). Reprinted by permission of the publisher.

Keck, Margaret E. and Kathryn Sikkink, pp. 1–2, 6–7, 8–10, 12–15, 16–17, 25–9, 32–4 from "Transnational Advocacy Networks in International Politics: Introduction" and pp. 122–6, 128–32, 134–49, 161–3 from "Environmental Advocacy Networks," in *Activists beyond Borders: Advocacy Networks in International Politics* (Ithaca and London: Cornell University Press, 1998). Copyright © 1998 by Cornell University. Reprinted by permission of Cornell University Press.

Marx, Karl and Engels, Friedrich, "Manifesto of the Communist Party" (1848) and "Alienated Labor" (1844).

McMichael, Philip, "Globalization: Myths and Realities," from *Rural Sociology*, 61:1 (1996). Reprinted by permission of the Rural Sociological Society.

Moghadam, Valentine M., from "Gender and the Global Economy," in Myra Marx Ferree, Judith Lorber, and Beth B. Hess (eds.), *Revisioning Gender* (Lanham, MD: Alta Mira Press,

1999). Copyright © 1999 by Alta Mira Press. Reprinted by permission of the Rowman & Littlefield Publishing Group.

Nash, Bradley, Jr., pp. 6–8, "Organizing a Global Labor Movement from Top and Bottom," in "Forum: Problems and Prospects for a Global Labor Movement," from *Journal of World Systems Research* 4:1 (Winter 1998). http://jwsr.ucr.edu/. Copyright 1998 by Bradley Nash, Jr.

Norberg, Johan, pp. 9–18, 25–9, 31–5, 38–46, 54–8, 60–1 and notes from *In Defense of Global Capitalism* (Washington, DC: The Cato Institute, 2003). Copyright © 2003 by the Cato Institute. Reprinted by permission of the Cato Institute.

Rodrik, Dani, "Introduction," from *Has Globalization Gone Too Far?* (Washington, DC: Institute for International Economics, 1997). Reprinted by permission of the Copyright Clearance Center, Inc. on behalf of the Institute for International Economics.

Rodrik, Dani, pp. 138–43, 147–52 from "Summary and Implications," in *The New Global Economy and Developing Countries: Making Openness Work (Policy Essay No. 24)* (Washington, DC/Baltimore: Overseas Development Council/distributed by Johns Hopkins University Press, 1998). Copyright © 1999 by Overseas Development Council, Washington, DC. Reprinted by permission of the author, Dani Rodrik.

Rostow, W. W. "The Five Stages-of-Growth – A Summary," from *The Stages of Economic Growth: A Non-Communist Manifesto* (2d ed., New York: Cambridge University Press, 1971). Copyright © 1971 by Cambridge University Press. Reprinted by permission of the publisher.

Sachs, Jeffrey, "The Anti-Globalization Movement," pp. 353–9 from *The End of Poverty: Economic Possibilities for Our Time* (New York: Penguin, 2005). Copyright © 2005 by Jeffrey D. Sachs. Reprinted by permission of The Penguin Press, a division of Penguin Group (USA) Inc., and The Wylie Agency.

Sassen, Saskia, pp. 1–7 from "Place and Production in the Global Economy," pp. 11–13, 16, 18–27, from "The Urban Impact of Economic Globalization," pp. 139–44 from "A New Geography of Center and Margins," and References in *Cities in a World Economy* (2d ed., Thousand Oaks, CA: Pine Forge Press, 2000). Copyright © 2000 by Pine Forge Press. Reprinted by permission of Pine Forge Press.

Sklair, Leslie, "Competing Conceptions of Globalization," pp. 144–63 from *Journal of World Systems Research*, 5:2 (summer, 1999). Copyright © 1999 by Leslie Sklair. Reprinted by permission of the author.

Stiglitz, Joseph, "Globalism's Discontents" (The American Prospect). Copyright © 2006 by The American Prospect. Reprinted by permission of the publisher.

Wade, Robert, "What Strategies are Viable for Developing Countries Today? The World Trade Organization and the Shrinking of 'Development Space'," pp. 1–15, 17–20 from *Crisis States Programme: Working Paper 31* (London School of Economics and Development Studies Institute: Crisis States Programme, 2003). Copyright © 2003 by Robert Hunter Wade. Reprinted by permission of the author and Crisis States Research Centre.

Development and Globalization: Recurring Themes

Amy Bellone Hite and J. Timmons Roberts

A luxury cruise ship the size of a small city steams into a tropical harbor where residents live in dirt-floored shacks equipped only with pit toilets. An Islamic woman doctor works in a hijab headscarf. Massive hydroelectric dams inundate vast fields and rainforests to fuel export factories and modern city life; its power lines pass directly over the heads of poor villagers in darkened hamlets. Taiwanese businesspeople pass hand-cultivated rice fields on their way to tour their athletic shoe factory in mainland China that produces for a major US brand. Street children without shoes polish a new Mercedes outside government and corporate high-rises, returning to shacks along drainage ditches or sleeping on discarded cardboard on downtown storefront steps. Masai herdsmen move their scrawny cattle across drought-stricken lands, past Land Rovers loaded with tourists on their way home to eco-tourist hotels in game preserve parks.

Throughout the world, the unevenness of economic development and cultural and social change presents us with stark paradoxes and contrasts.[1] While these visual contrasts defy expectations and seem sometimes irreconcilable, they are just microcosms of inequality between the two worlds that exist on our one planet: the so-called "developed" and the "underdeveloped" worlds, the "First World" and the "Third World,"[2] the poor and the rich nations, the "Global North" and "Global South," Americanization and Africanization, "McWorld" and Islam. Within most poor nations the great divide is more startling because the contrasts are so close together.

Why should people in wealthy nations, which also face many disparities and contradictions, care about these poorer countries and their economic and social development? A hundred people would give as many answers. Some people in the wealthier nations are excited about economic opportunities in what might be a booming market for export products in the "developing South"; some see a source of cheap imports to keep inflation down and of products to market here. Others want to know about development because they worry about the loss of jobs to those same new industries in the South and sense a loss of European and US control over the world's political and economic scenes. Some experts worry about political instability or extremism in developing countries threatening business interests abroad or security at home. There is grave concern in some places about large-scale illegal immigration from poorer areas of the world. Others still are troubled about the global environment and are aware of the crucial role poorer nations play in problems as diverse as global warming, biodiversity in rainforests, or the preservation of individual, treasured species such as elephants, macaws, and mountain gorillas. Others care about developing countries because they have experienced their warm beaches, jungles, mountains, pyramids, and temples. These are some concrete reasons to care.

Some people's concern springs from very different places, based in moral, religious or purely academic roots. Some specialists who have devoted their lives to "development studies" or who work in development agencies are aware that of the world's six billion people, almost five billion live in countries where the average income is less than $3 a day.[3] At the same time, on average, the people in the high-income countries get to live on 23 times that much, and the gap between the two groups has not disappeared and appears to be widening.[4] About one out of four people in the world today lives in absolute poverty, defined as "too poor to afford an adequate diet and other necessities." Malnutrition is said to stunt the growth and development of 40 percent of all 2-year-olds in poorer countries.[5]

Many religious groups have targeted these billions as the greatest potential growth areas for their churches, sending missionaries, money, and material aid. Some are concerned with converting all the world's major population groups to hasten or to be prepared for the Second Coming of Christ.[6] Other religious groups might be concerned with studying and documenting gaps in development, so that their populations might live without the daily indignities of poverty. Some people want to understand the roots and potential cures of the problems that cause the desperate poverty of which we are reminded on television ads for groups who bring aid.

Finally, a few people point out that in countries where our economic and social systems have not fully penetrated, there remains a possible alternative to the development model followed in the wealthy countries. Beyond the material level, many authors are now proposing that we can learn from aboriginal and other cultures not just their medicinal uses of plants and land use, but also their cosmology and non-materialist values. More concretely, education and health techniques have "trickled up" from Brazil and Central America to wider application in the rich nations. Under duress from the collapse of the Soviet empire and an embargo from the United States, for example, Cuban agriculture has conducted the largest experiment ever in organic farming. Innovative urban solutions of mass transit, recycling, and job training are coming from the city of Curitiba in the south of Brazil.[7]

People, then, have diverse and often multiple reasons to care about what happens to the poor nations, and it is critical to grasp the roots of their interest to understand the approach they take and the conclusions they reach. This volume puts at your fingertips the original words of brilliant people attempting to understand how societies are changing. The goal of this Introduction is to provide some context for new readers and some framework for old hands. It begins with a discussion of the deep divide in our society over whom people believe are to blame for the poverty of poor nations. This divide runs through the decades of debate about international development, which this reader attempts to chronicle. We then introduce the five parts of the book by briefly discussing their contexts, main questions, and approaches.

This book chronicles two major social revolutions and the transition between them: the industrial revolution and the shift to global economic production. Part I, which covers the earliest theories of social change and the development of capitalism, begins the volume with two "classic" pieces by pivotal thinkers on these questions: Karl Marx/Friedrich Engels and Max Weber, and then moves on to W. W. Rostow's influential piece refuting Marx and Engels and Samuel Huntington on politics and change. Part II includes five pieces by what some argue was the earliest "globalization" theorizing, by writers who developed what came to be called the "dependency" and "world systems" approaches. Parts III, IV, and V contain 18 path-breaking pieces on the relationship between globalization and development, of which 16 are new for this edition. The first of these three parts on globalization represents a segment of the array of conceptualizations of economic globalization, featuring selections by Manuel Castells, Saskia Sassen, Leslie Sklair, and Thomas Friedman. As globalization has unfolded, there have been strong, opposing viewpoints on the promise and risks of free trade and increasing integration among nations. The selections in Part IV are characteristic of these divergent views, with Johan Norberg and Dani Rodrik representing the "cautious optimists"; Robert Wade, Mark Duffield, and Giovanni Arrighi et al. offering three pessimistic perspectives. Joseph Stiglitz might be characterized as somewhere in between. The book concludes with a sampling of the varied chorus of voices opposing globalization, or as Peter Evans names them, counter-hegemonic movements. In addition to Evans' evaluative synthesis of these movements, Part V examines feminist movements, organized labor, and environmental movements as arenas where activists are working on a transnational basis to identify important methods for ameliorating the negative impacts of globalization.

This Introduction, then, seeks to set some of the historical stage for the current debate over globalization and development, and to provide background on where some of these debates originated and where they have been. To do a complete job of this is of course impossible, but we use a few themes to illustrate abiding, opposing positions in at least the broadest strokes. For some more detailed discussions of the distinctions among the theories represented in this volume, we have provided new introductory material at the start of each of the five parts. These commentaries are designed to quickly orient readers, tell them about the authors they are about to read, and summarize a few of each piece's key points. The limitations of culling excerpts is apparent throughout the book, since nearly every author has generated a lifetime of intricate, elaborate, and evolving ideas. Nonetheless, we hope that this introductory material will provide a simple but useful framework of the most basic ideas of each group, upon which readers can build the nuance these authors deserve. In turn, we hope that readers will someday explore the original works more fully to avoid the risks of oversimplifying the bodies of literature from the few small excerpts we were able to fit in this volume.[8]

Why Are the Poor Countries Poor? Diverging Opinions

"Why are the poor countries poor?" This seemingly simple question has elicited widely polarized views and driven starkly divergent national and international policies. Debates about developing countries reflect a similar chasm within most societies over whether individuals are poor owing to factors that are within or out of their control. Who is to blame: the poor or their society? This debate runs through not just the classic works of philosophy and religion, but also amongst politicians, business groups, labor unions, and advocates for the poor. In both Britain and the United States, the division often seems to split us along party lines. On one side are those who believe that poor people are lazy and will only improve their lot if they "pull themselves up by their own bootstraps," finding ways to make themselves rich by their own inventiveness. On the other side are those who see poor people as victims of their birth into bad conditions, of economic hard times like mass layoffs as industries close or move locations, or as victims of discrimination based on having the "wrong" skin color, gender, or ethnicity. There is a similarly deep disagreement among social scientists about the ability of individuals to change things.

It is difficult to overstate how profound this split's implications are for the role of national governments and international organizations. Should "the state" step in and try to overcome some of the structural barriers that create poverty? Or should states get out of the way and let ingenuity and the market solve the problem? Throughout the readings in this volume, the "proper" role and size of states are reverberating themes.

There are surprising parallels between these acrimonious national debates and those over why poor countries are poor and what we should do about them. This book is a vehicle for gaining familiarity with the most important of the many, complex theories that explain national poverty, development, and distributions of wealth. One guidepost for navigating this complexity is to consider whether authors believe national poverty or "backwardness" is due to *internal* or *external* factors. That is, are nations poor because their society lacks key elements like an efficient government or freely operating markets, or is their situation the product of centuries of colonial exploitation and continuing political and economic domination by more powerful imperialist nations like the Netherlands, Spain, Britain, the United States, and Japan? From the beginning to the end of this volume, you should see that debates about development are both stark and long raging. The "modernization theorists" we introduce in the following part of the volume, for example, see *internal* factors as what drives development; the authors represented in Part II, however, stress the importance of external factors in the development process. More recently, the "Washington consensus" of development policy during the 1980s and 1990s was driven by a belief that national policy and government effectiveness was the key to moving countries out of poverty. Parts IV and V show just how unsettled this debate is: the "consensus" is now openly being challenged.

Social Turmoil and the Classical Thinkers

To understand the startling contrasts and bewildering changes globalization foments, contemporary "development" thinkers often look back to earlier changes associated with the age of industrialization. Political, economic, scientific, and social turmoil served as the backdrop for the work of eighteenth- and nineteenth-century theorists such as Scottish economist Adam Smith (1723–90), German theorists Karl Marx (1818–83), Friedrich Engels (1820–95), and Max Weber (1864–1920), and the Frenchman Emile Durkheim (1858–1917). Albeit with many decades of layers of sophistication superimposed on their core ideas, these theorists' work serves as bedrock for many contemporary explanations of development and social change.

Adam Smith's landmark book *An Inquiry into the Nature and Causes of the Wealth of Nations*, published in 1776, is the classic treatise on economic liberalism (free markets), and that era's best description of what was the emerging capitalist system. In this work, Smith argued that human selfishness was universal and, left untouched in the area of production and trade, would create benefits for the whole society, as freely operating markets would lead selfish actors to seek the greatest profits, which they would make meeting the greatest human needs. At a time when the economy was based largely on merchants buying in one area and selling in another (mercantilism), nations were adding regulations, tariffs, and quotas to try to protect their own industries and raise money for their armies and growing bureaucracies. Smith suggested that the best way to meet the needs of the people was not through such regulation but through letting selfish human forces loose, while reserving policy making for non-market aspects of society. Smith called the impersonal force of markets creating an overall benefit to society the "invisible hand":

> [H]e intends only his own gain, and he is in this, as in many other cases, led by an invisible hand to promote an end which was no part of his intention. Nor is it always the worse for the society that it was no part of it. By pursuing his own interest he frequently promotes that of the society more effectually than when he really intends to promote it. I have never known much good done by those who affected to trade for the public good. (Book 4, Chapter 2)

Smith's book is the foundation for modern economics; its description of human action forms the basis for countless analyses of whether economic systems are working as they should or whether government interventions are distorting them.

On protecting national industries through the imposition of tariffs on imports – what he refers to above as affecting "trade for the public good," Smith argues that

> By restraining, either by high duties, or by absolute prohibitions, the importation of such goods from foreign countries as can be produced at home, the monopoly of the home-market is more or less secured to the domestic industry employed in producing them. Thus the . . . high duties upon the importation of corn, which in times of moderate plenty amount to a prohibition, give a like advantage to the growers of that commodity . . . That this monopoly of the home-market frequently gives great encouragement to that particular species of industry which enjoys it . . . cannot be doubted. But whether it tends either to increase the general industry of the society, or to give it the most advantageous direction, is not, perhaps, altogether so evident. (Book 4, Chapter 2)

Smith insists that areas should specialize in production according to their special endowments, what he termed a "comparative advantage": "The natural advantages which one country has over another in producing particular commodities are sometimes so great, that it is acknowledged by all the world to be in vain to struggle with them" (Book 4, Chapter 2).

In many ways, Smith's great book on the wealth of nations sought to reassure readers that capitalism, including the great disruptions and inequality that economic growth and free markets were bringing, would ultimately serve the greater good. His argument was clear: stay out of the way and allow humans to solve these problems. These same points will be made again and again as successive periods of change reverberate through the world economy, right up to the current debates over globalization. As the selections throughout this book illustrate, the nature of a society's specialization, or comparative advantage, has monumental consequences.

Many people were not so assured about the future as was Adam Smith. While factories, railroads, and cities were proliferating, centuries-old institutions such as religion, intimate communities, and the authority of traditional rulers like kings and lords were unraveling before everyone's eyes. As colonial rebellion and then industrial revolution rocked Europe, fear of its disruptions spread. Poor peasants lost their land to "enclosures" by capitalist ranchers. Old, moneyed, landowning classes saw their power to control government weaken as urban-based businesspeople gained influence in first economic, and then political circles. But, perhaps most frightening to many people were the masses of urban unemployed and industrial workers hired up in the sprawling new factories. These workers' brusque, unrefined ways offended many "proper" urbanites; and as living conditions were often tight and unsanitary, disease (both physical and social), promiscuity, and unrest were seen as deplorable or inevitable. Factory work and city life were changing peasants into a new type of proletarian laborer. Controlling them and planning for the future required understanding the fundamental but unknown implications of this enormous class.

Just as current efforts to explain "globalization" give a clear sense that society is in the midst of fundamental social, political, and economic change, during the mid- to late nineteenth century, there was a similar sense among these important theorists that fundamental change was happening before their very eyes. It was very apparent that modern Western society was fundamentally different from anything that had come before. The new developments seemed to correspond to eroding political, economic, and social structure, without there being a clear notion of what would emerge in place of the old. Social theorists asked how these social structures emerged and how they were engendering different ways of thinking, working, and organizing.

Addressing these big questions were two major German social theorists, whose works are presented in the first section of readings: Karl Marx, in collaboration with Friedrich Engels, and Max Weber. In addition to these major German theorists, Frenchman Emile Durkheim (1858–1917) also studied carefully and scientifically the division of labor in society and the process of social change. All three of these authors analyzed many of the same social processes, but there are two major differences between the work of Marx, Engels, and Weber, and that of Durkheim. First, Marx, Engels, and Weber are what we call "macro" theorists, meaning that they focused on "the big picture" and the major historical trends. Durkheim focused more on what we think of as the "micro" level, trying to understand how more intimate relationships work.

The authors whose words we print here and many others saw a sharp shift from "traditional" to "modern" ways of life that manifested in myriad ways. They documented a breakdown of the ties and institutions governing those "traditional" societies. These theorists observed and documented a process of *increased division of labor*. That is, they saw different members of a society increasingly specializing in specific tasks (such as trading, banking, carpentry, fishing, and so on). Perhaps most importantly, they observed that society was changing from one where authority and beliefs stemmed from traditions, superstitions, fatalism, or emotions, to one dominated by the application of reason and practicality, an appreciation of efficiency and the ability to explain the world scientifically. This new complex of beliefs – that nature could be understood and controlled and that life should be organized with a goal of efficiency – they termed "rationalization."

In general, all of these classic social theorists saw this shift to modernity in terms of increased complexity. In other words, what people do and how they do it, how people relate to one another, how people envision their universe, how individuals organize as a group, and how people make decisions all become more specialized, segmented, and complex. For example, someone working in a modern factory and living in a city might specialize in creating one thing in exchange for a daily wage and would use new technologies in production. This "modern" person might not know his or her neighbors. Instead of believing in natural forces, they would base faith and decisions on science, law, and accounting. Instead of knowing only a few people intimately, they might have daily but superficial contact with hundreds of individuals very different from themselves. Their interactions with these near-strangers would be based on their survival needs of making an exchange of money for goods, services, or work.

Factory work and city life were changing former peasants into a new type of laborer, one Marx labeled "proletarians." Controlling them and planning for the future required understanding the fundamental but unknown implications of these new relationships and the new enormous groups industrialization created. For Marx, this led to important questions about how economic relations created social and political groups, and how these groups negotiate capitalism. For Weber, these developments led him to attempt to explain how these changes arose, what the relationship between people's "mindsets" and their production was, and how changes in economic and social organization were associated with changes in the type of authority that controlled society. These are the perspectives reviewed in Part I. Marx and Weber's focus on the relationship between capitalism and social change brought us into the twentieth century, when social sciences began to flourish.

Becoming Modern

Why do some countries remain poor and "backward" despite exposure to capitalism and other aspects of modern life? What can be done to make capitalism develop further in these countries? These were the questions addressed by a group of theorists whose ideas heavily influenced US efforts to foster capitalist development in poorer nations, then called the "Third World."[9]

After World War II, the United States found itself alone at the top of the world power structure. It was the only nation on either side of the war that had its physical and economic infrastructure intact. It had a near-monopoly on new technology and the industry in place to produce goods that would sell for a high price around the world. Nevertheless, without functioning economies to buy these products, the growth of the US economy was limited. Not only was aiding the recovery of Europe and Asia through a massive aid program called "the Marshall Plan" a pragmatic solution to debilitated foreign markets, but it was also a mechanism to stem the spread of communism.

Coupled with a concern for the wellbeing of obvious trading and military partners in Europe was concern about what was to come of the billions of people living in the poor, sometimes newly independent nations in the southern hemisphere. On the one hand, there was a fear among people in wealthier countries of the kind of social unrest that could result from such widespread poverty in a world of modernity and late twentieth-century prosperity. On the other hand was an even larger, more evident threat: the Soviet Union. The Soviet Union offered a solution to development that had a strong mass appeal and had something of a proven track record. Politicians, development experts, academicians, and the public were afraid of people in Latin America and Africa deciding that Communism was a surer path to development than capitalism. In response, theories about development that were generated in the 1950s and 1960s in the United States provided an explicitly non-Communist solution to poverty and underdevelopment.

A group of influential development experts saw three obvious problems holding back the industrialization of the poor countries. First, companies there simply were not big enough to construct the modern factories needed to compete with the huge corporations of the big powers of Europe and North America. Secondly, access to great amounts of capital allowed corporations in these "developed" nations to continually build up and adapt new technologies, which was sorely lacking in the poor nations. Thirdly, and most important for our discussion here, they saw the cultural, institutional, and organizational features of poorer countries as roadblocks in their attempts to develop and democratize. Therefore, according to this group of "modernization theorists," poorer nations are poor because they lack big capital, technology, and modern social organization and values.[10] This group of theorists set out to explain the reasons for these absences and laid out policy recommendations to overcome them. The introduction to Part II reviews these theories in detail, and the readings that follow offer two classic examples: W. W. Rostow's description of the stages societies go through on their way to development, and Samuel Huntington's theory about the relationships among political, social, and economic change.

After two decades of dominance in development circles, modernization theory came under attack from several angles. First, it was as ahistorical: modernization theory failed to make distinctions between countries, regions, structural conditions, or specific historical experiences. For example, modernization theorists did not address the fact that these poorer regions exhibited not one situation of poverty or one type of society, but multiple "pre-modernities." Many of the countries that would be classified as "undeveloped" in fact already had "modern" industries, educational systems, or the other "precursors" that were thought necessary for modernity. A critique was increasingly lodged that the term "modernization" was only a euphemism for "Americanization," a point supported by a closer read of several early authors in the lineage. The field was therefore labeled ethnocentric and pro-capitalist, an explicit tool of the American Cold War anti-Communist effort. And by emphasizing nations' internal problems as the cause of underdevelopment, modernization theory seemed to blame the victims themselves for their poverty. Finally, critics claimed that important external causes of poverty and underdevelopment are ignored.

Some modernization ideas have come back into fashion both on what is called the Right, and from some surprising quarters of the Left. Two 1998 pieces serve as examples. On the right, Landes' monumental book *The Wealth and Poverty of Nations* (New York: Norton) concludes that "Some people [respond to markets] better than others, and culture can make all the difference." On the other side of the spectrum, Cristobal Kay endorses Sunkel's 1993 opinion that "The heart of development lies in the supply side: quality, flexibility, the efficient combination and utilization of productive resources, the adoption of technological development, an innovative spirit, creativity, the capacity for organization and social discipline."[11] Some postmodernists hold that culture has now become more important than economics in driving social change, and that in fact it probably always was so. As argued below, analyses of development which entirely ignore internal "cultural" variables between (and even within) nations will fail to provide complete answers to the question of why the different parts of the world are diverging under globalization. Finally, many theories of social change continue to include expectations that nations will move through a series of necessary stages, a central tenet of the modernizationists.

Dependency and World Systems Theories

By focusing on internal factors and arguing that poor nations lacked the right cultural values, were modernizationists "blaming the victims"? Beginning in the late 1950s, harsh refutation of the modernizationists' ideas came from a steadily growing group of scholars and planners in Latin America and Africa, a group whose formative critiques of colonial and neocolonial relationships would come to be called "dependency theory."

Dependency theorists, and the world systems researchers who were influenced by them, all tied "globalization" – referring not to the current term so much as to international political economy – to the colonial era starting around 1500, and to the long-term exploitation of the people and resources of Africa, South America, and Asia by wealthy countries in Europe and North America. Rather than saying global trade and its impacts are brand new, dependency theorists argued that this history goes back hundreds of years, at least to the rise of mercantile capitalism, which was reliant on trading goods across these regions of rich and poor, or imperialist and colonized. Thus, dependency-school theorists were reacting explicitly to "modernization theorists," who said that poor nations lacked the capital (investable piles of money in a few hands), values (of hard work and investment), and business practices (like modern accounting) to make firms and nations succeed. Dependency theorists considered this "blaming the victims."

The earliest ideas came from a group of economists working in Santiago, Chile in the Economic Commission for Latin America (ECLA), a United Nations agency that analyzed how development could be achieved in the region.[12] When Raul Prebisch led ECLA in the 1950s there emerged a theory that because of colonial and later neocolonial relationships, European powers had subordinated the "Third World," linking to them merely as a source for cheap raw materials and as a market for its more expensive manufactures.[13] The problem with this arrangement was that while the value of manufactures has a tendency to rise steadily over time, the value of raw materials and primary foodstuffs generally declines. ECLA identified this trend of *declining terms of trade* as a key reason Latin America remained less developed than wealthier nations: poor countries had to sell more and more goods to get less in return. The readings in this volume testify to the importance of terms of trade by consistently returning to this historical pattern of relationships and its impacts on development and social change.

Exports of raw materials and sale of cheap labor often led to "enclaves of modernity" in a sea of backwardness, such as those suggested by some of the contrasting scenes at the start of this Introduction. In cases of export enclaves, the internal market was unimportant for producers: the tiny class of wealthy people desired products not produced locally; the masses were too poor to buy more than the very bare necessities. Samir Amin, Alain de Janvry, and Carlos Garramón called these "disarticulated" economies because there was no connection between local producers and consumers, and because there often were no "multiplier" effects created by supplying the export enclaves with locally produced component parts.[14] Both Amin and de Janvry also made much of the "rural labor reserves," subsistence farming areas where workers could return when sick or old or unemployed, to recover and survive more cheaply than possible in cities or where employers might have to fully cover the costs of their workers' long-term survival. Neo-Marxist economists like Amin and de Janvry saw these rural reserves as providing a crucial invisible subsidy for businesses operating in poor nations, as well as to consumers of their products in the rich nations. Later authors have advanced this logic by pointing out that households that share survival expenses or participate in the urban informal sector (without a formal contract or sales/services without licenses) also provide similar subsidies.

Dependency theorists paid special attention to explaining the savage inequalities in poor nations, tying them to colonial histories of those regions and to current economic and political systems of exclusion and repression of the masses. They thought arguing that later industrialization should be as easy as early industrialization, while ignoring colonial legacies, was blatantly self-serving for the rich nations. Dependency theorists did not put all the blame for the poorer nations' poverty outside the nations, however. Cardoso, de Janvry, and several others identified local elites (meaning within the poorer nations) as agents of dependency and underdevelopment because they profit from paving the way for transnational corporations, maintaining unfavorable trade and banking arrangements. In other words, dependency theorists mainly saw foreign groups "feasting" at the table of poorer nations, but elites from those very poorer countries, they theorized, were the ones who "set the table."

By the late 1960s, the fusion of elements of ECLA's work with that of neo-Marxist theory emerged as a serious theoretical challenge to the US-led modernization theory.[15] Some members of this new "dependency school" were ECLA economists, others were academics, and some were members of a vibrant Latin American leftist movement. While dependency theory was already influencing policy in Latin America in the 1950s, it was not until the late 1960s that authors like Andre Gunder Frank "popularized" the theory and development scholars in the rich nations began to take note. Frank simplified many of the dependency group's ideas and was the first author widely published in English.[16] In the era of Vietnam and other military interventions by the United States around the world, the dependency theory's ideas were a welcome alternative approach that profoundly questioned the mainstream social science of the day.

Reviewed in much more depth at the beginning of Part II of this volume, dependency theory took many forms, ranging quite significantly in complexity and the degree to which the theorists saw the possibility of developing nations escaping this exploitative relationship. In particular, some dependency theorists, most notably Andre Gunder Frank, viewed a situation of dependency as inescapable as long as poorer nations participated in the capitalist world economy. Other dependency theorists, represented in this volume by Fernando Henrique Cardoso (Chapter 6), saw opportunities for various nations at various historical junctures to adjust this system of exploitation in their favor.

Emerging from this latter variant of dependency theory, and taking into account the many critiques of dependency is world systems theory. These criticisms centered on dependency theory's difficulty in generating testable hypotheses and lack of explanatory power. Furthermore, after dependency theory's initial splash in the development theory arena, many analysts sought to move beyond the rather crude dichotomy of core–periphery (as outsiders often mistakenly portrayed it) and to engage in more rigorous attention to the impact of historical contexts. The result of this splitting off from dependency theory (especially its initial variants) was an attempt to analyze development in a manner more comprehensive than ever before (perhaps with the exception of Weber's work). It also was the "Americanization" of a development theory that was quite opposite of the dominant, modernist, US theories of development. As such, world systems research became increasingly cross-sectional (using data about one point in time) and quantitative.[17] This was not always the case, as the historical works of Ferdinand Braudel and Immanuel Wallerstein attest.[18] World systems theory attempted a comprehensive analysis of the development process not only from a historical perspective, but also through systematic analyses of the operation of capitalism and the global economic system. While groups of sociologists and geographers using world systems and other political economy perspectives advanced their analysis of global systems of production and power, a new literature on "globalization" sprouted from other fields and the popular press.

From Development to Globalization

From the earliest social theorists all the way through the dependency theorists of the 1950s and 1960s, the literature on social change and development was largely associated with industrialization and the gaps between wealthier and poorer nations. Marx and Weber wrote about and analyzed the industrial revolution; modernization theorists thought an urban, industrial milieu was a sort of school for modernity; and many dependency theorists thought that if Latin America wished to become part of the "developed world," it would need to have more national industries. Since then, all this has been questioned. Contributions to the three latter parts of this volume perceive development differently. First, it is no longer a given that building factories and infrastructure means raising wellbeing for a nation or its people. Rather, power in the world is increasingly linked to control over information, technology, and international banking institutions. Second, much of the new literature on globalization moves beyond the "poor versus rich" image that nations are groups into distinct "worlds." Instead, this literature often argues how interdependent and integrated the world has become. The sentinel piece by Folker Fröbel, Jürgen Heinrichs, and Otto Kreye coined the term "the global assembly line" back in 1980, noticing how closing factories in Europe and the United States was tied to new strategies by large corporations of moving the labor-intensive stages of their production process overseas. Twenty-five years later, Thomas Friedman's bestselling 2005 book and article reprinted here insisted that this process had continued and accelerated after the year 2000, to the point where the world had become "flat." Friedman argues that quantum leaps in technology and advances in education and global sourcing had spread economic opportunity and risk everywhere to the point that old boundaries simply no longer apply. Peter Dicken, author of a very useful volume called *Global Shift*, would categorize Friedman's ideas as "hyperglobalist," that globalization is leveling the playing field and is inevitable.[19]

But the term "globalization" is often used without clarification. First and most broadly, globalization refers to a set of processes that increasingly make the parts of the world interdependently integrated.[20] Although the world has long had important international linkages, globalization refers to integration where firms are interdependent, production is linked on a global scale, there is a dramatic increase in visible and invisible trade, and national economies are connected. Beyond this increase in trade and globally organized production, for some authors globalization means also the control of decision making by a new "political and economic elite," or more critically and explicitly, the "Wall Street–US Treasury–IMF/World Bank Complex."[21] For these authors globalization is not just economic integration, but centralized, homogenized control. There is sharp debate about both of these dimensions of globalization.

Debt has played an important part in the globalization process, as Philip McMichael states very explicitly in his books and the piece we have included here. The poorer nations took on heavy debts in the 1960s and 1970s to try to build their industrial sectors and infrastructures to catch up with the core nations. Loans allowed these poor nations to finally do some development planning, building roads, airports, new capitals, dams, and oil refineries. But the rates for their loans were often adjustable, and like a credit card or house mortgage debt with an adjustable rate, an increase in US interest rates exponentially increased the total debt burden of these countries. In 1982 Mexico and then Brazil said they could not pay their debts, and soon the list of defaulting nations grew. To continue to get the money they needed to pay even just the interest they owed, these nations had to secure more loans, and usually it was only multinational agencies like the World Bank and IMF that agreed to lend to them. In exchange for these loans, the heavily indebted nations had to submit to a sweeping program of cuts in food, housing, and transport subsidies, privatization of state-run companies, and lowering tariff barriers to force local industries to face global competition.[22] These sweeping reforms (called structural adjustment programs by the banks) have been the subject of two decades of bitter debate, protests, riots, and even rebellions across the Third World.[23] Cutting government intervention in the economy, changing political and economic structures, and acting to stabilize macroeconomic indicators is more broadly called "neoliberalism," referencing the liberal economic policies long ago advocated by Adam Smith. This shift toward embracing free, global trade and promoting smaller, less intrusive states is the context to which the majority of the selections in the latter three parts of this volume are responding.

Part III offers readers various perspectives to clarify what globalization means, on how our world is changing. Reflecting this volume's focus on economic development and social change, we have limited these selections to those focused on *economic* globalization, so we have by necessity largely excluded the vast literature that explores globalization as a phenomenon with dimensions that are revolutionizing arenas as diverse as the media, culture, states, and international relations. Even so, readers can note how vast the linkages and effects associated with globalization are. From Sassen's analysis of the movement of capital among what she terms "global cities" to Castells' description of how we are encountering an entirely new mode of production based on the production and control over information, we can see that globalization's impacts are deep and surround us completely.

At the crux of economic globalization, of course, is trade. In recent decades, debates about the merit or menace of free trade have moved well beyond the category of esoteric, academic debates. While most nonspecialists are thinking more about trade policy, much less understood are the current global efforts to forge regulatory frameworks for what already is a completely global system of trade. Several selections in Part IV of this volume educate us about these International Trade Agreements such as the General Agreement on Tariffs and Trade (GATT). These selections explain what is at stake, outline the major debates surrounding these multilateral negotiations, take a critical look at who controls their outcomes, and describe their likely impacts on workers throughout the world.

What is unique about trade in this current era is that the depth of interactions (both direct and indirect) among the actors involved are far more complex than in previous eras. With the telephone, Internet, and cheaper and better express shipping, companies can place an order to a factory halfway round the world and have it met in as little or less time than a shop down the street. What's more, the goods from a complex web of suppliers around the world can be orchestrated to come together at precisely the right time at assembly sites which can be strategically located almost anywhere. Also unique is the expansion of world trade to not just goods, but services as well. Our phone calls are often answered a half a world away; our rebates and forms are processed anywhere in the world; and the money we set aside to invest could be at work for us in almost any place in the world.

Some have argued that by being so tightly reliant on people around the world, a more peaceful "global society" has emerged. Production is entirely globalized; this means that, to the extent that trade is a social process, we are intimately and continuously linked to people of nationalities, classes, social and cultural groups vastly different from our own in this "global society." In another sense, however, the vast differences that remain in the world between rich and poor, "Global North" and "Global South," or among "less developed"/developing and developed nations. Critics point out that this growing social inequality makes it difficult to conceptualize a "global society" as any sort of coherent social group. In what is perhaps the great paradox of our time, our economic lives are more interdependent than ever, yet these interdependencies coexist alongside vast differences in cultures, wealth, and social or political organization. Many argue that these material dependencies are also translating to a global homogenization of culture, a "McDonaldization" of the world.[24] And, if recent US foreign policy is any indicator, there are also strong believers in linking globalization to the global spread of democracy.

While Part IV presents the sides of the intellectual and policy debates over globalization, Part V offers a broad outline of several of the most vocal social movements' efforts to confront globalization: the antiglobalization movement, feminist movements, organized labor, and environmental movements. Many of these organized groups are those Dani Rodrik is referring to as he discusses why "losers" are uneasy about globalization. We are excited to be able to offer readers these insightful pieces, and we introduce their ideas in the section introductions to come. What we see in these readings is that, just like the media, trade, agriculture and food production, and culture, what we now have – albeit in a nascent and often weak form – is a globalization of activism. Beginning in 2001, the World Social Forum emerged as an international arena to organize critiques about globalization and for groups from around the world to share experiences in challenging globalization's impacts, as well as offering a long-standing, international, and heterogeneous infrastructure for those fighting to stem the consequences of globalization. In a path-breaking analysis that closes our volume, Peter Evans characterizes movements that organize transnationally and challenge free trade and other pillars of globalization as "counter-hegemonic movements." While he cautions us about being overly optimistic about the effectiveness of these movements, he highlights the novel ways they are linking across the globe, linking issues together, and coalescing grievances held by very heterogeneous groups. Also included in this section is another message of hope, this one from the world-renowned development economist Jeffrey Sachs. In this very brief excerpt from his latest book, he explains that for the first time in the history of human civilization, the world in which we now live is capable of lifting every person out of poverty.

Before concluding, we need to express one great hesitation. The modernizationists and dependency theorists agreed on far more than they might admit, Bob Sutcliffe once wrote in a piece called "Development after Ecology." He argues that both Left and Right shared the view "that development was desirable" (that it would solve human welfare needs of the majority), that whole nations develop or don't, and that any obstacles were human: social, economic, or political. While other critics were chiseling away at modernity and development, profound environmental concerns surfaced about the desire for nations to rise out of poverty. The most uncomfortable point for many of us is the realization that "the globalization of the characteristics of developed countries would surely make the planet uninhabitable." Sutcliffe stated flatly that "the development of underdevelopment has also been the development of unsustainability." This suggests simply that development is going in the wrong direction. It is the underdeveloped countries, he asserted, which provide better models for sustainable societies than do developed ones. Even as development agencies and firms have hijacked the term "sustainability" to their own ends and then moved on to the next fad, the profound ecological critique put forward by Sutcliffe is the 500-gorilla which is essentially ignored by virtually all social studies of development. The only encouraging sign is the dawning realization of the complex interweaving of climate change, development issues, and cultural survival.

We believe that social scientists working in the area of development need to be aware of the debates that preceded them so that they can glean insights and avoid repeating old mistakes. We hope this volume provides readers the opportunity to begin to examine this crucial debate over the past century and a half. Though helping the poor nations should be enough reason to care, social sciences of development are no longer only about helping the poor nations. The emerging work on globalization and on the environmental consequences of development has taken away any doubt from the proposition that our fate is intricately linked to those of the other six billion souls with whom we share the planet.

Why are the poor countries poor? Who are the winners and losers of globalization? Who's to blame for the unintended consequences of development? And what can be done? Should states step in and try to overcome some of the structural barriers that create poverty, or should they get out of the way and let ingenuity and the market solve the problem? These audacious questions – those of the wellbeing and survival of five or perhaps all six billion of the world's population – are the ones that the readings in this volume explicitly attempt to address.

NOTES

1   Many of the terms used here are highly debated, perhaps none so much as the term "development" itself. Rather than enter into that debate here, we follow Kincaid and Portes in conceptualizing national development as change in economic growth, social welfare, and citizenship (political rights). A. Douglas Kincaid and Alejandro Portes, *Comparative National Development: Society and Economy in the New Global Order*, Chapel Hill, NC: University of North Carolina Press, 1994, p. 2.

2   In what is now outdated, Cold War terminology, the first world consisted of Western Europe, the United States, and Canada, while the second world was the communist bloc of the Soviet Union and its allies. The rest was the Third World.

3   World Bank, *World Development Report 1997*, Oxford: Oxford University Press, 1997, pp. 214–15.

4   The World Bank admitted in 1995 that in spite of their 50-year effort to address the issue, "on average, countries that started rich grew faster . . . poor countries tend to grow more slowly." World Bank, *World Development Report 1995*, Oxford: Oxford University Press, 1995, p. 53.

5   UNRISD, *States of Disarray: The Social Effects of Globalization*, Geneva: UNRISD, 1997, p. 24; CARE Development Facts, 2 Sept. 1996: http://www.care.org/world/devfact.html. Six billion people total. One-third of 5 billion equals 1.5 billion, which equals 1 in 4.

6   We suggest readers visit the websites of major evangelical Christian groups.

7   Roberts and Thanos 2003.

8   Our goal in excerpting has been to maintain the central points of each reading while shortening them enough to fit the variety of authors in this volume. We regret the possible confusion and lost arguments that such excerpting requires; we also removed most of the footnotes with more nuanced arguments.

9   See note 2.

10   We acknowledge the excellent framework from lectures by Geographer Maria Patricia Fernandez-Kelly.

11   "Relevance of Structuralist and Dependency Theories in the Neoliberal Period: A Latin American Perspective," The Hague: Institute of Social Sciences, Working Paper Series No. 281, 1988, p. 18.

12   The group's Spanish acronym is CEPAL. "And the Caribbean" was later added to its English name: it is now named ECLAC.

13   African theorist Samir Amin called this "unequal exchange."

14   For de Janvry and Garramón's discussion of disarticulation see "The Dynamics of Rural Poverty in Latin America," *Journal of Peasant Studies* 4:3 (1977): 206–16. For Samir Amin's, see "Accumulation and Development: A Theoretical Model," *Review of African Political Economy* 1 (1974): 9–26.

15   Peter F. Klarén, "Lost Promise: Explaining Latin American Underdevelopment," *Promise of Development: Theories of Change in Latin America*, Boulder, CO: Westview, 1986, p. 14.

16   By contrast, Fernando Henrique Cardoso's more subtle analysis excerpted here was initially published in 1971 but didn't get published in English until 1979.

17   Instead of one or two cases, some world systems theory analyses used statistics to examine patterns among samples of dozens or over one hundred countries.

18   See Fernand Braudel, *Civilization and Capitalism, 15th–18th Century*, vols. I–III, New York: Harper & Row, 1982.

19   Peter Dicken, *Global Shift* (4th edn), New York: Guilford, 2003, p. 11.

20   Peter Dicken, *Global Shift* (3rd edn), New York: Guilford, 1998, p. 5.

21   The first quote is from McMichael's excerpt in this volume (Chapter 13). The second phrase is an adaptation of a coinage by Wade and Veneroso 1998, cited in Kay 1998.

22   McMichael 1996, pp. 36–7.

23   See, e.g., John Walton, "Debt, Protest, and the State in Latin America," in *Power and Popular Protest*, ed. Susan Eckstein, Berkeley: University of California Press, 1989, pp. 299–328.

24   E.g., George Ritzer, *The McDonaldization of Society*, Thousand Oaks, CA: Pine Forge, 1995.

Part I Formative Approaches to Development and Social Change

Introduction

Marx and Weber saw ample evidence that capitalism was an enormously powerful, efficient force capable of producing unprecedented wealth. Alongside this evidence, however, there was competing evidence of the poverty, social upheaval, inequality, and political crisis it seemed to bring. It was trying to understand these contradictions and consequences of capitalism that drove the theories of the "formative" authors represented in Part I. In the interests of expanding the variety of perspectives on globalization in this volume, the selection here is admittedly quite brief. Nonetheless, what follows demonstrates the distinctiveness of both Marx (and Engels) and Weber's theories, as well as their most notable conceptualizations about the relationship between social and economic change. The latter two selections are North Americans writing almost a century later and expressing views on the relationship between social and economic change, albeit from a very different perspective.

Karl Marx (1818–83), known as an historical materialist, once wrote: "Men make their own history, but they do not make it just as they please; they do not make it under circumstances chosen by themselves, but under circumstances directly encountered, given and transmitted from the past."[1] For Friedrich Engels (1820–95) and Marx, the point in studying history was not just memorizing the deeds of individuals or their actions, but understanding the evolving structure of things. They saw history as a series of types of production, each type corresponding to ways of organizing and thinking. Economic relationships structured people's lives; what and how they produce things, relationships among workers, tools, and ownership of inputs can all explain people's daily actions, choices, feelings, and even beliefs. Moreover, Marx and Engels viewed conflict over these relationships as omnipresent and a primary source of social change: the economy drives the system.

Marx and his longtime colleague Friedrich Engels were especially interested in the latest mode of economic organization, capitalism. In the capitalist system, they saw wage labor and exchange for profit as an overarching, all-encompassing structure that breeds exploitative economic relationships among individuals, classes, and regions. These economic relationships, in turn, determine how people think – they influence prevailing ideologies and behaviors. Marx's work is essentially a critique of capitalism. These critiques stem from one central idea: that the human relationships that capitalism requires do not allow people to reach their full, creative potentials, or to exercise free will, which he conceives as fundamental parts of human nature. Marx argued that one of the ways capitalist production exploits workers is by making them feel estranged from the products of their own hands. Alienation occurs when the systems of social relationships created by a system out of our control comes to dominate us. In "Alienated Labor" Marx explains how capitalism's negative effects extend well beyond the workplace.

Marx's greatest legacy is probably his contention that all history is a story of struggles between those who own factories and tools to produce goods (the bourgeoisie), and those who own so little that they must sell their labor in order to purchase the goods they need to survive (the proletariat). This separation of society into workers and owners means that in capitalist society there is a constant struggle over the difference between what workers are paid and the final price of what they create. For example, using modern production techniques workers might create 100 pairs of shoes per day, each of which might sell for, say, $75. Yet, each worker might only earn $3 a day. In capitalism, there is a constant struggle between workers and owners over the difference between the cost of production and the price that products command on the market. As long as workers are unable to capture the surplus value of what they produce (the difference between the cost to produce 100 shoes and the total price the shoes sell for), conflict permeates economic and social relationships. It is conflict in the form of exploitation of labor that both characterizes capitalism as a system and will, according to Marx and Engels, lead to its demise.

From the early twentieth century, the revolutionary message of *The Communist Manifesto* influenced billions of lives. Marx and Engels penned this "Manifesto" as a program for a new socialist league of German journeymen living in Paris, Brussels, and London. As with all of Marx's work (and that of Engels as well), the *Communist Manifesto* is a critique of modern (to him this was "capitalist") society. According to Marx and Engels, capitalism was merely an historical stage, albeit a crucial one, in which all relationships are mediated by the exchange of things that can be bought and sold. Confronted with what they saw as this dehumanizing and seemingly overwhelming force of capitalism, Marx and Engels were nonetheless hopeful that contradictions within capitalism would ultimately lead to its replacement by a new social order. Notwithstanding the political controversy this manifesto inspired, or its errant predictions on capitalism's demise and its replacement with a new order, this pamphlet has inspired both revolutionary leaders and social scientists for generations. As with Adam Smith's *Wealth of Nations*, in piece after piece in this book, the ideas in the clear, strident, and political *Communist Manifesto* are incorporated, expanded, refuted and directly critiqued by social scientists of all stripes that followed.

About a half-century after Marx and Engels, German sociologist Max Weber (1864–1920) wrote in response to Marx and Engels to demonstrate that social change goes beyond mere economic relationships. In his 1905 piece "The Protestant Ethic and the Spirit of Capitalism," Weber proposed that in addition to the economic system driving social change, religious ideas were crucial in the development of capitalism in Europe. In addition to this theoretical disagreement, Weber was less interested in presenting a political agenda and more interested in explaining the underlying forces that allowed the new society around him to develop. Because his project was more academic than polemical, Weber laid out a more complex and less deterministic theory of how societies were changing.

For centuries, sources of traditional authority – the church, the crown, or the landed elite – dominated European society. Virtue was independent of excelling in one's work, but rather work was not for "proper" people at all, who focused on fineries and "courtly love." Similarly, properly showing God's glory was through art, poetry, or music. As society urbanized and industrialized, the power of these traditional sources of authority eroded quickly, as an almost scientific pursuit of moneymaking emerged as the dominating force of the era. People were more interested in investing their surplus in productive investments than in spending it on luxury goods. Weber noted that this new approach to work and money brought with it profound attitudinal and behavioral changes, a veritable "Spirit of Capitalism."

In the excerpt from this work reprinted here, Weber traces how the initial development of Protestantism in Europe and North America contributed to economic arrangements of that specific era. For example, early Protestants advocated devoting one's life to a calling to demonstrate one's willingness to serve God's will. Therefore, hard work in a specific area was a virtue and laziness or idleness considered sinful. This devotion to a calling, coupled with the belief in the sinfulness of an unproductive accumulation of wealth (as it was evidence of a lack of grace), led to vocational specialization and the reinvestment of capital. It was only the Protestant attitude toward wealth, argued Weber, which resulted in capital being viewed as something to reinvest judiciously. Similarly, specialization according to one's calling infused work with religious meaning and made hard work, efficiency, and asceticism inherently virtuous, as the accumulation of wisely invested wealth demonstrated a state of grace. Ultimately, capitalism was no longer imbued with Protestantism but emerged as an independent force. Specifically, Weber argued that certain Protestant religious practices had become secularized and developed into a new type of authority.

This change following the Protestant reformation was a profound one. Weber explained how society went from valuing tradition toward being dominated by new, more objective practices and values such as the written contract, merit, expertise, universal standards, and established methods and procedures for completing tasks. In short, he explained that society had come to value rational procedures more than traditional authority. Weber asks: How did written rules, limited jurisdictions, limited powers, record-keeping, separation of public and private life, and the following of documented, comprehensive procedures come to almost replace religion and lineage as a source of authority? His answer is that the ideas accompanying the emergence of Protestantism and rational bureaucratic organization spilled over and even dominated an economic system, modern capitalism. In this sense Weber differs greatly from Marx: where Marx believed economic arrangements determined ideology (ideas) and nearly everything else, Weber believed in the possibility that the ideas of men could lead the process of economic development. In this case, Protestant ideas helped shape the rise of capitalism in its modern form.

The influence of Weber's observations cannot be overstated: "modernization theorists" writing on developing nations many decades later held the implicit assumption that there is something inherently morally superior in the investment of wealth, harder work, efficiency, and strict bureaucratic structures. They called these traits in a society "modern" and "rational," labeling the others as leftovers of previous social structures, as "irrational," or as impediments to progress. These ideas continue to hold sway in national and multilateral agency centers: billions of dollars in foreign assistance are currently being allotted based on whether nations fit this vision of what a "modern" society is. Many other ideas have been carried forward from Weber's work. For example, some authors included in the final sections of this volume take up Weber's assertion that power is based not just on relations of production (i.e., on money), but on factors like access to information, cultural identification, and organizational potential. And his attention to social status and the role of the state (the government) has informed a new generation of "neo-Weberian" scholarship on social change and development.

Following the examples of Marx and Weber's theories about capitalism and social change are two examples of "modernization theory," outlined briefly in the Editors' Introduction. To understand the gap between wealthier and poorer nations, modernization theorists explored the process of development and offered a composite portrait of what it means to be "modern." In short, "modernization" involves the adoption of new ways of material life – like how work and community are organized, or how technology or governments are dealt with – and it also changes, or rather "improves" our education system and our most basic values and attitudes. In modernization theory's dualistic schema, societies go from being one type of society (traditional or undeveloped) to another type of society (modern, or developed). Samuel Huntington, whose work ends this section of the reader, explained that modernization is an evolutionary process that changes societies in a revolutionary manner.[2]

Although different academic disciplines produced their own species of these theories, they all set up dichotomies and perceived development as a process that involved social, psychological, economic, cultural, political, or even biological sequences of changes from point A to point B along a single trajectory. Different theorists saw varied "motors" as the key to movement from traditional to modern. Some modernization theorists, such as W. W. Rostow, thought that an increased accumulation of capital would lead a modernization process that would then affect other elements of a society such as politics and values. Others considered noneconomic factors the most important in explaining why poorer countries are poor and why some countries have been unable to generate sufficient capital and technology to "modernize." Bert Hoselitz, for example, perceived entrepreneurs as key figures in a society's shift in attitude from traditional to modern.[3] In a traditional society, the entrepreneur is a social deviant because he is doing something new and different; in a modern society change is routine, innovation is valued, and the entrepreneur esteemed. D. C. McClelland saw the "need for achievement" as a key factor in distinguishing "modern" individuals.[4] For Daniel Lerner it was "projection" – the individual believing that others are like them, and "introjection" – an enlarged sense of oneself that includes new ideas and habits. Hagen's theory was also psychological – he said what motivates modern individuals were creativity and anxiety, the latter due to an uneasy feeling when they weren't being productive, a product of their mother's insatiable demands.

So what does modernization theory suggest nations should do to become more "developed"? Although the major thrust of modernization implied that nations should focus on changing their internal society by rationalizing it, many also believed that "developed" countries could play a pivotal role assisting and guiding the modernization of later developers. Rostow, for example, argued that investments and the transfer of technology by wealthier countries would allow "backward" societies to become modern at a faster rate than earlier developers. Lerner suggested that the media would act as an accelerator of change because it would expose people to abstract situations and force them to think beyond their own lives. Gino Germani thought that a process of diffusion and demonstration of innovations would accelerate the development in late modernizers.[5]

For these late modernizers the prescription was the same: borrow, import, imitate, and rationalize. To get investments flowing, to break the nation out of the cycle of poverty and lack of investment, nations should allow large firms from wealthy countries free access to their national markets, labor, and resources. Some of this production would be for local and some for export markets, but at least money would finally be flowing where before it was lacking entirely, or locked up in the overly cautious and fragmented hands of wealthy landed elites who had no experience in industry. This lack of concentrated industrial capital also suggested that borrowing money might be necessary to jump-start an economy.

The analyses this body of theorists produced carried weight in US foreign policy. W. W. Rostow, for example, served in both the Kennedy and Johnson administrations. The US Agency for International Development programs based policies on the concepts of modernization theory (e.g., the Alliance for Progress, the Peace Corps). And the ideas are still very much alive: many of the policy programs stemming from this era are still influential in policymaking circles today, including among planners in many poorer nations.

Economist Walt W. Rostow's (1916–) "The Stages of Economic Growth: A *Non-Communist Manifesto*" is based on a 1958 series of lectures for a nonprofessional audience. The theory he expresses in this selection posits that all nations pass through the same five stages of economic development: preconditions for takeoff, takeoff, the drive to maturity, the age of high mass consumption, and beyond consumption. Rostow's views were especially attractive to planners and countries who wished to increase productivity and achieve sustained economic growth. For Rostow, technology, savings, entrepreneurialism, and the correct political systems were all key motors in moving countries along this path. He also argues that countries that begin to achieve sustained economic growth later (i.e., poorer countries) may move through the stages much faster. Regardless of the influence Rostow's ideas had on policymakers in the United States and elsewhere, his ideas were severely critiqued by noneconomist academicians for making such gross generalizations about poorer countries and for only examining internal conditions as variables as obstacles to development. Despite theories of development moving drastically away from Rostow's early notions of comparative international development, his characterization of development as a relatively homogeneous experience still influences many policy recommendations for developing economies.

Harvard political scientist Samuel Huntington emphasized the disruptive nature of modernization. In the first section of the selection, "The Change to Change," Huntington outlines what he and others describe as "the Grand Process of Modernization." It occurs on many dimensions: it is an individual experience; it happens in many different arenas (social, educational, economic, and political); it is an interrelated process; and, although it is revolutionary in magnitude, it is a very slow process occurring in several stages. The second selection by Huntington, from his 1968 book *Political Order in Changing Societies*, suggests that a modern political system requires not only a high degree of political participation, but also a high level of political institutionalization and organization of politics. Huntington perceives these as the outcome of political modernization that goes well beyond parties, elections, and leaders. Political stability in a modernized political system is only the result of a multifaceted process of change that includes organization, education, a growing middle class, and economic development. The paradox of political modernization that Huntington identifies is that although the result is a stable political system that allows for universal participation, getting to that point means that in the process of doing so a society must pass through extremely disruptive and violent phases. He sees political systems that emerge in developing countries as symptoms of the disruption caused by rapid development. Again, while subsequent theorists have taken exception to the generalizations embedded in theories such as Huntington's, such assumptions still pervade many foreign policy and academic approaches to political modernization in the assumption that societies will ultimately "modernize" to liberal democracies.

NOTES

1   Karl Marx, *The Eighteenth Brumaire of Louis Napoleon*, 1852.
2   1971:288.
3   Bert F. Hoselitz, *Sociological Aspects of Economic Growth*, Chicago: The Free Press, 1964.
4   D. C. McClelland, *The Achieving Society*, New York: The Free Press, 1961.
5   Gino Germani, "Stages in Modernization in Latin America," *Studies in Comparative International Development* 5:8 (1969–70): 155–74.

1 Manifesto of the Communist Party (1848) and Alienated Labor (1844)

Karl Marx and Friedrich Engels

Manifesto of the Communist Party

Bourgeois and Proletarians

The history of all hitherto existing society is the history of class struggles.

Freeman and slave, patrician and plebeian, lord and serf, guild-master and journeyman, in a word, oppressor and oppressed, stood in constant opposition to one another, carried on an uninterrupted, now hidden, now open fight, a fight that each time ended, either in a revolutionary reconstitution of society at large, or in the common ruin of the contending classes.

In the earlier epochs of history, we find almost everywhere a complicated arrangement of society into various orders, a manifold gradation of social rank. In ancient Rome we have patricians, knights, plebeians, slaves; in the Middle Ages, feudal lords, vassals, guild-masters, journeymen, apprentices, serfs; in almost all of these classes, again, subordinate gradations.

The modern bourgeois society that has sprouted from the ruins of feudal society, has not done away with class antagonisms. It has but established new classes, new conditions of oppression, new forms of struggle in place of the old ones.

Our epoch, the epoch of the bourgeoisie, possesses, however, this distinctive feature; it has simplified the class antagonisms. Society as a whole is more and more splitting up into two great hostile camps, into two great classes directly facing each other: Bourgeoisie and Proletariat.

From the serfs of the Middle Ages sprang the chartered burghers of the earliest towns. From these burgesses the first elements of the bourgeoisie were developed.

The discovery of America, the rounding of the Cape, opened up fresh ground for the rising bourgeoisie. The East Indian and Chinese markets, the [colonization] of America, trade with the colonies, the increase in the means of exchange and in commodities generally, gave to commerce, to navigation, to industry, an impulse never before known, and thereby, to the revolutionary element in the tottering feudal society, a rapid development.

The feudal system of industry, under which industrial production was monopolized by close guilds, now no longer sufficed for the growing wants of the new markets. The manufacturing system took its place. The guild-masters were pushed on one side by the manufacturing middle class; division of labor between the different corporate guilds vanished in the face of division of labor in each single workshop.

Meantime the markets kept ever growing, the demand, ever rising. Even manufacture no longer sufficed. Thereupon, steam and machinery revolutionized industrial production. The place of manufacture was taken by the giant, Modern Industry, the place of the industrial middle class, by industrial millionaires, the leaders of whole industrial armies, the modern bourgeois.

Modern industry has established the world-market, for which the discovery of America paved the way. This market has given an immense development to commerce, to navigation, to communication by land. This development has, in its turn, reacted on the extension of industry; and in proportion as industry, commerce, navigation, railways extended, in the same proportion the bourgeoisie developed, increased its capital, and pushed into the background every class handed down from the Middle Ages.

We see, therefore, how the modern bourgeoisie is itself the product of a long course of development, of a series of revolutions in the modes of production and of exchange.

Each step in the development of the bourgeoisie was accompanied by a corresponding political advance of that class. An oppressed class under the sway of the feudal nobility, an armed and self-governing association in the mediaeval commune, here independent urban republic (as in Italy and Germany), there taxable "third estate" of the monarchy (as in France), afterwards, in the period of manufacture proper, serving either the semi-feudal or the absolute monarchy as a counterpoise against the nobility, and, in fact, cornerstone of the great monarchies in general, the bourgeoisie has at last, since the establishment of Modern Industry and of the world-market, conquered for itself, in the modern representative State, exclusive political sway. The executive of the modern State is but a committee for managing the common affairs of the whole bourgeoisie.

The bourgeoisie, historically, has played a most revolutionary part.

The bourgeoisie, wherever it has got the upper hand, has put an end to all feudal, patriarchal, idyllic relations. It has pitilessly torn asunder the motley feudal ties that bound man to his "natural superiors," and has left remaining no other nexus between man and man than naked self-interest, than callous "cash payment." It has drowned the most heavenly ecstasies of religious fervour, of chivalrous enthusiasm, of philistine sentimentalism, in the icy water of egotistical calculation. It has resolved personal worth into exchange value, and in place of the numberless indefensible chartered freedoms, has set up that single, unconscionable freedom – Free Trade. In one word, for exploitation, veiled by religious and political illusions, it has substituted naked, shameless, direct, brutal exploitation.

The bourgeoisie has stripped of its halo every occupation hitherto honoured and looked up to with reverent awe. It has converted the physician, the lawyer, the priest, the poet, the man of science, into its paid [wage-laborers].

The bourgeoisie has torn away from the family its sentimental veil, and has reduced the family relation to a mere money relation.

The bourgeoisie has disclosed how it came to pass that the brutal display of vigour in the Middle Ages, which Reactionists so much admire, found its fitting complement in the most slothful indolence. It has been the first to show what man's activity can bring about. It has accomplished wonders far surpassing Egyptian pyramids, Roman aqueducts, and Gothic cathedrals; it has conducted expeditions that put in the shade all former Exoduses of nations and crusades.

The bourgeoisie cannot exist without constantly revolutionizing the instruments of production, and thereby the relations of production, and with them the whole relations of society. Conservation of the old modes of production in unaltered form, was, on the contrary, the first condition of existence for all earlier industrial classes. Constant revolutionizing of production, uninterrupted disturbance of all social conditions, everlasting uncertainty and agitation distinguish the bourgeois epoch from all earlier ones. All fixed, fast-frozen relations, with their train of ancient and venerable prejudices and opinions, are swept away, all new-formed ones become antiquated before they can ossify. All that is solid melts into air, all that is holy is profaned, and man is at last compelled to face with sober senses, his real conditions of life, and his relations with his kind.

The need of a constantly expanding market for its products chases the bourgeoisie over the whole surface of the globe. It must nestle everywhere, settle everywhere, establish [connections] everywhere.

The bourgeoisie has through its exploitation of the world-market given a cosmopolitan character to production and consumption in every country. To the great chagrin of Reactionists, it has drawn from under the feet of industry the national ground on which it stood. All old-established national industries have been destroyed or are daily being destroyed. They are dislodged by new industries, whose introduction becomes a life and death question for all civilized nations, by industries that no longer work up indigenous raw material, but raw material drawn from the remotest zones; industries whose products are consumed, not only at home, but in every quarter of the globe. In place of the old wants, satisfied by the productions of the country, we find new wants, requiring for their satisfaction the products of distant lands and climes. In place of the old local and national seclusion and self-sufficiency, we have intercourse in every direction, universal interdependence of nations. And as in material, so also in intellectual production. The intellectual creations of individual nations become common property. National one-sidedness and narrowmindedness become more and more impossible, and from the numerous national and local literatures there arises a world-literature.

The bourgeoisie, by the rapid improvement of all instruments of production, by the immensely facilitated means of communication, draws all, even the most barbarian, nations into civilization. The cheap prices of its commodities are the heavy artillery with which it batters down all Chinese walls, with which it forces the barbarians' intensely obstinate hatred of foreigners to capitulate. It compels all nations, on pain of extinction, to adopt the bourgeois mode of production; it compels them to introduce what it calls civilization into their midst, i.e., to become bourgeois themselves. In a word, it creates a world after its own image.

The bourgeoisie has subjected the country to the rule of the towns. It has created enormous cities, has greatly increased the urban population as compared with the rural, and has thus rescued a considerable part of the population from the idiocy of rural life. Just as it has made the country dependent on the towns, so it has made barbarian and semi-barbarian countries dependent on the civilized ones, nations of peasants on nations of bourgeois, the East on the West.

The bourgeoisie keeps more and more doing away with the scattered state of the population, of the means of production, and of property. It has agglomerated population, centralized means of production, and has concentrated property in a few hands. The necessary consequence of this was political centralization. Independent, or but loosely connected provinces, with separate interests, laws, governments and systems of taxation, became lumped together in one nation, with one government, one code of laws, one national class-interest, one frontier and one customs-tariff.

The bourgeoisie, during its rule of scarce one hundred years, has created more massive and more colossal productive forces than have all preceding generations together. Subjection of Nature's forces to man, machinery, application of chemistry to industry and agriculture, steam-navigation, railways, electric telegraphs, clearing of whole continents for cultivation, canalization of rivers, whole populations conjured out of the ground – what earlier century had even a presentiment that such productive forces slumbered in the lap of social labor?

We see then: The means of production and of exchange on whose foundation the bourgeoisie built itself up, were generated in feudal society. At a certain stage in the development of these means of production and of exchange, the conditions under which feudal society produced and exchanged, the feudal organization of agriculture and manufacturing industry, in one word, the feudal relations of property became no longer compatible with the already developed productive forces; they became so many fetters. They had to burst asunder; they were burst asunder.

Into their places stepped free competition, accompanied by a social and political constitution adapted to it, and by the economical and political sway of the bourgeois class.

A similar movement is going on before our own eyes. Modern bourgeois society with its relations of production, of exchange and of property, a society that has conjured up such gigantic means of production and of exchange, is like the sorcerer, who is no longer able to control the powers of the nether world whom he has called up by his spells. For many a decade past the history of industry and commerce is but the history of the revolt of modern productive forces against modern conditions of production, against the property relations that are the conditions for the existence of the bourgeoisie and of its rule. It is enough to mention the commercial crises that by their periodical return put on its trial, each time more threateningly, the existence of the entire bourgeois society. In these crises a great part not only of the existing products, but also of the previously created productive forces, are periodically destroyed. In these crises there breaks out an epidemic that, in all earlier epochs, would have seemed an absurdity – the epidemic of overproduction. Society suddenly finds itself put back into a state of momentary barbarism; it appears as if a famine, a universal war of devastation had cut off the supply of every means of subsistence; industry and commerce seem to be destroyed; and why? Because there is too much civilization, too much means of subsistence, too much industry, too much commerce. The productive forces at the disposal of society no longer tend to further the development of the conditions of bourgeois property; on the contrary, they have become too powerful for these conditions, by which they are fettered, and so soon as they overcome these fetters, they bring disorder into the whole of bourgeois society, endanger the existence of bourgeois property. The conditions of bourgeois society are too narrow to comprise the wealth created by them. And how does the bourgeoisie get over these crises? On the one hand by enforced destruction of a mass of productive forces; on the other, by the conquest of new markets, and by the more thorough exploitation of the old ones. That is to say, by paving the way for more extensive and more destructive crises, and by diminishing the means whereby crises are prevented.

The weapons with which the bourgeoisie felled feudalism to the ground are now turned against the bourgeoisie itself.

But not only has the bourgeoisie forged the weapons that bring death to itself; it has also called into existence the men who are to wield those weapons – the modern working class – the proletarians.

In proportion as the bourgeoisie, i.e., capital, is developed, in the same proportion is the proletariat, the modern working class, developed, a class of laborers, who live only so long as they find work, and who find work only so long as their labor increases capital. These laborers, who must sell themselves piecemeal, are a commodity, like every other article of commerce, and are consequently exposed to all the vicissitudes of competition, to all the fluctuations of the market.

Owing to the extensive use of machinery and to division of labor, the work of the proletarians has lost all individual character, and, consequently, all charm for the workman. He becomes an appendage of the machine, and it is only the most simple, most monotonous, and most easily acquired knack that is required of him. Hence, the cost of production of a workman is restricted, almost entirely, to the means of subsistence that he requires for his maintenance, and for the propagation of his race. But the price of a commodity, and also of labor, is equal to its cost of production. In proportion, therefore, as the repulsiveness of the work increases, the wage decreases. Nay more, in proportion as the use of machinery and division of labor increases, in the same proportion the burden of toil also increases, whether by prolongation of the working hours, by increase of the work enacted a given time, or by increased speed of the machinery, etc.

Modern industry has converted the little workshop of the patriarchal master into the great factory of the industrial capitalist. Masses of laborers, crowded into the factory, are organized like soldiers. As privates of the industrial army they are placed under the command of a perfect hierarchy of officers and sergeants. Not only are they the slaves of the bourgeois class, and of the bourgeois State, they are daily and hourly enslaved by the machine, by the over-looker, and, above all, by the individual bourgeois manufacturer himself. The more openly this despotism proclaims gain to be its end aim, the more petty, the more hateful and the more embittering it is.

The less the skill and exertion or strength implied in manual labor, in other words, the more modern industry becomes developed, the more is the labor of men superseded by that of women. Differences of age and sex have no longer any distinctive social validity for the working class. All are instruments of labor, more or less expensive to use, according to their age and sex.

No sooner is the exploitation of the laborer by the manufacturer, so far, at an end, that he receives his wages in cash, than he is set upon by the other portions of the bourgeoisie, the landlord, the shopkeeper, the pawnbroker, etc.

The lower strata of the middle class – the small tradespeople, shopkeepers, and retired tradesmen generally, the handicraftsmen and peasants – all these sink gradually into the proletariat, partly because their diminutive capital does not suffice for the scale on which Modern Industry is carried on, and is swamped in the competition with the large capitalists, partly because their specialised skill is rendered worthless by new methods of production. Thus the proletariat is recruited from all classes of the population.

The proletariat goes through various stages of development. With its birth begins its struggle with the bourgeoisie. At first the contest is carried on by individual laborers, then by the work-people of a factory, then by the operatives of one trade, in one locality, against the individual bourgeois who directly exploits them. They direct their attacks not against the bourgeois conditions of production, but against the instruments of production themselves; they destroy imported wares that compete with their labor, they set factories ablaze, they seek to restore by force the vanished status of the workman of the Middle Ages.

At this stage the laborers still form an incoherent mass scattered over the whole country, and broken up by their mutual competition. If anywhere they unite to form more compact bodies, this is not yet the consequence of their own active union, but of the union of the bourgeoisie, which class, in order to attain its own political ends, is compelled to set the whole proletariat in motion, and is moreover yet, for a time, able to do so. At this stage, therefore, the proletarians do not fight their enemies, but the enemies of their enemies, the remnants of absolute monarchy, the landowners, the non-industrial bourgeois, the petty bourgeoisie. Thus the whole historical movement is concentrated in the hands of the bourgeoisie; every victory so obtained is a victory for the bourgeoisie.

But with the development of industry the proletariat not only increases in number; it becomes concentrated in greater masses, its strength grows, and it feels that strength more. The various interests and conditions of life with the ranks of the proletariat are more and more equalized, in proportion as machinery obliterates all distinctions of labor, and nearly everywhere reduces wages to the same low level. The growing competition among the bourgeois, and the resulting commercial crises, make the wages of the workers ever more fluctuating. The unceasing improvement of machinery, ever more rapidly developing, makes their livelihood more and more precarious; the collisions between individual workmen and individual bourgeois take more and more the character of collisions between two classes. Thereupon the workers begin to form combinations (Trades' Unions) against the bourgeois; they club together in order to keep up the rate of wages; they found permanent associations in order to make provision beforehand for these occasional revolts. Here and there the contest breaks out into riots.

Now and then the workers are victorious, but only for a time. The real fruit of their battles lies, not in the immediate result, but in the ever expanding union of the workers. This union is helped on by the improved means of communication that are created by modern industry, and that place the workers of different localities in contact with one another. It was just this contact that was needed to centralise the numerous local struggles, all of the same character, into one national struggle between classes. But every class struggle is a political struggle. And that union, to attain which the burghers of the Middle Ages, with their miserable highways, required centuries, the modern proletarians, thanks to railways, achieve in a few years.

This organization of the proletarians into a class, and consequently into a political party, is continually being upset again by the competition between the workers themselves. But it ever rises up again, stronger, firmer, mightier. It compels legislative recognition of particular interests of the workers, by taking advantage of the divisions among the bourgeoisie itself. Thus the ten-hours'-bill in England was carried.

Altogether collisions between the classes of the old society further, in many ways, the course of development of the proletariat. The bourgeoisie finds itself involved in a constant battle. At first with the aristocracy; later on, with those portions of the bourgeoisie itself, whose interests have become antagonistic to the progress of industry; at all times, with the bourgeoisie of foreign countries. In all these battles it sees itself compelled to appeal to the proletariat, to ask for its help, and thus, to drag it into the political arena. The bourgeoisie itself, therefore, supplies the proletariat with its own elements of political and general education, in other words, it furnishes the proletariat with weapons for fighting the bourgeoisie.

Further, as we have already seen, entire sections of the ruling classes are, by the advance of industry, precipitated into the proletariat, or are at least threatened in their conditions of existence. These also supply the proletariat with fresh elements of enlightenment and progress.

Finally, in times when the class-struggle nears the decisive hour, the process of dissolution going on within the ruling class, in fact with the whole range of old society, assumes such a violent, glaring character, that a small section of the ruling class cuts itself adrift, and joins the revolutionary class, the class that holds the future in its hands. Just as, therefore, at an earlier period, a section of the nobility went over to the bourgeoisie, so now a portion of the bourgeoisie goes over to the proletariat, and in particular, a portion of the bourgeois ideologists, who have raised themselves to the level of comprehending theoretically the historical movements as a whole.

Of all the classes that stand face to face with the bourgeoisie today, the proletariat alone is a really revolutionary class. The other classes decay and finally disappear in the face of modern industry; the proletariat is its special and essential product.

The lower-middle class, the small manufacturer, the shopkeeper, the artisan, the peasant, all these fight against the bourgeoisie, to save from extinction their existence as fractions of the middle class. They are therefore not revolutionary, but conservative. Nay more, they are reactionary, for they try to roll back the wheel of history. If by chance they are revolutionary, they are so, only in view of their impending transfer into the proletariat, they thus defend not their present, but their future interests, they desert their own standpoint to place themselves at that of the proletariat.

The "dangerous class," the social scum, that passively rotting mass thrown off by the lowest layers of old society, may, here and there, be swept into the movement by a proletarian revolution; its conditions of life, however, prepare it far more for the part of a bribed tool of reactionary intrigue.

In the conditions of the proletariat, those of old society at large are already virtually swamped. The proletarian is without property; his relation to his wife and children has no longer anything in common with the bourgeois family-relations; modern industrial labor, modern subjection to capital, the same in England as in France, in America as in Germany, has stripped him of every trace of national character. Law, morality, religion, are to him so many bourgeois prejudices, behind which lurk in ambush just as many bourgeois interests.

All the preceding classes that got the upper hand, sought to fortify their already acquired status by subjecting society at large to their conditions of appropriation. The proletarians cannot become masters of the productive forces of society, except by abolishing their own previous mode of appropriation, and thereby also every other previous mode of appropriation. They have nothing of their own to secure and to fortify; their mission is to destroy all previous securities for, and insurances of, individual property.

All previous historical movements were movements of minorities, or in the interest of minorities. The proletarian movement is the self-conscious, independent movement of the immense majority, in the interest of the immense majority. The proletariat, the lowest stratum of our present society, cannot stir, cannot raise itself up, without the whole super-incumbent strata of official society being sprung into the air.

Though not in substance, yet in form, the struggle of the proletariat with the bourgeoisie is at first a national struggle. The proletariat of each country must, of course, first of all settle matters with its own bourgeoisie.

In depicting the most general phases of the development of the proletariat, we traced the more or less veiled civil war, raging within existing society, up to the point where that war breaks out into open revolution, and where the violent overthrow of the bourgeoisie, lays the foundation for the sway of the proletariat.

Hitherto, every form of society has been based, as we have already seen, on the antagonism of oppressing and oppressed classes. But in order to oppress a class, certain conditions must be assured to it under which it can, at least, continue its slavish existence. The serf, in the period of serfdom, raised himself to membership in the commune, just as the petty bourgeois, under the yoke of feudal absolutism, managed to develop into a bourgeois. The modern laborer, on the contrary, instead of rising with the progress of industry, sinks deeper and deeper below the conditions of existence of his own class. He becomes a pauper, and pauperism develops more rapidly than population and wealth. And here it becomes evident, that the bourgeoisie is unfit any longer to be the ruling class in society, and to impose its conditions of existence upon society as an overriding law. It is unfit to rule, because it is incompetent to assure an existence to its slave within his slavery, because it cannot help letting him sink into such a state, that it has to feed him, instead of being fed by him. Society can no longer live under this bourgeoisie, in other words, its existence is no longer compatible with society.

The essential condition for the existence, and for the sway of the bourgeois class, is the formation and augmentation of capital; the condition for capital is wage-labor. Wage-labor rests exclusively on competition between the laborers. The advance of industry, whose involuntary promoter is the bourgeoisie, replaces the isolation of the laborers, due to competition, by their involuntary combination, due to association. The development of Modern Industry, therefore, cuts from under its feet the very foundation on which the bourgeoisie produces and appropriates products. What the bourgeoisie therefore produces, above all, are its own grave-diggers. Its fall and the victory of the proletariat are equally inevitable.

Alienated Labor

We shall begin from a *contemporary* economic fact. The worker becomes poorer the more wealth he produces and the more his production increases in power and extent. The worker becomes an ever cheaper commodity the more goods he creates. The *devaluation* of the human world increases in direct relation with the *increase in value* of the world of things. Labor does not only create goods; it also produces itself and the worker as a *commodity*, and indeed in the same proportion as it produces goods.

This fact simply implies that the object produced by labor, its product, now stands opposed to it as an *alien being*, as a *power independent* of the producer. The product of labor is labor which has been embodied in an object and turned into a physical thing; this product is an *objectification* of labor. The performance of work is at the same time its objectification. The performance of work appears in the sphere of political economy as a *vitiation* [debasement] of the worker, objectification as a *loss* and as *servitude to the object*, and appropriation as *alienation*.

So much does the performance of work appear as vitiation that the worker is vitiated to the point of starvation. So much does objectification appear as loss of the object that the worker is deprived of the most essential things not only of life but also of work. Labor itself becomes an object which he can acquire only by the greatest effort and with unpredictable interruptions. So much does the appropriation of the object appear as alienation that the more objects the worker produces the fewer he can possess and the more he falls under the domination of his product, of capital.

All these consequences follow from the fact that the worker is related to the *product of his labor* as to an *alien* object. For it is clear on this presupposition that the more the worker expends himself in work the more powerful becomes the world of objects which he creates in face of himself, the poorer he becomes in his inner life, and the less he belongs to himself. It is just the same as in religion. The more of himself man attributes to God the less he has left in himself. The worker puts his life into the object, and his life then belongs no longer to himself but to the object. The greater his activity, therefore, the less he possesses. What is embodied in the product of his labor is no longer his own. The greater this product is, therefore, the more he is diminished. The *alienation* of the worker in his product means not only that his labor becomes an object, assumes an *external* existence, but that it exists independently, *outside himself*, and alien to him, and that it stands opposed to him as an autonomous power. The life which he has given to the object sets itself against him as an alien and hostile force . . .

(The alienation of the worker in his object is expressed as follows in the laws of political economy: The more the worker produces the less he has to consume; the more value he creates the more worthless he becomes; the more refined his product the more crude and misshapen the worker; the more civilized the product the more barbarous the worker; the more powerful the work the more feeble the worker; the more the work manifests intelligence the more the worker declines in intelligence and becomes a slave of nature.)

Political economy conceals the alienation in the nature of labor insofar as it does not examine the direct relationship between the worker (work) and production. Labor certainly produces marvels for the rich but it produces privation for the worker. It produces palaces, but hovels for the worker. It produces beauty, but deformity for the worker. It replaces labor by machinery, but it casts some of the workers back into a barbarous kind of work and turns the others into machines. It produces intelligence, but also stupidity and cretinism for the workers.

The direct relationship of labor to its products is the relationship of the worker to the objects of his production. The relationship of property owners to the objects of production and to production itself is merely a *consequence* of this first relationship and confirms it.

2   The Protestant Ethic and the Spirit of Capitalism (1905)

Max Weber

In order to understand the connection between the fundamental religious ideas of ascetic Protestantism and its maxims for everyday economic conduct, it is necessary to examine with especial care such writings as have evidently been derived from ministerial practice. For in a time in which the beyond meant everything, when the social position of the Christian depended upon his admission to the communion, the clergyman, through his ministry, Church discipline, and preaching, exercised an influence . . . which we modern men are entirely unable to picture. In such a time the religious forces which express themselves through such channels are the decisive influences in the formation of national character.

For [present] purposes we can treat ascetic Protestantism as a single whole. But since that side of English Puritanism which was derived from Calvinism gives the most consistent religious basis for the idea of the calling, we shall place one of its representatives at the centre of the discussion. Richard Baxter stands out above many other writers on Puritan ethics.

[. . .]

Now, in glancing at Baxter's *Saints' Everlasting Rest*, or his *Christian Directory*, or similar works of others, one is struck at first glance by the emphasis placed, in the discussion of wealth and its acquisition, on the ebionitic elements of the New Testament. Wealth as such is a great danger; its temptations never end, and its pursuit is not only senseless as compared with the dominating importance of the Kingdom of God, but it is morally suspect. Here asceticism seems to have turned much more sharply against the acquisition of earthly goods than it did in Calvin, who saw no hindrance to the effectiveness of the clergy in their wealth, but rather a thoroughly desirable enhancement of their prestige. Hence he permitted them to employ their means profitably. Examples of the condemnation of the pursuit of money and goods may be gathered without end from Puritan writings, and may be contrasted with the late mediæval ethical literature, which was much more open-minded on this point.

Moreover, these doubts were meant with perfect seriousness; only it is necessary to examine them somewhat more closely in order to understand their true ethical significance and implications. The real moral objection is to relaxation in the security of possession, the enjoyment of wealth with the consequence of idleness and the temptations of the flesh, above all of distraction from the pursuit of a righteous life. In fact, it is only because possession involves this danger of relaxation that it is objectionable at all. For the saints' everlasting rest is in the next world; on earth man must, to be certain of his state of grace, "do the works of him who sent him, as long as it is yet day". Not leisure and enjoyment, but only activity serves to increase the glory of God, according to the definite manifestations of His will.

Waste of time is thus the first and in principle the deadliest of sins. The span of human life is infinitely short and precious to make sure of one's own election. Loss of time through sociability, idle talk, luxury, even more sleep than is necessary for health, six to at most eight hours, is worthy of absolute moral condemnation. It does not yet hold, with Franklin, that time is money, but the proposition is true in a certain spiritual sense. It is infinitely valuable because every hour lost is lost to labour for the glory of God. Thus inactive contemplation is also valueless, or even directly reprehensible if it is at the expense of one's daily work. For it is less pleasing to God than the active performance of His will in a calling. . . .

Accordingly, Baxter's principal work is dominated by the continually repeated, often almost passionate preaching of hard, continuous bodily or mental labour. It is due to a combination of two different motives. Labour is, on the one hand, an approved ascetic technique, as it always has been in the Western Church, in sharp contrast not only to the Orient but to almost all monastic rules the world over. It is in particular the specific defence against all those temptations which Puritanism united under the name of the unclean life, whose rôle for it was by no means small. The sexual asceticism of Puritanism differs only in degree, not in fundamental principle, from that of monasticism; and on account of the Puritan conception of marriage, its practical influence is more far-reaching than that of the latter. For sexual intercourse is permitted, even within marriage, only as the means willed by God for the increase of His glory according to the commandment, "Be fruitful and multiply." Along with a moderate vegetable diet and cold baths, the same prescription is given for all sexual temptations as is used against religious doubts and a sense of moral unworthiness: "Work hard in your calling." But the most important thing was that even beyond that labour came to be considered in itself the end of life, ordained as such by God. St Paul's "He who will not work shall not eat" holds unconditionally for everyone. Unwillingness to work is symptomatic of the lack of grace.

Here the difference from the mediæval view-point becomes quite evident. Thomas Aquinas also gave an interpretation of that statement of St Paul. But for him labour is only necessary *naturali ratione* for the maintenance of individual and community. Where this end is achieved, the precept ceases to have any meaning. Moreover, it holds only for the race, not for every individual. It does not apply to anyone who can live without labour on his possessions, and of course contemplation, as a spiritual form of action in the Kingdom of God, takes precedence over the commandment in its literal sense. Moreover, for the popular theology of the time, the highest form of monastic productivity lay in the increase of the *Thesaurus ecclesiæ* through prayer and chant.

Not only do these exceptions to the duty to labour naturally no longer hold for Baxter, but he holds most emphatically that wealth does not exempt anyone from the unconditional command. Even the wealthy shall not eat without working, for even though they do not need to labour to support their own needs, there is God's commandment which they, like the poor, must obey. For everyone without exception God's Providence has prepared a calling, which he should profess and in which he should labour. And this calling is not, as it was for the Lutheran, a fate to which he must submit and which he must make the best of, but God's commandment to the individual to work for the divine glory. This seemingly subtle difference had far-reaching psychological consequences, and became connected with a further development of the providential interpretation of the economic order which had begun in scholasticism.

The phenomenon of the division of labour and occupations in society had, among others, been interpreted by Thomas Aquinas, to whom we may most conveniently refer, as a direct consequence of the divine scheme of things. But the places assigned to each man in this cosmos follow *ex causis naturalibus* and are fortuitous (contingent in the Scholastic terminology). The differentiation of men into the classes and occupations established through historical development became for Luther, as we have seen, a direct result of the divine will. The perseverance of the individual in the place and within the limits which God had assigned to him was a religious duty. . . .

But in the Puritan view, the providential character of the play of private economic interests takes on a somewhat different emphasis. True to the Puritan tendency to pragmatic interpretations, the providential purpose of the division of labour is to be known by its fruits. On this point Baxter expresses himself in terms which more than once directly recall Adam Smith's well-known apotheosis of the division of labour. The specialization of occupations leads, since it makes the development of skill possible, to a quantitative and qualitative improvement in production, and thus serves the common good, which is identical with the good of the greatest possible number. So far, the motivation is purely utilitarian, and is closely related to the customary view-point of much of the secular literature of the time.

But the characteristic Puritan element appears when Baxter sets at the head of his discussion the statement that "outside of a well-marked calling the accomplishments of a man are only casual and irregular, and he spends more time in idleness than at work", and when he concludes it as follows: "and he [the specialized worker] will carry out his work in order while another remains in constant confusion, and his business knows neither time nor place . . . therefore is a certain calling the best for everyone". Irregular work, which the ordinary labourer is often forced to accept, is often unavoidable, but always an unwelcome state of transition. A man without a calling thus lacks the systematic, methodical character which is, as we have seen, demanded by worldly asceticism.

The Quaker ethic also holds that a man's life in his calling is an exercise in ascetic virtue, a proof of his state of grace through his conscientiousness, which is expressed in the care and method with which he pursues his calling. What God demands is not labour in itself, but rational labour in a calling. In the Puritan concept of the calling the emphasis is always placed on this methodical character of worldly asceticism, not, as with Luther, on the acceptance of the lot which God has irretrievably assigned to man.

Hence the question whether anyone may combine several callings is answered in the affirmative, if it is useful for the common good or one's own, and not injurious to anyone, and if it does not lead to unfaithfulness in one of the callings. Even a change of calling is by no means regarded as objectionable, if it is not thoughtless and is made for the purpose of pursuing a calling more pleasing to God, which means, on general principles, one more useful.

It is true that the usefulness of a calling, and thus its favour in the sight of God, is measured primarily in moral terms, and thus in terms of the importance of the goods produced in it for the community. But a further, and, above all, in practice the most important, criterion is found in private profitableness. For if that God, whose hand the Puritan sees in all the occurrences of life, shows one of His elect a chance of profit, he must do it with a purpose. Hence the faithful Christian must follow the call by taking advantage of the opportunity. "If God show you a way in which you may lawfully get more than in another way (without wrong to your soul or to any other), if you refuse this, and choose the less gainful way, you cross one of the ends of your calling, and you refuse to be God's steward, and to accept His gifts and use them for Him when He requireth it: you may labour to be rich for God, though not for the flesh and sin."

Wealth is thus bad ethically only in so far as it is a temptation to idleness and sinful enjoyment of life, and its acquisition is bad only when it is with the purpose of later living merrily and without care. But as a performance of duty in a calling it is not only morally permissible, but actually enjoined. The parable of the servant who was rejected because he did not increase the talent which was entrusted to him seemed to say so directly. To wish to be poor was, it was often argued, the same as wishing to be unhealthy; it is objectionable as a glorification of works and derogatory to the glory of God. Especially begging, on the part of one able to work, is not only the sin of slothfulness, but a violation of the duty of brotherly love according to the Apostle's own word.

The emphasis on the ascetic importance of a fixed calling provided an ethical justification of the modern specialized division of labour. In a similar way the providential interpretation of profit-making justified the activities of the business man. The superior indulgence of the *seigneur* and the parvenu ostentation of the *nouveau riche* are equally detestable to asceticism. But, on the other hand, it has the highest ethical appreciation of the sober, middle-class, self-made man. "God blesseth His trade" is a stock remark about those good men who had successfully followed the divine hints. The whole power of the God of the Old Testament, who rewards His people for their obedience in this life, necessarily exercised a similar influence on the Puritan who, following Baxter's advice, compared his own state of grace with that of the heroes of the Bible, and in the process interpreted the statements of the Scriptures as the articles of a book of statutes.

Of course, the words of the Old Testament were not entirely without ambiguity. We have seen that Luther first used the concept of the calling in the secular sense in translating a passage from Jesus Sirach. But the book of Jesus Sirach belongs, with the whole atmosphere expressed in it, to those parts of the broadened Old Testament with a distinctly traditionalistic tendency, in spite of Hellenistic influences. It is characteristic that down to the present day this book seems to enjoy a special favour among Lutheran German peasants, just as the Lutheran influence in large sections of German Pietism has been expressed by a preference for Jesus Sirach.

The Puritans repudiated the Apocrypha as not inspired, consistently with their sharp distinction between things divine and things of the flesh. But among the canonical books that of Job had all the more influence. On the one hand it contained a grand conception of the absolute sovereign majesty of God, beyond all human comprehension, which was closely related to that of Calvinism. With that, on the other hand, it combined the certainty which, though incidental for Calvin, came to be of great importance for Puritanism, that

God would bless His own in this life – in the book of Job only – and also in the material sense. The Oriental quietism, which appears in several of the finest verses of the Psalms and in the Proverbs, was interpreted away, just as Baxter did with the traditionalistic tinge of the passage in the 1st Epistle to the Corinthians, so important for the idea of the calling.

But all the more emphasis was placed on those parts of the Old Testament which praise formal legality as a sign of conduct pleasing to God. They held the theory that the Mosaic Law had only lost its validity through Christ in so far as it contained ceremonial or purely historical precepts applying only to the Jewish people, but that otherwise it had always been valid as an expression of the natural law, and must hence be retained. This made it possible, on the one hand, to eliminate elements which could not be reconciled with modern life. But still, through its numerous related features, Old Testament morality was able to give a powerful impetus to that spirit of self-righteous and sober legality which was so characteristic of the worldly asceticism of this form of Protestantism.

Thus when authors, as was the case with several contemporaries as well as later writers, characterize the basic ethical tendency of Puritanism, especially in England, as English Hebraism they are, correctly understood, not wrong. It is necessary, however, not to think of Palestinian Judaism at the time of the writing of the Scriptures, but of Judaism as it became under the influence of many centuries of formalistic, legalistic, and Talmudic education. Even then one must be very careful in drawing parallels. The general tendency of the older Judaism toward a naïve acceptance of life as such was far removed from the special characteristics of Puritanism. It was, however, just as far – and this ought not to be overlooked – from the economic ethics of mediæval and modern Judaism, in the traits which determined the positions of both in the development of the capitalistic ethos. The Jews stood on the side of the politically and speculatively oriented adventurous capitalism; their ethos was, in a word, that of pariah-capitalism. But Puritanism carried the ethos of the rational organization of capital and labour. It took over from the Jewish ethic only what was adapted to this purpose.

To analyse the effects on the character of peoples of the penetration of life with Old Testament norms – a tempting task which, however, has not yet satisfactorily been done even for Judaism – would be impossible within the limits of this sketch. In addition to the relationships already pointed out, it is important for the general inner attitude of the Puritans, above all, that the belief that they were God's chosen people saw in them a great renaissance. Even the kindly Baxter thanked God that he was born in England, and thus in the true Church, and nowhere else. This thankfulness for one's own perfection by the grace of God penetrated the attitude toward life of the Puritan middle class, and played its part in developing that formalistic, hard, correct character which was peculiar to the men of that heroic age of capitalism.

Let us now try to clarify the points in which the Puritan idea of the calling and the premium it placed upon ascetic conduct was bound directly to influence the development of a capitalistic way of life. As we have seen, this asceticism turned with all its force against one thing: the spontaneous enjoyment of life and all it had to offer. This is perhaps most characteristically brought out in the struggle over the *Book of Sports* which James I and Charles I made into law expressly as a means of counteracting Puritanism, and which the latter ordered to be read from all the pulpits. The fanatical opposition of the Puritans to the ordinances of the King, permitting certain popular amusements on Sunday outside of Church hours by law, was not only explained by the disturbance of the Sabbath rest, but also by resentment against the intentional diversion from the ordered life of the saint, which it caused. And, on his side, the King's threats of severe punishment for every attack on the legality of those sports were motivated by his purpose of breaking the anti-authoritarian ascetic tendency of Puritanism, which was so dangerous to the State. The feudal and monarchical forces protected the pleasure seekers against the rising middle-class morality and the anti-authoritarian ascetic conventicles, just as to-day capitalistic society tends to protect those willing to work against the class morality of the proletariat and the anti-authoritarian trade union.

As against this the Puritans upheld their decisive characteristic, the principle of ascetic conduct. For otherwise the Puritan aversion to sport, even for the Quakers, was by no means simply one of principle. Sport was accepted if it served a rational purpose, that of recreation necessary for physical efficiency. But as a means for the spontaneous expression of undisciplined impulses, it was under suspicion; and in so far as it became purely a means of enjoyment, or awakened pride, raw instincts or the irrational gambling instinct, it was of course strictly condemned. Impulsive enjoyment of life, which leads away both from work in a calling and from religion, was as such the enemy of rational asceticism, whether in the form of seigneurial sports, or the enjoyment of the dance-hall or the public-house of the common man.

Its attitude was thus suspicious and often hostile to the aspects of culture without any immediate religious value. It is not, however, true that the ideals of Puritanism implied a solemn, narrow-minded contempt of culture. Quite the contrary is the case at least for science, with the exception of the hatred of Scholasticism. Moreover, the great men of the Puritan movement were thoroughly steeped in the culture of the Renaissance. . . .

But the situation is quite different when one looks at non-scientific literature, and especially the fine arts. Here asceticism descended like a frost on the life of "Merrie old England." And not only worldly merriment felt its effect. The Puritan's ferocious hatred of everything which smacked of superstition, of all survivals of magical or sacramental salvation, applied to the Christmas festivities and the May Pole and all spontaneous religious art. . . .

The theatre was obnoxious to the Puritans, and with the strict exclusion of the erotic and of nudity from the realm of toleration, a radical view of either literature or art could not exist. The conceptions of idle talk, of superfluities, and of vain ostentation, all designations of an irrational attitude without objective purpose, thus not ascetic, and especially not serving the glory of God, but of man, were always at hand to serve in deciding in favour of sober utility as against any artistic tendencies. This was especially true in the case of decoration of the person, for instance clothing. That powerful tendency toward uniformity of life, which to-day so immensely aids the capitalistic interest in the standardization of production, had its ideal foundations in the repudiation of all idolatry of the flesh.

[. . .]

Although we cannot here enter upon a discussion of the influence of Puritanism in all these directions, we should call attention to the fact that the toleration of pleasure in cultural goods, which contributed to purely æsthetic or athletic enjoyment, certainly always ran up against one characteristic limitation: they must not cost anything. Man is only a trustee of the goods which have come to him through God's grace. He must, like the servant in the parable, give an account of every penny entrusted to him, and it is at least hazardous to spend any of it for a purpose which does not serve the glory of God but only one's own enjoyment. What person, who keeps his eyes open, has not met representatives of this view-point even in the present? The idea of a man's duty to his possessions, to which he subordinates himself as an obedient steward, or even as an acquisitive machine, bears with chilling weight on his life. The greater the possessions the heavier, if the ascetic attitude toward life stands the test, the feeling of responsibility for them, for holding them undiminished for the glory of God and increasing them by restless effort. The origin of this type of life also extends in certain roots, like so many aspects of the spirit of capitalism, back into the Middle Ages. But it was in the ethic of ascetic Protestantism that it first found a consistent ethical foundation. Its significance for the development of capitalism is obvious.

This worldly Protestant asceticism, as we may recapitulate up to this point, acted powerfully against the spontaneous enjoyment of possessions; it restricted consumption, especially of luxuries. On the other hand, it had the psychological effect of freeing the acquisition of goods from the inhibitions of traditionalistic ethics. It broke the bonds of the impulse of acquisition in that it not only legalized it, but (in the sense discussed) looked upon it as directly willed by God. The campaign against the temptations of the flesh, and the dependence on external things, was, as besides the Puritans the great Quaker apologist Barclay expressly says, not a struggle against the rational acquisition, but against the irrational use of wealth.

But this irrational use was exemplified in the outward forms of luxury which their code condemned as idolatry of the flesh, however natural they had appeared to the feudal mind. On the other hand, they approved the rational and utilitarian uses of wealth which were willed by God for the needs of the individual and the community. They did not wish to impose mortification on the man of wealth, but the use of his means for necessary and practical things. The idea of comfort characteristically limits the extent of ethically permissible expenditures. It is naturally no accident that the development of a manner of living consistent with that idea may be observed earliest and most clearly among the most consistent representatives of this whole attitude toward life. Over against the glitter and ostentation of feudal magnificence which, resting on an unsound economic basis, prefers a sordid elegance to a sober simplicity, they set the clean and solid comfort of the middle-class home as an ideal.

On the side of the production of private wealth, asceticism condemned both dishonesty and impulsive avarice. What was condemned as covetousness, Mammonism, etc., was the pursuit of riches for their own sake. For wealth in itself was a temptation. But here asceticism was the power "which ever seeks the good but ever creates evil"; what was evil in its sense was possession and its temptations, For, in conformity with the Old Testament and in analogy to the ethical valuation of good works, asceticism looked upon the pursuit of wealth as an end in itself as highly reprehensible; but the attainment of it as a fruit of labour in a calling was a sign of God's blessing. And even more important: the religious valuation of restless, continuous, systematic work in a worldly calling, as the highest means to asceticism, and at the same time the surest and most evident proof of rebirth and genuine faith, must have been the most powerful conceivable lever for the expansion of that attitude toward life which we have here called the spirit of capitalism.

When the limitation of consumption is combined with this release of acquisitive activity, the inevitable practical result is obvious: accumulation of capital through ascetic compulsion to save. The restraints which were imposed upon the consumption of wealth naturally served to increase it by making possible the productive investment of capital. How strong this influence was is not, unfortunately, susceptible of exact statistical demonstration. In New England the connection is so evident that it did not escape the eye of so discerning a historian as Doyle. But also in Holland, which was really only dominated by strict Calvinism for seven years, the greater simplicity of life in the more seriously religious circles, in combination with great wealth, led to an excessive propensity to accumulation.

That, furthermore, the tendency which has existed everywhere and at all times, being quite strong in Germany to-day, for middle-class fortunes to be absorbed into the nobility, was necessarily checked by the Puritan antipathy to the feudal way of life, is evident. English Mercantilist writers of the seventeenth century attributed the superiority of Dutch capital to English to the circumstance that newly acquired wealth there did not regularly seek investment in land. Also, since it is not simply a question of the purchase of land, it did not there seek to transfer itself to feudal habits of life, and thereby to remove itself from the possibility of capitalistic investment. The high esteem for agriculture as a peculiarly important branch of activity, also especially consistent with piety, which the Puritans shared, applied (for instance in Baxter) not to the landlord, but to the yeoman and farmer, in the eighteenth century not to the squire, but the rational cultivator. Through the whole of English society in the time since the seventeenth century goes the conflict between the squirearchy, the representatives of "merrie old England", and the Puritan circles of widely varying social influence. Both elements, that of an unspoiled naïve joy of life, and of a strictly regulated, reserved self-control, and conventional ethical conduct are even to-day combined to form the English national character. Similarly, the early history of the North American Colonies is dominated by the sharp contrast of the adventurers, who wanted to set up plantations with the labour of indentured servants, and live as feudal lords, and the specifically middle-class outlook of the Puritans.

As far as the influence of the Puritan outlook extended, under all circumstances – and this is, of course, much more important than the mere encouragement of capital accumulation – it favoured the development of a rational bourgeois economic life; it was the most important, and above all the only consistent influence in the development of that life. It stood at the cradle of the modern economic man.

To be sure, these Puritanical ideals tended to give way under excessive pressure from the temptations of wealth, as the Puritans themselves knew very well. With great regularity we find the most genuine adherents of Puritanism among the classes which were rising from a lowly status, the small bourgeois and farmers, while the *beati possidentes*, even among Quakers, are often found tending to repudiate the old ideals. It was the same fate which again and again befell the predecessor of this worldly asceticism, the monastic asceticism of the Middle Ages. In the latter case, when rational economic activity had worked out its full effects by strict regulation of conduct and limitation of consumption, the wealth accumulated either succumbed directly to the nobility, as in the time before the Reformation, or monastic discipline threatened to break down, and one of the numerous reformations became necessary.

In fact the whole history of monasticism is in a certain sense the history of a continual struggle with the problem of the secularizing influence of wealth. The same is true on a grand scale of the worldly asceticism of Puritanism. The great revival of Methodism, which preceded the expansion of English industry toward the end of the eighteenth century, may well be compared with such a monastic reform. We may hence quote here a passage from John Wesley himself which might well serve as a motto for everything which has been said above. . . .

"I fear, wherever riches have increased, the essence of religion has decreased in the same proportion. Therefore I do not see how it is possible, in the nature of things, for any revival of true religion to continue long. For religion must necessarily produce both industry and frugality, and these cannot but produce riches. But as riches increase, so will pride, anger, and love of the world in all its branches. How then is it possible that Methodism, that is, a religion of the heart, though it flourishes now as a green bay tree, should continue in this state? For the Methodists in every place grow diligent and frugal; consequently they increase in goods. Hense they proportionately increase in pride, in anger, in the desire of the flesh, the desire of the eyes, and the pride of life. So, although the form of religion remains, the spirit is swiftly vanishing away. Is there no way to prevent this – this continual decay of pure religion? We ought not to prevent people from being diligent and frugal; *we must exhort all Christians to gain all they can, and to save all they can; that is, in effect, to grow rich.*"

[. . .]

As Wesley here says, the full economic effect of those great religious movements, whose significance for economic development lay above all in their ascetic educative influence, generally came only after the peak of the purely religious enthusiasm was past. Then the intensity of the search for the Kingdom of God commenced gradually to pass over into sober economic virtue; the religious roots died out slowly, giving way to utilitarian worldliness.

[. . .]

A specifically bourgeois economic ethic had grown up. With the consciousness of standing in the fullness of God's grace and being visibly blessed by Him, the bourgeois business man, as long as he remained within the bounds of formal correctness, as long as his moral conduct was spotless and the use to which he put his wealth was not objectionable, could follow his pecuniary interests as he would and feel that he was fulfilling a duty in doing so. The power of religious asceticism provided him in addition with sober, conscientious, and unusually industrious workmen, who clung to their work as to a life purpose willed by God.

Finally, it gave him the comforting assurance that the unequal distribution of the goods of this world was a special dispensation of Divine Providence, which in these differences, as in particular grace, pursued secret ends unknown to men. Calvin himself had made the much-quoted statement that only when the people, i.e. the mass of labourers and craftsmen, were poor did they remain obedient to God. In the Netherlands (Pieter de la Court and others), that had been secularized to the effect that the mass of men only labour when necessity forces them to do so. This formulation of a leading idea of capitalistic economy later entered into the current theories of the productivity of low wages. Here also, with the dying out of the religious root, the utilitarian interpretation crept in unnoticed, in the line of development which we have again and again observed.

Mediæval ethics not only tolerated begging but actually glorified it in the mendicant orders. . . . It remained for Puritan Asceticism to take part in the severe English Poor Relief Legislation which fundamentally changed the situation. And it could do that, because the Protestant sects and the strict Puritan communities actually did not know any begging in their own midst.

On the other hand, seen from the side of the workers, the Zinzendorf branch of Pietism, for instance, glorified the loyal worker who did not seek acquisition, but lived according to the apostolic model, and was thus endowed with the *charisma* of the disciples. Similar ideas had originally been prevalent among the Baptists in an even more radical form.

Now naturally the whole ascetic literature of almost all denominations is saturated with the idea that faithful labour, even at low wages, on the part of those whom life offers no other opportunities, is highly pleasing to God. In this respect Protestant Asceticism added in itself nothing new. But it not only deepened this idea most powerfully, it also created the force which was alone decisive for its effectiveness: the psychological sanction of it through the conception of this labour as a calling, as the best, often in the last analysis the only means of attaining certainty of grace. And on the other hand it legalized the exploitation of this specific willingness to work, in that it also interpreted the employer's business activity as a calling. It is obvious how powerfully the exclusive search for the Kingdom of God only through the fulfilment of duty in the calling, and the strict asceticism which Church discipline naturally imposed, especially on the propertyless classes, was bound to affect the productivity of labour in the capitalistic sense of the word. The treatment of labour as a calling became as characteristic of the modern worker as the corresponding attitude toward acquisition of the business man. . . .

Calvinism opposed organic social organization in the fiscal-monopolistic form which it assumed in Anglicanism under the Stuarts, especially in the conceptions of Laud, this alliance of Church and State with the monopolists on the basis of a Christian-social ethical foundation. Its leaders were universally among the most passionate opponents of this type of politically privileged commercial, putting-out, and colonial capitalism. Over against it they placed the individualistic motives of rational legal acquisition by virtue of one's own ability and initiative. And, while the politically privileged monopoly industries in England all disappeared in short order, this attitude played a large and decisive part in the development of the industries which grew up in spite of and against the authority of the State. The Puritans (Prynne, Parker) repudiated all connection with the large-scale capitalistic courtiers and projectors as an ethically suspicious class. On the other hand, they took pride in their own superior middle-class business morality, which formed the true reason for the persecutions to which they were subjected on the part of those circles. Defoe proposed to win the battle against dissent by boycotting bank credit and withdrawing deposits. The difference of the two types of capitalistic attitude went to a very large extent hand in hand with religious differences. The opponents of the Nonconformists, even in the eighteenth century, again and again ridiculed them for personifying the spirit of shopkeepers, and for having ruined the ideals of old England. Here also lay the difference of the Puritan economic ethic from the Jewish; and contemporaries (Prynne) knew well that the former and not the latter was the bourgeois capitalistic ethic.

One of the fundamental elements of the spirit of modern capitalism, and not only of that but of all modern culture: rational conduct on the basis of the idea of the calling, was born

– that is what this discussion has sought to demonstrate – from the spirit of Christian asceticism. One has only to re-read the passage from Franklin, quoted at the beginning of this
essay, in order to see that the essential elements of the attitude which was there called the
spirit of capitalism are the same as what we have just shown to be the content of the Puritan
worldly asceticism, only without the religious basis, which by Franklin's time had died
away. . . .

The Puritan wanted to work in a calling; we are forced to do so. For when asceticism
was carried out of monastic cells into everyday life, and began to dominate worldly morality, it did its part in building the tremendous cosmos of the modern economic order. This
order is now bound to the technical and economic conditions of machine production which
to-day determine the lives of all the individuals who are born into this mechanism, not
only those directly concerned with economic acquisition, with irresistible force. Perhaps it
will so determine them until the last ton of fossilized coal is burnt. In Baxter's view the
care for external goods should only lie on the shoulders of the "saint like a light cloak,
which can be thrown aside at any moment". But fate decreed that the cloak should become
an iron cage.

Since asceticism undertook to remodel the world and to work out its ideals in the world,
material goods have gained an increasing and finally an inexorable power over the lives of
men as at no previous period in history. To-day the spirit of religious asceticism – whether
finally, who knows? – has escaped from the cage. But victorious capitalism, since it rests on
mechanical foundations, needs its support no longer. The rosy blush of its laughing heir,
the Enlightenment, seems also to be irretrievably fading, and the idea of duty in one's
calling prowls about in our lives like the ghost of dead religious beliefs. Where the fulfilment of the calling cannot directly be related to the highest spiritual and cultural values,
or when, on the other hand, it need not be felt simply as economic compulsion, the individual generally abandons the attempt to justify it at all. In the field of its highest development, in the United States, the pursuit of wealth, stripped of its religious and ethical
meaning, tends to become associated with purely mundane passions, which often actually
give it the character of sport.

No one knows who will live in this cage in the future, or whether at the end of this tremendous development entirely new prophets will arise, or there will be a great rebirth of
old ideas and ideals, or, if neither, mechanized petrification, embellished with a sort of
convulsive self-importance. For of the last stage of this cultural development, it might well
be truly said: "Specialists without spirit, sensualists without heart; this nullity imagines
that it has attained a level of civilization never before achieved."

But this brings us to the world of judgments of value and of faith, with which this purely
historical discussion need not be burdened. The next task would be rather to show the significance of ascetic rationalism, which has only been touched in the foregoing sketch, for
the content of practical social ethics, thus for the types of organization and the functions
of social groups from the conventicle to the State. Then its relations to humanistic rationalism, its ideals of life and cultural influence; further to the development of philosophical
and scientific empiricism, to technical development and to spiritual ideals would have to
be analysed. Then its historical development from the mediæval beginnings of worldly
asceticism to its dissolution into pure utilitarianism would have to be traced out through
all the areas of ascetic religion. Only then could the quantitative cultural significance of

ascetic Protestantism in its relation to the other plastic elements of modern culture be estimated.

Here we have only attempted to trace the fact and the direction of its influence to their motives in one, though a very important point. But it would also further be necessary to investigate how Protestant Asceticism was in turn influenced in its development and its character by the totality of social conditions, especially economic. The modern man is in general, even with the best will, unable to give religious ideas a significance for culture and national character which they deserve. But it is, of course, not my aim to substitute for a one-sided materialistic an equally one-sided spiritualistic causal interpretation of culture and of history. Each is equally possible, but each, if it does not serve as the preparation, but as the conclusion of an investigation, accomplishes equally little in the interest of historical truth.

3 The Stages of Economic Growth: A *Non*-Communist Manifesto (1960)

W. W. Rostow

The Five Stages-of-growth – A Summary

It is possible to identify all societies, in their economic dimensions, as lying within one of five categories: the traditional society, the preconditions for take-off, the take-off, the drive to maturity, and the age of high mass-consumption.

The Traditional Society

First, the traditional society. A traditional society is one whose structure is developed within limited production functions, based on pre-Newtonian science and technology, and on pre-Newtonian attitudes towards the physical world. Newton is here used as a symbol for that watershed in history when men came widely to believe that the external world was subject to a few knowable laws, and was systematically capable of productive manipulation.

The conception of the traditional society is, however, in no sense static; and it would not exclude increases in output. Acreage could be expanded; some *ad hoc* technical innovations, often highly productive innovations, could be introduced in trade, industry and agriculture; productivity could rise with, for example, the improvement of irrigation works or the discovery and diffusion of a new crop. But the central fact about the traditional society was that a ceiling existed on the level of attainable output per head. This ceiling resulted from the fact that the potentialities which flow from modern science and technology were either not available or not regularly and systematically applied.

Both in the longer past and in recent times the story of traditional societies was thus a story of endless change. The area and volume of trade within them and between them fluctuated, for example, with the degree of political and social turbulence, the efficiency of central rule, the upkeep of the roads. Population – and, within limits, the level of life – rose and fell not only with the sequence of the harvests, but with the incidence of war and of plague. Varying degrees of manufacture developed; but, as in agriculture, the level of productivity was limited by the inaccessibility of modern science, its applications, and its frame of mind.

Generally speaking, these societies, because of the limitation on productivity, had to devote a very high proportion of their resources to agriculture; and flowing from the agricultural system there was an hierarchical social structure, with relatively narrow scope – but some scope – for vertical mobility. Family and clan connexions played a large role in social organization. The value system of these societies was generally geared to what might be called a long-run fatalism; that is, the assumption that the range of possibilities open to one's grandchildren would be just about what it had been for one's grandparents. But this long-run fatalism by no means excluded the short-run option that, within a considerable range, it was possible and legitimate for the individual to strive to improve his lot, within his lifetime. In Chinese villages, for example, there was an endless struggle to acquire or to avoid losing land, yielding a situation where land rarely remained within the same family for a century.

Although central political rule – in one form or another – often existed in traditional societies, transcending the relatively self-sufficient regions, the centre of gravity of political power generally lay in the regions, in the hands of those who owned or controlled the land. The landowner maintained fluctuating but usually profound influence over such central political power as existed, backed by its entourage of civil servants and soldiers, imbued with attitudes and controlled by interests transcending the regions.

In terms of history then, with the phrase "traditional society" we are grouping the whole pre-Newtonian world: the dynasties in China; the civilization of the Middle East and the Mediterranean; the world of medieval Europe. And to them we add the post-Newtonian societies which, for a time, remained untouched or unmoved by man's new capability for regularly manipulating his environment to his economic advantage.

To place these infinitely various, changing societies in a single category, on the ground that they all shared a ceiling on the productivity of their economic techniques, is to say very little indeed. But we are, after all, merely clearing the way in order to get at the subject of this book; that is, the post-traditional societies, in which each of the major characteristics of the traditional society was altered in such ways as to permit regular growth: its politics, social structure, and (to a degree) its values, as well as its economy.

The Preconditions for Take-Off

The second stage of growth embraces societies in the process of transition; that is, the period when the preconditions for take-off are developed; for it takes time to transform a traditional society in the ways necessary for it to exploit the fruits of modern science, to fend off diminishing returns, and thus to enjoy the blessings and choices opened up by the march of compound interest.

The preconditions for take-off were initially developed, in a clearly marked way, in Western Europe of the late seventeenth and early eighteenth centuries as the insights of modern science began to be translated into new production functions in both agriculture and industry, in a setting given dynamism by the lateral expansion of world markets and the international competition for them. But all that lies behind the break-up of the Middle Ages is relevant to the creation of the preconditions for take-off in Western Europe. Among the Western European states, Britain, favoured by geography, natural resources, trading possibilities, social and political structure, was the first to develop fully the preconditions for take-off.

The more general case in modern history, however, saw the stage of preconditions arise not endogenously but from some external intrusion by more advanced societies. These invasions – literal or figurative – shocked the traditional society and began or hastened its undoing; but they also set in motion ideas and sentiments which initiated the process by which a modern alternative to the traditional society was constructed out of the old culture.

The idea spreads not merely that economic progress is possible, but that economic progress is a necessary condition for some other purpose, judged to be good: be it national dignity, private profit, the general welfare, or a better life for the children. Education, for some at least, broadens and changes to suit the needs of modern economic activity. New types of enterprising men come forward – in the private economy, in government, or both – willing to mobilize savings and to take risks in pursuit of profit or modernization. Banks and other institutions for mobilizing capital appear. Investment increases, notably in transport, communications, and in raw materials in which other nations may have an economic interest. The scope of commerce, internal and external, widens. And, here and there, modern manufacturing enterprise appears, using the new methods. But all this activity proceeds at a limited pace within an economy and a society still mainly characterized by traditional low-productivity methods, by the old social structure and values, and by the regionally based political institutions that developed in conjunction with them.

In many recent cases, for example, the traditional society persisted side by side with modern economic activities, conducted for limited economic purposes by a colonial or quasi-colonial power.

Although the period of transition – between the traditional society and the take-off – saw major changes in both the economy itself and in the balance of social values, a decisive feature was often political. Politically, the building of an effective centralized national state – on the basis of coalitions touched with a new nationalism, in opposition to the traditional landed regional interests, the colonial power, or both, was a decisive aspect of the preconditions period; and it was, almost universally, a necessary condition for take-off.

There is a great deal more that needs to be said about the preconditions period, but we shall leave it for chapter 3, where the anatomy of the transition from a traditional to a modern society is examined.

The Take-Off

We come now to the great watershed in the life of modern societies: the third stage in this sequence, the take-off. The take-off is the interval when the old blocks and resistances to steady growth are finally overcome. The forces making for economic progress, which yielded limited bursts and enclaves of modern activity, expand and come to dominate the society. Growth becomes its normal condition. Compound interest becomes built, as it were, into its habits and institutional structure.

In Britain and the well-endowed parts of the world populated substantially from Britain (the United States, Canada, etc.) the proximate stimulus for take-off was mainly (but not wholly) technological. In the more general case, the take-off awaited not only the build-up of social overhead capital and a surge of technological development in industry and agriculture, but also the emergence to political power of a group prepared to regard the modernization of the economy as serious, high-order political business.

During the take-off, the rate of effective investment and savings may rise from, say, 5 per cent of the national income to 10 per cent or more; although where heavy social overhead capital investment was required to create the technical preconditions for take-off the investment rate in the preconditions period could be higher than 5 per cent, as, for example, in Canada before the 1890s and Argentina before 1914. In such cases capital imports usually formed a high proportion of total investment in the preconditions period and sometimes even during the take-off itself, as in Russia and Canada during their pre-1914 railway booms.

During the take-off new industries expand rapidly, yielding profits a large proportion of which are reinvested in new plant; and these new industries, in turn, stimulate, through their rapidly expanding requirement for factory workers, the services to support them, and for other manufactured goods, a further expansion in urban areas and in other modern industrial plants. The whole process of expansion in the modern sector yields an increase of income in the hands of those who not only save at high rates but place their savings at the disposal of those engaged in modern sector activities. The new class of entrepreneurs expands; and it directs the enlarging flows of investment in the private sector. The economy exploits hitherto unused natural resources and methods of production.

New techniques spread in agriculture as well as industry, as agriculture is commercialized, and increasing numbers of farmers are prepared to accept the new methods and the deep changes they bring to ways of life. The revolutionary changes in agricultural productivity are an essential condition for successful take-off; for modernization of a society increases radically its bill for agricultural products. In a decade or two both the basic structure of the economy and the social and political structure of the society are transformed in such a way that a steady rate of growth can be, thereafter, regularly sustained.

As indicated in a later chapter, one can approximately allocate the take-off of Britain to the two decades after 1783; France and the United States to the several decades preceding 1860; Germany, the third quarter of the nineteenth century; Japan, the fourth quarter of the nineteenth century; Russia and Canada the quarter-century or so preceding 1914; while during the 1950s India and China have, in quite different ways, launched their respective take-offs.

The Drive to Maturity

After take-off there follows a long interval of sustained if fluctuating progress, as the now regularly growing economy drives to extend modern technology over the whole front of its economic activity. Some 10–20 per cent of the national income is steadily invested, permitting output regularly to outstrip the increase in population. The make-up of the economy changes unceasingly as technique improves, new industries accelerate, older industries level off. The economy finds its place in the international economy: goods formerly imported are produced at home; new import requirements develop, and new export commodities to match them. The society makes such terms as it will with the requirements of modern efficient production, balancing off the new against the older values and institutions, or revising the latter in such ways as to support rather than to retard the growth process.

Some sixty years after take-off begins (say, forty years after the end of take-off) what may be called maturity is generally attained. The economy, focused during the take-off around a relatively narrow complex of industry and technology, has extended its range into more refined and technologically often more complex processes; for example, there may be a shift in focus from the coal, iron, and heavy engineering industries of the railway phase to machine-tools, chemicals, and electrical equipment. This, for example, was the transition through which Germany, Britain, France, and the United States had passed by the end of the nineteenth century or shortly thereafter. But there are other sectoral patterns which have been followed in the sequence from take-off to maturity, which are considered in a later chapter.

Formally, we can define maturity as the stage in which an economy demonstrates the capacity to move beyond the original industries which powered its take-off and to absorb and to apply efficiently over a very wide range of its resources – if not the whole range – the most advanced fruits of (then) modern technology. This is the stage in which an economy demonstrates that it has the technological and entrepreneurial skills to produce not every-thing, but anything that it chooses to produce. It may lack (like contemporary Sweden and Switzerland, for example) the raw materials or other supply conditions required to produce a given type of output economically; but its dependence is a matter of economic choice or political priority rather than a technological or institutional necessity.

Historically, it would appear that something like sixty years was required to move a society from the beginning of take-off to maturity. Analytically the explanation for some such interval may lie in the powerful arithmetic of compound interest applied to the capital stock, combined with the broader consequences for a society's ability to absorb modern technology of three successive generations living under a regime where growth is the normal condition. But, clearly, no dogmatism is justified about the exact length of the interval from take-off to maturity.

The Age of High Mass-Consumption

We come now to the age of high mass-consumption, where, in time, the leading sectors shift towards durable consumers' goods and services: a phase from which Americans are beginning to emerge; whose not unequivocal joys Western Europe and Japan are beginning energetically to probe; and with which Soviet society is engaged in an uneasy flirtation.

As societies achieved maturity in the twentieth century two things happened: real income per head rose to a point where a large number of persons gained a command over consumption which transcended basic food, shelter, and clothing; and the structure of the working force changed in ways which increased not only the proportion of urban to total population, but also the proportion of the population working in offices or in skilled factory jobs – aware of and anxious to acquire the consumption fruits of a mature economy.

In addition to these economic changes, the society ceased to accept the further extension of modern technology as an overriding objective. It is in this post-maturity stage, for example, that, through the political process, Western societies have chosen to allocate increased resources to social welfare and security. The emergence of the welfare state is one manifestation of a society's moving beyond technical maturity; but it is also at this stage that resources tend increasingly to be directed to the production of consumers' dur-ables and to the diffusion of services on a mass basis, if consumers' sovereignty reigns. The sewing-machine, the bicycle, and then the various electric-powered household gadgets were gradually diffused. Historically, however, the decisive element has been the cheap mass automobile with its quite revolutionary effects – social as well as economic – on the life and expectations of society.

For the United States, the turning point was, perhaps, Henry Ford's moving assembly line of 1913–14; but it was in the 1920s, and again in the post-war decade, 1946–56, that this stage of growth was pressed to, virtually, its logical conclusion. In the 1950s Western Europe and Japan appear to have fully entered this phase, accounting substantially for a momentum in their economies quite unexpected in the immediate post-war years. The Soviet Union is technically ready for this stage, and, by every sign, its citizens hunger for it; but Communist leaders face difficult political and social problems of adjustment if this stage is launched.

Beyond Consumption

Beyond, it is impossible to predict, except perhaps to observe that Americans, at least, have behaved in the past decade as if diminishing relative marginal utility sets in, after a point, for durable consumers' goods; and they have chosen, at the margin, larger families – behaviour in the pattern of Buddenbrooks dynamics. Americans have behaved as if, having been born into a system that provided economic security and high mass-consumption, they placed a lower valuation on acquiring additional increments of real income in the conventional form as opposed to the advantages and values of an enlarged family. But even in this adventure in generalization it is a shade too soon to create – on the basis of one case – a new stage-of-growth, based on babies, in succession to the age of consumers' durables: as economists might say, the income-elasticity of demand for babies may well vary from society to society. But it is true that the implications of the baby boom along with the not wholly unrelated deficit in social overhead capital are likely to dominate the American economy over the next decade rather than the further diffusion of consumers' durables.

Here then, in an impressionistic rather than an analytic way, are the stages-of-growth which can be distinguished once a traditional society begins its modernization: the transitional period when the preconditions for take-off are created generally in response to the intrusion of a foreign power, converging with certain domestic forces making for modernization; the take-off itself; the sweep into maturity generally taking up the life of about two further generations; and then, finally, if the rise of income has matched the spread of technological virtuosity (which, as we shall see, it need not immediately do) the diversion of the fully mature economy to the provision of durable consumers' goods and services (as well as the welfare state) for its increasingly urban – and then suburban – population. Beyond lies the question of whether or not secular spiritual stagnation will arise, and, if it does, how man might fend it off: a matter considered in a later chapter.

In the four chapters that follow we shall take a harder, and more rigorous look at the preconditions, the take-off, the drive to maturity, and the processes which have led to the age of high mass-consumption. But even in this introductory chapter one characteristic of this system should be made clear.

A Dynamic Theory of Production

These stages are not merely descriptive. They are not merely a way of generalizing certain factual observations about the sequence of development of modern societies. They have an inner logic and continuity. They have an analytic bone-structure, rooted in a dynamic theory of production.

The classical theory of production is formulated under essentially static assumptions which freeze – or permit only once-over change – in the variables most relevant to the process of economic growth. As modern economists have sought to merge classical production theory with Keynesian income analysis they have introduced the dynamic variables: population, technology, entrepreneurship, etc. But they have tended to do so in forms so rigid and general that their models cannot grip the essential phenomena of growth, as they appear to an economic historian. We require a dynamic theory of production which isolates not only the distribution of income between consumption, saving, and investment (and the balance of production between consumers and capital goods) but which focuses directly and in some detail on the composition of investment and on developments within particular sectors of the economy. The argument that follows is based on such a flexible, disaggregated theory of production.

When the conventional limits on the theory of production are widened, it is possible to define theoretical equilibrium positions not only for output, investment, and consumption as a whole, but for each sector of the economy.[1]

Within the framework set by forces determining the total level of output, sectoral optimum positions are determined on the side of demand, by the levels of income and of population, and by the character of tastes; on the side of supply, by the state of technology and the quality of entrepreneurship, as the latter determines the proportion of technically available and potentially profitable innovations actually incorporated in the capital stock.[2]

In addition, one must introduce an extremely significant empirical hypothesis: namely, that deceleration is the normal optimum path of a sector, due to a variety of factors operating on it, from the side of both supply and demand.[3]

The equilibria which emerge from the application of these criteria are a set of sectoral paths, from which flows, as first derivatives, a sequence of optimum patterns of investment.

Historical patterns of investment did not, of course, exactly follow these optimum patterns. They were distorted by imperfections in the private investment process, by the policies of governments, and by the impact of wars. Wars temporarily altered the profitable directions of investment by setting up arbitrary demands and by changing the conditions of supply; they destroyed capital; and, occasionally, they accelerated the development of new technology relevant to the peacetime economy and shifted the political and social framework in ways conducive to peacetime growth.[4] The historical sequence of business-cycles and trend-periods results from these deviations of actual from optimal patterns; and such fluctuations, along with the impact of wars, yield historical paths of growth which differ from those which the optima, calculated before the event, would have yielded.

Nevertheless, the economic history of growing societies takes a part of its rude shape from the effort of societies to approximate the optimum sectoral paths.

At any period of time, the rate of growth in the sectors will vary greatly; and it is possible to isolate empirically certain leading sectors, at early stages of their evolution, whose rapid rate of expansion plays an essential direct and indirect role in maintaining the overall momentum of the economy.[5] For some purposes it is useful to characterize an economy in terms of its leading sectors; and a part of the technical basis for the stages of growth lies in the changing sequence of leading sectors. In essence it is the fact that sectors tend to have a rapid growth-phase, early in their life, that makes it possible and useful to regard economic history as a sequence of stages rather than merely as a continuum, within which nature never makes a jump.

The stages-of-growth also require, however, that elasticities of demand be taken into account, and that this familiar concept be widened; for these rapid growth phases in the sectors derive not merely from the discontinuity of production functions but also from high price- or income-elasticities of demand. Leading sectors are determined not merely by the changing flow of technology and the changing willingness of entrepreneurs to accept available innovations: they are also partially determined by those types of demand which have exhibited high elasticity with respect to price, income, or both.

The demand for resources has resulted, however, not merely from demands set up by private taste and choice, but also from social decisions and from the policies of governments – whether democratically responsive or not. It is necessary, therefore, to look at the choices made by societies in the disposition of their resources in terms which transcend conventional market processes. It is necessary to look at their welfare functions, in the widest sense, including the non-economic processes which determined them.

The course of birth-rates, for example, represents one form of welfare choice made by societies, as income has changed; and population curves reflect (in addition to changing death-rates) how the calculus about family size was made in the various stages; from the usual (but not universal) decline in birth-rates, during or soon after the take-off, as urbanization took hold and progress became a palpable possibility, to the recent rise, as Americans (and others in societies marked by high mass-consumption) have appeared to seek in larger families values beyond those afforded by economic security and by an ample supply of durable consumers' goods and services.

And there are other decisions as well that societies have made as the choices open to them have been altered by the unfolding process of economic growth; and these broad collective decisions, determined by many factors – deep in history, culture, and the active political process – outside the market-place, have interplayed with the dynamics of market demand, risk-taking, technology and entrepreneurship, to determine the specific content of the stages of growth for each society.

How, for example, should the traditional society react to the intrusion of a more advanced power: with cohesion, promptness, and vigour, like the Japanese; by making a virtue of fecklessness, like the oppressed Irish of eighteenth century; by slowly and reluctantly altering the traditional society, like the Chinese?

When independent modern nationhood is achieved, how should the national energies be disposed: in external aggression, to right old wrongs or to exploit newly created or perceived possibilities for enlarged national power; in completing and refining the political victory of the new national government over old regional interests; or in modernizing the economy?

Once growth is under way, with the take-off, to what extent should the requirements of diffusing modern technology and maximizing the rate of growth be moderated by the desire to increase consumption *per capita* and to increase welfare?

When technological maturity is reached, and the nation has at its command a modernized and differentiated industrial machine, to what ends should it be put, and in what proportions: to increase social security, through the welfare state; to expand mass-consumption into the range of durable consumers' goods and services; to increase the nation's stature and power on the world scene; or to increase leisure?

And then the question beyond, where history offers us only fragments: what to do when the increase in real income itself loses its charm? Babies, boredom, three-day week-ends, the moon, or the creation of new inner, human frontiers in substitution for the imperatives of scarcity?

In surveying now the broad contours of each stage-of-growth, we are examining, then, not merely the sectoral structure of economies, as they transformed themselves for growth, and grew; we are also examining a succession of strategic choices made by various societies concerning the disposition of their resources, which include but transcend the income- and price-elasticities of demand.

NOTES

1   W. W. Rostow, *The Process of Economic Growth* (Oxford, 1953), esp. ch. IV. Also "Trends in the Allocation of Resources in Secular Growth," ch. 15 of Leon H. Dupriez (ed.), with the assistance of Douglas C. Hague, *Economic Progress* (Louvain, 1955).
2   In a closed model, a dynamic theory of production must account for changing stocks of basic and applied science, as sectoral aspects of investment, which is done in Rostow, *Process of Economic Growth*, esp. pp. 22–5.
3   Ibid., pp. 96–103.
4   Ibid., ch. VII, esp. pp. 164–7.
5   For a discussion of the leading sectors, their direct and indirect consequences, and the diverse routes of their impact, see Rostow, "Trends in the Allocation of Resources in Secular Growth."

4 The Change to Change: Modernization, Development, and Politics (1971) and Political Order in Changing Societies (1968)

Samuel Huntington

The Change to Change: Modernization, Development, and Politics

I Political Science and Political Change

Change is a problem for social science. Sociologists, for instance, have regularly bemoaned their lack of knowledge concerning social change . . . Yet, as opposed to political scientists, the sociologists are relatively well off. Compared with past neglect of the theory of political change in political science, sociology is rich with works on the theory of social change. These more generalized treatments are supplemented by the extensive literature on group dynamics, planned change, organizational change, and the nature of innovation. Until very recently, in contrast, political theory in general has not attempted to deal directly with the problems of change. "Over the last seventy-five years," David Easton wrote in 1953, "political research has confined itself largely to the study of given conditions to the neglect of political change."[1] . . .

II The Context of Modernization

General Theory of Modernization

The new developments in comparative politics in the 1950s involved extension of the geographical scope of concern from Western Europe and related areas to the non-Western "developing" countries. It was no longer true that political scientists ignored change. Indeed, they seemed almost overwhelmed with the immensity of the changes taking place in the modernizing societies of Asia, Africa, and Latin America. The theory of modernization was embraced by political scientists, and comparative politics was looked at in the context of modernization. The concepts of modernity and tradition bid fair to replace many of the other typologies which had been dear to the hearts of political analysts: democracy, oligarchy, and dictatorship; liberalism and conservatism; totalitarianism and constitutionalism; socialism, communism, and capitalism; nationalism and internationalism. Obviously, these categories were still used. But by the late 1960s, for every discussion among political scientists in which the categories "constitutional" and "totalitarian" were employed, there must have been ten others in which the categories "modern" and "traditional" were used. . . .

The essential difference between modern and traditional society, most theorists of modernization contend, lies in the greater control which modern man has over his natural and social environment. This control, in turn, is based on the expansion of scientific and technological knowledge. . . . To virtually all theorists, these differences in the extent of man's control over his environment reflect differences in his fundamental attitudes toward and expectations from his environment. The contrast between modern man and traditional man is the source of the contrast between modern society and traditional society. Traditional man is passive and acquiescent; he expects continuity in nature and society and does not believe in the capacity of man to change or to control either. Modern man, in contrast, believes in both the possibility and the desirability of change, and has confidence in the ability of man to control change so as to accomplish his purposes.

At the intellectual level, modern society is characterized by the tremendous accumulation of knowledge about man's environment and by the diffusion of this knowledge through society by means of literacy, mass communications, and education. In contrast to traditional society, modern society also involves much better health, longer life expectancy, and higher rates of occupational and geographical mobility. It is predominantly urban rather than rural. Socially, the family and other primary groups having diffuse roles are supplanted or supplemented in modern society by consciously organized secondary associations having more specific functions. Economically, there is a diversification of activity as a few simple occupations give way to many complex ones; the level of occupational skill and the ratio of capital to labor are much higher than in traditional society. Agriculture declines in importance compared to commercial, industrial, and other nonagricultural activities, and commercial agriculture replaces subsistence agriculture. The geographical scope of economic activity is far greater in modern society than in traditional society, and there is a centralization of such activity at the national level, with the emergence of a national market, national sources of capital, and other national economic institutions . . .

The bridge across the Great Dichotomy between modern and traditional societies is the Grand Process of Modernization. The broad outlines and characteristics of this process are also generally agreed upon by scholars. Most writers on modernization implicitly or explicitly assign nine characteristics to the modernization process.

1　Modernization is a *revolutionary* process. This follows directly from the contrasts between modern and traditional society. The one differs fundamentally from the other, and the change from tradition to modernity consequently involves a radical and total change in patterns of human life. The shift from tradition to modernity, as Cyril Black says, is comparable to the changes from prehuman to human existence and from primitive to civilized societies. The changes in the eighteenth century, Reinhard Bendix echoes, were "Comparable in magnitude only to the transformation of nomadic peoples into settled agriculturalists some 10,000 years earlier."[2]

2   Modernization is a *complex* process. It cannot be easily reduced to a single factor or to a single dimension. It involves changes in virtually all areas of human thought and behavior. At a minimum, its components include: industrialization, urbanization, social mobilization, differentiation, secularization, media expansion, increasing literacy and education, expansion of political participation.

3   Modernization is a *systemic* process. Changes in one factor are related to and affect changes in the other factors. Modernization, as Daniel Lerner has expressed it in an oft-quoted phrase, is "a process with some distinctive *quality* of its own, which would explain why modernity is felt as a *consistent whole* among people who live by its rules." The various elements of modernization have been highly associated together "because, in some historic sense, they *had to* go together."[3]

4   Modernization is a *global* process. Modernization originated in fifteenth- and sixteenth-century Europe, but it has now become a worldwide phenomenon. This is brought about primarily through the diffusion of modern ideas and techniques from the European center, but also in part through the endogenous development of non-Western societies. In any event, all societies were at one time traditional; all societies are now either modern or in the process of becoming modern.

5   Modernization is a *lengthy* process. The totality of the changes which modernization involves can only be worked out through time. Consequently, while modernization is revolutionary in the extent of the changes it brings about in traditional society, it is evolutionary in the amount of time required to bring about those changes. Western societies required several centuries to modernize. The contemporary modernizing societies will do it in less time. Rates of modernization are, in this sense, accelerating, but the time required to move from tradition to modernity will still be measured in generations.

6   Modernization is a *phased* process. It is possible to distinguish different levels or phases of modernization through which all societies will move. Societies obviously begin in the traditional stage and end in the modern stage. The intervening transitional phase, however, can also be broken down into sub-phases. Societies consequently can be compared and ranked in terms of the extent to which they have moved down the road from tradition to modernity. While the leadership in the process and the more detailed patterns of modernization will differ from one society to another, all societies will move through essentially the same stages.

7   Modernization is a *homogenizing* process. Many different types of traditional societies exist; indeed, traditional societies, some argue, have little in common except their lack of modernity. Modern societies, on the other hand, share basic similarities. Modernization produces tendencies toward convergence among societies. Modernization involves movement "toward an interdependence among politically organized societies and toward an ultimate integration of societies." The "universal imperatives of modern ideas and institutions" may lead to a stage "at which the various societies are so homogeneous as to be capable of forming a world state. . . ."[4]

8   Modernization is an *irreversible* process. While there may be temporary breakdowns and occasional reversals in elements of the modernizing process, modernization as a whole is an essentially secular trend. A society which has reached

certain levels of urbanization, literacy, industrialization in one decade will not decline to substantially lower levels in the next decade. The rates of change will vary significantly from one society to another, but the direction of change will not.

9 Modernization is *a progressive* process. The traumas of modernization are many and profound, but in the long run modernization is not only inevitable, it is also desirable. The costs and the pains of the period of transition, particularly its early phases, are great, but the achievement of a modern social, political, and economic order is worth them. Modernization in the long run enhances human well-being, culturally and materially. . . .

Political Order in Changing Societies

1.1 Political Order and Political Decay

The Political Gap

The most important political distinction among countries concerns not their form of government but their degree of government. The differences between democracy and dictatorship are less than the differences between those countries whose politics embodies consensus, community, legitimacy, organization, effectiveness, stability, and those countries whose politics is deficient in these qualities. Communist totalitarian states and Western liberal states both belong generally in the category of effective rather than debile political systems. The United States, Great Britain, and the Soviet Union have different forms of government, but in all three systems the government governs. Each country is a political community with an overwhelming consensus among the people on the legitimacy of the political system. In each country the citizens and their leaders share a vision of the public interest of the society and of the traditions and principles upon which the political community is based. All three countries have strong, adaptable, coherent political institutions: effective bureaucracies, well-organized political parties, a high degree of popular participation in public affairs, working systems of civilian control over the military, extensive activity by the government in the economy, and reasonably effective procedures for regulating succession and controlling political conflict. These governments command the loyalties of their citizens and thus have the capacity to tax resources, to conscript manpower, and to innovate and to execute policy. If the Politburo, the Cabinet, or the President makes a decision, the probability is high that it will be implemented through the government machinery.

In all these characteristics the political systems of the United States, Great Britain, and the Soviet Union differ significantly from the governments which exist in many, if not most, of the modernizing countries of Asia, Africa, and Latin America. These countries lack many things. They suffer real shortages of food, literacy, education, wealth, income, health, and productivity, but most of them have been recognized and efforts made to do something about them. Beyond and behind these shortages, however, there is a greater shortage: a shortage of political community and of effective, authoritative, legitimate government. . . .

With a few notable exceptions, the political evolution of these countries after World War II was characterized by increasing ethnic and class conflict, recurring rioting and mob violence, frequent military coups d'état, the dominance of unstable personalistic leaders who often pursued disastrous economic and social policies, widespread and blatant corruption among cabinet ministers and civil servants, arbitrary infringement of the rights and liberties of citizens, declining standards of bureaucratic efficiency and performance, the pervasive alienation of urban political groups, the loss of authority by legislatures and courts, and the fragmentation and at times complete disintegration of broadly based political parties. . . .

During the 1950s and 1960s the numerical incidence of political violence and disorder increased dramatically in most countries on the world. The year 1958, according to one calculation, witnessed some 28 prolonged guerrilla insurgencies, four military uprisings, and two conventional wars. Seven years later, in 1965, 42 prolonged insurgencies were underway; ten military revolts occurred; and five conventional conflicts were being fought. Political instability also increased significantly during the 1950s and 1960s. Violence and other destabilizing events were five times more frequent between 1955 and 1962 than they were between 1948 and 1954. Sixty-four of 84 countries were less stable in the latter period than in the earlier one.[5] Throughout Asia, Africa, and Latin America there was a decline in political order, an undermining of the authority, effectiveness, and legitimacy of government. There was a lack of civic morale and public spirit and of political institutions capable of giving meaning and direction to the public interest. Not political development but political decay dominated the scene . . .

What was responsible for this violence and instability? The primary thesis of this book is that it was in large part the product of rapid social change and the rapid mobilization of new groups into politics coupled with the slow development of political institutions. "Among the laws that rule human societies," de Tocqueville observed, "there is one which seems to be more precise and clear than all others. If men are to remain civilized or to become so, the art of associating together must grow and improve in the same ratio in which the equality of conditions is increased."[6] The political instability in Asia, Africa, and Latin America derives precisely from the failure to meet this condition: equality of political participation is growing much more rapidly than "the art of associating together." Social and economic change – urbanization, increases in literacy and education, industrialization, mass media expansion – extend political consciousness, multiply political demands, broaden political participation. These changes undermine traditional sources of political authority and traditional political institutions; they enormously complicate the problems of creating new bases of political association and new political institutions combining legitimacy and effectiveness. The rates of social mobilization and the expansion of political participation are high; the rates of political organization and institutionalization are low. The result is political instability and disorder. The primary problem of politics is the lag in the development of political institutions behind social and economic change.

For two decades after World War II American foreign policy failed to come to grips with this problem. The economic gap, in contrast to the political gap, was the target of sustained attention, analysis, and action. Aid programs and loan programs, the World Bank and regional banks, the UN and the OECD, consortia and combines, planners and politicians, all shared in a massive effort to do something about the problem of economic development. Who, however, was concerned with the political gap? American officials recognized that the United States had a primary interest in the creation of viable political regimes in modernizing countries. But few, if any, of all the activities of the American government affecting those countries were directly concerned with the promotion of political stability and the reduction of the political gap. How can this astonishing lacuna be explained?

It would appear to be rooted in two distinct aspects of the American historical experience. In confronting the modernizing countries the United States was handicapped by its happy history. In its development the United States was blessed with more than its fair share of economic plenty, social well-being, and political stability. This pleasant conjuncture of blessings led Americans to believe in the unity of goodness: to assume that all good things go together and that the achievement of one desirable social goal aids in the achievement of others. In American policy toward modernizing countries this experience was reflected in the belief that political stability would be the natural and inevitable result of the achievement of, first, economic development and then of social reform. Throughout the 1950s the prevailing assumption of American policy was that economic development – the elimination of poverty, disease, illiteracy – was necessary for political development and political stability. In American thinking the causal chain was: economic assistance promotes economic development, economic development promotes political stability. This dogma was enshrined in legislation and, perhaps more important, it was ingrained in the thinking of officials in AID and other agencies concerned with the foreign assistance programs.

If political decay and political instability were more rampant in Asia, Africa, and Latin America in 1965 than they were fifteen years earlier, it was in part because American policy reflected this erroneous dogma. For in fact, economic development and political stability are two independent goals and progress toward one has no necessary connection with progress toward the other. In some instances programs of economic development may promote political stability; in other instances they may seriously undermine such stability. So also, some forms of political stability may encourage economic growth; other forms may discourage it. India was one of the poorest countries in the world in the 1950s and had only a modest rate of economic growth. Yet through the Congress Party it achieved a high degree of political stability. Per capita incomes in Argentina and Venezuela were perhaps ten times that in India, and Venezuela had a phenomenal rate of economic growth. Yet for both countries stability remained an elusive goal.

With the Alliance for Progress in 1961, social reform – that is, the more equitable distribution of material and symbolic resources – joined economic development as a conscious and explicit goal of American policy toward modernizing countries. This development was, in part, a reaction to the Cuban Revolution, and it reflected the assumption among policymakers that land and tax reforms, housing projects, and welfare programs would reduce social tensions and deactivate the fuse to Fidelismo. Once again political stability was to be the by-product of the achievement of another socially desirable goal. In fact, of course, the relationship between social reform and political stability resembles that between economic development and political stability. In some circumstances reforms may reduce tensions and encourage peaceful rather than violent change. In other circumstances, however, reform may well exacerbate tensions, precipitate violence, and be a catalyst of rather than a substitute for revolution.

A second reason for American indifference to political development was the absence in the American historical experience of the need to found a political order. Americans, de Tocqueville said, were born equal and hence never had to worry about creating equality; they enjoyed the fruits of a democratic revolution without having suffered one. So also, America was born with a government, with political institutions and practices imported from seventeenth-century England. Hence Americans never had to worry about creating a government. This gap in historical experience made them peculiarly blind to the problems of creating effective authority in modernizing countries. When an American thinks about the problem of government-building, he directs himself not to the creation of authority and the accumulation of power but rather to the limitation of authority and the division of power. Asked to design a government, he comes up with a written constitution, bill of rights, separation of powers, checks and balances, federalism, regular elections, competitive parties – all excellent devices for limiting government. The Lockean American is so fundamentally anti-government that he identifies government with restrictions on government. Confronted with the need to design a political system which will maximize power and authority, he has no ready answer. His general formula is that governments should be based on free and fair elections.

In many modernizing societies this formula is irrelevant. Elections to be meaningful presuppose a certain level of political organization. The problem is not to hold elections but to create organizations. In many, if not most, modernizing countries elections serve only to enhance the power of disruptive and often reactionary social forces and to tear down the structure of public authority. "In framing a government which is to be administered by men over men," Madison warned in *The Federalist*, No. 51, "the great difficulty lies in this: you must first enable the government to control the governed; and in the next place oblige it to control itself." In many modernizing countries governments are still unable to perform the first function, much less the second. The primary problem is not liberty but the creation of a legitimate public order. Men may, of course, have order without liberty, but they cannot have liberty without order. Authority has to exist before it can be limited, and it is authority that is in scarce supply in those modernizing countries where government is at the mercy of alienated intellectuals, rambunctious colonels, and rioting students.

It is precisely this scarcity that communist and communist-type movements are often able to overcome. History shows conclusively that communist governments are no better than free governments in alleviating famine, improving health, expanding national product, creating industry, and maximizing welfare. But the one thing communist governments can do is to govern; they do provide effective authority. Their ideology furnishes a basis of legitimacy, and their party organization provides the institutional mechanism for mobilizing support and executing policy. . . . The real challenge which the communists pose to modernizing countries is not that they are so good at overthrowing governments (which is easy), but that they are so good at making governments (which is a far more difficult task). They may not provide liberty, but they do provide authority; they do create governments that can govern . . .

Political Participation: Modernization and Political Decay

Modernization and Political Consciousness

. . . Those aspects of modernization most relevant to politics can be broadly grouped into two categories. First, social mobilization, in Deutsch's formulation, is the process by which "major clusters of old social, economic and psychological commitments are eroded or broken and people become available for new patterns of socialization and behavior."[7] It means a change in the attitudes, values, and expectations of people from those associated with the traditional world to those common to the modern world. It is a consequence of literacy, education, increased communications, mass media exposure, and urbanization. Secondly, economic development refers to the growth in the total economic activity and output of a society. It may be measured by per capita gross national product, level of industrialization, and level of individual welfare gauged by such indices as life expectancy, caloric intake, supply of hospitals and doctors. Social mobilization involves changes in the aspirations of individuals, groups, and societies; economic development involves changes in their capabilities. Modernization requires both. . . . the most crucial aspects of political modernization can be roughly subsumed under three broad headings. First, political modernization involves the rationalization of authority, the replacement of a large number of traditional, religious, familial, and ethnic political authorities by a single secular, national political authority. This change implies that government is the product of man, not of nature or of God, and that a well-ordered society must have a determinate human source of final authority, obedience to whose positive law takes precedence over other obligations. Political modernization involves assertion of the external sovereignty of the nation-state against transnational influences and of the internal sovereignty of the national government against local and regional powers. It means national integration and the centralization or accumulation of power in recognized national lawmaking institutions.

Secondly, political modernization involves the differentiation of new political functions and the development of specialized structures to perform those functions. Areas of particular competence – legal, military, administrative, scientific – become separated from the political realm, and autonomous, specialized, but subordinate organs arise to discharge those tasks. Administrative hierarchies become more elaborate, more complex, more disciplined. Office and power are distributed more by achievement and less by ascription. Thirdly, political modernization involves increased participation in politics by social groups throughout society. Broadened participation in politics may enhance control of the people by the government, as in totalitarian states, or it may enhance control of the government by the people, as in some democratic ones. But in all modern states the citizens become directly involved in and affected by governmental affairs. Rationalized authority, differentiated structure, and mass participation thus distinguish modern polities from antecedent polities.

It is, however, a mistake to conclude that in practice modernization means the rationalization of authority, differentiation of structure, and expansion of political participation. A basic and frequently overlooked distinction exists between political modernization defined as movement from a traditional to a modern polity and political modernization defined as the political aspects and political effects of social, economic, and cultural modernization. The former posits the direction in which political change theoretically should move. The latter describes the political changes which actually occur in modernizing countries. The gap between the two is often vast. Modernization in practice always involves change in and usually the disintegration of a traditional political system, but it does not necessarily involve significant movement toward a modern political system. Yet the tendency has been to assume that what is true for the broader social processes of modernization is also true for political changes. Social modernization, in some degree, is a fact in Asia, Africa, Latin America: urbanization is rapid, literacy is slowly increasing; industrialization is being pushed; per capita gross national product is inching upward; mass media circulation is expanding. All these are facts. In contrast progress toward many of the other goals which writers have identified with political modernization – democracy, stability, structural differentiation, achievement patterns, national integration – often is dubious at best. Yet the tendency is to think that because social modernization is taking place, political modernization also must be taking place . . .

In actuality, only some of the tendencies frequently encompassed in the concept "political modernization" characterized the "modernizing" areas. Instead of a trend toward competitiveness and democracy, there was an "erosion of democracy" and a tendency to autocratic military regimes and one-party regimes.[8] Instead of stability, there were repeated coups and revolts. Instead of a unifying nationalism and nation-building, there were repeated ethnic conflicts and civil wars. Instead of institutional rationalization and differentiation, there was frequently a decay of the administrative organizations inherited from the colonial era and a weakening and disruption of the political organizations developed during the struggle for independence. Only the concept of political modernization as mobilization and participation appeared to be generally applicable to the "developing" world. Rationalization, integration, and differentiation, in contrast, seemed to have only a dim relation to reality.

More than by anything else, the modern state is distinguished from the traditional state by the broadened extent to which people participate in politics and are affected by politics in large-scale political units. . . .

The disruptive effects of social and economic modernization on politics and political institutions take many forms. Social and economic changes necessarily disrupt traditional social and political groupings and undermine loyalty to traditional authorities. . . . Modernization thus tends to produce alienation and anomie, normlessness generated by the conflict of old values and new. The new values undermine the old bases of association and of authority before new skills, motivations, and resources can be brought into existence to create new groupings.

The breakup of traditional institutions may lead to psychological disintegration and anomie, but these very conditions also create the need for new identifications and loyalties. The latter may take the form of reidentification with a group which existed in latent or actual form in traditional society or they may lead to identification with a new set of symbols or a new group which has itself evolved in the process of modernization. Industrialization, Marx argued, produces class consciousness first in the bourgeoisie and then in the proletariat. Marx focused on only one minor aspect of a much more general phenomenon. Industrialization is only one aspect of modernization and modernization induces not just class consciousness but new group consciousness of all kinds: in tribe, region, clan, religion, and caste, as well as in class, occupation, and association. Modernization means that all groups, old as well as new, traditional as well as modern, become increasingly aware of themselves as groups and of their interests and claims in relation to other groups. One of the most striking phenomena of modernization, indeed, is the increased consciousness, coherence, organization, and action which it produces in many social forces which existed on a much lower level of conscious identity and organization in traditional society. . . . The same group consciousness, however, can also be a major obstacle to the creation of effective political institutions encompassing a broader spectrum of social forces. Along with group consciousness, group prejudice also "develops when there is intensive contact between different groups, such as has accompanied the movement toward more centralized political and social organizations."[9] And along with group prejudice comes group conflict. Ethnic or religious groups which had lived peacefully side by side in traditional society become aroused to violent conflict as a result of the interaction, the tensions, the inequalities generated by social and economic modernization. Modernization thus increases conflict among traditional groups, between traditional groups and modern ones, and among modern groups. The new elites based on Western or modern education come into conflict with the traditional elites whose authority rests on ascribed and inherited status. Within the modernized elites, antagonisms arise between politicians and bureaucrats, intellectuals and soldiers, labor leaders and businessmen. Many, if not most, of these conflicts at one time or another erupt into violence.

Modernization and Violence

[. . .]

The gap hypothesis.   Social mobilization is much more destabilizing than economic development. The gap between these two forms of change furnishes some measure of the impact of modernization on political stability. Urbanization, literacy, education, mass media, all expose the traditional man to new forms of life, new standards of enjoyment, new possibilities of satisfaction. These experiences break the cognitive and attitudinal barriers of the traditional culture and promote new levels of aspirations and wants. The ability of transitional society to satisfy these new aspirations, however, increases much more slowly than the aspirations themselves. Consequently, a gap develops between aspiration and expectation, want formation and want satisfaction, or the aspirations function and the level-of-living function.[10] This gap generates social frustration and dissatisfaction. In practice, the extent of the gap provides a reasonable index to political instability.

The reasons for this relationship between social frustration and political instability are somewhat more complicated than they may appear on the surface. The relationship is, in large part, due to the absence of two potential intervening variables: opportunities for social and economic mobility and adaptable political institutions. . . . Consequently, the extent to which social frustration produces political participation depends in large part on the nature of the economic and social structure of the traditional society. Conceivably this frustration could be removed through social and economic mobility if the traditional society is sufficiently "open" to offer opportunities for such mobility. In part, this is precisely what occurs in rural areas, where outside opportunities for horizontal mobility (urbanization) contribute to the relative stability of the countryside in most modernizing countries. The few opportunities for vertical (occupational and income) mobility within the cities, in turn, contribute to their greater instability. Apart from urbanization, however, most modernizing countries have low levels of social-economic mobility. In relatively few societies are the traditional structures likely to encourage economic rather than political activity. Land and any other types of economic wealth in the traditional society are tightly held by a relatively small oligarchy or are controlled by foreign corporations and investors. The values of the traditional society often are hostile to entrepreneurial roles, and such roles consequently may be largely monopolized by an ethnic minority (Greeks and Armenians in the ottoman Empire; Chinese in southeast Asia; Lebanese in Africa). In addition, the modern values and ideas which are introduced into the system often stress the primacy of government (socialism, the planned economy), and consequently may also lead mobilized individuals to shy away from entrepreneurial roles.

In these conditions, political participation becomes the road for advancement of the socially mobilized individual. Social frustration leads to demands on the government and the expansion of political participation to enforce those demands. The political backwardness of the country in terms of political institutionalization, moreover, makes it difficult if not impossible for the demands upon the government to be expressed through legitimate channels and to be moderated and aggregated within the political system. Hence the sharp increase in political participation gives rise to political instability. . . .

Political instability in modernizing countries is thus in large part a function of the gap between aspirations and expectations produced by the escalation of aspirations which particularly occurs in the early phases of modernization. . . . . Modernization affects economic inequality and thus political instability in two ways. First, wealth and income are normally more unevenly distributed in poor countries than in economically developed countries.[11] In a traditional society this inequality is accepted as part of the natural pattern of life. Social mobilization, however, increases awareness of the inequality and presumably resentment of it. The influx of new ideas calls into question the legitimacy of the old distribution and suggests the feasibility and the desirability of a more equitable distribution of income. The obvious way of achieving a rapid change in income distribution is through government. Those who command the income, however, usually also command the government. Hence social mobilization turns the traditional economic inequality into a stimulus to rebellion.

Secondly, in the long run, economic development produces a more equitable distribution of income than existed in the traditional society. In the short run, however, the immediate impact of economic growth is often to exacerbate income inequalities. The gains of rapid economic growth are often concentrated in a few groups while the losses are diffused among many; as a result, the number of people getting poorer in the society may actually increase. Rapid growth often involves inflation; in inflation prices typically rise faster than wages with consequent tendencies toward a more unequal distribution of wealth. The impact of Western legal systems in non-Western societies often encourages the replacement of communal forms of land ownership with private ownership and thus tends to produce greater inequalities in land ownership than existed in the traditional society. In addition, in less developed societies the distribution of income in the more modern, non-agricultural sector is typically more unequal than it is in the agricultural. In rural India in 1950, for instance, 5 per cent of the families received 28.9 per cent of the income; but in urban India 5 per cent of the families received 61.5 per cent of the income.[12] Since the overall distribution of income is more equal in the less agricultural, developed nations, the distribution of income within the nonagricultural sector of an underdeveloped country is much more unequal than it is in the same sector in a developed country. . . .

Economic development increases economic inequality at the same time that social mobilization decreases the legitimacy of that inequality. Both aspects of modernization combine to produce political instability.

NOTE

1   David Easton, *The Political System* (New York, 1953), p. 42.

2   Cyril E. Black, *The Dynamics of Modernization* (New York, 1966), pp. 1–5; Reinhard Bendix, "Tradition and Modernity Reconsidered," *Comparative Studies in Society and History*, IX (April 1967), 292–3.

3   Daniel Lerner, *The Passing of Traditional Society* (Glencoe, 1958), p. 438.

4   Black, *Dynamics of Modernization*, pp. 155, 174.

5   Wallace W. Conroe, "A Cross-national Analysis of the Impact of Modernization Upon Political Stability" (unpublished MA thesis, San Diego State College, 1965), pp. 52–4, 60–2; Ivo K. and Rosalind L. Feierabend, "Aggressive Behaviors Within Polities, 1948–1962: A Cross-National Study," *Journal of Conflict Resolution*, 10 (Sept. 1966), 253–4.

6   Alexis de Toqueville, *Democracy in America* (ed. Phillips Bradley, New York, Knopf, 1955), 2, 118.

7   Karl W. Deutsch, "Social Mobilization and Political Development," *American Political Science Review*, 55 (Sept. 1961), 494.

8   On the "erosion of democracy" and political instability, see Rupert Emerson, *From Empire to Nation* (Cambridge, Harvard University Press, 1960), ch. 5; and Michael Brecher, *The New States of Asia* (London, Oxford University Press, 1963), ch. 2.

9   Robert A. LeVine and Donald T. Campbell, "Report on Preliminary Results of Cross-Cultural Study of Ethnocentrism," *Carnegie Corporation of New York Quarterly* (Jan. 1966), 7.

10   These are terms employed by Deutsch, "Social Mobilization," pp. 493 ff.; James C. Davies, "Toward a Theory of Revolution," *American Sociological Review*, 27 (Feb. 1952), 5 ff.; Feierabend, "Aggressive Behaviors," pp. 256–62; Charles Wolf, *Foreign Aid: Theory and Practice in Southern Asia* (Princeton, Princeton University Press, 1960), pp. 296 ff.; and Manus Midlarsky and Raymond Tanter, "Toward a Theory of Political Instability in Latin America," *Journal of Peace Research*, 4 (1967), 271 ff.

11   See Simon Kuznets, "Qualitative Aspects of the Economic Growth of Nations: VIII. Distribution of Income by Size," *Economic Development and Cultural Change*, 11 (Jan. 1963), 68; UN Social Commission, *Preliminary Report on the World Social Situation* (New York, United Nations, 1952), pp. 132–3; Gunnar Myrdal, *An International Economy* (New York, Harper, 1956), p. 133.

12   Kuznets, "Qualitative Aspects," pp. 46–58.

Part II Dependency and Beyond

Introduction

Dependency theories conceptualize the world as consisting of two poles: wealthy countries are the "center" (core) of the global capitalist system, and poor countries are its "satellite" or "periphery." Peripheral countries have low wages enforced by coercive regimes that undermine independent labor unions and social movements. Because there are few members of dependent nations to make up a local market for a range of products, these nations depend on nations in the core for exporting their products. For its part, the core exploits them for cheap labor, raw materials, and larger markets they need to increase their own wealth. Moreover, class conflicts in the center nations are temporarily resolved by their (imperialistic) ability to exploit the periphery. For dependency theorists, underdevelopment in the periphery is the direct result of development in the center, and vice versa. The center–periphery hierarchy and its exploitation was repeated along a chain from wealthy nations to capital cities in poor nations, to their regional cities and then to the hinterlands. Flowing up the chain of unequal relations was power, natural resources, and "surplus value" from labor; flowing down were control, ideology, and expensive products.

Dependency theorists identified several key agents that promote and thrive on a situation of dependency: foreign capital such as multinational corporations based in core nations, elites within nations of the periphery, and national governments. In some cases, the state serves to assure cooperation by the masses. Gereffi's excerpt in this volume clearly demonstrates that the different paths Latin American and East Asian nations took to achieve development are substantially attributable to differences in how these peripheral nations were governed.

Dependency highlights the global nature of capitalism; the poor and wealthy countries are parts of the same global capitalist system, not similar entities at different stages of development (as modernizationists conceived). Dependency theory also illustrates that capitalist expansion is the result of not just economic growth, but specific relationships of economic development that have differential rewards. Furthermore, the center–periphery analogy emphasizes the inherently hierarchical nature of capitalist relationships, both on a global and national scale. While previous development theories treated capitalism as a homogeneous force, dependency and world systems theorists focus on the inequalities created by this set of international economic relationships.

This portion of the volume offers representative works of not only dependency theorists, but also later works representative of world systems theory. This section of readings begins with the work of Andre Gunder Frank. Born in Berlin, Gunder Frank (1929–2004) was educated in the United States and between 1963 and 1973 taught in universities in Brazil, Mexico, and Chile before returning to an academic career in the United States. Although scholars such as Raúl Prebisch, Paul Baran, and Fernando Henrique Cardoso, who all worked for the Chile-based United Nations Economic Commission for Latin America (ECLA), first developed dependency theory, Gunder Frank was the first to present these ideas in English. In the wake of the likes of Rostow, Huntington, and other influential "modernization theorists" of the 1960s, Gunder Frank imported a succinct and controversial set of ideas that were an attractive critique of both capitalism and the dominant perspectives on development as a path. Moreover, the ideas he popularized in dependency theory were the first explanations of why poorer nations are poor that actually originated in those nations whose development (or lack of development) had for years been explained thoroughly by US academics and policy makers.

It is the question of whether and how a situation of dependency can be "fixed" that roughly divides dependency theorists into two schools. The first, of which Gunder Frank's piece is exemplary, argues that underdevelopment is not a phase but a permanent, inescapable condition, only remedied by escaping the entire capitalist system. In this more radical camp Gunder Frank is joined by others, such as Paul Baran, Theotonio Dos Santos, and Samir Amin. These authors believe that the capitalist system is not a competitive one, but one based on monopolies. Therefore, poorer countries cannot expect to change their situation through competition. For example, Baran argues that places like Latin America are not engaged in a process of becoming more capitalistic. Instead, their historical experience resulted in their being stuck in what he calls an "imperialist" stage of capitalism.[1] Similarly, Gunder Frank claims, at the same time that capitalism produces wealth and furthers development in the "core" countries, it creates poverty and underdevelopment in the "satellite" countries. This underdevelopment, according to Gunder Frank, will not just dissipate with time or even with social change; the only recourse for poorer nations is to protect their markets strongly from relationships with richer ones, relationships that are ultimately exploitative.

These theorists have been widely criticized on the basis that they do not really offer any feasible solutions. This strain of dependency theory also seemed to lack mechanisms for analyzing change (especially upward mobility experienced by some peripheral countries), for recognizing heterogeneity within the periphery, or for acknowledging any vulnerability on the part of the world's center nations. For example, when dependency theory suggests that capitalism produces permanent unalterable relationships, it fails to explain why there appear to be different levels of exploitation over time or why there are significant differences among poorer countries. These theories may be more useful in furthering specific political agendas than actually explaining processes of development or underdevelopment.

The other school of dependency theory acknowledges the crucial impacts of situations of dependency, but envisions a *possibility* for some degree of development within this relationship, what is called "associated" and "dependent" development.[2] In such circumstances, poorer countries are subject to a situation of dependency, yet manage to develop to some extent. Through a set of policies known as Import Substitution Industrialization, ECLA advocated the development of domestic industries as a way to develop a comparative advantage in products with higher values and reduce Latin American countries' *dependency* on center countries. This type of policy was an effort to acknowledge dependency, but it attempts to ameliorate its effects by developing in only relative isolation from the damaging relations with the wealthy nations.

Representing this "structuralist" variant of dependency theory in this volume is the work of Brazilian sociologist Fernando Henrique Cardoso. As an exile in Chile following Brazil's military coup of 1964, Cardoso worked with other development theorists associated with ECLA. He took their economistic ideas in new social and political directions, with a more strongly historical approach than many dependency theorists. When he returned to Brazil in the 1980s, he served as a governor and senator, became Economic Minister, and was then elected President in 1995. In his work, Cardoso pays especially close attention to how elites in poorer nations have historically allied themselves with foreign interests to their benefit and to the detriment of the poorer masses in their countries. His historical analysis also shows how wealthier nations and wealthier people in poorer nations have used imperialist tactics to keep poorer countries producing cheaper things like minerals and food, so that these things are available to further economic development and industrialization in wealthier countries. Because he pays attention to the nuances within the economies and societies of poorer countries, Cardoso demonstrates how limited forms of development occur despite consistent subordination by wealthier nations. Believing that poorer nations must navigate toward what development they can within the global economy makes Cardoso an important intellectual and political leader of the more moderate "structuralist" group of dependency theorists.

Later North American authors such as Gary Gereffi and Peter Evans further developed the notion of dependent development by exploring how economic structure and/or specific state policies may perpetuate dependency or foment development within a context of dependency. They also worked toward more systematic comparisons of economic resource bases, elite actions, types of governance, and relationships among actors in the periphery to highlight key historical and indigenous differences among nations of the periphery. They found that differences among various types of elites in the periphery can help explain different political regimes, economies, and class relationships within the periphery. Evans even goes further in his perceptions of possibilities for autonomous action by asking what challenges to the situation of dependency have arisen, especially from peripheral economies (specifically, Brazil).[3] Ultimately, in response to critiques of dependency and under the leadership of theorists such as Immanuel Wallerstein, dependency theories were developed into a distinct "World Systems Theory." For example, Christopher Chase-Dunn, Peter Evans, and Gary Gereffi all did early work that could have been classified as dependency theory, and later became key contributors to world systems theory.

It was Immanuel Wallerstein's three-volume *The Modern World System* – the first of which was published in 1974 – that marked the birth of the subdiscipline in the United States. This work describes four core postulates of world systems theory. First, that there is one single underlying set of processes in the world system, to which all economies are subject. Any history of a location must include an understanding of that history of the whole. Therefore, the nation-state, although an important variable in development, is not the only level of analysis in understanding processes of development. Instead, there are worldwide processes that serve as key determinants of development and change at all levels.

Second, and elaborating on the work of the dependency theorists, this worldwide system is a hierarchy consisting of three situations, or zones: the core, semi-periphery, and periphery. Based on the unit of the nation state, as well as international and national class alliances, the core of the world system extracts wealth and controls, through various types of relationships, from nations in the periphery, which are dependent on trade and relationships with the core. The semi-peripheral zone includes nations like Brazil and South Africa which have features of both the rich and poor countries, and which act as intermediaries in the processes of exploitation of the periphery by the core. Wallerstein's approach to the "socialist" nations was that they were merely "state capitalist," that is, their governments were acting as the owners, and trading in a world capitalist system where markets were determining prices. It is important to note that unlike the crudest forms of dependency theory, world systems theory allows for the possibility of mobility in the hierarchy of this single global system, though most countries have not been able to move up.

Third, the processes by which wealth is extracted from the periphery are similar to those described by the dependency theorists: unequal exchange, active or subtle repression, and the control of marketing and the high-value ends of commodity chains (see Gereffi, Chapter 8). Finally, world systems theory proposes that in addition to cycles, capitalism has some crucial secular trends. These include the broadening of the areas of the world participating in capitalist exchange, and the deepening which goes on by attaching a price to everything (commodification), making everyone a wage-worker (proletarianization), mechanization, and the polarization of social classes.

Within a cadre of world systems theorists, Duke University sociologist Gary Gereffi (1948–) pioneered the "commodity chain" approach and has contributed enormously in recent decades to the comparative study of development. He argues that poorer countries were able to develop only so far because they were selling their goods on unfavorable terms, for example, in contracting arrangements, where US firms like Nike carried out the marketing of shoes produced cheaply in Korea or China. In "Rethinking Development Theory: Insights from East Asia and Latin America," first published in 1989, Gereffi points out the differences and similarities in the trajectories of Latin American and Asian developing nations, comparing Brazil and Mexico with Korea and Taiwan. He examines the question of why East Asian countries were able to maintain growth in the 1970s and 1980s when other nations endured the effects of a global recession. His work is useful in tracing the stages of policies taken by nations in the two regions, showing how production for export (Asia) or internal markets (Latin America) was based on and later influenced many aspects of the nation's social structure, such as income distribution or politics.

Despite their close attention to class inequalities, critiques of capitalism such as dependency and world systems have long been criticized for undertheorizing the relationships between capitalism and its parallel system of exploitation, patriarchy. Even though economic change and development can actively marginalize women's productive and reproductive labor, too often women's work is invisible in the academic literature explaining development. While many have documented how capitalist development affects women, efforts to explain how gender affects the biggest structures of the global economy are much less elaborated in mainstream world systems literature and instead somewhat marginalized in "feminist" literatures on women and development. We complete this section with an effort to address this failing by Valentine Moghadam, who is currently serving as the Chief of the Gender Equality and Development, Social and Human Sciences Sector at UNESCO (United Nations). In this piece, Moghadam attempts to integrate these efforts by mapping the relationship between gender and the global economy. She explains that not only does development and economic policy have gender-specific impacts, but also that gender roles support the global economy in many ways.

An additional critique of world systems theory is that it is too economistic, that is, the economy is assumed to be determining everything else. Research in recent decades, including that by Gereffi, exemplifies strong efforts by world systems researchers to incorporate the state more directly in their theorizing; but have yet to do much with culture as causation. Thomas Shannon also accuses world systems theory of bordering on teleology – assuming that the capitalist world system is driving toward some end, and ascribes agency and functionalist needs to the capitalist system itself. And finally, world systems theory, like many of the theories in this volume, is based on propositions that are still not especially testable. Sociologist Alejandro Portes levels a harsh critique of world systems theory for often remaining at high levels of abstraction and failing to capitalize on the burgeoning awareness that the economy had indeed gone global.[4] World systems theorists had been saying this for years.[5]

NOTES

1 Peter F. Klarén and Thomas J. Bossert, *The Promise of Development: Theories of Change in Latin America*, Boulder, CO: Westview, 1986, p. 17.

2 See Fernando Enrique Cardoso and Enzo Faletto, *Dependency and Development in Latin America* (Berkeley and Los Angeles: University of California Press, 1979) and Peter Evans, *Dependent Development: the Alliance of Multinational, State and Local Capital in Brazil* (Princeton: Princeton University Press, 1979). Cristóbal Kay reminds us that this line is "structuralism," while the more radical line is true "dependency" theory (see his "Relevance of Structuralist and Dependency Theories in the Neoliberal Period: A Latin American Perspective," Institute of Social Sciences, The Hague: Working Paper Series No. 281, 1998 and *Latin American Theories of Development and Underdevelopment*, New York: Routledge, 1989). A 2005 issue of the *Latin American Research Review* (40:3) includes a research forum reevaluating structuralism and its descendants.

3 Peter Evans, *Dependent Development: the Alliance of Multinational, State and Local Capital in Brazil*, Princeton, NJ: Princeton University Press, 1979.

4 Alejandro Portes, "Neoliberalism and the Sociology of Development: Emerging Trends and Unanticipated Facts," *Population and Development Review* 23:2 (1997): 229–59.

5 The field of world systems theory remains alive in sociology and political science in the United States, but its growth was curtailed by the postmodernist critique that *no* overarching theory of development could be possible (J. Timmons Roberts and Peter E. Grimes, "Extending the World-System to the Whole System: Towards a Political Economy of the Biosphere," in *The Global Environment and the World-System*, ed. Walter Goldfrank, David Goodman, and Andrew Szasz, Westport, CT: Greenwood Press, 1999, pp. 59–83). It should be pointed out that several of the authors presented under the following sections on globalization are in fact active in networks of world systems scholars; they are here attempting to explain globalization from world systems perspectives.

5 The Development of Underdevelopment (1969)

Andre Gunder Frank

I

We cannot hope to formulate adequate development theory and policy for the majority of the world's population who suffer from underdevelopment without first learning how their past economic and social history gave rise to their present underdevelopment. Yet most historians study only the developed metropolitan countries and pay scant attention to the colonial and underdeveloped lands. For this reason most of our theoretical categories and guides to development policy have been distilled exclusively from the historical experience of the European and North American advanced capitalist nations.

Since the historical experience of the colonial and underdeveloped countries has demonstrably been quite different, available theory therefore fails to reflect the past of the underdeveloped part of the world entirely, and reflects the past of the world as a whole only in part. More important, our ignorance of the underdeveloped countries' history leads us to assume that their past and indeed their present resembles earlier stages of the history of the now developed countries. This ignorance and this assumption lead us into serious misconceptions about contemporary underdevelopment and development. Further, most studies of development and underdevelopment fail to take account of the economic and other relations between the metropolis and its economic colonies throughout the history of the world-wide expansion and development of the mercantilist and capitalist system. Consequently, most of our theory fails to explain the structure and development of the capitalist system as a whole and to account for its simultaneous generation of underdevelopment in some of its parts and of economic development in others.

It is generally held that economic development occurs in a succession of capitalist stages and that today's underdeveloped countries are still in a stage, sometimes depicted as an original stage of history, through which the now developed countries passed long ago. Yet even a modest acquaintance with history shows that underdevelopment is not original or traditional and that neither the past nor the present of the underdeveloped countries resembles in any important respect the past of the now developed countries. The now developed countries were never *under*developed, though they may have been *un*developed. It is also widely believed that the contemporary underdevelopment of a country can be understood as the product or reflection solely of its own economic, political, social, and cultural characteristics or structure. Yet historical research demonstrates that contemporary underdevelopment is in large part the historical product of past and continuing economic and other relations between the satellite underdeveloped and the now developed metropolitan countries. Furthermore, these relations are an essential part of the structure and development of the capitalist system on a world scale as a whole. A related and also largely erroneous view is that the development of these underdeveloped countries and, within them of their most underdeveloped domestic areas, must and will be generated or stimulated by diffusing capital, institutions, values, etc., to them from the international and national capitalist metropoles. Historical perspective based on the underdeveloped countries' past experience suggests that on the contrary in the underdeveloped countries economic development can now occur only independently of most of these relations of diffusion.

Evident inequalities of income and differences in culture have led many observers to see "dual" societies and economics in the underdeveloped countries. Each of the two parts is supposed to have a history of its own, a structure, and a contemporary dynamic largely independent of the other. Supposedly, only one part of the economy and society has been importantly affected by intimate economic relations with the "outside" capitalist world; and that part, it is held, became modern, capitalist, and relatively developed precisely because of this contact. The other part is widely regarded as variously isolated, subsistence-based, feudal, or precapitalist, and therefore more underdeveloped.

I believe on the contrary that the entire "dual society" thesis is false and that the policy recommendations to which it leads will, if acted upon, serve only to intensify and perpetuate the very conditions of underdevelopment they are supposedly designed to remedy.

A mounting body of evidence suggests, and I am confident that future historical research will confirm, that the expansion of the capitalist system over the past centuries effectively and entirely penetrated even the apparently most isolated sectors of the underdeveloped world. Therefore, the economic, political, social, and cultural institutions and relations we now observe there are the products of the historical development of the capitalist system no less than are the seemingly more modern or capitalist features of the national metropoles of these underdeveloped countries. Analogously to the relations between development and underdevelopment on the international level, the contemporary underdeveloped institutions of the so-called backward or feudal domestic areas of an underdeveloped country are no less the product of the single historical process of capitalist development than are the so-called capitalist institutions of the supposedly more progressive areas. In this paper I should like to sketch the kinds of evidence which support this thesis and at the same time indicate lines along which further study and research could fruitfully proceed.

II

The Secretary General of the Latin American Center for Research in the Social Sciences writes in that Center's journal: "The privileged position of the city has its origin in the colonial period. It was founded by the Conqueror to serve the same ends that it still serves today; to incorporate the indigenous population into the economy brought and developed by that Conqueror and his descendants. The regional city was an instrument of conquest and is still today an instrument of domination."[1] The Instituto Nacional Indigenista (National Indian Institute) of Mexico confirms this observation when it notes that "the mestizo population, in fact, always lives in a city, a center of an intercultural region, which acts as the metropolis of a zone of indigenous population and which maintains with the underdeveloped communities an intimate relation which links the center with the satellite communities."[2] The Institute goes on to point out that "between the mestizos who live in the nuclear city of the region and the Indians who live in the peasant hinterland there is in reality a closer economic and social interdependence than might at first glance appear" and that the provincial metropoles "by being centers of intercourse are also centers of exploitation."[3]

Thus these metropolis–satellite relations are not limited to the imperial or international level but penetrate and structure the very economic, political, and social life of the Latin American colonies and countries. Just as the colonial and national capital and its export sector become the satellite of the Iberian (and later of other) metropoles of the world economic system, this satellite immediately becomes a colonial and then a national metropolis with respect to the productive sectors and population of the interior. Furthermore, the provincial capitals, which thus are themselves satellites of the national metropolis – and through the latter of the world metropolis – are in turn provincial centers around which their own local satellites orbit. Thus, a whole chain of constellations of metropoles and satellites relates all parts of the whole system from its metropolitan center in Europe or the United States to the farthest outpost in the Latin American countryside.

When we examine this metropolis–satellite structure, we find that each of the satellites, including now-underdeveloped Spain and Portugal, serves as an instrument to suck capital or economic surplus out of its own satellites and to channel part of this surplus to the world metropolis of which all are satellites. Moreover, each national and local metropolis serves to impose and maintain the monopolistic structure and exploitative relationship of this system (as the Instituto Nacional Indigenista of Mexico calls it) as long as it serves the interests of the metropoles which take advantage of this global, national, and local structure to promote their own development and the enrichment of their ruling classes.

These are the principal and still surviving structural characteristics which were implanted in Latin America by the Conquest. Beyond examining the establishment of this colonial structure in its historical context, the proposed approach calls for study of the development – and underdevelopment – of these metropoles and satellites of Latin America throughout the following and still continuing historical process. In this way we can understand why there were and still are tendencies in the Latin American and world capitalist structure which seem to lead to the development of the metropolis and the underdevelopment of the satellite and why, particularly, the satellized national, regional, and local metropoles in Latin America find that their economic development is at best a limited or underdeveloped development.

III

That present underdevelopment of Latin America is the result of its centuries-long participation in the process of world capitalist development, I believe I have shown in my case studies of the economic and social histories of Chile and Brazil. My study of Chilean history suggests that the Conquest not only incorporated this country fully into the expansion and development of the world mercantile and later industrial capitalist system but that it also introduced the monopolistic metropolis–satellite structure and development of capitalism into the Chilean domestic economy and society itself. This structure then penetrated and permeated all of Chile very quickly. Since that time and in the course of world and Chilean history during the epochs of colonialism, free trade, imperialism, and the present, Chile has become increasingly marked by the economic, social, and political structure of satellite underdevelopment. This development of underdevelopment continues today, both in Chile's still increasing satellization by the world metropolis and through the ever more acute polarization of Chile's domestic economy.

The history of Brazil is perhaps the clearest case of both national and regional development of underdevelopment. The expansion of the world economy since the beginning of the sixteenth century successively converted the Northeast, the Minas Gerais interior, the North, and the Center-South (Rio de Janeiro, São Paulo, and Paraná) into export economies and incorporated them into the structure and development of the world capitalist system. Each of these regions experienced what may have appeared as economic development during the period of its respective golden age. But it was a satellite development which was neither self-generating nor self-perpetuating. As the market or the productivity of the first three regions declined, foreign and domestic economic interest in them waned; and they were left to develop the underdevelopment they live today. In the fourth region, the coffee economy experienced a similar though not yet quite as serious fate (though the development of a synthetic coffee substitute promises to deal it a mortal blow in the not too distant future). All of this historical evidence contradicts the generally accepted theses that Latin America suffers from a dual society or from the survival of feudal institutions and that these are important obstacles to its economic development.

IV

During the First World War, however, and even more during the Great Depression and the Second World War, São Paulo began to build up an industrial establishment which is the largest in Latin America today. The question arises whether this industrial development did or can break Brazil out of the cycle of satellite development and underdevelopment which has characterized its other regions and national history within the capitalist system so far. I believe that the answer is no. Domestically the evidence so far is fairly clear. The development of industry in São Paulo has not brought greater riches to the other regions of Brazil. Instead, it converted them into internal colonial satellites, de-capitalized them further, and consolidated or even deepened their underdevelopment. There is little evidence to suggest that this process is likely to be reversed in the foreseeable future except insofar as the provincial poor migrate and become the poor of the metropolitan cities. Externally, the evidence is that although the initial development of São Paulo's industry was relatively autonomous it is being increasingly satellized by the world capitalist metropolis and its future development possibilities are increasingly restricted. This development, my studies lead me to believe, also appears destined to limited or underdeveloped development as long as it takes place in the present economic, political, and social framework.

We must conclude, in short, that underdevelopment is not due to the survival of archaic institutions and the existence of capital shortage in regions that have remained isolated from the stream of world history. On the contrary, underdevelopment was and still is generated by the very same historical process which also generated economic development: the development of capitalism itself. This view, I am glad to say, is gaining adherents among students of Latin America and is proving its worth in shedding new light on the problems of the area and in affording a better perspective for the formulation of theory and policy.

V

The same historical and structural approach can also lead to better development theory and policy by generating a series of hypotheses about development and underdevelopment such as those I am testing in my current research. The hypotheses are derived from the empirical observation and theoretical assumption that within this world-embracing metropolis–satellite structure the metropoles tend to develop and the satellites to underdevelop. The first hypothesis has already been mentioned above: that in contrast to the development of the world metropolis which is no one's satellite, the development of the national and other subordinate metropoles is limited by their satellite status. It is perhaps more difficult to test this hypothesis than the following ones because part of its confirmation depends on the test of the other hypotheses. Nonetheless, this hypothesis appears to be generally confirmed by the non-autonomous and unsatisfactory economic and especially industrial development of Latin America's national metropoles, as documented in the studies already cited. The most important and at the same time most confirmatory examples are the metropolitan regions of Buenos Aires and São Paulo whose growth only began in the nineteenth century, was therefore largely untrammelled by any colonial heritage, but was and remains a satellite development largely dependent on the outside metropolis, first of Britain and then of the United States.

A second hypothesis is that the satellites experience their greatest economic development and especially their most classically capitalist industrial development if and when their ties to their metropolis are weakest. This hypothesis is almost diametrically opposed to the generally accepted thesis that development in the underdeveloped countries follows from the greatest degree of contact with and diffusion from the metropolitan developed countries. This hypothesis seems to be confirmed by two kinds of relative isolation that Latin America has experienced in the course of its history. One is the temporary isolation caused by the crises of war or depression in the world metropolis. Apart from minor ones, five periods of such major crises stand out and seem to confirm the hypothesis. These are: the European (and especially Spanish) Depression of the seventeenth century, the Napoleonic Wars, the First World War, the Depression of the 1930's, and the Second World War. It is clearly established and generally recognized that the most important recent industrial development – especially of Argentina, Brazil, and Mexico, but also of other countries such as Chile – has taken place precisely during the periods of the two World

Wars and the intervening Depression. Thanks to the consequent loosening of trade and investment ties during these periods, the satellites initiated marked autonomous industrialization and growth. Historical research demonstrates that the same thing happened in Latin America during Europe's seventeenth-century depression. Manufacturing grew in the Latin American countries, and several of them such as Chile became exporters of manufactured goods. The Napoleonic Wars gave rise to independence movements in Latin America, and these should perhaps also be interpreted as confirming the development hypothesis in part.

The other kind of isolation which tends to confirm the second hypothesis is the geographic and economic isolation of regions which at one time were relatively weakly tied to and poorly integrated into the mercantilist and capitalist system. My preliminary research suggests that in Latin America it was these regions which initiated and experienced the most promising self-generating economic development of the classical industrial capitalist type. The most important regional cases probably are Tucumán and Asunción, as well as other cities such as Mendoza and Rosario, in the interior of Argentina and Paraguay during the end of the eighteenth and the beginning of the nineteenth centuries. Seventeenth- and eighteenth-century São Paulo, long before coffee was grown there, is another example. Perhaps Antioquia in Colombia and Puebla and Querétaro in Mexico are other examples. In its own way, Chile was also an example since, before the sea route around the Horn was opened, this country was relatively isolated at the end of the long voyage from Europe via Panama. All of these regions became manufacturing centers and even exporters, usually of textiles, during the periods preceding their effective incorporation as satellites into the colonial, national, and world capitalist system. . . .

VI

A corollary of the second hypothesis is that when the metropolis recovers from its crisis and re-establishes the trade and investment ties which fully re-incorporate the satellite into the system, or when the metropolis expands to incorporate previously isolated regions into the world-wide system, the previous development and industrialization of these regions is choked off or channelled into directions which are not self-perpetuating and promising. This happened after each of the five crises cited above. The renewed expansion of trade and the spread of economic liberalism in the eighteenth and nineteenth centuries choked off and reversed the manufacturing development which Latin America had experienced during the seventeenth century, and in some places at the beginning of the nineteenth. After the First World War, the new national industry of Brazil suffered serious consequences from American economic invasion. The increase in the growth rate of Gross National Product and particularly of industrialization throughout Latin America was again reversed and industry became increasingly satellized after the Second World War and especially after the post-Korean War recovery and expansion of the metropolis. Far from having become more developed since then, industrial sectors of Brazil and most conspicuously of Argentina have become structurally more and more underdeveloped and less and less able to generate continued industrialization and/or sustain development of the economy.

This process, from which India also suffers, is reflected in a whole gamut of balance-of-payments, inflationary, and other economic and political difficulties, and promises to yield to no solution short of far-reaching structural change.

Our hypothesis suggests that fundamentally the same process occurred even more dramatically with the incorporation into the system of previously unsatellized regions. The expansion of Buenos Aires as a satellite of Great Britain and the introduction of free trade in the interest of the ruling groups of both metropoles destroyed the manufacturing and much of the remainder of the economic base of the previously relatively prosperous interior almost entirely. Manufacturing was destroyed by foreign competition, lands were taken and concentrated into latifundia by the rapaciously growing export economy, intraregional distribution of income became much more unequal, and the previously developing regions became simple satellites of Buenos Aires and through it of London. The provincial centers did not yield to satellization without a struggle. This metropolis–satellite conflict was much of the cause of the long political and armed struggle between the Unitarists in Buenos Aires and the Federalists in the provinces, and it may be said to have been the sole important cause of the War of the Triple Alliance in which Buenos Aires, Montevideo, and Rio de Janeiro, encouraged and helped by London, destroyed not only the autonomously developing economy of Paraguay but killed off nearly all of its population which was unwilling to give in. Though this is no doubt the most spectacular example which tends to confirm the hypothesis, I believe that historical research on the satellization of previously relatively independent yeoman-farming and incipient manufacturing regions such as the Caribbean islands will confirm it further. These regions did not have a chance against the forces of expanding and developing capitalism, and their own development had to be sacrificed to that of others. The economy and industry of Argentina, Brazil, and other countries which have experienced the effects of metropolitan recovery since the Second World War are today suffering much the same fate, if fortunately still in lesser degree.

VII

A third major hypothesis derived from the metropolis–satellite structure is that the regions which are the most underdeveloped and feudal-seeming today are the ones which had the closest ties to the metropolis in the past. They are the regions which were the greatest exporters of primary products to and the biggest sources of capital for the world metropolis and which were abandoned by the metropolis when for one reason or another business fell off. This hypothesis also contradicts the generally held thesis that the source of a region's underdevelopment is its isolation and its precapitalist institutions.

This hypothesis seems to be amply confirmed by the former super-satellite development and present ultra-underdevelopment of the once sugar-exporting West Indies, Northeastern Brazil, the ex-mining districts of Minas Gerais in Brazil, highland Peru, and Bolivia, and the central Mexican states of Guanajuato, Zacatecas, and others whose names were made world famous centuries ago by their silver. There surely are no major regions in Latin America which are today more cursed by underdevelopment and poverty; yet all of these regions, like Bengal in India, once provided the life blood of mercantile and industrial capitalist development – in the metropolis. These regions' participation in the development of the world capitalist system gave them, already in their golden age, the typical structure of underdevelopment of a capitalist export economy. When the market for their sugar or the wealth of their mines disappeared and the metropolis abandoned them to their own devices, the already existing economic, political, and social structure of these regions prohibited autonomous generation of economic development and left them no alternative but to turn in upon themselves and to degenerate into the ultra-underdevelopment we find there today.

VIII

These considerations suggest two further and related hypotheses. One is that the latifundium, irrespective of whether it appears as a plantation or a hacienda today, was typically born as a commercial enterprise which created for itself the institutions which permitted it to respond to increased demand in the world or national market by expanding the amount of its land, capital, and labor and to increase the supply of its products. The fifth hypothesis is that the latifundia which appear isolated, subsistence-based, and semi-feudal today saw the demand for their products or their productive capacity decline and that they are to be found principally in the above-named former agricultural and mining export regions whose economic activity declined in general. These two hypotheses run counter to the notions of most people, and even to the opinions of some historians and other students of the subject, according to whom the historical roots and socio-economic causes of Latin American latifundia and agrarian institutions are to be found in the transfer of feudal institutions from Europe and/or in economic depression.

The evidence to test these hypotheses is not open to easy general inspection and requires detailed analyses of many cases. Nonetheless, some important confirmatory evidence is available. The growth of the latifundium in nineteenth-century Argentina and Cuba is a clear case in support of the fourth hypothesis and can in no way be attributed to the transfer of feudal institutions during colonial times. The same is evidently the case of the postrevolutionary and contemporary resurgence of latifundia particularly in the North of Mexico, which produce for the American market, and of similar ones on the coast of Peru and the new coffee regions of Brazil. The conversion of previously yeoman-farming Caribbean islands, such as Barbados, into sugar-exporting economies at various times between the seventeenth and twentieth centuries and the resulting rise of the latifundia in these islands would seem to confirm the fourth hypothesis as well. In Chile, the rise of the latifundium and the creation of the institutions of servitude which later came to be called feudal occurred in the eighteenth century and have been conclusively shown to be the result of and response to the opening of a market for Chilean wheat in Lima.[4] Even the growth and consolidation of the latifundium in seventeenth-century Mexico – which most expert students have attributed to a depression of the economy caused by the decline of mining and a shortage of Indian labor and to a consequent turning in upon itself and ruralization of the economy – occurred at a time when urban population and demand were growing, food shortages became acute, food prices skyrocketed, and the profitability of other economic activities such as mining and foreign trade declined. All of these and other factors rendered hacienda agriculture more profitable. Thus, even this case would seem to confirm the hypothesis that the growth of the latifundium and its feudal-seeming conditions of servi-tude in Latin America has always been and still is the commercial response to increased demand and that it does not represent the transfer or survival of alien institutions that have remained beyond the reach of capitalist development. The emergence of latifundia, which today really are more or less (though not entirely) isolated, might then be attributed to the causes advanced in the fifth hypothesis – i.e., the decline of previously profitable agricul-tural enterprises whose capital was, and whose currently produced economic surplus still is, transferred elsewhere by owners and merchants who frequently are the same persons or families. Testing this hypothesis requires still more detailed analysis, some of which I have undertaken in a study on Brazilian agriculture.

IX

All of these hypotheses and studies suggest that the global extension and unity of the capi-talist system, its monopoly structure and uneven development throughout its history, and the resulting persistence of commercial rather than industrial capitalism in the under-developed world (including its most industrially advanced countries) deserve much more attention in the study of economic development and cultural change than they have hitherto received. Though science and truth know no national boundaries, it is probably new generations of scientists from the underdeveloped countries themselves who most need to, and best can, devote the necessary attention to these problems and clarify the process of underdevelopment and development. It is their people who in the last analysis face the task of changing this no longer acceptable process and eliminating this miserable reality.

They will not be able to accomplish these goals by importing sterile stereotypes from the metropolis which do not correspond to their satellite economic reality and do not respond to their liberating political needs. To change their reality they must understand it. For this reason, I hope that better confirmation of these hypotheses and further pursuit of the proposed historic, holistic, and structural approach may help the peoples of the under-developed countries to understand the causes and eliminate the reality of their development of underdevelopment and their underdevelopment of development.

NOTES

1   *América Latina*, Año 6, No. 4 (Oct.–Dec. 1963), p. 8.
2   Instituto Nacional Indigenista, *Los centros coordinadores indigenistas* (Mexico City, 1962), p. 34.
3   *Ibid.*, pp. 33–4, 88.
4   Mario Góngora, *Origen de los "inquilinos" de Chile central* (Santiago: Editorial Universitaria, 1960); Jean Borde and Mario Góngora, *Evolución de la propriedad rural en el Valle del Puango* (Santiago: Instituto de Sociología de la Universidad de Chile); Sergio Sepúlveda, *El trigo chileno en el mercado mundial* (Santiago: Editorial Universitaria, 1959).

6 Dependency and Development in Latin America (1972)

Fernando Henrique Cardoso

The theory of imperialist capitalism, as is well known, has so far attained its most significant treatment in Lenin's works. This is not only because Lenin attempts to explain transformations of the capitalist economies that occurred during the last decade of the 19th century and the first decade of the 20th, but mainly because of the political and historical implications contained in his interpretations. In fact, the descriptive arguments of Lenin's theory of imperialism were borrowed from Hobson's analysis. Other writers had already presented evidence of the international expansion of the capitalist economies and nations. Nevertheless, Lenin, inspired by Marx's views, was able to bring together evidence to the effect that economic expansion is meaningless if we do not take into consideration the *political* and *historical* aspects with which economic factors are intimately related. From Lenin's perspective, imperialism is a new form of the capitalist mode of production. This new form cannot be considered as a *different* mode of economic organization, in so far as capital accumulation based on private ownership of the means of production and exploitation of the labour force remain the basic features of the system. But its significance is that of a new *stage* of capitalism. The historical "momentum" was a new one, with all the political consequences of that type of transformation: within the dominant capitalist classes, new sectors tried to impose their interests and ideologies; the State, the Army and all basic social and political institutions were redefined in order to assure expansion abroad. At the same time new types of liberation and social struggles came onto the historical scene – the colonial liberation movements and the fight against "trade unionism", the latter a struggle against an initial form of working-class compromise with the bourgeoisie made possible by the exploitation of the colonial world.

From that broad picture of a new historical stage of capitalist development Lenin inferred new political tasks, tactics and strategies for socialist revolution.

Lenin's Characterization of Imperialism

The main points of Lenin's characterization of imperialism that are essential to the present discussion can be summarized as follows:

(a)   the capitalist economy in its "advanced stages" involves a concentration of capital and production (points that were well established by Marx in *Capital*) in such a way that the competitive market is replaced in its basic branches by a monopolistic one.

(b)   this trend was historically accomplished through internal differentiation of capitalist functions, leading not only to the formation of a financial stratum among entrepreneurs but to the marked prominence of the banking system in the capitalist mode of production. Furthermore, the fusion of industrial capital with financial capital under the control of the latter turned out to be the decisive feature of the political and economic relations within capitalist classes, with all the practical consequences that such a system of relations has in terms of state organization, politics and ideology.

(c)   capitalism thus reached its "ultimate stage of development" both internally and externally. Internally, control of the productive system by financiers turned the productive forces and the capital accumulation process toward the search for new possibilities for investment. The problem of "capital realization" became in this way an imperative necessity to permit the continuing of capitalist expansion. In addition there were internal limits that impeded the continuous reinvestment of new capital (impoverishment of the masses, a faster rate of capital growth than that of the internal market, and so on.) *External outlets* had to be found to ensure the continuity of capitalist advance and accumulation.

(d)   the increased and increasing speed of the development of productive forces under monopolistic control also pushed the advanced capitalist countries toward the political control of foreign lands. The search for control over *raw materials* is yet another reason why capitalism in its monopolistic stage becomes expansionist.

In short, Lenin's explanations of why advanced capitalist economies were impelled toward the control of backward lands, was based on two main factors. One stressed movements of capital, the other outlined the productive process. Both were not only linked to each other but also related to the global transformation of the capitalist system that had led to the control of the productive system by financiers. It is not difficult to see that such modifications deeply affected state organization and functions as well as the relationships among nations, since a main thrust of capitalist development in the stage of imperialism was toward the territorial division of the world among the leading capitalist countries. This process guaranteed capital flows from the over-capitalized economies to backward countries and assured provision of raw materials in return.

Imperialism and Dependent Economies

From that perspective, the consequence of imperialism with respect to dependent economies and nations (or colonies) was the integration of the latter into the international market. Inequality among nations and economies resulted from imperialism's development to the extent that import of raw materials and export of manufactured goods were the bases of the imperialist-colonial relationship. The reproduction and amplification of inequality between advanced economies and dependent economies developed as a by-product of the very process of capitalist growth.

Certainly, Lenin was aware of particular types of interconnections, as in Argentina and other economies dependent on Great Britain, where local bourgeoisies controlled sectors of the productive system creating more complex patterns of exploitation. The same was true with respect to the political aspects of dependency in those countries where the state tried to defend the national bourgeoisie against imperialist pressures.

Nevertheless, from the theoretical point of view, as a mode of exploitation, imperialism should tend to restrict the economic growth of backward countries to mineral and agricultural sectors in order to assure raw materials for the advanced capitalist nations in their drive for further industrialization. For the same reasons the indigenous labour force could be kept at low wage and salary levels. By that means the dominant central economies were assured of cheap raw material prices. Consequently, in colonized or dependent nations, internal markets did not have any special strategic significance.

Of course, in terms of "capital realization", selling products abroad had importance. But even so, the main imperialistic tie in terms of direct capital investment was oriented toward the concession of loans to the dependent State or to private local entrepreneurs. In both cases, however, political and financial guarantees were assured by the State or the administration of the receiver country.

In short, imperialist profit was based on unequal trade and financial exploitation. The latter could be measured by the increasing indebtedness of exploited economies to the central economies. The former was evidenced through the different types of products exchanged, i.e. raw materials for manufactured goods. This process of exploitation of the indigenous labour force thus insured an unevenness in both types of economies. Moreover, technological advances in the industrial sectors of central economies provided a high level of exploitation, increasing the relative surplus value extracted through a continuously advancing technology of production (leading in turn to unevenness of the rate of organic composition of capital), while in the dominated economies the direct over-exploitation of labour prevailed in the productive system.

Politically, this type of economic expansion thus reinforced colonial links, through wars, repression and subjugation of peoples that previously were not only marginal to the international market, but were culturally independent and structurally did not have links with the Western world. Such were the African and Asian regions where nations, in spite of previous commercial–capitalist expansion, remained largely untouched in terms of their productive systems.

Latin America from the beginning was somewhat different in its links to the imperialist process. It is true that this process of colonialistic penetration obtained with respect to some countries (mainly the Caribbean nations). Yet throughout most of Latin America, the imperialistic upsurge occurred by way of a more complex process, through which Latin American countries kept their political independence, but slowly shifted from subordination to an earlier British influence to American predominance.

Ownership of the productive system was the site of the main differences. Some Latin American economies, even after imperialist predominance, were able to cope with the new situation by maintaining proprietorship of the local export economy in the hands of native bourgeoisies. Thus in some countries (such as Argentina, Brazil, Uruguay, Colombia, Chile), the export sector remained at least to some extent controlled by the local bourgeoisie and the links of dependence were based more on trade and financial relations than directly on the productive sectors. In some countries the internal financial system was itself mainly dominated by internal bankers, and financial dependence was based on international loans contracted, as noted above, by the State or under State guarantees.

In spite of numerous political and economic variations, Lenin's basic picture remained valid: the internal market of Latin American countries grew in a limited way during the period of the first imperialist expansion; the industrial sector was not significantly expanded; external financial dependence grew enormously; raw materials including foodstuffs constituted the basis of export economies.

At the same time not only were the majority of Latin American countries unable to keep control of the export sector, but some of the countries that had previously retained dominance of raw materials or food production, now lost that capacity (as in the Chilean mineral economy).

New Patterns of Capital Accumulation

In spite of the accuracy of Lenin's insights as measured against historical events during the first half of the century in many parts of the world, some important recent changes have deeply affected the pattern of relationship between imperialist and dependent nations. These changes demand a reappraisal of emergent structures and their main tendencies. Even if these modifications are not so deep as the shift that enabled Lenin to characterize a new stage of capitalism during the period of imperialist expansion, they are marked enough to warrant a major modification of the established analyses of capitalism and imperialism. Nevertheless, contemporary international capitalist expansion and control of dependent economies undoubtedly prove that this new pattern of economic relationships among nations remains imperialist. However, the main points of Lenin's characterization of imperialism and capitalism are no longer fully adequate to describe and explain the present forms of capital accumulation and external expansion.

With respect to changes that have occurred within the more advanced capitalist economies (chiefly the rise of monopoly capital and corporate enterprise) there are some consistent analyses. Baran and Sweezy's works, as well as those of Magdoff, Mandel and O'Connor, come to mind. These offer a comprehensive body of descriptive and explanatory material showing the differences between capitalism now and during Lenin's life.

In spite of some recent criticism, Baran and Sweezy argued convincingly (and Sweezy's article on "The Resurgence of Financial Control: Fact or Fancy?"[1] helps to affirm that conviction) that corporations operate as quasi-self-sufficient units of decision and action vis-à-vis capital accumulation. Hence previous notions of banking control over industry need to be rethought. Similarly, the conglomerate form of present big corporations and the multinational scope of the production and marketing adds considerable novelty to the capitalist form of production.[2]

These transformations (and we are only suggesting some of the principal ones which affect all processes of capitalist transformation) have led to important consequences that have been already analysed by the authors noted, as well as others. These writers stress, for instance, the increasing secular growth of profit rates under administered prices in a monopoly system. Of course, this is a central point in Marxian theory and in Lenin's analysis. Yet now important modifications, such as those mentioned, alter the type of political response that the capitalist system is able to produce in order to cope with the challenging situations created by its expansion.

It is equally necessary to approach the problem of surplus realization with a fresh perspective. In this connection some authors have considered the strengthened ties between militarist expansion and the reinforcement of military control over society, through a war economy, as the basic means of capital realization. As a second argument, but a still important factor, State expenditures in welfare are emphasized as alternative outlets for capital accumulation.

Though the adequacy of this analysis may be questioned, Marxist authors have carried out a fairly comprehensive *economic* reinterpretation of the mode of functioning of monopoly capitalism. The same is not true, however, when one considers the *political* aspects of the problem and especially the *politico-economic* consequences of monopoly capitalism in dependent economies. Let us start with the last aspect of the question.

New Forms of Economic Dependency

. . . [F]oreign investment in the new nations and in Latin America is moving rapidly away from oil, raw materials and agriculture and in the direction of the industrial sectors. Even where the bulk of assets continues to remain in the traditional sectors of imperialist investment, the rate of expansion of the industrial sector is rapid. This is true not only for Latin America but also for Africa and Asia.

The point is not only that multinational corporations are investing in the industrial sectors of dominated economies, instead of in the traditional agricultural and mineral sectors. Beyond that, even when "traditional" sectors of dependent economies, they are operating in technically and organizationally advanced modes, sometimes accepting local participation in their enterprises. Of course, these transformations do not mean that previous types of imperialistic investment, i.e. in oil or metals, are disappearing, even in the case of the most industrialized dependent economies, i.e., Argentina, Brazil and Mexico in Latin America. However, the dominant traits of imperialism in those countries, as the process of industrialization continues, cannot be adequately described and interpreted on the basis of frames of reference that posit the exchange of raw material for industrialized goods as the main feature of trade, and suppose virtually complete external ownership of the dependent economies' means of production.

Even the mineral sector (such as manganese in Brazil, copper in Chile during Frei's government, or petro-chemicals in various countries) is now being submitted to new patterns of economic ownership. The distinguishing feature of these new forms is the joint venture enterprise, comprising local state capital, private national capital and monopoly international investment (under foreign control in the last analysis).

As a consequence, in some dependent economies – among these, the so-called "developing countries" of Latin America – foreign investment no longer remains a simple zero-sum game of exploitation as was the pattern in classical imperialism. Strictly speaking – if we consider the purely economic indicators – it is not difficult to show that *development* and *monopoly penetration* in the industrial sectors of dependent economies are not incompatible. The idea that there occurs a kind of development of underdevelopment, apart from the play on words, is not helpful. In fact, *dependency, monopoly capitalism* and *development* are not contradictory terms: there occurs a kind of *dependent capitalist development* in the sectors of the Third World integrated into the new forms of monopolistic expansion.

As a result in countries like Argentina, Brazil, Mexico, South Africa, India, and some others, there is an internal structural fragmentation, connecting the most "advanced" parts of their economies to the international capitalist system. Separate although subordinated to these advanced sectors, the backward economic and social sectors of the dependent countries then play the role of "internal colonies". The gap between both will probably increase, creating a new type of dualism, quite different from the imaginary one sustained by some non-Marxist authors. The new structural "duality" corresponds to a kind of internal differentiation of the same unity. It results directly, of course, from capitalist expansion and is functional to that expansion, in so far as it helps to keep wages at a low level and diminishes political pressures inside the "modern" sector, since the social and economic position of those who belong to the latter is always better in comparative terms.

If this is true, to what extent is it possible to sustain the idea of *development* in tandem with dependence? The answer cannot be immediate. First of all I am suggesting that the present trend of imperialist investment allows some degree of local participation in the process of economic production. Let us indicate a crucial feature in which present and past forms of capitalism differ. During the previous type of imperialism, the market for goods produced in dependent economies by foreign enterprise was mostly, if not fully, the market of the advanced economies: oil, copper, coffee, iron bauxite, manganese, etc., were produced to be sold and consumed in the advanced capitalist countries. This explains why the internal market of dependent economies was irrelevant for the imperialist economies, excepting the modest portion of import goods consumed by the upper class in the dominated society.

Today for G.M. or Volkswagen, or General Electric, or Sears Roebuck, the Latin American market, if not the particular market in each country where those corporations are producing in Latin America, is the immediate goal in terms of profit. So, at least to some extent, a certain type of foreign investment needs some kind of internal prosperity. There are and there will be some parts of dependent societies, tied to the corporate system, internally and abroad, through shared interests.

On the other hand, and in spite of internal economic development, countries tied to international capitalism by that type of linkage remain economically dependent, insofar as the production of the means of production (technology) are concentrated in advanced capitalist economies (mainly in the US).

In terms of the Marxist scheme of capital reproduction, this means that sector I (the production of means of production) – the strategic part of the reproductive scheme – is virtually non-existent in dependent economies. Thus, from a broad perspective, the realization of capital accumulation *demands* a productive complementarity which does not exist within the country. In Lenin's interpretation the imperialist economies needed external expansion for the realization of capital accumulation. Conversely, within the dependent economies capital returns to the metropole in order to complete the cycle of capitalist reproduction. That is the reason why "technology" is so important. Its "material" aspect is less impressive than its significance as a form of maintenance of control and as a necessary step in the process of capital accumulation. Through technological advantage, corporations make secure their key roles in the global system of capital accumulation. Some degree of local prosperity is possible insofar as consumption goods locally produced by foreign investments can induce some dynamic effects in the dependent economies. But at the same time, the global process of capitalist development determines an interconnection between the sector of production of consumption goods and the capital goods sector, reproducing in this way the links of dependency.

One of the main factors which explained imperialist expansion in Lenin's theory was the search for capitalist investment. Now since foreign capital goes to the industrial sector of dependent economies in search of external markets, some considerable changes have occurred. First, in comparison with expanding assets of foreign corporations, the net amount of foreign capital actually invested in the dependent economies is decreasing: local savings and the reinvestment of profits realized in local markets provides resources for the growth of foreign assets with limited external flow of new capital. This is intimately related to the previously discussed process of expansion of the local market and it is also related to the mounting of "joint ventures" linking local capitalists and foreign enterprise.

Secondly, but no less important, statistics demonstrate that dependent economies during the period of monopolistic imperialist expansion are *exporting* capital to the dominant economies.

As a reaction against that process, some dependent countries have tried to limit exportable profits. Nevertheless, international corporations had the foresight to sense that the principal way to send returns abroad is through the payment of licenses, patents, royalties and related items. These institutional devices, together with the increasing indebtedness of the exploited nations vis-à-vis international agencies and banks (in fact controlled by the big imperialist countries), have altered the main forms of exploitation.

It is not the purpose of this presentation to discuss all the consequences of this for a monopoly capitalist economy. However, some repercussions of the new pattern of imperialism on the US and other central economies are obvious. If a real problem of capital realization exists under monopoly capitalism, the new form of dependency will increase the necessity to find new fields of application for the capital accumulated in the metropolitan economies. Witness the push toward more "technical obsolescence" administered by corporations. Military expenditures are another means of finding new outlets for capital.

Nevertheless, I am not considering the whole picture. In fact, some of these conclusions might change if the capital flows and trade interrelations among advanced capitalist economies were taken into consideration. Thus the preceding remarks are presented with the single aim of stressing that the present trend of capital export from the underdeveloped countries to the imperialist ones leads to a redefinition of the function of foreign expansion for capital realization.

The idea that the growth of capitalism depends on Third World exploitation requires some further elaboration. In fact, the main trends of the last decade show that Latin American participation in both the expansion of international trade and investment is decreasing. If we accept the distinction between two sectors of international trade – the

Centre and the Periphery – one finds that the trade rate of growth was 7.9 per cent per year in the central economies and 4.8 per cent in the peripheral ones. As a consequence, exports of the peripheral economies which reached a peak in 1948 (32 per cent of the international trade) decreased to 26 per cent in 1958 and to 21 per cent in 1968 (below the 28 per cent of the pre-war period). In the Latin American case this participation decreased from 12 per cent in 1948 to 6 per cent in 1968. The same is happening with respect to the importance that the periphery has for US investments. The periphery absorbed 55 per cent of the total US direct investment in 1950 and only 40 per cent in 1968. Latin American participation in this process fell in the same period from 39 per cent to 20 per cent.

Of course, these data do not show the increase of "loans and aid" which – as was stressed before – has been of increasing importance in economic imperialism. However, the fact that the interrelations among the most advanced economies are growing cannot be utilized as an argument to infer the "end of imperialism". On the contrary, the more appropriate inference is that the relations between advanced capitalist countries and dependent nations lead rather to a "marginalization" of the latter within the global system of economic development (as Anibal Pinto has outlined).

Some Political Consequences

The new forms of dependency will undoubtedly give rise to novel political and social adaptations and reactions inside the dependent countries. If my analysis is correct, the above-mentioned process of fragmentation of interests will probably lead to an internal differentiation that in very schematic terms can be suggested as follows. Part of the "national bourgeoisie", (the principal one in terms of economic power – agrarian, commercial, industrial or financial) is the direct beneficiary, as a junior partner, of the foreign interest. I refer not only to the direct associates, but also to economic groups that benefit from the eventual atmosphere of prosperity derived from dependent development (as is easily demonstrated in Brazil or Mexico). The process goes further and not only part of the "middle class" (intellectuals, state bureaucracies, armies, etc.) are involved in the new system, but even part of the working class. Those employed by the "internationalized" sector structurally belong to it.

Of course, structural dependence does not mean immediate political co-option. Effective political integration of groups and persons depends on the political processes, movements, goals and alternatives that they face.

Nevertheless, as the process of internationalization of dependent nations progresses, it becomes difficult to perceive the political process in terms of a struggle between the Nation and the anti-Nation, the latter conceived as the Foreign Power of Imperialism. The anti-Nation will be inside the "Nation" – so to speak, among the local people in different social strata. Furthermore, to perceive that, in these terms, the Nation is an occupied one, is not an easy process: there are very few "others" in cultural and national terms physically representing the presence of "the enemy".

I do not wish to give the impression that I conceive the political process in a mechanistic way. Consequently, my intention is not to "derive" some political consequences from a structural economic analysis. Rather, the point is that most socialist interpretations of the

Latin American political situation not only run in that direction but also assume the wrong structural point of departure.

Some more general remarks can be summarized thus:

(a) Analysis which is based on the naive assumption that imperialism unifies the interests and reactions of dominated nations is a clear oversimplification of what is really occurring. It does not take into consideration the internal fragmentation of these countries and the attraction that development exerts in different social strata, and not only on the upper classes.

(b) The term 'development of underdevelopment' (in A. G. Frank) summarizes another mistake. In fact, the assumption of a structural 'lack of dynamism' in dependent economies because of imperialism misinterprets the actual forms of economic imperialism and presents an imprecise political understanding of the situation. It is necessary to understand that in specific situations it is possible to expect *development* and *dependency*.

It would be wrong to generalize these processes to the entire Third World. They only occur when corporations reorganize the international division of labour and include parts of dependent economies in their plans of productive investment.

Thus the majority of the Third World is not necessarily involved in this specific structural situation. To assume the contrary will lead to political mistakes equivalent to those derived from, for instance, Debray's analysis of Latin America. Debray once accepted the view that imperialism homogenized all Latin American countries (with one or two exceptions) and assumed a frame of reference which stressed the old fashioned type of imperialist exploitation with its attendant reinforcement of oligarchic and landlord-based types of dominance.

Now, I am assuming that there are different forms of dependency in Latin America and that in some of them, development produces a shift in internal power, displacing the old oligarchical power groups and reinforcing more "modern" types of political control. In that sense, the present dictatorships in Latin America, even when militarily based, do not express, by virtue of pure structural constraints, a traditional and "anti-developmentalist" (I mean anti-modern capitalism) form of domination.

It is hardly necessary to repeat that from the left's point of view there are strong arguments to maintain its denunciation of both new forms of imperialism or dependency and political authoritarianism. But clearly, new political analyses are needed to explain the bureaucratic-technocratic form of authoritarian state which serves the interests of the internationalized bourgeoisie and their allies.

In this context, and in order to avoid a mechanistic approach, a correct orientation of the struggles against capitalist imperialism demands special attention to cultural problems and the different forms of alienation.

If the capitalist pattern of development in industrialized dependent countries pushes toward internal fragmentation and inequalities, values related to national integrity and social participation might be transformed into instruments of political struggle. To permit the State and bourgeois groups to command the banner of nationalism – conceived not only in terms of sovereignty but also of internal cohesion and progressive social integration –

would be a mistake with deep consequences. I am not supporting the idea that the strategic (or revolutionary) side of dependent industrialized societies is the "marginalized sector". But denunciation of marginalization as a consequence of capitalist growth, and the organization of unstructured masses, are indispensable tasks of analysis and practical politics.

For this reason it is not very realistic to expect the national bourgeoisie to lead resistance against external penetration. Consequently, denunciation of the dependency perspective cannot rest on values associated with bourgeois nationalism. National integrity as cited above means primarily popular integration in the nation and the need to struggle against the particular form of development promoted by the large corporations.

In the same way that trade unionism may become a danger for workers in advanced capitalist societies, development is a real ideological pole of attraction for middle class *and workers'* sectors in Latin American countries. The answer to that attractive effect cannot be a purely ideological denial of economic progress, when it occurs. A reply must be based on values and political objectives that enlarge the awareness of the masses with respect to social inequalities and national dependency.

NOTES

1   See P. Sweezy, "The Resurgence of Financial Control: Fact or Fancy?," *Socialist Revolution*, 8:2:2 (Mar.–Apr. 1972), 157–92.
2   See H. Magdoff and P. Sweezy, "Notes on the Multinational Corporation," in K.T. Fann and D.C. Hodges, *Readings in U.S. Imperialism* (Boston, 1972), pp. 93–116.

7 The Rise and Future Demise of the World Capitalist System: Concepts for Comparative Analysis (1979)

Immanuel Wallerstein

The growth within the capitalist world-economy of the industrial sector of production, the so-called "industrial revolution", was accompanied by a very strong current of thought which defined this change as both a process of organic development and of progress. There were those who considered these economic developments and the concomitant changes in social organization to be some penultimate stage of world development whose final working out was but a matter of time. These included such diverse thinkers as Saint-Simon, Comte, Hegel, Weber, Durkheim. And then there were the critics, most notably Marx, who argued, if you will, that the nineteenth-century present was only an antepenultimate stage of development, that the capitalist world was to know a cataclysmic political revolution which would then lead in the fullness of time to a final societal form, in this case the classless society.

One of the great strengths of Marxism was that, being an oppositional and hence critical doctrine, it called attention not merely to the contradictions of the system but to those of its ideologists, by appealing to the empirical evidence of historical reality which unmasked the irrelevancy of the models proposed for the explanation of the social world. The Marxist critics saw in abstracted models concrete rationalization, and they argued their case fundamentally by pointing to the failure of their opponents to analyze the social whole. As Lukács put it, "it is not the primacy of economic motives in historical explanation that constitutes the decisive difference between Marxism and bourgeois thought, but the point of view of totality".[1] . . .

Shall we then turn to . . . Marxism, to give us a better account of social reality? In principle yes; in practice there are many different, often contradictory, versions extant of "Marxism". But what is more fundamental is the fact that in many countries Marxism is now the official state doctrine. Marxism is no longer exclusively an oppositional doctrine as it was in the nineteenth century.

The social fate of official doctrines is that they suffer a constant social pressure towards dogmatism and apologia, difficult although by no means impossible to counteract, and that they thereby often fall into the same intellectual dead end of ahistorical model building. . . .

Nothing illustrates the distortions of ahistorical models of social change better than the dilemmas to which the concept of stages gives rise. If we are to deal with social transformations over long historical time (Braudel's "the long term"), and if we are to give an explanation of both continuity and transformation, then we must logically divide the long term into segments in order to observe the structural changes from time A to time B. These segments are however not discrete but continuous in reality; *ergo* they are "stages" in the "development" of a social structure, a development which we determine however not *a priori* but *a posteriori*. That is, we cannot predict the future concretely, but we can predict the past.

The crucial issue when comparing "stages" is to determine the units of which the "stages" are synchronic portraits (or "ideal types", if you will). And the fundamental error of ahistorical social science (including ahistorical versions of Marxism) is to reify parts of the totality into such units and then to compare these reified structures.

For example, we may take modes of disposition of agricultural production, and term them subsistence cropping and cash cropping. We may then see these as entities which are "stages" of a development. We may talk about decisions of groups of peasants to shift from one to the other. We may describe other partial entities, such as states, as having within them two separate "economies", each based on a different mode of disposition of agricultural production. If we take each of these successive steps, all of which are false steps, we will end up with the misleading concept of the "dual economy" as have many liberal economists dealing with the so-called underdeveloped countries of the world. Still worse, we may reify a misreading of British history into a set of universal "stages" as Rostow does.

Marxist scholars have often fallen into exactly the same trap. If we take modes of payment of agricultural labor and contrast a "feudal" mode wherein the laborer is permitted to retain for subsistence a part of his agricultural production with a "capitalist" mode wherein the same laborer turns over the totality of his production to the landowner, receiving part of it back in the form of wages, we may then see these two modes as "stages" of a development. We may talk of the interests of "feudal" landowners in preventing the conversion of their mode of payment to a system of wages. We may then explain the fact that in the twentieth century a partial entity, say a state in Latin America, has not yet industrialized as the consequence of its being dominated by such landlords. If we take each of these successive steps, all of which are false steps, we will end up with the misleading concept of a "state dominated by feudal elements", as though such a thing could possibly exist in a capitalist world-economy. . . .

Not only does the misidentification of the entities to be compared lead us into false concepts, but it creates a non-problem: can stages be skipped? This question is only logically meaningful if we have "stages" that "coexist" within a single empirical framework. If within a capitalist world-economy, we define one state as feudal, a second as capitalist, and a third as socialist, then and only then can we pose the question: can a country "skip" from the feudal stage to the socialist stage of national development without "passing through capitalism"?

But if there is no such thing as "national development" (if by that we mean a natural history), and if the proper entity of comparison is the world system, then the problem of stage skipping is nonsense. If a stage can be skipped, it isn't a stage. And we know this *a posteriori*.

If we are to talk of stages, then – and we should talk of stages – it must be stages of social systems, that is, of totalities. And the only totalities that exist or have historically existed are minisystems and world-systems, and in the nineteenth and twentieth centuries there has been only one world-system in existence, the capitalist world-economy.

We take the defining characteristic of a social system to be the existence within it of a division of labor, such that the various sectors or areas within are dependent upon economic exchange with others for the smooth and continuous provisioning of the needs of the area. Such economic exchange can clearly exist without a common political structure and even more obviously without sharing the same culture.

A minisystem is an entity that has within it a complete division of labor, and a single cultural framework. Such systems are found only in very simple agricultural or hunting and gathering societies. Such minisystems no longer exist in the world. Furthermore, there were fewer in the past than is often asserted, since any such system that became tied to an empire by the payment of tribute as "protection costs"[2] ceased by that fact to be a "system", no longer having a self-contained division of labor. For such an area, the payment of tribute marked a shift, in Polanyi's language, from being a reciprocal economy to participating in a larger redistributive economy.[3]

Leaving aside the now defunct minisystems, the only kind of social system is a world-system, which we define quite simply as a unit with a single division of labor and multiple cultural systems. It follows logically that there can, however, be two varieties of such world-systems, one with a common political system and one without. We shall designate these respectively as world-empires and world-economies.

It turns out empirically that world-economies have historically been unstable structures leading either towards disintegration or conquest by one group and hence transformation into a world-empire. Examples of such world-empires emerging from world-economies are all the so-called great civilizations of premodern times, such as China, Egypt, Rome (each at appropriate periods of its history). On the other hand, the so-called nineteenth-century empires, such as Great Britain or France, were not world-empires at all, but nation-states with colonial appendages operating within the framework of a world-economy.

World-empires were basically redistributive in economic form. No doubt they bred clusters of merchants who engaged in economic exchange (primarily long-distance trade), but such clusters, however large, were a minor part of the total economy and not fundamentally determinative of its fate. Such long-distance trade tended to be, as Polanyi argues, "administered trade" and not market trade, utilizing "ports of trade".

It was only with the emergence of the modern world-economy in sixteenth-century Europe that we saw the full development and economic predominance of market trade. This was the system called capitalism. Capitalism and a world-economy (that is, a single division of labor but multiple polities and cultures) are obverse sides of the same coin. One does not cause the other. We are merely defining the same indivisible phenomenon by different characteristics. . . .

On the "feudalism" debate, we take as a starting point Frank's concept of "the development of underdevelopment", that is, the view that the economic structures of contemporary underdeveloped countries is not the form which a "traditional" society takes upon contact with "developed" societies, not an earlier stage in the "transition" to industrialization. It is rather the result of being involved in the world-economy as a peripheral, raw material producing area, or as Frank puts it for Chile, "underdevelopment . . . is the necessary product of four centuries of capitalism itself".[4]

This formulation runs counter to a large body of writing concerning the underdeveloped countries that was produced in the period 1950–70, a literature which sought the factors that explained "development" within non-systems such as "states" or "cultures" and, once having presumably discovered these factors, urged their reproduction in underdeveloped areas as the road to salvation.

Frank's theory also runs counter, as we have already noted, to the received orthodox version of Marxism that had long dominated Marxist parties and intellectual circles, for example in Latin America. This older "Marxist" view of Latin America as a set of feudal societies in a more or less prebourgeois stage of development has fallen before the critiques of Frank and many others as well as before the political reality symbolized by the Cuban revolution and all its many consequences. Recent analysis in Latin America has centered instead around the concept of "dependence".[5]

However, recently, Ernesto Laclau has made an attack on Frank which, while accepting the critique of dualist doctrines, refuses to accept the categorization of Latin American states as capitalist. Instead Laclau asserts that "the world capitalist system . . . includes, *at the level of its definition*, various modes of production". He accuses Frank of confusing the two concepts of the "capitalist mode of production" and "participation in a world capitalist economic system".[6]

Of course, if it's a matter of definition, then there can be no argument. But then the polemic is scarcely useful since it is reduced to a question of semantics. Furthermore, Laclau insists that the definition is not his but that of Marx, which is more debatable. . . .

There is . . . a substantive issue in this debate. It is in fact the same substantive issue that underlay the debate between Maurice Dobb and Paul Sweezy in the early 1950s about the "transition from feudalism to capitalism" that occurred in early modern Europe.[7] The substantive issue, in my view, concerns the appropriate unit of analysis for the purpose of comparison. Basically, although neither Sweezy nor Frank is quite explicit on this point, and though Dobb and Laclau can both point to texts of Marx that seem clearly to indicate that they more faithfully follow Marx's argument, I believe both Sweezy and Frank better follow the spirit of Marx if not his letter[8] and that, leaving Marx quite out of the picture, they bring us nearer to an understanding of what actually happened and is happening than do their opponents.

What is the picture, both analytical and historical, that Laclau constructs? The heart of the problem revolves around the existence of free labor as the defining characteristic of a capitalist mode of production:

> The fundamental economic relationship of capitalism is constituted by the *free* [italics mine] labourer's sale of his labour-power, whose necessary precondition is the loss by the direct producer of ownership of the means of production . . .[9] . . .

There in a nutshell it is. Western Europe, at least England from the late seventeenth century on, had primarily landless, wage-earning laborers. In Latin America, then and to some extent still now, laborers were not proletarians, but slaves or "serfs". If proletariat, then capitalism. Of course. To be sure. But is England, or Mexico, or the West Indies a unit of analysis? Does each have a separate "mode of production"? Or is the unit (for the six-teenth–eighteenth centuries) the European world-economy, including England *and* Mexico, in which case what was the "mode of production" of this world-economy?

Before we argue our response to this question, let us turn to quite another debate, one between Mao Tse-Tung and Liu Shao-Chi in the 1960s concerning whether or not the Chinese People's Republic was a "socialist state". This is a debate that has a long background in the evolving thought of Marxist parties.

Marx, as has been often noted, said virtually nothing about the post-revolutionary politi-cal process. Engels spoke quite late in his writings of the "dictatorship of the proletariat". It was left to Lenin to elaborate a theory about such a "dictatorship", in his pamphlet *State and Revolution*, published in the last stages before the Bolshevik takeover of Russia, that is, in August 1917. The coming to power of the Bolsheviks led to a considerable debate as to the nature of the regime that had been established. Eventually a theoretical distinction emerged in Soviet thought between "socialism" and "communism" as two stages in histori-cal development, one realizable in the present and one only in the future. In 1936 Stalin proclaimed that the USSR had become a socialist (but not yet a communist) state. Thus we now had firmly established *three* stages after bourgeois rule: a post-revolutionary govern-ment, a socialist state, and eventually communism. When, after the Second World War, various regimes dominated by the Communist Party were established in various east European states, these regimes were proclaimed to be "peoples' democracies", a new name then given to the post-revolutionary stage one. At later points, some of these countries, for example Czechoslovakia, asserted they had passed into stage two, that of becoming a socialist republic.

In 1961, the 22nd Congress of the CPSU invented a fourth stage, in between the former second and third stages: that of a socialist state which had become a "state of the whole people", a stage it was contended the USSR had at that point reached. The Programme of the Congress asserted that "the state as an organization of the entire people will survive until the complete victory of communism".[10] One of its commentators defines the "intrinsic substance (and) chief distinctive feature" of this stage: "The state of the whole people is the first state in the world with no class struggle to contend with and, hence, with no class domination and no suppression."[11]

One of the earliest signs of a major disagreement in the 1950s between the Communist Party of the Soviet Union and the Chinese Communist Party was a theoretical debate that revolved around the question of the "gradual transition to Communism". Basically, the CPSU argued that different socialist states would proceed separately in effectuating such a transition whereas the CCP argued that all socialist states would proceed simultaneously.

As we can see, this last form of the debate about "stages" implicitly raised the issue of the unit of analysis, for in effect the CCP was arguing that "communism" was a character-istic not of nation-states but of the world-economy as a whole. This debate was transposed onto the internal Chinese scene by the ideological debate, now known to have deep and long-standing roots, that gave rise eventually to the Cultural Revolution.

One of the corollaries of these debates about "stages" was whether or not the class struggle continued in post-revolutionary states prior to the achievement of communism. The 22nd Congress of the CPSU in 1961 had argued that the USSR had become a state without an internal class struggle, there were no longer existing antagonistic classes within it. Without speaking of the USSR, Mao Tse-Tung in 1957 had asserted in China:

> The class struggle is by no means over . . . It will continue to be long and tortuous, and at times will even become very acute . . . Marxists are still a minority among the entire population as well as among the intellectuals. Therefore, Marxism must still develop through struggle . . . Such struggles will never end. This is the law of development of truth and, naturally, of Marxism as well.[12]

If such struggles *never* end, then many of the facile generalizations about "stages" which "socialist" states are presumed to go through are thrown into question.

During the Cultural Revolution, it was asserted that Mao's report *On the Correct Handling of Contradiction Among the People* cited above, as well as one other, "entirely repudiated the 'theory of the dying out of the class struggle' advocated by Liu Shao-Chi . . ."[13] Specifically, Mao argued that "the elimination of the system of ownership by the exploiting classes through socialist transformation is not equal to the disappearance of struggle in the political and ideological spheres".[14]

Indeed, this is the logic of a *cultural* revolution. Mao is asserting that even if there is the achievement of *political* power (dictatorship of the proletariat) and *economic* transformation (abolition of private ownership of the means of production), the revolution is still far from complete. Revolution is not an event but a process. This process Mao calls "socialist society" – in my view a somewhat confusing choice of words, but no matter – and "socialist society covers a fairly long historical period".[15] Furthermore, "there are classes and class struggle throughout the period of socialist society".[16] The Tenth Plenum of the 8th Central Committee of the CCP, meeting from 24 to 27 September 1962, in endorsing Mao's views, omitted the phrase "socialist society" and talked instead of "the historical period of proletarian revolution and proletarian dictatorship, . . . the historical period of transition from capitalism to communism", which it said "will last scores of years or even longer" and during which "there is a class struggle between the proletariat and the bourgeosie and struggle between the socialist road and the capitalist road".[17]

We do not have directly Liu's counter arguments. We might however take as an expression of the alternative position a recent analysis published in the USSR on the relationship of the socialist system and world development. There it is asserted that at some unspecified point after the Second World War, "socialism outgrew the bounds of one country and became a world system . . ."[18] It is further argued that: "Capitalism, emerging in the 16th century, became a world economic system only in the 19th century. It took the bourgeois revolutions 300 years to put an end to the power of the feudal elite. It took socialism 30 or 40 years to generate the forces for a new world system."[19] Finally, this book speaks of "capitalism's international division of labor"[20] and "international socialist cooperation of labor"[21] as two separate phenomena, drawing from this counterposition the policy conclusion: "Socialist unity has suffered a serious setback from the divisive course being pursued by the incumbent leadership of the Chinese People's Republic", and attributes this to "the great-power chauvinism of Mao Tse-Tung and his group".[22]

Note well the contrast between these two positions. Mao Tse-Tung is arguing for viewing "socialist society" as process rather than structure. Like Frank and Sweezy, and once again implicitly rather than explicitly, he is taking the world-system rather than the nation-state as the unit of analysis. The analysis by USSR scholars by contrast specifically argues the existence of *two* world-systems with two divisions of labor existing side by side, although the socialist system is acknowledged to be "divided". If divided politically, is it united economically? Hardly, one would think; in which case what is the substructural base to argue the existence of the system? Is it merely a moral imperative? And are then the Soviet scholars defending their concepts on the basis of Kantian metaphysics?

Let us see now if we can reinterpret the issues developed in these two debates within the framework of a general set of concepts that could be used to analyze the functioning of world-systems, and particularly of the historically specific capitalist world-economy that has existed for about four or five centuries now.

We must start with how one demonstrates the existence of a single division of labor. We can regard a division of labor as a grid which is substantially interdependent. Economic actors operate on some assumption (obviously seldom clear to any individual actor) that the totality of their essential needs – of sustenance, protection, and pleasure – will be met over a reasonable time span by a combination of their own productive activities and exchange in some form. The smallest grid that would substantially meet the expectations of the overwhelming majority of actors within those boundaries constitutes a single division of labor.

The reason why a small farming community whose only significant link to outsiders is the payment of annual tribute does not constitute such a single division of labor is that the assumptions of persons living in it concerning the provision of protection involve an "exchange" with other parts of the world-empire.

This concept of a grid of exchange relationships assumes, however, a distinction between *essential* exchanges and what might be called "luxury" exchanges. This is to be sure a distinction rooted in the social perceptions of the actors and hence in both their social organization and their culture. These perceptions can change. But this distinction is crucial if we are not to fall into the trap of identifying *every* exchange activity as evidence of the existence of a system. Members of a system (a minisystem or a world-system) can be linked in limited exchanges with elements located outside the system, in the "external arena" of the system. . . .

We are, as you see, coming to the essential feature of a capitalist world-economy, which is production for sale in a market in which the object is to realize the maximum profit. In such a system production is constantly expanded as long as further production is profitable, and men constantly innovate new ways of producing things that will expand the profit margin. The classical economists tried to argue that such production for the market was somehow the "natural" state of man. But the combined writings of the anthropologists and the Marxists left few in doubt that such a mode of production (these days called "capitalism") was only one of several possible modes.

Since, however, the intellectual debate between the liberals and the Marxists took place in the era of the industrial revolution, there has tended to be a *de facto* confusion between industrialism and capitalism. This left the liberals after 1945 in the dilemma of explaining how a presumably non-capitalist society, the USSR, had industrialized. The most sophisticated response has been to conceive of "liberal capitalism" and "socialism" as two variants of an "industrial society", two variants destined to "converge". This argument has been trenchantly expounded by Raymond Aron.[23] But the same confusion left the Marxists, including Marx, with the problem of explaining what was the mode of production that predominated in Europe from the sixteenth to the eighteenth centuries, that is before the industrial revolution. Essentially, most Marxists have talked of a "transitional" stage, which is in fact a blurry non-concept with no operational indicators. This dilemma is heightened if the unit of analysis used is the state, in which case one has to explain why the transition has occurred at different rates and times in different countries.

Marx himself handled this by drawing a distinction between "merchant capitalism" and "industrial capitalism". This I believe is unfortunate terminology, since it leads to such conclusions as that of Maurice Dobb who says of this "transitional" period:

> But why speak of this as a stage of capitalism at all? The workers were generally not proletarianized: that is, they were not separated from the instruments of production, nor even in many cases from occupation of a plot of land. Production was scattered and decentralized and not concentrated. *The capitalist was still predominantly a merchant* [italics mine] who did not control production directly and did not impose his own discipline upon the work of artisan-craftsmen, who both laboured as individual (or family) units and retained a considerable measure of independence (if a dwindling one).[24]

One might well say: why indeed? Especially if one remembers how much emphasis Dobb places a few pages earlier on capitalism as a mode of *production* – how then can the capitalist be primarily a merchant? – on the concentration of such ownership in the hands of a few, and on the fact that capitalism is not synonymous with private ownership, capitalism being different from a system in which the owners are "small peasant producers or artisan-producers". Dobb argues that a defining feature of private ownership under capitalism is that some are "obliged to [work for those that own] since [they own] nothing and [have] no access to means of production [and hence] have no other means of livelihood".[25] Given this contradiction, the answer Dobb gives to his own question is in my view very weak: "While it is true that at this date the situation was transitional, and capital-to-wage-labour relations were still immaturely developed, the latter were already beginning to assume their characteristic features".[26]

If capitalism is a mode of production, production for profit in a market, then we ought, I should have thought, to look to whether or not such production was or was not occurring. It turns out in fact that it was, and in a very substantial form. Most of this production, however, was not industrial production. What was happening in Europe from the sixteenth to the eighteenth centuries is that over a large geographical area going from Poland in the northeast westwards and southwards throughout Europe and including large parts of the Western Hemisphere as well, there grew up a world-economy with a single division of labor within which there was a world market, for which men produced largely agricultural products for sale and profit. I would think the simplest thing to do would be to call this agricultural capitalism.

This then resolves the problems incurred by using the pervasiveness of *wage* labor as a defining characteristic of capitalism. An individual is no less a capitalist exploiting labor because the state assists him to pay his laborers low wages (including wages in kind) and denies these laborers the right to change employment. Slavery and so-called "second serfdom" are not to be regarded as anomalies in a capitalist system. Rather the so-called serf in Poland or the Indian on a Spanish *encomienda* in New Spain in this sixteenth-century world-economy were working for landlords who "paid" them (however euphemistic this term) for cash crop production. This is a relationship in which labor power is a commodity (how could it ever be more so than under slavery?), quite different from the relationship of a feudal serf to his lord in eleventh-century Burgundy, where the economy was not oriented to a world market, and where labor power was (therefore?) in no sense bought or sold.

Capitalism thus means labor as a commodity to be sure. But in the era of agricultural capitalism, wage labor is only one of the modes in which labor is recruited and recompensed in the labor market. Slavery, coerced cash-crop production (my name for the so-called "second feudalism"), sharecropping, and tenancy are all alternative modes. It would be too long to develop here the conditions under which differing regions of the world-economy tend to specialize in different agricultural products. I have done this elsewhere.[27]

What we must notice now is that this specialization occurs in specific and differing geographic regions of the world-economy. This regional specialization comes about by the attempts of actors in the market to avoid the normal operation of the market whenever it does not maximize their profit. The attempts of these actors to use nonmarket devices to ensure short-run profits makes them turn to the political entities which have in fact power to affect the market – the nation-states. . . .

. . . In any case, the local capitalist classes – cash-crop landowners (often, even usually, nobility) and merchants – turned to the state, not only to liberate them from non-market constraints (as traditionally emphasized by liberal historiography) but to create new constraints on the new market, the market of the European world-economy.

By a series of accidents – historical, ecological, geographic – northwest Europe was better situated in the sixteenth century to diversify its agricultural specialization and add to it certain industries (such as textiles, shipbuilding, and metal wares) than were other parts of Europe. Northwest Europe emerged as the core area of this world-economy, specializing in agricultural production of higher skill levels, which favored (again for reasons too complex to develop) tenancy and wage labor as the modes of labor control. Eastern Europe and the Western Hemisphere became peripheral areas specializing in export of grains, bullion, wood, cotton, sugar – all of which favored the use of slavery and coerced cash-crop labor as the modes of labor control. Mediterranean Europe emerged as the semiperipheral area of this world-enconomy specializing in high-cost industrial products (for example, silks) and credit and specie transactions, which had as a consequence in the agricultural arena sharecropping as the mode of labor control and little export to other areas.

The three structural positions in a world-economy – core, periphery, and semiperiphery – had become stabilized by about 1640. How certain areas became one and not the other is a long story. The key fact is that given slightly different starting points, the interests of various local groups converged in northwest Europe, leading to the development of strong state mechanisms, and diverged sharply in the peripheral areas, leading to very weak ones. Once we get a difference in the strength of the state machineries, we get the operation of "unequal exchange"[28] which is enforced by strong states on weak ones, by core states on peripheral areas. Thus capitalism involves not only appropriation of the surplus value by an owner from a laborer, but an appropriation of surplus of the whole world-economy by core areas. And this was as true in the stage of agricultural capitalism as it is in the stage of industrial capitalism. . . .

Capitalism was from the beginning an affair of the world-economy and not of nation-states. It is a misreading of the situation to claim that it is only in the twentieth century that capitalism has become "world-wide", although this claim is frequently made in various writings, particularly by Marxists. . . . capital has never allowed its aspirations to be determined by national boundaries in a capitalist world-economy, and that the creation of "national" barriers – generically, mercantilism – has historically been a defensive mechanism of capitalists located in states which are one level below the high point of strength in the system.

. . . In the process a large number of countries create national economic barriers whose consequences often last beyond their initial objectives. At this later point in the process the very same capitalists who pressed their national governments to impose the restrictions now find these restrictions constraining. This is not an "internationalization" of "national" capital. This is simply a new political demand by certain sectors of the capitalist classes who have at all points in time sought to maximize their profits within the real economic market, that of the world-economy.

If this is so, then what meaning does it have to talk of structural positions within this economy and identify states as being in one of these positions? And why talk of three positions, inserting that of "semiperiphery" in between the widely used concepts of core and periphery? The state machineries of the core states were strengthened to meet the needs of capitalist landowners and their merchant allies. . . .

The strengthening of the state machineries in core areas has as its direct counterpart the decline of the state machineries in peripheral areas. . . . In peripheral countries, the interests of the capitalist landowners lie in an opposite direction from those of the local commercial bourgeoisie. Their interests lie in maintaining an open economy to maximize their profit from world-market trade (no restrictions in exports and access to lower-cost industrial products from core countries) and in elimination of the commercial bourgeoisie in favor of outside merchants (who pose no local political threat). Thus, in terms of the state, the coalition which strengthened it in core countries was precisely absent.

The second reason, which has become ever more operative over the history of the modern world-system, is that the strength of the state machinery in core states is a function of the weakness of other state machineries. Hence intervention of outsiders via war, subversion, and diplomacy is the lot of peripheral states.

All this seems very obvious. I repeat it only in order to make clear two points. One cannot reasonably explain the strength of various state machineries at specific moments of the history of the modern world-system primarily in terms of a genetic-cultural line of argumentation, but rather in terms of the structural role a country plays in the world-economy at that moment in time. To be sure, the initial eligibility for a particular role is often decided by an accidental edge a particular country has, and the "accident" of which one is talking is no doubt located in part in past history, in part in current geography. But once this relatively minor accident is given, it is the operations of the world-market forces which accentuate the differences, institutionalize them, and make them impossible to surmount over the short run.

The second point we wish to make about the structural differences of core and periphery is that they are not comprehensible unless we realize that there is a third structural position: that of the semiperiphery. This is not the result merely of establishing arbitrary cutting-points on a continuum of characteristics. . . . The semiperiphery is needed to make a capitalist world-economy run smoothly. Both kinds of world-system, the world-empire with a redistributive economy and the world-economy with a capitalist market economy, involve markedly unequal distribution of rewards. Thus, logically, there is immediately posed the question of how it is possible politically for such a system to persist. Why do not the majority who are exploited simply overwhelm the minority who draw disproportionate benefits? The most rapid glance at the historic record shows that these world-systems have been faced rather rarely by fundamental system-wide insurrection. While internal discontent has been eternal, it has usually taken quite long before the accumulation of the erosion of power has led to the decline of a world-system, and as often as not, an external force has been a major factor in this decline.

There have been three major mechanisms that have enabled world-systems to retain relative political stability (not in terms of the particular groups who will play the leading roles in the system, but in terms of systemic survival itself). One obviously is the concentration of military strength in the hands of the dominant forces. The modalities of this obviously vary with the technology, and there are to be sure political prerequisites for such a concentration, but nonetheless sheer force is no doubt a central consideration.

A second mechanism is the pervasiveness of an ideological commitment to the system as a whole. I do not mean what has often been termed the "legitimation" of a system, because that term has been used to imply that the lower strata of a system feel some affinity with or loyalty towards the rulers, and I doubt that this has ever been a significant factor in the survival of world-systems. I mean rather the degree to which the staff or cadres of the system (and I leave this term deliberately vague) feel that their own well-being is wrapped up in the survival of the system as such and the competence of its leaders. It is this staff which not only propagates the myths; it is they who believe them.

But neither force nor the ideological commitment of the staff would suffice were it not for the division of the majority into a larger lower stratum and a smaller middle stratum. Both the revolutionary call for polarization as a strategy of change and the liberal encomium to consensus as the basis of the liberal polity reflect this proposition. The import is far wider than its use in the analysis of contemporary political problems suggests. It is the normal condition of either kind of world-system to have a three-layered structure. When and if this ceases to be the case, the world-system disintegrates.

In a world-empire, the middle stratum is in fact accorded the role of maintaining the marginally desirable long-distance luxury trade, while the upper stratum concentrates its resources on controlling the military machinery which can collect the tribute, the crucial mode of redistributing surplus. By providing, however, for an access to a limited portion of the surplus to urbanized elements who alone, in premodern societies, could contribute political cohesiveness to isolated clusters of primary producers, the upper stratum effectively buys off the potential leadership of coordinated revolt. And by denying access to political rights for this commercial-urban middle stratum, it makes them constantly vulnerable to confiscatory measures whenever their economic profits become sufficiently swollen so that they might begin to create for themselves military strength.

In a world-economy, such "cultural" stratification is not so simple, because the absence of a single political system means the concentration of economic roles vertically rather than horizontally throughout the system. The solution then is to have three *kinds* of states, with pressures for cultural homogenization within each of them – thus, besides the upper stratum of core states and the lower stratum of peripheral states, there is a middle stratum of semiperipheral ones.

This semiperiphery is then assigned as it were a specific economic role, but the reason is less economic than political. That is to say, one might make a good case that the world-economy as an economy would function every bit as well without a semiperiphery. But it would be far less *politically* stable, for it would mean a polarized world-system. The existence of the third category means precisely that the upper stratum is not faced with the *unified* opposition of all the others because the *middle* stratum is both exploited and exploiter. It follows that the specific economic role is not all that important, and has thus changed through the various historical stages of the modern world-system. . . .

Where then does class analysis fit in all of this? And what in such a formulation are nations, nationalities, peoples, ethnic groups? First of all, without arguing the point now, I would contend that all these latter terms denote variants of a single phenomenon which I will term "ethno-nations".

Both classes and ethnic groups, or status groups, or ethno-nations are phenomena of world-economies and much of the enormous confusion that has surrounded the concrete analysis of their functioning can be attributed quite simply to the fact that they have been analyzed as though they existed within the nation-states of this world-economy, instead of within the world-economy as a whole. This has been a Procrustean bed indeed.

The range of economic activities being far wider in the core than in the periphery, the range of syndical interest groups is far wider there.[29] Thus, it has been widely observed that there does not exist in many parts of the world today a proletariat of the kind which exists in, say, Europe or North America. But this is a confusing way to state the observation. Industrial activity being disproportionately concentrated in certain parts of the world-economy, industrial wage workers are to be found principally in certain geographic regions. Their interests as a syndical group are determined by their collective relationship to the world-economy. Their ability to influence the political functioning of this world-economy is shaped by the fact that they command larger percentages of the population in one sovereign entity than another. The form their organizations take have, in large part, been governed too by these political boundaries. The same might be said about industrial capitalists. Class analysis is perfectly capable of accounting for the political position of, let us say, French skilled workers if we look at their structural position and interests in the world-economy. Similarly with ethno-nations. The meaning of ethnic consciousness in a core area is considerably different from that of ethnic consciousness in a peripheral area precisely because of the different class position such ethnic groups have in the world-economy.

Political struggles of ethno-nations or segments of classes within national boundaries of course are the daily bread and butter of local politics. But their significance or consequences can only be fruitfully analyzed if one spells out the implications of their organizational activity or political demands for the functioning of the world-economy. . . .

The functioning then of a capitalist world-economy requires that groups pursue their economic interests within a single world market while seeking to distort this market for their benefit by organizing to exert influence on states, some of which are far more powerful than others but none of which controls the world market in its entirety. Of course, we shall find on closer inspection that there are periods where one state is relatively quite powerful and other periods where power is more diffuse and contested, permitting weaker states broader ranges of action. We can talk then of the relative tightness or looseness of the world-system as an important variable and seek to analyze why this dimension tends to be cyclical in nature, as it seems to have been for several hundred years.

We are now in a position to look at the historical evolution of this capitalist world-economy itself and analyze the degree to which it is fruitful to talk of distinct stages in its evolution as a system. The emergence of the European world-economy in the "long" sixteenth century (1450–1640) was made possible by an historical conjuncture: on those long-term trends which were the culmination of what has been sometimes described as the "crisis of feudalism" was superimposed a more immediate cyclical crisis plus climatic changes, all of which created a dilemma that could only be resolved by a geographic expansion of the division of labor. Furthermore, the balance of intersystem forces was such as to make this realizable. Thus a geographic expansion did take place in conjunction with a demographic expansion and an upward price rise. . . .

Each of the states or potential states within the European world-economy was quickly in the race to bureaucratize, to raise a standing army, to homogenize its culture, to diversify its economic activities. By 1640, those in north-west Europe had succeeded in establishing themselves as the core states; Spain and the northern Italian city-states declined into being semiperipheral; northeastern Europe and Iberian America had become the periphery. At this point, those in semiperipheral status had reached it by virtue of decline from a former more pre-eminent status.

It was the system-wide recession of 1650–1730 that consolidated the European world-economy and opened stage two of the modern world-economy. For the recession forced retrenchment, and the decline in relative surplus allowed room for only one core state to survive. The mode of struggle was mercantilism . . . In this struggle England first ousted the Netherlands from its commercial primacy and then resisted successfully France's attempt to catch up. As England began to speed up the process of industrialization after 1760, there was one last attempt of those capitalist forces located in France to break the imminent British hegemony. This attempt was expressed first in the French Revolution's replacement of the cadres of the regime and then in Napoleon's continental blockade. But it failed.

Stage three of the capitalist world-economy begins then, a stage of industrial rather than of agricultural capitalism. Henceforth, industrial production is no longer a minor aspect of the world market but comprises an ever larger percentage of world gross production – and even more important, of world gross surplus. This involves a whole series of consequences for the world-system.

First of all, it led to the further geographic expansion of the European world-economy to include now the whole of the globe. This was in part the result of its technological feasibility both in terms of improved military firepower and improved shipping facilities which made regular trade sufficiently inexpensive to be viable. But, in addition, industrial production *required* access to raw materials of a nature and in a quantity such that the needs could not be supplied within the former boundaries. At first, however, the search for new markets was not a primary consideration in the geographic expansion since the new markets were more readily available within the old boundaries, as we shall see.

The geographic expansion of the European world-economy meant the elimination of other world-systems as well as the absorption of the remaining minisystems. The most important world-system up to then outside of the European world-economy, Russia, entered in semiperipheral status, the consequence of the strength of its state machinery (including its army) and the degree of industrialization already achieved in the eighteenth century. The independences in the Latin American countries did nothing to change their peripheral status. They merely eliminated the last vestiges of Spain's semiperipheral role and ended pockets of noninvolvement in the world-economy in the interior of Latin America. Asia and Africa were absorbed into the periphery in the nineteenth century, although Japan, because of the combination of the strength of its state machinery, the poverty of its resource base (which led to a certain disinterest on the part of world capitalist forces), and its geographic remoteness from the core areas, was able quickly to graduate into semiperipheral status. . . .

The creation of vast new areas as the periphery of the expanded world-economy made possible a shift in the role of some other areas. Specifically, both the United States and Germany (as it came into being) combined formerly peripheral and semiperipheral regions. The manufacturing sector in each was able to gain political ascendancy, as the peripheral subregions became less economically crucial to the world-economy. Mercantilism now became the major tool of semiperipheral countries seeking to become core countries, thus still performing a function analogous to that of the mercantilist drives of the late seventeenth and eighteenth centuries in England and France. To be sure, the struggle of semiperipheral countries to "industrialize" varied in the degree to which it succeeded in the period before the First World War: all the way in the United States, only partially in Germany, not at all in Russia.

The internal structure of core states also changed fundamentally under industrial capitalism. For a core area, industrialism involved divesting itself of substantially all agricultural activities (except that in the twentieth century further mechanization was to create a new form of working the land that was so highly mechanized as to warrant the appellation industrial). Thus whereas, in the period 1700–40, England not only was Europe's leading industrial exporter but was also Europe's leading agricultural exporter – this was at a high point in the economy-wide recession – by 1900, less than 10 percent of England's population were engaged in agricultural pursuits.

At first under industrial capitalism, the core exchanged manufactured products against the periphery's agricultural products – hence, Britain from 1815 to 1873 as the "workshop of the world". Even to those semiperipheral countries that had some manufacture (France, Germany, Belgium, the US), Britain in this period supplied about half their needs in manufactured goods. As, however, the mercantilist practices of this latter group both cut Britain off from outlets and even created competition for Britain in sales to peripheral areas, a competition which led to the late nineteenth-century "scramble for Africa", the world division of labor was reallocated to ensure a new special role for the core: less the provision of the manufactures, more the provision of the machines to make the manufactures as well as the provision of infrastructure (especially, in this period, railroads).

The rise of manufacturing created for the first time under capitalism a large-scale urban proletariat. And in consequence for the first time there arose what Michels has called the "anti-capitalist mass spirit",[30] which was translated into concrete organizational forms (trade unions, socialist parties). This development intruded a new factor as threatening to the stability of the states and of the capitalist forces now so securely in control of them as the earlier centrifugal thrusts of regional anti-capitalist landed elements had been in the seventeenth century.

At the same time that the bourgeoisies of the core countries were faced by this threat to the internal stability of their state structures, they were simultaneously faced with the economic crisis of the latter third of the nineteenth century resulting from the more rapid increase of agricultural production (and indeed of light manufactures) than the expansion of a potential market for these goods. Some of the surplus would have to be redistributed to someone to allow these goods to be bought and the economic machinery to return to smooth operation. By expanding the purchasing power of the industrial proletariat of the core countries, the world-economy was unburdened simultaneously of two problems: the bottleneck of demand, and the unsettling "class conflict" of the core states – hence, the social liberalism or welfare-state ideology that arose just at that point in time.

The First World War was, as men of the time observed, the end of an era; and the Russian Revolution of October 1917 the beginning of a new one – our stage four. This stage was to be sure a stage of revolutionary turmoil but it also was, in a seeming paradox, the stage of the *consolidation* of the industrial capitalist world-economy. The Russian Revolution was essentially that of a semiperipheral country whose internal balance of forces had been such that as of the late nineteenth century it began on a decline towards a peripheral status. . . . The Revolution brought to power a group of state managers who reversed each one of these trends by using the classic technique of mercantilist semiwithdrawal from the world-economy. In the process of doing this, the now USSR mobilized considerable popular support, especially in the urban sector. At the end of the Second World War, Russia was reinstated as a very strong member of the semiperiphery and could begin to seek full core status. . . .

It was the Second World War that enabled the United States for a brief period (1945–65) to attain the same level of primacy as Britain had in the first part of the nineteenth century. United States growth in this period was spectacular and created a great need for expanded market outlets. The Cold War closure denied not only the USSR but eastern Europe to US exports. And the Chinese Revolution meant that this region, which had been destined for much exploitative activity, was also cut off. Three alternative areas were available and each was pursued with assiduity. First, western Europe had to be rapidly "reconstructed", and it was the Marshall Plan which thus allowed this area to play a primary role in the expansion of world productivity. Secondly, Latin America became the reserve of US investment from which now Britain and Germany were completely cut off. Thirdly, southern Asia, the Middle East and Africa had to be decolonized. On the one hand, this was necessary in order to reduce the share of the surplus taken by the western European intermediaries, as Canning covertly supported the Latin American revolutionaries against Spain in the 1820s.[31]

But also, these countries had to be decolonized in order to mobilize productive potential in a way that had never been achieved in the colonial era. Colonial rule after all had been an *inferior* mode of relationship of core and periphery, one occasioned by the strenuous late-nineteenth-century conflict among industrial states but one no longer desirable from the point of view of the new hegemonic power.[32]

But a world capitalist economy does not permit true imperium. Charles V could not succeed in his dream of world-empire. The Pax Britannica stimulated its own demise. So too did the Pax Americana. . . .

Such a decline in US state hegemony has actually *increased* the freedom of action of capitalist enterprises, the larger of which have now taken the form of multinational corporations which are able to maneuver against state bureaucracies whenever the national politicians become too responsive to internal worker pressures. Whether some effective links can be established between multinational corporations, presently limited to operating in certain areas, and the USSR remains to be seen, but it is by no means impossible.

This brings us back to one of the questions with which we opened this paper, the seemingly esoteric debate between Liu Shao-Chi and Mao Tse-Tung as to whether China was, as Liu argued, a socialist state, or whether, as Mao argued, socialism was a *process* involving continued and continual class struggle. No doubt to those to whom the terminology is foreign the discussion seems abstrusely theological. The issue, however, as we said, is real. If the Russian Revolution emerged as a reaction to the threatened further decline of Russia's structural position in the world-economy, and if fifty years later one can talk of the USSR as entering the status of a core power in a *capitalist* world-economy, what then is the meaning of the various so-called socialist revolutions that have occurred on a third of the world's surface? First let us notice that it has been neither Thailand nor Liberia nor Paraguay that has had a "socialist revolution" but Russia, China and Cuba. That is to say, these revolutions have occurred in countries that, in terms of their internal economic structures in the pre-revolutionary period, had a certain minimum strength in terms of skilled personnel, some manufacturing, and other factors which made it plausible that, within the framework of a capitalist world-economy, such a country could alter its role in the world division of labor within a reasonable period (say 30–50 years) by the use of the technique of mercantilist semi-withdrawal. (This may not be all that plausible for Cuba, but we shall see.) Of course, other countries in the geographic regions and military orbit of these revolutionary forces had changes of regime without in any way having these characteristics (for example, Mongolia or Albania). It is also to be noted that many of the countries where similar forces are strong or where considerable counterforce is required to keep them from emerging also share this status of minimum strength. I think of Chile or Brazil or Egypt – or indeed Italy.

Are we not seeing the emergence of a political structure for *semiperipheral* nations adapted to stage four of the capitalist world-system? The fact that all enterprises are nationalized in these countries does not make the participation of these enterprises in the world-economy one that does not conform to the mode of operation of a capitalist market system: seeking increased efficiency of production in order to realize a maximum price on sales, thus achieving a more favorable allocation of the surplus of the world-economy. If tomorrow US Steel became a worker's collective in which all employees without exception received an identical share of the profits and all stockholders are expropriated without compensation, would US Steel thereby cease to be a capitalist enterprise operating in a capitalist world-economy?

What then have been the consequences for the world-system of the emergence of many states in which there is no private ownership of the basic means of production? To some extent, this has meant an internal reallocation of consumption. It has certainly undermined the ideological justification in world capitalism, both by showing the political vulnerability of capitalist entrepreneurs and by demonstrating that private ownership is irrelevant to the rapid expansion of industrial productivity. But to the extent that it has raised the ability of the new semiperipheral areas to enjoy a larger share of the world surplus, it has once again depolarized the world, re-creating the triad of strata that has been a fundamental element in the survival of the world-system.

Finally, in the peripheral areas of the world-economy, both the continued economic expansion of the core (even though the core is seeing some reallocation of surplus internal to it) and the new strength of the semiperiphery has led to a further weakening of the political and hence economic position of the peripheral areas. The pundits note that "the gap is getting wider", but thus far no one has succeeded in doing much about it, and it is not clear that there are very many in whose interests it would be to do so. Far from a strengthening of state authority, in many parts of the world we are witnessing the same kind of deterioration Poland knew in the sixteenth century, a deterioration of which the frequency of military coups is only one of many signposts. And all of this leads us to conclude that stage four has been the stage of the *consolidation* of the capitalist world-economy.

Consolidation, however, does not mean the absence of contradictions and does not mean the likelihood of long-term survival. . . .

There are two fundamental contradictions, it seems to me, involved in the workings of the capitalist world-system. In the first place, there is the contradiction to which the nineteenth-century Marxian corpus pointed, which I would phrase as follows: whereas in the short run the maximization of profit requires maximizing the withdrawal of surplus from immediate consumption of the majority, in the long run the continued production of surplus requires a mass demand which can only be created by redistributing the surplus withdrawn. Since these two considerations move in opposite directions (a "contradiction"), the system has constant crises which in the long run both weaken it and make the game for those with privilege less worth playing.

The second fundamental contradiction, to which Mao's concept of socialism as process points, is the following: whenever the tenants of privilege seek to coopt an oppositional movement by including them in a minor share of the privilege, they may no doubt eliminate opponents in the short run; but they also up the ante for the next oppositional movement created in the next crisis of the world-economy. Thus the cost of "cooption" rises ever higher and the advantages of cooption seem ever less worthwhile.

There are today no socialist systems in the world-economy any more than there are feudal systems because there is only *one* world-system. It is a world-economy and it is by definition capitalist in form. Socialism involves the creation of a new kind of *world*-system, neither a redistributive world-empire nor a capitalist world-economy but a socialist world-government. I don't see this projection as being in the least utopian but I also don't feel its institution is imminent. It will be the outcome of a long struggle in forms that may be familiar and perhaps in very few forms, that will take place in *all* the areas of the world-economy (Mao's continual "class struggle"). Governments may be in the hands of persons, groups or movements sympathetic to this transformation but *states* as such are neither progressive nor reactionary. It is movements and forces that deserve such evaluative judgment.

NOTES

1   George Lukács, "The Marxism of Rosa Luxemburg," in *History and Class Consciousness* (London: Merlin Press, 1968), p. 27.

2   See Frederic Lane's discussion of "protection costs" which is reprinted in part 3 of *Venice and History* (Baltimore: Johns Hopkins University Press, 1966). For the specific discussion of tribute, see pp. 389–90, 416–20.

3   See Karl Polanyi, "The Economy as Instituted Process," in Karl Polanyi, Conrad M. Arsenberg and Harry W. Pearson (eds), *Trade and Market in the Early Empire* (Glencoe: Free Press, 1957), pp. 243–70.

4   Andre Gunder Frank, "The Myth of Feudalism," in *Capitalism and Under-development in Latin America* (New York: Monthly Review Press, 1967), p. 3.

5   See Theotonio Dos Santos, *La Nueva Dependencia* (Buenos Aires: s/ediciones, 1968).

6   Ernesto Laclau, "Feudalism and Capitalism in Latin America," *New Left Review*, 67 (May–June 1971), 37–8.

7   The debate begins with Maurice Dobb, *Studies in the Development of Capitalism* (London: Routledge & Kegan Paul, 1946). Paul Sweezy criticized Dobb in "The Transition from Feudalism to Capitalism," *Science and Society*, 14: 2 (Spring 1950), 134–57, with a "Reply" by Dobb in the same issue. From that point on many others got into the debate in various parts of the world. I have reviewed and discussed this debate *in extenso* in *The Modern World-System: Capitalist Agriculture and the Origins of the European World-Economy in the Sixteenth Century* (New York: Academic Press, 1974), ch. 1.

8   It would take us into a long discursus to defend the proposition that, like all great thinkers, there was the Marx who was the prisoner of his social location and the Marx, the genius, who could on occasion see from a wider vantage point. The former Marx generalized from British history. The latter Marx is the one who has inspired a critical conceptual framework of social reality. W. W. Rostow incidentally seeks to refute the former Marx by offering an alternative generalization from British history. He ignores the latter and more significant Marx. See *The Stages of Economic Growth: A Non-Communist Manifesto* (Cambridge: University Press, 1960).

9   Laclau, "Feudalism and Capitalism," pp. 25, 30.

10   Cited in F. Burlatsky, *The State and Communism* (Moscow: Progress Publishers, n.d. [1961]), p. 95.

11   Ibid., p. 97.

12   Mao Tse-Tung, *On The Correct Handling of Contradictions Among The People*, 7th edn, revised translation (Peking: Foreign Languages Press, 1966), pp. 37–8.

13   *Long Live The Invincible Thought of Mao Tse-Tung!*, undated pamphlet, issued between 1967 and 1969, translated in *Current Background*, 884 (18 July 1969), 14.

14   This is the position taken by Mao Tse-Tung in his speech to the Work Conference of the Central Committee at Peitaiho in August 1962, as reported in the pamphlet, *Long Live . . .* , p. 20. Mao's position was subsequently endorsed at the 10th Plenum of the 8th CCP Central Committee in September 1962, a session this same pamphlet describes as "a great turning point in the violent

struggle between the proletarian headquarters and the bourgeois headquarters in China." *Ibid.*, p. 21.

15   Remarks made by Mao at 10th Plenum, cited in *ibid.*, p. 20.

16   Mao Tse-Tung, "Talk on the Question of Democratic Centralism," 30 Jan. 1962, in *Current Background*, 891 (8 Oct. 1969), 39.

17   "Communiqué of the 10th Plenary Session of the 8th Central Committee of the Chinese Communist Party," *Current Background*, 691 (5 Oct. 1962), 3.

18   Yuri Sdobnikov (ed.), *Socialism and Capitalism: Score and Prospects* (Moscow: Progress Publications, 1971), p. 20.

19   Ibid., p. 21.

20   Ibid., p. 26.

21   Ibid., p. 24.

22   Ibid., p. 25.

23   Say Raymond Aron, *Dix-huit leçons de la société industrielle* (Paris: Gallimard, 1962).

24   Maurice Dobb, *Capitalism Yesterday and Today* (London: Lawrence & Wishart, 1958), p. 21.

25   Ibid., pp. 6–7.

26   Ibid., p. 21.

27   See my *The Modern World-System*, ch. 2.

28   See Arghiri Emmanuel, *Unequal Exchange* (New York: Monthly Review Press, 1972).

29   "Range" in this sentence means the number of different occupations in which a significant proportion of the population is engaged. Thus peripheral society typically is overwhelmingly agricultural. A core society typically has its occupations well-distributed over all of Colin Clark's three sectors. If one shifted the connotation of range to talk of style of life, consumption patterns, even income distribution quite possibly one might reverse the correlation. In a typical peripheral society, the differences between a subsistence farmer and an urban professional are probably far greater than those which could be found in a typical core state.

30   Robert Michels, "The Origins of the Anti-Capitalist Mass Spirit", in *Man in Contemporary Society* (New York: Columbia University Press, 1955), vol. 1, pp. 740–65.

31   See William W. Kaufman, *British Policy and the Independence of Latin America, 1804–28* (New Haven: Yale University Press, 1951).

32   Cf. Catherine Coquery-Vidrovitch, "De l'impérialisme britannique à l'impérialisme contemporaine – l'avatar colonial," *L'Homme et la société*, 18 (Oct.–Dec. 1970), 61–90.

8 Rethinking Development Theory: Insights from East Asia and Latin America (1989/1994)

Gary Gereffi

Introduction

[. . .]

The highly industrialized countries in East Asia and Latin America have been a fertile spawning ground for a variety of theories and concepts dealing with Third World development. However, the weight of the evidence used in support of these approaches typically has been quite uneven across the two regions. The theories and concepts often are biased because they reflect events in only some of the East Asian and Latin American nations, leading them to misrepresent the reality of the others.

This essay is an effort to rethink some of the key suppositions of development theory and to identify the fallacies that have been generated by a selective reading of the evidence from East Asia and Latin America. Although the East Asian and Latin American nations by no means cover the entire spectrum of development possibilities in the Third World, they are a good base from which to build solid comparative generalizations because they embody different routes to industrial success. This suggests that there are a number of alternative paths of national development.

The first part of this essay outlines several theoretical perspectives on development that highlight key features of the East Asian and Latin American experiences. While these perspectives offer some important insights, each one is flawed by attempts to generalize beyond the cases that gave rise to the insight itself. These misperceptions are dealt with in the remainder of the study, which presents cross-regional evidence from East Asia and Latin America leading to a reformulation and synthesis of some of these earlier approaches.

Theoretical Perspectives on East Asian and Latin American Development: Perceptions and Misconceptions

The development theories related to East Asia and Latin America are at several different levels of generality, including new trends in the global economy, distinct conceptual categories used to describe and analyze the highly industrialized nations in the two regions, and the roles of domestic institutions and sociocultural factors that shape the process of national development. The literature on *the new international division of labor* traces the recent surge of manufactured exports from the Third World to the emergence of a global manufacturing system based on labor-intensive export platforms established by transnational corporations in low-wage areas. This new international division of labor was created in order to exploit reserve armies of labor on a world scale by using the advanced transport and communication technologies that permit the spatial segmentation of the production process (Fröbel et al., 1981).

An extension of this approach, the *globalization of production* perspective, argues that the shift of manufacturing capacity toward decentralized production sites is occurring in both the advanced and the developing countries, and it reflects the increasingly centralized control and coordination by transnational corporations (TNCs) of these decentralized production units. This has fostered both greater international interdependence and enhanced TNC leverage over national governments and domestic labor (Gordon, 1988).

The most widely used term in referring to the high-growth, diversified economies of East Asia and Latin America is *newly industrializing countries* (or NICs). The expression was coined in the mid-1970s by the advanced capitalist nations, which were concerned that a number of developing countries were significantly expanding their world share in the production and export of manufactured goods. (See OECD, 1979. The NICs included are South Korea, Taiwan, Hong Kong, Singapore, Brazil, Mexico, Spain, Portugal, Greece, and Yugoslavia.) The specter of "other Japans" was a worry to the slumping Western industrial economies, giving rise in some circles to strident calls for protectionism.

Once the economic trends in the NICs became well established, the World Bank and prominent neoclassical economists in a variety of other institutions began to offer unambiguous policy prescriptions regarding the *development strategies* of these Third World nations. They argued that the outward-oriented development strategies of the East Asian NICs led to better economic performance in terms of exports, economic growth, and employment than did the inward-oriented development strategies of the Latin American NICs (see Balassa, 1981: 1–26; Balassa et al., 1986; World Bank, 1983: chap. 5). The clear implication was that the East Asian NICs should serve as a model to be emulated by the rest of the developing world.

World-systems theory employs the concept of *semiperipheral countries* to identify an intermediate stratum between core and peripheral nations that promotes the stability and legitimacy of the three-tiered world economy. The countries within the semiperipheral zone, which includes the East Asian and Latin American NICs, supposedly have the capacity to resist peripheralization but not the capability to move into the upper tier (Wallerstein, 1974; Arrighi and Drangel, 1986).

Dependency theory uses the term *dependent development* to indicate that structural dependency on foreign capital and external markets in rapidly industrializing Third World nations like the Latin American and East Asian NICs constrains and distorts, but is not incompatible with, capitalist economic development (Evans, 1979; Cardoso and Faletto, 1979; Gold, 1981; Lim, 1985). This was a striking departure from earlier "stagnationist" views that claimed dependency could only lead to underdevelopment and revolution (see Gereffi, 1983: chap. I, for an overview of this debate).

Some political scientists argue that one of the key institutional features of successful late industrializers is the rise of a *developmental state* oriented to selective but substantial intervention in their economies in order to promote rapid capital accumulation and industrial progress. In Latin America as well as East Asia, the state has tended to be strong, centralized, authoritarian (often under military control), and actively involved in economic affairs (O'Donnell, 1973; Collier, 1979; Johnson, 1987; Wade, 1990). This literature raises the question of whether a developmental state is a prerequisite for capitalist industrialization on the periphery.

The rapid growth of the East Asian NICs has refocused attention on the role of *cultural factors* in national development. Various writers have recently argued that Confucianism confers certain advantages over other traditions in the quest for economic development. Because Confucian beliefs place a high value on hard work, loyalty, respect for authority, and punctuality, these characteristics are thought to have facilitated the national consensus around high-speed economic growth evident in Japan and the East Asian NICs since the 1950s and 1960s. This culturally derived capacity for cooperation led political elites, industrial leaders, workers, and other citizens to agree on the primacy of economic objectives for the society as a whole and on the means to achieve those objectives (Johnson, 1983: 6–10). . . . . In Latin America, a divergent set of cultural norms based upon an Ibero-Catholic heritage has been identified as impeding the economic advancement of the region (see Valenzuela and Valenzuela, 1978, for a review of this approach).

Each of these theoretical perspectives contains valuable observations about the development of the East Asian and Latin American NICs. Recent comparative research, however, suggests that some of these prior generalizations may be too sweeping. They often fit one region or time period reasonably well but falter when their scope is expanded. To facilitate efforts at reformulating the earlier theoretical approaches, I will highlight the fallacies or misperceptions embedded in each of these perspectives.

1   The early discussions of the new international division of labor place an undue emphasis on labor-intensive, assembly-oriented export production in the NICs, which in retrospect characterizes only the initial phase of their export efforts. Since the 1970s, both the East Asian and the Latin American NICs have moved toward more technology- and skill-intensive exports focusing on high-vlaue-added products. Furthermore, these newer export industries are not "export enclaves" but instead promote high levels of integration with a well-developed local industrial base.

2   The globalization of production approach correctly highlights the emergence of a decentralized global manufacturing system in which production capacity is dispersed to an unprecedented number of developing as well as industrialized countries. However, this does not rest solely on a base of increasingly centralized and coordinated control by TNCs. Local private firms are the main exporters in many of the Third World nations today, but their ability to effectively capture the economic surplus in these export industries tends to be restricted by the kinds of subcontracting relationships in which they are enmeshed.

3   The East Asian and Latin American NICs are not really "newly" industrializing, nor have they developed in response to the same kinds of global dynamics.

Because these NICs originated in the mid-1970s as a defensive reaction by OECD (Organization for Economic Cooperation and Development) countries to increasing Third World exports, many studies of the NICs tend to focus too narrowly on manufactured exports and implicitly or explicitly marginalize the opportunities for countries that have a rich endowment of natural resources. To understand the emergence of the NICs we need to adopt a broader historical and world-systems perspective that is sensitive to different kinds of economic capabilities in Third World nations.

4   The contrast between the outward-oriented and inward-oriented development strategies of the East Asian and Latin American NICs, respectively, is overdrawn. Each of the countries in the two regions has pursued a combination of inward- and outward-oriented strategies. Furthermore, it is this mix of development strategies that helps us understand how industrial diversification has led to enhanced export flexibility and competitiveness in both sets of NICs in the 1980s.

5   The semiperipheral zone encompasses an extremely diverse range of countries. In order to understand the actual roles played by semiperipheral nations in the world economy today, we need to disaggregate this concept and focus on the specific characteristics of the NICs in different geographical regions like East Asia and Latin America.

6   Dependent development is applicable to the NICs in East Asia as well as Latin America. The nature and consequences of dependency are quite different in the two regions, however. Dependency in the East Asian NICs is a product of their heavy reliance on foreign aid and foreign trade, while dependency in the Latin American NICs is an outgrowth of their extensive involvement with transnational corporations and transnational banks. The developmental consequences of these different types of dependency turn, in large degree, on the ability of the state to convert these external linkages to national advantage. Successful "dependency management" depends on the historical timing of these efforts as well as institutional factors.

7   While there is a substantial degree of state intervention in the economies of the Latin American and East Asian NICs (with the exception of Hong Kong), the developmental state is not a singular phenomenon in the two regions. The objectives, social bases, and policy instruments of the state are quite different in each country, with major implications for the exercise of state autonomy in areas like industrial policy.

8   Simplistic cultural arguments run into a variety of problems. First, regions are not culturally homogeneous; this is particularly true of East Asia. In Taiwan and South Korea, for example, Taoism and Buddhism as well as Confucianism have important followings, and there is a significant Christian minority in some East Asian countries like South Korea. More importantly in terms of the timing of high-speed growth, both the Confucian and Ibero-Catholic traditions have existed for centuries. In both regions, but especially in East Asia, however, the dynamic shifts in economic performance have occurred primarily in recent decades. A more sophisticated cultural interpretation would see culture as historically situated, emergent, and mediated through institutions (see Swidler, 1986). The impact

of cultural variables probably is most important in outlining an acceptable range of solutions to development problems, rather than in determining specific economic outcomes.

The following sections of this essay address some of these themes in greater detail. In closing, I will outline the elements for a new theoretical synthesis, with some suggestions for future research.

The NICs in Historical and World-Systems Context[1]

The East Asian and Latin American NICs are a very heterogeneous group, with major differences in population size, land area, resource endowments, cultural legacies, political regimes, social structures, per capita income, and economic policies. Nonetheless, these nations tend to have several dynamic features in common that lead them to be widely perceived as industrial "success stories": rapid and generally sustained economic growth, based on a sharp increase in the manufacturing sector's share of total output and employment; a growing diversification of industrial production that permits each nation to make ever broader ranges of manufactured goods; and a fast expansion of exports with an emphasis on manufacturers.

The Latin American and East Asian NICs are at relatively advanced levels of industrial development. They are all upper-middle- or upper-income countries by World Bank standards, although the average gross national product (GNP) per capita in 1990 was considerably higher in the East Asian nations . . . However, while the East Asian NICs grew rapidly during the 1980s, the Latin American NICs suffered an absolute as well as a relative decline. The 1981 GNP per capita figures highlight both trends. The Latin American NICs had similar or, in the case of Argentina, substantially lower per capita incomes in 1990 than nine years earlier. The East Asian NICs, on the other hand, doubled or tripled their average incomes in the 1980s.

Manufacturing has been a cornerstone of development for the Latin American and East Asian NICs, while the role of agriculture has declined in these economies since 1965. The manufacturing sector's share of gross domestic product (GDP) in 1990 was 18 percent in Hong Kong; it ranged between 23 percent and 29 percent in Mexico, Brazil, and Singapore; and it reached peak levels of 31 to 35 percent in South Korea, Taiwan, and Argentina. The prominence of manufacturing activities in the NICs is much higher than in the United States (17 percent) and comparable to many of the other advanced industrial economies, including Japan (29 percent). In all of the core nations, and Hong Kong as well, the service sector now is the most dynamic sector of the economy.

The East Asian and Latin American NICs have launched major export drives since 1980. By 1990, the East Asian NICs had clearly established themselves as the Third World's premier exporters. Taiwan and South Korea topped the list in 1990 with $67 and $65 billion in exports, respectively, followed by Singapore with an export total (including re-exports) of nearly $53 billion. Hong Kong, Brazil, and Mexico occupied a second tier with exports in the $27 to $31 billion range, while Argentina ($12 billion) lagged well behind the rest of the pack. The East Asian "super-exporters" thus tended to surge well ahead of the other NICs in export volume.

The NICs also vary considerably in the priority given to external trade. The East Asian nations are export-led economies in which exports in 1990 accounted for 43 percent and 27 percent of GDP in Taiwan and South Korea, respectively, and for 100 percent or more of GDP in the entrepôt city states of Hong Kong and Singapore when their re-exports are included. This compares with export/GDP ratios of only 8 percent to 13 percent in the much larger Latin American NICs. To put these figures in a broader perspective, Japan, which oftern is seen as a model for its East Asian neighbors, had an export/GDP ratio of 10 percent in 1990, while the export ratio for the United States was only 7 percent. The East Asian NICs, partly because of their smaller size, thus are far more dependent on external trade than are their Latin American counterparts or Japan.

In exports as in production, manufactures are the chief source of growth in the NICs. While the role of primary commodity exports decreased sharply in all these economies between 1965 and 1990, manufactured items in 1990 constituted well over 90 percent of all exports in the East Asian NICs (except Singapore, where petroleum refining is highly significant) and for between one-third and one-half of the export total in the Latin American NICs.

The maturity or sophistication of a country's industrial structure can be measured by the complexity of the products it exports. Here again, the East Asian NICs are relatively advanced. In Singapore and South Korea, overseas sales of machinery and transport equipment, which utilize capital- and skill-intensive technology, grew by 18 and 34 percent, respectively, from 1965 to 1990 as a share of total merchandise exports. Taiwan's exports in this sector increased by 21 percent and Hong Kong's by 16 percent. In Latin America, Mexico (24 percent) and Brazil (16 percent) also made machinery and transport equipment a dynamic export base, while both Brazil and Argentina achieved solid export gains in the "other manufactures" category. Textiles and clothing, the most important export sector in the East Asian NICs in the 1960s, actually shrank as a proportion of total exports in these four nations during the past 25 years, reflecting their transition from traditional to more advanced forms of manufacturing.

The economic growth of the Latin American and East Asian NICs has occurred at different historical phases and in different rhythms. Furthermore, changes in the world system profoundly shaped the patterns of industrialization in the developing world.

The phrase *newly industrializing countries* actually is a misnomer when applied to Argentina, Brazil, and Mexico, since they established their first major wave of import-substituting industries in the 1930s and 1940s in response to the international economic dislocations caused by the Great Depression and World War II. In fact, the process of industrial growth in the larger Latin American countries already was well under way in the interwar period. The deterioration of the terms of trade for agricultural exports began in the 1920s, reflecting falling demand and rising supplies of agricultural goods throughout the industrialized nations and the adoption of protectionism in many countries of Continental Europe. This led to the demise of the primary product export model and served as an incentive for import-substituting industrialization (see Thorp, 1984; Cortes Conde and Hunt, 1985). Instead of representing a sudden mutation, then, the 1929 crisis brought into high relief trends that originated in the years immediately after World War I.

In Latin America, "the world slump of 1929–33 cut the purchasing power of the continent's exports by 60 percent, and ended the possibility of much borrowing abroad. Most countries were obliged to suspend the convertibility of their currencies, cut imports radically and take measures to stimulate the production of domestic substitutes" (Harris, 1987: 17). While the manufacturing output of the advanced countries declined precipitously during the 1930s, World War II production demands actually had an expansive impact on the Third World countries that helped supply the bellicose powers (Gordon, 1988: 34–5).

The postwar economic expansion of the United States as the hegemonic leader of the capitalist world economy was fueled by a decade of reconstruction in Europe and Asia. The revitalization of direct foreign investment (DFI) and international trade laid the groundwork for a new international division of labor, based on increasingly complex networks of industrial production and sourcing, and new forms of geographical specialization (Fröbel et al., 1981).

The Latin American NICs sought to deepen their industrialization in the mid-1950s by opening their doors to new waves of DFI from the United States, Western Europe, and eventually Japan. Whereas foreign investors in Latin America traditionally had concentrated on export-oriented projects in mining, oil, and agriculture, postwar DFI emphasized import-substituting investments in advanced manufacturing industries like automobiles, chemicals, machinery, and pharmaceuticals whose output was destined primarily for the relatively large domestic markets in Latin America.

The East Asian NICs followed a contrasting sequence. They did not begin their rapid economic growth until the mid-1960s, after an extended period of colonization by Japan prior to 1945 and with a heavy infusion of American aid during the next two decades. Hong Kong, Singapore, South Korea, and Taiwan pursued policies of outward-oriented industrialization in the 1960s in order to generate foreign exchange via manufactured exports. During this initial phase of export expansion, the rapid growth of the East Asian NICs was founded on light, labor-intensive industries like textiles, garments, and electronic equipment. In subsequent phases, however, South Korea, Taiwan, and Singapore achieved success in much heavier industries like steel, petrochemicals, shipbuilding, vehicle manufacture, and computers that were less well suited to their original factor endowments (i.e., limited raw materials, unskilled labor, and small markets). The East Asian NICs thus were motivated by the principle of dynamic competitive advantage rather than by their static comparative advantage in cheap, disciplined labor.

The emergence and evolution of the NICs has been a product of cyclical shifts in the world economy. When the conditions that made import substitution a viable and appealing option for many countries changed, there was increased general interest in export promotion. The turn outward by the East Asian NICs in the 1960s foreshadowed similar efforts in the following decades by a wide range of developing nations, including the Latin American NICs. To gain a better picture of the dynamic relationship between these patterns of inward- and outward-oriented industrialization, we need to examine more closely the paths of industrialization followed by the Latin American and East Asian NICs.

The Dynamic Interplay of Inward- and Outward-Oriented Industrialization

Based on a broad historical view of industrialization in the Latin American and East Asian NICs, one can identify five main phases of industrial development. Three of these are

Mexico and Brazil: 1880–1930	Mexico and Brazil: 1930–55	Mexico: 1955–70 Brazil: 1955–68	Mexico: 1970–present Brazil: 1968–present

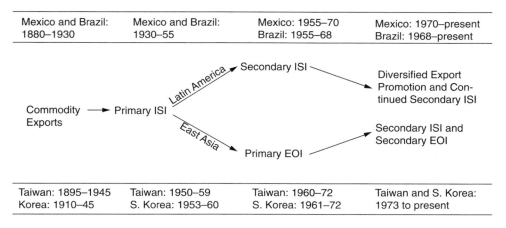

Taiwan: 1895–1945 Korea: 1910–45	Taiwan: 1950–59 S. Korea: 1953–60	Taiwan: 1960–72 S. Korea: 1961–72	Taiwan and S. Korea: 1973 to present

Figure 1   Paths of Industrialization in Latin America and East Asia: Commonalities, Divergence, and Convergence

outward looking: a commodity export phase, and primary and secondary export-oriented industrialization (EOI). The other two are inward looking: primary and secondary import-substituting industrialization (ISI). The subtypes within the outward and inward approaches are distinguished by the kind of products involved in each.

In the commodity export phase, the output typically is unrefined or semiprocessed raw materials (agricultural goods, minerals, oil, etc.). Primary ISI entails the shift from imports to the local manufacture of basic consumer goods, and in almost all countries the key industries during this phase are textiles, clothing, footwear, and food processing. Secondary ISI involves using domestic production to substitute for imports of a variety of capital- and technology-intensive manufactures: consumer durables (e.g., automobiles), intermediate goods (e.g., petrochemicals and steel), and capital goods (e.g., heavy machinery).

Both phases of EOI involve manufactured exports. In primary EOI these tend to be labor-intensive products, while secondary EOI includes higher-value-added items that are skill intensive and require a more fully developed local industrial base.

Following this schema, the principal sequences of industrial development in Mexico, Brazil, South Korea, and Taiwan are outlined in Figure 1. For convenience, I use the phrase *paths of industrialization to* refer to these economic outcomes. The varied role of government policies, incentives, and explicit development strategies in bringing about these industrial shifts is an important but separate issue that I will not address here. (This topic is analyzed in Cheng and Haggard, 1987; Cheng, 1990; Kaufman, 1990; and Wade, 1990.)

Each of the two regional pairs of NICs has followed a distinctive industrial trajectory that includes the ISI and EOI ideal types mentioned above, plus a "mixed" phase in the most recent period. An analysis of these trajectories, as shown in Figure 1, suggests the following conclusions (see Gereffi and Wyman, 1989).

First, the contrast often made between the Latin American and the East Asian NICs as representing inward- and outward-oriented industrial paths, respectively, is oversimplified. While this distinction is appropriate for some periods, a historical perspective shows that each of these NICs has pursued both inward- and outward-oriented approaches.

Every nation, with the exception of Britain at the time of the Industrial Revolution, went through an initial stage of ISI in which protection was extended to incipient manufacturing industries producing for domestic markets. Even Hong Kong, the most laissez-faire of the NICs, benefited from a period of "disguised ISI" on the Chinese mainland. Refugees to Hong Kong from the mainland included a significant segment of the Shanghai capitalist class and a huge supply of politically unorganized labor, and they brought with them technical know-how, skills, and even machinery (Haggard and Cheng, 1987: 106–10). Furthermore, each of the NICs subsequently has combined both advanced ISI and different types of EOI in order to avoid the inherent limitations of an exclusive reliance on domestic or external markets, and also to facilitate the industrial diversification and upgrading that are required for these nations to remain competitive in the world economy. Rather than being mutually exclusive alternatives, the ISI and EOI development paths in fact have been complementary and interactive (Gereffi and Wyman, 1990).

Second, the early phases of industrialization – commodity exports and primary ISI – were common to all of the Latin American and East Asian NICs, although the timing and specific products involved varied considerably. The subsequent divergence in the regional sequences stems from the ways in which each country responded to the basic problems associated with the continuation of primary ISI. These problems included balance of payments pressures, rapidly rising inflation, high levels of dependence of intermediate and capital goods imports, and low levels of manufactured exports.

Third, the duration and timing of these development patterns vary by region. Primary ISI began earlier, lasted longer, and was more populist in Latin America than in East Asia. Timing helps explain these sequences because the opportunities and constraints that shape development choices are constantly shifting. The East Asian NICs began their accelerated export of manufactured products during a period of extraordinary dynamism in the world economy. The two decades that preceded the global economic crisis of the 1970s saw unprecedented annual growth rates of world industrial production (approximately 5.6 percent) and world trade (around 7.3 percent), relatively low inflation and high employment rates in the industrialized countries, and stable international monetary arrangements. The expansion of world trade was fastest between 1960 and 1973, when the average annual growth rate of exports reached almost 9 percent.

Starting in 1973, however, the international economy entered a troublesome phase. From 1973 to the end of the decade, the annual growth in world trade fell to 4.5 percent as manufactured exports from the developing countries encountered stiffer protectionist measures in the industrialized markets. These new trends were among the factors that led the East Asian NICs to modify their EOI approach in the 1970s (see Cheng and Haggard, 1987).

Fourth, the development trajectories of the Latin American and East Asian NICs show some signs of convergence in the 1970s and 1980s. To support this convergence thesis, it is necessary to distinguish two subphases during the most recent period. In the 1970s Mexico and Brazil began to expand both their commodity exports (oil, soybeans, minerals, etc.) and their manufactured exports, as well as to accelerate their foreign borrowing, in order to acquire enough foreign exchange to finance the imports necessary for furthering secondary ISI. This "diversified exports" approach, which became even more prominent in the

1980s in the face of sharply curtailed foreign borrowing, was an important addition to Mexico's and Brazil's earlier emphasis on industrial deepening.

South Korea and Taiwan, on the other hand, emphasized heavy and chemical industrialization from 1973 to 1979, with a focus on steel, automobiles, shipbuilding, and petrochemicals. The objective of heavy and chemical industrialization in East Asia was twofold: to develop national production capability in these sectors, justified by national security as well as import substitution considerations, and to lay the groundwork for more diversified exports in the future. China's reentry into the international community, ushered in by its détente with the United States in the early 1970s, not only made South Korea's and Taiwan's domestic defense concerns more credible, but China also presented a long-term threat to labor-intensive industries in the region. South Korea and Taiwan have used the secondary ISI industries established during the 1970s as a base for launching a far more variegated array of technology- and skill-intensive manufactured exports in the 1980s (Gereffi, 1989).

It is clear that neither inward-oriented nor outward-oriented paths of industrialization are self-sufficient models of development. Both are susceptible to systemic constraints or vulnerabilities such as recurring balance of payments problems, persistent inflation, and the disruption of key trading relationships (see Gereffi, 1990b). However, the NICs in each region have adapted or switched their development trajectories in response to these problems, and thus they succeeded in moving to a more diversified pattern of export growth in the 1980s.

Dependent Development in Latin America and East Asia

Dependency theory has been flawed by its historically close association with the development of the Latin American NICs. The "dependent development" literature drew heavily on the experience of Latin American nations, and it looked at the problems of Third World development with an eye toward investment and debt dependency. Therefore it has been claimed that dependency theory has little, if any, relevance to East Asian NICs (Amsden, 1979; Barrett and Whyte, 1982; Berger, 1986). In fact, the East Asian NICs have experienced two distinct kinds of dependency: the dependency on American aid in the 1950s, and trade dependency, again largely on the United States, since the 1960s. The internal and external consequences of each kind of dependency are quite different.

To approach the issue of dependent development in a cross-regional setting, the concept of transnational economic linkages (TNELs) is quite useful. There are four main TNELs: foreign aid, foreign trade, direct foreign investment, and foreign loans. They affect development strategies and outcomes in several ways (see Gereffi and Wyman, 1989).

First, they represent economic resources that may be used, singly or in diverse combinations and sequences, to finance development. For example, DFI sustained secondary ISI in Latin America, much as massive foreign aid flows made primary ISI possible in East Asia.

Second, the availability of these resources is conditioned by factors beyond as well as within the control of nation states. Factors beyond the control of individual countries include global economic conditions (e.g., trends in world trade) as well as geopolitical

Table 1 The Structure of Dependent Development in Latin America and East Asia

Transitional Economic Linkages	Development Strategies, Brazil and Mexico				Development Strategies, South Korea and Taiwan			
	Commodity Exports	Primary ISI	Secondary ISI	Diversified Exports and Secondary ISI	Commodity Exports	Primary ISI	Primary EOI	Secondary ISI and EOI
Foreign aid	Low	Low	Medium	Low	Low	High	Medium	Medium
Foreign trade	High	Low	Low (exports) Medium (imports)	Medium (imports) High (exports)	High	Low (exports) Medium (imports)	High	High
Direct foreign investment	Medium (Brazil) High (Mexico)	Low	High	Medium	Medium	Low	Low (S. Korea) Medium (Taiwan)	Medium (S. Korea) High (Taiwan)
Foreign borrowing	Medium	Low	Medium	High	Low	Low	Low (Taiwan) Medium (S. Korea)	Medium (Taiwan) High (S. Korea)

Source: Gereffi and Wyman (1989).

pressures that help channel capital toward some countries and away from others. National policies regarding domestic wage levels, foreign investment, and the degree of political stability in a country, on the other hand, can also shape the performance to TNELs.

Third, the destination and use of TNELs in a country directly affect the power of domestic actors. It matters, for example, whether these economic resources are used to finance luxury imports for the wealthy or irrigation systems and public transportation for the masses, just as it matters whether the presence of these resources strengthens or weakens agrarian elites vis-à-vis the peasantry or the industrial bourgeoisie rather than the urban working class.

Table 1 identifies the relative importance of each of the TNELs in Brazil, Mexico, South Korea, and Taiwan during the different phases of industrialization discussed earlier. The high, medium, and low weights in Table 1 are based on estimates of the relative significance of the TNELs in each economy, compared with other developing countries at similar stages in their industrialization process.

There is considerable variation among the NICs in the role played by TNELs. First, the salience of TNELs varies markedly over time within each region, since each phase of the industrial trajectories of the Latin American and East Asian NICs is associated with a different mix of external resources used to finance development. In East Asia, for example, primary ISI relied on a great deal of foreign aid and little export trade; conversely, the subsequent phase of primary EOI was defined by extensive exports and virtually no foreign aid.

Second, the salience of TNELs also varies between the two regions within the same phase of industrialization. For example, both regions went through a period of primary ISI, but the dynamics were quite different. In East Asia primary ISI was financed by massive amounts of foreign economic assistance, whereas in Latin America the same phase tended to be carried out by local industrialists with the support of the state and with limited participation by transnational corporations. It is widely acknowledged that the South Korean and Taiwanese economies could not have survived the 1950s without American assistance. Between 1951 and 1965, $1.5 billion in economic aid and $2.5 billion in military aid were sent to Taiwan by the United States. South Korea received a similar amount of U.S. aid in the 1953–61 period, with $2.6 billion earmarked for economic assistance and $1.6 billion for military expenditures. Aid financed 40 percent of fixed investment in Taiwan and 80 percent in South Korea. Concessional capital flows were used to purchase 70 percent of the imports coming into South Korea, as well as to pay 90 percent of the balance of trade deficit in Taiwan (Jacoby, 1966; Cole, 1980).

Third, the contrast with regard to TNELs is sharpest during the 1960s, when Latin America's secondary ISI is juxtaposed with East Asia's primary EOI. The former phase relied heavily on DFI and external loans but was oriented toward supplying local markets; the latter phase depended on access to overseas markets but was implemented in large part by domestic entrepreneurs who drew mainly on local financial resources (this was especially true in Taiwan, whereas in South Korea local capitalists became heavily indebted to foreign creditors in the 1970s).

Fourth and finally, Latin America and East Asia differ in terms of the overall weight that TNELs have had in the two regions. Historically DFI and foreign loans represented the most important external economic resources for the Latin American NICs; in contrast, export trade and foreign aid have been the key forms of East Asian linkage to the international economy. A main reason why dependency has been such a thorny issue for the Latin American countries is that DFI tends to create greater frictions than other types of foreign capital in Third World countries (see Stallings, 1990). In the East Asian NICs, on the other hand, trade dependency on the United States has been declining since the early 1970s, and their export profile has become more diversified (Barrett and Chin, 1987), thus reducing but not eliminating some of the deleterious consequences of export partner and product concentration.

The dependency perspective can be enriched by dealing more explicitly with issues of dependency management. This approach focuses attention on the capacity of domestic institutions to use external economic resources productively and selectively to serve local interests. A key to understanding the success of the East Asian NICs' export strategy, for example, is the performance of locally owned exporting firms that aggressively sought and exploited opportunities for profitable overseas sales. These local exporters established close ties with foreign buyers, who assisted in matters of product design and technology transfer. The adaptation of available modern technology has enabled the East Asian NICs to move from conventional labor-intensive exports like textiles, clothing, and footwear to heavier and high-technology industries like transportation equipment, electrical machinery, and computer components. Joint-venture research projects, as well as locally owned companies, have been set up in South Korea and Taiwan to give these countries greater flexibility in developing their own production and technological capabilities (Schive, 1990). The success of both primary and secondary EOI in the East Asian NICs thus is explained in large part by the ability of domestic firms to manage effectively their dependency relationships in the areas of international trade and investment.

The Emergent Global Manufacturing System: Toward a Theoretical Synthesis

This comparative overview of industrialization in the East Asian and Latin American NICs provides the elements for a new synthesis in development theory. This theoretical synthesis is based on a modified world-systems perspective, in which my focus is the changing parameters for mobility by the NICs in the emergent global manufacturing system.

I will discuss three related themes to illustrate the direction this approach might take: (1) the declining significance of industrialization, (2) the position of core and peripheral capital in contemporary commodity chains and export/marketing networks, and (3) a framework for differentiating the roles of the NICs in the world economy. My concluding remarks will address issues for future research on this topic.

The Declining Significance of Industrialization

Since the 1950s, the gap between developed and developing countries has been narrowing in terms of industrialization. Industry as a share of GDP has increased substantially in the vast majority of Third World nations, not only in absolute terms but also relative to that of the core countries (see Harris, 1987). By the late 1970s, the NICs as a whole not only caught up with but overtook the core countries in terms of their degree of industrialization (Arrighi and Drangel, 1986: 54–5).

By 1986, all of the NICs in Latin America and East Asia, with the exception of Hong Kong, had industry/GDP ratios that exceeded the industrial market countries' average level of 35 percent. The same pattern holds true for manufacturing, which is generally the most dynamic part of the industrial sector. The manufacturing/GDP ratio in 1990 for the United States, for example, was 17 percent, which was lower than that of any of the seven Latin American and East Asian NICs.

While industry and manufacturing as a share of GDP are on the decline in the most developed nations of the world economy, this trend is counterbalanced by the core's emphasis on the service sector and on the most productive, high-value-added segments of manufacturing. Ironically, as more and more countries in the world are becoming industrialized, industrialization itself is losing the key status it once had as an ultimate hallmark of national development.

These observations lead to two basic conclusions about the theoretical status of industrialization in the contemporary world economy. First, *industrialization* and *development* are not synonymous. This is apparent in the disparate social and economic consequences of industrial growth in the Latin American and East Asian NICs over the past couple of decades. Despite similarly high levels of industrialization in the NICs from both regions, the East Asian nations have performed significantly better than their Latin American counterparts in terms of standard indicators of development such as GNP per capita, income distribution, literacy, health, and education (see Gereffi and Fonda, 1992).

Second, just as industrialization cannot be equated with development, neither does it guarantee proximity to core status in the world system. Although the NICs are now more industrialized than most of the core countries, this achievement generally has not led to a substantial change in the relative position of the NICs in the hierarchy of nations in the world economy. Arrighi and Drangel (1986: 44), who measured upward and downward mobility in the world system over the past fifty years in terms of national changes in per capita GNP, found that 95 percent of the states classified in one of the three world-system zones (core, semiperiphery, and periphery) in 1938–50 were in the same zone in 1975–83. Among the few exceptional cases of upward mobility in the world system were Japan and Italy, which moved from the semiperiphery to the core, and South Korea and Taiwan, which moved from the periphery to the semiperiphery.

Therefore, while industrialization may be a necessary condition for core status in the world system, it no longer is sufficient. Mobility from the semiperiphery to the core, or from the periphery to the semiperiphery, should not be defined simply in terms of a country's degree of industrialization, but rather by a nation's success in upgrading its mix of economic activities toward technology- and skill-intensive products and techniques with higher levels of local value added. Continued innovations by the most developed countries tend to make core status an ever receding frontier.

Commodity Chains and Export/Marketing Networks

In the global manufacturing system of today, production of a single good commonly spans several countries, with each nation performing tasks in which it has a cost advantage. This is true for traditional manufactures, such as garments and footwear, as well as for modern products, like automobiles and computers (Gereffi, 1989). To analyze the implications of this globalization of production for specific sets of countries like the East Asian and Latin American NICs, it is helpful to utilize the concept of commodity chains.

A "commodity chain," as defined by Hopkins and Wallerstein (1986: 159), refers to "a network of labor and production processes whose end result is a finished commodity." To delineate the anatomy of the chain, one typically starts with the final production operation for a consumable good and moves sequentially backward until one reaches the raw material inputs. However, the complexity of commodity chains for the kinds of export-oriented manufacturing industries that the NICs are predominant in today requires us to extend the model proposed by Hopkins and Wallerstein in several ways (see Gereffi and Korzeniewicz, 1994).

First, the dynamic growth of the NICs has revolved around their success in expanding their production and exports of a wide range of consumer products destined mainly for core-country markets. This means that it is extremely important to include forward as well as backward linkages from the production stage in the commodity chain. Most commodity chains are composed of four major segments: (1) raw material supply, (2) production, (3) exporting, and (4) marketing and retailing. In the footwear industry, for example, a full commodity chain takes us across the entire spectrum of activities in the world economy: the agro-extractive sector (cattle for leather, and crude oil as the basis for plastic and synthetic rubber inputs), the industrial sector (footwear manufacturing), and the service sector (the activities associated with the export, marketing, and retailing of shoes). Commodity chains in most other manufacturing industries today are similar in their broad scope.

Second, the extension of commodity chains beyond production to include the flow of products to the final consumer is essential for our ability to detect where economic surplus is concentrated in a global industry. The comparative advantage of the NICs lies primarily at the production stage because of the low labor costs in these countries relative to the core and their high productivity relative to the periphery. An important corollary of this fact, however, is that the distribution and retail marketing segments of these commodity chains tend to be more profitable than manufacturing per se. Furthermore, the economic surplus that accrues to distributors and retailers in core countries generally is much higher when production is done overseas rather than domestically.

The distributors' margins in the footwear industry in the United States, for example, averaged 50 percent in the mid-1970s but were closer to 60 percent for imported goods (Gereffi and Korzeniewicz, 1990: 54–5). Product differentiation by means of heavily advertised brand names (e.g., Nike, Reebok, or Florsheim in shoes) and the use of diverse retail outlets allow core-country firms rather than those in the semiperiphery to capture the lion's share of economic rents in a diverse range of consumer goods industries.

For semiperipheral countries to ascend in the world economy, they will have to find new ways to move to the most profitable end of commodity chains. This requires a fundamental shift from manufacturing in the semiperiphery to marketing in the core, a daunting task that will require new patterns of investment in research and development, advertising, and retail distribution by the NICs.

Differentiating the Roles of the NICs in the World Economy

The foregoing analysis of the Latin American and East Asian NICs allows us to identify a differentiated set of roles that semiperipheral nations play in the world economy. These roles reflect the mix of core-peripheral economic activities in the NICs, as well as the significance of core and peripheral capital in carrying out these development efforts. These roles are not mutually exclusive, and their importance for a given country or set of countries may undergo fairly dramatic shifts over time. From the perspective of world-systems theory, it is essential to note that these roles in the world economy are largely determined by domestic conditions, such as the pattern of economic, social, and political organization within the NICs.

This framework focuses on export production in the NICs, since this is the best indicator of a country's international competitive advantage. The NICs can be characterized in terms of at least four basic types of economic roles: (1) the commodity-export role, (2) the export-platform role, (3) the specification-contracting role, and (4) the component-supplier role.

The *commodity-export role* is of prime importance for the Latin American NICs, where natural resources account for two-thirds or more of total exports, and also for Singapore, which processes and re-exports a large volume of petroleum-related products. Peripheral capital controls most of these natural-resource industries at the production stage in Latin America, with the petroleum and mining industries usually being run by state-owned enterprises, while the agricultural and livestock industries generally are owned by local capital. In Singapore, by contrast, TNCs are the proprietors of most of the petroleum-related industries. These commodity exports are sent to a wide range of nations, with the predominant share going to core countries. The export and distribution networks are usually controlled by core capital.

The *export-platform role* corresponds to those nations that have foreign-owned, labor-intensive assembly of manufactured goods in export-processing zones. These zones offer special incentives to foreign capital and tend to attract firms in a common set of industries: garments, footwear, and electronics. Virtually all of the East Asian and Latin American NICs have engaged in this form of labor-intensive production, although its significance tends to wane as wage rates rise and countries become more developed. In Taiwan and South Korea, export-processing zones have been on the decline during the past two decades, largely because labor costs have been rapidly increasing. These nations have been trying to upgrade their mix of export activities by moving toward more skill- and technology-intensive products. The export-platform role in Asia is now being occupied by low-wage countries like China, the Philippines, Thailand, Indonesia, and Malaysia.

In Latin America, on the other hand, export-platform industries are on the upswing because the wage levels in most countries of the region are considerably below those of the East Asian NICs, and recent currency devaluations in the Latin American NICs make the price of their exports more competitive internationally. The export platforms in Latin America also have the advantage of geographical proximity to the most important core-country markets in comparison with Asian export platforms. Mexico's *maquiladora* industry, which was set up in 1965 as an integral part of Mexico's Northern Border Industrialization Program, is probably the largest and most dynamic of these export areas. . . . There are similar zones in Brazil, Colombia, Central America, and the Caribbean. Core capital controls the production, export, and marketing stages of the commodity chains for these consumer goods. The main contribution of peripheral nations is cheap labor.

The *specification-contracting role* refers to the production of finished consumer goods by locally owned firms, where the output is distributed and marketed by core capital or its agents. This is the major niche filled by the East Asian NICs in the contemporary world economy. . . . In East Asia, peripheral capital controls the production stage of the finished consumer-goods commodity chains (see Haggard and Cheng, 1987; Gereffi, 1990a), while core capital tends to control the more profitable export, distribution, and retail marketing stages. While the international subcontracting of finished consumer goods is growing in Latin America, it tends to be subordinated to the export-platform and component-supplier forms of production.

The *component-supplier role* refers to the production of component parts in capital- and technology-intensive industries in the periphery, for export and usually final assembly in the core country. This has been the major niche for the manufactured exports of the Latin American NICs during the past two decades. Brazil and Mexico have been important production sites for vertically integrated exports by TNCs to core-country markets, especially the United States, since the late 1960s. This is most notable in certain industries like motor vehicles, computers, and pharmaceuticals (see Newfarmer, 1985). American, European, and Japanese automotive TNCs, for example, have advanced manufacturing facilities in Mexico and Brazil for the production of engines, auto parts, and even completed vehicles for the US and European markets.

In Latin America, the manufacturing stage of the commodity chain in component-supplier production typically is owned and run by core capital, sometimes in conjunction with a local partner. The export, distribution, and marketing of the manufactured items are handled by the TNC. A major advantage of this production arrangement is that it is most likely to result in a significant transfer of technology from the core nations.

In East Asia there are two variants of the component-supplier role. The first is similar to the Latin American arrangement in which foreign subsidiaries manufacture parts or subunits in East Asia for products like television sets, radios, sporting goods, and consumer appliances that are assembled and marketed in the country of destination (most often the United States).

The second variant of the component-supplier role involves production of components by East Asian firms for sale to diversified buyers on the world market. This is illustrated in the semiconductor industry. South Korean companies have focused almost exclusively on the mass production of powerful memory chips, the single largest segment of the semiconductor industry, which are sold as inputs to a wide range of domestic and international manufacturers of electronic equipment. Taiwan, on the other hand, has targeted the highest-value-added segment of the semiconductor market: tailor-made "designer chips" that perform special tasks in toys, video games, and other machines. Taiwan was reported to have forty chip-design houses that specialize in finding export niches and then developing products for them (*Far Eastern Economic Review*, 1988).

Taiwan, with its technological prowess, is acquiring the flexibility to move into the high-value-added field of product innovation. However, without their own internationally recognized company brand names, a substantial advertising budget, and appropriate marketing and retail networks, Taiwan's ingenious producers will find it difficult to break free of the international subcontracting role. South Korea probably has more potential to enter core-country markets successfully because the *jaebols* have the capital and technology to set up overseas production facilities and marketing networks. Thus South Korea's leading auto manufacturer, Hyundai Motor Company, has become one of the top importers into both Canada and the United States since the mid-1980s (see Gereffi, 1990a).

This typology of the different roles that the Latin American and East Asian NICs play in the world economy shows that the standard development literature has presented an oversimplified picture of the semiperiphery. The East Asian NICs have been most success-ful in the areas of international subcontracting and component supply, with secondary and declining importance given to the export-platform role emphasized in "the new international division of labor" literature. The Latin American NICs, on the other hand, have a different kind of relationship to the world economy. They are prominent in the commodity-export, export-platform, and component-supplier forms of production, but they lag far behind the East Asian NICs in the international-subcontracting type of manufactured exports.

Although each of these roles has certain advantages and disadvantages in terms of mobil-ity in the world system, the prospects for the NICs can only be understood by looking at the interacting sets of roles in which these nations are enmeshed. If development theory is to be relevant for the 1990s, it will have to become flexible enough to incorporate both increased specialization at the commodity and geographical levels, along with new patterns of regional and global integration.

[. . .]

Development theory needs to incorporate and integrate the global, national, and local levels of analysis if we are to understand the challenges and choices that confront industrial-izing nations. The false dilemma of outward- versus inward-oriented development must be replaced by a more comprehensive approach that sees countries as occupying differentiated roles in the world economy requiring a combination of export industries as well as those producing for domestic markets. A multidisciplinary view of development issues offers the best hope for a theory that is responsive to concrete problems and can also provide the basis for useful generalizations.

EDITOR'S NOTE

1   Figures in this section are from World Bank (1982, 1983, and 1992). These figures are cited in the following two tables, which are omitted here: "Table 1: The East Asian and Latin American NICs: Basic Indicators" and "Table 2: Exports by the East Asian and Latin American NICs, 1965 to 1900."

REFERENCES

Amsden, Alice H., 1979, "Taiwan's economic history: A case of étatisme and a challenge to depen-dency theory." *Modern China* 5:341–80.

Arrighi, Giovanni, and Jessica Drangel, 1986, "The stratification of the world economy: An explora-tion of the semiperipheral zone." *Review* 10:9–74.

Balassa, Bela, 1981, *The Newly Industrializing Countries in the World Economy*. New York: Pergamon Press.

Balassa, Bela, Gerardo M. Bueno, Pedro-Pablo Kuczynski, and Mario Henrique Simonsen, 1986, *Toward Renewed Economic Growth in Latin America*. Washington, DC: Institute of International Economics.

Barrett, Richard E., and Soomi Chin, 1987, "Export-oriented industrializing states in the capitalist world system: Similarities and differences." In *The Political Economy of the New Asian Industrialism*, edited by Frederic C. Deyo, 23–43. Ithaca, NY: Cornell University Press.

Barrett, Richard E., and Martin King Whyte, 1982, "Dependency theory and Taiwan: Analysis of a deviant case." *American Journal of Sociology* 87:1064–89.

Berger, Peter L., 1986, *The Capitalist Revolution*. New York: Basic Books.

Cardoso, Fernando Henrique, and Enzo Faletto, 1979, *Dependency and Development in Latin America*. Berkeley: University of California Press.

Cheng, Tun-jen, 1990, "Political regimes and development strategies: South Korea and Taiwan." In *Manufacturing Miracles: Paths of Industrialization in Latin America and East Asia*, edited by Gary Gereffi and Donald Wyman, 139–78. Princeton, NJ: Princeton University Press.

Cheng, Tun-jen, and Stephan Haggard, 1987, *Newly Industrializing Asia in Transition: Policy Reform and American Response*. Berkeley: Institute of International Studies, University of California.

Cole, David C., 1980, "Foreign assistance and Korean development." In *The Korean Economy – Issues of Development*, edited by David C. Cole, Youngil Lim, and Paul W. Kuznets, 1–29. Berkeley: Institute of East Asian Studies, University of California.

Collier, David, ed., 1979, *The New Authoritarianism in Latin America*. Princeton, NJ: Princeton University Press.

Cortes Conde, Roberto, and Shane J. Hunt, eds., 1985, *The Latin American Economies Growth and the Export Sector, 1880–1930*. New York; Holmes and Mejer.

Evans, Peter, 1979, *Dependent Development: The Alliance of Multinationals, State and Local Capital in Brazil*. Princeton, NJ: Princeton University Press.

Far Eastern Economic Review, 1988, "Sizzling hot chips: Asia is the source of the semiconductor industry's spectacular growth." August 18, pp. 80–6.

Fröbel, Folker, Jurgen Heinrichs, and Otto Kreye, 1981, *The New International Division of Labor*. New York: Cambridge University Press.

Gereffi, Gary, 1983, *The Pharmaceutical Industry and Dependency in the Third World*. Princeton, NJ: Princeton University Press.

—— 1989, "Development strategies and the global factory." *Annals of the American Academy of Political and Social Science* 505:92–104.

—— 1990a, "Big business and the state." In *Manufacturing Miracles: Paths of Industrialization in Latin America and East Asia*, edited by Gary Gereffi and Donald Wyman, 90–109. Princeton, NJ: Princeton University Press.

—— 1990b, "International economics and domestic policies." In *Economy and Society: Overviews in Economic Sociology*, edited by Alberto Martinelli and Neil J. Smelser, 231–58. Newbury Park, Calif.: Sage.

Gereffi, Gary, and Stephanie Fonda, 1992, "Regional paths of development." *Annual Review of Sociology* 18:419–48.

Gereffi, Gary, and Miguel Korzeniewicz, 1990, "Commodity chains and footwear exports in the semiperiphery." In *Semiperipheral States in the World-Economy*, edited by William Martin, 45–68. Westport, CT: Greenwood Press.

Gereffi, Gary, and Miguel Korzeniewicz, eds., 1994, *Commodity Chains and Global Capitalism*. Westport, Conn.: Greenwood Press.

Gereffi, Gary, and Donald Wyman, 1989, "Determinants of development strategies in Latin America and East Asia." In *Pacific Dynamics: The International Politics of Industrial Change*, edited by Stephan Haggard and Chung-in Moon, 23–52. Boulder, Colo.: Westview Press.

Gereffi, Gary, and Donald Wyman, eds., 1990, *Manufacturing Miracles: Paths of Industrialization in Latin America and East Asia*. Princeton, NJ: Princeton University Press.

Gold, Thomas B., 1981, "Dependent development in Taiwan." Ph.D. diss., Harvard University, Cambridge, Mass.

Gordon, David M., 1988, "The global economy: New edifice or crumbling foundations?" *New Left Review* 168:24–64.

Haggard, Stephan, and Tunjen Cheng, 1987, "State and foreign capital in the East Asian NICs." In *The Political Economy of the New Asian Industrialism*, edited by Frederic C. Deyo, 84–135, Ithaca, NY: Cornell University Press.

Harris, Nigel, 1987, *The End of the Third World: Newly Industrializing Countries and the Decline of an Ideology*. New York: Viking Penguin.

Hopkins, Terence K., and Immanuel Wallerstein, 1986, "Commodity chains in the world-economy prior to 1800." *Review* 10:157–70.

Jacoby, Neil H., 1966, *U.S. Aid to Taiwan*. New York: Praeger.

Johnson, Chalmers, 1983, "The 'internationalization' of the Japanese economy." *California Management Review* 25:5–26.

—— 1987, "Political institutions and economic performance: The government–business relationship in Japan, South Korea, and Taiwan." In *The Political Economy of the New Asian Industrialism*, edited by Frederic C. Deyo, 136–64. Ithaca, NY: Cornell University Press.

Kaufman, Robert, 1990, "How societies change development strategies or keep them: Reflections on the Latin American experience in the 1930s and the post-war world." In *Manufacturing Miracles: Paths of Industrialization in Latin America and East Asia*, edited by Gary Gereffi and Donald Wyman, 110–38. Princeton, NJ: Princeton University Press.

Lim, Hyun-Chin, 1985, *Dependent Development in Korea, 1963–1979*. Seoul: Seoul National University Press.

Newfarmer, Richard, 1985, *Profits, Progress and Poverty: Case Studies of International Industries in Latin America*. Notre Dame, Ind.: University of Notre Dame Press.

O'Donnell, Guillermo, 1973, *Modernization and Bureaucratic Authoritarianism: Studies in South American Politics*. Berkeley: Institute of International Studies, University of California.

OECD (Organization for Economic Cooperation and Development), 1979, *The Impact of the Newly Industrializing Countries on Production and Trade in Manufactures*. Paris: OECD.

Schive, Chi, 1990, "The next stage of industrialization in Taiwan and South Korea." In *Manufacturing Miracles: Paths of Industrialization in Latin America and East Asia*, edited by Gary Gereffi and Donald Wyman, 267–91. Princeton, NJ: Princeton University Press.

Stallings, Barbara, 1990, "The role of foreign capital and economic development." In *Manufacturing Miracles: Paths of Industrialization in Latin America and East Asia*, edited by Gary Gereffi and Donald Wyman, 55–89. Princeton, NJ: Princeton University Press.

Swidler, Ann, 1986, "Culture in action: Symbols and strategies." *American Sociological Review* 51:273–86.

Thorp, Rosemary, ed., 1984, *Latin America in the 1930's: The Role of the Periphery in the World Crisis*. Oxford: Macmillan.

Valenzuela, J. Samuel, and Arturo Valenzuela, 1978, "Modernization and dependency: Alternative perspectives in the study of Latin American underdevelopment." *Comparative Politics* 10:535–57.

Wade, Robert, 1990, "Industrial policy in East Asia – Does it lead or follow the market?" In *Manufacturing Miracles: Paths of Industrialization in Latin America and East Asia*, edited by Gary Gereffi and Donald Wyman, 231–66. Princeton, NJ: Princeton University Press.

Wallerstein, Immanuel, 1974, "Dependence in an interdependent world: The limited possibilities of transformation within the capitalist world economy." *African Studies Review* 17:1–26.

World Bank, 1982, *World Development Report 1982*. New York: Oxford University Press.

—— 1983, *World Development Report 1983*. New York: Oxford University Press.

—— 1992, *World Development Report 1992*. New York: Oxford University Press.

9 Gender and the Global Economy (1999)

Valentine M. Moghadam

In what way does a gender perspective deepen our understanding of global economic processes? How has the recognition that women and men are differently situated in and affected by socioeconomic processes influenced economic thinking and policy making? As sociologists, how do we approach gender *theoretically* in relation to the global economy, and in terms of its intersection with class, race/ethnicity, and the state? In what sense are economic restructuring and globalization *gendered*?

The scholarship on gender and the global economy has advanced considerably since the early 1980s. It is produced mainly by researchers working in the interdisciplinary field originally known as women-in-development and now called gender and development. It builds on earlier research – carried out largely within national frameworks, utilizing ethnographic methods, and focused on underdeveloped or Third World societies – on the way the gender division of labor shapes women's roles in production and reproduction (e.g., Afshar 1985; Boserup 1987; Young, Walkowitz, and McCollough 1981). Advancement in the field has occurred partly because the dramatic economic changes of structural adjustment and globalization have forced researchers to examine the implications of those changes for women and gender relations, and partly because feminists are beginning to theorize the way that gender shapes some of these processes and is in turn affected by them.[1] The now prodigious body of knowledge produced by feminist social scientists on development, women, and gender has not only shaped the evolution of the field itself, but is having some influence on practitioners and policy makers in international development agencies such as the United Nations and, to a lesser degree, the World Bank. Moreover, gender issues are being considered by some development economists (e.g., Collier 1989; Drèze and Sen 1989; Haddad et al. 1995; Karshenas 1997; Taylor 1995) and macrosociologists (especially Sklair 1991; see also Chase-Dunn 1989).

Theoretical work on gender and the world economy is only in its early stages – and necessarily so, as empirical research documenting gender-specific effects has had to be carried out first in order to provide evidence for the generalizations and larger theoretical claims. Many more studies exist on the effects of economic processes on women (e.g., Afshar and Dennis 1992; Beneria and Feldman 1992; Joekes and Weston 1995) than on the way that gender is inscribed in the macroeconomy or in the social structure, hence shaping socioeconomic outcomes. Still, researchers have sought explanations for economic impacts in terms of gender relations, ideologies, or bias (e.g., Elson 1991; Fernandez-Kelly 1989;

Moghadam 1993; Pearson 1992; Redclift and Stewart 1991). Feminist economists are beginning to engage their more conventional colleagues with theoretical models and empirical evidence about the gendered nature of macroeconomic policies and especially structural adjustment (see the contributions in "Gender and Structural Adjustment," 1995). Sociologists are also producing important works that explore the gender aspects of economic restructuring, the way that gender shapes the labor process, and the impact of women's employment on gender relations (Blumberg et al. 1995; Feldman 1992; Moghadam 1995; Tiano 1994; Ward 1990). Feminists are working individually and collectively on gender processes in a (capitalist) *world* economy, or they are explicitly situating their national studies in global developments.

The objective of this chapter is to show how a gender perspective deepens our understanding of the global economy and of how women and men are involved in and affected by the global economy. By *gender*, I mean an asymmetrical social relationship between women and men based on perceived sex differences, and an ideology regarding their roles, rights, and values as workers, owners, citizens, and parents. The differential positions of women and men in the spheres of production and reproduction reflect the social relations of gender and are perpetuated by gender ideologies, whereas economic differences among women result from the inequalities of class and ethnicity, structured by the mode of production. By *global economy*, I mean the increasingly integrated and interdependent system of capital-labor flows across regions, between states, and through transnational corporations and international financial institutions, in the form of capital investments, technology transfer, financial exchanges, and increased trade, as well as the various forms of the deployment of labor, by which global accumulation takes place. The regions across and within which capital accumulation takes place may be understood in terms of geographic units (e.g., Latin America, sub-Saharan Africa, Southeast Asia, North America), in terms of income levels (high-, middle-, and low-income countries) or stages of industrialization (developing/industrializing countries – the South; developed/postindustrial countries – the North), or in terms of the economic zones of the world-system (core, periphery, and semi-periphery). All of these imply uneven development and unequal power relations. In illuminating the gender dynamics of economic and employment processes at the global level, I will focus in this chapter on *structural adjustment* in developing countries, the transition to a market economy in the former socialist world, recession and unemployment in the developed countries, the increasing labor force participation of women, and the growing informalization of labor arrangements. This focus on structure will be complemented in the final section by attention to expressions of women's agency, including the emergence of women's organizations and transnational networks that are responding to global economic issues.

The Global Economy: Economic Restructuring and Globalization

It may be useful to begin this discussion by outlining the main features of the contemporary global economy, in order that the gender aspects, as well as the contributions of gender analysis, be understood in their context. What follows is a descriptive account.

The term *global economy* has gained currency because of the increasingly integrated processes of production and trade and the rapidity with which financial transactions occur across borders and regions. These are made possible by advances in information technologies and in transportation, by expanded forms of investment, and by the end of protectionist trade regimes through new agreements such as the Uruguay Round and the formation of the World Trade Organization. There has been much discussion in recent years of two dimensions of the global economy: economic restructuring and globalization. *Economic restructuring* refers to changes in the organization of production, and may take place at the global, regional, national, or firm level. *Globalization* refers to the outward-oriented and transnational nature of economic activity, the importance of national competitiveness, and the increasing integration of markets, all of which have employment, price, and wage implications. These processes have taken place through a number of interrelated processes at the regional and national levels.

In developing countries there has been a shift from an exclusive concentration on the extraction and export of raw materials and on agricultural production to the production of manufactured goods and the growth of the services sector. The earlier strategy of import-substitution industrialization, which favored the production of intermediate-level capital goods and consumer products for the home market, has been replaced by a strategy that favors the production of goods for export to world markets. In particular, newly industrialized countries (NICs) have effected the transition from agrarian, peasant, and low-income countries to industrialized, proletarianized, and upper middle-income countries. The first generation of these countries – South Korea, Taiwan, Hong Kong, and Singapore – began as producers of cheap and sometimes low-quality goods but now export sophisticated products. They are also investing in other developing countries; for example, Vietnam is now a site for capital investments from South Korea, Hong Kong, and Taiwan, mainly in textiles, handicrafts, and tourism. Among developing countries, the industrializing countries are the most integrated in the global economy, but other Asian economies that are advancing rapidly include Malaysia, Thailand, the Philippines, and China. There, qualified but cheap labor and competitive goods attract considerable foreign investment from the North as well as from the NICs. The first- and second-generation NICs have formed their own regional economic institution, the Association of Southeast Asian Nations. In other regions, such as Latin America, foreign investments and domestic capital investments have contributed to the expansion of competitive industries, such as Brazil's shoe manufacturers, who export to world markets.

A principal player in the global economy is the transnational corporation, now numbering some 40,000 parent firms and some 250,000 foreign affiliates. Most of the stock of foreign direct investment flows among the United States and the North American Free Trade Agreement (NAFTA) countries (Canada and Mexico), the countries of the European Union, and Japan, with significant flows also between Japan and Southeast Asia. China receives a substantial amount of foreign investment, accounting for 40 percent of all flows into developing countries in 1994, and worth $34 billion (United Nations Conference on Trade and Development [UNCTAD] 1995:103).

Elsewhere in the developing world, and especially in sub-Saharan Africa and the Middle East, countries are less integrated into the global economy or remain on the periphery because their trade regimes are still restricted and intraregional trade is limited, or because of political instability or the relative underdevelopment of human resources. In addition, these two regions have suffered the consequences of high interest rates on loans from international commercial banks, the fall of commodities prices (e.g., oil and cocoa), and huge military expenditures. Africa has experienced deindustrialization as well as a number of debilitating civil conflicts. The Middle East and North Africa have seen the rise of fundamentalist movements that claim to offer religiously derived solutions to socioeconomic difficulties and cultural changes, including the reinstitutionalization of patriarchal gender relations (Moghadam 1994). Africa and the Middle East receive far smaller shares of total world investment than do other regions. In 1994, the value of foreign investment in the Middle East and Africa (including North African as well as sub-Saharan countries) was $34.5 billion and $53.1 billion, respectively. This compares with $186.2 billion in Latin America and the Caribbean and $305.1 billion in East, South, and Southeast Asia (see UNCTAD 1995, table 5:112–13).

Integration into the global economy is being touted as the only solution to economic crisis and as the only path to economic growth open to developing countries, given the end of the communist bloc and its alternative socialist economic system. As a first step toward global economic integration, countries are encouraged to implement structural adjustment policies, which aim to balance budgets and increase competitiveness through trade and price liberalization. In order to reduce the public sector wage bill and encourage growth of the private sector, developing countries have denationalized state holdings, privatized social services, invited foreign investment, and promoted exports. The international financial institutions, especially the World Bank and the International Monetary Fund, are the chief instigators of this free market policy shift, known as neoliberal economics. These institutions have clout because of the very favorable terms they offer when extending loans to developing countries. Structural adjustment policies were first implemented in some African and Latin American countries as a result of the debt crisis of the early 1980s. They were extended to other countries, including Malaysia, in the mid-1980s, and they were adopted in a number of Middle Eastern countries, including Jordan and Egypt, in the 1990s.

Structural adjustment has been a very controversial topic in the development studies literature; some development economists find that it has worked in some places but not in others, whereas other economists have regarded the entire turn to be a disaster for national sovereignty and for people's well-being. The feminist literature on development has been especially critical, charging structural adjustment with carrying out its objectives on the backs of the poor and especially poor women. They have had to assume extra productive and reproductive activities in order to survive the austerities of adjustment and stabilization policies, including higher prices, and to compensate for the withdrawal or reduction of government subsidies of food and services.

Integration into the global economy has also extended to the former socialist world. The centrally planned economies of Eastern Europe and the Soviet Union once had their own system of production, trade, and assistance, along with their own economic institutions. These extended benefits not only to socialist developing countries such as Vietnam and Cuba, but also to a number of friendly developing countries. That system was dissolved between 1989 and 1991, and the former socialist countries began the process of transition to a market economy and integration in the capitalist global economy.

In the developed world, integration has meant increased foreign investments to developing countries through bilateral and multilateral agreements, the formation of regional blocs such as NAFTA and the European Union (EU), the relocation of production sites to developing countries, and the shift from assembly-line manufacturing to postindustrial, high-tech service economies. Inequalities have widened in many developed countries, most dramatically in the United States, and unemployment has increased in EU countries. These developments have led to calls for more protection of declining industries and regulation of immigration, and opposing calls for the free flow of capital and of immigrant labor.

The adverse effects of economic restructuring have been felt within all regions, and especially by their respective labor forces. With increased trade, the prices of imported goods often compete with the prices of domestic products, forcing domestic capitalists to attempt to cut labor costs. In the developed countries, as plants relocate to sites elsewhere in search of cheaper costs of labor and production, jobs disappear and wages erode in the declining industrial sectors. As the developed countries shift from manufacturing to high-tech services, blue-collar unemployment grows, along with the expansion of part-time and temporary jobs at the expense of the kind of stable employment that men came to expect during "the golden age of capitalism" (Marglin and Schor 1990). Developing countries have seen a shift from internally oriented to externally oriented growth strategies and the shrinkage of large public sectors and nationalized industries. The result has been an expansion of informal sectors and self-employment. In both developing and developed regions, the stable, organized, and mostly male labor force has become increasingly "flexible" and "feminized." . . .

Restructuring, Women's Labor, and Gender Ideology

Through institutions such as the transnational corporation and the state, the global economy generates capital largely through the exploitation of labor, but it is not indifferent to the gender and ethnicity of that labor. Gender and racial ideologies have been deployed to favor White male workers and exclude others, but they have also been used to integrate and exploit the labor power of women and of members of disadvantaged racial and ethnic groups in the interest of profit making. In the current global environment of open economies, new trade regimes, and competitive export industries, global accumulation relies heavily on the work of women, both waged and unwaged, in formal sectors and in the home, in manufacturing, and in public and private services. This phenomenon has been termed the "feminization of labor." Standing (1989) has hypothesized that the increasing globalization of production and the pursuit of flexible forms of labor to retain or increase competitiveness, as well as changing job structures in industrial enterprises, favor the feminization of employment in the dual sense of an increase in the numbers of women in the labor force and a deterioration of work conditions (labor standards, income, and employment status). Women have been gaining an increasing share of many kinds of jobs, but in the context of a decline in the social power of labor and growing unemployment, their labor market participation has not been accompanied by a redistribution of domestic, household, and child-care responsibilities. Moreover, women are still disadvantaged in the new labor markets in terms of wages, training, and occupational segregation. They are also disproportionately involved in forms of employment increasingly used to maximize profits: temporary, part-time, casual, and home-based work. Generally speaking, the situation is better or worse for women depending on the type of state and the strength of the economy. . . . Vast numbers of economically active women in the developing world lack formal training, work in the informal sector, have no access to social security, and live in poverty.

Proletarianization

As world markets have expanded, a process of female proletarianization has taken place. In developing countries – and especially in Southeast and East Asia, parts of Latin America and the Caribbean, and Tunisia and Morocco – more and more women have been drawn into the labor-intensive and low-wage textile and garment industries, as well as into electronics and pharmaceuticals, which produce both for the home market and for export. The surge in women's waged employment in developing countries began in the 1970s, following an earlier period of capitalist development and economic growth that was characterized by the displacement of labor and craft work, commercialization of agriculture, and rural-urban migration (see Boserup 1987). Some have called the earlier marginalization of women "housewife-ization" (Mies 1986); others have described it as the "U pattern" of female labor force participation in early modernization.

During the 1970s, it was observed that export processing zones along the US-Mexico border and in Southeast Asia, established by transnational corporations to take advantage of low labor costs in developing countries, were hiring mainly women (Elson and Pearson 1981; Nash and Fernandez-Kelly 1983). By the early 1980s, it was clear that the new industrialization in what was then called the Third World was drawing heavily on women workers. Many studies by women-in-development specialists and socialist feminists centered on the role played by the available pool of relatively cheap female labor. Gender ideologies emphasizing the "nimble fingers" of young women workers and their capacity for hard work, especially in the Southeast Asian economies (Heyzer 1986; Lim 1985), facilitated the recruitment of women for unskilled and semiskilled work in labor-intensive industries at wages lower than men would accept, and in conditions that unions would not permit. In South Korea in 1985, women's earnings were only 47 percent of equivalent men's earnings; in Singapore, the figure was 63 percent (Pearson 1992:231). In Latin America, women entered the labor force at a time when average wages were falling dramatically. Around the world, women's share of total industrial labor rarely exceeds 30 to 40 percent, but "the percentage of women workers in export processing factories producing textiles, electronics components and garments is much higher, with figures as high as 90% in some cases" (Pearson 1992:231). A 1984 study of the export promotion zone in Bombay, India, showed that 98 percent of its workers were women (Shah et al. 1994:WS-42). Studies commissioned by INSTRAW, a UN agency, led Joekes to conclude that "exports of manufactures from developing countries have been made up in the main of the kinds of goods normally produced by female labor: industrialization in the post-war period has been as much *female* led as *export* led" (Joekes and INSTRAW 1987:81).

Professionalization

The process of the feminization of labor continued throughout the recessionary 1980s, not only in the manufacturing sector, but also in public services, where throughout the world women's share has grown to 30 to 50 percent – at a time when public sector wages, like industrial wages, have been declining. It is significant that in Iran, Egypt, and Turkey, women's share of public service employment (including jobs as teachers and university professors in public schools and state universities, nurses and doctors in state hospitals, and workers and administrators across the ministries) has increased at a time when salaries have eroded tremendously. At the same time, the more lucrative and expanding private sector is absorbing more men (Moghadam 1998).

The proletarianization and professionalization of women have cultural repercussions and sometimes entail gender conflicts. During the 1980s, the increasing participation of women in the labor force in Middle Eastern countries was accompanied by subtle and overt pressures on them to conform to religious dictates concerning dress. Hence in Egypt, many professional women came to don modest dress and to cover their heads. One may hypothesize that in the earlier stage of the Islamist movement, the influx of women in the workforce raised fears of competition with men, leading to calls for the redomestication of women, as occurred immediately after the Iranian revolution. In the current stage, with the labor force participation of women now a fait accompli, Islamists in Turkey, Iran, Egypt, Sudan, and Yemen are not calling on women to withdraw from the labor force – indeed, many of their female adherents are educated and employed – but they do insist on veiling and on spatial and functional segregation. Only the most determined and secular women resist these pressures as they seek employment in public and private services.

As world trade in services has increased and global firms engage in outsourcing, the involvement of women in various occupations and professions of the service sector has grown. Women around the world have made impressive inroads into professional services such as law, banking, accounting, computing, and architecture; into tourism-related occupations; and into information services, as offshore airline booking agents, mail order and credit card service operators, word processors for publishers, telephone operators, and so on. The world trade in services also favors women's labor migration, in contrast to the demand for men manufacturing workers during the earlier periods of industrialization in Europe and the United States. Mexican, Central American, and Caribbean women have migrated to the United States to work as nurses, nannies, and domestics; Filipinas and Sri Lankans have gone to neighboring countries as well as to the Middle East to work as waitresses, nurses, nannies, and domestics; Argentine women have traveled to Italy to work as nurses; and an increasing number of Moroccan, Tunisian, and Algerian women have migrated alone to work in various occupations in France, Italy, and Spain.

[. . .]

The Informal Sector

At the same time that women have been entering the formal labor force in record numbers in the developed countries, much of the increase in female labor force participation in developing countries has occurred in the informal sectors of the economy. The informal sector is usually defined as that which is outside the purview of the state and social security. Unregistered and small-scale urban enterprises, homework, and self-employment may fall into this category, and they include an array of commercial and productive activities. The extent of the urban informal sector and its links to the formal sector are matters of dispute, and women's involvement in it have not always been captured in the official statistics. Official statistics have traditionally overlooked women in the agricultural sector, and only in recent years have developing countries corrected this. . . .

In the urban areas of developing countries, many formal jobs have become "informalized" as employers seek to increase "flexibility" and lower labor and production costs through subcontracting, as Beneria and Roldán (1987) show in their study of Mexico City. The growth of informalization is observed also in developed countries (Fernandez-Kelly and Garcia 1989). Drawing on existing gender ideologies regarding women's roles, their attachment to family, and the perceived lower value of their work, subcontracting arrangements encourage the persistence of home-based work. Many women accept this kind of work – with its insecurity, low wages, and absence of benefits – as a convenient form of income generation that allows them to carry out domestic responsibilities and care for children; some deny that it is "work," preferring to call it a hobby or a form of amusement, in order not to counter cultural codes or gender ideologies that idealize housewifery (see Cinar 1994; Dangler 1994; MacLeod 1996). . . . Informalization in developed and developing countries requires a gender perspective to understand "the process whereby employers seeking competitive edges in domestic and international markets can tap into not only 'cheap labor,' which is both female and male, but also into a substratum of labor, predominantly female, that is outside of formal relationships" (Fernandez-Kelly 1989:13). . . .

The Income Gap

The social relations of gender account for the pervasive income gap between men and women workers, a gap that is detrimental to women but lucrative to employers. On average, women earn 75 percent of men's wages (United Nations Development Program [UNDP] 1995:36), with Sweden, Sri Lanka, and Vietnam at the upper and more egalitarian end (90 percent) and Bangladesh, Chile, China, Cyprus, South Korea, the Philippines, and Syria at the lower and more unequal end (42–61 percent). The gender-based income gap is found mainly in the private sector, whereas the public sector tends to reward women more equitably. In Egypt, women's wages in the private sector are about half those of comparable men workers, whereas in the government sector women are paid the same as men (World Bank 1995:73). Some of the difference in the income gap is certainly based on lower education and intermittent employment among women workers, yet gender bias accounts for much of the difference in earnings. In some countries, women earn less than men despite higher qualifications, a problem that is especially acute in the private sector. For example, in Ecuador, Jamaica, and the Philippines, "women actually have more education and experience, on average, than men, but get paid between 20 and 30 percent less" (World Bank 1995:45). Labor market segmentation along gender lines perpetuates the income gap. For example, in the computing and information processing sectors, the majority of high-skilled jobs go to male workers, and women are concentrated in low-skilled jobs (Pearson and Mitter 1993:50).

Unemployment

Considering the social relations of gender and the function of gender ideologies, it should come as no surprise that despite women's key role in the global economy, unemployment rates of women are very high. Global unemployment is partly a function of the nature of global economic restructuring itself, which has entailed massive retrenchment of labor in many developing countries, in the former socialist countries now undergoing marketization, and in the developed countries. Unemployment rates are especially high in Algeria, Jamaica, Jordan, Egypt, Morocco, Nicaragua, Poland, the Slovak Republic, and Turkey (World Bank 1995:29). Yet although men's unemployment is high, it is often higher for women (Moghadam 1995). In many developing countries unemployed women are new entrants to the labor force, who are seeking but not finding jobs (as in Egypt, Iran, Turkey, and Chile, where women's unemployment can be as high as 30 percent, compared with 10 percent for men). In certain countries where restructuring has occurred in enterprises employing large numbers of women, or in export sectors that have lost markets, the unemployment rates of women may also reflect job losses by previously employed women – as in Malaysia in the mid-1980s; Vietnam in the late 1980s; Poland, Bulgaria, and Russia in the early 1990s; and Morocco, Tunisia, and Turkey more recently. . . .

A gender perspective also allows us to understand changes in the skill-designation and downgrading of jobs resulting from technical improvements. As noted above, many enterprises producing textiles and electronics, especially those for export, rely heavily on women workers. And yet as more sophisticated technology is used to produce these goods, women workers tend to be replaced by men or recruited at a slower pace, as appears to have been occurring in the Mexican *maquiladoras* (Sklair 1993) and in the textiles industries of Spain and Italy.

In all regions, high unemployment represents the downside of globalization and economic restructuring, especially for women workers, who must contend with not only the class biases but also the gender biases of free market economics. The feminization of unemployment, therefore, is as much a characteristic of the global economy as is the feminization of labor.

[. . .]

Structural Adjustment and the Feminization of Poverty: Making Gender Visible

Much of the development and economics literature on globalization and restructuring is largely devoid of any consideration of gender. In the sociology of development, standard texts do not integrate a gender dimension into their analyses (see, e.g., Booth 1994; Evans and Stephens 1998; Kincaid and Portes 1994). It has been up to feminist researchers to make women visible, and to show how women have been marginalized, segregated, and exploited by the development process. Subsequently, they have demonstrated the adverse implications for development projects of ignoring women's productive and reproductive roles. Currently, they are theorizing the relationship between gender and macroeconomic processes and mapping out strategies for transformation. Their contributions to a gender analysis of structural adjustment, which have come to influence policy makers, represent an important case in point.

As mentioned above, structural adjustment policies have been controversial in the development community. The now-classic UNICEF study *Adjustment with a Human Face* (Cornia, Jolly, and Stewart 1987) highlighted the social costs of adjustment and provided empirical evidence of the deterioration of social conditions in 10 countries undergoing adjustment. Subsequent studies found that there have been differential impacts on the various categories of the poor, including the "chronic" poor, the "borderline" poor, and the "new" or "working" poor. In the early 1980s, critical voices argued that adjustment and stabilization programs in developing countries were having particularly adverse effects on women. In September 1982, the UN Division for the Advancement of Women organized a meeting on "women and the international development strategy." One of the participants, Margarida da Gama Santos, a senior economist with the Ministry of Industry in Portugal, presented a prescient paper outlining the likely impacts of adjustment policies on women's employment patterns and on their household responsibilities (da Gama Santos 1985). She recognized that the gender division of labor and the differential positions of women and men in the spheres of production and reproduction would mean that the new policy shifts would lead to very different outcomes for women and men, although these gender differences would differ further by social class and by economic sector. In sum, the burden of adjustment falls on the urban poor, the working class, and women (see Elson 1991).

Structural adjustment policies – with their attendant price increases, elimination of subsidies, social service decreases, and introduction or increase of "user fees" for "cost recovery" in the provision of schooling and health care – heighten the risk and vulnerability of women and children in households where the distribution of consumption and the provision of health care and education favor men or income-earning adults. Structural adjustment causes women to bear most of the responsibility of coping with increased prices and shrinking incomes, because in most instances they are responsible for household budgeting and maintenance. Rising unemployment and reduced wages for men in a given household lead to increased economic activity on the part of women and children. This occurs also in households headed by women – an increasing proportion of all households in most regions. Household survival strategies include increases in the unpaid as well as paid labor of women, as discussed in the previous section. In Guayaquil, Ecuador, the proportion of wives working outside the household jumped from 45 percent to 95 percent during structural adjustment (World Bank 1995:106). In Ghana, women working in the informal sector saw their wages decline as excess labor released from formal employment moved into informal activities (World Bank 1995:107). In the Philippines, mean household size increased as relatives pooled their resources. . . . This global economic context was the focus of Standing's (1989) seminal paper on the feminization of labor and subsequent studies on the "feminization of poverty" (see Moghadam 1997; United Nations 1995).

The literature dealing with structural adjustment and women consists of empirical studies focusing on the unequal distribution of the burden of adjustment between men and women within households and labor markets (e.g., Afshar and Dennis 1992; Bakker 1994b;

Beneria and Feldman 1992; Elson 1991; Sparr 1994; UNICEF 1989) and theoretical studies that challenge the presumed gender neutrality of theoretical and policy models (see Bakker 1994a; "Gender and Structural Adjustment" 1995). Why do economic crises and structural adjustment hurt women more than they do men? The reasons have to do with both the social relations of gender and the nature of market reforms. Intrahousehold inequalities, unequal allocation of resources, and the traditional gender division of labor within the home all contribute to the outcome. In some parts of the world, and especially in large patriarchal households, women do not enjoy the same relationship to their own labor as do men. They cannot organize and distribute their labor time as they see fit, they engage in considerable unpaid domestic labor, they may receive unequal amounts of food, and the products of their labor (including handicrafts and rugs) are often appropriated and disposed of by their husbands or fathers (see, e.g., Morvaridi 1992, on women agricultural workers in Turkey). Elsewhere, the decline in men's wages and increases in household poverty force women to seek employment or informal-type work. Poor parents may remove daughters from school to help at home or to bring in income. Labor market segmentation, low wages, and the lack of help for child rearing add to women's plight. Market reforms by their very nature place the burden of adjustment and change on labor; most vulnerable are women workers, whether they work in the formal or informal economy or in the home. Empirical evidence from Latin America, South Asia, sub-Saharan Africa, the Middle East, China, Vietnam, Central and Eastern Europe, and Russia confirms feminist criticisms of the gender bias in structural adjustment and economic liberalization more broadly. The effects of gender on the economy, and the effects of globalization and restructuring on women, include the following:

- Customary biases and intrahousehold inequalities lead to lower consumption by and fewer benefits for women and girls among lower-income groups.
- The mobility of labor that is assumed by free market economics and encouraged by structural adjustment policies does not take into account that women's geographic and occupational mobility is constrained by family and child-rearing responsibilities.
- The legal and regulatory framework often does not treat women as autonomous citizens, but rather as dependents or minors – with the result that in many countries women cannot own or inherit property, seek jobs, or take out loans without the permission of their husbands or fathers.
- Structural adjustment policies overstretch women's labor time by increasing women's productive activities (higher labor force participation due to economic need and household survival strategy) and reproductive burdens (in that women have to compensate in care-giving for cutbacks in social services). Working-class women and urban poor women are particularly hard hit.
- Because of women's concentration in government jobs in many developing countries, and because the private sector discriminates against women or is otherwise "unfriendly" to women and unwilling to provide support structures for working mothers, middle-class women may suffer disproportionately from policies that aim to contract the public sector wage bill by slowing down public sector hiring.

- Industrial restructuring or privatization affects women adversely, because women tend to be laid off first due to gender bias, but also because women workers tend to be concentrated in the lower rungs of the occupational ladder, in unskilled production jobs, or in overstaffed administrative and clerical positions.
- The poverty-inducing aspect of structural adjustment hits women hard and is especially hard on female-headed households with children.
- Labor market discrimination and job segregation result in women's being concentrated in the low-wage employment sectors, in the informal sector, and in the contingent of "flexible labor."

[. . .]

Gender Dynamics of the Global Economy: A Theoretical Framework

In this section I return to the questions raised at the outset by tying together the theoretical strands that have been woven into this essay. I use a world-system theoretical framework, which, despite its rigidity and inattention to gender, has several advantages. First, it is a pertinent point of departure for a development social scientist, as it consists of concepts and methods, including its historical, global, and comparative sweep, that are consonant with non-West-centered social theories. Second, its insistence on the existence of a *world* system, integrated unevenly across economic zones and incorporating commodity chains and different forms of labor, has stood the test of time, given today's consensus, described above, concerning the global economy, globalization, integration of markets, informalization of labor markets, and so on. Third, world-system theory may be more amenable to the integration of gender analysis because of its built-in premises regarding social inequalities and its studies of class, race, gender, and households in the world-system (see Berquist 1984; Chase-Dunn 1989; Smith, Wallerstein, and Evers 1984; Smith et al. 1988; Smith and Wallerstein 1992; Timberlake 1985; Ward 1984, 1990). Fourth, because the theory concerns not only a world *economy* but also a system of states and cultures (Wallerstein 1991), it is better equipped to explain such phenomena as the rise of "identity politics" (including fundamentalisms) and the social and economic bases of cultural revivalist movements. Fifth, world-system theory provides a useful framework for understanding the links among structural adjustment in developing countries, privatization in the former socialist countries, competition between states and economies, and the changing fortunes of labor. It also provides an adequate explanation for global inequalities, economic crises, the hegemonic role of certain ("core") states and international financial institutions, the peripheralization of other states, and the significance of middle-income industrializing ("semiperipheral") states. . . .

Although class has been elaborated, the place of *gender* in the world-system perspective remains undertheorized. However, at a very general level of analysis, one may begin to explain gender hierarchies and positions of women across the globe and within societies in terms of core, periphery, and semiperiphery locations. For example, in an early study, Ward (1984) found that peripheral status negatively affects women's share of the labor force and increases pressures for fertility. Defining peripheral status as "economic dependency" and a concentration of foreign investments in commodities, and utilizing 1960s and 1970s data sets, Ward found that this status leads to greater inequalities – not only between countries and between classes within countries, but between women and men. Women have limited job opportunities in the formal sector (the jobs go to men), are relegated to unpaid work in the informal sector, and are encouraged to have more children. Ward's most significant contribution, in my view, is her demonstration that fertility increases in the periphery because women's socioeconomic position vis-à-vis men is low, because women have less control over their fertility, and because children are needed as labor inputs and for old-age security, especially in agrarian settings.

In contrast, greater diversity in the structure of production and trade positively affects women's share of the labor force and decreases fertility rates, the pattern in the core and the semiperiphery. Most countries within the semiperiphery have seen dramatic declines in fertility, as more and more women have assumed nonagricultural employment, as described in preceding sections. In core countries, too, mass education, salaried employment, and social security programs have led to low birthrates. Within a society, differences in fertility are explained by the different class positions of women, which is why fertility behavior differs among poor, peasant, proletarian, and professional women. Thus location within economic zone and location within class structure are strong predictors of fertility behavior and child-care needs of women, and of their patterns of employment.

More recently, Ward (1993) has been critical of world-system theory for its overemphasis on exchange, accumulation, and class, and for its inability or unwillingness to theorize the gendered nature of production and the links between the formal sector and women's informal and domestic labor. She also takes issue with the recent work on households by Smith and Wallerstein (1992), who argue that "the appropriate operational unit for analyzing the ways in which people fit into the 'labor force' is not the individual but the 'household', defined for these purposes as the social unit that effectively over long periods of time enables individuals, of varying ages of both sexes, to pool income coming from multiple sources in order to ensure their individual and collective reproduction and well-being" (p. 13). Wallerstein, Smith, and their collaborators feel that this approach will explain how people respond to economic stagnation, expansion, and other cycles and trends; it recognizes the contribution of unwaged labor to the reproduction of the labor force and the capitalist system, and it offers a "micro" perspective on antisystemic movements. Ward (1993), however, finds that the household perspective "ignores the divergent interests of men and women within households"; it "obscures how women's socioeconomic roles in waged and nonwaged labor and housework are intertwined"; it "ignores how women have been systematically denied access to formal waged labor under the global economy"; and it leads to "male biases in how work and households are defined in their theories" (pp. 52–5). . . . If the concept of household is to be useful, it should incorporate the existence of gender differences, for, as shown earlier in this chapter, intrahousehold inequalities and the traditional gender division of labor are critical factors in explaining differential effects and responses to economic crises and new economic policies for women and men. At the same time, one may dispute Ward's contention that women have been "systematically denied access to formal waged labor under the global economy." As this chapter has shown, there has been a tremendous increase in women's employment, not only in core countries but in semiperipheral countries as well – at the same time that informalization and

ᵧment have been expanding. World-system theorists correctly recognize the _dif-_
__ᵤₜ modes of remuneration of labor_, which they explain in terms of interconnections among
various production processes, or "commodity chains," some of which are core-like and
some of which are peripheral (see Wallerstein and Smith 1992:16).

The capitalist world-economy functions by means of the deployment of labor that is both
waged and nonwaged. In recent decades, the involvement of women in both kinds of labor
arrangements has been striking, as I have emphasized here. Capitalist accumulation is
achieved through the surplus extraction of labor, and this includes the paid and unpaid
economic activities of women, whether in male-headed or female-headed households.
Global accumulation as the driving force of the world-system not only hinges on class and
regional differences across economic zones, it is a gendered process as well, predicated upon
gender differences in the spheres of production and reproduction. The various forms of the
deployment of women's labor reflect asymmetrical gender relations and patriarchal gender
ideologies – but the involvement of women in the global economy and in national labor
forces has also served to interrogate and modify gender relations and ideologies.

[. . .]

NOTE

1   For discussions of the evolution of the WID/GAD framework, see Rathgeber (1990), Scott (1986),
and Razavi and Miller (1995).

REFERENCES

Afshar, Haleh, ed. 1985. _Women, Work and Ideology in the Third World_. London: Tavistock.

Afshar, Haleh and Carolyne Dennis, eds. 1992. _Women and Adjustment Policies in the Third World_.
London: Macmillan.

Bakker, Isabella, ed. 1994a. "Introduction: Engendering Macro-economic Policy Reform in the Era
of Global Restructuring and Adjustment." Pp. 1–29 in _The Strategic Silence: Gender and Economic
Policy_, edited by Isabella Bakker. London: Zed.

——. 1994b. _The Strategic Silence: Gender and Economic Policy_. London: Zed.

Beneria, Lourdes and Shelley Feldman, eds. 1992. _Unequal Burden: Economic Crises, Persistent Poverty,
and Women's Work_. Boulder, CO: Westview.

Beneria, Lourdes and Martha Roldán. 1987. _The Crossroads of Class and Gender: Industrial Homework,
Subcontracting, and Household Dynamics in Mexico City_. Chicago: University of Chicago Press.

Berquist, Charles, ed. 1984. _Labor in the Capitalist World-Economy_. Newbury Park, CA: Sage.

Blumberg, Rae Lesser, Cathy A., Rakowski, Irene Tinker, and Michael Monteon, eds. 1995. _Engender-
ing Wealth and Well-Being_. Boulder, CO: Westview.

Booth, David, ed. 1994. _Rethinking Social Development: Theory, Research and Practice_. Harlow, UK:
Longman Scientific and Technical.

Boserup, Ester. 1987. _Women and Economic Development_. 2d ed. New York: St. Martin's.

Chase-Dunn, Christopher. 1989. _Global Formation: Structures of the World-Economy_. New York: Basil
Blackwell.

Cinar, Mine. 1994. "Unskilled Urban Migrant Women and Disguised Employment: Homeworking
Women in Istanbul, Turkey." _World Development_ 22:369–80.

Collier, Paul. 1989. _Women and Structural Adjustment_. Oxford: Oxford University, Unit for the Study
of African Economies.

Cornia, Giovanni A., Richard Jolly, and Frances Stewart, eds. 1987. *Adjustment with a Human Face.* Oxford: Clarendon.

da Gama Santos, Margarida. 1985. "The Impact of Adjustment Programmes on Women in Developing Countries." *Public Enterprise* 5:287–97.

Dangler, Jaimie Fricella. 1994. *Hidden in the Home: The Role of the Waged Homework in the Modern World-Economy.* Albany: State University of New York Press.

Drèze, Jean and Amartya Sen. 1989. *Hunger and Public Action.* Oxford: Clarendon.

Elson, Diane, ed. 1991. *Male Bias in the Development Process.* London: Macmillan.

Elson, Diane, and Ruth Pearson. 1981. "Nimble Fingers Make Cheap Workers: An Analysis of Women's Employment in Third World Export Manufacturing." *Feminist Review* (Spring):87–107.

Evans, Peter and John Stephens. 1988. "Development in the World Economy." In *The Handbook of Sociology,* edited by Neil J. Smelser. Newbury Park, CA: Sage.

Feldman, Shelley. 1992. "Crisis, Islam, and Gender in Bangladesh: The Social Construction of a female Labor Force." In *Unequal Burden: Economic Crises, Persistent Poverty, and Women's Work,* edited by Lourdes Beneria and Shelley Feldman. Boulder, CO: Westview.

Fernandez-Kelly, Patricia. 1989. "Broadening the Scope: Gender and the Study of International Economic Development." *Sociological Forum* 4, no. 4:11–35.

Fernandez-Kelly, Patricia and Anna M. Garcia. 1989. "Informalization at the Core: Hispanic Women, Homework, and the Advanced Capitalist State." In *The Informal Economy: Studies in Advanced and Less Developed Countries,* edited by Alejandro Portes, M. Castells, and L. Benton. Baltimore: Johns Hopkins University Press.

"Gender and Structural Adjustment." 1995. Symposium. *World Development* 23, no. 11.

Haddad, Lawrence et al. 1995. "The Gender Dimensions of Economic Adjustment Policies: Potential Interactions and Evidence to Date." *World Development* 23:881–96.

Heyzer, Noeleen. 1986. *Working Women in South East Asia.* London: Open University Press.

Joekes, Susan and INSTRAW. 1987. *Women in the Global Economy: An INSTRAW Study.* New York: Oxford University Press.

Joekes, Susan and Ann Weston. 1995. *Women and the New Trade Agenda.* New York: UNIFEM.

Karshenas, Massoud. 1997. "Female Employment, Economic Liberalization, and Competitiveness in the Middle East." Economic Research Forum Working Paper, Cairo.

Kincaid, Douglas and Alejandro Portes, eds. 1994. *Comparative National Development: Society and Economy in the New World Order.* Chapel Hill: University of North Carolina Press.

Lim, Linda. 1985. *Women Workers in Multinational Enterprises in Developing Countries.* Geneva: International Labor Organization.

MacLeod, Arlene Elowe. 1996. "Transforming Women's Identity: The Intersection of Household and Workplace in Cairo." In *Development, Change and Gender in Cairo: A View from the Household,* edited by Diane Singerman and Homa Hoodfar. Bloomington: Indiana University Press.

Marglin, Stephen and Juliet Schor, eds. 1990. *The Golden Age of Capitalism.* Oxford: Clarendon.

Moghadam, Valentine M. 1993. "Bringing the Third World In: A Comparative Analysis in Gender and Restructuring in the Third World and in State Socialist Societies." In *Democratic Reform and the Position of Women in Transitional Economies,* edited by Valentine M. Moghadam. Oxford: Clarendon.

——. 1994. "Women and Identity Politics in Theoretical and Comparative Perspective." In *Identity Politics and Women: Cultural Reassertions and Feminisms in International Perspective,* edited by Valentine M. Moghadam. Boulder, CO: Westview.

——. 1995. "Gender Aspects of Employment and Unemployment in a Global Perspective." In *Global Employment: An Investigation into the Future of Work,* edited by Mihaly Simai. London: Zed.

——. 1997. "The Feminization of Poverty? Notes on a Concept and Trends." Occasional Paper No. 2 (August), Illinois State University, Women's Studies Program.

——. 1998. *Women, Work, and Economic Reform in the Middle East and North Africa*. Boulder, CO: Lynne Rienner.

Morvaridi, Behrooz. 1992. "Gender Relations in Agriculture: Women in Turkey." *Economic Development and Cultural Change* 40:567–86.

Nash, June and Maria Fernandez-Kelly, eds. 1983. *Women, Men, and the International Division of Labor*. Albany: State University of New York Press.

Pearson, Ruth. 1992. "Gender Issues in Industrialization." In *Industrialization and Development*, edited by Tom Hewitt, Hazel Johnson, and David Wield. Oxford: Oxford University Press.

Pearson, Ruth and Swasti Mitter. 1993. "Employment and Working Conditions of Low-Skilled Information-Processing Workers in Less-Developed Countries." *International Labour Review* 132, no. 1:49–64.

Rathgeber, Eva. 1990. "WID, WAD, GAD: Trends in Research and Practice." *Journal of Developing Areas* 24:489–502.

Razavi, Shahrashoub and Carole Miller. 1995. "From WID to GAD: Conceptual Shifts in the Women and Development Discourse." Occasional Paper 1, United Nations Research Institute for Social Development, Geneva.

Redclift, Nanneke and M. Thea Stewart, eds. 1991. *Working Women: International Perspectives on Women and Gender Ideology*. London: Routledge.

Scott, Alison MacEwan. 1986. "Women and Industrialization: Examining the 'Female Marginalisation' Thesis." *Journal of Development Studies* 22:649–80.

Shah, Nandita et al. 1994. "Structural Adjustment, Feminisation of Labor Force and Organisational Strategies." *Economic and Political Weekly* 29, no. 18: WS-39–WS-48.

Sklair, Leslie. 1991. *A Sociology of the Global System*. Baltimore: Johns Hopkins University Press.

——. 1993. *Assembling for Development: The Maquila Industry in Mexico and the United States*. San Diego: University of California, Center for U.S.-Mexican Studies.

Smith, Joan et al., eds. 1988. *Racism and Sexism in the World-System*. Westport, CT: Greenwood.

Smith, Joan and Immanuel Wallerstein, eds. 1992. *Creating and Transforming Households: The Constraints of the World-Economy*. Cambridge: Cambridge University Press and Maison des Sciences de l'Homme.

Smith, Joan Immanuel Wallerstein, and Harry Evers, eds. 1984. *Households and the World-Economy*. Beverly Hills, CA: Sage.

Sparr, Pam, ed. 1994. *Mortgaging Women's Lives: Feminist Critiques of Structural Adjustment*. London: Zed.

Standing, Guy. 1989. "Global Feminization through Flexible Labor." *World Development* 17:1077–95.

Taylor, Lance. 1995. "Environmental and Gender Feedbacks in Macroeconomics." *World Development* 23, no. 11.

Tiano, Susan. 1994. *Patriarchy on the Line: Labor, Gender, and Ideology in the Mexican Maquila Industry*. Philadelphia: Temple University Press.

Timberlake, Michael, ed. 1985. *Urbanization in the World-Economy*. New York: Academic Press.

UNICEF. 1989. *The Invisible Adjustment: Poor Women and the Economic Crisis*. Santiago: Americas and Caribbean Regional Office, UNICEF.

United Nations. 1995. *The World's Women 1995: Trends and Statistics*. New York: United Nations.

United Nations Conference on Trade and Development (UNCTAD). 1995. "World Investment Report 1995: Transnational Corporations and Competitiveness." *Transnational Corporations* 4, no. 3:101–65.

United Nations Development Program (UNDP). 1995. *The Human Development Report 1995*. New York: Oxford University Press.

Wallerstein, Immanuel. 1991. *Geopolitics and Geoculture: Essays on the Changing World System*. Cambridge: Cambridge University Press.

Wallerstein, Immanuel and Joan Smith. 1992. "Households as an Institution in the World-Economy." In *Creating and Transforming Households: The Constraints of the World-Economy*, edited by Joan Smith and Immanuel Wallerstein. Cambridge: Cambridge University Press.

Ward, Kathryn. 1984. *Women in the World-System: Its Impact on Status and Fertility*. New York: Praeger.

———, ed. 1990. *Women Workers and Global Restructuring*. Ithaca, NY: ILR.

———. 1993. "Reconceptualizing World System Theory to Include Women." In *Theory on Gender/ Feminism on Theory*, edited by Paula England. New York: Aldine.

World Bank. 1995. *World Development Report 1995: Workers in an Integrating World*. New York: Oxford University Press.

Young, Kate, C. Walkowitz, and R. McCollough, eds. 1981. *Of Marriage and the Market: Women's Subordination in International Perspective*. London: CSE.

Part III   What is Globalization? Attempts to Understand Economic Globalization

Introduction

As the title suggests, this part of the book addresses understanding what is meant by globalization, and in particular, economic globalization. These six pieces are likely representing thousands of others. In addition to presenting various perspectives on what constitutes economic globalization, we are also illustrating the evolution of conceptualizations about globalization, ranging from Fröbel, Heinrichs, and Kreye's embryonic conceptualization in the early 1980s, to Thomas Friedman's 2005 reaffirmation of the magnitude of the transformation to globalization.

Writing at the Max Planck Institute in the late 1970s, Germans Folker Fröbel, Jurgen Heinrichs, and Otto Kreye described what was emerging as a "New International Division of Labour" (NIDL). In their book that coined this now common and centrally important term, they described a pattern of firms shutting down manufacturing plants in the developed countries and investing in the poor countries, devastating economies in regions where labor unions and worker protections were strong. The social effects they saw in wealthy nations were devastating: "more and more workers are losing not only their jobs but also their acquired profession . . . they are thrown onto the labour market where . . . they are obliged to sell their labour-power as unskilled or semiskilled workers at considerably worse terms than before."[1] They describe these adjustments by individual workers as "rapid and psychologically exhausting," while the government suffers a "long-term fiscal crisis."[2] These governments were caught between a shrinking tax base and employment on the one hand, and rising demands for unemployment and retirement benefits on the other.

Meanwhile, the cities of the world's poor nations were "overcrowded with [millions of] landless rural immigrants . . . [who] are forced to seek employment regardless of the level of remuneration and under the most inhuman conditions merely to ensure their sheer physical survival."[3] They and a series of other researchers documented how employers selected those workers according to age, sex, and skill, most frequently choosing to exploit young women because they worked hard and tended not to quit or unionize. In contrast to the optimism of the modernizationists, Fröbel, Heinrichs, and Kreye saw no likely improvement of living conditions as a result of the industrial work by these people in factories set up for producing exports. Like dependency theorists Gunder Frank and Cardoso, they saw complicity by local elites as largely to blame for dependency on world markets and widespread poverty. They argue forcefully that workers in both regions were being impoverished by the change, thus echoing the alarm of once-protected workers and observers in the developed world, that something had changed and that their security was gone: they could no longer act without concern for the poor nations.

Their work spurred a new and vast literature showing how productive shifts in wealthier countries dating from the 1970s, such as closing factories, were linked to the opening of new industries, sweatshops, and economic relationships in the periphery. While aware of the pioneering work of many economic geographers of the time, in this volume we designate *The New International Division of Labor in the World Economy* as the start of the *literature* on globalization as a distinct social phenomenon, because this work demonstrates how new ways of organizing production processes globally has differential effects in different places and on different people, all of which are linked.

Like the excerpt from *The New International Division of Labor in the World Economy*, Manuel Castells' contribution to this volume, "The Informational Mode of Development and the Restructuring of Capitalism," builds macro-level theories about social change by analyzing and comparing empirical evidence. Castells is a Spanish-born, French-educated sociologist who has spent time in Latin America and has served on various US faculties. While he is an incredibly prolific author, the short excerpt we reprint here is from his 1990s trilogy that identified and explained a new form of capitalism, which he calls the "Informational Mode of Development." Closely associated with economic restructuring, this global, highly coordinated, and flexible form of capitalism is characterized by the production of information, revolutionary changes in various processes, unprecedented flexibility in production, and fundamentally altered roles and capabilities for traditional states. Castells seeks to clarify this new post-industrial phase of the global economy and its implications. Communications and information technology drives the creation of an endless series of new products, which drives economic growth. (One need only consider the social transformations wrought by the personal computer.) The implications for social organization are stunning: they are "transforming the way we produce, consume, manage, live, and die" (pp. 177–8).[4] The most productive cultures, Castells argues, are those most proficient at creating and manipulating the symbols of these technologies; neither totalitarian states nor those without state interventions in the economy seem well adapted to this future competition. These technologies create and require *flexibility of organization*, but ironically, perhaps, this flexibility tends to be most effectively taken advantage of by large corporations and organizations – this "complex, interacting system of technology and organizational processes, underlying economic growth and social change, that we call a *mode of development*." Castells lists a series of critical implications of the emergence of this new mode of development, including the increasing internationalization of production and consumption, the weakening of labor owing to increased flexibility arrangements for management, and the restructuring of the state as more tasks can be privatized. Finally, he argues that rather than huge corporations being most adapted to this new world, decentralized networks "made up of a plurality of sizes and forms of organizational units" will emerge.

Writing about how global flows of capital and economic restructuring impact urban life is Saskia Sassen. Originally published in 1991, the excerpt reprinted here is from her 2000 second edition of *Cities in a World Economy*, in which her empirical evidence is updated from the first edition. Sassen emerged in the 1990s as not only one of the formative thinkers on globalization, but the foremost thinker about how globalization affects urban life. She coined the term "global city," referring to the places in the world that have specializations in massive financial operations and sophisticated service industries, giving them unusually large roles in managing the global economy. Sassen identifies a major paradox associated with the physical and economic aspects of global economic integration: Global cities, such as London, Tokyo, New York, and Paris arise as clear areas of concentration of key functions in a global economy, at the same time that globalization of the economy involves increasing geographic dispersal of economic activities such as production (p. 22). Sassen concludes that these spatial and economic shifts constitute a fundamentally novel organization of "center" and "margin." "Global cities become the sites of immense concentrations of economic power while cities that were once major manufacturing centers suffer inordinate declines; highly educated workers see their incomes rise to unusually high levels while low- or medium-skilled workers see theirs sink. Financial services produce superprofits while industrial services barely survive" (p. 140).

The three preceding contributions, without explicitly taking "globalization" as their topic, portray the fundamental changes in social and political organization and relationships that economic restructuring, increased information technology, and the increasing flexibility of production and trade engender. There are several currents running through these works, namely that centers of control are more concentrated and often less identifiable, that changes in capitalism have deep and widespread impacts outside economic activities, and that confronting these changes requires new modes of organization. In slight contrast to the first three selections in this section, the subsequent three selections explicitly take up the task of establishing what we mean by globalization and building theories about its operation and implications.

In his article, "Globalization: Myths and Realities" from *Rural Sociology*, Australian-born Cornell sociologist Philip McMichael argues that we cannot simply describe globalization in terms of economic integration. Rather, "a qualitative shift in the mode of social organization that marks an historic transition in the capitalist world order" is occurring. This qualitative shift has at least one profound implication, which is that local people and their governments no longer have control over the key decisions that will shape their lives. Speculative financial capital investors and traders use globally uniform indicators of "creditworthiness" to decide which firms and even governments will get to borrow money and on what terms. This global uniformity puts tremendous power in the hands of a new "global ruling class." In this new elite McMichael puts three groups of managers: bureaucrats and politicians willing to cut government spending and play by the new global rules of relentless efficiency; owners and executives of transnational corporations and international banks; and those who run the multilateral organizations like the IMF, the World Bank, and the World Trade Organization.[4] Now firms and states cannot make policy without always considering how their decisions will be seen by global creditors who could quickly make their lives miserable with poor credit ratings, disinvestment, or savage speculation on the demise of their currency. Many indebted nations (the list includes almost the whole world, but especially the poor nations) have been forced to cut food, housing assistance, and medical aid to their poor citizens, and to take away trade protections that helped their local industries. As a result, this global management means that local people and their governments no longer have first say in controlling key decisions. These are increasingly the central issues of our day and the tensions that result are obvious. With globalization, individual actors are certainly important, but it is often hard to tell who is involved or in charge because everything has become so extensively integrated. This situation is made all the more acute because the proliferation of information and the rate at which it can be exchanged makes the pace of economic change and financial markets faster than ever. At the same time, however, the Zapatista rebellion in Chiapas, Mexico arose just before McMichael wrote this piece, and by examining it he sees the possibilities of strong local resistance to the crushing demands of global capitalism.

Emeritus Professor of Sociology at the London School of Economics, Leslie Sklair has published several landmark pieces on globalization since the mid-1990s, including the book *Globalization: Capitalism and its Alternatives* (2002) and *The Transnational Capitalist Class* (2001). For those yearning for a "taxonomy" of globalization theory, in this 1999 piece from the *Journal of World-System Research* Sklair critically reviews the four ways the term globalization has been used by social scientists: the world systems approach, global cultures, global society, and global capitalism. Echoing Weber, Sklair says most of these place too much emphasis on either economy, culture, or politics. He argues that much of that literature is confusing globalization with internationalization, and that these two concepts need to be carefully distinguished. He is more favorable to the view that there is a transnational class of business, political, and cultural elites, who use their control of leading institutions like the huge transnational corporations and institutions such as the WTO (World Trade Organization) and IMF (International Monetary Fund). Sklair argues in his books that these groups use their power to influence economics and politics everywhere, and they drive global values of consumerism and free trade. He concludes by evaluating the possibilities of new social movements to disrupt this capitalist globalization.

Thomas Friedman, foreign affairs columnist at the *New York Times*, largely popularized the term globalization and shaped the way many people thought about it with his 1999 book *The Lexus and the Olive Tree: Understanding Globalization*. His 2005 bestseller, *The World is Flat: A Brief History of the Twenty-First Century*, is largely summarized in the piece here, which ran first in the *New York Times Magazine*. Friedman focuses on the dramatic changes which have taken place just since 2000, with the sharply increased and nearly instantaneous ability of firms to globally manage the planning, supply, production, and marketing of their products and services. This is Fröbel, Heinrichs, and Kreye at hyperspeed, "on steroids." Friedman describes ten Earth "flatteners," the top one being new communication technologies. With the construction of a huge amount of broadband fiber optic infrastructure, phone, e-mail and Web communication is instantaneous, from Beijing (China) to Bangalore (India) to Bristol (England) to the Bronx (United States), and back again. Friedman argues that something new happens when it is possible to communicate across the world: that individuals gain power "to collaborate and compete globally." Given the contentions of other writers in this volume, this is Friedman's most debatable point: that these technologies speeding globalization are creating greater equality of opportunity around the world. Friedman means the article and book to wake up readers to the fact that the world is changing very quickly indeed, and that they risk being left behind. He argues that non-Western, non-white individuals "from every corner of the flat world are being empowered" by these changes. "It is time we got focused."

NOTES

1   Folker Fröbel, Jürgen Heinrichs, and Otto Kreye, *The New International Division of Labour* (Cambridge: Cambridge University Press, 1980), p. 3.

2   Ibid., p. 4.

3   Ibid., p. 5.

4   Philip McMichael, "Globalization: Myths and Realities," *Rural Sociology* 61:1 (1996): 32. Leslie Sklair has called this the new "Transnational Capitalist Class."

10 The New International Division of Labor in the World Economy (1980)

Folker Fröbel, Jürgen Heinrichs, and Otto Kreye

Two fundamental issues confront corporate management in 1977. They are:

- the probability that the post-war era of unusual rapid economic expansion is over, and
- the probability that the post-war era of unprecedented world economic and political cooperation is coming to an end.

The world's departure from these patterns could force companies into the most radical and painful reassessments of their plans and strategies in living memory . . . Growth, translated into improved living conditions, has . . . become one of the basic expectations of all the world's citizens, including the poorest. These assumptions clearly must now be challenged. The recent world recession will, hopefully, prove to have been merely an extremely severe one, but 1977 may reveal the recession as the sign-off of an exceptional period in world economic history. Within many nations, the tensions from a prolonged era of no or low growth could ultimately prove explosive . . . The turmoil within and between nations resulting from the frustration of mass expectations would, in many instances, bring revolution and war to the fore.[1]

A blueprint for a new economic era published today outlines profound changes in life-styles that will be needed over the next five years to put capitalist societies back on the track for sustained economic growth. The most significant change is a shift away from the consumer-oriented growth that has marked the post-war period to a model more akin to the Communist bloc countries with the emphasis on improving and expanding plant and equipment. This shift would be achieved in part through a reduction in real wages and limits on the growth of living standards. One of the major tools to effect these changes would be a sustained level of unemployment well over post-war norms although below the record level seen in the just ended recession. . . . The author of this blueprint is the secretariat of the Organisation for Economic Cooperation and Development, the economic clearing house for the 24 largest industrialised states outside the Communist bloc. . . . [The OECD notes] "that it would be tempting to consider a more favourable scenario. . . . Unfortunately, there are few grounds for believing that this is a realistic alternative unless economic policies prove much more effective than in the past."[2]

1.1 The Phenomenon

Business International is one of the world's largest business consultancy firms. The OECD is the supranational institution which was established by the Western industrialised countries for the purpose of observing and coordinating their economies. What is the empirical evidence of recent changes in the world economy which has induced these two institutions to proffer such gloomy forecasts?

In the Western *industrialised countries* the rate of unemployment has reached its highest level for many years. In 1975 the official rate of unemployment, which always understates the real volume of unemployment, averaged 5 percent for the OECD countries (USA = 8.5 percent, Japan = 1.9 percent, Federal Germany = 4.7 percent) and has remained at this high level with no indications that it will decrease. The number of people in OECD countries officially registered as unemployed has hovered around the fifteen million mark since 1975 and there is no reason to suppose that it will fall in the immediate future.

An increasing number of the industrial branches of the OECD countries are reporting declining output, overcapacities, short-time working and mass redundancies. For example, the garment, textile and synthetic fibres industries in the most highly industrialised countries have, almost without exception, drastically cut back the production of their respective products at the traditional manufacturing sites as production there is becoming increasingly less competitive in the world market. Employees in many branches of industry are threatened with redundancy and the devaluation of their professional skills – victims of spreading automation and, in particular, of the recent leap forward in the rationalisation of the production process made possible by technical developments in the electrical engineering industry, especially the shift from electro-mechanical to electronic components in the production both of consumer goods and components to be used in other sectors of the economy.

Domestic investment in the largest industrialised countries (USA, Japan, Federal Germany, France, United Kingdom) has not only been stagnating but has even fallen in Japan and Federal Germany as a proportion of gross national product in the first half of the 1970s. In the face of the decreasing profitability of domestic investments, companies in the OECD countries have expanded and justified their policy of investment directed towards rationalisation on the grounds that they cannot expect any change in the current trends for the foreseeable future. In many countries the increase in the share of domestic investment which has been directed towards rationalisation schemes over recent years has resulted in a substantial loss of local jobs, without any reduction in productive capacity.

By contrast, *foreign* investments originating from the Western industrialised countries have been steadily increasing for a number of years. An ever-increasing share of these investments is flowing into the developing countries. Foreign investment for the purpose of industrial relocation is gaining in importance, both that undertaken in industrialised countries, as well as in developing countries.

Stagnating output, short-time working and mass redundancies in numerous countries do not, however, necessarily reflect the fates of individual companies. On the contrary, many companies, both large and small, from the industrialised countries are expanding their investments, production capacities and employment abroad, especially in developing countries, whilst their investments, production capacities and employment at home are stagnating or even declining.

The primacy given to investment for rationalisation instead of for expansion in the Western industrialised countries implies increased "mobility" for workers. More and more workers are losing not only their jobs but also their acquired profession as a result of rationalisation schemes. They are thrown onto the labour market where, because they lack relevant qualifications or training, they are obliged to sell their labour-power as unskilled or semiskilled workers at considerably worse terms than before. Given the rapid changes in the specifications and qualifications demanded of the labour-force by current economic developments and the concurrent increase in occupational "mobility", it is hardly surprising that the rationale and usefulness of professional training is becoming more and more questionable, and that companies are increasingly cutting back on comprehensive programmes of industrial training. More and more workers are being forced to make rapid and psychologically exhausting adjustments to the changing demands of the labour market – changes which are both abrupt and more or less unforeseeable.

In addition, the Western industrialised countries are experiencing a long-term fiscal crisis of the state. High unemployment and short-time working have forced the state to increase its expenditure, while at the same time the state's tax receipts have fallen because high unemployment has reduced the revenue from personal taxation and the threat or reality of industrial relocation has reduced the ability of the state to tax private companies. It is becoming more and more difficult to provide adequate funds for public pension and health programmes. Outlays on social services are being cut, while at the same time higher social security contributions and taxes threaten employees with a decrease in real incomes. On the other hand, the state has been compelled to provide grants, loans and tax concessions to private business on an increasing scale, hoping that this will stimulate domestic investment, reduce the rate of unemployment, and thus avert the danger of potentially explosive social tensions. This policy of curbing real wages and of promoting the so-called growth industries by official massive backing from the state has nonetheless so far failed to yield any noticeable success in making domestic industrial sites attractive again. "The horses have been led to the water, but are refusing to drink."

These economic, social and political problems in each of the Western industrialised countries are occurring in the context of world-wide higher turnovers and profits by individual companies. The annual reports of most large companies show that, even in the years of the world recession, these companies have been operating very successfully.

A remarkable contrast then exists between the success of individual private companies and the failure of the economic policies of the industrialised countries to attain their declared principal policy aim, namely the reduction in unemployment. The panacea of the last few decades, high rates of growth in gross national product, no longer appears to be available. In fact, whether the extensive elimination of unemployment is seriously the prime objective of the economic policies of the industrial nations is far from certain when one considers the OECD "scenario" cited at the beginning of this chapter. One cannot avoid the question: Are the politicians simply incapable, or have the structures of national economies recently undergone such profound changes that the present problem of chronic unemployment is simply so much more intractable than formerly? We shall return to this question later.

The number of un- and underemployed in the *developing countries* is even greater: they constitute an enormous mass of people who are either not at all or only partially integrated as productive labour into the so-called modern sector. This reservoir of potential labour amounts to hundreds of millions of workers. It is an oversimplification to say that it is the traditionally bad living conditions in underdeveloped countries which produced an ever-increasing flow of people seeking work and incomes from the countryside into the cities, the potential sites of the industry which can grant these things. Paradoxically the cause must be looked for in the modernisation of agriculture which can only attain its declared goal of increasing food production by the destruction of small subsistence farming, the traditional modest basis of survival for large sections of the rural population who are then forced to migrate to the cities where they are not usually able to obtain an income sufficient to provide them with a decent living.

The contemporary slums and similar poverty-stricken districts of the underdeveloped countries' cities are overcrowded with these landless rural immigrants. (By 1970 population statistics from at least ten cities in the so-called Third World showed that more than a million people in each of them were living in such areas.) Transformed into proletarianised wage workers they are forced to seek employment regardless of the level of remuneration and under the most inhuman conditions merely to ensure their sheer physical survival. They constitute a nearly inexhaustible source of the cheapest and most exploitable labour in the underdeveloped countries.

This vast industrial reserve army of extremely cheap labour feeds a process of industrialisation which can be observed in many contemporary developing countries. But this process of industrialisation rarely absorbs any significant proportion of the local labour-force. It is oriented to production for export, as the purchasing power of the mass of the local population is too low to constitute an effective demand on the local market for the products of the country's own industry. The markets supplied by the industrialisation of the developing countries are therefore predominantly overseas, primarily in the traditional industrial countries.

This process of export-oriented industrialisation in developing countries is not only highly dependent on foreign companies but also extremely fragmented. Only very rarely do developing countries end up with the establishment of reasonably complex industrial branches (e.g. textile and garment industry in some cases complemented by synthetic fibre production). And even in the very few developing countries where such centres of partial industrialisation have been established there are no signs that they are being supplemented by a wider industrial complex which would enable them to free themselves eventually from their dependency on the already industrialised countries for imports of capital- and other goods, and for the maintenance of their industrial installations.

However, in the overwhelming majority of developing countries not even the beginnings of this partial industrialisation process can be observed, that is, a process which would at least serve to develop a few individual branches of industry. Instead, industrial production is confined to a few highly specialised manufacturing processes: inputs are imported from outside the country, are worked on by the local labour-force in "world market factories" (for example, sewing, soldering, assembling and testing) and are then exported in their processed form. In other words, these world market factories are industrial enclaves with no connection to the local economy except for their utilisation of extremely cheap labour and occasionally some local inputs (energy, water and services for example), and are isolated from the local economy in almost all other respects. The labour-force recruited for production in these industrial enclaves is equipped with the necessary training in a period that rarely lasts for more than a few weeks, is exploited for a time-span which is optimal for the companies, and is then replaced by a newly recruited and freshly trained labour-force. Under such conditions there is no such thing as a skilled labour-force, or, at best, the skills which the workers do acquire are very minimal. Likewise there is no observable transfer of technology, despite the euphoric claims made by firms which relocate their manufacturing processes in the developing countries. The technology which is employed in these world market factories is not only in most cases quite simple, but also dependent on the expertise of foreign specialists and managers. This technology is often quite useless for the development of any form of industrialisation which would serve the basic needs of the local population.

So far export-oriented industrialisation has failed to achieve any improvement in the social conditions of the mass of the populations of the developing countries, not even as far as their most fundamental needs such as food, clothing, health, habitation and education are concerned. Nor can any improvement be expected in the foreseeable future. Quite the opposite – the social tensions and struggles between the tiny privileged minority which benefits from export-oriented industrialisation, and the vast majority of the population which derives no benefits from it will intensify in the future. It is such predictable developments as these which have occasioned Business International to take account of war and revolution in many countries. The increasing militarisation of the so-called Third World is a clear indication that increasingly overt and repressive force is needed to prevent the violent eruption of social tensions. South Africa, Chile and Thailand are but three especially well-known examples of military repression – but there are very many others. The "preventive counter-revolution", to use an expression coined by Herbert Marcuse, is well under way in most parts of the so-called Third World (and not only there).

After decades and centuries of the underdevelopment of the so-called developing countries the recent export-oriented industrialisation of these countries offers but faint hope that living standards and conditions of the mass of their populations will undergo any substantial improvements in the foreseeable future. Moreover there is no reason to assume that the main goal of the policies pursued by the governments of many developing countries is, in fact, the improvement of the material conditions of the mass of their populations. But even in those developing countries whose governments appear to be actively pursuing this goal, little progress can be discerned, except in very rare instances. Again, are the politicians of these developing countries simply incapable, or are the economic and social structures of the developing countries – the stark contrast between élite and masses, and debilitating economic dependency – so rigid that the goal of improving the living standards of the masses of the populations is unattainable under present circumstances? We shall come back to this question also.

Even the most superficial description of the *world economy* in the 1970s cannot be confined to a consideration of the situation of the industrialised countries on one hand, and of developing countries on the other, each looked at in artificial isolation. (The "socialist" countries will be taken into account in our study only inasmuch as they are also integrated into the world market.) The world economy is not simply the sum total of national economies, each of which functions essentially according to its own laws of motion, with only marginal interconnections, such as those established by external trade. These national economies are, rather, organic elements of one all-embracing system, namely a world economy which is in fact a single world-wide capitalist system. As our cursory survey has already shown, the structural changes in individual national economies are interrelated within this single world economy and mutually determine one another.

The most striking manifestation of the world economy is international trade. Well over 15 percent of all commodities and services which are produced every year in Western industrialised and developing countries enter international trade, and this percentage has been steadily increasing for at least the last fifteen years. Recognition of this fact is a first step towards understanding the increase of world-wide economic interpenetration.

The industrialised countries handle 70 percent of international trade and the developing countries only 20 percent. Seventy per cent of exports from both developing and industrialised countries are destined for industrialised countries and only 20 percent for the developing countries. In other words, whereas the foreign trade of the industrialised countries is mostly with each other, the foreign trade of the developing countries is mostly with the industrialised countries, and not their fellow developing countries. Recognition of this fact is a first step towards understanding the economic dependency of the developing countries on the industrialised countries.

The developing countries' exports to the industrialised countries still consist overwhelmingly of raw materials, whereas the vast bulk of the exports of the industrialised countries to the developing countries are still manufactures. In recent years, however, there has been a marked, slow but steady increase in manufactures exported from developing countries as a proportion of total world exports of manufactured goods. Recognition of this fact is a first important step towards understanding a potential change in the structure not only of world trade, but also, and more importantly, of the world economy itself. This change is especially evident in the rapid expansion of textile and garment exports from the developing countries to the industrialised countries.

International trade and world-wide industrial production, however, provide only a very superficial picture of the increasing interpenetration of national economies. World trade is increasingly becoming a flow of commodities between the plants of the same company spread throughout the world, or at least a flow between companies and their partners in subcontracting agreements. (For instance company A in Federal Germany delivers semi-processed products for further manufacturing to a subcontractor B abroad; the finished manufactures are subsequently re-imported into Federal Germany.) In this case, foreign trade is not just simply an exchange of commodities between two national economies, but more precisely, a concrete manifestation of the international division of labour, consciously planned and utilised by individual companies.

One, albeit incomplete, expression of this international division of labour, which has been organised by private companies in pursuit of their own profit maximisation, is foreign investment. Figures for Federal German investment show that in recent years investment abroad by Federal German companies has exceeded investment by foreign companies in Federal Germany. Taken together with the fact that investment policy in Federal Germany has concentrated on rationalisation schemes for a number of years, this would suggest that Federal Germany has now apparently become less "interesting" as a site for the expansion of industrial production. (Figures on the development of industrial assets of Federal German companies, including the re-invested profits, both at home and abroad would, in all probability, if available, demonstrate this phenomenon even more clearly.)

However, perhaps the clearest expression of the structural changes in the world economy which can be observed in the mid-1970s is the relocation of production. One form of this relocation (among other equally important ones) is the closing down of certain types of manufacturing operations in undertakings in the industrial nations and the subsequent installation of these parts of the production process in the foreign subsidiaries of the same company. The Federal German textile and garment industries represent one of the best-known examples of such relocations. Trousers for the Federal German market are no longer produced for example in Mönchengladbach, but in the Tunisian subsidiary of the same Federal German company. The process of relocation is also gaining momentum in other branches of industry. Injection pumps which were formerly made for the Federal German market by a Federal German company in Stuttgart, are now manufactured partly to the same end by the same company at a site in India. Television sets are produced on the same basis by another company in Taiwan; car radio equipment in Malaysia, car engines in Brazil, watches in Hong Kong, electronic components in Singapore and Malaysia all fall into the same category.

The Federal German worker rendered unemployed by the relocation of production has been replaced by a newly hired worker in a foreign subsidiary of "his" or "her" company.

1.2   Main Tendencies in the Contemporary World Economy

The question which we began with was the following: What has happened in the world economy to have occasioned the forecasts published by the OECD and Business International? To answer this we started with an outline of the economic situation of both the industrialised and the developing countries and we were occasionally obliged to resort to the vague term "the rest of the world". We have tried, however, to correct some of the misleading implications of this initial procedure by subsequent reference to some of the mutual relations and dependencies between the economies of the industrialised countries and the developing countries, which make up one world economy. We have chosen this descriptive procedure by way of introduction in order not to have to use more information, where possible, than is already available to any newspaper reader who is interested in political and economic matters.

Our next step is to undertake a *systematic presentation of essentially the same observable facts* and to show how they can only be understood as an *expression of the development of a single world economy.* ([Later] we try to explain the development of the world economy over the last five centuries showing how this development can only be understood as a necessary expression of the development of a *capitalist* world system.)

The origins of the present-day world economy are to be found in the sixteenth century. Its genesis was inextricably connected with the simultaneous emergence of a regional division of labour which affected the whole world. Different forms of the organisation of labour were used in different regions of the world (or introduced from outside the region itself) for different types of production. The following represent some characteristic examples:

From the Sixteenth Century to the Eighteenth Century

(a) Independent crafts and domestic labour (the putting-out system) formed the basis in Western Europe of manufactures such as textiles and metals, ship-building and arms production. Wage labour was also already used in individual large-scale manufacturing enterprises.

(b) Forced or slave labour formed the basis of silver mining in Peru and Mexico, and also of sugar plantations established by European colonial masters in Brazil and the West Indies. Serf labour formed the basis of grain production in Eastern Europe; the "second serfdom", a reversal in the trend towards the disintegration of landlord/serf relations, was utilised and even intensified owing to the demand for corn from Western Europe.

Eighteenth and Nineteenth Centuries

(a) Wage labour supplanted other forms of labour as the basis of the industrial revolution, which spread from England where cotton manufacturing, the steam engine and railways were developed.

(b) Slave labour became the basis of raw cotton production in the West Indies and in the Southern United States; India's indigenous cotton manufacturing which had initially been stimulated by world trade was destroyed; China and Japan were "opened up" for world trade (the Opium Wars etc.).

First Half of the Twentieth Century

(a) Wage labour formed the basis of manufacturing in Europe, USA and Japan.

(b) A peculiar form of wage labour (which will be discussed below) formed the basis of the extraction and production of raw materials in the enclaves of Latin America, Africa and Asia (coffee in Brazil, saltpetre and copper in Chile, gold and diamonds in South Africa). These were primarily for export onto the world market. A partial industrialisation process was established in a small number of developing countries through a policy of import-substitution.

The regions of Latin America, Africa and Asia have therefore been integrated for centuries into the developing world economy chiefly as producers of agricultural and mineral raw materials, sometimes as the suppliers of a labour-force (e.g. African slaves). This integration was enforced wherever it was feasible and necessary by the military, technological and economic superiority which the West European nations and rulers developed after the sixteenth century.

Some countries of the so-called Third World have, under certain very specific conditions, experienced a weak process of industrialisation based on a policy of import-substitution: for instance, parts of Latin America during the partial disintegration of the world economy between 1930 and 1945. During this period it was possible for a modest local industry to develop in some underdeveloped countries for the purpose of supplying a very restricted domestic market. This development was possible only behind a barrier of selective import restrictions and was facilitated by the preoccupation of the most powerful industrialised nations with their "own" problems during this period, a preoccupation which prevented them from intervening in the so-called Third World. This modest profitable local industry, however, very quickly reached the limits of local effective demand, and since it was non-competitive on the world market, receded into stagnation almost everywhere after the Second World War, and even in some cases, such as Argentina, collapsed into agony.

Our earlier descriptive sketch of some typical aspects of the contemporary world economy has already indicated that the old or "classical" international division of labour is now open for replacement. The decisive evidence for this hypothesis is the fact that developing countries have increasingly become sites for manufacturing – producing manufactured goods which are competitive on the world market. The three case studies presented in this book provide extensive documentation of this world market oriented production of manufactures which is now being established and developed on new industrial sites, especially those in the developing countries.

This world market oriented industrialisation which is emerging today in many developing countries is not the result of positive decisions made by individual governments or companies. Industry only locates itself at those sites where production will yield a certain profit, sites which have been determined by five centuries of development of the world economy. In the "classical" international division of labour which developed over this period, industrial sites for manufacturing basically only existed in Western Europe, and later in the USA and Japan. Since it is evident that the developing countries are now providing sites for the profitable manufacture of industrial products destined for the world market to an ever-increasing extent, we quickly come up against the question: What changes are responsible for this development?

Three preconditions taken together seem to be decisive for this new development.

Firstly, a practically inexhaustible reservoir of disposable labour has come into existence in the developing countries over the last few centuries. This labour-force is extremely cheap; it can be mobilized for production for practically the whole of the year, and all hours of the day, on shift work, night work and Sunday work; in many cases it can reach levels of labour productivity comparable with those of similar processes in the developed countries after a short period of training; companies can afford to exhaust the labour-force by overwork as it can easily be replaced, and they can also select their employees very specifically according to age, sex, skill, discipline and other relevant factors as there is an oversupply of people who are forced to take any job which is available.

Secondly, the division and subdivision of the production process is now so advanced that most of these fragmented operations can be carried out with minimal levels of skill easily learnt within a very short time.

Thirdly, the development of techniques of transport and communication has created the possibility, in many cases, of the complete or partial production of goods at any site in the world – a possibility no longer ruled out by technical, organisational and cost factors.

The coincidence of these three preconditions (which are supplemented by other, less important ones) has brought into existence a world market for labour and a real world industrial reserve army of workers, together with a world market for production sites. Workers in the already industrialised countries are now placed on a world-wide labour market and forced to compete for their jobs with their fellow workers in the developing countries. Today, with the development of a world-wide market in production sites, the traditional industrialised and the developing countries have to compete against one another to attract industry to their sites.

In other words, for the first time in the history of the 500-year-old world economy, the profitable production of manufactures for the world market has finally become possible to a significant and increasing extent, not only in the industrialised countries, but also now in the developing countries. Furthermore, commodity production is being increasingly subdivided into fragments which can be assigned to whichever part of the world can provide the most profitable combination of capital and labour.

The term which we shall use to designate this qualitatively new development in the world economy is the *new international division of labour.*

Of those countries which were able to supply vast reserve armies of potential industrial workers and to offer these workers' labour-power at a low price, the first to attract the relocation of parts of the production process were countries with close geographical and commercial links to existing industrial centres. The first shifts of US industry were to Western Europe and to countries "south of the border"; West European companies transferred production to other regions in Europe, such as Eire, Greece, Portugal and the south of Italy; Japanese industry moved into South Korea and Taiwan. At the same time, industrial firms recruited labour from countries with high rates of unemployment and drew it in to the traditional sites of industrial production. Hence the appearance of *Gastarbeiter* in Western Europe, and Mexican and Puerto Rican immigrant workers in the USA.

Since then, sites for relocated manufacturing are not only being supplied in the border areas of Western Europe, Central America, North Africa, and South East Asia, but increasingly in Eastern Europe, South America, Central Africa and South Asia. The transfer of production to places with cheap labour not only affects the more or less labour-intensive production processes but also processes which are heavily dependent on raw materials and energy, and those which are a source of environmental pollution, given that the new sites can also offer favourable conditions as far as other factors of production are concerned. It has even affected capital-intensive production processes, contrary to the unsubstantiated prejudices of a number of international economists. Not only are investments, production capacities and output expanded and developed at these new sites, but existing facilities at the traditional sites which have become obsolete in terms of profitability are closed down.

This means that any company, almost irrespective of its size, which wishes to survive is now forced to initiate a transnational reorganisation of production to adapt to these qualitatively new conditions.

By far the most important means by which companies have secured their continued survival in the past has been through "investment in rationalisation" – the installation of more efficient machinery and a reduction in the size and skills of the labour force. This device alone (along with other "classical" devices) is no longer adequate. The development of the world economy has increasingly created conditions (forcing the development of the new international division of labour) in which the survival of more and more companies can only be assured through the relocation of production to new industrial sites, where labour-power is cheap to buy, abundant and well-disciplined; in short, through the transnational reorganisation of production.

[. . .]

The results of our empirical studies are presented in Parts I, II and III [omitted here]. Some of the results are presented in summary form immediately below. If read without being placed in the context of our later more extensive presentation they may lead to distorted interpretations. The figures mentioned in this summary should therefore only be taken as approximate indications of the extent to which the new international division of labour has already developed.

Case Study I is a survey of 214 textile and 185 garment companies from Federal Germany. In 1974 these companies accounted for roughly 60 percent of turnover and employment in the Federal German textile industry and 40 percent in the Federal German garment industry. In each of these samples about a hundred companies had *subsidiaries* producing abroad by 1974/5. These figures do not include production abroad by a quite significant number of nominally independent foreign producers, in particular through subcontracting and export-processing cooperation agreements with Eastern European and East Asian firms. These figures should be compared with those of other studies which identified about thirty firms from each industry in 1966, and forty firms from each in 1970 producing either in wholly or partly owned subsidiaries abroad.

A breakdown of our findings by region shows that in 1974 foreign production in the subsidiaries of the companies covered by our case study was concentrated in the industrialised countries (chiefly, the EEC countries, Austria and Switzerland) on the one hand, with a share of 50–60 percent, and in certain of the developing countries on the other hand (the textile industry in Africa and the Mediterranean countries, and the garment industry in the Mediterranean countries and Asia). The concentration of production in these regions is confirmed statistically regardless of whether we look at the number of foreign subsidiaries or the number of employees.

The following figures are the numbers of employees in the foreign subsidiaries of the Federal German textile and garment industries. In the textile industry, the numbers of employed increased from 8000 in 1966 to 14,200 in 1970 and finally to 29,500 in 1974: these are minimum estimates. In the garment industry, the equivalent figures are 15,000, 24,800 and 31,000. The sizes of the labour-force employed in foreign subsidiaries as a proportion of these industries' domestic employment in the Federal Republic of Germany are as follows: in the textile industry, 1.5 percent in 1966, 2.8 percent in 1970 and 7.5 percent in 1974/5; in the garment industry, 3.7 percent in 1966, 6.5 percent in 1970 and 10.0 percent in 1974/5. Foreign employment in Federal German subsidiaries in the "low wage countries" as proportion of the total foreign labour employed by Federal German subsidiaries abroad in the textile and garment industries has increased from approximately 25 percent in 1966 to approximately 45 percent by 1974/5.

A breakdown of employment abroad by sex and age group reveals that the subsidiaries of Federal German garment companies in the "low wage countries" employ an extremely high percentage of young female workers. Roughly 43 percent of the employed are younger than twenty, and more than 90 percent are female.

If one includes *subcontracting arrangements* with foreign firms, then the Federal German textile and garment industries are employing at least 69,000 workers in subsidiaries and subcontracted firms abroad, and very probably significantly more; a figure of over 80,000 employees for the Federal German textile and garment industry abroad is not an improbable estimate for 1974/5.

In short, the foreign employment of the Federal German textile and garment industries has more than doubled between 1966 and 1974/5, whereas domestic employment has decreased by roughly a quarter over the same period. An estimate for 1977 would show that for every hundred workers employed by the Federal German textile and garment industries in Federal Germany itself, there are more than ten foreign workers employed abroad.

In 1974/5, some 30,000 employees in the foreign production facilities of the Federal German textile and garment industry were producing either exclusively or predominantly for the Federal German market. This is an indication of the extent to which companies have relocated production for the domestic market from production sites in Federal Germany to sites abroad.

The case study analyses in some detail the following indicators of the new international division of labour in the sphere of the textile and garment industries: the drastically increased negative balance of trade in textiles and clothing of Federal Germany; the structural unemployment in the traditional industrial centres which has been caused by this development in the world economy; the export-oriented industrialisation of the developing countries; the corresponding relocations of production as industry is moved from sites in the "centre" to the "periphery"; and the increasing subdivision of the production process into fragmented routines which can be distributed throughout the world. The growing significance of these factors over the last ten to fifteen years in the sphere of the textile and garment industries provides incontrovertible evidence of the fact that the economic pressure of the world-wide labour market and the world market for industrial sites is forcing companies to undertake a global reorganisation of their own production processes. Rationalisation schemes, both at home and abroad, and industrial relocation abroad (especially to "low wage countries") go hand in hand.

What this process means for those it directly affects is, first and foremost, unemployment and the devaluation of skills for workers in the traditional industrial countries, and the subjection of the populations of the developing countries to inhuman working conditions, with no hope for improvement in the foreseeable future. Furthermore, the inevitable development of this process means that in the years to come working people will be threatened even more drastically than in the past with the degradation and rigid discipline which reduces them to the status of mere appendages of the machine.

Case Study II surveys 602 Federal German manufacturing companies (excluding the textile and garment industries) which have had at least one subsidiary producing abroad (outside the EEC) between 1961 and 1976. The sum total of these subsidiaries (Federal German formal share-in-capital between 25 percent and 100 percent) of these companies producing outside the EEC is 1,760. Of these companies, 339 have one subsidiary abroad, 528 companies have up to four subsidiaries abroad, and twelve companies have twenty or more. These subsidiaries are located in a total of seventy-seven countries, with Brazil, Spain, the USA and Austria each accounting for more than a hundred. Of the 602 companies in our survey, 335 have 709 subsidiaries in industrialised countries, and 444 have 1,051 subsidiaries in developing countries.

It was possible to collect employment figures for 1,178 of the 1,760 subsidiaries surveyed; in 1975 these subsidiaries employed 560,788 persons. If the EEC countries and the textile and garment industries are included, our estimate of the total employment abroad by Federal German manufacturing companies amounts to 1.5 million workers. That is, the number of workers directly employed by Federal German manufacturing companies in foreign countries amounts to 20 percent of the total domestic labour-force in Federal German manufacturing industry. This figure, which is based on quite conservative estimates, is considerably higher than any other estimate published to date.

Foreign production is fairly well distributed over the different branches of industry. The mechanical engineering branch has the highest number of companies involved in production abroad, the chemicals industry has the most subsidiaries, and the electrical engineering industry has the most employees abroad. The data collected shows that nearly all branches of Federal German industry participate to a significant degree in production abroad and industrial relocation.

Between 1961 and 1976 the number of foreign subsidiaries belonging to the companies surveyed in this case study increased fourfold, with much of this increase first starting at the end of the 1960s. The increase in the number of employees abroad has been even more striking since many existing foreign subsidiaries have expanded their production and employment during the period of time under investigation. Complete data is available for a subsample of the companies surveyed, and reveals that the number of employees employed abroad by these companies increased fivefold between 1961 and 1974.

The above figures represent only a fraction of all foreign production by Federal German industry. This is due not so much to lack of information on the companies producing abroad but more significantly to our operational definition of what constitutes Federal German production abroad, i.e. production where the Federal German share in the subsidiaries' capital was at least 25 percent, which therefore excludes instances of Federal German foreign production where the direct holding is low or non-existent. However, it is possible for Federal German industry to use foreign production facilities without any direct capital participation, as evidenced by such cooperative arrangements as international subcontracting, management, supply and licence agreements. Our case study does not provide statistical data on the extent of this type of foreign production, and it is difficult to estimate how widespread it is. In some parts of the world, at least, this type of foreign production is more important than that controlled through direct capital holdings (e.g. in Eastern Europe and India).

These complexities must be taken into account in estimating the amount of industrial relocation. The procedure must start not only with individual companies and take note of all changes in industrial sites for the totality of production organised by those companies, but must add to this processes of relocation at the level of whole branches of industry which are not organised by domestic companies alone; for example, if domestic production in a given company is cut back or shut down completely because the product is now obtained from non-Federal German companies producing abroad. An assessment of the tendencies towards the relocation of industry throughout the world, and hence of the structural changes in the world economy and its subeconomies, can only be obtained by a global estimate of the redistribution of industrial sites.

The results of case study II (the study of industry in one major industrial country) testify to the changed conditions for the world-wide valorisation of capital which are forcing industrial undertakings, regardless of size and industrial branch, to reorganise their production. In an increasing number of cases, this reorganisation involves the relocation of production abroad. To conclude: the new international division of labour is manifested in the changing world distribution of, in this case, Federal German production facilities. The high level of structural unemployment in Federal Germany is an inevitable result of the transfer of industrial employment elsewhere in the world.

Case Study III is based on data embracing 103 countries in Asia, Africa and Latin America. Whereas in the mid-1960s manufacturing for the markets of the industrialised countries was virtually non-existent in the underdeveloped countries, ten years later, there were literally thousands of factories in production in the underdeveloped countries producing goods almost exclusively for the markets of the industrialised countries. Such factories existed in at least thirty-nine underdeveloped countries; fifteen of these countries were in Asia, eight in Africa and sixteen in Latin America. This spread of industrial production in the so-called Third World is tied up with the creation of a new type of industrial site – the free production zone – and with the creation of a new type of factory – the world market factory.

Free production zones are industrial areas which are separated off from the rest of the country, located at places where labour is cheap and designated as sites for world market oriented industry; world market factories are factories which are built on these sites, but can also be situated elsewhere, and intended for the industrial utilisation of the available labour and the processing of goods destined essentially for the markets of the industrialised countries. In 1975, seventy-nine free production zones were in operation in twenty-five underdeveloped countries; eleven of these countries were in Asia, five in Africa and nine in Latin America.

As far as the structure of production at these sites is concerned, nearly all branches of manufacturing industry are represented. On the other hand, as far as individual zones and countries are concerned, there is a tendency for the development of industrial mono-structures. In 1975 the bulk of production was accounted for by the products of the textiles and garment industry on one hand, and those of the electrical engineering industry on the other. Production in world market factories is highly vertically integrated into the transnational operations of the individual companies and involves non-complex production operations; as regards the processing of each product or product group, the production process is largely confined to part operations: the manufacturing of parts, assembling of parts, or final assembly. Only in the case of a few product groups, and in a few countries, can one identify anything resembling complex manufacture; textiles and garments are one example.

The employment structure in free production zones and world market factories is extremely unbalanced. Given a virtually unlimited supply of unemployed labour, world market factories at the free production zones, or other sites, select one specific type of worker, chiefly women from the younger age groups. The criteria used for the selection of workers are quite unambiguous: the labour which is employed is that which demands the least remuneration, provides the maximum amount of energy (i.e. fresh labour which can be expected to work at a high intensity) and which is predominantly unskilled or semiskilled.

The case study attempts to provide an answer to the question as to whether the aims of development policy, which are allegedly linked with world market oriented industrialisation, are being attained. These are: reduction in unemployment, training of skilled personnel, access to modern technology, and increases in the foreign currency earned by the country concerned. The historical record up to now and the foreseeable future both indicate that the answer to this question is an unequivocal "no".

NOTES

1   Business International Corporation, *Business International – Weekly Report to Managers of Worldwide Operations*, 7 January 1977, p. 1.
2   "Changes in West life-styles expected. OECD sees tough capitalist road ahead," *Herald Tribune*, 28 July 1976; cf. OECD, *Economic Outlook*, 19 July 1976, Special Supplement, "A growth scenario to 1980".

11 The Informational Mode of Development and the Restructuring of Capitalism (1989)

Manuel Castells

[. . .]

The New Technological Revolution and the Informational Mode of Development

The New Technological Paradigm

During the two decades from the late 1960s to the late 1980s a series of scientific and technological innovations have converged to constitute a new technological paradigm.[1] The scientific and technical core of this paradigm lies in microelectronics, building on the sequential discoveries of the transistor (1947), the integrated circuit (1957), the planar process (1959), and the microprocessor (1971).[2] Computers, spurred on by exponential increases in power and dramatic decreases in cost per unit of memory, were able to revolutionize information processing, in both hardware and software. Telecommunications became the key vector for the diffusion and full utilization of the new technologies by enabling connections between processing units, to form information systems. Applications of these microelectronics-based information systems to work processes in factories and offices created the basis for CAD/CAM (computer aided design/computer aided manufacturing) and flexible integrated manufacturing, as well as for advanced office automation, paving the way for the general application of flexible integrated production and management systems. Around this nucleus of information technologies, a number of other fundamental innovations took place, particularly in new materials (ceramics, alloys, optical fiber), and more recently, in superconductors, in laser, and in renewable energy sources. In a parallel process, which benefited from the enhanced capacity to store and analyze information, genetic engineering extended the technological revolution to the realm of living matter. This laid the foundations for biotechnology, itself an information technology with its scientific basis in the ability to decode and reprogram the information embodied in living organisms.[3]

Although the scientific foundations of these discoveries had already come into existence, over timescales varying from field to field, the relatively simultaneous emergence of these various technologies, and the synergy created by their interaction, contributed to their rapid diffusion and application, and this in turn expanded the potential of each technology and induced a broader and faster development of the new technological paradigm.[4] A key factor in this synergistic process relates to the specific nature of this process of innovation: because it is based on enhanced ability to store, retrieve, and analyze information, every single discovery, as well as every application, can be related to developments in other fields and in other applications, by continuous interactions through the common medium of information systems, and communicating by means of the common language of science, in spite of the persistence of specialization in different scientific fields.

Social, economic, and institutional factors have, as I will argue, been decisive in the coming together of these different scientific innovations under the form of a new technological paradigm.[5] However, the specificity of the new technologies plays a major role in the structure and evolution of this paradigm, and imposes the materiality of their internal logic on the articulation between the process of innovation and the process of social organization. The new technological paradigm is characterized by two fundamental features.[6] First, the core new technologies are *focused on information processing*. This is the primary distinguishing feature of the emerging technological paradigm. To be sure, information and knowledge have been crucial elements in all technological revolutions, since technology ultimately boils down to the ability to perform new operations, or to perform established practices better, on the basis of the application of new knowledge. All major technological changes are in fact based on new knowledge. However, what differentiates the current process of technological change is that *its raw material itself is information, and so is its outcome*. What an integrated circuit does is to speed up the processing of information while increasing the complexity and the accuracy of the process. What computers do is to organize the sets of instructions required for the handling of information, and, increasingly, for the generation of new information, on the basis of the combination and interaction of stored information. What telecommunications does is to transmit information, making possible flows of information exchange and treatment of information, regardless of distance, at lower cost and with shorter transmission times. What genetic engineering does is to decipher and, eventually, program the code of the living matter, dramatically expanding the realm of controllable information processing.

The output of the new technologies is also information. Their embodiment in goods and services, in decisions, in procedures, is the result of the application of their informational output, not the output itself. In this sense, the new technologies differ from former technological revolutions, and justify calling the new paradigm the "informational technological paradigm," in spite of the fact that some of the fundamental technologies involved in it (for example, superconductivity) are not information technologies. But the paradigm itself exists and articulates a convergent set of scientific discoveries by focusing on information processing and by using the newly found informational capacity to enable articulation and communication throughout the whole spectrum of technological innovations. Furthermore, with the progress of the new technological revolution, the machines themselves take second place to the creative synergy made possible by their use as sources of productivity. This trend is often referred to in the literature as the growing importance of software over hardware, a theme stimulated by the promise of research in such fields as artificial intelligence. However, this is still an open debate in scientific terms. Better design of integrated circuits, ever larger-scale integration, enhanced telecommunications capability, and the use of new material in the manufacturing of information-processing devices, are in the medium-term perspective probably more important than artificial intelligence as a basis for information-handling and information-generation capacity. The fundamental trend overall seems to depend not so much on the somewhat obsolete idea of the growing dominance of software over hardware, as on the ability of new information technologies to generate new information, thus emphasizing the specific nature of their output *vis-à-vis* former technological paradigms.

The second major characteristic of the new technologies is in fact common to all major technological revolutions.[7] The main effects of their innovations are on *processes*, rather than on *products*.[8] There are, of course, major innovations in products, and the surge of new products is a fundamental factor in spurring new economic growth. However, the deepest impact of innovation is associated with the transformation of processes.[9] This was also the case with the two industrial revolutions associated with technical paradigms organized respectively around the steam engine and around electricity.[10] In both cases, energy was the pivotal element which, by gradually penetrating all processes of production, distribution, transportation, and management, revolutionized the entire economy and the whole society, not so much because of the new goods and services being produced and distributed, but because of the ways of performing the processes of production and distribution, on the basis of a new source of energy that could be decentralized and distributed in a flexible manner. The new energy-based industrial and organizational processes gave birth to goods and services, hence products, that could not even have been imagined before the diffusion of energy-processing devices. But it was the revolution in energy, with its influence on all kinds of processes, that created the opportunity for the surge in new products. Process commands products, although functional, economic, and social feedback effects are crucial to an understanding of the historical process.

Similarly, in the current informational revolution, what new information technologies are about in the first place is process. A chip has value only as a means of improving the performance of a machine for an end-use function. A computer is a tool for information handling, whose usefulness for the organization or individual using it depends on the purpose of the information-processing activity. A genetically modified cell will take on its actual significance in its interaction with the whole body. While all social and biological activities are in fact processes, some elements of these processes crystallize in material forms that constitute goods and services, the usual content of economic products. Technological revolutions are made up of innovations whose products are in fact processes.

These two major characteristics of the informational technological paradigm[11] have fundamental effects on its impact on society. (Society itself, as stated above, frames and influences technological innovation in a dialectical relationship of which, at this point, we are only examining one factor, namely, the influence of new technologies on social organization.)

A fundamental consequence is derived from the essential process-orientation of technological innovation. Because processes, unlike products, enter into all spheres of human activity, their transformation by such technologies, focusing on omnipresent flows of information, leads to modification in the material basis of the entire social organization. Thus, new information technologies are transforming the way we produce, consume, manage, live, and die; not by themselves, certainly, but as powerful mediators of the broader set of factors that determines human behavior and social organization.

The fact that new technologies are focused on information processing has far-reaching consequences for the relationship between the sphere of sociocultural symbols and the productive basis of society. Information is based upon culture, and information processing is, in fact, symbol manipulation on the basis of existing knowledge; that is, codified information verified by science and/or social experience. Thus, the predominant role of new information technologies in the process of innovation is to establish ever more intimate relationships among the culture of society, scientific knowledge, and the development of productive forces. If information processing becomes the key component of the new productive forces, the symbolic capacity of society itself, collectively as well as individually, is tightly linked to its developmental process. In other words, the structurally determined capacity of labor to process information and generate knowledge is, more than ever, the material source of productivity, and therefore of economic growth and social well-being. Yet this symbolic capacity of labor is not an individual attribute. Labor has to be formed, educated, trained, and retrained, in flexible manipulation of symbols, determining its ability constantly to reprogram itself. In addition, productive organizations, social institutions, and the overall structure of society, including its ideology, will be key elements in fostering or stalling the new information-based productive forces. The more a society facilitates the exchange of information flows, and the decentralized generation and distribution of information, the greater will be its collective symbolic capacity. It is this capacity which underlies the enhancement and diffusion of information technologies, and thus the development of productive forces.

In this sense, the new informational technological paradigm emphasizes the historical importance of the Marxian proposition on the close interaction between productive forces and social systems.[12] Perhaps it is only in the current historical period, because of the close connection between information and culture through the human mind, and thus between productivity and social organization, that such inspired anticipation bears its full meaning. However, if this perspective is to be intellectually fruitful it must be purified both from any ideological assumption of historical directionality and from any value judgment. The development of productive forces by the liberation of information flows does not require that capitalism be superseded. In fact, state-planned societies have proved more resistant to the new technological revolution than market-based economies, in contradiction of Marx's prophecy that socialism possessed a superior ability to develop productive forces. Equally unfounded is the opposite ideological position which states that market forces are innately superior in steering development in information technologies. Japan's leadership in the field has been built on strong, systematic state intervention in support of national companies, to raise their technological level in pursuit of the national goal of establishing Japan as a world power on non-military grounds.

The key mechanism for the development of productive forces in the new informational technological paradigm seems to be the ability of a given social organization to educate and motivate its labor force while at the same time setting up an institutional framework that maximizes information flows and connects them to the developmental tasks. The social and political means of achieving such goals vary historically, as do the societal outcomes of the development processes. However, not all these processes are undetermined, and relationships can certainly be found between social structures, technoeconomic development, and institutional goals. Nevertheless, the present purpose is more limited and more focused. It is sufficient here to pinpoint the fact that because the new productive forces are information based, their development is more closely related than ever to the characteristics of symbolic production and manipulation in every society, actually fulfilling the hypothesis proposed by Marx on the relationship between social structure and technoeconomic development.

From the characteristics of the process-orientation of information-based technology derives a third fundamental effect of the new technological paradigm on social organization: namely, increased *flexibility* of organizations in production, consumption, and management. Flexibility, in fact, emerges as a key characteristic of the new system taking shape;[13] yet it takes place within a context of large-scale production, consumption, and management, generally associated with large organizations and/or extended organizational networks. What happens is that new technologies build on the organizational capacity resulting from the industrial form of production and consumption, particularly during its mature stage (generally associated with what has been labeled in the literature as "Fordism," a very misleading term);[14] but they contribute both to transforming this system and enhancing that organizational capacity by preserving the economies of scale and the depth of organizational power, while overcoming rigidity and facilitating constant adaptation to a rapidly changing context. In this way, the historical oppositions between craft production and large-scale manufacture, between mass consumption and customized markets, between powerful bureaucracies and innovative enterprises, are dialectically superseded by the new technological medium, which ushers in an era of adaptive organizations in direct relationship with their social environments.[15] By increasing the flexibility of all processes, new information technologies contribute to minimizing the distance between economy and society.

The Organizational Transition from Industrialism to Informationalism

The new technological paradigm has fundamental social consequences linked to the specific logic of its basic characteristic. Yet, the new technologies are themselves articulated into a broader system of production and organization, whose ultimate roots are social, but to whose development new technologies powerfully contribute.[16] It is this complex, interacting system of technology and organizational processes, underlying economic growth and social change, that we call a *mode of development*. It is not the product of new technologies, nor are the new technologies a mechanical response to the demands of the new organizational system. It is the convergence between the two processes that changes the technical relationships of production, giving rise to a new mode of development. The previous section presented in summary form the relatively autonomous evolution of technological innovation which has led to the emergence of the informational technological paradigm. This section will examine, even more succinctly, the main organizational and structural trends that characterize the transition from the industrial to the informational mode of development.

The main process in this transition is not the shift from goods to services but, as the two main theorists of the "post-industrial society"[17] proposed many years ago, Alain Touraine in 1969 and Daniel Bell in 1973, the emergence of information processing as the core, fundamental activity conditioning the effectiveness and productivity of all processes of production, distribution, consumption, and management. The new centrality of information processing results from evolution in all the fundamental spheres of the industrial mode of development, under the influence of economic and social factors and structured largely by the mode of production. Specifically, the secular trend toward the increasing role of information results from a series of developments in the spheres of production, of consumption, and of state intervention.

In the sphere of *production*, two major factors have fostered information-processing activities within the industrial mode of development. The first is the emergence of the large corporation as the predominant organizational form of production and management.[18] An economy based on large-scale production and centralized management generated the growing number of information flows that were needed for efficient articulation of the system. The second resides within the production process itself (considering production in the broad sense, that is including production of both goods and services), and is the shift of the productivity sources from capital and labor to "other factors" (often associated with science, technology, and management), as shown by the series of econometric analyses in the tradition best represented by Robert Solow.[19] The hard core of these information-processing activities is composed of knowledge, which structures and provides adequate meaning to the mass of information required to manage organizations and to increase productivity.

In the sphere of *consumption*, two parallel processes have emphasized the role of information. On the one hand, the constitution of mass markets, and the increasing distance between buyers and sellers, have created the need for specific marketing and effective distribution by firms, thus triggering a flurry of information-gathering systems and information-distributing flows, to establish the connection between the two ends of the market.[20] On the other hand, under the pressure of new social demands, often expressed in social movements, a growing share of the consumption process has been taken over by collective consumption, that is, goods and services directly or indirectly produced and/or managed by the state,[21] as a right rather than as a commodity, giving rise to the welfare state. The formation of the welfare state has produced a gigantic system of information flows affecting most people and most activities, spurring the growth of bureaucracies, the formation of service delivery agencies, and consequently the creation of millions of jobs in information handling.[22]

In the sphere of *state intervention*, the past half-century has seen a huge expansion of government regulation of economic and social activities that has generated a whole new administration, entirely made up of information flows and information-based decision processes.[23] Although variations in the mode of production lead to a bureaucratic cycle, with upswings and downturns in the trend toward regulation, state intervention is in more subtle ways a structural feature of the new mode of development, in a process that Alain Touraine has characterized as "la société programmée."[24] This is the process by which the state sets up a framework within which large-scale organizations, both private and public, define strategic goals, which may be geared toward international economic competitiveness or military supremacy, that permeate the entire realm of social activities without necessarily institutionalizing or formalizing the strategic guidance of these activities. To be able to steer a complex society without suffocating it, the modern state relies on a system of "neo-corporatist" pacts, in Philippe Schmitter's terms,[25] which mobilize and control society through a system of incentives and disincentives made up of storage of information, emission of signals, and management of instructions. The state of the informational mode of development, be it under capitalism or under statism, exercises more intervention than ever, but it does so by controlling and manipulating the network of information flows that penetrate all activities. It does not follow that society is doomed to the Orwellian vision, since the intervention of the state will be informed by the political values emerging from the dynamics of the civil society, and thus its enhanced power could be used to counteract the built-in bureaucratic tendencies of state apparatuses.[26] As Nicos Poulantzas wrote ten years ago: "This statism does not refer to the univocal reinforcement of the State, but it is rather the effect of one tendency, whose two poles develop unevenly, toward the simultaneous reinforcing–weakening of the State."[27] The attempt by the state to override the contradiction between its increasing role and its decreasing legitimacy by diffusing its power through immaterial information flows greatly contributes to the dramatic explosion of information-processing activities and organizations. This is because the state sets up a series of information systems that control activities and citizens' lives through the codes and rules determined by those systems.

These structural trends, emerging and converging in a society largely dominated by the industrial mode of development, pave the way for the transformation of that mode, as information processing, with its core in knowledge generation, detracts from the importance of energy in material production, as well as from the importance of goods-producing in the overall social fabric. However, this transformation of the mode of development could not be accomplished without the surge of innovation in information technologies which, by creating the material basis from which information processing can expand its role, contributes to the change both in the structure of the production process and in the organization of society. It is in this sense that I hypothesize the formation of a new, informational mode of development: on the basis of the convergence through interaction of information technologies and information-processing activities into an articulated techno-organizational system.

The Interaction between Technological Innovation and Organizational Change in the Constitution of the Informational Mode of Development

The convergence between the revolution in information technology and the predominant role of information-processing activities in production, consumption, and state regulation leads to the rise of the new, informational mode of development. This process triggers a series of new structural contradictions which highlight the relative autonomy of technological change in the process of social transformation. In fact, the diffusion of new technologies under the new mode of development calls into question the very processes and organizational forms that were at the basis of the demand for information technologies. This is because these organizational forms were born within the industrial mode of development, under the influence of the capitalist mode of production, and generally reflect the old state of technology. As the new technologies, and the realm of the possibilities they offer, expand, those same organizational forms that were responsible for the demand for new technologies are being rendered obsolete by their development. For instance, the large corporation was critical in fostering the demand for computers. But as microcomputers increase in power and become able to constitute information systems in harness with advanced telecommunications, it is no longer the large, vertical conglomerate but the network which is the most flexible, efficient form of management.

In another crucial development, the old form of the welfare state loses relevance. Previously, its operation had called for the expansion of information-processing activities: but as information itself becomes a productive force, so the social characteristics of labor reproduction (and thus of collective consumption: education, health, housing, etc.) become key elements in the development of productive forces, embodied in the cultural capacity of labor to process information. Thus, the old, redistributive welfare state becomes obsolete, not so much because it is too expensive (this is the capitalist critique, not the informational challenge), as because it has to be restructured to connect its redistributional goals with its new role as a source of productivity by means of the investment in human capital.

A third manifestation of the process of institutional change set in motion by the new technologies concerns the role of the state. The expansion of state regulatory intervention underlay the explosion of government-led information activities, enhancing its dominant role, within the limits of its legitimacy. However, rapid innovation in information technologies has created the facility for two-way information flows, making it possible for civil society to control the state on democratic principles, without paralyzing its effectiveness as a public interest agency. In this situation, the persistence of bureaucratic aloofness, once deprived of its former technical justification, emphasizes authoritarian tendencies within the state, delegitimizes its power, and prompts calls for institutional reform toward more flexible and more responsive government agencies.

The organizational transformation of the mode of development, then, leads to the expansion of information technologies, whose effect triggers pressure for further organizational change. The informational mode of development is not a rigid structure, but a constant process of change based on the interaction between technology and organization. Yet the logic of this process of change does not depend primarily on the interaction between these two planes, for modes of development are conditioned in their historical evolution by the dynamics of specific societies, themselves largely conditioned by the contradictions and transformations of the modes of production that characterize them. More specifically, the evolution of the informational mode of development, with its changing interaction between technology and organizational structures, depends, in our societies, on the restructuring of the capitalist mode of production that has taken place in the past decade. The transition between modes of development is not independent of the historical context in which it takes place; it relies heavily on the social matrix initially framing the transition, as well as on the social conflicts and interests that shape the transformation of that matrix. Therefore, the newly emerging forms of the informational mode of development, including its spatial forms, will not be determined by the structural requirements of new technologies seeking to fulfil their developmental potential, but will emerge from the interaction between its technological and organizational components, and the historically determined process of the restructuring capitalism.

The Restructuring of Capitalism in the 1980s

When social systems experience a structural crisis, as a result of historical events acting on their specific contradictions, they are compelled either to change their goals, or to change their means in order to overcome the crisis. When the system changes its goals (or structural principles of performance), actually becoming a different system, there is a process of social transformation. When the system changes the institutionalized means by which it aims to achieve its systemic goals, there is a process of social restructuring. Each restructuring process leads to a new manifestation of the system, with specific institutional rules which induce historically specific sets of contradictions and conflicts, developing into new crises that potentially trigger new restructuring processes. This sequence goes on until the social equation underlying both structures and processes makes possible historical change to replace the old system by a new one.

The transformation of the capitalist mode of production on a global scale follows, in general terms, this social logic. The Great Depression of the 1930s, followed by the dislocation of World War II, triggered a restructuring process that led to the emergence of a new form of capitalism very different from the *laissez-faire* model of the pre-Depression era.[28] This new capitalist model, often characterized by the misleading term "Keynesianism,"[29] relied on three major structural modifications:[30]

1   A social pact between capital and labor which, in exchange for the stability of capitalist social relationships of production and the adaptation of the labor process to the requirements of productivity, recognized the rights of organized labor, assured steadily rising wages for the unionized labor force, and extended the realm of entitlements to social benefits, creating an ever-expanding welfare state.

2   Regulation and intervention by the state in the economic sphere: key initiatives in the accumulation process, stimulation of demand through public expenditures, and absorption of surplus labor by increasing public employment.

3   Control of the international economic order by intervention in the sphere of circulation via a set of new international institutions, organized around the International Monetary Fund and under the hegemony of the United States, with the imposition of the dollar (and to some extent the pound) as the standard international currency. The ordering of world economic processes included the control by the center of the supply and prices of key raw materials and energy sources, most of these being produced by a still largely colonized Third World.

This state-regulated capitalism assured unprecedented economic growth, gains in productivity, and prosperity in the core countries for about a quarter of a century. In retrospect, history will probably consider these years as the golden age of western capitalism.

As I have shown elsewhere,[31] these same structural elements that accounted for the dynamism of this model were the very factors that led to its crisis in the 1970s, under the stress of its contradictions, expressed through rampant inflation that disrupted the circulation process, and under the pressure of social movements and labor struggles whose successful social and wage demands lowered the rate of profit. The oil shocks of 1974 and 1979 were precipitant events which, acting on structurally determined inflation, drove the circulation of capital out of control, prompting the need for austerity policies and fiscal restraint, and thus undermining the economic basis for state intervention. Although in strictly economic terms the increase in oil prices was not the cause of the structural crisis, its impact was crucial in calling into question the post-World War II model of capitalism, because of the pervasive effects of energy cost and supply in an economic system relying on an industrial mode of development based upon energy.

The crisis of the system in the 1970s revealed the declining effectiveness of the mechanisms established in the 1930s and 1940s in ensuring the fulfillment of the basic goals of the capitalist economy.[32] Labor was steadily increasing its share of the product. Social movements outside the workplace were imposing growing constraints on the ability of capital and bureaucracies to organize production and society free from social control. The state entered a fiscal crisis brought on by the contradiction between growing expenditures (determined by social demands) and comparatively decreasing revenues (limited by the need to preserve corporate profits).[33] The international order was disrupted by the surge of Third World nationalism (simultaneously opposed, supported, and manipulated by the strategies of the superpowers), and by the entry into the international economy of new competitive actors. The structural difficulty of making hard choices led companies to pass costs on into prices, the state to finance its intervention through debt and money supply, and the international economy to prosper through financial speculation and irresponsible lending in the global markets. After a series of unsuccessful stop-and-go policies, the second oil shock of 1979 revealed the depth of the crisis and necessitated a restructuring process that was undertaken simultaneously by both governments and firms, while international institutions such as the IMF imposed the new economic discipline throughout the world economy.

A new model of socio-economic organization had to be established which would be able to achieve the basic aims of a capitalist system, namely: to enhance the rate of profit for private capital, the engine of investment, and thus of growth; to find new markets, both through deepening the existing ones and by incorporating new regions of the world into an integrated capitalist economy; to control the circulation process, curbing structural inflation; and to assure the social reproduction and the economic regulation of the system through mechanisms that would not contradict those established to achieve the preceding goals of higher profit rates, expanding demand, and inflation control.

On the basis of these premises, a new model of capitalism emerged which, with national variations and diverse fortunes, actually characterizes most of the international system in the late 1980s. Reducing the new model to its essentials, we can summarize it in three major features which simultaneously address the four goals stated above as the fundamental requirements for the restructuring of capitalism to operate successfully.

(1) *The appropriation by capital of a significantly higher share of surplus from the production process.* This is a reversal of the historical power relationship between capital and labor, and

a negation of the social pact achieved in the 1930s and 1940s. This fundamental goal is achieved by combining increases in productivity and increases in exploitation, by means of a fundamental restructuring of the work process and of the labor market which includes the following aspects:

(a) Higher productivity derived from technological innovation, combined with the uneven distribution of the productivity gains in favor of capital.

(b) Lower wages, reduced social benefits, and less protective working conditions.

(c) Decentralization of production to regions or countries characterized by lower wages and more relaxed regulation of business activities.

(d) Dramatic expansion of the informal economy, at both the core and the periphery of the system. By the informal economy is meant income-generating activities that are unregulated by the institutional system, in a context where similar activities are regulated. Much of the development of the informal economy has to do with the dismantling in practice of many provisions of the welfare state, for example, avoiding payment of social benefits and contravening the legislation protecting workers.[34]

(e) A restructuring of labor markets to take in growing proportions of women, ethnic minorities, and immigrants, namely, those social groups which, because of institutionalized discrimination and social stigma, are most vulnerable in society and thus in the marketplace.[35] However, it is important to observe that such vulnerability is socially determined. Should the social context change, this supposedly docile labor would not be incorporated into the new labor markets. For example, while immigration has boomed during the restructuring process in the US, it has been practically halted in western Europe. Although part of the difference has to lie in the ability of the US to create millions of new unskilled jobs, a substantial factor is the unionization and rising consciousness of immigrant workers in Europe during the 1970s, to the point where, in countries such as Switzerland and Germany, they have become the militant vanguard among factory wokers.[36] It makes little sense for European management to continue to import labor which, despite its social vulnerability, could turn into a focus for militancy while not being responsive to the same mechanisms of integration that are operative with respect to native workers.

(f) The weakening of trade unions – a fundamental, explicit goal of the restructuring process in most countries, and in fact, probably the most important single factor in achieving the overall objective of restoring the rate of profit at a level acceptable for business. By and large this objective has been achieved. Organized labor in most capitalist countries, with the exception of Scandinavia, is at the lowest point of its power and influence in the past thirty years, and its situation is still deteriorating rapidly. Some of the reasons for this decline are structural: for example, the fading away of traditional manufacturing, where the strength of the unions was concentrated, and the parallel expansion of a weakly unionized service economy. Other factors have to do directly with the transformation of labor markets, as noted under (e) above: women, often because of the sexism of the labor unions, are less unionized; many immigrants do not feel that the unions represent them; the informal economy detracts from the social-izing effects of the workplace. However, organized labor has also been weak-ened as a result of targeted policies by both governments and firms, engaging in a deliberate effort at achieving what is perceived as a historical objective that would dramatically increase the freedom of capital to steer the economy and society.[37] Thus, Reagan's tough handling of the 1981 air traffic controllers' strike in the US, ending up with the de-registration of their union (PATCO), and the placement of the names of all the strikers in a blacklist to ban them from future Federal government employment, sent out a powerful signal that was well heard by business. Similarly, Thatcher's merciless repression of the coal miners' strike in the UK ushered in a new era of management–labor relations that put the British Trades Union Congress on the defensive. The historical reversal of the capital-labor power relationship, encapsulated in the gradual decline of the trade union movement, is the cornerstone of the restructuring of capitalism in the 1980s.

(2)   *A substantial change in the pattern of state intervention, with the emphasis shifted from political legitimation and social redistribution to political domination and capital accumulation.*[38] Although in the "Keynesian" model regulation of capitalist growth was also a key objective, the means by which such regulation was exercised included widespread expansion of the welfare state, as well as both direct and indirect creation of public sector jobs, stimulating demand and contributing to the reproduction of labor power. The new forms of state inter-vention are much more directly focused on capital accumulation, and give priority to domination over legitimation in the relationship between state and society, in response to the emergency situation in which the system found itself in the 1970s. However, in contra-diction of the ideological self-representation of the restructuring process by its main pro-tagonists, what we are witnessing is not the withdrawal of the state from the economic scene, but the emergence of a new form of intervention, whereby new means and new areas are penetrated by the state, while others are deregulated and transferred to the market. This simultaneous engagement and disengagement of the state in the economy and society is evident in several mechanisms that express the new form of state support of capitalism:

(a)   Deregulation of many activities, including relaxation of social and environmen-tal controls in the work process.
(b)   Shrinkage of, and privatization of productive activities in, the public sector.
(c)   Regressive tax reform, favoring corporations and upper-income groups.
(d)   State support for high-technology R&D and leading industrial sectors which form the basis of the new informational economy. This support usually takes the dual form of financing infrastructure and research, and favorable fiscal policies.
(e)   Accordance of priority status to defense and to defense-related industries, com-bining, in pursuit of the objectives of the new state, the reinforcement of mili-tary power and the stimulation of a high-technology dominated defense sector.

Following an old formula of Herbert Marcuse, I will call this trend the rise of the "warfare state." Defense spending and the development of new defense industries is also a fundamental way of creating new markets to compensate for retrenchment in other public-sector expenditures, as well as for the loss of demand resulting from the lowering of wages in the production process.

(f) Shrinkage of the welfare state, with variations within and between countries according to the relative power of affected groups.

(g) Fiscal austerity, with the goal of a balanced budget, and tight monetary policy. These are key policies for the new model of capitalism, as the fundamental means of controlling inflation. However, while fiscal conservatism is an integral component of the new capitalism, recent historical experience shows the possibility of huge budget deficits resulting from the contradictions consequent on the implementation of the model in given country, in particular in the US.

(3) *The third major mechanism of the restructuring of capitalism is the accelerated internationalization of all economic processes, to increase profitability and to open up markets through the expansion of the system.* The capitalist economy has been, since its beginnings, a world economy, as Braudel and Wallerstein have reminded us.[39] However, what is new is the increasing interpenetration of all economic processes at the international level with the system working as a unit, worldwide in real time. This is a process that has grown steadily since the 1950s and has accelerated rapidly in the 1970s and 1980s as an essential element of the restructuring process. It embraces capital movements, labor migration, the process of production itself, the interpenetration of markets, and the use of nation states as elements of support in an international competition that will ultimately determine the economic fate of all nations.

The internationalization of capitalism enhances profitability at several levels:

(a) It allows capital to take advantage of the most favourable conditions for investment and production anywhere in the world. Sometimes this translates into low wages and lack of government regulation. In other instances, penetration of key markets or access to technology are more important considerations for the firm. But the fact remains that the increasing homogenization of the economic structure across nations allows for a variable geometry of production and distribution that maximizes advantages in terms of opportunity costs.

(b) By allowing round-the-clock capital investment opportunities worldwide, internationalization dramatically increases the rate of turnover of capital, thus enhancing profit levels for a given profit rate, although at the cost of increasing instability built into the system.

(c) The internationalization process also opens up new markets, and connects segments of markets across borders, increasingly differentiating societies vertically while homogenizing markets horizontally. This expansion of demand through new markets is absolutely crucial in a model that relies on the reduction of wages in the core countries, since the loss in potential demand has to be made up by the incorporation of whichever new markets may exist anywhere in the world.

This is particularly important in the transitional period of restructuring, when wages have to be kept at the lowest possible level to increase profits and attract investment, while keeping demand high enough to justify new investment.

The process of internationalization offers dynamic expansion possibilities that could substantially benefit the capitalist system. But it can also pose fundamental problems to individual units of that system, be they firms or countries, which are faced with new, tougher competition from the new actors which are incorporated into the system and quickly learn the ruthlessness of the game. This has been the case for the US which has lost market share, in both its domestic market and the international economy, to Japan and the newly industrialized countries. Given the interdependence of economic processes and national policies, the internationalization process prepares the ground for future major crises: on the one hand, any significant downturn has immediate repercussions worldwide, and is thus amplified; on the other hand, competition constantly provokes the threat of protectionism which could wreck the very basis of the system. A system in which the interests of the totality are not necessarily the interests of each competitive unit in every moment in time could become increasingly disruptive. When the "creative destruction" process[40] takes place at the international level, the intermixing of national interests with competitive strategies becomes explosive.

The overpowering of labor by capital, the shift of the state toward the domination–accumulation functions of its intervention in economy and society, and the internationalization of the capitalist system to form a worldwide interdependent unit working in real time are the three fundamental dimensions of the restructuring process that has given birth to a new model of capitalism, as distinct from the "Keynesian" model of the 1945–75 era as that one was from *"laissez-faire"* capitalism.[41]

These three processes are present in most countries' recent economic policies, but their relative importance may vary considerably according to each country's history, institutions, social dynamics, and place in the world economy. Thus, the UK has emphasized the over-powering of labor as the rallying cry of the Thatcher government; the US has made the emergence of a new "warfare state," based upon high-technology development, the center-piece of its economic recovery; Japan has saved itself much of the pain of the restructuring process by riding the crest of the internationalization wave. However, since the capitalist system is a world system at the level of the mode of production (although certainly not at the level of societies), the different dimensions of the restructuring process are intercon-nected across the various regions of the international economy.

Also, the actual practice of restructuring is full of contradictions. Not only social but economic as well. For instance, in the case of the Reagan administration in the US the dra-matic defense build up, combined with a regressive tax reform and the political inability to dismantle social security, led to the biggest budget deficit in American history, under one of the most ideologically committed administrations to fiscal conservatism. The budget deficit was financed to a large extent by foreign capital, attracted by high interest rates, driving up the dollar's exchange rate. Together with declining competitiveness of American manufacturing, this evolution resulted in catastrophic trade deficits that weakened the American economy. The twin mega-deficits have spoiled to a large extent the benefits of restructuring for American capitalism and will, most likely, lead to austerity policies in the

1989–91 period that could trigger a world recession. While our purpose here goes far beyond economic forecasting we want to emphasize that the process of restructuring is by no means exempt of contradictions. While fiscal austerity was a must of the new model, and as such was formulated by its supply-side defenders, it could not actually be implemented because the political support for the boldest extremes of restructuring could not be marshalled. The artificial implementation of the model (on the basis of debt-financed military expenditures, a policy we have labeled "perverted Keynesianism")[42] could lead to its demise or to its sharpening through reinforced austerity policies, ushering in a new crisis.

However, in spite of these contradictory trends, a new model of capitalism has emerged that could outlast the forthcoming crises. One of the reasons for its likely durability, we hypothesize, is that it has encompassed in its expansion the informational mode of development that was bursting into life in a process of historical simultaneity. It is the interaction and the articulation between the informational mode of development and the restructuring of capitalism that creates the framework shaping the dynamics of our society and our space.

The Articulation between the Informational Mode of Development and the Restructuring of Capitalism: Reshaping the Techno-Economic Paradigm

The historical coincidence of the restructuring of capitalism and the rise of the informational mode of development has created a structural convergence resulting in the formation of a specific techno-economic paradigm at the very roots of our social dynamics. Because political and organizational decision-makers are always primarily concerned to perpetuate the interests they represent, and therefore concerned with the process of restructuring, it is under the dominance of that process that the merger has taken place. However, the two components of the paradigm are distinguishable only analytically, because while informationalism has now been decisively shaped by the restructuring process, restructuring could never have been accomplished, even in a contradictory manner, without the unleashing of the technological and organizational potential of informationalism.

Given the complexity of the articulation process, I will differentiate between the two dimensions that compose the informational mode of development: the *technological* and the *organizational*. Both have been fundamental in giving rise to a new form of capitalism which, in turn, has stimulated and supported the technological revolution and has adopted new organizational forms.

New *information technologies* have been decisive in the implementation of the three fundamental processes of capitalist restructuring

(1) *Increasing the rate of profit* by various means:

(a) Enhancing productivity by the introduction of microelectronics-based machines that transform the production process.
(b) Making possible the decentralization of production, and the spatial separation of different units of the firm, while reintegrating production and management

at the level of the firm by using telecommunications and flexible manufacturing systems.

(c)   Enabling management to automate those processes employing labor with a sufficiently high cost level and a sufficiently low skill level to make automation both profitable and feasible. These jobs happened to be those concentrated in the large-scale factories that had become the strongholds of labor unions, and better remunerated labor, during the industrial era.

(d)   Positioning capital in a powerful position *vis-à-vis* labor. Automation, flexible manufacturing, and new transportation technologies provide management with a variety of options that considerably weaken the bargaining position of the unions. Should the unions insist on preserving or improving their levels of wages and benefits, the company can automate or move elsewhere, or both, without losing its connections with the market or with the network of production. Thus, either by using automation to substitute for labor, or by extracting concessions by wielding the threat to automate or relocate, capital uses new technologies to free itself from the constraints of organized labor.

(2)   New technologies are also a powerful instrument in weighting the accumulation and domination functions of state intervention. This occurs on two main levels:

(a)   On the one hand, rapid technological change makes obsolete the entire existing weapons system, creating the basis for the expansion of the "warfare state" in a political environment characterized by states striving for military supremacy and therefore engaging in a technological arms race that can only be supported by the resources of the state.

(b)   On the other hand, the strategic role played by high technology in economic development draws the state to concentrate on providing the required infrastructure, downplaying its role in redistributional policies.

(3)   The process of *internationalization of the economy* could never take place without the dramatic breakthroughs in information technologies. Advances in telecommunications, flexible manufacturing that allows simultaneously for standardization and customization, and new transportation technologies emerging from the use of computers and new materials, have created the material infrastructure for the world economy, as the construction of the railway system provided the basis for the formation of national markets in the nineteenth century. In addition, the economic effects of new technologies are also crucial in the formation of an international economy. Their effects on process condition the international competitiveness of countries and firms. Their effects on new products create new markets in which the harshest competitive battles are fought, with new economic actors trying to short-circuit the sequence of development by leapfrogging into state-of-the-art high-technology markets through dramatic efforts of national development. The new technological division of labor is one of the fundamental lines of cleavage in the emerging international economic order.

The *organizational* components of the informational mode of development are also fundamental features in the restructuring process. Three major organizational characteristics of informationalism may be distinguished, each one of them affecting the three dimensions of the restructuring process.

(1)   There is a growing *concentration of knowledge-generation and decision-making processes in high-level organizations* in which both information and the capacity of processing it are concentrated. The informational world is made up of a very hierarchical functional structure in which increasingly secluded centers take to its extreme the historical division between intellectual and manual labor. Given the strategic role of knowledge and information control in productivity and profitability, these core centers of corporate organizations are the only truly indispensable components of the system, with most other work, and thus most other workers, being potential candidates for automation from the strictly functional point of view. How far this tendency toward widespread automation is actually taken in practice is a different matter, depending on the dynamics of labor markets and social organization.

This concentration of information power in selected segments of the corporate structure greatly favors the chances of the restructuring process in the three dimensions presented:

(a)   Productive labor can be reduced to its essential component, thus downgrading the objective bargaining power of the large mass of functionally dispensable labor.

(b)   The rise of the technocracy within the state displaces the traditional integrative functions of the politically determined bureaucracy, establishing a tight linkage between the high levels of the state and the corporate world through the intermediary of the scientific establishment. The rise of the meritocracy, using the notion advanced by Daniel Bell, establishes new principles of legitimacy in the state, further removing it from the political controls and constituencies represented by the diversity of social interests.

(c)   As technology transfer becomes the key to competition in the international economy, that process is controlled by knowledge holders in the centers of the dominant scientific and corporate organizations. It follows that the effective accomplishment of the internationalization process requires access to these knowledge centers, ruling out the adoption of an isolationist stance, which would only lead to the technological obsolescence of those economies and firms holding it.

(2)   The second major organizational characteristic of informationalism concerns the *flexibility* of the system and of the relationships among its units, since flexibility is both a requirement of and a possibility offered by new information technologies.[43] Flexibility acts powerfully as a facilitator of the restructuring process in the following ways:

(a)   It changes capital–labor relationships, transforming a potentially permanent and protected worker status into a flexible arrangement generally adapted to the momentary convenience of management. Thus, temporary workers, part-time jobs, homework, flexitime schedules, indefinite positions in the corporate structure, changing assignments, varying wages and benefits according to performance, etc., are all creative expedients of management that, while they increase tremendously the flexibility and thus the productivity of the firm, undermine the collective status of labor *vis-à-vis* capital.

(b)   In the restructuring of the state, organizational flexibility contributes to the formation of public–private partnerships and to the blurring of the distinction between the public and private spheres. Segments of the welfare state are being shifted to the private sector, corporations are being brought into the formulation of public polities, and a selective interpenetration of state and capital is diminishing the autonomy of the state, along the lines of the "recapitalization" of the state, characteristic of the restructuring process.[44]

(c)   Flexibility is also a necessary condition for the formation of the new world economy, since it is the only organizational form that allows constant adaptation of firms to the changing conditions of the world market.[45]

(3)   A third fundamental organizational characteristic of informationalism is the shift from *centralized* large corporations to *decentralized* networks made up of a plurality of sizes and forms of organizational units.[46]

[. . .]

NOTES

1   For a summary, informed presentation of the rise and implications of information technology, see, for instance, Tom Forester, *High Tech Society. The Story of the Information Technology Revolution* (Oxford: Blackwell, 1987); also Bruce R. Guile (ed.), *Information Technologies and Social Transformation* (Washington, DC: National Academy Press, 1985).

2   See E. Braun and S. MacDonald, *Revolution in Miniature* (Cambridge: Cambridge University Press, 1982).

3   See Edward J. Sylvester and Lynn C. Klotz, *The Gene Age: Genetic Engineering and the Next Industrial Revolution* (New York: Scribner, 1983).

4   See John S. Mayo, "The evolution of information technologies," in Guile (ed.), *Information Technologies*, pp. 7–33.

5   Nathan Rosenberg, "The impact of historical innovation: a historical view," in Ralph Landau and Nathan Rosenberg (eds), *The Positive Sum Strategy: Harnessing Technology for Economic Growth* (Washington, DC: National Academy Press, 1986).

6   See Melvin Kranzberg, "The information age: evolution or revolution," in Guile (ed.), *Information Technologies*, pp. 35–55.

7   See Melvin Kranzberg and Carroll W. Pursell, Jr. (eds), *Technology in Western Civilization*, 2 vols (New York: Oxford University Press, 1967).

8   I. Mackintosh, *Sunrise Europe: The Dynamics of Information Technology* (Oxford: Blackwell, 1986).

9   Nathan Rosenberg, *Perspectives in Technology* (Cambridge: Cambridge University Press, 1976).

10   See Eugene S. Ferguson, "The steam engine before 1830;" John R. Brae, "Energy conversion;" and Harold J. Sharlin, "Applications of electricity;" in Kranzberg and Pursell (eds), *Technology in Western Civilization*.

11   For the notion of "technical paradigm" see the analysis in Carlota Perez, "Structural change and the assimilation of new technologies in the economic and social systems," *Futures*, 15 (1983), pp. 357–75.

12 Marx developed his most far-reaching analysis of the social implications of technology in the *Grundrisse*.

13 See Robert Boyer and Benjamin Coriat, "Technical flexibility and macro stabilisation," paper presented at the Venice Conference on Innovation Diffusion, 17–21 March 1986 (Paris: CEPREMAP, 1986).

14 For an analysis of "Fordism," see Robert Boyer, *Technical Change and the Theory of Regulation* (Paris: CEPREMAP, 1987).

15 Michael Piore and Charles Sabel, *The Second Industrial Divide* (New York: Basic Books, 1984).

16 See the fundamental work on the whole series of issues discussed in this chapter, Peter Hall and Paschal Preston, *The Carrier Wave: New Information Technology and the Geography of Innovation, 1846–2003* (London: Unwin Hyman, 1988).

17 For a discussion of post-industrialism, see Manuel Castells, The *Economic Crisis and American Society* (Oxford: Blackwell, 1980), pp. 164–78.

18 Alfred D. Chandler, *The Visible Hand* (Cambridge: Cambridge University Press, 1977).

19 Robert Solow, "Technical changes and the aggregate production function," *Review of Economics and Statistics*, August 1957. For a summary of the debate on the sources of productivity, see Richard R. Nelson, "Research on productivity growth and productivity differences: dead ends and new departures," *Journal of Economic Literature*, 19 (September 1981), pp. 1029–64.

20 I have relied for this analysis on Nicole Woolsey-Biggart, *Charismatic Capitalism* (Chicago, IL: University of Chicago Press, 1990).

21 Manuel Castells, "Collective consumption and urban contradictions in advanced capitalism," in Leo Lindberg et al. (eds), *Stress and Contradiction in Modern Capitalism* (Lexington, MA: Health, 1974).

22 Morris Janowitz, *Social Control of the Welfare State* (Chicago, IL: University of Chicago Press, 1976).

23 Michel Aglietta, *Une théorie de la regulation économique: le cas des Etats-Unis* (Paris: Calmann-Levy, 1976).

24 Alain Touraine, *La voix et le regard* (Paris: Seuil, 1978).

25 Philippe Schmitter, *Interest Conflict and Political Change in Brazil* (Stanford: Stanford University Press, 1981).

26 Gordon Clark and Michael Dear, *State Apparatus* (Boston: Allen and Unwin, 1984).

27 Nicos Poulantzas, *L'etat, le pouvoir, le socialisme* (Paris: Presses University de France, 1978), p. 226 (my translation).

28 See James O'Connor, *Accumulation Crisis* (Oxford: Blackwell, 1984).

29 Post-Depression capitalism did not actually follow the policies proposed by Keynes: the state acted on supply as much as on demand. It would be more appropriate to refer to this form of capitalism as state-regulated capitalism.

30 See Michel Aglietta, *Regulation et crises du capitalisme* (Paris: Calmann-Levy, 1976).

31 For an analysis of the causes of the economic crisis of the 1970s and of the potential way out of it through the restructuring process, see Castells, *Economic Crisis and American Society*.

32 Samuel Bowles et al., *Beyond the Wasteland* (New York: Doubleday, 1983).

33 See James O'Connor's classic, *The Fiscal Crisis of the State* (New York: St Martin's Press, 1973).

34 See Manuel Castells and Alejandro Portes, "World underneath: the origins, dynamics, and consequences of the informal economy," in Alejandro Portes, Manuel Castells, and Lauren Benton (eds), *The Informal Economy* (Baltimore, MD: The Johns Hopkins University Press, 1989).

35 Michael Reich, *Discrimination in Labor Markets* (Princeton, NJ: Princeton University Press, 1982).

36 Manuel Castells, "Immigrant workers and class struggle in Western Europe," *Politics and Society*, 2 (1975).

37   Joel Krieger, *Reagan, Thatcher and the Politics of Decline* (New York: Oxford University Press, 1986).

38   I rely here on an analysis of the state, adapted from Nicos Poulantzas's work, that sees the state's relatively autonomous actions taking place within a dialectical process of ensuring domination and accumulation on the one hand, while trying to maintain legitimation and redistribution on the other. For an attempt at using these concepts in empirical research, see Manuel Castells and Francis Godard, *Monopolville* (Paris: Mouton, 1974).

39   Fernand Braudel, *Capitalisme et civilisation materielle* (Paris: Armand Colin, 1979); Immanuel Wallerstein, *The Modern World System* (New York: Academic Press, 1974).

40   By the "creative destruction" of capitalism I refer, of course, to the notion proposed by Schumpeter in his *Business Cycles: A Theoretical, Historical, and Statistical Analysis of the Capitalist Process* (Mansfield Centre, CT: Martino, 2006 [1939]).

41   Robert Boyer (ed.), *Capitalismes fin de siècle* (Paris: Presses Universitaires de France, 1986).

42   See our analysis of "Reaganomics" in Martin Carnoy and Manuel Castells, "After the crisis?," *World Policy Journal*, May 1984.

43   On the role of flexibility, see Boyer and Coriat, "Technical flexibility."

44   The notion of the "recapitalization" of the state has been proposed by S.M. Miller.

45   For an analysis of flexibility in enhancing competitiveness in the international economy, see Manuel Castells et al., *The Shek Kip Mei Syndrome: Economic Development and Public Housing in Hong Kong and Singapore* (London: Pion, 1990).

46   On the analysis of networks, see Piore and Sabel, *The Second Industrial Divide* and Woolsey-Biggart, "The economic history of direct selling" in *Charismatic Capitalism*, pp. 20–47.

12 Cities in a World Economy (2000)

Saskia Sassen

Place and Production in the Global Economy

At the end of the 20th century, massive developments in telecommunications and the ascendance of information industries led analysts and politicians to proclaim the end of cities. Cities, they told us, would become obsolete as economic entities. With large-scale relocations of offices and factories to less congested and lower-cost areas than central cities, computerized workplaces can be located anywhere: in a clerical "factory" in the Bahamas or in a home in the suburbs. The growth of information industries means that more and more outputs can be transmitted around the globe instantaneously. And the globalization of economic activity suggests that place – particularly the type of place represented by cities – no longer matters.

But this is a partial account. These trends are indeed all taking place, yet they represent only half of what is happening. Alongside the well-documented spatial dispersal of economic activities, we are seeing the growth of new forms of territorial centralization in top-level management and control operations. National and global markets, as well as globally integrated operations, require central places where the work of running global systems gets done. Furthermore, information industries require a vast physical infrastructure containing strategic nodes with a hyper-concentration of facilities. Finally, even the most advanced information industries have a production process that is partly place-bound.

Once these processes are brought into the analysis, funny things happen; secretaries become part of it, and so do the cleaners of the buildings where professionals work. An economic configuration very different from that suggested by the concept of **information economy** emerges. We recover the material conditions, production sites, and place-boundedness that are also part of globalization and the information economy. A detailed examination of the activities, firms, markets, and physical infrastructure involved in globalization, and concentrated in cities, allows us to see the actual role played by cities in a global economy. Thus, when telecommunications were introduced on a large scale in all advanced industries in the 1980s, we saw the central business districts of the leading cities and international business centers of the world – New York, Los Angeles, London, Tokyo,

Paris, Frankfurt, São Paulo, Hong Kong, and Sydney, among others – reach their highest density of firms ever. This explosion in the numbers of firms located in the downtown areas of major cities in the 1980s and 1990s goes against what should have been expected according to models emphasizing territorial dispersal; this is especially true when one considers the high cost of locating in a major downtown area.

If telecommunications have not made cities obsolete, have they at least altered the economic function of cities in a global economy? And if this is so, what does it tell us about the importance of place and locale in an era dominated by the imagery and language of economic globalization and information flows? Is there a new and strategic role for major cities, a role linked to the formation of a truly global economic system, a role not sufficiently recognized by analysts and policymakers? And could it be that the reason this new and strategic role has not been sufficiently recognized is that economic globalization – what it actually takes to implement global markets and processes – is misunderstood?

The notion of a global economy has become deeply entrenched in political and media circles all around the world. Yet its dominant images – the instantaneous transmission of money around the globe, the information economy, the neutralization of distance through **telematics** – are partial, and hence profoundly inadequate, representations of what globalization and the rise of information economies actually entail for the concrete life of cities. Missing from this abstract model are the actual material processes, activities, and infrastructures crucial to the implementation of globalization. Overlooking the spatial dimension of economic globalization and overemphasizing the information dimensions both have served to distort the role played by major cities in the current phase of economic globalization.

The last 20 years have seen pronounced changes in the geography, composition, and institutional framework of economic globalization. Although a world economy has been in existence for several centuries, it has been repeatedly reconstituted over time. A key starting point for this book is the fact that in each historical period, the world economy has consisted of a distinct configuration of geographic areas, industries, and institutional arrangements. One of the most important changes over the last 20 years has been the increase in mobility of capital at both the national and especially the transnational levels. This transnational mobility of capital has brought about specific forms of articulation among different geographic areas and transformations in the role played by these areas in the world economy. This trend in turn has produced several types of locations for international transactions, the most familiar of which are **export processing zones** and **offshore banking centers**. One question for us, then, is the extent to which major cities are yet another type of *location* for international transactions in our world economy, although clearly one at a very high level of complexity.

Increased capital mobility not only brings about changes in the geographic organization of manufacturing production and in the network of financial markets, but it also generates a demand for types of production needed to ensure the management, control, and servicing of this new organization of manufacturing and finance. These new types of production range from the development of telecommunications to specialized services that are key inputs for the management of a global network of factories, offices, and financial markets. The mobility of capital also includes the production of a broad array of innovations in these sectors. These types of production have their own locational patterns; they tend toward high levels of agglomeration. We will want to ask whether a focus on the *production* of these service inputs illuminates the question of place in processes of economic globalization, particularly the kind of place represented by cities.

Specialized services for firms and financial transactions, as well as the complex markets connected to these regions of the economy, are a layer of activity that has been central to the organization of major global processes beginning in the 1980s. To what extent is it useful to think in terms of the broader category of cities as key locations for such activities – in addition to the more narrowly defined locations represented by headquarters of transnational corporations or offshore banking centers – to further our understanding of major aspects of the world economy's organization and management?

Much of the scholarly literature on cities has focused on internal aspects of the urban social, economic, and political systems, and it has considered cities to be part of national urban systems. International aspects typically have been considered the preserve of nation-states, not of cities. The literature on international economic activities, moreover, has traditionally focused on the activities of multinational corporations and banks and has seen the key to globalization in the *power* of multinational firms. Again, this conceptualization has had the effect of leaving no room for a possible role for cities.

Including cities in the analysis adds three important dimensions to the study of economic internationalization. First, it breaks down the nation-state into a variety of components that may be significant in understanding international economic activity. Second, it displaces our focus from the power of large corporations over governments and economies to the range of activities and organizational arrangements necessary for the implementation and maintenance of a global network of factories, service operations, and markets; these are all processes only partly encompassed by the activities of transnational corporations and banks. Third, it contributes to a focus on place and on the urban social and political order associated with these activities of the global network. Processes of economic globalization are thereby reconstituted as concrete production complexes situated in specific places containing a multiplicity of activities and interests, many unconnected to global processes. Focusing on cities allows us to specify a geography of strategic places on a global scale, as well as the microgeographies and politics unfolding within these places.

A central thesis organizing this book is that the last two decades have seen transformations in the composition of the world economy, accompanied by the shift to services and finance, that have renewed the importance of major cities as sites for certain types of activities and functions. In the current phase of the world economy, it is precisely the combination of the global dispersal of economic activities *and* global integration – under conditions of continued concentration of economic ownership and control – that has contributed to a strategic role for certain major cities. These I call **global cities** (Sassen 1991). Some have been centers for world trade and banking for centuries. Yet beyond these long-standing functions, today's global cities are (1) command points in the organization of the world economy; (2) key locations and marketplaces for the leading industries of the current period – finance and specialized services for firms; and (3) major sites of production for these industries, including the production of innovations in these industries. Several cities also fulfill equivalent functions on the smaller geographic scales of both trans- and subnational regions. Furthermore, whether at the global or at the regional level, these cities must inevitably engage each other in fulfilling their functions, as the new forms of growth seen in these cities are a result of these networks of cities. There is no such entity as a single global city.

Alongside these new global and regional hierarchies of cities is a vast territory that has become increasingly peripheral, increasingly excluded from the major processes that fuel economic growth in the new global economy. Many formerly important manufacturing centers and port cities have lost functions and are in decline, not only in the less developed countries but also in the most advanced economies. This is yet another meaning of economic globalization. We can think of these developments as constituting new geographies of centrality that cut across the old divide of poor/rich countries, and of new geographies of marginality that also cut across the poor/rich country divide.

The most powerful of these new geographies of centrality binds together the major international financial and business centers: New York, London, Tokyo, Paris, Frankfurt, Zurich, Amsterdam, Sydney, and Hong Kong, among others. But this geography now also includes cities such as São Paulo, Mexico City, Bombay, Buenos Aires, and Seoul. The intensity of transactions among these cities, particularly through financial markets, flows of services, and investment has increased sharply, and so have the orders of magnitude involved. At the same time, there has been a sharpening inequality in the concentration of strategic resources and activities between each of these cities and others in their respective countries. For instance, Paris now concentrates a larger share of leading economic sectors and wealth in France than it did 20 years ago, whereas Marseilles, once a major economic center, has lost its own share and is suffering severe decline. Some national capitals, for example, have lost central economic functions and power to the new global cities, which have taken over some of the coordination functions, markets, and production processes once concentrated in national capitals or in major regional centers. A case in point, São Paulo has gained immense strength as a business and financial center in Brazil over Rio de Janeiro – once the capital and most important city in the country – and over the once powerful axis represented by Rio and Brasilia, the current capital. This is one of the meanings, or consequences, of the formation of a globally integrated economic system.

What is the impact of this type of economic growth on the broader social and economic order of these cities? A vast literature on the impact of a dynamic, high-growth manufacturing sector in highly developed countries shows that it raises wages, reduces economic inequality, and contributes to the formation of a middle class. There is much less literature about the impact on the service economy, especially the rapidly growing specialized services.

Specialized services, which have become a key component of all developed economies, are not usually analyzed in terms of a production or work process. Such services are usually seen as a type of output – that is, high-level technical expertise. Thus, insufficient attention has been paid to the actual array of jobs, from high paying to low paying, involved in the production of these services. A focus on production displaces the emphasis from expertise to work. Services need to be produced, and the buildings that hold the workers need to be built and cleaned. The rapid growth of the financial industry and of highly specialized services generates not only high-level technical and administrative jobs but also low-wage unskilled jobs. Together with the new interurban inequalities mentioned above, we are also seeing new economic inequalities within cities, especially within global cities and their regional counterparts.

The new urban economy is in many ways highly problematic. This is perhaps particularly evident in global cities and their regional counterparts. The new growth sectors of specialized services and finance contain capabilities for profit making vastly superior to those of more traditional economic sectors. The latter are essential to the operation of the urban economy and the daily needs of residents, but their survival is threatened in a situation in which finance and specialized services can earn superprofits. This sharp polarization in the profit-making capabilities of different sectors of the economy has always existed. But what we see happening today takes place on a higher order of magnitude, and it is engendering massive distortions in the operations of various markets, from housing to labor. We can see this effect, for example, in the unusually sharp increase in the beginning salaries of MBAs and lawyers in the corporate sector and in the fall, or stagnation, in the wages of low-skilled manual workers and clerical workers. We can see the same effect in the retreat of many real estate developers from the low- and medium-income housing market who are attracted to the rapidly expanding housing demand by the new highly paid professionals and the possibility for vast overpricing of this housing supply.

The rapid development of an international property market has made this disparity even worse. It means that real estate prices at the center of New York City are more connected to prices in London or Frankfurt than to the overall real estate market in the city. In the 1980s, powerful institutional investors from Japan, for instance, found it profitable to buy and sell property in Manhattan or central London. In the 1990s, this story has multiplied many times. German, Dutch, French, and US investors are buying properties in central London and in major cities around the world. They force prices up because of the competition and raise them even further to sell at a profit. How can a small commercial operation in these cities compete with such investors and the prices they can command?

The high profit-making capability of the new growth sectors rests partly on speculative activity. The extent of this dependence on speculation can be seen in the crisis of the early 1990s that followed the unusually high profits in finance and real estate in the 1980s. That real estate and financial crisis, however, seems to have left the basic dynamic of the sector untouched, and we saw prices and stock market values reach new highs by the mid-1990s – only to have yet another crisis in 1997–98 and, once again, enormous increases as the decade closes. These crises can thus be seen as a temporary adjustment to more reasonable (i.e., less speculative) profit levels. The overall dynamic of polarization in profit levels in the urban economy remains in place, as do the distortions in many markets.

The typical informed view of the global economy, cities, and the new growth sectors does not incorporate these multiple dimensions. Elsewhere, I have argued that we could think of the dominant narrative or mainstream account of economic globalization as a narrative of eviction (Sassen 1996). In the dominant account, the key concepts of globalization, information economy, and telematics all suggest that place no longer matters and that the only type of worker that matters is the highly educated professional. This account favors (1) the capability for global transmission over the concentrations of material infrastructure that make transmission possible; (2) information outputs over the workers producing those outputs, from specialists to secretaries; and (3) the new transnational corporate culture over the multiplicity of cultural environments, including reterritorialized "immigrant" cultures within which many of the "other" jobs of the global information economy take place. In brief, the dominant narrative concerns itself with the upper circuits of capital, not the lower ones.

This narrow focus has the effect of excluding from the account the *place*-boundedness of significant components of the global information economy; it thereby also excludes a whole array of activities and types of workers from the story of globalization that are in their own way as vital to it as international finance and global telecommunications are. Failing to include these activities and workers ignores the variety of cultural contexts within which they exist, a diversity as present in processes of globalization as is the new international corporate culture. When we focus on place and production, we can see that globalization is a process involving not only the corporate economy and the new transnational corporate culture but also, for example, the immigrant economies and work cultures evident in our large cities.

[. . .]

The subject of the city in a world economy is extremely broad. The literature on cities is inevitably vast, but it focuses mostly on single cities. It is also a literature that is mostly domestic in orientation. International studies of cities tend to be comparative. What is lacking is a transnational perspective on the subject: that is to say, one that takes as its starting point a dynamic system or set of transactions that by its nature entails multiple locations involving more than one country. This contrasts with a comparative international approach, which focuses on two or more cities that may have no connections between each other.

[. . .]

The Urban Impact of Economic Globalization

Profound changes in the composition, geography, and institutional framework of the global economy have had major implications for cities. In the 1800s, when the world economy consisted largely of trade, the crucial sites were harbors, plantations, factories, and mines. Cities were already servicing centers at that time: The major cities of the time typically developed alongside harbors, and trading companies depended on multiple industrial, banking, and other commercial services located in cities. Cities, however, were not the key production sites for the leading industries in the 1800s; the production of wealth was centered elsewhere. Today, international trade continues to be an important fact in the global economy, but it has been overshadowed both in value and in power by international financial flows, whether loans and equities or foreign currency transactions. In the 1980s, finance and specialized services emerged as the major components of international transactions. The crucial sites for these transactions are financial markets, advanced corporate service firms, banks, and the headquarters of transnational corporations (TNCs). These sites lie at the heart of the process for the creation of wealth, and they are located in cities.

Thus, one of the factors influencing the role of cities in the new global economy is the change in the composition of international transactions, a factor often not recognized in standard analyses of the world economy. The current composition of international transactions shows this transformation very clearly. For instance, foreign direct investment (FDI) grew three times faster in the 1980s than the growth of the export trade. Furthermore, by the mid-1980s, investment in services had become the main component in FDI flows, whereas before it had been in manufacturing or raw materials extraction. These trends became even sharper in the 1990s. By 1999, the monetary value of international financial flows was vastly larger than the value of international trade and FDI. The sharp growth of international financial flows has raised the level of complexity of transactions. This new circumstance demands a highly advanced infrastructure of specialized services and top-level concentrations of telecommunications facilities. Cities are central locations for both. . . .

The Global Economy Today

Here we emphasize new investment patterns and dominant features of the current period. The purpose is not to present an exhaustive account of all that constitutes the world economy today. It is rather to discuss what distinguishes the current period from the immediate past.

Geography

A key feature of the global economy today is the geography of the new types of international transactions. When international flows consist of raw materials, agricultural products, or mining goods, the geography of transactions is in part determined by the location of natural resources. Historically, this has meant that a large number of countries in Africa, Latin America, and the Caribbean were key sites in this geography. When finance and specialized services became the dominant component of international transactions in the early 1980s, the role of cities was strengthened. At the same time, the sharp concentration in these industries means that now only a limited number of cities play a strategic role.

The fact of a new geography of international transactions becomes evident in FDI flows – that is, investors acquiring a firm, wholly or in part, or building and setting up new firms in a foreign country (see UNCTAD 1993). FDI flows are highly differentiated in their destination and can be constituted through many different processes. During the last two decades, the growth in FDI has been embedded in the internationalization of production of goods and services. The internationalization of production in manufacturing is particularly important in establishing FDI flows into developing countries.

Compared with the 1950s, the 1980s saw a narrowing of the geography of the global economy and a far stronger East–West axis. This is evident in the sharp growth of investment and trade within what is often referred to as the *triad*: the United States, Western Europe, and Japan. FDI flows to developed countries grew at an average annual rate of 24% from 1986 to 1990, reaching a value of US$129.6 billion in 1991, out of a total worldwide FDI inflow of US$159.3 billion. By the mid-1980s, 75% of all FDI stock and 84% of FDI stock in services was in developed countries. There was a sharp concentration even among developed countries in these patterns: The top four recipient countries (United States, United Kingdom, France, and Germany) accounted for half of world inflows in the 1980s; the five major exporters of capital (United States, United Kingdom, Japan, France, and Germany) accounted for 70% of total outflows. In the early 1990s, there were declines in most of these figures due to the financial crisis, but by the late 1990s, levels of investment had grown sharply, reaching US$233.1 billion in developed countries and US$148.9 in developing countries. Overall, worldwide FDI inflows went from US$175.8 billion in 1992 to US$400.5 billion in 1997. Financial concentration is evident in a ranking of the top banks in the world, with only eight countries represented.

Although investment flows in developing countries in the 1990s were lower than in developed countries, they were high in historic terms – a fact that reflects the growing internationalization of economic activity. International investment in developing countries lost share in the 1980s, although it increased in absolute value and regained share by the early 1990s. Since 1985, FDI has been growing at an annual rate of 22%, compared with 3% from 1980 to 1984, and 13% from 1975 to 1979. Yet the share of worldwide flows going to developing countries as a whole fell from 26% to 17% between the early 1980s and the late 1980s, pointing to the strength of flows within the triad (United States, Western Europe, and Japan); it grew in the 1990s, reaching 37.2% by 1997 before the financial crisis of the late 1990s. Most of the flow to developing countries has gone into East, South, and Southeast Asia, where the annual rate of growth rose on the average by over 37% a year in the 1980s and 1990s.

There was a time when Latin America was the single largest recipient region of FDI. Between 1985 and 1989, Latin America's share of total flows to developing countries fell from 49% to 38%, and Southeast Asia's share rose from 37% to 48%. However, the absolute increase in FDI has been so sharp that, notwithstanding a falling share, Latin America has actually experienced increases in the amount of FDI, especially toward the end of the 1980s and in the 1990s (although these increases are mostly concentrated in a few countries). These figures point to the emergence of Southeast Asia as a crucial transnational space for production. The Asian region has surpassed Latin America and the Caribbean for the first time ever as the largest host region for FDI in developing countries.

The other two major components of the global economy are trade and financial flows other than FDI. By its very nature, the geography of trade is less concentrated than that of direct foreign investment. Wherever there are buyers, sellers are likely to go. Finance, on the other hand, is enormously concentrated.

Composition

In the 1950s, the major international flow was world trade, concentrated in raw materials, other primary products, and resource-based manufacturing. In the 1980s, the gap between the growth rate of exports and that of financial flows widened sharply. Although there are severe problems with measurement, the increase in financial and service transactions, especially the former, is so sharp as to leave little doubt. For instance, worldwide outflows of FDI nearly tripled between 1984 and 1987, grew another 20% in 1988, and grew yet another 20% in 1989. By 1990, total worldwide stock of FDI stood at US$1.5 trillion and at US$2 trillion by 1992. After the 1981–82 slump and up to 1990, global FDI grew at an average of 29% a year, a historic high. Furthermore, the shares of the tertiary sector grew consistently over the 1980s and 1990s while that of the primary sector fell. Between 1992 and 1997, worldwide FDI inflows grew by 56%. FDI worldwide outward stock stood at US$3.5 trillion in 1997.

Many factors have fed the growth of FDI: (1) Several developed countries became major capital exporters, most notably Japan; (2) the number of cross-border mergers and acquisitions grew sharply; and (3) the flow of services and transnational service corporations have emerged as major components in the world economy. Services, which accounted for about 24% of worldwide stock in FDI in the early 1970s, had grown to 50% of stock and 60% of annual flows by the end of the 1980s. The single largest recipient of FDI in services in the 1980s – the decade of high growth of these flows – was the European Community, yet another indication of a very distinct geography in world transactions. But it should be noted that these flows have also increased in absolute terms in the case of less developed countries.

Another major transformation has been the sharp growth in the numbers and economic weight of TNCs – firms that operate in more than one country through affiliates, subsidiaries, or other arrangements. The central role played by TNCs can be seen in the fact that US and foreign TNCs accounted for 80% of international trade in the United States in the late 1980s (UNCTC 1991: chap. 3). By 1997, global sales generated by foreign affiliates of TNCs were valued at US$9.5 trillion, while worldwide exports of goods and services were at US$7.4 trillion, of which one-third was intra-firm trade (UNCTAD 1998). More than 143 countries have adopted special FDI regimes to attract FDI, up from 20 in 1982 (UNCTAD 1998: chap. 3).

Institutional Framework

How does the "world economy" cohere as a system? We cannot take the world economy for granted and assume that it exists simply because international transactions do. One question raised by the developments described above is whether the global economic activities occurring today represent a mere quantitative change or actually entail a change in the international regime governing the world economy. Elsewhere, I have argued that the ascendance of international finance and services produces a new regime with distinct consequences for other industries, especially manufacturing, and for regional development, insofar as regions tend to be dominated by particular industries (Sassen 1991). One consequence of this new regime is that TNCs have become even more central to the organization of the world economy, and the new, or vastly expanded older, global markets are now an important element in the institutional framework.

In addition to financing huge government deficits, the financial credit markets that exploded into growth in the 1980s served the needs of TNCs to a disproportionate extent. TNCs also emerged as a source for financial flows to developing countries, both through direct inflows of FDI and indirectly, insofar as FDI stimulates other forms of financial flows. In some respects, TNCs replaced banks.[1] The bank crisis of 1982 sharply cut bank loans to developing countries to the point that the aggregate net flow of financial resources to developing countries was negative during much of the 1980s. For better or for worse, the TNC is now a strategic organizer of what we call the world economy.

Global financial markets have emerged as yet another crucial institution organizing the world economy. The central role of markets in international finance, a key component of the world economy today, was in part brought about by the so-called Third World bank crisis formally declared in 1982. This was a crisis for the major transnational banks in the

United States, which had made massive loans to Third World countries and firms incapable of repayment. The crisis created a space into which small, highly competitive financial firms moved, launching a whole new era in the 1980s in speculation, innovation, and levels of profitability. The result was a highly unstable period but one with almost inconceivably high levels of profits that fed a massive expansion in the volume of international financial transactions. Deregulation was another key mechanism facilitating this type of growth, centered in internationalization and in speculation. Markets provided an institutional framework that organized these massive financial flows. Notwithstanding two financial crises, one in 1990–91 and the second in 1997–98, the end of the 1990s saw a sharp growth in the value of financial transactions.

The formation of transnational trading blocs is yet another development that contributes to the new institutional framework. The two major blocs are the North American Free Trade Agreement (NAFTA) and the European Economic Community (EEC). According to the World Trade Organization (WTO), there were over 70 regional trade agreements by the late 1990s. The specifics of each of the two major trading blocs currently being implemented vary considerably, but both strongly feature the enhanced capability for capital to move across borders. Crucial to the design of these blocs is the free movement of financial services. Trade, although it has received far more attention, is less significant; there already is a lot of trade among the countries in each bloc, and tariffs are already low for many goods. The NAFTA and EEC blocs represent a further formalization of capital as a transnational category, one that operates on another level from that represented by TNCs and global financial markets. Finally, in 1993, the WTO was set up to oversee cross-border trade. It has the power to adjudicate in cross-border disputes between countries and represents potentially a key institutional framework for the governance of the global economy.

Considerable effort and resources have gone into the development of a framework for governing global finance. This includes the development of new institutional accounting and financial reporting standards, minimum capital requirements for banks, and efforts to institute greater transparency in corporate governance.

These realignments have had pronounced consequences. One consequence of the extremely high level of profitability in the financial industry, for example, was the devaluing of manufacturing as a sector – although not necessarily in all subbranches. Much of the policy around deregulation had the effect of making finance so profitable that it took investment away from manufacturing. Finance also contains the possibility for superprofits by maximizing the circulation of and speculation in money – that is, buying and selling – in a way that manufacturing does not (e.g., securitization, multiple transactions over a short period of time, selling debts). Securitization, which played a crucial role, refers to the transformation of various types of financial assets and debts into marketable instruments. The 1980s saw the invention of numerous ways to securitize debts, a trend that has continued in the 1990s with the invention of ever more complex and speculative instruments. A simple illustration is the bundling of a large number of mortgages that can be sold many times, even though the number of houses involved stays the same. This option is basically not available in manufacturing. The good is made and sold; once it enters the realm of circulation, it enters another set of industries, or sector of the economy, and the profits from subsequent sales accrue to these sectors.

These changes in the geography and in the composition of international transactions, and the framework through which these transactions are implemented, have contributed to the formation of new strategic sites in the world economy. This is the subject of the next section.

Strategic Places

Three types of places above all others symbolize the new forms of economic globalization: export processing zones, offshore banking centers, high-tech districts, and global cities. There are also many other locations where international transactions materialize. Certainly, harbors continue to be strategic in a world of growing international trade and in the formation of regional blocs for trade and investment. And massive industrial districts in major manufacturing export countries, such as the United States, Japan, and Germany, are in many ways strategic sites for international activity and specifically for production for export. None of these locations, however, captures the prototypical image of today's global economy the way the first four do. Some geographers now speak of global city regions to capture this development.

[. . .]

Global Cities

Global cities are strategic sites for the management of the global economy and the production of the most advanced services and financial operations. They are key sites for the advanced services and telecommunications facilities necessary for the implementation and management of global economic operations. They also tend to concentrate the headquarters of firms, especially firms that operate globally. The growth of international investment and trade and the need to finance and service such activities have fed the growth of these functions in major cities. The erosion of the role of the government in the world economy, which was much larger when trade was the dominant form of international transaction, has displaced some of the organizing and servicing work from governments and major headquarters to specialized service firms and global markets in services and finance. Here we briefly examine these developments, first by presenting the concept of the global city and then by empirically describing the concentration of major international markets and firms in various cities.

The specific forms assumed by globalization over the last decade have created particular organizational requirements. The emergence of global markets for finance and specialized services, along with the growth of investment as a major type of international transaction, has contributed to the expansion in command functions and in the demand for specialized services for firms. Much of this activity is not encompassed by the organizational form of the TNC or bank, even though these types of firms account for a disproportionate share of international flows. Nor is much of this activity encompassed by the power of transnationals, a power often invoked to explain the fact of economic globalization. It involves work and workers. Here some of the hypotheses developed in our recent work are of interest, especially those that examine the spatial and organizational forms of economic globalization and the actual work of running transnational economic operations (Sassen 1991). This way of framing the inquiry has the effect of recovering the centrality of place and work in processes of economic globalization.

A central proposition in the global city model (Sassen 1991) is that the *combination* of geographic dispersal of economic activities and system integration that lies at the heart of the current economic era has contributed to a strategic role for major cities. Rather than becoming obsolete because of the dispersal made possible by information technologies, cities instead concentrate command functions. In a somewhat different vocabulary, Friedmann and Wolff (1982) posited this long before it exploded into the research literature it is now (see also Friedmann 1986; Sassen-Koob 1982).[2] To this role, I have added two additional functions: (1) Cities are postindustrial production sites for the leading industries of this period – finance and specialized services – and (2) cities are transnational marketplaces where firms and governments from all over the world can buy financial instruments and specialized services.

The territorial dispersal of economic activity at the national and world scale implied by globalization has created new forms of concentration. This territorial dispersal and ongoing concentration in ownership can be inferred from some of the figures on the growth of transnational enterprises and their affiliates. Table 1 shows how vast the numbers of affiliates of TNCs are. This raises the complexity of management functions, accounting, and legal services, and hence the growth of these activities in global cities.

In the case of the financial industry, we see a similar dynamic of global integration: a growth in the number of cities integrated in the global financial network and a simultaneous increase of concentration of value managed at the top of the hierarchy of centers. We can identify two distinct phases. Up to the end of the 1982 Third World debt crisis, the large transnational banks dominated the financial markets in terms of both the volume and the nature of financial transactions. After 1982, this dominance was increasingly challenged by other financial institutions and the major innovations they produced. These challenges led to a transformation in the leading components of the financial industry, a proliferation of financial institutions, and the rapid internationalization of financial markets. The marketplace and the advantages of agglomeration – and hence, cities – assumed new significance beginning in the mid-1980s. These developments led simultaneously to (1) the incorporation of a multiplicity of markets all over the world into a global system that fed the growth of the industry after the 1982 debt crisis and (2) new forms of concentration, specifically the centralization of the industry in a few leading financial centers. Hence, in the case of the financial industry, to focus only on the large transnational banks would exclude precisely those sectors of the industry where much of the new growth and production of innovations has occurred. Also, it would again leave out an examination of the wide range of activities, firms, and markets that compose the financial industry beginning in the 1980s.

The geographic dispersal of plants, offices, and service outlets and the integration of a growing number of stock markets around the world could have been accompanied by a corresponding decentralization in control and central functions. But this has not happened.

If we organize some of the evidence on financial flows according to the places where the markets and firms are located, we can see distinct patterns of concentration. The

Table 1 Number of Parent Transnational Corporations and Foreign Affiliates, by Region and Country, Selected Years (1990–1997)

	Year	Parent Corporations Based in Country	Foreign Affiliates Located in Country
All Developed Countries	1990	33,500	81,800
	1996	43,442	96,620
Select countries			
Australia	1992	1,306	695
	1997	485	2,371
Canada	1991	1,308	5,874
	1996	1,695	4,541
Federal Republic of Germany	1990	6,984	11,821
	1996	7,569	11,445
France	1990	2,056	6,870
	1996	2,078	9,351
Japan	1992	3,529	3,150
	1996	4,231	3,014
Sweden	1991	3,529	2,400
	1997	4,148	5,551
Switzerland	1985	3,000	2,900
	1995	4,506	5,774
United Kingdom	1991	1,500	2,900
	1996	1,059	2,609
United States	1990	3,000	14,900
	1995	3,379	18,901
All Developing Countries	1990	2,700	71,300
	1996	9,323	230,696
Select countries			
Brazil	1992	566	7,110
	1995	797	6,322
China	1989	379	15,966
	1997	379	145,000
Colombia	1987	–	1,041
	1995	302	2,220
Hong Kong, China	1991	500	2,828
	1997	500	5,067
Indonesia	1988	–	1,064
	1995	313	3,472
Philippines	1987	–	1,952
	1995	–	14,802
Republic of Korea	1991	1,049	3,671
	1996	4,806	3,878
Singapore	1986	–	10,709
	1995	–	18,154
Central and Eastern Europe	1990	400	21,800
	1996	842	121,601
World Total	1990	36,600	174,900
	1996	53,607	448,917

Source: Based on UNCTAD, *World Investment Report* (1998: 3, 4).

evidence on the locational patterns of banks and securities houses points to sharp concentration. For example, the worldwide distribution of the 100 largest banks and 25 largest securities houses in 1991 shows that Japan, the United States, and the United Kingdom accounted for 39 and 23 of each, respectively. This pattern persists in the late 1990s, notwithstanding multiple financial crises in the world and in Japan particularly.

The stock market illustrates this pattern well. From Bangkok to Buenos Aires, governments deregulated their stock markets to allow their participation in a global market system. And they have seen an enormous increase in the value of transactions. Yet there is immense concentration in leading stock markets in terms of worldwide capitalization – that is, the value of publicly listed firms. The market value of equities in domestic firms confirms the leading position of a few cities. In September 1987, before the stock market crisis, this value stood at US$2.8 trillion in the United States and at US$2.89 trillion in Japan. Third ranked was the United Kingdom, with US$728 billion. The extent to which these values represent extremely high levels is indicated by the fact that the next largest value was for West Germany, a major economy where capitalization stood at US$255 billion, a long distance from the top three. What these levels of stock market capitalization represent in the top countries is indicated by a comparison with gross national product (GNP) figures: in Japan, stock market capitalization was the equivalent of 64%; in the United States, the equivalent of 119%; in the United Kingdom, the equivalent of 118% of GNP; and in Germany, 23% of GNP. The full impact of deregulation and the growth of financial markets can be seen in the increases in value and in number of firms listed in all the major stock markets in the world by 1997 (see Figures 1 and 2). The market value of listings rose between 1990 and 1997 from US$2.8 trillion to US$9.4 trillion in New York City and from US$1 trillion to US$2 trillion in London. Similar patterns, although at lower orders of magnitude, are evident in the other stock markets listed in Figures 1 and 2.

The concentration in the operational side of the financial industry is made evident in the fact that most of the stock market transactions in the leading countries are concentrated in a few stock markets. The Tokyo exchange accounts for 90% of equities trading in Japan. New York accounts for about two-thirds of equities trading in the United States; and London accounts for most trading in the United Kingdom. There is, then, a disproportionate concentration of worldwide capitalization in a few cities.

Certain aspects of the territorial dispersal of economic activity may have led to some dispersal of profits and ownership. Large firms, for example, have increased their subcontracting to smaller firms worldwide, and many national firms in the newly industrializing countries have grown rapidly, thanks to investment by foreign firms and access to world markets, often through arrangements with transnational firms. Yet this form of growth is ultimately part of a chain in which a limited number of corporations continue to control the end product and reap most of the profits associated with selling on the world market. Even industrial homeworkers in remote rural areas are now part of that chain (Sassen 1988: chap. 4).

Under these conditions, the territorial dispersal of economic activity creates a need for expanded central control and management if this dispersal is to occur along with continued economic concentration. This in turn has contributed to the strategic role played by major cities in the world economy today.

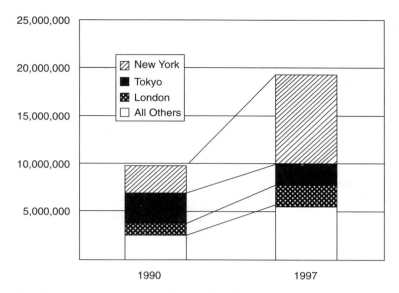

Figure 1　New York, Tokyo, and London: Share of World Stock Market Value, 1990 and 1997 (US$ millions and number)

Note: All others includes Frankfurt, Paris, Zurich, Toronto, Amsterdam, Milan, Sydney, Hong Kong, Singapore, Taiwan, and Seoul stock exchanges.

Source: Based on Meridian Securities Markets, *World Stock Exchange Fact Book* (1998).

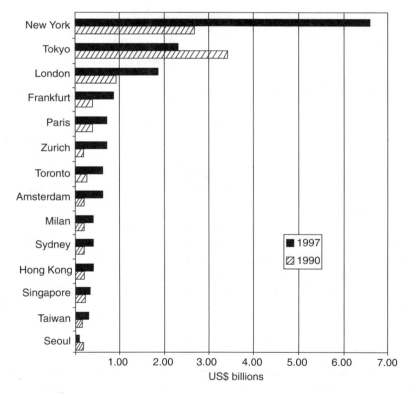

Figure 2　Top Cities Ranked by Stock Market Value, 1990 and 1997 (US$ billions)

Note: For Australia 1997, the number of listed companies is from 1996; when only domestic is listed, it represents the total market value.

Source: Based on Meridian Securities Markets, *World Stock Exchange Fact Book* (1998).

1.3   A New Geography of Centers and Margins: Summary and Implications

Three important developments over the last 25 years laid the foundation for the analysis of cities in the world economy presented in this book. They are captured in the three broad propositions organizing the preceding chapters.

1   *The territorial dispersal of economic activities, of which globalization is one form, contributes to the growth of centralized functions and operations.* We find here a new logic for agglomeration and key conditions for the renewed centrality of cities in advanced economies. Information technologies, often thought of as neutralizing geography, actually contribute to spatial concentration. They make possible the geographic dispersal and simultaneous integration of many activities. But the particular conditions under which such facilities are available have promoted centralization of the most advanced users in the most advanced telecommunications centers. We see parallel developments in cities that function as regional nodes – that is, at smaller geographic scales and lower levels of complexity than global cities.

2   *Centralized control and management over a geographically dispersed array of economic operations does not come about inevitably as part of a "world system."* It requires the production of a vast range of highly specialized services, telecommunications infrastructure, and industrial services. Major cities are centers for the servicing and financing of international trade, investment, and headquarters operations. And in this sense, they are strategic production sites for today's leading economic sectors. This function is reflected in the ascendance of these activities in their economies. Again, cities that serve as regional centers exhibit similar developments. This is the way in which the spatial effects of the growing service intensity in the organization of all industries materialize in cities.

3   *Economic globalization has contributed to a new geography of centrality and marginality.* This new geography assumes many forms and operates in many terrains, from the distribution of telecommunications facilities to the structure of the economy and of employment. Global cities become the sites of immense concentrations of economic power while cities that were once major manufacturing centers suffer inordinate declines; highly educated workers see their incomes rise to unusually high levels while low- or medium-skilled workers see theirs sink. Financial services produce superprofits while industrial services barely survive.

Let us look more closely now at this last and most encompassing of the propositions.

The Locus of the Peripheral

The sharpening distance between the extremes evident in all major cities of developed countries raises questions about the notion of "rich" countries and "rich" cities. It suggests that the geography of centrality and marginality, which in the past was seen in terms of the duality of highly developed and less developed countries, is now also evident within developed countries and especially within their major cities.

One line of theorization posits that the intensified inequalities described in the preceding chapters represent a transformation in the geography of center and periphery. They signal that peripheralization processes are occurring inside areas that were once conceived of as "core" areas – whether at the global, regional, or urban level – and that alongside the sharpening of peripheralization processes, centrality has also become sharper at all three levels.

The condition of being peripheral is installed in different geographic terrains depending on the prevailing economic dynamic. We see new forms of peripheralization at the center of major cities in developed countries not far from some of the most expensive commercial land in the world: "inner cities" are evident not only in the United States and large European cities, but also now in Tokyo (Komori 1983; Nakabayashi 1987; KUPI [Kobe Urban Problems Institute] 1981; Sassen 1991: chap. 9). Furthermore, we can see peripheralization operating at the center in organizational terms as well (Sassen-Koob 1982; Wilson 1987). We have long known about segmented labor markets, but the manufacturing decline and the kind of devaluing of nonprofessional workers in leading industries that we see today in these cities go beyond segmentation and in fact represent an instance of peripheralization.

Furthermore, the new forms of growth evident at the urban perimeter also mean crisis: violence in the immigrant ghetto of the *banlieues* (the French term for *suburbs*), exurbanites clamoring for control over growth to protect their environment, new forms of urban governance (Body-Gendrot 1993; Pickvance and Preteceille 1991). The regional mode of regulation in many of these cities is based on the old center/suburb model and may hence become increasingly inadequate to deal with intraperipheral conflicts – conflicts between different types of constituencies at the urban perimeter or urban region. Frankfurt, for example, is a city that cannot function without its region's towns; yet this particular *urban region* would not have emerged without the specific forms of growth in Frankfurt's center. Keil and Ronneberger (1992) note the ideological motivation in the call by politicians to officially *recognize* the region so as to strengthen Frankfurt's position in the global interurban competition. This call also provides a rationale for coherence and the idea of common interests among the many objectively disparate interests in the region: It displaces the conflicts between unequally advantaged sectors onto a project of regional competition with other regions. Regionalism then emerges as the concept for bridging the global orientation of leading sectors with the various local agendas of various constituencies in the region.

In contrast, the city discourse rather than the ideology of regionalism dominates in cities such as New York or São Paulo (see Toulouse 1992). The challenge is how to bridge the inner city, or the squatters at the urban perimeter, with the center. In multiracial cities, multiculturalism has emerged as one form of this bridging. A "regional" discourse is perhaps beginning to emerge, but it has until now been totally submerged under the suburbanization banner, a concept that suggests both escape from and dependence on the city. The notion of conflict within the urban periphery between diverse interests and constituencies has not really been much of a factor in the United States. The delicate point at the level of the region has rather been the articulation between the residential suburbs and the city.

Contested Space

Large cities have emerged as strategic territories for these developments. *First, cities are the sites for concrete operations of the economy.* For our purposes, we can distinguish two forms of such concrete operations: (1) In terms of economic globalization and place, cities are strategic places that concentrate command functions, global markets, and production sites for the advanced corporate service industries. (2) In terms of day-to-day work in the leading industrial complex, finance, and specialized services, a large share of the jobs involved are low paid and manual, and many are held by women and immigrants. Although these types of workers and jobs are never represented as part of the global economy, they are in fact as much a part of globalization as international finance is. We see at work here a dynamic of valorization that has sharply increased the distance between the devalorized and the valorized – indeed overvalorized – sectors of the economy. These joint presences have made cities a contested terrain.

The structure of economic activity has brought about changes in the organization of work that are reflected in a pronounced shift in the job supply, with strong polarization occurring in the income distribution and occupational distribution of workers. Major growth industries show a greater incidence of jobs at the high- and low-paying ends of the scale than do the older industries now in decline. Almost half the jobs in the producer services are lower-income jobs, and the other half are in the two highest earnings classes. On the other hand, a large share of manufacturing workers were in middle-earning jobs during the postwar period of high growth in these industries in the United States and most of western Europe.

One particular concern here was to understand how new forms of inequality actually are constituted into new social forms, such as gentrified neighborhoods, informal economies, or downgraded manufacturing sectors. To what extent these developments are connected to the consolidation of an economic complex oriented to the global market is difficult to say. Precise empirical documentation of the linkages or impacts is impossible; the effort here is focused, then, on a more general attempt to understand the consequences of both the ascendance of such an international economic complex and the general move to a service economy.

Second, the city concentrates diversity. Its spaces are inscribed with the dominant corporate culture but also with a multiplicity of other cultures and identities, notably through immigration. The slippage is evident: The dominant culture can encompass only part of the city. And while corporate power inscribes noncorporate cultures and identities with "otherness," thereby devaluing them, they are present everywhere. The immigrant communities and informal economy are only two instances. Diverse cultures and ethnicities are especially strong in major cities in the United States and Western Europe; these also have the largest concentrations of corporate power.

We see here an interesting correspondence between great concentrations of corporate power and large concentrations of "others." It invites us to see that globalization is not only constituted in terms of capital and the new international corporate culture (international finance, telecommunications, information flows) but also in terms of people and noncorporate cultures. There is a whole infrastructure of low-wage, nonprofessional jobs and activities that constitutes a crucial part of the so-called corporate economy.

A focus on the *work* behind command functions, on *production* in the finance and services complex, and on market*places* has the effect of incorporating the material facilities underlying globalization and the whole infrastructure of jobs and workers typically not seen as belonging to the corporate sector of the economy: secretaries and cleaners, the truckers who deliver the software, the variety of technicians and repair workers, and all the jobs having to do with the maintenance, painting, and renovation of the buildings where it is all housed.

This expanded focus can lead to the recognition that a multiplicity of economies is involved in constituting the so-called global information economy. It recognizes types of activities, workers, and firms that have never been installed in the "center" of the economy or that have been evicted from that center in the restructuring of the 1980s and have therefore been devalued in a system that puts too much weight on a narrow conception of the center of the economy. Globalization can, then, be seen as a process that involves multiple economies and work cultures.

The preceding chapters have tried to demonstrate that cities are of great importance to the dominant economic sectors. Large cities in the highly developed world are the places where globalization processes assume concrete, localized forms. These localized forms are, in good part, what globalization is about. We can then think of cities also as the place where the contradictions of the internationalization of capital either come to rest or conflict. If we consider, further, that large cities also concentrate a growing share of disadvantaged populations – immigrants in both Europe and the United States, African Americans and Latinos in the United States – then we can see that cities have become a strategic terrain for a whole series of conflicts and contradictions.

On one hand, they concentrate a disproportionate share of corporate power and are one of the key sites for the overvalorization of the corporate economy; on the other, they concentrate a disproportionate share of the disadvantaged and are one of the key sites for their devalorization. This joint presence happens in a context in which (1) the internationalization of the economy has grown sharply and cities have become increasingly strategic for global capital and (2) marginalized people have come into representation and are making claims on the city as well. This joint presence is further brought into focus by the sharpening of the distance between the two. The center now concentrates immense power, a power that rests on the capability for global control and the capability to produce superprofits. And marginality, notwithstanding weak economic and political power, has become an increasingly strong presence through the new politics of culture and identity.

If cities were irrelevant to the globalization of economic activity, the center could simply abandon them and not be bothered by all of this. Indeed, this is precisely what some politicians argue – that cities have become hopeless reservoirs for all kinds of social despair. It is interesting to note again how the dominant economic narrative argues that place no longer matters, that firms can be located anywhere thanks to telematics, that major industries now are information-based and hence not place-bound. This line of argument devalues cities at a time when they are major sites for the new cultural politics. It also allows the corporate economy to extract major concessions from city governments under the notion that firms can simply leave and relocate elsewhere, which is not quite the case for a whole complex of firms, as much of this book sought to show.

In seeking to show that (1) cities are strategic to economic globalization because they are command points, global marketplaces, and production sites for the information economy and (2) many of the devalued sectors of the urban economy actually fulfill crucial functions for the center, this book attempts to recover the importance of cities specifically in a globalized economic system and the importance of those overlooked sectors that rest largely on the labor of women, immigrants, and in the case of large US cities, African Americans and Latinos. In fact it is the intermediary sectors of the economy (such as routine office work, headquarters that are not geared to the world markets, the variety of services demanded by the largely suburbanized middle class) and of the urban population (the middle class) that can and have left cities. The two sectors that have stayed, the center and the "other," find in the city the strategic terrain for their operations.

NOTES

1   FDI by transnationals may be financed through transnational banks or through the international credit markets. The mid-1980s saw a sharp increase in the share of the latter and a sharp decline in the former (see Sassen 1991: chap. 4).
2   I have traced this emerging scholarly lineage in Sassen (2000). Some of the texts are Castells (1989); Fainstein (1993); Knox and Taylor (1995); Allen, Massey, and Pryke (1999); Short and Kim (1999); and Eade (1997).

REFERENCES

Allen, John, Doreen Massey and Michael Pryke, eds. 1999. *Unsettling Cities*. New York: Routledge.
Body-Gendrot, S. 1993. *Ville et violence*. Paris: Presses Universitaires de France.
Castells, Manuel. 1989. *The Informational City: Information Technology, Economic Restructuring, and the Urban – Regional Process*. Cambridge, MA: Blackwell.
Eade, John. 1997. *Living the Global City: Globalization as a Local Process*. New York: Routledge.
Fainstein, S. 1993. *The City Builders*. Oxford: Blackwell.
Friedmann, John. 1986. "The World City Hypothesis." *Development and Change* 17:69–84.
Friedmann, J. and G. Wolff. 1982. "World City Formation: An Agenda for Research and Action." *International Journal of Urban and Regional Research* 15(1):269–83.
Keil, Roger and Klaus Ronneberger. 1992. "Going up the Country: Internationalization and Urbanization on Frankfurt's Northern Fringe." Presented at the UCLA International Sociological Association, Research Committee 29, *A New Urban and Regional Hierarchy? Impacts of Modernization, Restructuring and the End of Bipolarity*, April 24–26, Los Angeles, CA.
Knox, P. and P. Taylor, eds. 1995. *World Cities in a World-System*. New York: Cambridge University Press.
Komori, S. 1983. "Inner City in Japanese Context." *City Planning Review* 125:11–17.
KUPI (Kobe Urban Problems Institute). 1981. *Policy for Revitalization of Inner City*. Kobe: KUPI.
Meridian Securities Markets. 1998. *World Stock Exchange Fact Book*. Morris Plains, NJ: Electronic Commerce.
Nakabayashi, Itsuki. 1987. "Social-Economic and Living Conditions of Tokyo's Inner City." *Geographical Reports of Tokyo Metropolitan University* 22.
Pickvance, C. and E. Preteceille, eds. 1991. *State Restructuring and Local Power: A Comparative Perspective*. London: Pinter.

Sassen, Saskia. 1988. *The Mobility of Labor and Capital: A Study in International Investment and Labor Flow.* New York: Cambridge University Press.

——. 1991. *The Global City: New York, London, Tokyo.* Princeton, NJ: Princeton University Press.

——. 1996. *Losing Control? Sovereignty in an Age of Globalization.* The 1995 Columbia University Leonard Hastings Schoff Memorial Lectures. New York: Columbia University Press.

——, ed. 2000. *Cities and Their Crossborder Networks.* Tokyo: United Nations.

Sassen-Koob, Saskia. 1982. "Recomposition and Peripheralization at the Core." Pp. 88–100 *Immigration and Change in the International Division of Labor.* San Francisco: Synthesis. (Reprinted in *Contemporary Marxism,* Vol. 4.)

Short, J.R. and Y.-H. Kim. 1999. *Globalization and the City.* New York: Longman.

Toulouse, Christopher. 1992. "Thatcherism, Class Politics and Urban Development in London." *Critical Sociology* 18(1):57–76.

UN Center on Transnational Corporations (UNCTC). 1991. *World Investment Report: The Triad in Foreign Direct Investment.* New York: United Nations.

UN Conference on Trade and Development (UNCTAD), Programme on Transnational Corporations. 1993. *World Investment Report 1993: Transnational Corporations and Integrated International Production.* New York: United Nations.

——. 1998. *World Investment Report 1998: Trends and Determinants.* New York: United Nations.

Wilson, W. J. 1987. *The Truly Disadvantaged: The Inner City, the Underclass and Public Policy.* Chicago: University of Chicago Press.

13 Globalization: Myths and Realities (1996)

Philip McMichael

Introduction

The late 20th century offers rural sociology a unique opportunity for revitalization in the crisis of the development paradigm – the modernist project associated with nation-building. The development paradigm subordinated rural populations, and hence rural studies, to the higher authority of industrialism. Development theorists extrapolated from the example of modern states, whose rural populations had diminished drastically as agriculture industrialized. Remaining rural populations, across the world, were cast essentially as "unlimited supplies of labor" for an industrial future (Lewis 1954). In this way, rural issues were marginalized in the social scientific agenda. But marginalization has not eliminated them; if anything, it has magnified their significance. The consequences of agro-industrialism – landlessness, hyper-urbanization, and environmental deterioration – reveal the short-comings of the development paradigm's underlying belief in inexorable technological progress. Sustainability has become the new catchword.

The rising concern with sustainability reveals the limits of the development paradigm in guaranteeing the survival of the human species and the natural world. In addition, the growing unsustainability of the institutions of the development paradigm confounds this crisis, as globalization undermines social protections. This argument is based on the following premises: First, development is perhaps the "master" concept of the social sciences, and has been understood as an evolutionary movement bringing rising standards of living – a logical outcome of human rationality, as revealed in the European experience; second, the development project was a political strategy to institute nationally managed economic growth as a replicable pattern across the expanding system of states in the post-World War II world order; third, the paradigm of developmentalism offered a broadly acceptable interpretation of how to organize states and international institutions around the goal of maximizing national welfare via technological advances in industry and agriculture; fourth, this paradigm has collapsed with the puncturing of the illusion of development in the 1980s debt crisis, the management of which dismantled development institutions; and fifth, debt management instituted a new organizing principle of "globalization" as an alternative institutional framework, with the underlying message that nation-states no longer "develop;" rather, they position themselves in the global economy.

This paradigmatic shift resonates globally. It registers in the demise of welfarist regimes in the First World, of socialist regimes of central planning in the Second World, and of the Third World as a political collectivity of post-colonial states. All are subsumed within the big tent of globalism, which displaces simultaneously their institutional and ideological legacies. In a general reversal of thinking, the present is no longer the logical development of the past; rather it is increasingly the hostage of the future: a future defined by globalists as one of inexorable efficiency.

In this essay, I elaborate this interpretation of the origins of post-developmentalism, and then consider some consequences for rural sociology. In particular, the connection between local, rural processes and globalization needs clarification. Globalization tends to be understood as a process of economic integration – observed through local prisms, or "grounded" in local terms, giving a local face to processes of globalization. But these processes (such as proliferating commodity chains or transnational firm expansion) are routinely taken as given contexts, to be observed on the "ground," where agency and culture enter in. An alternative approach is first to ground globalization as a historical project, and, as such, to problematize it as a set of institutional and ideological relations constructed by powerful social forces (e.g., managers of international agencies, states and firms, academic ideologues). Local processes, and local expressions of globalization,[1] are then situated in an historically concrete, rather than an abstract context.

Globalization

Global exchanges predate the capitalist era. Why should they only now take on the appearance of being the governing force of the late-20th century world? Advocates of globalization claim, for example, that "the world's needs and desires have been irrevocably homogenized," and technology "drives consumers relentlessly towards the same common goals – alleviation of life's burdens and the expansion of discretionary time and spending power" (Levitt 1983: 99). Global economic integration is an empirical fact, but it is hardly the only reality. About 80 percent of the more than five billion people in the world live outside global consumer networks (Barnet and Cavanagh 1994: 383).

Nevertheless, globalization has become consequential by virtue of its institutional force within the state system, and from there it reaches out to subject populations. Its most palpable impact has been through the worldwide process of restructuring of states and economies, brining diverse populations and regions into the realm of a common dynamic. This dynamic is not simply a quantitative extension of commodity relations. It is, rather, a qualitative shift in the mode of social organization that marks a historic transition in the capitalist world order.

Arrighi (1994) links this shift to the onset of "financialization" – a contagious preference for liquid rather than fixed capital on the part of private and institutional investors under specific historical conditions (usually associated with the decline of a hegemonic state). Most recently, the (relative) decline of the United States is pegged to the rise of offshore money markets in the 1970s (discussed below). These currency markets stimulated the rise of unregulated financial institutions alongside of traditional (nationally regulated) banking systems. Heightened mobility of capital has privileged, and rewarded, financial speculation at the expense of fixed investment. Arrighi characterizes this as the subordination of the "territorial" principle to the "capitalist" principle. It marks a new stage of competition among states and firms in an unstable, post-hegemonic world order. When the center of accumulation (the US home market) erodes, speculation on an unknown financial future heightens.

As money capital decoupled from productive capital, financiers consolidated power and reshaped modern political and economic institutions in the 1980s, including farming (Bienefield 1989; Marsden and Whatmore 1994). Growing financial securitization (i.e., trading in securities, including debt) heightened the authority of debt security rating institutions, which meant in effect that all firms and states found their credit ratings subject to a global "information standard" (Sinclair 1994). Corporate downsizing and relocation, and state restructuring programs, in the service of credit-worthiness, have rippled across the global social landscape.

The new power of financial institutions has been at the expense of the sovereignty of state monetary authorities. In 1992, the former Chairman of Citicorp described the 200,000 currency traders across the world, as conducting "a kind of global plebiscite on the monetary and fiscal policies of the governments using currency. [This system] is far more draconian than any previous arrangement, such as the gold standard of the Bretton Woods system, since there is no way for a nation to opt out" (quoted in Brecher and Costello 1994: 30). In other words, precisely because of the non-territorial character of financialization, all states are constrained to manage their finances according to global criteria.

Under these circumstances, state organizations transmitted the effects of financial restructuring through the relatively circumscribed institutions of the "formal" economy and beyond, where communities depend on "informal" markets, subsidies, public lands, and casual employment on the fringes of the "formal" economy. In order to justify, or discount, the divisive consequences of restructuring – notably the social concentration of resources and the fragmentation of previously coherent social systems (e.g., economic arrangements, social protections, communities) – globalization advocates appeal to a higher good, namely, efficiency, and stress the importance of discipline in the global economy. Since some of these advocates are policymakers, they claim the discipline is imposed by the debt managers. . . .

In short, as the rationale for recent restructuring of states and economies, "globalization" is an historically specific project of global economic (financial) management. Prosecuted by a powerful global elite of financiers, international and national bureaucrats, and corporate leaders, the globalist project grows out of the dissolution of the development project.

The Development Project

The development project was a postwar construct through which the world capitalist economy was stabilized. Like any social construct, the institutions of market economy are historically specific. Just as early capitalism emerged within distinct political frameworks – pre-19th century mercantilism (trade organized to enlarge national wealth), 19th century liberalism (free trade imperialism to enlarge capitalist markets) – so mid-20th century capitalism was organized within the framework of the (now universal) nation-state system (McMichael 1987). The completed nation-state system *combined* the principles of mercantilist and liberal organization into a new international regime of "embedded liberalism" (Ruggie 1982). This regime subordinated trade to systems of national economic management, anchored in strategic economic sectors like steel and farming. Together, international and national institutions regulated monetary and wage relations to stabilize national capitalisms within a liberal trade regime. Its extension to the so-called Third World, as the decolonization process unfolded, generated the paradigm of "developmentalism."

Under the project of developmentalism, states were responsible for managing national economic growth, with trade as a stimulus. How individual states accomplished this was generally their own concern, giving rise to a clear range of national political-economies (e.g., Japanese state capitalism, German corporatism, and US liberal capitalism underwritten by military spending). The macroeconomic goal was to consolidate national welfare, through a context of stable monetary relations. Again, with rich variation, this principle of nationally-managed economic growth was the adopted form of political economy in the multiplicity of new states that formed during this period. Economic Commission for Latin America (ECLA) prescriptions for import-substitution industrialization dovetailed with the green revolution (providing essentially urban wage foods) to shape national economic growth in Third World countries.

Development was a universal project, also inspiring accelerated industrialization in the Second World. It took its cue from the European experience, understood as superior economic performance and/or living standards vis-à-vis the non-European world. It was an ideal that we know, at least from hindsight, was unrealizable. But development was not just an ideal (as idealized history, and prescription). It was thoroughly institutionalized in the post-war world.

The institutionalization of development, as the central postwar project, required a stable international monetary regime and a uniform political entity such as the nation-state. It was a matter of historical choice. When pan-Africanists demanded territorial federations during the decolonization movement, they were overridden by the European powers and their fellow nationalists – both groups seeing in the nation-state form a vehicle for stable accumulation of wealth and extraction of economic resources on the national and the international scale (see Davidson 1992).

The monetary regime, instituted through the Bretton Woods agreements in 1944, established the principle of fixed exchange rates and mechanisms whereby the IMF could maintain stable currency exchange by extending short-term loans to those states with payments imbalances (Block 1977). National economies, geared to stabilizing the wage relation through rising investment (in mass production) and state subsidies (to promote full employment and rising consumption), were supported by a stable trade environment. This formula, despite its uneven implementation, is often characterized as a mix of Keynesian/Fordist political-economy (Harvey 1989).

Alongside of this multilateral arrangement were the geopolitical realities of the Cold War. The United States, in particular, deployed Marshall aid to redistribute dollars to capital-poor regions of the world (from Europe, through East Asia to Africa). This established the dollar as the international reserve currency and promoted freedom of enterprise, which became the litmus test of the so-called free world (Arrighi 1982). Export credits, extended to Marshall Plan recipients, facilitated the transfer of American technology. In turn, the World Bank (along with other such multilateral financial assistance institutions) disbursed long-term loan funds to encourage the habit of developmentalism (Rich 1994).

Without further elaboration, the point remains that in the mid-20th century the foundations of capitalism were reformulated through a massive restructuring of the world order. In other words, not only is "restructuring" not unique to the late 20th century, but it has an essential institutional dimension. In the postwar era, it combined forms of international (monetary relations) with national (wage relation) regulation. Developmentalism emerged within this institutional framework. First World (and Cold War) planners perceived their goal as raising and protecting living standards, and to this end pursued massive (military and economic) assistance programs. Developmentalism thus instrumentalized the nation-state, and bilateral and multilateral institutions, as its appropriate vehicles and agents.

Developmentalism was, indeed, a project originating in the stabilization of world capitalism after the inter-war crisis and in the context of the Cold War. It was a constructed order, even though planners presented development in ideal terms: as an evolutionary progression along a linear trajectory of modernization. In this respect, not only would each state replicate the modernity of the First World (with the US at the apex), but there were expectations that the development gap between First and Third Worlds would be progressively closed. Despite some apparent successes (e.g., the newly industrializing countries of East Asia and some Latin American states for a time), the development gap across these world divisions remained. The development project was unsuccessful in its own universalist terms. Its failure is both cause and consequence of the rise of a new, alternative project: the globalization project.

The Globalization Project

As suggested, globalization is not specific to our era. But globalization as a view of ordering the world is. It is a historical project, just as the development project was. The development project was a view of ordering the world, but it was understood, institutionalized, and embraced as a process to be replicated in nation-states. Postwar capitalism was stabilized through national economic management. Alternatively, the globalization project seeks to stabilize capitalism through global economic management – this time along the lines of specialization, rather than replication. Specialization differentiates states and regions (and includes marginalization), whereas replication was a universalist project (in the sense that all nation-states were expected to follow and realize the ideal Western path). Many of the same institutions obtain (e.g., states, multilaterals, banks, aid institutions, even nongovernmental organizations). But they operate in a transformed world. Their character, role and significance in the world order are different.

The concept of a "globalization project" allows an analogous, and related, view of a particular institutional form of capitalism. It replaced the development project as an organizing principle, growing out of the dissolution of that project. Its enunciation as a vision by new global elites is quite distinct from the developmentalist vision elaborated in the postwar world. The developmentalist elites were essentially state managers who shared an interest in stabilizing the world capitalist order, one in which First World working classes, and colonial and post-colonial populist movements were demanding inclusion. . . .

The elites associated with the globalization project are a different kettle of fish. In addition to state managers (those embracing liberalization), there are the new financial and transnational corporate elites combined with the managers of newly-empowered multilateral institutions like the IMF, the World Bank and the World Trade Organization. As proponents of globalization – formed through the conjunction of the Trilateral Commission (a 1970s global think-tank), debt crisis management and Uruguay Round negotiations regarding global trade and investment regulation – these elites constitute what is arguably an incipient global ruling class.

Global Integration Trends

The globalization project grew out of the development project because developmentalism included specific international relations. In particular, the US emphasis on the principle of freedom of enterprise, and the use of bilateral measures (i.e., dollar credits and investment and market guarantees) to underwrite this, encouraged transnational economic integration. . . .

As this transnational dimension extended to firms from Europe and Japan and some Third World countries, a series of global exchanges began to overlay national economies. In the late 1960s and 1970s, Third World newly industrializing countries (NICs) actively participated in these global exchanges through a strategy of export-oriented industrialization (EOI). Under these circumstances, the World Bank in its 1980 *World Development Report* redefined development as "participation in the world market" (Hoogvelt 1987: 58). Symbolically this marked the demise of the development regime as a global economy emerged alongside of declining national economies. This is not to say, however, that all consumers and producers were now "global," but that the global economy itself became consequential in reshaping the conditions under which states made economic policy.

Transnational economic integration depended ultimately on the role of the dollar as a reserve international currency. Postwar disbursements of the dollar, via export credits and foreign investment, allowed an offshore dollar market to form, beyond the reach of national banking and currency controls – the origins of financialization. This "Eurodollar" market promoted the rise of transnational corporate activity, and especially the rise of global banks. But as the offshore capital market expanded (from $3 billion in 1960, to $75 billion in 1970, and eventually to over $1 trillion in 1984), it undercut the Bretton Woods monetary regime (Strange 1994: 107). This occurred as mounting pressure on the dollar from offshore holdings forced President Nixon to end the gold-dollar standard and declare the dollar nonconvertible in 1971 – initiating a destabilizing shift from fixed to floating currency exchange rates. The foundational monetary relations of the development project unraveled.

In the 1970s, Third World developmentalist states and global banks entered into a loan binge, where unsecured funds flowed into extravagant public developmentalist projects sponsored by Third World states bent on pursuing the goal of catch-up with the First World. In this sense, borrowing amplified the central purpose of the development project:

industrialization. The debt-based development of the 1970s coincided with First World profitability declines and recession. Under these circumstances, the Third World, especially the newly industrializing countries, became the engine of growth for the global economy. The stimulus of a substantial decentralization of industrial investment encouraged a "new international division of labor" to form as First World firms relocated unskilled production offshore and sold components and products on the world market (Fröbel, Heinrichs, and Kreye 1979).

By the end of the 1970s, debt became a liability rather than a vehicle of development. Monetarism had gained legitimacy as a mechanism of restructuring the balance of power within First World states, putting labor and social programs on the defensive. When the US Federal Reserve Board reduced the money supply in 1980 to stem the fall in the value of the dollar, lending to Third World countries slowed, and came on shorter terms. By 1986, Third World debt totalled $1 trillion, and even though it was only half of that of the US national debt in that year, it was now a debt crisis. Third World countries were devoting new loans entirely to servicing previous loans, whereas the US (given its sheer global power) was able to continue the fiction of a paper dollar standard.

The Debt Regime

The debt crisis marked the reversal of the development project. Debt management served to reconstruct global, and hence national, monetary relations. The IMF assumed a de facto role of banker to the world, determining, with the World Bank, conditions by which states could renegotiate their outstanding loans and/or service their debt. These conditions were universally imposed and adopted, as states privatized public assets, slashed social budgets, cut wages, devalued national currencies, and promoted exporting. In short, the goals of the development project of nationally-managed economic growth with a view to enhancing national welfare yielded to a new principle: globally-managed economic growth with a view to sustaining the integrity of the global financial system and the conditions for transnational corporate capitalism.

Structural adjustment measures were adopted across the so-called "three worlds," and those states that did not formally undergo structural adjustment have done so informally in order to compete in the global economy. The conditions of the 1980s debt crisis suggested that developmentalism was an illusion (Arrighi 1990), ending the Second and Third Worlds as geo-political categories. Commentators spoke of the "lost decade" for the Third World, and political and economic liberalization spread across the socialist world (Friedmann 1998; Harris 1987). The definition of development was further refined to encompass a comprehensive policy of economic liberalization – especially privatization of public functions and the application of market principles to the administration of wages, prices, trade and investment.

Structural adjustment programs allowed the multilateral institutions combined with state managers and financial classes to reformulate the role of the state. States found they were under pressure to pursue credit-worthiness and competitiveness in the global economy by downgrading their national priorities – especially welfare enhancement and sustaining political constituencies supportive of national economic integration around an industrial base. Boosting export production and offering attractive conditions for foreign investment became the new priorities alongside an extraordinary roll-back of public investment in the former Third World, as privatization increased tenfold across the decade (Crook 1993: 16). Shrinking the state reduced its capacity as a national institution at the same time as it privileged the financial and trade ministries that survived and managed the cuts in other ministries, such as education, agriculture, health and social services. This means that state agencies that support and regulate economic and social sectors affecting the lives of the majority of the citizenry, especially poorer classes, have lost resources. And they have lost them to agencies more concerned with the sectors that connect with global enterprise. Hence global-economic criteria cast a shadow over the social criteria that defined the national project.

In structurally adjusting countries on a case-by-case basis but with a standard package of adjustments, this debt regime transformed the discourse of development in two distinct ways. First, the conditions imposed on debtors for renewal of credit enabled the debt managers to reframe the national project. It was no longer a question of pursuing the goals of the development project; rather, wholesale restructuring (to compete in the global economy) was necessary to guarantee repayment of debt. Indeed, the World Bank's traditional focus on project loans yielded to a new focus in the 1980s on policy loans, that is, loans linked to policies of liberalization. Second, austerity measures, privatization and export expansion renewed the global economy (or the global financial system) rather than individual national economies. Austerity measures lowered wages to encourage foreign investment, privatization ensured renewal of the principle of the global freedom of enterprise, and export expansion sustained the flow of products to the wealthier zones of the global economy.

Each measure potentially undermined the coherence and sovereignty of national economies. Lowered wages reduced local purchasing power. Wage-earners had to tighten their belts, which meant that the market for locally produced goods contracted. Privatization of public enterprises reduced the capacity of states. This meant they were no longer in a position to enter into joint ventures with private firms, using this to set production priorities. Reduction in public expenditure generally reduced states' capacity for coordination of national economic and social programs. As parts of national economies became embedded more deeply in global enterprise, they weakened as nationally-coordinated units themselves, and strengthened the reach of the global economy. This was not unique to the 1980s, but the mechanisms of the debt regime institutionalized the power and authority of global management within states' very organizations and procedures, as illustrated in the following case study.

The Mexican Dress Rehearsal for NAFTA

Perhaps the most dramatic case of state restructuring in recent years is that of the Mexican dress rehearsal for the implementation of NAFTA in the 1990s. The Mexican state sponsored agro-industrialization in the form of irrigated commercial agriculture through the postwar development era, at the same time regulating a basic grains sector. Despite the agro-industrial priority, President Echeverría's 1971 revision of the agrarian reform code, under pressure from *campesinos* (peasants and farmworkers) for greater participation, renewed financial and institutional support for the *ejido* sector (community controlled land holdings deriving from the Mexican Revolution of 1910). Basic grain prices were subsidized and various forms of agricultural credit assisted the small farm sector. In other words, the state managed an extensive rural social system based on *campesino* agriculture supplying foods to domestic markets, alongside a profitable commercial agribusiness sector. But the government supported the *campesino* sector with multilateral loans, rather than a national progressive tax.

When Mexico's oil prices fell in 1981, the debt financing of the basic grains sector could no longer continue, and the Mexican crisis triggered the so-called debt crisis. The national food security system (i.e., grain production and distribution scheme) that had begun the previous year under the López Portillo government was scrapped. Between 1980 and 1991, Mexico negotiated 13 adjustment loans with the World Bank, and six agreements with the IMF. The World Bank proposed an agricultural Structural Adjustment Loan in 1986 to assist in the elimination of imported food subsidies, privatization of rural parastatal agencies, the liberalization of trade and domestic food prices, "sound" public investment, and cutbacks in the size of the agricultural ministry (McMichael and Myhre 1991).

These were the conditions of multilateral loans, and the Mexican government's submission to them (eschewing joining a Latin American debtor's cartel) became the model of restructuring. Rural social services were subordinated to economic criteria which focused on expanding agro-industrial exports to service the debt and thereby assist in stabilizing the global financial system. In 1991, a follow-up sectoral adjustment loan for Mexican agriculture further liberalized food importing, privatized state-owned monopolies and eliminatd price guarantees on corn – a drastic step. The social repercussions were sufficiently severe that the World Bank subsequently supported the government's Pronasol and Procampo programs, which offered financial assistance to poor rural producers (Barry 1995: 36, 43–4, 144).

Through a decade of liberal reforms mandated by the global managers and pursued by the Mexican government to maintain its credit-worthiness, the state abandoned its role as manager and regulator of the enormous agricultural sector. It shed agencies, and withdrew its financial support from the *campesinos*, at the same time as funds shifted into expanding agro-exports. This overall priority shift prepared the ground for NAFTA. During the debates preceding the signing of NAFTA, the opposition candidate, Cuauhtémoc Cárdenas, argued that "exploitation of cheap labor, energy, raw materials, technological dependency, and lax environmental protection should not be the premises upon which Mexico establishes links with the United States, Canada, and the world economy" (quoted in Resource Center 1993: 2).

As a result of this drastic shrinking of state involvement in the rural sector, the percentage of *campesinos* with access to official credit fell from 50 to less than 20 percent at the end of the 1980s. Under these conditions, *campesino* organizations have mobilized to create new and locally controlled credit systems to replace the vacuum left by the state. Their dilemma is that this vacuum compels them to negotiate with the National Banking Commission, which regulates credit arrangements and which is increasingly geared to the new principles of global competitiveness – clearly quite distinct from the principles on which *campesino* communities run (Myhre 1994). In sum, when states restructure, they may improve their financial standing and their export sectors, but the majority of citizens and poorer classes find their protections shorn away in the rush to participate in the world market.

Global Economic Management

The globalization project is not simply an external imposition on states from global agencies. State managers collaborate in the restructuring of state organs under the dictates of the new rules of the multilateral agencies to improve the efficiency of the economic enterprise under their jurisdiction. The South Commission noted that the "most powerful countries in the North have become a de facto board of management for the world economy, protecting their interests and imposing their will on the South" (South Centre 1993: 3). While this is a Third Worldist perspective – as it is not Northern countries, but instead regulators and business executives from the North and the South that do the managing – it does draw attention to the new project of managing the world economy as a singular entity.

Not only has the globalist regime-in-the-making actively reorganized states, but this reorganization has been profoundly unrepresentative. Bureaucrats in global agencies exert a growing influence as makers or custodians of the new market rules – this much is clear from the imposition of liberalization measures on indebted states with little or no scrutiny by the citizens of those states. And this practice is to be extended in the newly created World Trade Organization (WTO), which has independent jurisdiction and oversees trade in manufactures, agriculture, services, investment, and intellectual property protection. The WTO has global governing power insofar as its rules are binding on all members, and it has the potential to overrule state and local powers regulating environment, product and food safety. Its staff are unelected bureaucrats, who have no constituency to answer to other than an abstract set of free trade rules and their proponents. Proceedings are secret, denying citizen participation.

Through the WTO, global managers assume extraordinary powers to manage the web of global economic relations overlaying states, at the expense of those state organizations, including their democratic achievements. What is remarkable is that the reach of real economic globalization itself is so limited in terms of the populations it includes, and yet its impact is so extensive. The impact is extensive precisely because states have been absorbed into the project. Just as nation-states were the ideal vehicle of the development project, so restructured states convey the globalization project to their populations. A similar configuration of undemocratic power defines numerous free trade agreements (e.g., NAFTA, APEC, the European Union) springing up as global regionalist arrangements and reflecting what Stephen Gill (1992) has termed "the internationalization of political authority."

The internationalization of political authority includes both the centralization of power in multilateral institutions to set global rules and the internalization of those rules in national policymaking, as our discussion of Mexico suggests. The definition of an international regime – adherence to internationally agreed upon rules through multilateral consent – is thereby refined to include the actual determination, or at least implementation, of those rules by global agencies. In other words, the potential global regime is only formally multilateral, as states lose capacity as sovereign rule makers.

The centralization of state power in global institutions means, in effect, the ability to shape state administrative priorities. This tendency is exemplified by the World Bank's new lending criteria. The World Bank's 1992 *World Development Report* stated that, "Good governance, for the World Bank, is synonymous with sound development management" (George and Sabelli 1994: 150). As the most influential development agency in the world, the World Bank now insists on shaping governments rather than simply economic trajectories – a practice it refined during the 1980s by way of its Structural Adjustment Loans (Cahn 1993).

The globalization project represents a new institutional form for stabilizing capitalism. It is emerging out of the contradictions of the development project that came to a head in the 1980s. Although it could be said that the Third World was a proving ground, this new project of economic management is thoroughly global, as all states submit to the new market rules. In addition, the restructuring of the former Third World has a recursive effect, as it has accelerated the movement of refugees from south to north and driven down wages across the world, in what is termed the "race to the bottom" (Brecher and Costello 1994). Both of these trends are spawning a politics of racial intolerance as employment conditions decline, dividing labor and civilian populations in states across the world. First World national politics, for example, are increasingly framed in exclusive, or "status," terms, rather than the inclusive citizenship terms associated with social democracy.

Restructuring the Wage Relation

In this shift we can see the restructuring of the wage relation along global lines. Certainly states still manage the wage relation, but the conditions under which they do so are increasingly globally defined. Labor protections, achieved over decades of political struggle and compromise and providing the social foundation for the welfare state, are steadily eroded under the new dictates of global market efficiency – just as labor organization itself has steadily eroded since the onslaught of monetarism in the 1970s.

Returning to the NAFTA example, free trade has a "harmonizing" effect on policies regarding levels of wages and social services, which means reducing the differential towards the minimal standard, typically found in the lower cost regions. This is known as "downward leveling." Consider the recent process of "harmonization" from the US side. Industries that shift to Mexico are those in which women are disproportionately employed, such as apparel, consumer electronics, and food processing. Many of these women entered the workforce in the late 1970s and 1980s, because families could no longer get by on a single wage. Once their already low-wage jobs move south, the possibility of regaining equivalent work lessens. The pressure on family livelihood increases. This only adds to the general downward pressure on the US wage, as Mexico's cheaper labor comes on line. . . .

In the global economy, product cycles are unstable, as consumer fashions and sourcing sites change relentlessly. The loss of jobs is not simply an economic transfer from one nation to another; more fundamentally, it represents the "hollowing out" of a nation's economic base, and the erosion of social institutions that stabilize the conditions of employment and habitat associated with those jobs. A century of institution-building in labor markets, in corporate/union relations, and in communities, can disappear overnight when the winds of the market are allowed to blow across national boundaries. Those who have work find they are often working longer hours to make ends meet. Wage labor as we know it is undergoing a profound transformation, signalled by the increasingly unstable terms on which people are hired across the world, and the growing range of forms of labor in industry and agriculture – from stable cores of wage work through contract- and piece-work to new forms of indentured, slave and child labor – incorporated into global commodity chains under the conditions of restructuring of the global economy.

Globalization is ultimately an institutional transformation. It has no single face, as institutions and institutional change vary across the world. Former categories like the Three Worlds, and "core" and "periphery," lose their salience, as chains of commodity production and exchange operate above, below, and across national and regional boundaries, generating their own time-compressed spatial relations as the velocity of economic transactions intensifies (Mittelman 1995). State organizations restructure accordingly, complemented by emerging global and regional institutions.

Elsewhere, I have suggested that globalization is a formative and contradictory process with no clear structural imperative (McMichael 1994). Its only unifying dimension, I would argue, is the political project of restructuring to secure or stabilize market conditions for corporate expansion on a world scale. Following the Third World "lost decade" of the 1980s, this has been pursued with draconian effect in Eastern Europe since the collapse of the Berlin Wall (Gowan 1995). Financial regulation is ad hoc – managed politically through the multilateral institutions, meetings of the powerful Group of Seven (G-7) states, and macro-regional free trade agreements.

The global regulation of monetary relations, however fragile, is necessary under circumstances where nation-states have lost the ability to regulate their own currency values, and vast amounts of currency cross national borders daily. At the national level, states continue to regulate wage relations, but increasingly under global, rather than national, terms – which often means under the terms of the firms that organize commodity complexes. This "global wage relation" combines a mosaic of quite different forms of labor (paid and unpaid) contributing to the global production and circulation of value under increasingly casual, insecure, globally competitive conditions.

In short, the extensive transition in economic and political arrangements that we term "restructuring" has its roots in the displacement of the development project (the management of national economic growth and welfare) by the globalization project (the management of global economic growth and the global commons). It is not simply a quantitative economic trend; rather it involves substantive changes in institutional and ideological relations – generating the new paradigm of "post-developmentalism."

The World of Post-Developmentalism: The Possibilities of Localism

The post-developmentalist paradigm is shared by globalists and anti-globalists alike, because of the differentiating effects of global integration. The erosion of state capacities to manage national economic growth and welfare disorganizes class coalitions formed around developmentalism, including the dismantling of public patronage systems. The series of IMF food riots in the last two decades attests to this (Walton & Seddon 1994). As states decentralize, the opportunity for local political renewal presents itself, often quite compellingly. As global integration intensifies, the currents of multiculturalism swirl faster. Under these conditions, which include the juxtaposition of ethnically distinct labor forces and communities, the politics of identity tends to substitute for the civic (universalist) politics of nation-building. Also, regions and communities see self-determination as more than a political goal. It extends to the idea of cultural renewal, which includes recovering local knowledges. . . .

The new forms of imagination embody what Wolfgang Sachs (1992: 112) terms "cosmopolitan localism," that is, the assertion of diverse localism as a universal right. Cosmopolitan localism questions the assumption of uniformity in the global project. It is by definition part of the contradictory dynamics of globalization, often being a protective response where communities try to avoid the marginalization or disruption of unpredictable global markets. Such questioning also asserts the need to respect alternative cultural traditions as a matter of global survival. Finally, it is a question of preserving or asserting human and democratic rights within broader settings, whether a world community or individual national arenas.

The Chiapas Rebellion

The most potent recent example of cosmopolitan localism was the 1994 peasant revolt in Mexico's southern state of Chiapas. Chiapas is a region in which small peasant farms are surrounded by huge cattle ranches and coffee plantations. A third of the unresolved land reforms in the Mexican agrarian reform department, going back more than half a century, are here. To alleviate this situation, the government allowed landless *campesinos* to colonize the Lacandon jungle and produce subsistence crops, coffee, and cattle. Coffee, cattle, and corn prices all fell during the 1980s, but *campesinos* were prohibited from logging despite the fact that timber companies continued the practice (Fox 1994). The revolt, therefore, had these deepening class inequities as its foundation. But the source of these deepening inequities transcended the region.

The January 1, 1994 revolt was timed to symbolize the conjunction of these inequities with another set of inequities, this time on a macro-regional scale. The revolt coincided with the day of implementation of the North American Free Trade Agreement (NAFTA). To the Chiapas rebels, NAFTA completed the undermining of the revolutionary heritage in the Mexican national Constitution of 1917. In particular, under this constitution, communal lands (*ejido*) were protected from alienation. In 1992, under the pretext of structural adjustment policies and the promise of NAFTA, the Mexican government began opening these lands for sale to Mexican and foreign agribusinesses. In addition, the terms of the NAFTA included a provision to deregulate commodity markets – especially for maize, the staple peasant food. Not only was the government deciding the fate of local communities such as those in Chiapas; it was also proceeding without representation from those communities.

The *Zapatistas* perceive the Mexican state as the chief agent exploiting the region's cultural and natural wealth, especially through dismantling the communal tradition of the Mexican national state symbolized in the infamous reform of Article 27 of the Constitution. The Article now privileges private (foreign) investment in land over the traditional rights of *campesinos* to petition for land redistribution within the framework of the *ejido* (Indian community land held in common). The *Zapatistas* argue that this reform, along with NAFTA liberalizations, seriously threatens the Mexican smallholder and the basic grains sector. They understand that the US "comparative advantage" in maize production

(6.9 US tons vs 1.7 Mexican tons per hectare, including infrastructural disparities) would swamp Mexican producers, especially since under NAFTA the Mexican government has agreed to phase out guaranteed prices for staples such as maize and beans (Harvey 1994: 14). Herman Daly, former World Bank senior economist, warned: "US corn subsidized by depleting topsoil, aquifers, oil wells and the federal treasury can be freely imported [to Mexico, and] it is likely that NAFTA will ruin Mexican peasants" (quoted in Chomsky 1994: 180).

The *Zapatistas'* demands for inclusion in the political process signify the movement for local political renewal. This addresses the absence of free and fair elections in Chiapas (and elsewhere in Mexico), adequate political representation of *campesino* interests (as against those of Chiapas planters and ranchers), and the elimination of violence and authoritarianism in local government. The Ejército Zapatista de Liberación Nacional (EZLN) demands included a formal challenge to a centuries-old pattern of *caciquismo* (local strongman tradition) in which federal government initiatives have been routinely thwarted by local, too often venal, political and economic interests.

The Chiapas revolt has had a clear demonstration effect, as communities throughout Mexico have since mobilized around similar demands, especially as they face common pressures, such as market reforms. In challenging local patronage politics, the *Zapatistas* elevated national demands for inclusion of *campesino* organizations in political decisions regarding rural reforms. These include equity demands for small farmers as well as farm workers. They also advanced the cause of local and/or indigenous development projects that sustain local ecologies and cultures (Fox 1994: 18; Harvey 1994: 36–7). Nevertheless, aside from demanding indigenous cogovernors, the rebellion assumed a pan-Mayan identity rather than a specific ethnic identity.

The Chiapas rebellion is distinguished by the texture of its political action. Timed to coincide with the implementation of NAFTA, it wove together a powerful and symbolic critique of the politics of globalization. This critique had two objectives: first, opposing the involvement of national elites and governments in implementing neo-liberal (economic) reforms on a global or regional scale (which undo the institutionalized social entitlements associated with political liberalism); and second, asserting a new political agenda of renewal of a politics of rights that goes beyond individual (property) rights to human, and therefore, community rights. The push for regional autonomy challenged local class inequalities, and demanded the empowerment of *campesino* communities. These communities have created a "fabric of cooperation," woven from the various threads of local groupings. They substitute fluid organizational patterns for the bureaucratic organizational forms associated with modernist politics – such as political parties, trade unions, and hierarchical state structures (Cleaver 1994: 150). In that sense they express an emerging post-developmentalist politics.

In addition, the timing of this revolt to coincide with NAFTA's implementation implicitly addressed the broader movement to reform global economic rules, via the GATT Uruguay Round. While the revolt contributes to long-term resistance to a global economic regime, it has already destabilized the monetary system, as evidenced in the Mexican *peso* crisis of December 1994. Impatient with economic and political instabilities in Mexico, a sudden outflow of capital depressed the *peso*, creating the *tequila effect*, which rippled through regional money markets. In the space of a decade, a second Mexican bailout was necessary, to the tune of more than $40 billion.

In June of 1995, the G–7 powers created a worldwide emergency fund to bail out states on the verge of national bankruptcy. . . . In this way, the *Zapatista* uprising has indirectly contributed to new initiatives to stabilize global monetary relations. Global and local processes are thoroughly intertwined. This contradictory and unpredictable dynamic, rather than some trend or scenario of progressive homogenization of the world's social landscape, is the essence of "globalization." . . .

Unless we specify the historical relations in our concepts they remain abstract. "Levels," or units of analysis cannot be taken as empirically given. Social units are self-evident in neither space nor time: they form relationally. In this sense, the opposition of local and global analysis is a false opposition, as each template is a condition of the other. On their own, conceived in non-relational terms, global and local "units" can only exist as reified levels of analysis. Global relations are inconceivable without local "faces" (e.g., states, micro-regions, communities), just as the "local" has no meaning without context (whether it is a community with exchange relations beyond its boundaries or a community resisting the reach of states and markets). The very definitions of "global" or "local" are not only mutually conditioning, they continually change. For this reason, the use of "local" and/or "global" terms of reference needs problematizing. This essay has attempted this in regard to the concept of globalization and its expression, through restructuring processes, in local contexts. . . .

. . . [P]ost-developmentalism is not simply a new phase of capitalism or social organization – it is the consequence of an active project of globalization, involving a drastic restructuring of political and economic relations. Rather than concede the process of economic globalization as inevitable context, we are better served by problematizing it. . . .

In this essay, I used the Mexican case to illustrate the mutual conditioning of local and global relations. This case demonstrates that it is difficult to isolate local relations, as "localism" expresses itself precisely in historical, and therefore, global terms. Arguably, this is likely to be the case, one way or another, with most local entities, since their boundaries are ultimately social rather than geographical. In other words, it is not the entity itself so much as the entity in its relational field that concretizes restructuring. And in order to concretize, we need to have some understanding of the way in which relational fields are constructed historically.

As a broad relational field, developmentalism was constructed as a transnational project designed to integrate the postwar world, and is now undergoing dramatic revision via globalization. I conceptualize this project as the global reconstitution of the monetary and wage relations of capitalism across the state system. As such, it provides a fluid institutional context within which particular cases and entities can be examined. That is, while it does interpret the broad shift in organizing principles in the world economy, it can only initiate, rather than prefigure, analysis of particular cases and entities that negotiate this relational field.

NOTE

1   The term "local expressions" is shorthand for the process by which local communities negotiate their social context, which includes global relations as embedded in institutions that condition local communities.

REFERENCES

Arrighi, Giovanni. 1982. "A Crisis of Hegemony." Pp. 55–109 in *Dynamics of Global Crisis*, edited by S. Amin, G. Arrighi, A. G. Frank, and I. Wallerstein. New York: Monthly Review.

———. 1990. "The Developmentalist Illusion: A Reconceptualization of the Semiperiphery." Pp. 18–25 in *Semiperipheral States in the World Economy*, edited by W.G. Martin. Westport, CT: Greenwood.

———. 1994. *The Long Twentieth Century: Money, Power, and the Origins of Our Times*. London: Verso.

Barnet, Richard J., and John Cavanagh. 1994. *Global Dreams: Imperial Corporations and the New World Order*. New York, NY: Touchstone.

Barry, Tom. 1995. *Zapata's Revenge: Free Trade and the Farm Crisis in Mexico*. Boston, MA: South End.

Bienefeld, Manfred. 1989. "The Lessons of History." *Monthly Review* 3: 9–41.

Block, Fred L. 1977. *The Origins of International Economic Disorder: A Study of United States International Monetary Policy from World War II to the Present*. Berkeley & Los Angeles, CA: University of California Press.

Brecher, Jeremy, and Tim Costello. 1994. *Global Village or Global Pillage: Economic Reconstruction From the Bottom Up*. Boston, MA: South End.

Cahn, Jonathan. 1993. "Challenging the New Imperial Authority: the World Bank and the Democratization of Development." *Harvard Human Rights Journal* 6: 159–94.

Chomsky, Noam. 1994. *World Orders Old and New*. New York, NY: Columbia University Press.

Cleaver, Harry. 1994. "The Chiapas Uprising." *Studies in Political Economy* 44: 141–57.

Crook, Clive. 1993. "New Ways to Grow. A Survey of World Finance." *The Economist*. Special Supplement. 25 September.

Davidson, Basil. 1992. *The Black Man's Burden: Africa and the Curse of the Nation-State*. New York: Random House.

Fox, Jonathan. 1994. "The Challenge of Democracy." *Akwe:kon* 11(2): 13–19.

Friedmann, Harriet. 1998. "Warsaw Pact Socialism: Detente and Economic Tensions in the Soviet Bloc." In *Rethinking the Cold War: Essays on Its Dynamic, Meaning and Morality*, edited by Allen Hunt. Philadelphia, PA: Temple University Press.

Fröbel, Folker, Jürgen Heinrichs, and Otto Kreye. 1979. *The New International Division of Labor*. New York: Cambridge University Press.

George, Susan, and Fabrizio Sabelli. 1994. *Faith and Credit: The World Bank's Secular Empire*. Boulder, CO: Westview Press.

Gill, Stephen. 1992. "Economic Globalization and the Internationalization of Authority: Limits and Contradictions." *Geoforum* 23: 269–83.

Gowan, Peter. 1995. "Neo-Liberal Theory and Practice for Eastern Europe." *New Left Review* 213: 3–60.

Harris, Nigel. 1987. *The End of the Third World: Newly Industrializing Countries and the Decline of an Ideology*. Harmondsworth: Penguin.

Harvey, David. 1989. *The Condition of Postmodernity*. Oxford: Basil Blackwell.

Harvey, Neil. 1994. *Rebellion in Chiapas: Rural Reforms, Campesino Radicalism, and the Limits to Salinismo*. San Diego, CA: Center for US-Mexican Studies.

Hoogvelt, Ankie M. M. 1987. *The Third World in Global Development*. London: Macmillan.

Levitt, Theodore. 1983. "The Globalization of Markets." *Harvard Business Review* 61(3): 92–102.

Lewis, W. Arthur. 1954. "Economic Development with Unlimited Supplies of Labor." *Manchester School of Economics and Social Studies* 22: 139–91.

Marsden, Terry, and Sarah Whatmore. 1994. "Finance Capital and Food System Restructuring: Global Dynamics and their National Incorporation." Pp. 107–28 in *The Global Restructuring of Agro-Food Systems*, edited by P. McMichael. Ithaca, NY: Cornell University Press.

McMichael, Philip. 1987. "State Formation and the Construction of a World Market." Pp. 187–237 in *Political Power and Social Theory*, Vol. 6, edited by M. Zeitlin. Greenwich, CT: JAI.

———. 1994. "Global Restructuring: Some Lines of Inquiry." Pp. 277–300 in *The Global Restructuring of Agro-Food Systems*, edited by P. McMichael. Ithaca, NY: Cornell University Press.

McMichael, Philip, and David Myhre. 1991. "Global Regulation vs. the Nation-State: Agro-Food Systems and the New Politics of Capital." *Capital and Class* 43: 83–106.

Mittelman, James H. 1995. "Rethinking the International Division of Labour in the Context of Globalisation." *Third World Quarterly* 16(2): 273–95.

Myhre, David. 1994. "The Politics of Globalization in Rural Mexico: Campesino Initiatives to Restructure the Agricultural Credit System." Pp. 145–69 in *The Global Restructuring of Agro-Food Systems*, edited by P. McMichael. Ithaca, NY: Cornell University Press.

Resource Center. 1993. "Free Trade: The Ifs, Ands, and Buts." *Resource Center Bulletin*, pp. 31–2.

Rich, Bruce. 1994. *Mortgaging the Earth: The World Bank, Environmental Impoverishment and the Crisis of Development*. Boston, MA: Beacon.

Ruggie, John Gerard. 1982. "International Regimes, Transactions and Change: Embedded Liberalism in the Post-War Economic Order." *International Organization* 36: 397–415.

Sachs, Wolfgang. 1992. "One World." Pp. 102–15 in *The Development Dictionary*, edited by W. Sachs. London: Zed.

Sinclair, Timothy J. 1994. "Passing Judgement: Credit Rating Processes as Regulatory Mechanisms of Governance in the Emerging World Order." *Review of International Political Economy* 1: 133–59.

South Centre. 1993. *Facing the Challenge: Responses to the Report of the South Commission*. London: Zed.

Strange, Susan. 1994. *States and Markets*. London, New York: Pinter.

Walton, John, and David Seddon. 1994. *Free Markets and Food Riots: The Politics of Global Adjustment*. Oxford: Blackwell.

14 Competing Conceptions of Globalization (1999)

Leslie Sklair

Introduction

Globalization is a relatively new idea in the social sciences, although people who work in and write about the mass media, transnational corporations and international business have been using it for some time. . . . The purpose of this paper is to critically review the ways in which sociologists and other social scientists use ideas of globalization and to evaluate the fruitfulness of these competing conceptions.

The central feature of the idea of globalization is that many contemporary problems cannot be adequately studied at the level of nation-states, that is, in terms of each country and its inter-national relations, but instead need to be seen in terms of global processes. Some globalists (for example, Ohmae 1990) have even gone so far as to predict that global forces, by which they usually mean transnational corporations and other global economic institutions, global culture or globalizing belief systems/ ideologies of various types, or a combination of all of these, are becoming so powerful that the continuing existence of the nation-state is in serious doubt. This is not a necessary consequence of most theories of globalization, though many argue that the significance of the nation-state is declining (even if the ideology of nationalism is still strong in some places).

There is no single agreed definition of globalization, indeed, some argue that its significance has been much exaggerated, but as the ever-increasing numbers of books and articles discussing different aspects of it suggest, it appears to be an idea whose time has come in sociology in particular and in the social sciences in general. The author of the first genuine textbook on globalization suggests that it may be 'the concept of the 1990s' (Waters 1995, p. 1; see also Robertson 1992, Albrow 1996).

The argument of this paper is that the central problem in understanding much of the globalization literature is that not all those who use the term distinguish it clearly enough from internationalization, and some writers appear to use the two terms interchangeably. I argue that a clear distinction must be drawn between the inter-national and the global. The hyphen in inter-national is to signify confusing conceptions of globalization founded on the existing even if changing system of nation-states, while the global signifies the emergence of processes and a system of social relations not founded on the system of nation-states.

This difficulty is compounded by the fact that most theory and research in sociology is based on concepts of society that identify the unit of analysis with a particular country (for example, sociology of Britain, of Japan, of the USA, of Russia, of India, etc.), sub-systems within countries (British education, the Japanese economy, American culture, politics in Russia, religion in India) or comparisons between single countries and groups of them (modern Britain and traditional India, declining America and ascendent Japan, rich and poor countries, the West and the East). This general approach, usually called state-centrism, is still useful in many respects and there are clearly good reasons for it. Not the least of these is that most historical and contemporary sociological data sets have been collected on particular countries. However, most globalization theorists argue that the nation-state is no longer the only important unit of analysis. Some even argue that the nation-state is now less important in some fundamental respects than other, global, forces; examples being the mass media and the corporations that own and control them, transnational corporations (some of which are richer than the majority of nation-states in the world today) and even social movements that spread ideas such as universal human rights, global environmental responsibility and the world-wide call for democracy and human dignity. Yearley (1996, chapter 1) identifies two main obstacles to making sociological sense of globalization, namely 'the tight connection between the discipline of sociology and the nation-state' (p. 9) and the fact that countries differ significantly in their geographies. Despite these difficulties (really elaborations of the local-global problem which will be discussed below) he makes the telling point that a focus on the environment encourages us to 'work down to the global' from the universal, a necessary corrective to state-centrist conceptions which work up to the global from the nation-state or even, as we shall see, from individualistic notions of 'global consciousness'.

The study of globalization in sociology revolves primarily around two main classes of phenomena which have become increasingly significant in the last few decades. These are the emergence of a globalized economy based on new systems of production, finance and consumption; and the idea of 'global culture'. While not all globalization researchers entirely accept the existence of a global economy or a global culture, most accept that local, national and regional economies are undergoing important changes as a result of processes of globalization even where there are limits to globalization (see, for example, Scott 1997).

Researchers on globalization have focused on two phenomena, increasingly significant in the last few decades:

(i) the ways in which transnational corporations (TNC) have facilitated the globalization of capital and production (Dunning 1993, Barnet and Cavanagh 1994, Dicken 1998);

(ii) transformations in the global scope of particular types of TNC, those who own and control the mass media, notably television channels and the transnational advertising agencies. This is often connected with the spread of particular patterns of consumption and a culture and ideology of consumerism at the global level (Featherstone 1990, Dowmunt 1993, Sklair 1995, Barker 1997).

The largest TNCs have assets and annual sales far in excess of the Gross National Products of most of the countries in the world. The World Bank annual publication *World Development Report* reports that in 1995 only about 70 countries out a total of around 200 for which there is data, had GNPs of more than ten billion US dollars. By contrast, the *Fortune* Global 500 list of the biggest TNCs by turnover in 1995 reports that over 440 TNCs had annual sales greater than $10 billion. Thus, in this important sense, such well-known names as General Motors, Shell, Toyota, Unilever, Volkswagen, Nestle, Sony, Pepsico, Coca Cola, Kodak, Xerox and the huge Japanese trading houses (and many other corporations most people have never heard of) have more economic power at their disposal than the majority of the countries in the world. These figures prove little in themselves, they simply indicate the *gigantism* of TNCs relative to most countries.

Not only have TNCs grown enormously in size in recent decades but their 'global reach' has expanded dramatically. Many companies, even from large rich countries, regularly earn a third or more of their revenues from 'foreign' sources (see Sklair 1998). Not all *Fortune* Global 500 corporations are headquartered in the First World: some come from what was called the Third World or those parts of it known as the Newly Industrializing Countries (NICs). Examples of these are the 'national' oil companies of Brazil, India, Mexico, Taiwan and Venezuela (some owned by the state but most run like private corporations), banks in Brazil and China, an automobile company from Turkey, and the Korean manufacturing and trading conglomerates (*chaebol*), a few of which have attained global brand-name status (for example, Hyundai and Samsung).

Writers who are sceptical about economic globalization argue that the facts that most TNCs are legally domiciled in the USA, Japan and Europe and that they trade and invest mainly between themselves means that the world economy is still best analyzed in terms of national corporations and that the global economy is a myth (see, for example, Hirst and Thompson 1996). But this deduction entirely ignores the well-established fact that an increasing number of corporations operating outside their 'home' countries see themselves as developing global strategies, as is obvious if we read their annual reports and other publications rather than focus exclusively on aggregate data on foreign investment. You cannot simply assume that all 'US', 'Japanese' and other 'national' TNCs somehow express a 'national interest'. They do not. They primarily express the interests of those who own and control them, even if historical patterns of TNC development have differed from place to place, country to country and region to region. Analysing globalization as a relatively recent phenomenon, originating from the 1960s, allows us to see more clearly the tensions between traditional 'national' patterns of TNC development and the new global corporate structures and dynamics. It is also important to realize that, even in state-centrist terms, a relatively small investment for a major TNC can result in a relatively large measure of economic presence in a small, poor country or a poor region or community in a larger and less poor country.

The second crucial phenomenon for globalization theorists is the global diffusion and increasingly concentrated ownership and control of the electronic mass media, particularly television (Barker 1997). The number of TV sets per capita has grown so rapidly in Third World countries in recent years (from fewer than 10 per thousand population in 1970 to 60 per 1,000 in 1993, according to UNESCO) that many researchers argue that a 'globalizing effect' due to the mass media is taking place even in the Third World (Sussman and Lent 1991, Sklair 1995).

Ownership and control of television, including satellite and cable systems, and associated media like newspaper, magazine and book publishing, films, video, records, tapes, compact discs, and a wide variety of other marketing media, are concentrated in relatively few very large TNCs. The predominance of US-based corporations is being challenged by others based in Japan, Europe and Australia and even by 'Third World' corporations like the media empires of TV Globo, based in Brazil and Televisa, based in Mexico (Nordenstreng and Schiller 1993).

Main Approaches to Globalization

As with other topics in sociology, there are several ways to categorize theory and research on globalization. One common approach is to compare mono-causal with multi-causal explanations of the phenomenon, as does McGrew (1992). This is a useful way of looking at the problem but it has two main drawbacks. First, it ends up by putting thinkers with entirely different types of explanations – for example those who see globalization as a consequence of the development of material-technological forces and those who see it as a consequence of ideological and/or cultural forces – in the same bag. Second, few thinkers present an entirely mono-causal explanation of anything; most of the thinkers McGrew identifies as mono-causal do try to show the relevance of a variety of factors even if they tend to prioritize some factors over others, while those he identifies as multi-causal do not always argue that everything causes everything else. Globalization, by its very nature, is a big and complex subject.

A second approach is to compare the disciplinary focus of globalization studies. This is certainly an interesting and fruitful avenue to explore: several disciplines have made distinctive contributions to the study of globalization (to some extent all the social sciences have contributed to the debate, but anthropology, geography and international political economy in addition to sociology, can be singled out). These contributions are commonly borrowed by sociologists of globalization, and *vice versa*, and this will be reflected in my own categorization. I have chosen to categorize globalization studies on the basis of four research clusters in which groups of scholars are working on similar research problems, either in direct contact with each other or, more commonly, in rather indirect contact. Accordingly, I identify the following four sources of globalization research in contemporary sociology:

1   The world-systems approach;
2   The global culture approach;
3   The global society approach;
4   The global capitalism approach.

I   The World-Systems Approach

This approach is based on the distinction between core, semiperipheral and peripheral countries in terms of their changing roles in the international division of labour dominated by the capitalist world-system. World-systems as a model in social science research, inspired by the work of Immanuel Wallerstein, has been developed in a large and continually expanding body of literature since the 1970s (see Wallerstein 1979 and Shannon 1989 for a good overview).

The world-systems approach is, unlike the others to be discussed, not only a collection of academic writings but also a highly institutionalized academic enterprise. It is based at the Braudel Center at SUNY Binghamton, supports various international joint academic ventures, and publishes the journal, *Review*. Though the work of world-systems theorists cannot be said to be fully a part of the globalization literature as such (see King 1991), the institutionalization of the world-systems approach undoubtedly prepared the ground for globalization in the social sciences.

In some senses, Wallerstein and his school could rightly claim to have been 'global' all along – after all, what could be more global than the 'world-system'? However, there is no specific concept of the 'global' in most world-systems literature. Reference to the 'global' comes mainly from critics and, significantly, can be traced to the long-standing problems that the world-system model has had with 'cultural issues'. Wallerstein's essay on 'Culture as the Ideological Battleground of the Modern World-System', the critique by Boyne, and Wallerstein's attempt to rescue his position under the title of 'Culture is the World-System' (all in Featherstone 1990), illustrate the problem well.

Chase-Dunn, in his suggestively titled book *Global Formation* (1989), does try to take the argument a stage further by arguing for a dual logic approach to economy and polity. At the economic level, he argues, a global logic of the world-economy prevails whereas at the level of politics a state-centred logic of the world-system prevails. However, as the world-economy is basically still explicable only in terms of national economies (countries of the core, semiperiphery and periphery), Chase-Dunn's formulation largely reproduces the problems of Wallerstein's state-centrist analysis.

There is, therefore, no distinctively 'global' dimension in the world-systems model apart from the inter-national focus that it has always emphasized. Wallerstein himself rarely uses the word 'globalization'. For him, the *economics* of the model rests on the inter-national division of labour that distinguishes core, semiperiphery and periphery countries. The *politics* are mostly bound up with antisystemic movements and 'superpower struggles'. And the *cultural*, insofar as it is dealt with at all, covers debates about the 'national' and the 'universal' and the concept of 'civilization(s)' in the social sciences. Many critics are not convinced that the world-systems model, usually considered to be 'economistic' (that is, too locked into economic factors) can deal with cultural issues adequately. Wolff tellingly comments on the way in which the concept of 'culture' has been inserted into Wallerstein's world-system model: 'An economism which gallantly switches its attentions to the operations of culture is still economism' (in King 1991, p. 168). Wallerstein's attempts to theorize 'race', nationality and ethnicity in terms of what he refers to as different types of 'peoplehood' in the world-system (Wallerstein 1991) might be seen as a move in the right direction, but few would argue that cultural factors are an important part of the analysis.

While it would be fair to say that there are various remarks and ideas that do try to take the world-systems model beyond state-centrism[1], any conceptions of the global that world-system theorists have tend to be embedded in the world-economy based on the system of nation-states. The 'global' and the 'inter-national' are generally used interchangeably by world-systems theorists. This is certainly one possible use of 'global' but it seems quite superfluous, given that the idea of the 'inter-national' is so common in the social science literature. Whatever the fate of the world-systems approach, it is unlikely that ideas of globalization would have spread so quickly and deeply in sociology without the impetus it gave to looking at the whole world.

II   Global Culture Model

A second model of globalization derives specifically from research on the 'globalization of culture'. The global culture approach focuses on the problems that a homogenizing mass media-based culture poses for national identities. As we shall see below, this is complementary to, rather than in contradiction with, the global society approach, which focuses more on ideas of an emerging global consciousness and their implications for global community, governance and security.

This is well illustrated in the collection of articles in book-form from the journal *Theory, Culture and Society* (*TCS*) edited by Featherstone (1990) under the title *Global Culture*. *TCS* has brought together groups of like-minded theorists through the journal and conferences, which has resulted in an institutional framework and an intellectual critical mass for the development of a culturalist approach to globalization. Of the writers associated with *TCS* who have made notable contributions to this effort, Robertson – who has been credited with introducing the term globalization into sociology (Waters 1995, p. 2) – is probably the most influential.

Although these researchers cannot be identified as a school in the same way as world-system researchers can be, their works do constitute a relatively coherent whole. First, they tend to prioritize the cultural over the political and/or the economic. Second, there is a common interest in the question of how individual and/or national identity can survive in the face of an emerging 'global culture'.

A distinctive feature of this model is that it problematises the existence of 'global culture', as a reality, a possibility or a fantasy. This is based on the very rapid growth that has taken place over the last few decades in the scale of the mass media of communication and the emergence of what Marshall McLuhan famously called 'the global village'. The basic idea is that the spread of the mass media, especially television, means that everyone in the world can be exposed to the same images, almost instantaneously. This, the argument goes, turns the whole world into a sort of 'global village'.

Of considerable interest to sociologists theorizing and researching globalization is the distinctive contribution of anthropologists to these debates. Friedman, a Swedish anthropologist, argues, for example, that: 'Ethnic and cultural fragmentation and modernist homogenization are not two arguments, two opposing views of what is happening in the world today, but two constitutive trends of global reality. The dualist centralized world of the double East–West hegemony is fragmenting, politically, and culturally, but the homogeneity of capitalism remains as intact and as systematic as ever' (in Featherstone 1990:311). While not all would agree either that capitalism remains intact and systematic or that it is, in fact, the framework of globalization, the fragmentation of 'the double East–West hegemony' is beyond doubt. Ideas such as hybridization and creolization have been proposed in the effort to try to conceptualize what happens when people and items from different (sometimes, but not always, dominant and subordinate) cultures interact.[2]

Some 'globalization of culture' theorists have also contributed to current debates on postmodernity in which transformations in the mass media and media representations of reality and so-called 'hyperreality' play a central role. Indicative of similar interests is a compilation of articles edited by Albrow and King (1990) which raised several central issues relevant to the ideas of global sociology, global society and globalization, as new problem areas in the social sciences. One important emphasis has been the 'globalization' of sociology itself as a discipline. This connects in some important ways with the debate about the integrity of national cultures in a globalizing world. While the classical sociological theorists, notably Marx, Weber and Durkheim, all tried to generalize about how societies changed and tried to establish some universal features of social organization, none of them saw the need to theorize on the global level. This connects in some important ways with the debate about the integrity of national cultures in a globalizing world, and particularly the influence of 'Western' economic, political, military and cultural forms on non-Western societies.

Globo-localism

A subset of the global culture approach, characterised as 'globo-localism', derives from a group of scholars from various countries and social science traditions whose main concern is to try to make sense of the multifaceted and enormously complex web of local-global relations. There is a good deal of overlap between this and the 'globalization of culture' model, but the globo-local researchers tend to emphasize the 'territorial' dimension.

This view has been actively developed within the International Sociological Association (ISA). The ISA 12th World Congress of Sociology in Madrid in 1990 was organized around the theme 'Sociology for One World: Unity and Diversity'. Mlinar (1992) reports that 'the issue of globalization was readily accepted' and his edited volume of papers from the conference illustrates the variety of issues raised in Madrid. The 1994 ISA Congress in Bielefeld, Germany, continued the theme under the title: 'Contested Boundaries and Shifting Solidarities' and again discussions of globalization were quite prominently featured on the agenda, and the 1998 Conference in Montreal continues the trend. It is not surprising that globalization and territory attracted attention, for in the background to the 1990 and 1994 conferences the wars in the former Yugoslavia were raging (Mlinar himself is from Slovenia, formerly part of Yugoslavia) and, of course, the first shocks of the end of the communist state system were giving way to new territorial issues created by an explosive mix of local and global forces.

If Mlinar is a European progenitor of the globo-local model, then the American progenitor is Alger (1998) who developed the concept of the 'local-global nexus'. There is no single common theoretical position in the work of Mlinar, Alger and the others involved in this enterprise. What unites them is the urge to theorize and research questions of what happens to *territorial identities* (within and across countries) in a globalizing world. Thus, it is part of the more general global culture model, but with a distinct territorial focus.

The main research question for all these writers is the autonomy of local cultures in the face of an advancing 'global culture'. Competing claims of local cultures against the forces of 'globalization' have forced themselves onto the sociological, cultural and political agendas all over the world. This is largely continuous with the focus of the third globalization model, based on the idea of global society.

III   Global Society Models

Inspiration for this general conception of globalization is often located in the pictures of planet earth sent back by space explorers. A classic statement of this was the report of Apollo XIV astronaut Edgar Mitchell in 1971:

> It was a beautiful, harmonious, peaceful-looking planet, blue with white clouds, and one that gave you a deep sense . . . of home, of being, of identity. It is what I prefer to call instant global consciousness.[3]

Had astronaut Mitchell penetrated a little through the clouds, he would also have seen horrific wars in Vietnam and other parts of Asia, bloody repression by various dictatorial regimes in Africa and Latin America, dead and maimed bodies as a result of sectarian terrorism in Britain and Ireland, as well as a terrible toll of human misery from hunger, disease, drug abuse and carnage on roads all round the world as automobile cultures intensified their own peculiar structures of globalization. Nevertheless, some leading globalization theorists, for example Giddens (1991) and Robertson (1992), do attribute great significance to ideas like 'global awareness' and 'planetary consciousness'.

Historically, global society theorists argue that the concept of world or global society has become a believable idea only in the modern age and, in particular, science, technology, industry and universal values are increasingly creating a twentieth century world that is different from any past age. The globalization literature is full of discussions of the decreasing power and significance of the nation-state and the increasing significance (if not actually power) of supra-national and global institutions and systems of belief. Ideas of space-time distanciation (see Giddens 1991) and of time-space compression (see Harvey 1989) illustrate how processes of globalization compress, stretch and deepen space-time for people all over the world thus creating some of the conditions for a global society.

In his attempt to order the field of globalization studies, Spybey (1996) contrasts the view that 'modernity is inherently globalizing' (Giddens 1991, p. 63) with the view that globalization predates modernity (Robertson 1992). While Spybey comes down in favour of Giddens' thesis that globalization is best conceptualized as 'reflexive modernization', he is less clear about why these differences matter and, in the end, as with so many debates in the social sciences, the main protagonists seem to be saying more or less the same things in rather different languages. However, it is important to establish whether globalization is a new name for a relatively old phenomenon (which appears to be the argument of Robertson), or whether it is relatively new, a phenomenon of late modenity (the argument of Giddens) or whether it is very new and primarily a consequence of post-1960s capitalism (the argument of Sklair). Why does this matter? It matters because if we want to understand our own lives and the lives of those around us, in our families, communities, local regions, countries, supra-national regions and, ultimately how we relate to the global, then it is absolutely fundamental that we are clear about the extent to which the many different structures within which we live are the same in the most important respects as they have been or are different. Two critics, in their attempt to demonstrate that globalization is a myth because the global economy does not really exist, argue that there is 'no fundamental difference between the international submarine telegraph cable method of financial trans-actions [of the early twentieth century] and contemporary electronic systems' (Hirst and Thompson 1996, p. 197). They are entirely mistaken. The fundamental difference is, pre-cisely, in the way that the electronics revolution (a post-1960s phenomenon) has trans-formed the quantitative possibilities of transferring cash and money capital into qualitatively new forms of corporate and personal financing, entrepreneurship and, crucially, the system of credit on which the global culture and ideology of consumerism largely rests. Some globalization theorists argue forcefully that these phenomena are all new and fundamental for understanding not only what is happening in the rich countries, but in social groups anywhere who have a part to play in this global system. In this sense the idea of a global society is a very provocative one but, while it is relatively easy to establish empirically the objective dimensions of globalization as they involve the large majority of the world's popu-lation, the idea of a global society based on subjective relationships to globalization, plane-tary consciousness and the like, is highly speculative.

There appears to be, however, a real psychological need for many writers to believe in the possibilities of a global society (which I share).[4] As McGrew (1992) shows, this theme is elaborated by scholars grappling with the apparent contradictions between globalization and local disruption and strife based on ethnic and other particularistic loyalties. It is in this type of approach that a growing appreciation of the ethical problems of globalization is particularly to be found. The reason for this is simple: now that humankind has the capacity to destroy itself through war and toxic accidents of various types, a democratic and just human society on the global level, however utopian, seems to be the best long-term guarantee of the continued survival of humanity (Held 1995).

IV   Global Capitalism Model

A fourth model of globalization locates the dominant global forces in the structures of an ever-more globalizing capitalism (for example, Ross and Trachte 1990, Sklair 1995, McMichael 1996; see also Robinson 1996). While all of these writers and others who could be identified with this approach develop their own specific analyses of globalization, they all strive towards a concept of the 'global' that involves more than the relations between nation-states and state-centrist explanations of national economies competing against each other.

Ross and Trachte focus specifically on capitalism as a social system which is best ana-lyzed on three levels, namely the level of the internal logic of the system (inspired by Marx and Adam Smith), the structural level of historical development and the level of the specific social formation, or society. They explain the deindustrialization of some of the heartland regions of capitalism and the transformations of what we still call the Third World in these terms and argue that the globalization of the capitalist system is deeply connected to the capitalist crises of the 1970s and after (oil price shocks, rising unemployment, and increasing insecurity as the rich countries experience problems in paying for their welfare states). This leads them to conclude that: 'We are only at the beginning of the global era' (Ross and Trachte 1990, p. 230).

Sklair proposes a more explicit model of the global system based on the concept of *transnational practices*, practices that originate with non-state actors and cross state borders. They are analytically distinguished in three spheres: economic, political and cultural-ideological. Each of these practices is primarily, but not exclusively, characterized by a major institution. The *transnational corporation* (TNC) is the most important institution for economic transnational practices; the *transnational capitalist class* (TCC) for political transnational practices; and the *culture-ideology of consumerism* for transnational cultural-ideological practices (Sklair 1995). The research agenda of this theory is concerned with how TNCs, transnational capitalist classes and the culture-ideology of consumerism operate to transform the world in terms of the global capitalist project.

The culture-ideology of consumerism prioritizes the exceptional place of consumption and consumerism in contemporary capitalism, increasing consumption expectations and aspirations without necessarily ensuring the income to buy. The extent to which economic and environmental constraints on the private accumulation of capital challenge the global capitalist project in general and its culture-ideology of consumerism in particular, is a central issue for global system theory (Sklair in Redclift and Benton 1994; see also Durning 1992).

McMichael (1996) focuses on the issue of Third World development and provides both theoretical and empirical support for the thesis that globalization is a qualitatively new phenomenon and not simply a quantitative expansion of older trends. . . .

To these writers on globalization and capitalism we can add other Marxist and Marx-inspired scholars who see capitalism as a global system, but do not have any specific concepts of globalization. The most important of these is the geographer, David Harvey, whose Marxist analysis of modernity and postmodernity is significant for the attempt to build a bridge between the debates around economic and cultural globalization (Harvey 1989, especially chapter 15).

Summing up the Approaches

Each of the four approaches to globalization has its own distinctive strengths and weaknesses. The world-system model tends to be economistic (minimizing the importance of political and cultural factors), but as globalization is often interpreted in terms of economic actors and economic institutions, this does seem to be a realistic approach. The globalization of culture model, on the other hand, tends to be culturalist (minimizing economic factors), but as much of the criticism of globalization comes from those who focus on the negative effects of homogenizing mass media and marketing on local and indigenous cultures, the culturalist approach has many adherents. The world society model tends to be both optimistic and all-inclusive, an excellent combination for the production of world-views, but less satisfactory for social science research programmes. Finally, the global capitalism model, by prioritising the global capitalist system and paying less attention to other global forces, runs the risk of appearing one-sided. However, the question remains: how important is that 'one side' (global capitalism)?

Resistances to Globalization

Globalization is often seen in terms of impersonal forces wreaking havoc on the lives of ordinary and defenceless people and communities. It is not coincidental that interest in globalization over the last two decades has been accompanied by an upsurge in what has come to be known as New Social Movements (NSM) research. NSM theorists, despite their substantial differences, argue that the traditional response of the labour movement to global capitalism, based on class politics, has generally failed, and that a new analysis based on identity politics (of gender, sexuality, ethnicity, age, community, belief systems) is necessary to mount effective resistance to sexism, racism, environmental damage, warmongering, capitalist exploitation and other forms of injustice.

The globalization of identity politics involves the establishment of global networks of people with similar identities and interests outside the control of international, state and local authorities. There is a substantial volume of research and documentation on such developments in the women's, peace and environmental movements, some of it in direct response to governmental initiatives (for example, alternative and NGO organization shadowing official United Nations and other conferences) but most theorists and activists tend to operate under the slogan: think global, act local (Ekins 1992).

The main challenges to global capitalism in the economic sphere have also come from those who 'think global and act local'. This normally involves disrupting the capacity of TNCs and global financial institutions to accumulate private profits at the expense of their workforces, their consumers and the communities which are affected by their activities. An important part of economic globalization today is the increasing dispersal of the manufacturing process into many discrete phases carried out in many different places. Being no longer so dependent on the production of one factory and one workforce gives capital a distinct advantage, particularly against the strike weapon which once gave tremendous negative power to the working class. Global production chains can be disrupted by strategically planned stoppages, but these generally act more as inconveniences than as real weapons of labour against capital. The international division of labour and its corollary, the globalization of production, builds flexibility into the system so that not only can capital migrate anywhere in the world to find the cheapest reliable productive sources of labour but also few workforces can any longer decisively 'hold capital to ransom' by withdrawing their labour. At the level of the production process, globalizing capital has all but defeated labour. In this respect, the global organization of the TNCs and allied institutions like globalizing government agencies and the World Bank have, so far, proved too powerful for the local organization of labour and communities.

Nevertheless, the global capitalists, if we are to believe their own propaganda, are continuously beset by opposition, boycott, legal challenge and moral outrage from the consumers of their products and by disruptions from their workers. There are also many ways to be ambivalent or hostile about global capitalism and cultures and ideologies of consumerism, some of which have been successfully exploited by the 'Green' movement (see Mander and Goldsmith 1996).

The issue of democracy is central to the advance of the forces of globalization and the practices and the prospects of social movements that oppose them, both local and global. The rule of law, freedom of association and expression, freely contested elections, as minimum conditions and however imperfectly sustained, are as necessary in the long run for mass market based global consumerist capitalism as they are for alternative social systems.[5]

Conclusion

This account of the state of globalization studies to date has focused on what distinguishes global from inter-national forces, processes and institutions. It is almost exclusively based on the European and North American literature and it does not preclude the possibility of other and quite different conceptions of globalization being developed elsewhere. Despite the view, particularly evident in the accounts of 'global culture' theorists that globalization is more or less the same as Westernization or Americanization or McDonaldization (Ritzer 1995), more and more critics are beginning to question this one-way traffic bias in the globalization literature. This critique is well-represented in the the empirical cases and analytical points of those who are 'Interrogating Theories of the Global' (in King 1991, chapter 6) and the work of African and Asian scholars represented in Albrow and King (1990), all of whom provide some necessary correctives to European-North American orthodoxies. These scholars, and others, are doing important research relevant for the study of globalization, and their work does not necessarily fit into the four approaches identified above. It is very likely that an introduction to globalization studies to be written ten years from now will reflect non-Western perspectives much more strongly. Nevertheless, although of quite recent vintage, it is undeniable that globalization as a theoretical issue and an object of research, is now firmly on the agenda of the social sciences.

NOTES

1   For example, research on the idea of commodity chains, networks of labour, production and marketing of goods, has shifted attention away from national economies to global forces, to some extent (see Gereffi in Sklair 1994, chapter 11).

2   See Stuart Hall's chapter 6 in Hall et al. (1992). Also relevant here are Appadurai's five dimensions of global cultural flows: ethnoscapes, mediascapes, technoscapes, financescapes, and ideoscapes (in Featherstone 1990, pp. 295–310).

3   This is quoted in many different places. My source is, significantly, from the back page of the 25th Anniversary Issue of *Earthmatters*, the magazine of Friends of the Earth, UK. The quote is superimposed on a very cloudy map of a rather polluted planet earth.

4   For example, Strauss and Falk argue 'For a Global People's Assembly' in the *International Herald Tribune*, (14 November 1997), a publication that advertises itself as the newspaper for global elites!

5   I say in the long run. In the short-term, authoritarian regimes can ignore demands for democratization and push forward consumerist market reforms. It is by no means obvious that everyone in the world prefers 'democracy' to 'economic prosperity', if that is the choice they are persuaded to accept.

REFERENCES

(place of publication is London unless otherwise indicated)

Albrow, M. (1996) *The Global Age*, Cambridge: Polity Press.

Albrow, M. and King, E. eds. (1990) *Globalization, Knowledge and Society*, Sage.

Alger, C. (1998) 'Perceiving, analysing and coping with the local-global nexus', *International Social Science Journal* 117, August: 321–40.

Barker, Chris (1997) *Global Television*, Oxford: Blackwell.

Barnet, R. and Cavanagh, J. (1994) *Global Dreams*, New York: Simon and Schuster.

Chase-Dunn, C. (1989) *Global Formation*, Oxford: Blackwell.

Dicken, P. (1998) *Global Shift: Transforming the World Economy*, Paul Chapman, third edition.

Dowmunt, T. ed. (1993) *Channels of Resistance: Global Television and Local Empowerment*, BFI/Channel Four.

Dunning, J. (1993) *Multinational Enterprises and the Global Economy*, Wokingham: Addison-Wesley.

Durning, A. (1992) How Much is Enough, *Earthscan*.

Ekins, P. (1992) *A new world order: grassroots movements for global change*, Routledge.

Featherstone, M. ed. (1990) *Global Culture: Nationalism, Globalization and Identity*, Sage.

Giddens, A. (1991) *The Consequences of Modernity*, Cambridge: Polity Press.

Hall, S., Held, D. and McGrew, T. eds. (1992) *Modernity and its Futures*, Cambridge: Polity Press.

Harvey, D. (1989) *The Condition of Postmodernity*, Oxford: Basil Blackwell.

Held, D. (1995) *Democracy and the Global Order*, Cambridge: Polity Press.

Hirst, P. and Thompson, G. (1996) *Globalization in Question: The International Economy and the Possibilities of Governance*, Cambridge: Polity Press.

King, A.D. ed. (1991) *Culture, Globalization and the World-System*, Macmillan.

Mander, Jerry and Goldsmith, Edward eds. (1996) *The Case against the Global Economy*, San Francisco: Sierra Club.

McGrew, T. (1992) 'A Global Society?', in Hall et al. eds, op. cit.

McMichael, P. (1996) *Development and Social Change: A Global Perspective*, Thousand Oaks: Pine Forge Press.

Mlinar, Z. ed. (1992) *Globalization and Territorial Identities*, Aldershot: Avebury.

Nordenstreng, K. and Schiller, H. eds. (1993) *Beyond National Sovereignty: International Communication in the 1990s*, Norwood: Ablex.

Ohmae, K. (1990) *The Borderless World. Power and Strategy in the Interlinked Economy*. New York: Harper Business.

Redclift, M. and Benton, T. eds. (1994) *Social Theory and the Global Environment*, Routledge.

Ritzer, G. (1995) *The McDonaldization of Society*, Thousand Oaks: Pine Forge, second edition.

Robertson, R. (1992) *Globalization: Social Theory and Global Culture*, Sage.

Robinson, William (1996) 'Globalisation: nine theses on our epoch', *Race and Class* 38(2): 13–31.

Ross, R. and Trachte, K. (1990) *Global Capitalism: The New Leviathan*, Albany, NY: State University of New York Press.

Scott, Alan ed. (1997) *The Limits of Globalization*, Routledge.

Shannon, T. (1989) *An Introduction to the World-System Perspective*, Boulder: Westview.

Sklair, L. (1998) 'Globalization and the Corporations: The case of the California Fortune Global 500', *International Journal of Urban and Regional Research* (June).

—— (1995) *Sociology of the Global System*, Baltimore: Johns Hopkins UP, second edition (first ed. 1991).

—— ed. (1994) *Capitalism and Development*, Routledge.

Spybey, T. (1996) *Globalization and World Society*, Cambridge: Polity Press.

Sussman, G. and Lent, J. eds. (1991) *Transnational Communications: Wiring the Third World*, Sage.

Wallerstein, I. (1979) *The Capitalist World-Economy*, Cambridge: Cambridge University Press.

—— (1991) 'The construction of peoplehood: racism, nationalism, ethnicity'. In E. Balibar and I. Wallerstein, eds. *'Race', Nation, Class*, Verso.

Waters, M. (1995) *Globalization*, Routledge.

Yearley, S. (1996) *Sociology, Environmentalism, Globalization: Reinventing the Globe*, Sage.

15　It's a Flat World, After All (2005)

Thomas L. Friedman

In 1492 Christopher Columbus set sail for India, going west. He had the Niña, the Pinta and the Santa María. He never did find India, but he called the people he met "Indians" and came home and reported to his king and queen: "The world is round." I set off for India 512 years later. I knew just which direction I was going. I went east. I had Lufthansa business class, and I came home and reported only to my wife and only in a whisper: "The world is flat."

And therein lies a tale of technology and geoeconomics that is fundamentally reshaping our lives – much, much more quickly than many people realize. It all happened while we were sleeping, or rather while we were focused on 9/11, the dot-com bust, and Enron – which even prompted some to wonder whether globalization was over. Actually, just the opposite was true, which is why it's time to wake up and prepare ourselves for this flat world, because others already are, and there is no time to waste.

I wish I could say I saw it all coming. Alas, I encountered the flattening of the world quite by accident. It was in late February of last year, and I was visiting the Indian high-tech capital, Bangalore, working on a documentary for the Discovery Times channel about outsourcing. In short order, I interviewed Indian entrepreneurs who wanted to prepare my taxes from Bangalore, read my X-rays from Bangalore, trace my lost luggage from Bangalore and write my new software from Bangalore. The longer I was there, the more upset I became – upset at the realization that while I had been off covering the 9/11 wars, globalization had entered a whole new phase, and I had missed it. I guess the eureka moment came on a visit to the campus of Infosys Technologies, one of the crown jewels of the Indian outsourcing and software industry. Nandan Nilekani, the Infosys CEO, was showing me his global videoconference room, pointing with pride to a wall-size flat-screen TV, which he said was the biggest in Asia. Infosys, he explained, could hold a virtual meeting of the key players from its entire global supply chain for any project at any time on that supersize screen. So its American designers could be on the screen speaking with their Indian software writers and their Asian manufacturers all at once. That's what globalization is all about today, Nilekani said. Above the screen there were eight clocks that pretty well summed up the Infosys workday: 24/7/365. The clocks were labeled US West, US East, GMT, India, Singapore, Hong Kong, Japan, Australia.

"Outsourcing is just one dimension of a much more fundamental thing happening today in the world," Nilekani explained. "What happened over the last years is that there was a massive investment in technology, especially in the bubble era, when hundreds of millions of dollars were invested in putting broadband connectivity around the world, undersea cables, all those things." At the same time, he added, computers became cheaper and dispersed all over the world, and there was an explosion of e-mail software, search engines like Google, and proprietary software that can chop up any piece of work and send one part to Boston, one part to Bangalore, and one part to Beijing, making it easy for anyone to do remote development. When all of these things suddenly came together around 2000, Nilekani said, they "created a platform where intellectual work, intellectual capital, could be delivered from anywhere. It could be disaggregated, delivered, distributed, produced and put back together again – and this gave a whole new degree of freedom to the way we do work, especially work of an intellectual nature. And what you are seeing in Bangalore today is really the culmination of all these things coming together."

At one point, summing up the implications of all this, Nilekani uttered a phrase that rang in my ear. He said to me, "Tom, the playing field is being leveled." He meant that countries like India were now able to compete equally for global knowledge work as never before – and that America had better get ready for this. As I left the Infosys campus that evening and bounced along the potholed road back to Bangalore, I kept chewing on that phrase: "The playing field is being leveled."

"What Nandan is saying," I thought, "is that the playing field is being flattened. Flattened? Flattened? My God, he's telling me the world is flat!"

Here I was in Bangalore – more than 500 years after Columbus sailed over the horizon, looking for a shorter route to India using the rudimentary navigational technologies of his day, and returned safely to prove definitively that the world was round – and one of India's smartest engineers, trained at his country's top technical institute and backed by the most modern technologies of his day, was telling me that the world was flat, as flat as that screen on which he can host a meeting of his whole global supply chain. Even more interesting, he was citing this development as a new milestone in human progress and a great opportunity for India and the world – the fact that we had made our world flat!

This has been building for a long time. Globalization 1.0 (1492 to 1800) shrank the world from a size large to a size medium, and the dynamic force in that era was countries globalizing for resources and imperial conquest. Globalization 2.0 (1800 to 2000) shrank the world from a size medium to a size small, and it was spearheaded by companies globalizing for markets and labor. Globalization 3.0 (which started around 2000) is shrinking the world from a size small to a size tiny and flattening the playing field at the same time. And while the dynamic force in Globalization 1.0 was countries globalizing and the dynamic force in Globalization 2.0 was companies globalizing, the dynamic force in Globalization 3.0 – the thing that gives it its unique character – is individuals and small groups globalizing. Individuals must, and can, now ask: where do I fit into the global competition and opportunities of the day, and how can I, on my own, collaborate with others globally? But Globalization 3.0 not only differs from the previous eras in how it is shrinking and flattening the world and in how it is empowering individuals. It is also different in that Globalization 1.0 and 2.0 were driven primarily by European and American companies and countries. But going forward, this will be less and less true. Globalization 3.0 is not only going to be driven more by individuals but also by a much more diverse – non-Western, nonwhite – group of individuals. In Globalization 3.0, you are going to see every color of the human rainbow take part.

"Today, the most profound thing to me is the fact that a 14-year-old in Romania or Bangalore or the Soviet Union or Vietnam has all the information, all the tools, all the software easily available to apply knowledge however they want," said Marc Andreessen, a co-founder of Netscape and creator of the first commercial Internet browser. "That is why I am sure the next Napster is going to come out of left field. As bioscience becomes more computational and less about wet labs and as all the genomic data becomes easily available on the Internet, at some point you will be able to design vaccines on your laptop."

Andreessen is touching on the most exciting part of Globalization 3.0 and the flattening of the world: the fact that we are now in the process of connecting all the knowledge pools in the world together. We've tasted some of the downsides of that in the way that Osama bin Laden has connected terrorist knowledge pools together through his al-Qaeda network, not to mention the work of teenage hackers spinning off more and more lethal computer viruses that affect us all. But the upside is that by connecting all these knowledge pools we are on the cusp of an incredible new era of innovation, an era that will be driven from left field and right field, from West and East, and from North and South. Only 30 years ago, if you had a choice of being born a B student in Boston or a genius in Bangalore or Beijing, you probably would have chosen Boston, because a genius in Beijing or Bangalore could not really take advantage of his or her talent. They could not plug and play globally. Not anymore. Not when the world is flat, and anyone with smarts, access to Google, and a cheap wireless laptop can join the innovation fray.

When the world is flat, you can innovate without having to emigrate. This is going to get interesting. We are about to see creative destruction on steroids.

How did the world get flattened, and how did it happen so fast?

It was a result of 10 events and forces that all came together during the 1990s and converged right around the year 2000. Let me go through them briefly. The first event was 11/9. That's right – not 9/11, but 11/9. November 9, 1989, is the day the Berlin Wall came down, which was critically important because it allowed us to think of the world as a single space. "The Berlin Wall was not only a symbol of keeping people inside Germany; it was a way of preventing a kind of global view of our future," the Nobel Prize-winning economist Amartya Sen said. And the wall went down just as the windows went up – the breakthrough Microsoft Windows 3.0 operating system, which helped to flatten the playing field even more by creating a global computer interface, shipped six months after the wall fell.

The second key date was 8/9. August 9, 1995, is the day Netscape went public, which did two important things. First, it brought the Internet alive by giving us the browser to display images and data stored on Web sites. Second, the Netscape stock offering triggered the dot-com boom, which triggered the dot-com bubble, which triggered the massive overinvestment of billions of dollars in fiber-optic telecommunications cable. That overinvestment, by companies like Global Crossing, resulted in the willy-nilly creation of a global undersea-underground fiber network, which in turn drove down the cost of transmitting voices, data, and images to practically zero, which in turn accidentally made Boston, Bangalore, and Beijing next-door neighbors overnight. In sum, what the Netscape revolution did was bring people-to-people connectivity to a whole new level. Suddenly more people could connect with more other people from more different places in more different ways than ever before.

No country accidentally benfited more from the Netscape moment than India. "India had no resources and no infrastructure," said Dinakar Singh, one of the most respected hedge-fund managers on Wall Street, whose parents earned doctoral degrees in biochemistry from the University of Delhi before emigrating to America. "It produced people with quality and by quantity. But many of them rotted on the docks of India like vegetables. Only a relative few could get on ships and get out. Not anymore, because we built this ocean crosser, called fiber-optic cable. For decades you had to leave India to be a professional. Now you can plug into the world from India. You don't have to go to Yale and go to work for Goldman Sachs." India could never have afforded to pay for the bandwidth to connect brainy India with high-tech America, so American shareholders paid for it. Yes, crazy overinvestment can be good. The overinvestment in railroads turned out to be a great boon for the American economy. "But the railroad overinvestment was confined to your own country and so, too, were the benefits," Singh said. In the case of the digital railroads, "it was the foreigners who benefited." India got a free ride.

The first time this became apparent was when thousands of Indian engineers were enlisted to fix the Y2K – the year 2000 – computer bugs for companies from all over the world. (Y2K should be a national holiday in India. Call it "Indian Interdependence Day," says Michael Mandelbaum, a foreign-policy analyst at Johns Hopkins.) The fact that the Y2K work could be outsourced to Indians was made possible by the first two flatteners, along with a third, which I call "workflow." Workflow is shorthand for all the software applications, standards, and electronic transmission pipes, like middleware, that connected all those computers and fiber-optic cable. To put it another way, if the Netscape moment connected people to people like never before, what the workflow revolution did was connect applications to applications so that people all over the world could work together in manipulating and shaping words, data, and images on computers like never before.

Indeed, this breakthrough in people-to-people and application-to-application connectivity produced, in short order, six more flatteners – six new ways in which individuals and companies could collaborate on work and share knowledge. One was "outsourcing." When my software applications could connect seamlessly with all of your applications, it meant that all kinds of work – from accounting to software writing – could be digitized, disaggregated, and shifted to any place in the world where it could be done better and cheaper. The second was "offshoring." I send my whole factory from Canton, Ohio, to Canton, China. The third was "open-sourcing." I write the next operating system, Linux, using engineers collaborating together online and working for free. The fourth was "insourcing." I let a company like UPS come inside my company and take over my whole logistics operation – everything from filling my orders online to delivering my goods to repairing them for customers when they break. (People have no idea what UPS really does today. You'd be amazed!) The fifth was "supply-chaining." This is Wal-Mart's specialty. I create a global supply chain down to the last atom of efficiency so that if I sell an item in Arkansas, another is immediately made in China. (If Wal-Mart were a country, it would be China's eighth largest trading partner.) The last new form of collaboration I call "informing" – this is Google, Yahoo, and MSN Search, which now allow anyone to collaborate with, and mine, unlimited data all by themselves.

So the first three flatteners created the new platform for collaboration, and the next six are the new forms of collaboration that flattened the world even more. The tenth flattener I call "the steroids," and these are wireless access and voice over Internet protocol (VoIP). What the steroids do is turbocharge all these new forms of collaboration, so you can now do any one of them, from anywhere, with any device.

The world got flat when all 10 of these flatteners converged around the year 2000. This created a global, Web-enabled playing field that allows for multiple forms of collaboration on research and work in real time, without regard to geography, distance or, in the near future, even language. "It is the creation of this platform, with these unique attributes, that is the truly important sustainable breakthrough that made what you call the flattening of the world possible," said Craig Mundie, the chief technical officer of Microsoft.

No, not everyone has access yet to this platform, but it is open now to more people in more places on more days in more ways than anything like it in history. Wherever you look today – whether it is the world of journalism, with bloggers bringing down Dan Rather; the world of software, with the Linux code writers working in online forums for free to challenge Microsoft; or the world of business, where Indian and Chinese innovators are competing against and working with some of the most advanced Western multinationals – hierarchies are being flattened and value is being created less and less within vertical silos and more and more through horizontal collaboration within companies, between companies, and among individuals.

Do you recall "the IT revolution" that the business press has been pushing for the last 20 years? Sorry to tell you this, but that was just the prolog. The last 20 years were about forging, sharpening, and distributing all the new tools to collaborate and connect. Now the real information revolution is about to begin as all the complementarities among these collaborative tools start to converge. One of those who first called this moment by its real name was Carly Fiorina, the former Hewlett-Packard CEO, who in 2004 began to declare in her public speeches that the dot-com boom and bust were just "the end of the beginning." The last 25 years in technology, Fiorina said, have just been "the warm-up act." Now we are going into the main event, she said, "and by the main event, I mean an era in which technology will truly transform every aspect of business, of government, of society, of life."

As if the flattening wasn't enough, another convergence coincidentally occurred during the 1990s that was equally important. Some three billion people who were out of the game walked, and often ran, onto the playing field. I am talking about the people of China, India, Russia, Eastern Europe, Latin America, and Central Asia. Their economies and political systems all opened up during the course of the 1990s so that their people were increasingly able to join the free market. And when did these three billion people converge with the new playing field and the new business processes? Right when it was being flattened, right when millions of them could compete and collaborate more equally, more horizontally, and with cheaper and more readily available tools. Indeed, thanks to the flattening of the world, many of these new entrants didn't even have to leave home to participate. Thanks to the 10 flatteners, the playing field came to them!

It is this convergence – of new players, on a new playing field, developing new processes for horizontal collaboration – that I believe is the most important force shaping global economics and politics in the early twenty-first century. Sure, not all three billion can collaborate and compete. In fact, for most people the world is not yet flat at all. But even if we're talking about only 10 percent, that's 300 million people – about twice the size of the American workforce. And be advised: the Indians and Chinese are not racing us to the bottom. They are racing us to the top. What China's leaders really want is that the next generation of underwear and airplane wings not just be "made in China" but also be "designed in China." And that is where things are heading. So in 30 years we will have gone from "sold in China" to "made in China" to "designed in China" to "dreamed up in China" – or from China as collaborator with the worldwide manufacturers on nothing to China as a low-cost, high-quality, hyperefficient collaborator with worldwide manufacturers on everything. Ditto India. Said Craig Barrett, the CEO of Intel, "You don't bring three billion people into the world economy overnight without huge consequences, especially from three societies" – like India, China, and Russia – "with rich educational heritages."

That is why there is nothing that guarantees that Americans or Western Europeans will continue leading the way. These new players are stepping onto the playing field legacy-free, meaning that many of them were so far behind that they can leap right into the new technologies without having to worry about all the sunken costs of old systems. It means that they can move very fast to adopt new, state-of-the-art technologies, which is why there are already more cellphones in use in China today than there are people in America.

If you want to appreciate the sort of challenge we are facing, let me share with you two conversations. One was with some of the Microsoft officials who were involved in setting up Microsoft's research center in Beijing, Microsoft Research Asia, which opened in 1998 – after Microsoft sent teams to Chinese universities to administer IQ tests in order to recruit the best brains from China's 1.3 billion people. Out of the 2,000 top Chinese engineering and science students tested, Microsoft hired 20. They have a saying at Microsoft about their Asia center, which captures the intensity of competition it takes to win a job there and explains why it is already the most productive research team at Microsoft: "Remember, in China, when you are one in a million, there are 1,300 other people just like you."

The other is a conversation I had with Rajesh Rao, a young Indian entrepreneur who started an electronic-game company from Bangalore, which today owns the rights to Charlie Chaplin's image for mobile computer games. Rao said:

> We can't relax. I think in the case of the United States that is what happened a bit. Please look at me: I am from India. We have been at a very different level before in terms of technology and business. But once we saw we had an infrastructure that made the world a small place, we promptly tried to make the best use of it. We saw there were so many things we could do. We went ahead, and today what we are seeing is a result of that. There is no time to rest. That is gone. There are dozens of people who are doing the same thing you are doing, and they are trying to do it better. It is like water in a tray: you shake it, and it will find the path of least resistance. That is what is going to happen to so many jobs – they will go to that corner of the world where there is the least resistance and the most opportunity. If there is a skilled person in Timbuktu, he will get work if he knows how to access the rest of the world, which is quite easy today. You can make a Web site and have an e-mail address and you are up and running. And if you are able to demonstrate your work, using the same infrastructure, and if people are comfortable giving work to you and if you are diligent and clean in your transactions, then you are in business.

Instead of complaining about outsourcing, Rao said, Americans and Western Europeans would "be better off thinking about how you can raise your bar and raise yourselves into doing something better. Americans have consistently led in innovation over the last century. Americans whining – we have never seen that before."

Rao is right. And it is time we got focused. As a person who grew up during the Cold War, I'll always remember driving down the highway and listening to the radio, when suddenly the music would stop and a grim-voiced announcer would come on the air and say: "This is a test. This station is conducting a test of the Emergency Broadcast System." And then a high-pitched siren would sound for 20 seconds. Fortunately, we never had to live through a moment in the Cold War when the announcer came on and said, "This is not a test."

That, however, is exactly what I want to say here: "This is not a test."

The long-term opportunities and challenges that the flattening of the world puts before the United States are profound. Therefore, our ability to get by doing things the way we've been doing them – which is to say not always enriching our secret sauce – will not suffice any more. "For a country as wealthy we are, it is amazing how little we are doing to enhance our natural competitiveness," says Dinakar Singh, the Indian-American hedge-fund manager. "We are in a world that has a system that now allows convergence among many billions of people, and we had better step back and figure out what it means. It would be a nice coincidence if all the things that were true before were still true now, but there are quite a few things you actually need to do differently. You need to have a much more thoughtful national discussion."

If this moment has any parallel in recent American history, it is the height of the Cold War, around 1957, when the Soviet Union leapt ahead of America in the space race by putting up the Sputnik satellite. The main challenge then came from those who wanted to put up walls; the main challenge to America today comes from the fact that all the walls are being taken down and many other people can now compete and collaborate with us much more directly. The main challenge in that world was from those practicing extreme Communism, namely Russia, China, and North Korea. The main challenge to America today is from those practicing extreme capitalism, namely China, India, and South Korea. The main objective in that era was building a strong state, and the main objective in this era is building strong individuals.

Meeting the challenges of flatism requires as comprehensive, energetic, and focused a response as did meeting the challenge of Communism. It requires a president who can summon the nation to work harder, get smarter, attract more young women and men to science and engineering, and build the broadband infrastructure, portable pensions, and health care that will help every American become more employable in an age in which no one can guarantee you lifetime employment.

We have been slow to rise to the challenge of flatism, in contrast to Communism, maybe because flatism doesn't involve ICBM missiles aimed at our cities. Indeed, the hot line, which used to connect the Kremlin with the White House, has been replaced by the help line, which connects everyone in America to call centers in Bangalore. While the other end of the hot line might have had Leonid Brezhnev threatening nuclear war, the other end of the help line just has a soft voice eager to help you sort out your AOL bill or collaborate with you on a new piece of software. No, that voice has none of the menace of Nikita

Khrushchev pounding a shoe on the table at the United Nations, and it has none of the sinister snarl of the bad guys in *From Russia With Love*. No, that voice on the help line just has a friendly Indian lilt that masks any sense of threat or challenge. It simply says: "Hello, my name is Rajiv. Can I help you?"

No, Rajiv, actually you can't. When it comes to responding to the challenges of the flat world, there is no help line we can call. We have to dig into ourselves. We in America have all the basic economic and educational tools to do that. But we have not been improving those tools as much as we should. That is why we are in what Shirley Ann Jackson, the 2004 president of the American Association for the Advancement of Science and president of Rensselaer Polytechnic Institute, calls a "quiet crisis" – one that is slowly eating away at America's scientific and engineering base.

"If left unchecked," said Jackson, the first African American woman to earn a PhD in physics from MIT, "this could challenge our pre-eminence and capacity to innovate." And it is our ability to constantly innovate new products, services, and companies that has been the source of America's horn of plenty and steadily widening middle class for the last two centuries. This quiet crisis is a product of three gaps now plaguing American society. The first is an "ambition gap." Compared with the young, energetic Indians and Chinese, too many Americans have gotten too lazy. As David Rothkopf, a former official in the Clinton Commerce Department, puts it, "The real entitlement we need to get rid of is our sense of entitlement." Second, we have a serious numbers gap building. We are not producing enough engineers and scientists. We used to make up for that by importing them from India and China, but in a flat world, where people can now stay home and compete with us, and in a post-9/11 world, where we are insanely keeping out many of the first-round intellectual draft choices in the world for exaggerated security reasons, we can no longer cover the gap. That's a key reason companies are looking abroad. The numbers are not here. And finally we are developing an education gap. Here is the dirty little secret that no CEO wants to tell you: they are not just outsourcing to save on salary. They are doing it because they can often get better skilled and more productive people than their American workers.

These are some of the reasons that Bill Gates, the Microsoft chairman, warned the governors' conference in a February 26 speech that American high-school education is "obsolete." As Gates put it:

> When I compare our high schools to what I see when I'm traveling abroad, I am terrified for our workforce of tomorrow. In math and science, our fourth graders are among the top students in the world. By eighth grade, they're in the middle of the pack. By 12th grade, US students are scoring near the bottom of all industrialized nations . . . The percentage of a population with a college degree is important, but so are sheer numbers. In 2001, India graduated almost a million more students from college than the United States did. China graduates twice as many students with bachelor's degrees as the US, and they have six times as many graduates majoring in engineering. In the international competition to have the biggest and best supply of knowledge workers, America is falling behind.

We need to get going immediately. It takes 15 years to train a good engineer, because, ladies and gentlemen, this really is rocket science. So parents, throw away the Game Boy, turn off the television, and get your kids to work. There is no sugar-coating this: in a flat world, every individual is going to have to run a little faster if he or she wants to advance his or her standard of living. When I was growing up, my parents used to say to me: "Tom, finish your dinner – people in China are starving." But after sailing to the edges of the flat world for a year, I am now telling my own daughters: "Girls, finish your homework – people in China and India are starving for your jobs."

I repeat, this is not a test. This is the beginning of a crisis that won't remain quiet for long. And as the Stanford economist Paul Romer so rightly says, "A crisis is a terrible thing to waste."

Part IV   The Opportunities and Limits of Unfettered Globalization

Introduction

An important common focus in the readings in Part III was that we are witnessing a centralization of control over finance and trade. The institutional epicenters of this global concentration of power include international financial institutions such as the IMF and World Bank, as well as global regulatory agencies such as the WTO. The six readings in Part IV constitute a debate over this pattern, identifying the winners and losers in global reorganization of capitalism and discussing whether this trajectory allows for genuine possibilities for development among poorer, less industrialized nations. Our goal in selecting these excerpts was to represent a continuum along this debate, but exclude works that are not academic or that are overly polemical.

One common focus among these selections is the role of bureaucratic structures that are emerging as de facto, quasi-global governance. Through these descriptions and debates we are reminded of the older debates surrounding Adam Smith's advocacy of free trade. Proponents of minimal state intrusion, principally Johan Norberg, argue that the world has greatly benefited from unfettered global trade. Opponents implicitly agree that there is nothing "value-free" about free trade or refraining from activist development policies. Giovanni Arrighi, Beverly Silver, and Benjamin Brewer, as well as Robert Wade and Dani Rodrik argue that value-free development policies are not really value-free if they constrain developing countries from making important choices about what types of trade and government policies to pursue in order to meet their particular challenges with development. Instead, as Joseph Stiglitz's description of how the global economy is controlled from the "commanding heights" of international financial institutions and the world's most powerful governments demonstrates, the bureaucratic organizations' advocacy of free trade is a clear ideology. If development policies systematically privilege the same groups and routinely favor economic development over environmental protection or human rights, then free trade as a development policy is neither "value-free" nor "free." Instead, they argue, free trade represents the interests of the dominant global classes, reflected in international financial institutions, trade policy communities, and large, global corporate interests.

Johan Norberg, whose blog can be found on the Web at johannorberg.net, describes himself as a reformed left-wing anarchist who has swung over to become a spokesperson for liberalism in the classical European sense – free-trade "libertarianism" as used in the United States. Norberg is a Fellow at Timbro, the Swedish think tank, and his book from which our extract comes was published by the Washington, DC libertarian lobby, the Cato Institute. It describes itself as "the first book to rebut, systematically and thoroughly, the claims of the anti-globalization movement." By stepping back and using data to describe sharply positive global trends in poverty, hunger, education, democratization, oppression of women, and inequality, Norberg shows "why capitalism is in the process of creating a better world." He acknowledges that "the world [still] has more than its share of serious problems," but argues that where free-trade and small-state policies have been allowed to operate the longest, "the fantastic thing is that the spread of democracy and capitalism has reduced them so dramatically" (p. 61).

Counterbalancing Norberg's enthusiasm for globalization is Wade's "What Strategies are Viable for Developing Countries Today? The World Trade Organization and the Shrinking of 'Development Space,'" which appeared in the *Review of International Political Economy* in 2003. Wade, who is a native of New Zealand, is Professor of Development Studies at the London School of Economics. In this selection he presents a stark and troubling image: that the wealthy nations have "kicked out the development ladder" after climbing up, and systematically tipped "the playing field against developing countries." Wade describes the urgency of the issue, on moral grounds and, like Mark Duffield (discussed below), as an issue of security, because "globalization erodes the insulation of the North" from the responses of the South. Major treaties being negotiated under the WTO structure will hamstring poor nations in ways that now-developed nations never had to deal with. Wade describes how the WTO staff who drafted these agreements was "driven by a mixture of ideological conviction and intense corporate lobbying." Worse, Wade explains, are bilateral investment treaties, like the North American Free Trade Agreement (NAFTA) and others, which establish arbitration boards dominated by "private sector adjudicators naturally sympathetic to the needs of the firm." By contrast, Wade cites severe protectionism in Britain, Germany, and the United States during their periods of advancement in the world system. He calls the current round of agreements (with a self-admitted touch of hyperbole) "a slow motion Great Train Robbery." Wade suggests that import substitution was rejected too summarily, and that when carefully applied could be an important part of national development strategies that build "articulated" national economies (a rebirth of issues discussed by Amin and de Janvry and Garramón long ago, as described in the editors' introduction to this volume, pp. 1–16). Wade ends with a call for a new coalition of developing nations, social movements, responsible corporations, and "epistemic communities" of scholars rethinking development strategies.

Nobel Prize-winning economist Joseph Stiglitz was Chairman of the Council of Economic Advisors in the 1990s Clinton White House and then Senior Vice-President and Chief Economist at the World Bank in the late 1990s. His increasingly critical remarks led to his removal from the bank, after which he became professor at Columbia University. Acknowledging the critics of globalization, Stiglitz's main point is that "the problem is not with globalization, but how it has been managed." That is precisely what Stiglitz chronicles in *Globalization and its Discontents*, and in this piece published in Web-magazine *The American Prospect* from around the time of that book's publication. In addition to stinging critiques of the World Bank, the IMF, and the WTO, Stiglitz recommends specific major changes for these organizations. This piece lays out his plan for reform, focusing on voting rules and governance on the one hand, and on a far humbler mindset. For example, rather than standing behind ideologically driven orthodoxy and unrealistically positive predictions, Stiglitz argues that the IMF should drop its inflexible prescriptions for poor nations. Stiglitz lays out seven points of reform for these global institutions to "address the legitimate concerns of those who have expressed a discontent with globalization."

In an interview on the *Boston Review* Web page, Dani Rodrik, an expert on globalization with the Institute for International Economics at Harvard University, once said that "globalization has become a bogeyman – a topic about which it is futile to expect to have a rational conversation." In earlier work, he suggests that negative assessments of globalization are merely the complaints of those who have lost out in the process: labor unions, retired persons, and environmentalists, for example. Politicians and employers are making the situation worse for workers, Rodrik argued, by using globalization as an excuse to take advantage of workers' perceived vulnerability. The new excerpt we have chosen for this edition begins with a "modern-day fable" of an imagined Martian landing in Washington who is unable to find any evidence supporting the "accepted knowledge" among economists on what developing nations should do to ensure their success. The piece is a sustained plea for allowing poorer nations more flexibility in choosing their model of development for themselves – free of demands, they open their markets to free trade and slash their government spending. He also pleads for accountability of governments to their national citizens, and argues against the excessive power over these nations by "foreign investors, country-fund managers in London and New York, and a relatively small group of domestic exporters." Like Wade, Rodrik blasts several of the key agreements proposed under the WTO treaties, especially the TRIPS (Trade-related Aspects of Intellectual Property Rights) and TRIMS (Trade-related Investment Measures). The first of these would force poor nations to enforce copyright laws from wealthy nations, which Rodrik argues would block their progress and mean the transfer of billions of dollars from poor to rich nations. The TRIMS agreement makes it even harder for nations to plan their nations' development and assure benefits from investments and government spending. In short, Rodrik persists in seeking "rational conversation" on globalization, calls for caution against undermining national governments, and suggests great skepticism on the value of free-trade approaches for most nations. Perhaps Adam Smith would not be pleased.

Norberg, Rodrik, Stiglitz, and Jeffrey Sachs (who is represented in Part V) all agree that globalization is here to stay, that globalization has brought incalculable improvements for people in poor countries, and that there are serious and real impacts of globalization for societies throughout the world. The latter three argue that the mantra of unfettered trade has been pushed too far as an ideology, that the state *is* important, and that globalization has real problems; they also concur that neither proponents nor opponents rightly identify or address those challenges. The answer, for all three, are better policies, both economic and public, as well as stronger democracies and better access to education. They criticize opponents of globalization for pushing isolationist, or statist measures, when those measures will not necessarily improve the livelihoods of those in the poorest parts of the world. They identify secrecy, the blind following of one ideology, and bad leadership in international financial institutions (like the World Bank and the IMF) as serious obstacles.

Johns Hopkins University sociology professors Giovanni Arrighi and Beverly Silver and their doctoral student Benjamin Brewer directly address some of the contentions about globalization made by authors such as Friedman, Norberg, Stiglitz, and Rodrik. They document how nations of the global "South" imitated the industrialization of nations in the North, assuming that it would bring benefits and allow them to catch up. They describe how the costs of industrialization have almost never been taken into account, including devastating environmental damage, social disruptions, and most importantly, a steady increase in inequality. For reasons of space we have cut from the piece many tables describing this enduring inequality, and refer readers to the original piece which appeared in the journal *Studies in Comparative International Development* in 2003. These show, among other things, that in spite of massive industrialization drives around the world, the gap between income per capita in the global North and South has persisted overall, and grown far wider in most of the "developing" world. Overall, in 1998 "Third World" nations had incomes less than one-twentieth those of the wealthy "First World," just as they did in 1960. Sub-Saharan Africa, Latin America, and West Asia and North Africa all saw the gap widen between their wealth and that of the First World over those four decades. Only China and the rest of East Asia gained ground. Arrighi, Silver, and Brewer argue that there is very little "development" that now comes with industrialization, that the "creative destruction" of capitalism's global reorganization is creating very few nations one can call winners.

Finally, "The New Development–Security Terrain" is Mark Duffield's fascinating introduction to his 2001 book *Global Governance and the New Wars: The Merging of Development and Security*. Duffield, now Professor in the Institute for Politics and International Studies at the University of Leeds in the UK, has had a ground-level view from having worked for Oxfam in the Sudan for four years. He takes on many common assumptions about the role of aid and how to keep "stability" and peace in the parts of the world left behind by modernization and development. Published in the United States just days before the September 11, 2001 attacks there, Duffield's book argues that the exclusion of many nations from the global economy has led them to "perverse" incorporation in the global economy and "network wars." The piece's premonitions on this last point are striking: "The question of security has almost gone full circle: from being concerned with the biggest economies and war machines in the world to an interest in some of its smallest." This is a powerful reason for wealthy nations to care about places well down the "hierarchy of compassion," to attempt to address issues in nations that are not easy to work with, and who do not play by our rules of transparency, democracy, or free trade. Also clairvoyant was Duffield's descriptions of the privatization of war and the blurring of state–nonstate, military–civilian, and public–private lines. What may be most original here, however, is Duffield's critique of international aid, and the focus by the international community on avoiding conflicts and creating stability. Citing David Held (excerpted in the next section below), Duffield reminds us of war being "an axis of social reordering . . . a powerful mechanism for the globalisation of economic, political and scientific relations." Duffield's distinct focus on the linkages between development and national security reminds us of how vast the implications of globalization and the regulatory structures attempting to govern it really are.

16   In Defense of Global Capitalism (2003)

Johan Norberg

Introduction

[. . .]

I love what is rather barrenly termed "globalization," the process by which people, information, trade, investments, democracy, and the market economy are tending more and more to cross national borders. This internationalization has made us less constricted by mapmakers' boundaries.

Political power has always been a creature of geography, based on physical control of a certain territory. Globalization is enabling us more and more to override these territories, by traveling in person and by trading or investing across national borders. Our options and opportunities have multiplied as transportation costs have fallen, as we have acquired new and more efficient means of communication, and as trade and capital movements have been liberalized.

We don't have to shop with the big local company; we can turn to a foreign competitor. We don't have to work for the village's one and only employer; we can seek out alternative opportunities. We don't have to make do with local cultural amenities; the world's culture is at our disposal. We don't have to spend our whole lives in one place; we can travel and relocate.

Those factors lead to a liberation of our thinking. We no longer settle for following the local routine; we want to choose actively and freely. Companies, politicians, and associations have to exert themselves to elicit interest or support from people who have a whole world of options to choose from. Our ability to control our own lives is growing, and prosperity is growing with it.

[. . .]

In the past few years, more and more people have been complaining that the new liberty and internationalism have gone too far, giving rise to a "hypercapitalism." The protest movement against this more global capitalism may call itself radical and profess to stand for exciting new ideas, but its arguments actually represent the same old opposition to free markets and free trade that has always been shown by national rulers. Many groups – authoritarian Third World regimes and Eurocrats, agrarian movements and monopoly corporations, conservative intellectuals and new left movements – are afraid of a globalized humanity acquiring more power at the expense of political institutions. All of them are united in viewing globalization as a monster completely out of control, a monster that has to be rounded up and restrained.

Much of the criticism of globalization is based on portraying it as something big and menacing. Often such criticism is not reasoned argument, but flat statements of fact. Critics may say, for example, that 51 of the world's biggest economies are corporations or that something like $1.5 trillion are moved around in financial markets every day, as if size itself were intrinsically dangerous and terrifying. But that is arithmetic, not argument. It remains to be proved that big businesses or high turnover are problems in themselves. Frequently, the detractors forget to prove any such thing. In this book I argue for the opposite view: as long as we are at liberty to pick and choose, there is nothing wrong with certain forms of voluntary cooperation growing large through success.

Such imposing numbers and the abstract term "globalization" – coined in the early 1960s but in common use only since the 1980s – conjure up the image of an anonymous, enigmatic, elusive force. Simply because globalization is governed by people's individual actions across different continents, and not from a central control booth, it seems unchecked, chaotic. Political theorist Benjamin Barber echoed the thoughts of a host of like-minded intellectuals when he bemoaned the apparent absence of "viable powers capable of opposing, subduing, and civilizing the anarchic forces of the global economy."[1]

Many feel powerless in the face of globalization, and that feeling is understandable when we consider how much is determined by the decentralized decisions of millions of people. If others are free to run their own lives, we have no power over them. But in return, we acquire a new power over our own lives. That kind of powerlessness is a good thing. No one is in the driver's seat, because all of us are steering.

The Internet would wither and die if we did not send e-mails, order books, and download music every day through this global computer network. No company would import goods from abroad if we didn't buy them, and no one would invest money over the border if there weren't entrepreneurs there willing to expand existing businesses or launch new ones in response to customer demand. Globalization consists of our everyday actions. We eat bananas from Ecuador, drink wine from France, watch American movies, order books from Britain, work for export companies selling to Germany and Russia, vacation in Thailand, and save money for retirement in funds investing in South America and Asia. Capital may be channeled by finance corporations, and goods may by carried across borders by business enterprises, but they only do these things because we want them to. Globalization takes place from beneath, even though politicians come running after it with all sorts of abbreviations and acronyms (EU, IMF, UN, WTO, UNCTAD, OECD) in a bid to structure the process.

Of course, keeping up with the times doesn't always come easily, especially to intellectuals in the habit of having everything under control. . . . But how complex and confusing everything is becoming now that the other continents are awakening and developments are also beginning to be affected by ordinary people's everyday decisionmaking. No wonder, then, that influential people, decisionmakers, and politicians claim that "we" (meaning they) lose power because of globalization. *They* have lost some of it to *us* – to ordinary citizens.

Not all of us are going to be global jet-setters, but we don't have to be in order to be a part of the globalization process. In particular, the poor and powerless find their well-being vastly improved when inexpensive goods are no longer excluded by tariff barriers and when foreign investments offer employment and streamline production. Those still living in the place where they were born stand to benefit enormously from information being allowed to flow across borders, and from being free to choose their political representatives. But that requires more in the way of democratic reforms and economic liberalization.

Demanding more liberty to pick and choose may sound trivial, but it isn't. To those of us in the affluent world, the availability of nonlocal options may seem like a luxury, or even an annoyance. . . . The existence from which globalization delivers people in the Third World really is intolerable. For the poor, existence means abject poverty, filth, ignorance, and powerlessness; it means always wondering where the next meal is coming from; it means walking many miles to collect water that may not be fit to drink.

When globalization knocks at the door of Bhagant, an elderly agricultural worker and "untouchable" in the Indian village of Saijani, it leads to houses being built of brick instead of mud, to people getting shoes on their feet and clean clothes – not rags – on their backs. Outdoors, the streets now have drains, and the fragrance of tilled earth has replaced the stench of refuse. Thirty years ago Bhagant didn't know he was living in India. Today he watches world news on television.[2]

The new freedom of choice means that people are no longer consigned to working for the village's only employers, the large and powerful farmers. When the women get work away from home, they also become more powerful within the family. New capital markets mean that Bhagant's children are not compelled to borrow money from usurers who collect payment in future labor. The yoke of usury, by which the whole village was once held in thrall, vanishes when people are able to go to different banks and borrow money from them instead.

Everyone in Bhagant's generation was illiterate. In his children's generation, just a few were able to attend school, and in his grandchildren's generation, *everyone* goes to school. Things have improved, Bhagant finds. Liberty and prosperity have grown. Today the children's behavior is the big problem. When he was young, children were obedient and helped in the home. Now they have grown so terribly independent, making money of their own. Such things can cause tensions, of course, but it isn't quite the same thing as the risk of having to watch your children die, or having to sell them to a loan shark.

The stand that you and I and other people in the privileged world take on the burning issue of globalization can determine whether more people are to share in the development that has taken place in Bhagant's village or whether that development is to be reversed.

Critics of globalization often try to paint a picture of neo-liberal market marauders having secretly plotted for capitalism to attain world mastery. . . .

Deregulation, privatization, and trade liberalization, however, were not invented by ultra-liberal ideologues. True, there were political leaders – Reagan and Thatcher, for instance – who had been inspired by economic liberalism. But the biggest reformers were communists in China and the Soviet Union, protectionists in Latin America, and nationalists in Asia. In many other European countries, the progress has been spurred by Social Democrats. In short, the notion of conspiratorial ultra-liberals making a revolution by shock therapy is completely off the mark. Instead, it is pragmatic, often anti-liberal politicians, realizing that their governments have gone too far in the direction of control-freakery, who have for this very reason begun liberalizing their economies. The allegation of liberal-capitalist world dominion has to be further tempered by the observation that today we probably have the biggest public sectors and the highest taxes the world has ever known. The liberalization measures that have been introduced may have abolished some of the past's centralist excesses, but they have hardly ushered in a system of laissez faire. And because the rulers have retreated on their own terms and at their own speed, there is reason to ask whether things really have gone too far, or whether they have not gone far enough.

When I say that I mean to defend capitalism, what I have in mind is the capitalistic freedom to proceed by trial and error, without having to ask rulers and border officials for permission first. . . . I want everyone to have that liberty in abundance. If the critics of capitalism feel that we already have a superabundance of that liberty today, I would like to have more still – a superduper abundance if possible – especially for the poor of the world's population, who as things now stand have little say regarding their work and consumption. That is why I do not hesitate to call this book *In Defense of Global Capitalism*, even though the "capitalism" I celebrate is really more a possible future than a currently existing system.

By capitalism I do not specifically mean an economic system of capital ownership and investment opportunities. Those things can also exist in a command economy. What I mean is the liberal market economy, with free competition based on the right to use one's property and the freedom to negotiate, to conclude agreements, and to start up business activities. What I am defending, then, is individual liberty in the economy. Capitalists are dangerous when, instead of seeking profit through competition, they join forces with the government. If the state is a dictatorship, corporations can easily be parties to human rights violations, as a number of Western oil companies have been in African states.[3] By the same token, capitalists who stalk the corridors of political power in search of benefits and privileges are not *true* capitalists. On the contrary, they are a threat to the free market and as such must be criticized and counteracted. Often, businessmen want to play politics, and politicians want to play at being businessmen. That is not a market economy; it is a mixed economy in which entrepreneurs and politicians have confused their roles. Free capitalism exists when politicians pursue liberal policies and entrepreneurs do business.

What I really believe in, first and foremost, isn't capitalism or globalization. It isn't the systems or regulatory codes that achieve all we see around us in the way of prosperity, innovation, community, and culture. Those things are created by people. What I believe in is man's capacity for achieving great things, and the combined force that results from our interactions and exchanges. I plead for greater liberty and a more open world, not because I believe one system happens to be more efficient than another, but because those things provide a setting that unleashes individual creativity as no other system can. They spur the dynamism that has led to human, economic, scientific, and technical advances. Believing in capitalism does not mean believing in growth, the economy, or efficiency. Desirable as they may be, those are only the results. At its core, belief in capitalism is belief in mankind. . . . My aim is not for economic transactions to supplant all other human relations. My aim is freedom and voluntary relations in all fields. In the cultural arena, that means freedom of expression and of the press. In politics, it means democracy and the rule of law. In social life, it means the right to live according to one's own values and to choose one's own company. And in the economy, it means capitalism and free markets.

It is not my intention that we should put price tags on everything. The important things in life – love, family, friendship, one's own way of life – cannot be assigned a dollar value. Those who believe that, to the liberal mind, people always act with the aim of maximizing their income know nothing about liberals, and any liberal who does think that way knows nothing of human nature.

[. . .]

Poverty Reduction

Between 1965 and 1998, the average world citizen's income practically doubled, from $2,497 to $4,839, adjusted for purchasing power and inflation. That increase has not come about through the industrialized nations multiplying their incomes. During this period the richest fifth of the world's population increased their average income from $8,315 to $14,623, or by roughly 75 percent. For the poorest fifth of the world's population, the increase has been faster still, with average income more than doubling during that same period from $551 to $1,137.[4] World consumption today is more than twice what it was in 1960.

Thanks to material developments in the past half century, the world has over three billion more people living above the poverty line. This is historically unique. The United Nations Development Program (UNDP) has observed that, all in all, world poverty has fallen more during the past 50 years than during the preceding 500. In its *Human Development Report 1997*, the UNDP writes that humanity is in the midst of "the second great ascent." The first began in the 19th century, with the industrialization of the United States and Europe and the rapid spread of prosperity. The second began during the post-war era and is now in full swing, with first Asia and then the other developing countries scoring ever-greater victories in the war against poverty, hunger, disease, and illiteracy.

> The great success in reducing poverty in the 20th century shows that eradicating severe poverty in the first decades of the 21st century is feasible.[5]

Poverty is still rapidly diminishing. "Absolute poverty" is usually defined as the condition of having an income less than one dollar a day. In 1820 something like 85 percent of the world's population were living on the equivalent of less than a dollar a day. By 1950 that figure had fallen to about 50 percent and by 1980 to 31 percent. According to World Bank figures, absolute poverty has fallen since 1980 from 31 to 20 percent (a figure of 24 percent is often mentioned, meaning 24 percent of the population of the developing countries). The radical reduction of the past 20 years is unique in that not only the proportion but also the total number of people living in absolute poverty has declined – for the first time in world history. During these two decades the world's population has grown by a billion and a half, and yet the number of absolute poor has fallen by about 200 million. That decrease is connected with economic growth. In places where prosperity has grown faster, poverty has been most effectively combated. In East Asia (China excluded), absolute poverty has fallen from 15 to just over 9 percent, in China from 32 to 17 percent. Six Asians in 10 were absolutely poor in 1975. Today's figure, according to the World Bank, is fewer than 2 out of 10.

[. . .]

"But," the skeptic asks, "what do people in the developing countries want consumption and growth for? Why must we force our way of life upon them?" The answer is that we must not force a particular way of life on anyone. Whatever their values, the great majority of people the world over desire better material conditions, for the simple reason that they will then have more options, regardless of how they then decide to use that increased wealth. As Indian economist and Nobel laureate Amartya Sen has emphasized, poverty is not just a material problem. Poverty is something wider: it is about powerlessness, about being deprived of basic opportunities and freedom of choice. Small incomes are often symptomatic of the absence of these things, of people's marginalization or subjection to coercion. Human development means enjoying a reasonably healthy and secure existence, with a good standard of living and freedom to shape one's own life. It is important to investigate material development because it suggests how wealth can be produced and because it contributes to development in this broader sense. Material resources, individual and societal, enable people to feed and educate themselves, to obtain health care, and to be spared the pain of watching their children die. Those are pretty universal human desires, one finds, when people are allowed to choose for themselves.

The worldwide improvement in the human condition is reflected in a very rapid growth of average life expectancy. At the beginning of the 20th century, average life expectancy in the developing countries was under 30 years, by 1960 it had risen to 46, and in 1998 it was 65. Longevity in the developing countries today is nearly 15 years higher than it was a century ago in the world's *leading* economy at the time, Britain. Development has been slowest in sub-Saharan Africa, but even there life expectancy has risen, from 41 to 51 years since the 1960s. Average life expectancy remains highest in the most affluent countries – in the Organization for Economic Cooperation and Development (OECD) countries it is 78 – but the *fastest improvement* has been in the poor countries. In 1960, their average life expectancy was 60 percent of that of the affluent countries. Today it is more than 80 percent. Nine out of every 10 people in the world today can expect to live beyond 60, which is more than twice the average only a hundred years ago.

[. . .]

The improvement in health has been partly because of better eating habits and living conditions, but also because of improved health care. Twenty years ago there was one doctor for every thousand people; today there are 1.5. In the very poorest countries, there was 0.6 of a doctor per thousand inhabitants in 1980; this statistic has almost doubled to 1.0. Perhaps the most dependable indicator of the living conditions of the poor is infant mortality, which in the developing countries has fallen drastically. Whereas 18 percent of newborns – almost one in five! – died in 1950, by 1976 this figure had fallen to 11 percent and in 1995 was only 6 percent. In the past 30 years alone, mortality has been almost halved, from 107 deaths per thousand births in 1970 to 59 per thousand in 1998. More and more people, then, have been able to survive despite poverty. And even as more people in poor countries survive, a progressively smaller proportion of the world's population is poor, which in turn suggests that the reduction of poverty has been still greater than is apparent from a superficial study of the statistics.

Hunger

Longer lives and better health are connected with the reduction of one of the cruelest manifestations of underdevelopment – hunger. Calorie intake in the Third World has risen by 30 percent per capita since the 1960s. According to the UN Food and Agriculture Organization, 960 million people in the developing countries were undernourished in 1970. In 1991 the figure was 830 million, falling by 1996 to 790 million. In proportion to population, this is an immensely rapid improvement. Thirty years ago nearly 37 percent of the population of the developing countries were afflicted with hunger. Today's figure is less than 18 percent. Many? Yes. Too many? Of course. But the number is rapidly declining. It took the first two decades of the 20th century for Sweden to be declared free from chronic malnutrition. In only 30 years the proportion of hungry in the world has been reduced by half, and it is expected to decline further, to 12 percent by 2010. There have never been so many of us on earth, and we have never had such a good supply of food. During the 1990s, the ranks of the hungry diminished by an average of 6 million every year, at the same time as the world's population grew by about 800 million.

Things have moved fastest in East and Southeast Asia, where the proportion of the hungry has fallen from 43 to 13 percent since 1970. In Latin America, it has fallen from 19 to 11 percent, in North Africa and the Middle East from 25 to 9 percent, in South Asia from 38 to 23 percent. The worst development has occurred in Africa south of the Sahara, where the number of hungry has actually increased, from 89 to 180 million people. But even there the proportion of the population living in hunger has declined, albeit marginally, from 34 to 33 percent.

Global food production has doubled during the past half century, and in the developing countries it has tripled. Global food supply increased by 24 percent, from 2,257 to 2,808 calories per person daily, between 1961 and 1999. The fastest increase occurred in the developing countries, where consumption rose by 39 percent, from 1,932 to 2,684 calories daily.[6] Very little of this development is due to new land having been converted to agricultural use. Instead, the old land is being farmed more efficiently. The yield per acre of arable land has virtually doubled. Wheat, maize, and rice prices have fallen by more than 60 percent. Since the beginning of the 1980s alone, food prices have halved and production from a given area of land has risen by 25 percent – a process that has been swifter in poor countries than in affluent ones.

Such is the triumph of the "green revolution." Higher-yield, more-resistant crops have been developed, at the same time as sowing, irrigation, manuring, and harvesting methods have improved dramatically. New, efficient strains of wheat account for more than 75 percent of wheat production in the developing countries, and farmers there are estimated to have earned nearly $5 billion as a result of the change. In southern India, the green revolution is estimated to have boosted farmers' real earnings by 90 percent and those of landless peasants by 125 percent over 20 years. Its impact has been least in Africa, but even there the green revolution has raised maize production per acre by between 10 and 40 percent. Without this revolution, it is estimated that world prices of wheat and rice would be nearly 40 percent higher than they are today and that roughly another 2 percent of the world's children – children who are now getting enough to eat – would have suffered from chronic malnourishment. Today's food problem has nothing to do with overpopulation. Hunger today is a problem of access to the available knowledge and technology, to wealth, and to the secure background conditions that make food production possible. Many researchers believe that if modern farming techniques were applied in all the world's agriculture, we would already be able, here and now, to feed another billion or so people.[7]

The incidence of major famine disasters has also declined dramatically, largely as a result of the spread of democracy. Starvation has occurred in states of practically every kind – communist regimes, colonial empires, technocratic dictatorships, and ancient tribal societies. In all cases they have been centralized, authoritarian states that suppressed free debate and the workings of the market. As Amartya Sen observes, there has never been a famine disaster in a democracy. Even poor democracies like India and Botswana have avoided starvation, despite having a poorer food supply than many countries where famine *has* struck. By contrast, communist states like China, the Soviet Union, Cambodia, Ethiopia, and North Korea, as well as colonies like India under the British Raj, have experienced starvation. This shows that famine is caused by dictatorship, not by food shortage. Famine is induced by leaders destroying production and trade, making war, and ignoring the plight of the starving population.

Sen maintains that democracies are spared starvation for the simple reason that it is easily prevented if the rulers of a society wish to prevent it. Rulers can refrain from impeding the distribution of food, and they can create jobs for people who would not be able to afford food purchases in times of crisis. But dictators are under no pressure: they can eat their fill however badly off their people are, whereas democratic leaders will be unseated if they fail to address food distribution problems. Additionally, a free press makes the general public aware of the problems, so that they can be tackled in time. . . .[8]

At the same time as more people are getting the food they need, the supply of potable drinking water has doubled, which is hugely important for the reduction of disease and infection in developing countries. Worldwide, 8 people in 10 now have access to pure water. A generation ago, 90 percent of the world's rural population were without pure water. Today that applies to only 25 percent. At the beginning of the 1980s, little more than half of India's population had access to pure water, while 10 years later the figure was more than 80 percent. In Indonesia that percentage rose from 39 to 62. Countries like Kuwait and Saudi Arabia today derive large parts of their water supply from desalination of seawater, which is available in practically unlimited quantities. Desalination is a costly process, but it shows that growing prosperity can solve problems of scarce resources.

Democratization

The accelerating spread of information and ideas throughout the world, coupled with rising education standards and growing prosperity, is prompting demands for genuine political rights. Critics of globalization maintain that a dynamic market and international capital are a threat to democracy, but what they really see threatened is the use that *they* would like to make of democracy. Never before in human history have democracy, universal suffrage, and the free formation of opinion been as widespread as they are today.

A hundred years ago, no country on earth had universal and equal suffrage. The world was ruled by empires and monarchies. Even in the West, women were excluded from the democratic process. During the 20th century, large parts of the world were subjugated by communism, fascism, or National Socialism, ideologies that led to major wars and the political murder of more than a hundred million people. With just a few exceptions, those systems have fallen. The totalitarian states have collapsed, the dictatorships have been democratized, and the absolute monarchies have been deposed. A hundred years ago, one-third of the world's population was governed by remote colonial powers. Today the colonial empires have been dismantled. In the past few decades alone, dictatorships have fallen like bowling pins, especially following the tearing down of the communist Iron Curtain. The end of the Cold War also put an end to the unpleasant American strategy of supporting Third World dictatorships as long as they opposed the Soviet bloc.

According to the think tank Freedom House, there were 121 democracies with multiparty systems and with universal, equal suffrage in 2002. Living in those democracies are some 3.5 billion people, or roughly 60 percent of the world's population. Freedom House regards 85 countries, with a total of 2.5 billion inhabitants, as "free" (i.e., democratic countries with civil rights). That is more than 40 percent of the world's inhabitants, the biggest proportion ever. That many, in other words, are living in states that guarantee the rule of law and permit free debate and an active opposition.

In 2002, there were 47 states that violated basic human rights. Worst among them were Burma, Cuba, Iraq, Libya, North Korea, Saudi Arabia, Sudan, Syria, and Turkmenistan – that is, the countries least affected by globalization and least oriented in favor of the market economy and liberalism. While deploring and combating their oppression, suppression of opinion, government-controlled media, and wiretapping, we should still remember that such was the normal state of affairs for most of the world's population only a few decades ago. In 1973, only 20 countries with populations of more than a million were democratically governed.[9] . . .

Now and then it is alleged that democracy is hard to reconcile with Islam, and so it may seem in the world today. But we should remember that many researchers were saying the same about Catholicism as recently as the 1970s, when Catholic countries included, for example, the military regimes of Latin America, the communist states of eastern Europe, and dictatorships like the Philippines under Ferdinand Marcos.

The number of wars has diminished by half during the past decade, and today less than 1 percent of the world's population are directly affected by military conflicts. One reason is that democracies simply do not make war on each other; another is that international exchange makes conflict less interesting. With freedom of movement and free trade, citizens are not all that interested in the size of their country. People create prosperity, not by annexing land from another country, but by carrying on trade with that land and its resources. If, on the other hand, the world consists of self-contained nation states, the land of other countries has no value until one is able to seize it.

. . . In the trenchant words of the 19th-century French liberal Frédéric Bastiat, "If goods do not cross borders, soldiers will." Mutual dependence means fewer potential causes of conflict between states. Cross-ownership, multinational corporations, investment, and privately owned natural resources make it hard to tell where one country really ends and another begins. Several centuries ago, when the Swedes pillaged Europe, it was other people's resources they wrecked and stole. If they were to do the same thing today, the victims would include many Swedish companies, not to mention Swedish capital and Swedish export markets.

It has been asserted that the globalist challenge to nation-states leads to separatism and to local and ethnic conflicts. There is indeed a risk of separatist activity when national power is called into question, and the tragedy of the former Yugoslavia is evidence of the bloody conflicts that can follow. But the number of major internecine conflicts – those costing more than a thousand lives – fell from 20 to 13 between 1991 and 1998. Nine of those conflicts occurred in Africa, the world's least democratized, least globalized, and least capitalist continent. The conflicts that follow the collapse of totalitarian states are primarily power struggles in temporary power vacuums. In several countries, centralization has prevented the evolution of stable, democratic institutions and civil societies, and when centralization disappears, chaos ensues pending the establishment of new institutions. There is no reason for believing this to be a new trend in a more internationalized and democratic world.

Oppression of Women

One of the world's cruelest injustices is the oppression of women. There are parts of the world where women are regarded as the property of men. A father is entitled to marry off his daughters, and it is the husband who decides what work his wife is to do. In many countries, a husband owns his wife's passport or ID card, with the result that she cannot even travel freely in her own country. Laws disqualify women from divorce, from ownership of property, and from work outside the home. Daughters are denied the rights of inheritance enjoyed by sons. Girls receive nothing like the same education as boys, and very often no education at all. Women are abused and subjected to genital mutilation and rape without any intervention by the authorities.

It is true, as many complain, that globalization upsets old traditions and habits. How, for example, do you maintain patriarchal family traditions when children are suddenly earning more than the head of the family? One of the traditions challenged by globalization is the long-standing subjugation of women. Through cultural contacts and the interchange of ideas, new hopes and ideals are disseminated. Indian women who can see on television that women are not necessarily housewives begin to contemplate careers in law or medicine. Some Chinese women who had previously been isolated have been inspired to press demands for greater autonomy and to make decisions of their own by the website gaogenxie.com. The site's name, which means "high-heeled shoes," is a symbol of freedom contrasting with the tradition of bound feet. When women begin making their own decisions about their consumer behavior or their employment, they become more insistent in demanding equal liberty and power in other fields. Growing prosperity gives women more opportunity to become independent and provide for themselves. Experience from Africa and elsewhere shows that women are often leading entrepreneurs for various kinds of small-scale production and exchange in the informal sector, which suggests that, absent discrimination and regulation by the government, the market is their oyster. And indeed, the worldwide spread of freer conditions of service and freer markets has made it increasingly difficult for women to be kept out. Women today constitute 42 percent of the world's work force, compared with 36 percent 20 years ago. Capitalism doesn't care whether the best producer is a man or a woman. On the contrary, discrimination is expensive because it involves the rejection of certain people's goods and labor. All studies have shown that respect for women's rights and their ability to exert influence in the home are closely bound up with their ability to find employment outside the home and earn an independent income.

Technological progress can expedite social progress. Women in Saudi Arabia are prevented from showing themselves in public unless they cover their whole bodies except the hands, eyes, and feet. They are also disqualified from driving cars and from doing other things. The practical effect of this has been to exclude them from all economic activity. But now the Internet and the telephone have suddenly made it possible for women to carry on business from home, at the computer. . . .[10]

Democratization gives women a voice in politics, and in more and more countries the laws have been reformed to establish greater equality between the sexes. Divorce laws and rights of inheritance are becoming less and less biased. Equality before the law spreads with democracy and capitalism. The idea of equal human dignity spreads, knocking out discrimination.

[. . .]

Better education and extra earnings for a mother quickly result in better nourishment and education for her children, whereas the connection between paternal income and child welfare is less strong. In South Asia, where an inhuman attitude concerning the value of women resulted – and still does – in high mortality rates among girls during the first years of life, girls now have a greater life expectancy at birth than boys. The average life expectancy of women in the developing countries has increased by 20 years during the past half century. Development is also giving women more power over their own bodies. Increased power for women in poor countries, and improved availability of contraception, go hand in hand with reduced birthrates.

[. . .]

Global Inequality

This progress is all very well, many critics of globalization will argue, but even if the majority are better off, gaps have widened and wealthy people and countries have improved their lot more rapidly than others. So inequality has grown. The critics point to the fact that the combined per capita GDP of the 20 richest countries was 15 times greater than that of the 20 poorest countries 40 years ago and is now about 30 times greater.

There are two reasons why this objection to globalization does not hold up. First, even if this were true it would not matter very much. If everyone is coming to be better off, what does it matter that the improvement comes faster for some than for others? Surely the important thing is for everyone to be as well off as possible, not whether one group is better off than another. . . . It is better to be poor in the inegalitarian United States, where the poverty line for individuals in 2001 was about $9,039 per year, than to be equal in countries like Rwanda, where in 2001 GDP per capita (adjusted for purchasing power) was $1,000, or Bangladesh ($1,750), or Uzbekistan ($2,500). . . .[11] Second, the allegation of increased inequality is just wrong. The notion that global inequality has increased is largely based on figures from the UN Development Program, in particular its *Human Development Report* from 1999. But the problem with these figures is that they are not adjusted for purchasing power. That is, the UNDP numbers don't take into account what people can actually buy for their money. Without that adjustment the figures mainly show the level of a country's official exchange rate and what its currency is worth on the international market, which is a poor yardstick of poverty. Poor people's actual living standard, needless to say, hinges far more on the cost of their food, clothing, and housing than on what they would get for their money when vacationing in Europe. The odd thing is that the UNDP itself uses purchasing power-adjusted figures in its Human Development Index (HDI), which is its universal yardstick of living standards. It only resorts to the unadjusted figures in order to prove a thesis of inequality.

A report from the Norwegian Institute for Foreign Affairs investigated global inequality by means of figures adjusted for purchasing power. Their data show that, contrary to the conventional wisdom, inequality between countries has been continuously *declining* ever since the end of the 1970s. This decline was especially rapid between 1993 and 1998, when globalization really gathered speed.[12] More recently, similar research by Columbia University development economist Xavier Sala-i-Martin has confirmed those findings. When the UNDP's own numbers are adjusted for purchasing power, Sala-i-Martin found that world inequality declined sharply by any of the common ways of measuring it.[13] Bhalla and Sala-i-Martin also independently found that if we focus on inequality between *persons*, rather than inequality between *countries*, global inequality at the end of 2000 was at its lowest point since the end of World War II. Estimates that compare countries rather than individuals, as both authors note, grossly overestimate real inequality because they allow gains for huge numbers of people to be outweighed by comparable losses for far fewer. Country aggregates treat China and Grenada as data points of equal weight, even though China's population is 12,000 times Grenada's. Once we shift our focus to people rather than nations, the evidence is overwhelming that the past 30 years have witnessed a global equalization.[14] Comparing just the richest and poorest tenths, inequality has increased, suggesting that a small group has lagged behind, . . . but a study of all countries clearly points to a general growth of equality. If, for example, we compare the richest and poorest fifth or the richest and poorest third, we find the differences diminishing.

Economists usually measure the degree of inequality by means of the "Gini coefficient." If that number is zero, complete equality prevails, and everyone owns the same amount. If it is one, there is total inequality, with one person owning everything. The Gini coefficient for the whole world declined from 0.6 in 1968 to 0.52 in 1997, a reduction of more than 10 percent.

Because equality between the rich and poor *within* these countries appears to have been roughly constant during this time (having increased in half and diminished in half), global equality, quite contrary to popular supposition, is increasing. The 1998/99 World Bank report reviews among other things the difference in incomes going to the richest and poorest 20 percent in the developing countries. The review shows, of course, that the difference is very great, but it also shows that the difference is diminishing on all continents! The real exception is post-communist Eastern Europe, where inequality has grown fastest in the countries where reform has been slowest.[15]

The 1999 UNDP report appears to contradict this finding, but its conclusions are doubtful, not least because the UNDP omitted its own statistics for the years when inequality declined fastest, 1995–97. Furthermore, their own welfare statistics, as aggregated in the HDI, point to an even faster reduction of inequality in the world than is indicated by the Norwegian report. HDI adds together various aspects of welfare – the income, education standard, and life expectancy of the population. This index ranges from 0, representing the profoundest misery, to 1, representing complete welfare. The HDI has increased in all groups of countries over the past 40 years, but fastest of all in the poorest countries. In the OECD countries, HDI rose from 0.8 to 0.91 between 1960 and 1993, and in the developing countries it rose faster still, from 0.26 to 0.56.

One sometimes hears it said, on the basis of that same UNDP report, that the richest fifth of the world's population is 74 times wealthier than the poorest fifth. But if we measure wealth in terms of what these groups get for their money – that is, if we use figures adjusted for purchasing power – then the richest fifth is only 16 times richer than the poorest.[16]

Reservations

This is not by any means to say that all is well with the world, or even that everything is getting better and better. AIDS deaths in 2000 totaled 3 million, the highest figure ever. One of the cruel consequences of the epidemic is that it leaves children without parents: more than 13 million have been orphaned by AIDS, the vast majority in sub-Saharan Africa.[17] In several African countries, more than 15 percent of the adult population are suffering from HIV or AIDS. Something like 20 million people are now living as fugitives from oppression, conflicts, or natural disasters. Even though forecasts concerning the world's water supply have grown more optimistic, we still risk a huge shortage of pure water, possibly resulting in disease and conflicts. About 20 countries, most of them in southern Africa, have grown poorer since 1965. Illiteracy, hunger, and poverty may be diminishing, but many hundreds of millions of people are still afflicted by them. Armed conflicts are growing fewer, but this is cold comfort to the hundreds of thousands of people who are still being beaten, raped, and murdered.

The remaining problems are made all the more intolerable by our knowledge that something can actually be done about them. When underdevelopment appears to be a natural and inevitable part of the human condition, it is considered a tragic fate. But when we realize that it is not at all necessary, it becomes a problem that can and should be solved. This phenomenon is not unfamiliar: the same thing happened when the Industrial Revolution started to improve living standards in the West more than 200 years ago. When misery is everywhere, we can easily become oblivious to it. When it is contrasted with something else, with abundance and prosperity, our eyes are opened to it – a good thing, because our new awareness spurs our efforts to do something about the problems that remain. But this must not deceive us into thinking that the world has actually grown worse, for it has not.

No one can doubt that the world has more than its share of serious problems. The fantastic thing is that the spread of democracy and capitalism has reduced them so dramatically. Where liberal policies have been allowed to operate longest, they have made poverty and deprivation the exception instead of the rule – and they had previously been the rule everywhere in the world, at all times in history. Colossal changes await all of us, but at the same time our eyes have been opened to the political and technical solutions now available to us. And so, all things considered, there is no reason why we should not be optimistic.

NOTES

1   Benjamin R. Barber, "Globalizing Democracy," *The American Prospect* 11, no. 20, September 11, 2000, p. 16.

2   Lasse Berg and Stlg T. Karlsson, *I Asiens tid: Indien, Kina, Japan 1966–1999* (Stockholm: Ordfront, 2000), chap. 1.

3   See, for example, Human Right Watch, *The Price of Oil: Corporate Responsibility and Human Rights Violations in Nigeria's Oil Producing Communities* (New York: Human Rights Watch, 1999), http://www.hrw.org/reports/1999/nigeria/index.htm.

4   Arne Melchior, Kjetil Telle, and Henrik Wilg, *Globalisering och ulikhet: Verdens inntektsfordeling og levestandard, 1960–1998* (Oslo: Royal Norwegian Ministry of Foreign Affairs, 2000). Also available in an abridged English version: *Globalization and Inequality: World Income Distribution and Living Standards, 1960–1998*, Studies on Foreign Policy Issues, Report 6:B, 2000, chap. 2, http://xodin.dep.no/ud/engelsk/pub/rapporter/032001-990349/index-dok000-b-n-a.html.

5   UNDP, *Human Development Report 1997* (New York: Oxford University Press for the United Nations Development Program, 1997), "Overview," p. 12.

6   Indur M. Goklany, "The Globalization of Human Well-Being," Cato Institute Policy Analysis no. 447, 2002, p. 7, http://www.cato.org/pubs/pas/pa447.pdf.

7   *Forbes*, November 16, 1998, p. 36; World Bank, *World Development Report 2000/2001: Attacking Poverty* (New York: Oxford University Press/World Bank, 2000), p. 184, http://www.worldbank.org/poverty/wdrpoverty/report/index.htm.

8   Amartya Sen, *Development as Freedom* (New York: Anchor Books, 1999), chap. 7.

9   Freedom House, *Freedom in the World 2002* (New York: Freedom House, 2000), http://www.freedomhouse.org/research/freeworld/2002/web.pdf.

10   "How Women Beat the Rules," *The Economist*, October 2, 1999.

11   Central Intelligence Agency, *CIA World Factbook 2002*, http://www.cia.gov/cia/publications/factbook.

12   Melchior, Telle, and Wilg, This development toward greater equality will be even faster in coming decades, with the world's workforce growing older and thus earning more equally; see Tomas Larsson, *Falska mantran: globaliseringsdebatten efter Seattle* (Stockholm: Timbro, 2001), p. 11f, http://www. timbro.se/bokhandel/pejling/pdf/75664801.pdf.

13   Xavier Sala-i-Martin, "The Disturbing 'Rise' of Global Income Inequality," National Bureau of Economic Research Working Paper no. 8904, http://www.nber.org/papers/w8904.

14   Bhalla.

15   World Bank, *Marking Transition Work for Everyone: Poverty and inequality in Europe and Central Asia* (Washington: World Bank, 2000).

16   Larsson, *Falska mantran: globaliseringsdebatten efter Seattle*, p. 11f.

17   UNICEF, "Children Orphaned by AIDS: Front-Line Responses From Eastern and Southern Africa," http://www.unicef.org/pubsgen/aids.

17 What Strategies Are Viable for Developing Countries Today? The World Trade Organization and the Shrinking of 'Development Space' (2003)

Robert Hunter Wade

Developing countries as a group are being more tightly constrained in their national development strategies by proliferating regulations formulated and enforced by international organizations. These regulations are not about limiting companies' options, as 'regulation' normally connotes. Rather, they are about limiting the options of developing country governments to constrain the options of companies operating or hoping to operate within their borders. In effect, the new regulations are designed to expand the options of developed country firms to enter and exit markets more easily, with fewer restrictions and obligations, and to lock-in their appropriation of technological rents.

Developed country governments, led by the United States and the United Kingdom, are driving this proliferation of international market-opening and technology-rent-protecting regulations, using multilateral economic organizations, international treaties and bilateral agreements. They have come together to legitimise a level of intrusion into the economies and polities of developing countries hitherto frowned upon by the international community, framing the intrusion in the shape of international agreements. Ironically in view of the common belief that globalization is weakening the power of states to regulate, they are requiring developing country governments to regulate – themselves and their national firms – more, not less. At the same time the United States and the EU have not followed through on their general commitments to improve market access for developing countries.[1] Both have kept large parts of their economies off the negotiating table.[2]

The net result is that the 'development space' for diversification and upgrading policies in developing countries is being shrunk behind the rhetorical commitment to universal liberalization and privatisation. The rules being written into multilateral and bilateral agreements actively prevent developing countries from pursuing the kinds of industrial and technology policies adopted by the newly developed countries of East Asia and by the older developed countries when they were developing, policies aimed at accelerating the 'internal' articulation of the economy (about which more below). At the same time, developed country tariff escalation in sectors of interest to developing country exporters limits their export growth and their rise up the value chain.[3] All this constitutes a shrinkage not only of development space, but also of 'self-determination' space. It ties the hands of developing country governments 'forever' to the North's interpretation of a market opening agenda ('you open your markets and remove restrictions on incoming investment, in return for [promises of] improved access to our markets').

Here I shall show how the main international agreements from the Uruguay Round – TRIPS, TRIMS and GATS – systematically tip the playing field against developing countries. The agreements do not do for developing countries what their sponsors, the G7 states (Group of Seven major economies), say they will do, and they do help to lock in the economic, political and military dominance of these and other states in the core of the world economy. Why does this matter? Partly for moral reasons. I describe a system in which bargains are struck between strong players and weak players. They each need – see advantage in having – the cooperation of the others, so they reach agreements. But to the extent that bargaining is steered by morality, the balance of advantage in the agreements depends on which of two moralities prevails. One is the a-bit-better-than-the-jungle morality of 'tit-for-tat', or reciprocity, which sanctions that the agreements reflect relative bargaining strengths; thus the strong do best. The second is the all-men-are-brothers morality, which says that the strong have a duty to restrain themselves to help the weaker. This is the morality behind the decision of early 20th-century British judges to give trade unions legal privileges in order to force a degree of restraint on the part of employers. In what follows I bring out the extent to which the recent round of World Trade Organisation (WTO) agreements on intellectual property, investment, and trade in services expresses the a-bit-better-than-the-jungle morality, and show the implications of applying the all-men-are-brothers morality.

But the basis for not accepting the present agreements is not only moral. The case for 'development space' also rests on the costs to the world, including the citizens of the prosperous democracies, of making the creation of dynamic capitalisms in the non-core zone of the world economy even more difficult than it has been to date. The fear of the social instability caused by the unrestrained power of employers over employees drove the decision of those early 20th-century British judges to choose the second morality over the first. Developed world policy makers would do well to keep this precedent in mind. Globalization erodes the insulation of the North from the responses to poverty, inequality and subordination in the South – including migration, imploding states, civil wars, religious fundamentalism, and destruction of symbols of the structure of domination.

Shrinking the Development Space 1: The TRIPS Agreement

The Agreement on Trade-related Aspects of Intellectual Property Rights (TRIPS) was forged in the course of the Uruguay Round (1986–1994), and entered into operation in 1994.[4] It covers protection of trademarks, copyrights, industrial designs, data secrets, and patents (on drugs, electronic and mechanical devices, etc.). The big two are copyrights and patents. The agreement seems innocent enough. Under patents, all it does is to oblige WTO members to introduce minimum standards for intellectual property protection, and it provides a dispute resolution and enforcement mechanism. The minimum standards include: limits on states' abilities to deny patents to certain types of products; a period of 20 years for all patents (many countries granted patents for shorter periods); and limits on states' flexibility in the use of technologies or products patented in their territory, including states' ability to insist on compulsory licensing.[5]

The agreement handicaps developing countries through both economic and political mechanisms.

TRIPS Economic Handicaps

The economic handicaps operate through the market for knowledge. The North is a net producer of patentable knowledge, the South a net consumer. Even in the case of Mexico, an advanced developing country and member of the OECD, domestic residents made only 389 patent applications in 1996, compared to over 30,000 from foreign residents.[6] TRIPS raises the price of patentable knowledge to consumers, and so raises the flow of rents from South to North. According to World Bank estimates, US companies would pocket an additional net $19 billion a year in royalties from full application of TRIPS. They own many patents in many countries required to tighten intellectual property protection, while TRIPS does not require tightening of US patent law.

TRIPS defenders say that the higher returns to knowledge generation in the North will yield even more innovation, which will diffuse, to the South. There is no credible evidence that this is the case.[7] In the case of copyright, tougher copyright protections raise the cost of scientific publications. Research libraries around the world paid out 66 percent more for scientific monographs in 2001 than they did in 1986 and got 9 percent fewer monographs for their money, and paid out 210 percent more for 5 percent fewer periodicals. These price escalations widen the North/South gap in access to scientific knowledge.

But it is not just a matter of the rising cost of knowledge in relation to the not-rising ability to pay of the South. It is also that as most natural science research is being privatised, less and less research is being done on issues from which the researchers and right holders are unlikely to receive a significant economic pay-off. This includes many problem areas of primary interest to populations in developing countries.

TRIPS Political Handicaps

The political handicaps operate through two main mechanisms. First, *developing countries' rights and developed countries' obligations are unenforceable*, while developing countries' obligations and developed countries' rights are enforceable. On paper, the rights and obligations of members look to be balanced between patent-holding (developed) and patent-using (developing) countries. In practice the agreement is skewed in favour of the developed countries, because of the difference in enforceability.

For example, the developing countries have a wide array of obligations about what they allow to be patented and how they treat and enforce patents. If they do not meet their obligations they may be taken to the dispute settlement mechanism (DSM) of the WTO. The developed countries supposedly have obligations too, directed at ensuring that their governments and firms do provide technology to developing countries. But the agreement gives no recourse: nothing happens if they do not meet their obligations. No developing

country has taken a developed country to the dispute settlement mechanism for not transferring technology. Why not? Because the costs of mounting a case are high for a developing
country, the US and the EU may threaten reprisals, and the obligations of developed countries with regard to technology transfer and everything else are vague.

The second political mechanism is *the use of the TRIPS' standards by the US and EU as
merely the starting point for negotiating even tougher 'TRIPS-plus' standards of patent protection
in bilateral trade and investment treaties* (although the agreement's minimum standards are
themselves typically much tougher in favour of patent holders than developing countries
had in place before the agreement). This will give the developing countries even less protection under TRIPS than they have already.

Developing country representatives have argued for years that TRIPS must be revisited.
The response from the US and EU has been, 'We are happy to renegotiate, but there can
be no change between [a favourite phrase] *the balance of rights and obligations struck in the
Uruguay Round*.' This is a good wheeze – because the developed countries effectively placed
themselves under no obligations in the TRIPS agreement.

Indeed, the US has been active in trying to re-open the TRIPS negotiations – so as to
secure even stronger protections for intellectual property. But in the face of developing
country resistance it has recently abandoned this strategy, and is relying more on tighter
enforcement of the existing rules: making more use of the threat to take a country through
the WTO dispute resolution process; more use of TRIPS review procedures to press countries to enforce intellectual property rules; more use of informal bilateral pressure, including threats to withdraw aid and to support rival states in geopolitical disputes, complaints
to ministries or prime ministers about unconstructive or 'aggressive' ambassadors in
Geneva, and sweet deals for those who cooperate;[8] more intensive monitoring of countries
under the US's Super 301 trade sanctions process; and more use of bilateral and regional
trade negotiations to require countries to implement even stronger national intellectual
property legislation than called for by TRIPs.

Tightening the Noose: Doha and Brazil

Were the negotiations over TRIPS at the Doha Ministerial meeting of the WTO, in 2001,
not intended to improve the position of developing countries? The Doha Declaration on
'TRIPS and Public Health' is widely understood to have modified TRIPS sufficiently to
improve developing countries' access to certain drugs. To this extent it could expand – if
developed countries deliver on their promise – developing countries' TRIPS-consistent
options in a *humanitarian* direction. But it does not expand their options in industrial
transformation.

Even after the Doha modifications TRIPS leaves in place a much more restrictive environment for technology transfer than the older industrialized countries enjoyed during the
early stages of industrialization and the new industrialized countries of East Asia enjoyed
during theirs. Recall that Japan, Taiwan, and South Korea were each known as 'the coun-
terfeit capital' of the world in their time.[9] And the 19th-century United States, then a rapidly
industrializing country, was known – to Charles Dickens, among many other aggrieved
foreign authors – as a bold pirate of intellectual property. In all these cases foreign firms
had little legal redress against patent- or copyright-infringers in those countries of the kind

that they did have against infringers at home. But today, reverse-engineering, imitation, and many strategies of innovation to develop technology are either outlawed or made significantly more difficult by the high level of patent and copyright protection mandated by TRIPS. Thus, TRIPS raises significant development obstacles for many countries that the earlier developers did not face. These issues were not on the table at Doha.

The nub of the issue is caught in a recent pharmaceuticals dispute between the US and Brazil (which resembles the 1980s dispute between the US and Brazil over computers). Brazil has taken the lead among developing countries in developing domestic capacity to produce HIV/AIDS drugs at low cost. It has thereby helped to avoid a catastrophe on the scale afflicting many African and Asian countries.

Brazil's efforts have generated controversy regarding its intellectual property law. The government has relied on two particular articles of its 1997 industrial property law to advance the fulfilment of its national health objectives. Article 71 authorizes compulsory licenses in the case of national health emergencies – it allows the government to authorize local producers to produce generic drugs needed to fight a national health emergency or to import from a generic producer elsewhere, despite patent protection. This article is generally understood to be consistent with TRIPS. While Brazil has not actually used this law to issue a compulsory license, it has frequently used the threat of a compulsory license to facilitate fairer negotiations with pharmaceutical companies regarding the terms of licensing to Brazilian companies and the prices of drugs in Brazil.

The Brazilian law also contains an article (article 68) that authorizes licenses when manufactured goods are not produced locally. If a foreign company has obtained a patent for a product or process in Brazil but does not establish local production within three years the law authorizes the Brazilian government to license local producers to produce the good (the term of art here is 'local working'). This is the 'industrial policy' article, with application far beyond pharmaceuticals. By spurring foreign firms to establish local production it contributes to a more developmental foreign investment regime. But it is arguably in violation of TRIPS, and has been strongly opposed by the US.

The US brought a WTO panel dispute against Brazil in 2000. In June 2001 the two countries signed a communiqué announcing the withdrawal of the US challenge, but they also affirmed that the fundamental conflict over Article 68 remains unresolved. The US threatens that if the Brazilians use Article 68 to issue a compulsory license for non-pharmaceutical products (as part of a wider industrial policy) the WTO case would be restarted.

The signal sent to other developing countries is that emulating Brazil's program for distributing AIDS medicines is acceptable, but emulating Brazil's efforts to use intellectual property rights policy as a tool of industrial strategy is not acceptable. This demonstrates the point made earlier, that expanded opportunities for TRIPS-consistent developing country action secured at Doha are for humanitarian relief, not industrial transformation.

Shrinking the Development Space 2: The TRIMS Agreement

The Agreement on Trade-Related Investment Measures (TRIMS), another product of the Uruguay Round, limits the development space of developing countries even more than

TRIPS, because it covers a broader swathe of their economic activity.[10] The central point about TRIMS is that it moves trade rules from the principle of 'avoid discrimination' between countries (the 'most favoured nation' principle of the old General Agreement on Trade and Tariffs), to 'avoid trade and investment distortions.' It interprets more 'performance requirements' on foreign firms as distortions, and bans or aspires to ban them.[11]

The TRIMS agreement bans performance requirements related to local content, trade balancing, export requirements, and it also bans requirements on public agencies to procure goods from local suppliers. A country that tries to impose such requirements can be taken to the Dispute Settlement Mechanism, and will surely lose the case. In theory the complainant (normally the US or the EU) has to provide *evidence* that the specific requirement is distorting, but in practice the US and the EU do not; they simply assert that such requirements are distorting *by definition*, and – being dominant actors – their assertions generally prevail.

Moreover the US and the EU want to modify the current TRIMS agreement so as to ban *all* performance requirements, including for joint venturing, technology transfer, and research and development. At the Doha Ministerial meeting of the WTO in 2001 the US and the EU pressed this agenda, but India and Brazil prevented the ban being approved. However, the language in the relevant part of the current TRIMS is not legally clear, and many developing countries fear that if they do use such non-banned performance requirements the US or the EU will still threaten to take them to the DSM – whose rulings, they have seen, are almost always in favour of the most restrictive interpretation of allowable performance requirements; and the threat to take them to the DSM may well be reinforced by other threats, such as to cut foreign aid, as noted earlier. What is more, states currently negotiating to join the WTO (the 'accession countries') are finding that the rules they are being asked to sign on to are even more restrictive than those for existing members. There is not a standard set of rules.

TRIMS defenders point to the exemption clauses that allow categories of developing countries 'special and differential treatment'. The catch is that the exemptions are defined only in terms of the *time period* for complying. The time period has to do with administrative and legal handicaps in getting up to speed on TRIMS enforcement. It has nothing to do with the time needed to nurture infant industries, nothing to do with competitiveness. In this fundamental respect the TRIMS agreement narrows the scope of 'special and differential treatment' allowable for developing countries, compared to the scope of pre-TRIMS.[12]

Shrinking the Development Space 3: The GATS Agreement

The General Agreement on Trade in Services (GATS) also came out of the Uruguay Round, and has been in a new round of intensified negotiations at the WTO since 2000. GATS represents the extension of WTO rules from trade in products to trade in services – including everything from banking, to education, to rubbish collection, tourism, health delivery, water supply and sanitation. 'Trade' includes companies setting up in a foreign country to provide services there, so GATS is also an investment agreement. Foreign investment in services accounts for roughly half of world foreign direct investment, and developing countries have been assured that complying with GATS commitments will boost Foreign Direct Investment (FDI) inflows.

The central thrust of the GATS, as with TRIMS (but not TRIPS), is market liberalization. The articles of the agreement are a list of ways in which governments should not interfere in the market, should not place barriers in the way of service trade between countries; and should not regulate the behaviour of multinational corporations operating in their country.[13] Because the responsibility for affordable provision of public services is fundamental to a government's responsibility to its citizens – to the whole idea of social compact between government and taxpayers – the GATS agreement is intruding even further into domestic political economy than the other two. It makes it next to impossible for developing country governments to protect their own service industries from competition from well-established foreign firms, in the way that virtually all the successful developers have done in the past.

For example, GATS requires 'most favoured nation' treatment, such that a government must treat firms from all WTO members equally. GATS also requires 'national treatment', such that all foreign service providers must be treated at least as well as domestic firms. They cannot be required to use local suppliers, managers or staff, unless local firms are under the same requirement. And GATS requires 'market access', which prevents a government from putting a limit on the number of service suppliers or outlets and on where they operate. All this in the name of fairness.

However, GATS has a larger exemption provision than the other two agreements. Governments can specify limitations on *some* of the commitments they make in a particular service sector, and hence wall off particular government laws or regulations from GATS. Governments list which sectors and which requirements they wish to exclude (though not all requirements can be excluded – the most favoured nation principle, for example, cannot be excluded in any sector). The presumption is that anything not on their list is subject to the full commitments. In actuality however, this exemption procedure is less than meets the eye. The exemptions have to be signalled at the beginning, because it is almost impossible for governments to get them introduced later. Yet it is also almost impossible to predict what limitations should be put on commitments in advance.

As for the promised benefits to developing countries, a United Nations Conference on Trade and Development (UNCTAD) study concludes, 'There is no empirical evidence to link any significant increase in FDI flows to developing countries with the conclusion of GATS.'[14] The World Bank reports similar findings. FDI location decisions are much less sensitive to the protections of GATS than they are to factors like physical infrastructure and nests of local support services.

What the New Agreements Mean for Development

The new agreements must be seen in the context of the norms underlying the pre-Uruguay Round regime. At that time the 'development' norm carried some weight in trade negotiations, even if mainly when it could be deployed as a tool of Cold War and post-colonial objectives. The general push towards trade liberalization was conditioned by recognition that developing countries, and particularly least developed countries, needed 'special and differentiated' (S&D) treatment by definition of their being developing countries. The answer to the question, 'what do countries need to do (need to be permitted by international rules to do) to achieve equitable development' was not assumed to boil down to 'liberalize' and 'integrate'. Many poor countries were allowed to maintain protection.

As noted earlier, the past decade has ushered in an era of new market access dynamics much more favourable to the developed countries. Now, in the 'globalization plus' paradigm pushed from the North, the route to development is seen to be the route of liberalization and unmediated integration into the world economy, supplemented by domestic institutional reforms to make deep integration viable. As Dani Rodrik observes, 'Global integration has become, for all practical purposes, a substitute for a development strategy' despite its 'shaky empirical ground' and the serious distortion it gives to policymakers' priorities.[15]

Taken together, the three agreements greatly restrict the right of a government to carry though policies that favour the growth and technological upgrading of domestic industries and firms. The sanction is market access: a country that implemented such policies can now be legally handicapped in its access to developed country markets, and the US and EU do not even have to provide serious evidence in the Dispute Settlement Mechanism that a developing country's use of specific industrial policy instruments is 'trade distorting'. To quote Dani Rodrik again, 'The rules for admission into the world economy not only reflect little awareness of development priorities, they are often completely unrelated to sensible economic principles. For instance, WTO agreements on anti-dumping, subsidies and countervailing measures, agriculture, textiles, and trade-related intellectual property rights lack any economic rationale beyond the mercantilist interests of a narrow set of powerful groups in advanced industrial countries'.[16] With a touch of hyperbole the agreements could be called a slow motion Great Train Robbery.

How Do We Know that the Agreements Are – on the Whole – Bad for Development?

Seen in the round the agreements are bad for development for at least two reasons. One is that they are vague at points where vagueness benefits the developed countries, and precise at points where precision works against developing countries. Vagueness allows the developed countries to raise the level of threat to developing countries – threats to bring a case before the DSM and threats to take other punitive actions justified on the claim that the developing country is breaking the (vaguely defined) rules of the WTO.

The second reason concerns the gulf between the agreements' constraints on public policies in developing countries and the public policies adopted by the successful developers.[17] Almost all now-developed countries went through stages of protectionist policy before the capabilities of their firms reached the point where a policy of (more or less) free trade was declared to be in the national interest. Britain was protectionist when it was trying to catch up with Holland. Germany was protectionist when it was trying to catch up with Britain. The United States was protectionist when trying to catch up with Britain and Germany. Japan was protectionist for most of the twentieth century right up to the 1970s,

Korea and Taiwan to the 1990s. And none of them came close to matching our criteria for 'democracy' till the late stages of their catch ups.[18]

Today's fast growers – including China, India and Vietnam – began their fast economic growth well before their fast trade growth and even longer before their trade liberalizations. They have constrained their trade liberalization by considerations of the capacities of domestic firms to compete against imports. But today the World Bank would be first to denounce the amount of protection in their current trade policies – if they were not growing so fast. If nothing else, their experience shows how little we understand the root causes of economic growth.

On the other hand, the development experience of Latin America and Africa over the whole of the twentieth century shows that regions that integrate into the world economy as commodity supply regions – in line with their 'comparative advantage' – and that rely on 'natural' import replacement in response to transport costs, growing skills, and shifting relative costs, are only too likely to remain stuck in the role of commodity supply regions, their level of prosperity a function of access to rich country markets and terms of trade for their commodities.

When Latin American countries did go beyond 'natural' import replacement during the post-Second World War 'import substituting industrialization' decades their growth performance was in fact better by several measures than it has been during the subsequent era of liberalization and privatisation.

As for the argument that the agreements benefit developing countries by raising the inflow of FDI, the share of developing countries in world FDI is small and falling (from the 1990s peak of 40% in 1994 to less than 20% in 2000), and the concentration of FDI on a very small number of developing countries remains as high as in 1980, meaning that there has been no 'evolutionary' spreading out to more and more countries.[19] Moreover, there is no evidence that GATS has lifted the inflow, as noted earlier.

Bilateral investment treaties, which have been proliferating since the early 1990s (the US has now signed 42) take the TRIPS, TRIMS and GATS obligations of host governments as merely the starting point. They require the host government to lift even more restrictions on foreign firms hoping to operate in their territory, to give even more concessions, in return for better access to the US or other powerful-party market. And they establish firm-state arbitration boards, which allow a private firm to take a government to arbitration by a body dominated by private-sector adjudicators naturally sympathetic to the needs of the firm, using private contract law rather than public law, which allows damages against the government to be levied retroactively. The WTO's dispute settlement mechanism, where states deal with states under public law, looks evenly balanced by comparison.

Why Are Developed Country States Pushing this Agenda?

In the light of this evidence we should be sceptical of claims by representatives of developed countries that 'ever-freer trade and investment benefits just about everybody'. The claims are better understood in the light of Friedrich List's observations about how states with head-start advantages behave. Writing in the 1840s and generalizing from the behaviour of first Holland and then Britain in the face of manufacturing competition from elsewhere he observed:

> It is a very clever common device that when anyone has attained the summit of greatness, he kicks away the ladder by which he has climbed up, in order to deprive others of the means of climbing up after him. . . . Any nation which by means of protective duties and restrictions on navigation has raised her manufacturing power and her navigation to such a degree of development that no other nation can sustain free competition with her, can do nothing wiser than to throw away these ladders of her greatness, to preach to other nations the benefits of free trade, and to declare in penitent tones that she has hitherto wandered in the paths of error, and has now for the first time succeeded in discovering the truth.[20]

Perhaps the starkest example of developed countries precluding developing countries from using an array of measures that they themselves used to protect themselves from unwanted competition is the Multi-Fiber Agreement (MFA). The developed countries through the MFA put quotas on the import of textiles and apparel in order to protect their own – employment-intensive, therefore voter-sensitive – textile industries. Developing countries that tried to do something similar today would face serious trade sanctions under WTO rules. Moreover, even though the MFA has been abolished, western textile and apparel markets remain heavily protected through both tariffs and quotas. And agricultural subsidies remain infamously high. Each EU cow receives an average net subsidy of $2.50 per year, while European wheat farmers derive half of their income from subsidies, thanks to which they are able to cripple the export prospects of rivals like Argentina, which has defaulted on its debt because it cannot export enough to keep to its repayment schedule.

The apparatus of economic analysis has been deployed to affirm that largely free and open markets work best for all – which from a Listian perspective amounts to legitimising kicking away the ladder. But there is a odd twist. Since the 1980s much work on the frontiers of economics investigates the heterodox world of increasing returns, linkages, technological learning, oligopolistic pricing, herding behaviour, irrational exuberance and the like, which at least in principle provide justifications for governments to implement industrial policy measures and restrictions on capital flows. On the other hand, the dominant 'structural adjustment' prescriptions of the World Bank and the International Monetary Fund (IMF) assume orthodox decreasing returns, stable equilibria, and no significant non-market linkage effects. Sometimes the same economists straddle both worlds, setting aside their knowledge of the heterodox world when they deal with development policy in order to hammer home the orthodox 'fundamentals'.

The efforts of developed country states to hard-wire in the head-start advantages of their firms through the WTO agreements have been complemented by efforts to establish open capital accounts and free capital mobility as a principle of participation in the world economy. Notwithstanding all the evidence of the huge costs that free capital mobility can inflict on developing countries, especially after the East Asian financial crisis of 1997–8,[21] IMF Managing Director Michel Camdessus said in 1999:

> I believe it is now time for momentum to be re-established. . . . Full liberalization of capital movements should be promoted in a prudent and well-sequenced fashion . . . the liberalization of capital movements [should be made] one of the purposes of the Fund.[22]

US Under Secretary of Treasury John Taylor declared in 2003 that the free transfer of capital in and out of a country without delay is a 'fundamental right.'[23]

What Is to Be Done?

The new trade and investment rules and the old techniques of legitimation – to 'preach to other nations the benefits of free trade' – join with other features of the world system to tip the playing field even more against most developing countries. One is China's surging manufactured exports, which are hurting exporters in most other developing countries and sending a deflationary impulse through the world economy. Another is the skill-biased immigration policies of developed countries, which erode production and governance capabilities in many developing countries. And in a class of its own is HIV/AIDs, which is destroying lives, communities, economies and governments across Africa, South Asia and parts of East Asia, with no end in sight.

If the world is probably not moving in the right direction, as trends in world poverty and inequality suggest,[24] then the precautionary principle – applied to the likely costs to the world of having a large proportion of the world's population still at a small fraction of the living standards of North America and Western Europe half a century from now – suggests the need for non-market measures of intervention and for refocusing international cooperation around 'development' principles rather than 'reciprocity' and 'no distortions' principles.

Concretely, this would entail stronger one-way trade preferences for poor countries, and more legitimate scope for protection.[25] This was List's central prescription for a catch-up country like Germany:

> In order to allow freedom of trade to operate naturally, the less advanced nation must first be raised *by artificial measures* to that stage of cultivation to which the English nation has been artificially elevated.[26]

Of course, there is plenty of evidence of import substitution going awry in Latin America, Africa, South Asia, and Australasia. But this no more discredits import replacement as a principle than the failure of democracy in many developing countries discredits the principle of democracy. The policy response should be to do import replacement better, not do it less.[27]

It is clear from post Second World War experience that protection alone is not enough. Protection has to be made part of a larger industrial strategy to nurture the capabilities of domestic firms and raise the rate of domestic investment, in the context of a private enterprise, market-based economy. And as part of this larger strategy, government-led import replacement has to go with government-encouraged export development. The East Asian experience shows that trade policy restrictions on some imports need not stop the fast growth of other imports – and hence raise the demand for foreign exchange. Trade protection, in other words, need not be 'anti trade'.[28]

The problem in many developing countries – in Latin America and South Asia, for example, also in the formerly heavily protected economies of Australasia – has been the absence of this larger industrial strategy and implementing organizations, and the unwillingness of the 'aid' community, including the World Bank, to help them do industrial strategy sensibly.

The standard dismissal from economists is that even if protection and other forms of industrial policy could be justified in some circumstances, developing country states do not have the capacity to implement it effectively. This response rests on an unexamined assumption about low 'state capacity' in developing countries. But ironically, the world is proceeding on the assumption, in the TRIPS agreement, that developing country states do have a considerable capacity to enforce patents and copyrights. It is not obvious that a state that can do this would not also be able to implement effective protection and other forms of industrial policy.[29]

Rearticulating 'Articulation'

Today we use the word 'integration' to refer exclusively to integration into the world economy, and we assume that more integration is always good for development. One of the strangest silences of development thinking is the silence about internal integration. We should distinguish between 'external integration' and 'internal integration' (or articulation), and recognize that the development of a national economy is more about internal integration than about external integration.

An internally integrated economy has a dense set of input-output linkages between sectors (a high level of sectoral articulation between, for example, rural and urban, and consumer goods and intermediate goods), and a structure of demand such that a high proportion of domestic production is sold to domestic wage earners (a high level of social articulation between wages, consumption, and production). Export demand is not the main source of economic growth. Robust political coalitions between capitalists and employees become possible in this type of economy, because capitalists, employees and the government recognize a common interest in wages as a source of sales and economic growth, not just as a cost of production.

In unarticulated economies, by contrast, wages are viewed simply as a cost, not also a source of demand. Domestic production is not well connected to domestic consumption, leaving exports as the main stimulus to economic growth. Industrial and agricultural sectors producing for foreign markets remain enclaves. This socially and sectorally unintegrated structure limits the creation of class alliances, which handicaps democratic regimes.

The key question, then, is how can developing countries create more articulated economies? The starting point is to recognize that more external integration does not automatically generate more internal integration; on the contrary, it can erode internal integration. But it is also true that more internal integration, if fostered by high and unstrategic protection, can undermine external integration, at the cost of future internal integration at higher income levels.

Development strategy has to operate in the zone where the two forms of integration reinforce rather than undermine each other. But the fact is that the issues of internal integration – including practical nuts-and-bolts issues like nurturing supply links between domestic firms and the subsidiaries of multinational corporations, and designing arrangements to protect exports from protection – have largely dropped out of the development agenda as promulgated by western development organizations. And the WTO agreements make it much more difficult than in the past for development strategy to capture the synergies between internal and external integration.

To put the same point in more familiar terms, today's development theory assumes that the principle of comparative advantage – specialization between countries in line with the location preferences of firms in free and competitive markets – should be the ur-principle of development policy. Conversely it assumes that the principle of import replacement – government encouragement of local production of some items currently imported – is not to be followed, because such policies have seemingly been discredited by the evidence of what happens when it guides the policy framework. In fact, the central challenge of national development strategy is to combine the principle of comparative advantage with the principle of import replacement in a way that generates pressure for upgrading and diversifying national production. This does not always imply protection. Strategic economics prescribes free trade, protection, subsidies, or some combination, depending on a country's circumstances and level of industrialization. In some sectors and at some times, a country should give little weight to import replacement and a lot to comparative advantage; and vice versa. There are a number of small and non-growing countries which, even if untrammelled by international rules, could not hope in the foreseeable future to do more than provide a low-wage platform for rich-country outsourcing, and whose domestic markets are too small to offer more than very limited possibilities for import replacement. There are others, particularly in Latin America, where the scope for import replacement is much bigger but where rapacious oligarchs have long used import replacement policy as yet another means of monopolizing opportunities and exploiting their populations. Here, more trade liberalization and more foreign direct investment can plausibly be seen as a way to force the oligarchs to cede their control over the economy – after which it may make sense to promote another round of concerted import replacement. Meanwhile, China is currently doing both at once, aggressively exporting in line with changing comparative advantage and aggressively replacing some current imports, following in the footsteps of Japan, Korea and Taiwan.

[. . .]

The Unpromising Politics

It is easy to say that 'the international economic regime must be changed, developing countries should be given . . .' The politics are another matter. The developed country negotiators and the 500-strong WTO staff are being driven by a mixture of ideological conviction and intense corporate lobbying. A former WTO negotiator commented, that 'without the enormous pressure generated by the American financial services sector . . . there would have been no [GATS] services agreement'. The pressure came especially from the US Coalition of Service Industries, the European Services Forum, and the UK's Liberalisation of Trade in Services (LOTIS) group.[30] The TRIPS agreement was propelled by a few industries – mainly pharmaceuticals, software and Hollywood – that stand to gain a lot from the protections, whose interests the US government championed. It is not obvious that agreements written to suit western pharmaceutical companies, software companies, the Motion Picture Association, and Wall Street/City of London are good for the world.[31]

On the other hand, developing country governments are not cooperating closely enough to push for the sorts of changes suggested here. For the most part their trade negotiators accept the legitimacy of the idea that 'market access' is the key to development – but they emphasise their access to the North's markets, while the North's 'market access' agenda emphasises the North's access to their market, presented as being in *their* own best interest. They negotiate for better market access (for their exports) as an end in itself, not for 'development space'. And they do not see the critical importance of retaining the policy option of being able to constrain the inflow and outflow of capital by means of quantitative restrictions.

The vested interests are so strong, the legitimacy of the 'globalization plus' paradigm so well defended in the centres of power, that only economic crisis is likely to shift thinking. How many more crashes like those of the 1990s and the early 2000s will the world endure before we conclude that the project of constructing a single integrated world market with universal standards – the culmination of the European Enlightenment ideal – is a mistake? Many, quite likely, provided that the populations of the G7 states are not seriously affected. But small changes are possible even outside of crisis conditions, generated by some combination of, global social movements of NGOs, companies slowly expanding their social responsibility charters, 'epistemic communities' of scholars rethinking development strategies, and developing country governments pushing quietly ahead to encourage new activities (import replacement, new exports) in ways that by-pass or go under-the-radar of the international agreements.[32] From among these various entities it may be possible to organize coalitions for a determined push to revise specific and harmful clauses in existing agreements, such as article 27.1 of TRIPS.

And now that the WTO has come to affect central aspects of people's lives around the world, we should work right now to make it more open. At present the negotiations to create new trade agreements are opaque, and disputes about existing rules are mostly resolved in secret. Governments of developing countries are often left out of the horse-trading sessions and presented with *fait accompli*. We should press the WTO to reduce the current vagueness of the capstone agreements, which rebounds to the advantage of the developed countries; to adopt clearer operating rules and procedures; to publish a record of voting and discussions; to require the chairs of negotiating committees to explain why they include some proposals and reject others from the text of the draft declaration, rather than, as at present, being able occultly to make a 'magic text'.[33] After all, several monetary authorities, including the Bank of England and the Federal Reserve, have started to publish full minutes soon after decision-making meetings, and the experience is generally considered to be successful; and judges in many countries are required to give reasons for their decisions. We need the WTO to be subject to much closer scrutiny by NGOs, in much the way that the World Bank is watched by the Bank Information Center (BIC), an NGO based in Washington DC, and by the Bretton Woods Project, based in London.[34] And it would surely help if the WTO staff – which is an active policy maker, far from a mere facilitator of negotiations among representatives of member states – was more representative. Some

80 percent of the staff are nationals of developed countries, whose population comprises less than 20 percent of the population of the member states.[35] As what the Bush administration calls the US's 'strategic competitor', China, begins to inject its nationals into the WTO and other international organizations, and as China acquires the technological and even military capacity to be a competitor to the dominance of the west, it will be interesting to see how the international development agenda changes.

NOTES

1 These commitments were made in the Uruguay Round of 1986–94, and remade in the Doha agreement of November 2001 to start a new round of multilateral trade talks.
2 The United States has raised its agricultural and steel subsidies since the Doha agreement, and is more likely to raise trade barriers for textiles and garments, footwear, and several farm products than to lower them. These are sectors that are vulnerable to import competition from developing countries and important for the US political support system. The EU deploys protection about as much as the US, and has flouted its Doha commitments even more blatantly than the US by failing to commit to a timetable for reducing its subsidies.
3 Tariff escalation refers to higher tariffs on imports of more highly processed commodities.
4 The section on TRIPS is co-written with Kenneth Shadlen; see his 'Patents and public health: developing countries and the WTO', typescript, DESTIN, LSE, November 2002.
5 Compulsory licensing laws allow states to sidestep patents, to insist that a firm holding a patent on a technology or product of general importance license it to other firms.
6 'Intellectual property: balancing incentives with competitive access', in *Global Economic Prospects 2002*, The World Bank, Washington DC, 2002, p. 136.
7 Elhanan Helpman, 'Innovation, imitation, and intellectual property rights', *Econometrica*, 61, 6 November, 1993, pp. 1247–80.
8 The scope for sweet deals is enhanced by the 'single undertaking' nature of the WTO. Countries may decide that they have to accept a bad deal on some matters (e.g., TRIPS) in order to get what they want on other issues (e.g., agriculture). US appeals to the agriculture minister may elicit governmental pressure on the Geneva ambassador to give way on TRIPS.
9 Robert Wade, *Governing the Market*, Princeton, NJ: Princeton University Press, 1990 (reprinted 2003), pp. 268–9.
10 TRIPS relates mainly to patentable or copyrightable activity.
11 Performance requirements cover not only obligations but also incentives for investors/producers to do certain things. For example, the government might offer a tax incentive in return for a certain proportion of 'local content', locally procured inputs. Or in return for 'trade balancing', exports worth a certain proportion of imports; or exporting a certain proportion of total production; or joint venturing with a local firm.
12 Mari Pangestu, 'Industrial policy and developing countries', in *Development, Trade and the WTO: A Handbook*, World Bank, 2002.
13 'Out of service: the development dangers of the General Agreement on Trade in Services', World Development Movement, London, March 2002. See further, Chakravarthi Raghavan, *Developing Countries and Services Trade: Chasing A Black Cat in a Dark Room, Blindfolded*, Penang: Third World Network, 2002; Scott Sinclair, *Facing the Facts: A Guide to the GATS debate*, Canadian Center for Policy Alternatives, 2002.
14 UNCTAD, *A Positive Agenda for Developing Countries: Issues for Future Trade Negotiations*, New York and Geneva, 2000, p. 172.

15 Dani Rodrik, 'Trading in illusions', *Foreign Policy*, March–April 2001, available at www. foreignpolicy.com/issue_marapr_2001/rodrik.

16 Dani Rodrik (2001).

17 Richard Kozul-Wright, 'The myth of Anglo-Saxon capitalism: reconstructing the history of the American state', in Ha-Joon Chang & Robert Rowthorn (eds.), *The Role of the State in Economic Change*, Clarendon Press, Oxford, 1995, pp. 81–113; Ha-Joon Chang, *Kicking Away the Ladder: Development Strategy in Historical Perspective*, London, Anthem, 2002.

18 Hong Kong and Singapore are the great exceptions on the trade front, in that they did have free trade and they did catch up – but they are city-states and not to be treated as countries. In any case Singapore did place performance requirements/incentives on foreign subsidiaries and mounted an industrial policy to provide them with needed factor inputs.

19 See Wade, 'Reply', in 'Symposium on infant industries', *Oxford Development Studies*, 31, 1, 2003, pp. 8–14.

20 Friedrich List, *The National System of Political Economy*, New York: Augustus Kelley, 1966 [1885], p. 368.

21 Robert Wade, 'From "miracle" to "cronyism": explaining the Great Asian Slump', *Cambridge Journal of Economics*, 22/6, November, 1998; 'The gathering world slump and the battle over capital controls', *New Left Review*, 231, September–October 1998, with Frank Veneroso, pp. 13–42; 'Wheels within wheels: rethinking the Asian crisis and the Asian model', *Annual Review of Political Science 2000*, v.3, 2000, pp. 85–115; 'The US role in the long Asian crisis of 1990–2000', in F. Batista-Rivera and A. Lukauskis (eds.), *The East Asian Crisis and Its Aftermath*, Edward Elgar, 2001.

22 Michel Camdessus, speech, 17 May 1999. But a recent paper by IMF staff economists, including Chief Economist Kenneth Rogoff, finds no evidence that opening the capital account is good for growth and good evidence that it raises the volatility of national consumption; E. Prasad, K. Rogoff, S-J Wie, M.A. Kose, 'Effects of financial globalization on developing countries', typescript, March 13, 2003.

23 John Taylor, testimony before the subcommittee on domestic and international monetary policy, trade and technology, Committee on Financial Services, US House of Representatives, 1 April 2003.

24 I spell out the grounds for this contentious conclusion in 'Is globalization reducing poverty and inequality?', *World Development*, 32, 4, 2004, pp. 567–89; also in John Ravenhill (ed.), *Global political Economy*, Oxford University Press, New York.

25 The effectiveness of nonreciprocal trade preferences for poor countries is suggested by Andrew Rose's finding that – contrary to general assumption – being a member of the GATT/WTO as such made no statistical difference to how much trade a country did with others, but receiving trade preferences under GATT's Generalised System of Preferences (GSP) – preferences that rich countries gave to poor ones – roughly doubled a poor country's trade compared to what it would have been otherwise. Andrew Rose, 'Do we really know that the WTO increases trade?' CEPR Discussion Paper 3538, 2002.

26 List (1966), chapter 11, p. 131, emphasis added.

27 Henry Bruton, 'A reconsideration of import substitution', *Journal of Economic Literature*, 36(2), June 1998, pp. 903–36.

28 Robert Wade (1990), chapters 5 and 11; 'How to protect exports from protection: Taiwan's duty drawback scheme', *The World Economy*, 14, 3, 1991, pp. 299–309; Jane Jacobs, *Cities and the Wealth of Nations: Principles of Economic Life*, Random House, New York, 1984.

29 My thanks to Ken Shadlen for this point.

30 World Development Movement (2002), pp. 15–16.

31 See Kwa (2002).

32 As Korea and Taiwan beefed up covert trade controls even as they announced bold trade liberalizations.

33 A South Asian delegate said about the process of formulating the Draft Declaration for Doha, 'In the process of negotiations, we would object to a text, but it would still appear. We would state we wanted a text added in, and still it would not appear. It was like a magic text'. Quoted in Kwa (2002), p. 21.

34 A small WTO-watching NGO called the International Center for Trade and Sustainable Development (ICTSD) already exists, now in its sixth year. It publishes a regular bulletin of WTO news of particular interest to developing countries, *Bridges*. Others include WTO WATCH, Our World Is Not For Sale Network, Third World Network, the Trade Information Project which focus on getting information to NGOs and social movements to enable them to engage in advocacy with their governments and with the WTO. On WTO openness see 'Open up the WTO', editorial, *The Washington Post*, reprinted in *International Herald Tribune*, 23 December 2002. For a different view see Andrew Walter, 'NGOs, business, and international investment: the Multilateral Agreement on Investment, Seattle, and beyond', *Global Governance*, 7, 2001, pp. 51–73. On international organizations more generally, Ngaire Woods, 'Holding intergovernmental institutions to account', *Ethics and International Affairs*, 17, 1, 2003, pp. 69–80. For UK-based NGOs' opposition to a new investment agreement at the WTO see Oxfam, 'Unwanted, unproductive and unbalanced: six arguments against an investment agreement at the WTO', Joint Policy Paper, May 2003.

35 Kwa (2002), p. 43.

BIBLIOGRAPHY

Bruton, Henry, "A reconsideration of import substitution," *Journal of Economic Literature*, 36(2), June 1998, pp. 903–36.

Chang, Ha-Joon, *Kicking Away the Ladder: Development Strategy in Historical Perspective*, London, Anthem, 2002.

Helpman, Elhanan, "Innovation, imitation, and intellectual property rights," *Econometrica*, 61, November 6, 1993, pp. 1247–80.

Jacobs, Jane, *Cities and the Wealth of Nations: Principles of Economic Life*, New York, Random House, 1984.

Kozul-Wright, Richard, "The myth of Anglo-Saxon capitalism: reconstructing the history of the American state," in Ha-Joon Chang & Robert Rowthorn (eds.), *The Role of the State in Economic Change*, Clarendon Press, Oxford, 1995, pp. 81–113.

Kwa, Aileen, "Power politics in the WTO," Focus on the Global South, Chulalongkorn University, Bangkok, November 2002.

List, Friedrich, *The National System of Political Economy*, New York: Augustus Kelley, 1966 (first published 1885).

Oxfam, "Unwanted, unproductive and unbalanced: six arguments against an investment agreement at the WTO," Joint Policy Paper, May 2003.

Pangestu, Mari, "Industrial policy and developing countries," in *Development, Trade and the WTO: A Handbook*, World Bank, 2002.

Prasad, E., Rogoff, K., Wie, S-J. & Kose, M. A., "Effects of financial globalization on developing countries," typescript, March 13, 2003.

Raghavan, Chakravarthi, *Developing Countries and Services Trade: Chasing A Black Cat in a Dark Room, Blindfolded*, Penang: Third World Network, 2002.

Ravenhill, John (ed.), *Global Political Economy*, Oxford: Oxford University Press.

Rodrik, Dani, "Trading in illusions," *Foreign Policy*, March–April 2001.

Rose, Andrew, "Do we really know that the WTO increases trade?," CEPR Discussion Paper 3538, 2002.

Shadlen, Kenneth, "Patents and public health: developing countries and the WTO," typescript, DESTIN, LSE, November 2002.

Sinclair, Scott, *Facing the Facts: A Guide to the GATS debate*, Ganadian Center for Policy Alternatives, 2002.

UNCTAD, *A Positive Agenda for Developing Countries: Issues for Future Trade Negotiations*, New York and Geneva, 2000.

Wade, Robert, *Governing the Market*, Princeton, NJ: Princeton University Press, 1990 (reprinted 2003).

——, "How to protect exports from protection: Taiwan's duty drawback scheme," *The World Economy*, 14(3), 1991, pp. 299–309.

——, "From 'miracle' to 'cronyism': explaining the Great Asian Slump," *Cambridge Journal of Economics*, 22(6), November 1988.

——, "Wheels within wheels: Rethinking the Asian crisis and the Asian model," *Annual Review of Political Science 2000*, 3, 2000, pp. 85–115.

——, "The US role in the long Asian crisis of 1990–2000," in F. Batista-Rivera & A. Lukauskis (eds.), *The East Asian Crisis and Its Aftermath*, Edward Elgar, 2001.

——, "Reply," in "Symposium on infant industries," *Oxford Development Studies*, 31(1), 2003, pp. 8–14.

——, "Is globalization reducing poverty and inequality?," *World Development*, 32, 4, 2004, pp. 567–89.

Wade, Robert & Veneroso, Frank, "The gathering world slump and the battle over capital controls," *New Left Review*, 231, September–October 1998, pp. 13–42.

Walter, Andrew, "NGOs, business, and international investment: the Multilateral Agreement on Investment, Seattle, and beyond," *Global Governance*, 7, 2001, pp. 51–73.

Washington Post (editorial), "Open up the WTO," reprinted in *International Herald Tribune*, December 23, 2002.

Woods, Ngaire, "Holding intergovernmental institutions to account," *Ethics and International Affairs*, 17(1), 2003, pp. 69–80.

World Bank, "Intellectual property: balancing incentives with competitive access," *Global Economic Prospects 2002*, Washington, DC: World Bank, 2002.

World Development Movement, "Out of service: the development dangers of the General Agreement on Trade in Services," London, March 2002.

18   Globalism's Discontents (2002)

Joseph E. Stiglitz

Few subjects have polarized people throughout the world as much as globalization. Some see it as the way of the future, bringing unprecedented prosperity to everyone, everywhere. Others, symbolized by the Seattle protestors of December 1999, fault globalization as the source of untold problems, from the destruction of native cultures to increasing poverty and immiseration. In this article, I want to sort out the different meanings of globalization. In many countries, globalization has brought huge benefits to a few with few benefits to the many. But in the case of a few countries, it has brought enormous benefit to the many. Why have there been these huge differences in experiences? The answer is that globalization has meant different things in different places.

The countries that have managed globalization on their own, such as those in East Asia, have, by and large, ensured that they reaped huge benefits and that those benefits were equitably shared; they were able substantially to control the terms on which they engaged with the global economy. By contrast, the countries that have, by and large, had globalization managed for them by the International Monetary Fund and other international economic institutions have not done so well. The problem is thus not with globalization but with how it has been managed.

The international financial institutions have pushed a particular ideology – market fundamentalism – that is both bad economics and bad politics; it is based on premises concerning how markets work that do not hold even for developed countries, much less for developing countries. The IMF has pushed these economic policies without a broader vision of society or the role of economics within society. And it has pushed these policies in ways that have undermined emerging democracies.

More generally, globalization itself has been governed in ways that are undemocratic and have been disadvantageous to developing countries, especially the poor within those countries. The Seattle protestors pointed to the absence of democracy and of transparency, the governance of the international economic institutions by and for special corporate and financial interests, and the absence of countervailing democratic checks to ensure that these informal and *public* institutions serve a general interest. In these complaints, there is more than a grain of truth.

Beneficial Globalization

Of the countries of the world, those in East Asia have grown the fastest and done most to reduce poverty. And they have done so, emphatically, via "globalization." Their growth has been based on exports – by taking advantage of the global market for exports and by closing the technology gap. It was not just gaps in capital and other resources that separated the developed from the less-developed countries, but differences in knowledge. East Asian countries took advantage of the "globalization of knowledge" to reduce these disparities. But while some of the countries in the region grew by opening themselves up to multinational companies, others, such as Korea and Taiwan, grew by creating their own enterprises. Here is the key distinction: Each of the most successful globalizing countries determined its own pace of change; each made sure as it grew that the benefits were shared equitably; each rejected the basic tenets of the "Washington Consensus," which argued for a minimalist role for government and rapid privatization and liberalization.

In East Asia, government took an active role in managing the economy. The steel industry that the Korean government created was among the most efficient in the world – performing far better than its private-sector rivals in the United States (which, though private, are constantly turning to the government for protection and for subsidies). Financial markets were highly regulated. My research shows that those regulations promoted growth. It was only when these countries stripped away the regulations, under pressure from the US Treasury and the IMF, that they encountered problems.

During the 1960s, 1970s, and 1980s, the East Asian economies not only grew rapidly but were remarkable stable. Two of the countries most touched by the 1997–1998 economic crisis had had in the preceding three decades not a single year of negative growth; two had only one year – a better performance than the United States or the other wealthy nations that make up the Organization for Economic Cooperation and Development (OECD). The single most important factor leading to the troubles that several of the East Asian countries encountered in the late 1990s – the East Asian crisis – was the rapid liberalization of financial and capital markets. In short, the countries of East Asia benefited from globalization because they made globalization work for them; it was when they succumbed to the pressures from the outside that they ran into problems that were beyond their own capacity to manage well.

Globalization can yield immense benefits. Elsewhere in the developing world, globalization of knowledge has brought improved health, with life spans increasing at a rapid pace. How can one put a price on these benefits of globalization? Globalization has brought still other benefits: Today there is the beginning of a globalized civil society that has begun to succeed with such reforms as the Mine Ban Treaty and debt forgiveness for the poorest highly indebted countries (the Jubilee movement). The globalization protest movement itself would not have been possible without globalization.

The Darker Side of Globalization

How then could a trend with the power to have so many benefits have produced such opposition? Simply because it has not only failed to live up to its potential but frequently has had very adverse effects. But this forces us to ask, why has it had such adverse effects? The answer can be seen by looking at each of the economic elements of globalization as pursued by the international financial institutions and especially by the IMF.

The most adverse effects have arisen from the liberalization of financial and capital markets – which has posed risks to developing countries without commensurate rewards. The liberalization has left them prey to hot money pouring into the country, an influx that has fueled speculative real-estate booms; just as suddenly, as investor sentiment changes, the money is pulled out, leaving in its wake economic devastation. Early on, the IMF said that these countries were being rightly punished for pursuing bad economic policies. But as the crisis spread from country to country, even those that the IMF had given high marks found themselves ravaged.

The IMF often speaks about the importance of the discipline provided by capital markets. In doing so, it exhibits a certain paternalism, a new form of the old colonial mentality: "We in the establishment, we in the North who run our capital markets, know best. Do what we tell you to do, and you will prosper." The arrogance is offensive, but the objection is more than just to style. The position is highly undemocratic: There is an implied assumption that democracy by itself does not provide sufficient discipline. But if one is to have an external disciplinarian, one should choose a good disciplinarian who knows what is good for growth, who shares one's values. One doesn't want an arbitrary and capricious taskmaster who one moment praises you for your virtues and the next screams at you for being rotten to the core. But capital markets are just such a fickle taskmaster; even ardent advocates talk about their bouts of irrational exuberance followed by equally irrational pessimism.

Lessons of Crisis

Nowhere was the fickleness more evident than in the last global financial crisis. Historically, most of the disturbances in capital flows into and out of a country are not the result of factors inside the country. Major disturbances arise, rather, from influences outside the country. When Argentina suddenly faced high interest rates in 1998, it wasn't because of what Argentina did but because of what happened in Russia. Argentina cannot be blamed for Russia's crisis.

Small developing countries find it virtually impossible to withstand this volatility. I have described capital-market liberalization with a simple metaphor: Small countries are like small boats. Liberalizing capital markets is like setting them loose on a rough sea. Even if the boats are well captained, even if the boats are sound, they are likely to be hit broadside by a big wave and capsize. But the IMF pushed for the boats to set forth into the roughest parts of the sea before they were seaworthy, with untrained captains and crews, and without life vests. No wonder matters turned out so badly!

To see why it is important to choose a disciplinarian who shares one's values, consider a world in which there were free mobility of skilled labor. Skilled labor would then provide discipline. Today, a country that does not treat capital well will find capital quickly with-drawing; in a world of free labor mobility, if a country did not treat skilled labor well, it too would withdraw. Workers would worry about the quality of their children's education and their family's health care, the quality of their environment and of their own wages and working conditions. They would say to the government: If you fail to provide these essentials, we will move elsewhere. That is a far cry from the kind of discipline that free-flowing capital provides.

The liberalization of capital markets has not brought growth: How can one build factories or create jobs with money that can come in and out of a country overnight? And it gets worse: Prudential behavior requires countries to set aside reserves equal to the amount of short-term lending; so if a firm in a poor country borrows $100 million at, say, 20 percent interest rates short-term from a bank in the United States, the government must set aside a corresponding amount. The reserves are typically held in US Treasury bills – a safe, liquid asset. In effect, the country is borrowing $100 million from the United States and lending $100 million to the United States. But when it borrows, it pays a high interest rate, 20 percent; when it lends, it receives a low interest rate, around 4 percent. This may be great for the United States, but it can hardly help the growth of the poor country. There is also a high *opportunity* cost of the reserves; the money could have been much better spent on building rural roads or constructing schools or health clinics. But instead, the country is, in effect, forced to lend money to the United States.

Thailand illustrates the true ironies of such policies: There, the free market led to investments in empty office buildings, starving other sectors – such as education and transportation – of badly needed resources. Until the IMF and the US Treasury came along, Thailand had restricted bank lending for speculative real estate. The Thais had seen the record: Such lending is an essential part of the boom-bust cycle that has characterized capitalism for 200 years. It wanted to be sure that the scarce capital went to create jobs. But the IMF nixed this intervention in the free market. If the free market said, "Build empty office buildings," so be it! The market knew better than any government bureaucrat who mistakenly might have thought it wiser to build schools or factories.

The Costs of Volatility

Capital-market liberalization is inevitably accompanied by huge volatility, and this volatility impedes growth and increases poverty. It increases the risks of investing in the country, and thus investors demand a risk premium in the form of higher-than-normal profits. Not only is growth not enhanced but poverty is increased through several channels. The high volatility increases the likelihood of recessions – and the poor always bear the brunt of such downturns. Even in developed countries, safety nets are weak or nonexistent among the selfemployed and in the rural sector. But these are the dominant sectors in developing countries. Without adequate safety nets, the recessions that follow from capital-market liberalization lead to impoverishment. In the name of imposing budget discipline and reassuring investors, the IMF invariably demands expenditure reductions, which almost inevitably result in cuts in outlays for safety nets that are already threadbare.

But matters are even worse – for under the doctrines of the "discipline of the capital markets," if countries try to tax capital, capital flees. Thus, the IMF doctrines inevitably lead to an increase in tax burdens on the poor and the middle classes. Thus, while IMF bailouts enable the rich to take their money out of the country at more favorable terms (at the overvalued exchange rates), the burden of repaying the loans lies with the workers who remain behind.

The reason that I emphasize capital-market liberalization is that the case against it – and against the IMF's stance in pushing it – is so compelling. It illustrates what can go wrong with globalization. Even economists like Jagdish Bhagwati, strong advocates of free trade, see the folly in liberalizing capital markets. Belatedly, so too has the IMF – at least in its official rhetoric, though less so in its policy stances – but too late for all those countries that have suffered so much from following the IMF's prescriptions.

But while the case for trade liberalization – when properly done – is quite compelling, the way it has been pushed by the IMF has been far more problematic. The basic logic is simple: Trade liberalization is supposed to result in resources moving from inefficient protected sectors to more efficient export sectors. The problem is not only that job destruction comes before the job creation – so that unemployment and poverty result – but that the IMF's "structural adjustment programs" (designed in ways that allegedly would reassure global investors) make job creation almost impossible. For these programs are often accompanied by high interest rates that are often justified by a single-minded focus on inflation. Sometimes that concern is deserved; often, though, it is carried to an extreme. In the United States, we worry that small increases in the interest rate will discourage investment. The IMF has pushed for far higher interest rates in countries with a far less hospitable investment environment. The high interest rates mean that new jobs and enterprises are not created. What happens is that trade liberalization, rather than moving workers from low-productivity jobs to high-productivity ones, moves them from low-productivity jobs to unemployment. Rather than enhanced growth, the effect is increased poverty. To make matters even worse, the unfair trade-liberalization agenda forces poor countries to compete with highly subsidized American and European agriculture.

The Governance of Globalization

As the market economy has matured within countries, there has been increasing recognition of the importance of having rules to govern it. One hundred fifty years ago, in many parts of the world, there was a domestic process that was in some ways analogous to globalization. In the United States, government promoted the formation of the national economy, the building of the railroads, and the development of the telegraph – all of which reduced transportation and communication costs within the United Sates. As that process occurred, the democratically elected national government provided oversight: supervising and regulating, balancing interests, tempering crises, and limiting adverse consequences of this very large change in economic structure. So, for instance, in 1863 the US government established the first financial-banking regulatory authority – the Office of the Comptroller of Currency – because it was important to have strong national banks, and that requires strong regulation.

The United States, among the least statist of the industrial democracies, adopted other policies. Agriculture, the central industry of the United Stated in the mid-nineteenth century, was supported by the 1862 Morrill Act, which established research, extension, and teaching programs. That system worked extremely well and is widely credited with playing a central role in the enormous increases in agricultural productivity over the last century and a half. We established an industrial policy for other fledgling industries, including radio and civil aviation. The beginning of the telecommunications industry, with the first tele-graph line between Baltimore and Washington, DC, was funded by the federal government. And it is a tradition that has continued, with the US government's founding of the Internet.

By contrast, in the current process of globalization we have a system of what I call global governance without global government. International institutions like the World Trade Organization, the IMF, the World Bank, and others provide an ad hoc system of global governance, but it is a far cry from global government and lacks democratic accountability. Although it is perhaps better than not having any system of global governance, the system is structured not to serve general interests or assure equitable results. This not only raises issues of whether broader values are given short shrift; it does not even promote growth as much as an alternative might.

Governance through Ideology

Consider the contrast between how economic decisions are made inside the United States and how they are made in the international economic institutions. In this country, eco-nomic decisions within the administration are undertaken largely by the National Eco-nomic Council, which includes the secretary of labor, the secretary of commerce, the chairman of the Council of Economic Advisers, the treasury secretary, the assistant attor-ney general for antitrust, and the US trade representative. The Treasury is only one vote and often gets voted down. All of these officials, of course, are part of an administration that must face Congress and the democratic electorate. But in the international arena, only the voices of the financial community are heard. The IMF reports to the ministers of finance and the governors of the central banks, and one of the important items on its agenda is to make these central banks more independent – and less democratically accountable. It might make little difference if the IMF dealt only with matters of concern to the financial com-munity, such as the clearance of checks; but in fact, its policies affect every aspect of life. It forces countries to have tight monetary and fiscal policies: It evaluates the trade-off between inflation and unemployment, and in that trade-off it always puts far more weight on inflation than on jobs.

The problem with having the rules of the game dictated by the IMF – and thus by the financial community – is not just a question of values (though that is important) but also a question of ideology. The financial community's view of the world predominates – even when there is little evidence in its support. Indeed, beliefs on key issues are held so strongly that theoretical and empirical support of the positions is viewed as hardly necessary.

Recall again the IMF's position on liberalizing capital markets. As noted, the IMF pushed a set of policies that exposed countries to serious risk. One might have thought, given the evidence of the costs, that the IMF could offer plenty of evidence that the policies also did some good. In fact, there was no such evidence; the evidence that was available suggested that there was little if any positive effect on growth. Ideology enabled IMF officials not only to ignore the absence of benefits but also to overlook the evidence of the huge costs imposed on countries.

An Unfair Trade Agenda

The trade-liberalization agenda has been set by the North, or more accurately, by special interests in the North. Consequently, a disproportionate part of the gains has accrued to the advanced industrial countries, and in some cases the less-developed countries have actually been worse off. After the last round of trade negotiations, the Uruguay Round that ended in 1994, the World Bank calculated the gains and losses to each of the regions of the world. The United States and Europe gained enormously. But sub-Saharan Africa, the poorest region of the world, lost by about 2 percent because of terms-of-trade effects: The trade negotiations opened their markets to manufactured goods produced by the industrialized countries but did not open up the markets of Europe and the United States to the agricultural goods in which poor countries often have a comparative advantage. Nor did the trade agreements eliminate the subsidies to agriculture that make it so hard for the developing countries to compete.

The US negotiations with China over its membership in the WTO displayed a double standard bordering on the surreal. The US trade representative, the chief negotiator for the United States, began by insisting that China was a developed country. Under WTO rules, developing countries are allowed longer transition periods in which state subsidies and other departures from the WTO strictures are permitted. China certainly wishes it were a developed country, with Western-style per capita incomes. And since China has a lot of "capitas," it's possible to multiply a huge number of people by very small average incomes and conclude that the People's Republic is a big economy. But China is not only a developing economy; it is a low-income developing country. Yet the United States insisted that China be treated like a developed country! China went along with the fiction; the negotiations dragged on so long that China got some extra time to adjust. But the true hypocrisy was shown when US negotiators asked, in effect, for developing-country status for the United States to get extra time to shelter the American textile industry.

Trade negotiations in the service industries also illustrate the unlevel nature of the playing field. Which service industries did the United States say were *very* important? Financial services – industries in which Wall Street has a comparative advantage. Construction industries and maritime services were not on the agenda, because the developing countries would have a comparative advantage in these sectors.

Consider also intellectual-property rights, which are important if innovators are to have incentives to innovate (though many of the corporate advocates of intellectual property exaggerate its importance and fail to note that much of the most important research, as in basic science and mathematics, is not patentable). Intellectual-property rights, such as patents and trademarks, need to balance the interests of producers with those of users – not only users in developing countries, but researchers in developed countries. If we underprice the profitability of innovation to the inventor, we deter invention. If we overprice its cost to the research community and the end user, we retard its diffusion and beneficial effects on living standards.

In the final stages of the Uruguay negotiations, both the White House Office of Science and Technology Policy and the Council of Economic Advisers worried that we had not got the balance right – that the agreement put producers' interests over users'. We worried that, with this imbalance, the rate of progress and innovation might actually be impeded. After all, knowledge is the most important input into research, and overly strong intellectual-property rights can, in effect, increase the price of this input. We were also concerned about the consequences of denying lifesaving medicines to the poor. This issue subsequently gained international attention in the context of the provision of AIDS medicines in South Africa. The international outrage forced the drug companies to back down – and it appears that, going forward, the most adverse consequences will be circumscribed. But it is worth noting that initially, even the Democratic US administration supported the pharmaceutical companies.

What we were not fully aware of was another danger – what has come to be called "biopiracy," which involves international drug companies patenting traditional medicines. Not only do they seek to make money from "resources" and knowledge that rightfully belong to the developing countries, but in doing so they squelch domestic firms who long provided these traditional medicines. While it is not clear whether these patents would hold up in court if they were effectively challenged, it is clear that the less-developed countries may not have the legal and financial resources required to mount such a challenge. The issue has become the source of enormous emotional, and potentially economic, concern throughout the developing world. This fall, while I was in Ecuador visiting a village in the high Andes, the Indian mayor railed against how globalization had led to biopiracy.

Globalization and September 11

September 11 brought home a still darker side of globalization – it provided a global arena for terrorists. But the ensuing events and discussions highlighted broader aspects of the globalization debate. It made clear how untenable American unilateralist positions were. President Bush, who had unilaterally rejected the international agreement to address one of the long-term global risks perceived by countries around the world – global warming, in which the United States is the largest culprit – called for a global alliance against terrorism. The administration realized that success would require concerted action by all.

One of the ways to fight terrorists, Washington soon discovered, was to cut off their sources of funding. Ever since the East Asian crisis, global attention had focused on the secretive offshore banking centers. Discussions following that crisis focused on the importance of good information – transparency, or openness – but this was intended for the developing countries. As international discussions turned to the lack of transparency shown by the IMF and the offshore banking centers, the US Treasury changed its tune. It is not because these secretive banking havens provide better services than those provided by banks in New York or London that billions have been put there; the secrecy serves a variety of nefarious purposes – including avoiding taxation and money laundering. These institutions could be shut down overnight – or forced to comply with international norms – if the United States and the other leading countries wanted. They continue to exist because they serve the interests of the financial community and the wealthy. Their continuing existences is no accident. Indeed, the OECD drafted an agreement to limit their scope – and before September 11, the Bush administration unilaterally walked away from this agreement too.

How foolish this looks now in retrospect! Had it been embraced, we would have been further along the road to controlling the flow of money into the hands of the terrorists.

There is one more aspect to the aftermath of September 11 worth noting here. The United States was already in recession, but the attack made matters worse. It used to be said that when the United States sneezed, Mexico caught a cold. With globalization, when the United States sneezes, much of the rest of the world risks catching pneumonia. And the United States now has a bad case of the flu. With globalization, mismanaged macroeconomic policy in the United States – the failure to design an effective stimulus package – has global consequences. But around the world, anger at the traditional IMF policies is growing. The developing countries are saying to the industrialized nations: "When you face a slowdown, you follow the precepts that we are all taught in our economic courses: You adopt expansionary monetary and fiscal policies. But when we face a slowdown, you insist on contractionary policies. For you, deficits are okay; for us, they are impermissible – even if we can raise the funds through 'selling forward,' say, some natural resources." A heightened sense of inequity prevails, partly because the consequences of maintaining contractionary policies are so great.

Global Social Justice

Today, in much of the developing world, globalization is being questioned. For instance, in Latin America, after a short burst of growth in the early 1990s, stagnation and recession have set in. The growth was not sustained – some might say, was not sustainable. Indeed, at this juncture, the growth record of the so-called post-reform era looks no better, and in some countries much worse, than in the widely criticized import-substitution period of the 1950s and 1960s when Latin countries tried to industrialize by discouraging imports. Indeed, reform critics point out that the burst of growth in the early 1990s was little more than a "catch-up" that did not even make up for the lost decade of the 1980s.

Throughout the region, people are asking: "Has reform failed or has globalization failed?" The distinction is perhaps artificial, for globalization was at the center of the reforms. Even in those countries that have managed to grow, such as Mexico, the benefits have accrued largely to the upper 30 percent and have been even more concentrated in the top 10 percent. Those at the bottom have gained little; many are even worse off. The reforms have exposed countries to greater risk, and the risks have been borne disproportionately by those least able to cope with them. Just as in many countries where the pacing and sequencing of reforms has resulted in job destruction outmatching job creation, so too has the exposure to risk outmatched the ability to create institutions for coping with risk, including effective safety nets.

In this bleak landscape, there are some positive signs. Those in the North have become more aware of the inequities of the global economic architecture. The agreement at Doha to hold a new round of trade negotiations – the "Development Round" – promises to rectify some of the imbalances of the past. There has been a marked change in the rhetoric of the international economic institutions – at least they talk about poverty. At the World Bank, there have been some real reforms; there has been some progress in translating the rhetoric into reality – in ensuring that the voices of the poor are heard and the concerns of the developing countries are listened to. But elsewhere, there is often a gap between the rhetoric and the reality. Serious reforms in governance, in who makes decisions and how they are made, are not on the table. If one of the problems at the IMF has been that the ideology, interests, and perspectives of the financial community in the advanced industrialized countries have been given disproportionate weight (in matters whose effects go well beyond finance), then the prospects for success in the current discussions of reform, in which the same parties continue to predominate, are bleak. They are more likely to result in slight changes in the shape of the table, not changes in who is *at* the table or what is on the agenda.

September 11 has resulted in a global alliance against terrorism. What we now need is not just an alliance *against* evil, but an alliance *for* something positive – a global alliance for reducing poverty and for creating a better environment, an alliance for creating a global society with more social justice.

19 The New Global Economy and Developing Countries: Making Openness Work (1999) and Has Globalization Gone too Far? (1997)

Dani Rodrik

A Modern-Day Fable

Imagine that a Martian lands in Washington and is captured by a group of mischievous economists. The economists make a deal with her. They will release her if she can prove her intelligence by correctly answering an economics question: Which government policies are most likely to predict how well different countries did over the last two decades? To make the deal fair, the economists agree to provide the Martian with a briefing book containing a set of readings drawn from the current literature on trade and development. After this crash course on contemporary economic thought, the Martian provides her answer. The countries that grew most rapidly, she replies, were the ones with low tariffs, few nontariff barriers, and no restrictions on international capital flows. The economists look at each other and realize that they have no choice but to release her. They conclude that intelligent life exists outside Planet Earth.

Bit by the economics bug, the Martian decides to learn a bit more before returning home. She reads up on statistics and gets hold of some cross-national data. She calculates the correlation coefficients between various indicators of trade policy and growth of GDP per capita across countries. But the results are puzzling. None of the indicators of policy toward trade and capital flows that she can lay her hands on – average tariff levels, nontariff coverage ratios, or indexes of capital-account liberalization – correlate statistically significantly with per capita GDP growth.[1] Either economics is a lot more complicated than she sensed, or else humans are not nearly as intelligent as they seem. In either case, she figures it is best to leave Earth before her captors change their minds.

Table 1 Determinants of Per Capita GDP Growth, 1975–1994[1]

	(1)	(2)	(3)	(4)	(5)	(6)	(7)	(8)	(9)	(10)
Investment										
Investment/GDP, 1975–1994[a]		0.095* (0.025)								
Excluding Lesotho[a]			0.110** (0.050)							
Macroeconomic stability										
Index of macromismanagement[b]				-0.026* (0.007)						
Openness										
Average tariff rate (×100)					-0.024 (0.031)					
Nontariff barrier (NTB) coverage ratio[c]						-0.009 (0.009)				
Trade[d]							0.000 (0.000)			
Capital-account liberalization[e]								0.002 (0.005)		
Government size										
Government consumption/GDP									-0.040 (0.025)	
Total government expenditures/GDP										-0.011 (0.021)
N	91	84	83	83	82	73	73	90	91	76
R²	0.45	0.56	0.56	0.53	0.42	0.61	0.59	0.43	0.47	0.40

Notes:

a This regression is run with and without Lesotho, as this country looks like an outlier that could distort the results.

b This index is constructed by taking a simple average of the inflation rate and the log of (1 plus) the black market premium during 1975–1990.

c Sources: World Development Indicators 1998 (average import duty rate, 1975–1994) and Barro and Lee (1994) for NTBs.

d The volume of trade in excess of predicted volume, with the predicted values coming from a cross-country regression of trade on geographical determinants (population, distance from major trading partners, and regional dummies).

e The proportion of years during 1975–1994 without restrictions on the capital account, as coded by Kim (1997) from IMF sources.

Editors' Note

1 Five rows of data have been omitted here (Latin America, East Asia, Sub-Saharan Africa, "Log per capita GDP, 1975," and "Log secondary enrollment, 1975"). Their values were all significant throughout, except per capita GDP, which was not significant in models 1, 5, 9, and 10, but was still in the same negative direction. The coefficient for "Log secondary enrollment" in model 10 was also not significant.

The Promise and Perils of Openness

For policymakers around the world, the appeal of opening up to global markets is based on a simple but powerful promise: international economic integration will improve economic performance. As countries reduce their tariff and nontariff barriers to trade and open up to international capital flows, the expectation is that economic growth will increase thus, in turn, will reduce poverty and improve the quality of life for the vast majority of the residents of developing nations.

The trouble, as the Martian discovered, is that there is no convincing evidence that openness, in the sense of low barriers to trade and capital flows, systematically produces these consequences. In practice, the links between openness and economic growth tend to be weak, and to be contingent on the presence of complementary policies and institutions; the benefits of openness lie on the import side: the ability to import ideas, investment goods, and intermediate inputs from more advanced countries can significantly boost economic growth. But to realize this potential, developing nations need other things too. They need to create an environment that is conducive to private investment – to follow what I have called an investment strategy. They need to improve their institutions of conflict management – legally guaranteed civil liberties and political freedoms, social partnerships, and social insurance – so that they can maintain macroeconomic stability and adjust to rapid changes in external circumstances. In the absence of these complements to a strategy of external liberalization, openness will not yield much. At worst, it will cause instability, widening inequalities, and social conflict.

The evidence from the experience of the last two decades is clear: the countries whose economies have grown most rapidly since the mid-1970s are those that have invested a large share of GDP and maintained macroeconomic stability. This is the bottom line of the cross-national econometric exercise summarized in Table 1. The exercise is the type of effort that the Martian might have undertaken, had she a bit more knowledge and time. Her findings with regard to the relative insignificance of trade policy, however, would remain unchanged.

Table 1 shows the consequences of regressing per capita GDP growth over the 1975–1994 period on initial income, initial education levels, regional dummies, and additional explanatory variables. As the table shows, there is only a weak correlation over this period between economic growth and indicators of openness. Whether based on tariff and nontariff restrictions or on trade volumes, none of the measures of trade openness exhibit a statistically significant relationship with growth (columns 5, 6, and 7).[2]

Openness to capital flows – captured by an indicator of capital-account liberalization – does not exert any influence either (column 8). Neither is the size of government a significant factor (columns 9 and 10). What matters most are investment rates (columns 2 and 3) and macroeconomic stability (column 4).

[. . .]

Such findings should caution policymakers against buying too readily into current development fashions. The evidence in favor of the small government/free trade orthodoxy is less than overwhelming. Investment and macroeconomic policies remain key. There is no magic formula for surmounting the challenges of economic growth – and if there is, openness is not it.

From a broader historical perspective, there should be nothing surprising about these conclusions, and in particular about the argument that the relationship between trade barriers and economic performance is ambiguous. After all, most of the countries that successfully followed Britain into the Industrial Revolution did so under trade regimes that would be classified as highly restrictive by today's standards. In the United States, to take a prominent example, import tariffs averaged around 40 percent in the half century following the Civil War, a period in which the United States caught up with and overtook Britain and the rest of Europe. To put this number in perspective, note that only one country in our sample (among those for which there is data) had an average tariff rate during 1975–1994 exceeding 40 percent (Seychelles) – although nontariff barriers are more common these days than they were during the 19th century. Neither history nor recent evidence provides support for a straightforward association between the level of trade barriers and long-term growth.

[. . .]

As I have discussed throughout this book, the economies that have done well in the postwar period have all succeeded through their own particular brand of heterodox policies. Macroeconomic stability and high investment rates have been common, but beyond that, many details differ. This too should be a warning against trying to fit all developing nations into a straitjacket of policies that have only recently become conventional wisdom.

International Constraints on National Policy

But do developing countries really have a choice? Can small nations still pursue their own distinctive agendas and govern their economies in ways that differ from the prevailing precepts? To hear many policymakers speak, the answer in no. It has become a common refrain that there is little choice but to privatize, open up, and attract DFI.

As I have argued before, exports and DFI are means to an end, not ends in themselves. Gearing economic policy toward performance in the external sectors of the economy, at the expense of other objectives, amounts to mixing up the ends and the means of economic policy. Furthermore, there is nothing more conducive to trade and DFI than strong economic growth itself. Foreign investors care little about Botswana's huge public sector, and neither are they much deterred by Chinese-style socialism. Policies that are successful in igniting growth are also likely to pay off in terms of "international competitiveness."

As I have argued above, external constraints can sometimes be useful in fostering economic development if policymakers use these constraints wisely and creatively. For a government that would otherwise make a mess of its tariff code, the ability to bind tariffs in the World Trade Organization represents a useful opportunity. In an economy with a tendency toward large fiscal deficits, the discipline imposed by international financial markets can enhance the prospects for macroeconomic stability. The harmonization of regulatory standards with those in the advanced industrial countries can impart the rule of law and increase transparency in developing countries.

Yet such externally induced disciplines can also backfire if they are inappropriate to the economy in question or are viewed as serving the needs of particular social groups at the expense of others. Two conditions must be met to ensure that this does not happen:

1   The decision to submit to external discipline – by signing on to international agreements, opening up markets to international competition, or accepting World Bank/IMF conditionality – must be the product of a democratic decision-making process, with broad participation from major social groups.
2   There must be solid evidence that the discipline in question will improve economic performance in the country submitting to it.

International policy regimes that significantly constrain the ability of national policymakers to choose their own paths are likely to prove counter-productive in the absence of these preconditions.

Many international agreements fail one or both of these tests. Some of the agreements negotiated during the Uruguay Round can be cited in this connection. Consider, for example, the international agreement on trade-related aspects of intellectual property rights (TRIPs), which sets minimum standards of protection in patents, copyrights, and trademarks, and the agreement on trade-related investment measures (TRIMs), which requires the phasing out of performance requirements such as local-content and export-import linkage requirements. These represent cases of "forced" harmonization despite the absence of convincing evidence of benefits to developing nations. TRIPs is a particularly egregious instance, in that what the governments of the developed countries really obtained was the transfer of billions of dollars' worth of monopoly profits from poor countries to rich countries under the guise of protecting the property rights of inventors.[3] The draft Multilateral Agreement on Investment, which was under negotiation until recently at the OECD, contains many other doubtful restrictions on policy actions.

Some of the proposals to link the strengthening of labor standards in developing countries to trade privileges are problematic from the same perspective. In principle, there is nothing wrong with the international community requiring developing-country governments to protect basic worker rights. At times, this simply amounts to requiring that governments live up to commitments they have already made in the relevant International Labour Organisation (ILO) conventions they have ratified, such as those on the freedom of association and the minimum working age. The freedoms to associate and to organize are basic civil rights, and there is some evidence, as I have shown in previous chapters, that such freedoms are associated with superior economic performance. But often the demands from labor advocates in the developed countries go beyond basic civil rights and political liberties, and prescribe outcomes that may lead to inferior economic performance. The requirement that workers in developing countries be paid a "living wage" or the implementation of specific prohibitions on child labor may well end up doing more harm than good. The argument for international discipline is considerably weaker in such instances.[4]

The proposal to enshrine capital-account convertibility in the IMF's Articles of Agreement is another idea that lacks empirical justification. If recent evidence teaches us anything, it is that there is a compelling case for maintaining controls on short-term borrowing. The three countries hardest hit by the Asian financial crisis – Indonesia, Thailand, and South Korea – were the three in the region with the largest short-term obligations (in relation to reserves or exports). It is not that capital controls are necessarily the remedy for boom-and-bust cycles in international financial markets; they are not. But capital-account liberalization fills the bill even less. We can imagine cases in which the judicious application of capital controls could have prevented a crisis or greatly reduced its magnitude. Thailand and Indonesia would have been far better off restricting borrowing from abroad than encouraging it. South Korea just might have avoided a run on its reserves if controls on short-term borrowing had kept its short-term exposure to foreign banks, say, at 30 percent of its liabilities, rather than 70 percent.

Admittedly, we know too little about what kinds of controls work best in these circumstances. The evidence on the effectiveness of controls on short-term borrowing is patchy. But incomplete knowledge of this sort is an argument for allowing countries to follow their own preferred paths, selecting their own trade-offs between risk and reward.

A common argument in favor of capital market integration is that this serves to discipline governments, forcing them to follow sound fiscal and monetary policies. For governments with a penchant for populist macroeconomic policies, such market discipline can serve a useful role, much the same way that tariff bindings under the WTO help prevent excessive responsiveness to lobbying by industry groups at home. But this argument can be taken too far. In most democratic societies, the discipline needed by governments is provided by electoral accountability and by a constitutional system of checks and balances. Governments that mess up the economy are punished at the polls. It is not at all clear that international markets systematically improve the incentives faced by democratic governments. Certainly, the availability of financial resources on easy terms during periods of market euphoria can encourage fiscal profligacy – rather than penalize it – and result in quite the opposite effect. Moreover, market discipline empowers financial markets – domestic and foreign – over other constituencies in society, creating serious problems for democratic governance. Hence, in practice, the potential value of market discipline has to be traded off against the downside risks.

In sum, policymaking at the international level has to create space for national development efforts that are divergent in their philosophy and content. Forcing all countries into a single, neoliberal developmental model would be unwise – in light of the potential political backlash from national groups – even if there were serious grounds to believe that the model is economically advantageous. It is absurd when the evidence on the model's economic superiority is itself in doubt.

The lesson of history is that ultimately all successful countries develop their own brand of national capitalism. As Alexander Gerschenkron (1965) demonstrated, the patterns of development during the nineteenth century were quite diverse, and more recent economic history provides little evidence of convergence. The United States, Sweden, Germany, and Japan, to name just a few instances, are alike in that they are market-based economies that uphold private property and monetary stability. But the economic systems in these countries also differ on many important dimensions, including the organization of the labor market, the style of corporate governance, the extent of social insurance and safety nets, the intrusiveness of the government, and the regulatory framework in product and labor markets. Developing countries can choose among these and, no doubt, many other paths; they should be left free to do so.

A Question of Accountability

The internationalization of production and investment raises a fundamental question of accountability: to whom will national economic policymakers be accountable? The implicit answer provided by the globalization model is that they will be accountable to foreign investors, country-fund managers in London and New York, and a relatively small group of domestic exporters. In the globalized economy, these are the groups that determine whether an economy is judged a success or not, and whether it will prosper.

This would not necessarily be a bad thing if the invisible hand of global markets could always be relied upon to produce desirable outcomes. The reality is considerably more murky. It takes too much blind faith in markets to believe that the global allocation of resources is enhanced by the twenty-something-year-olds in London who move hundreds of millions of dollars around the globe in a matter of an instant, or by the executives of multinational enterprises who make plant location decisions on the basis of the concessions they can extract from governments. . . .

What is wrong, therefore, with the first chapter's parable of the fictional finance minister is that the minister is spending the vast majority of his time worrying about how the rest of the world evaluates his management of the economy. Traditional developmental concerns have been all but squeezed out. For this minister, it is global markets that dictate policy, not domestic priorities.

The fundamental dilemma of accountability in today's world economy is that it is domestic voters who choose national governments – and appropriately so – and not global markets. International markets, particularly financial ones, do not always get things right with respect to economic efficiency. They are even less likely to get things right with regard to societal outcomes suitable to each nation's aspirations. The structure of social institutions in a country, the extent of inequality that is tolerated, the types of public goods to be provided by governments – these are issues that are, and should be, resolved at the national level. Choices about social arrangements will vary across nations because of differences in norms, historical traditions, and levels of development. It is national governments that are held responsible for producing outcomes that are consonant with national aspirations. If governments can no longer be responsive to these aspirations, they can no longer be accountable to their electorates.

It may be true, as the conventional wisdom has it, that the information revolution and the globalization of production necessitate novel forms of governance. We need to figure out what these forms of governance are and how we can institute them. But national governments are all we have at present. It would be unwise to give them up without knowing what will replace them. A suitable international economic system is one that allows different styles of national capitalism to coexist with each other – not one that imposes a uniform model of economic governance.

NOTES

1 The Martian is smart enough to realize that richer countries – regardless of growth rate – have fewer restrictions on trade in goods and capital, and she controls for that.

2 It bears repeating the reasons why this finding departs from the conventional wisdom, especially given that conventional wisdom appears to be grounded in a large number of empirical studies. One reason is that many of the leading studies confound the trade regime with an economy's macroeconomic stability by using measures that are based on black-market premiums or exchange rates. When more appropriate indicators, that is, tariff and nontariff barriers to trade, are substituted for these hybrid measures, the strong results typically vanish. A second reason is that some studies use measures of openness that are based on actual volumes of trade or foreign investment. The results from these studies are uninformative on the role of openness because countries that grow fast also tend to experience rapid growth in trade and are more attractive to foreign investors.

3 The most direct consequence of the TRIPs agreement is an increase in prices of items such as pharmaceuticals for which patent treatment in the developing nations has been traditionally weak. The magnitude of the price increase one can expect is indicated by an exercise carried out by Subramanian (1994), who compares the prices for patented drugs in Malaysia (where patent protection for pharmaceuticals is reasonably tight) with those in India (where it is not). He finds that Malaysian prices are significantly higher than Indian ones, with the premium ranging from 17 percent (for Pentoxyphyllin 400 mg tablets) to 767 percent (for Atenolol 50 mg tablets). Insofar as the owners of patents in such drugs are foreign-owned firms (as is the case almost always), developing countries are faced not only with monopoly distortions in the home market, but, more important, with a potentially huge transfer of rents abroad.

4 Indeed, the United States has ratified very few of the ILO's conventions, citing the US federal structure (and the role of the states in regulatory policy) and other special circumstances.

Has Globalization Gone too Far?

Labor strikes in France at the end of 1995, which were aimed at reversing the French government's efforts to bring its budget in line with the Maastricht criteria, threw the country into its worst crisis since 1968. Around the same time in the United States, a prominent Republican was running a vigorous campaign for the presidency on a plank of economic nationalism, promising to erect trade barriers and tougher restrictions on immigration. In the countries of Eastern Europe and in Russia, former communists have won most of the parliamentary elections held since the fall of the Berlin Wall, and communist candidate Gennady Zyuganov garnered 40 percent of the vote in the second round of the Russian presidential election held in July 1996.

These apparently disparate developments have one common element: the international integration of markets for goods, services, and capital is pressuring societies to alter their traditional practices, and in return broad segments of these societies are putting up a fight. The pressures for change are tangible and affect all societies: In Japan, large corporations have started to dismantle the postwar practice of lifetime employment, one of Japan's most distinctive social institutions. In Germany, the federal government has been fighting union opposition to cuts on pension benefits aimed at improving competitiveness and balancing the budget. In South Korea, trade unions have gone on nation-wide strikes to protest new legislation making it easier for firms to lay off workers. Developing countries in Latin America have been competing with each other in opening up to trade, deregulating their economies, and privatizing public enterprises. Ask business executives or government officials why these changes are necessary, and you will hear the same mantra repeatedly: "We need to remain (or become) competitive in a global economy."

The opposition to these changes is no less tangible and sometimes makes for strange bedfellows. Labor unions decrying unfair competition from underage workers overseas and environmentalists are joined by billionaire businessmen Ross Perot and Sir James Goldsmith in railing against the North American Free Trade Agreement (NAFTA) and the World Trade Organization (WTO). In the United States, perhaps the most free-market-oriented of advanced industrial societies, the philosophical foundations of the classical liberal state have come under attack not only from traditional protectionists but also from the new communitarian movement, which emphasizes moral and civic virtue and is inherently suspicious of the expansion of markets.

The process that has come to be called "globalization" is *exposing a deep fault line between groups who have the skills and mobility to flourish in global markets and those who either don't have these advantages or perceive the expansion of unregulated markets as inimical to social stability and deeply held norms.* The result is severe tension between the market and social groups such as workers, pensioners, and environmentalists, with governments stuck in the middle.

This book argues that the most serious challenge for the world economy in the years ahead lies in making globalization compatible with domestic social and political stability – or to put it even more directly, in ensuring that international economic integration does not contribute to domestic social *dis*integration.

Attuned to the anxieties of their voters, politicians in the advanced industrial countries are well aware that all is not well with globalization. The Lyon summit of the Group of seven, held in June 1996, gave the issue central billing: its communiqué was titled "Making a Success of Globalization for the Benefit of All." The communiqué opened with a discussion of globalization – its challenges as well as its benefits. The leaders recognized that globalization raises difficulties for certain groups, and they wrote:

> In an increasingly interdependent world we must all recognize that we have an interest in spreading the benefits of economic growth as widely as possible and in diminishing the risk either of excluding individuals or groups in our own economies or of excluding certain countries or regions from the benefits of globalization.

But how are these objectives to be met?

An adequate policy response requires an understanding of the sources of the tensions generated by globalization. Without such an understanding, the reactions are likely to be of two kinds. One is of the knee-jerk type, with proposed cures worse than the disease. Such certainly is the case with blanket protectionism à la Patrick Buchanan or the abolition of the WTO à la Sir James Goldsmith. Indeed, much of what passes as analysis (followed by condemnation) of international trade is based on faulty logic and misleading empirics. To paraphrase Paul Samuelson, there is no better proof that the principle of comparative advantage is the only proposition in economics that is at once true *and* nontrivial than the long history of misunderstanding that has attached to the consequences of trade. The problems, while real, are more subtle than the terminology that has come to dominate the debate, such as "low-wage competition," or "leveling the playing field," or "race to the bottom." Consequently, they require nuanced and imaginative solutions.

The other possible response, and the one that perhaps best characterizes the attitude of much of the economics and policy community, is to downplay the problem. Economists' standard approach to globalization is to emphasize the benefits of the free flow of goods, capital, and ideas and to overlook the social tensions that may result. A common view is that the complaints of nongovernmental organizations or labor advocates represent nothing but old protectionist wine in new bottles. Recent research on trade and wages gives strength to this view: the available empirical evidence suggests that trade has played a somewhat minor role in generating the labor-market ills of the advanced industrial countries – that is, in increasing income inequality in the United States and unemployment in Europe.

While I share the idea that much of the opposition to trade is based on faulty premises, I also believe that economists have tended to take an excessively narrow view of the issues. To understand the impact of globalization on domestic social arrangements, we have to go beyond the question of what trade does to the skill premium. And even if we focus more narrowly on labor-market outcomes, there are additional channels, which have not yet come under close empirical scrutiny, through which increased economic integration works to the disadvantage of labor, and particularly of unskilled labor. This book attempts to offer such a broadened perspective. As we shall see, this perspective leads to a less benign outlook than the one economists commonly adopt. One side benefit, therefore, is that it serves to reduce the yawning gap that separates the views of most economists from the gut instincts of many laypeople.

Sources of Tension

I focus on three sources of tension between the global market and social stability and offer a brief overview of them here.

First, reduced barriers to trade and investment accentuate the asymmetry between groups that can cross international borders (either directly or indirectly, say through outsourcing) and those that cannot. In the first category are owners of capital, highly skilled workers, and many professionals, who are free to take their resources where they are most in demand. Unskilled and semiskilled workers and most middle managers belong in the second category. Putting the same point in more technical terms, globalization makes the demand for the services of individuals in the second category *more elastic* – that is, the services of large segments of the working population can be more easily substituted by the services of other people across national boundaries. Globalization therefore fundamentally transforms the employment relationship.

The fact that "workers" can be more easily substituted for each other across national boundaries undermines what many conceive to be a postwar social bargain between workers and employers, under which the former would receive a steady increase in wages and benefits in return for labor peace. This is because increased substitutability results in the following concrete consequences:

- Workers now have to pay a larger share of the cost of improvements in work conditions and benefits (that is, they bear a greater incidence of nonwage costs).
- They have to incur greater instability in earnings and hours worked in response to shocks to labor demand or labor productivity (that is, volatility and insecurity increase).
- Their bargaining power erodes, so they receive lower wages and benefits whenever bargaining is an element in setting the terms of employment.

These considerations have received insufficient attention in the recent academic literature on trade and wages, which has focused on the downward shift in demand for unskilled workers rather than the increase in the elasticity of that demand.

Second, globalization engenders conflicts within and between nations over domestic norms and the social institutions that embody them. As the technology for manufactured goods becomes standardized and diffused internationally, nations with very different sets of values, norms, institutions, and collective preferences begin to compete head on in markets for similar goods. And the spread of globalization creates opportunities for trade between countries at very different levels of development.

This is of no consequence under traditional multilateral trade policy of the WTO and the General Agreement on Tariffs and Trade (GATT): the "process" or "technology" through which goods are produced is immaterial, and so are the social institutions of the trading partners. Differences in national practices are treated just like differences in factor endowments or any other determinant of comparative advantage. However, introspection and empirical evidence both reveal that most people attach values to processes as well as outcomes. This is reflected in norms that shape and constrain the domestic environment in which goods and services are produced – for example, workplace practices, legal rules, and social safety nets.

Trade becomes contentious when it unleashes forces that undermine the norms implicit in domestic practices. Many residents of advanced industrial countries are uncomfortable with the weakening of domestic institutions through the forces of trade, as when, for example, child labor in Honduras displaces workers in South Carolina or when pension benefits are cut in Europe in response to the requirements of the Maastricht treaty. This sense of unease is one way of interpreting the demands for "fair trade." Much of the discussion surrounding the "new" issues in trade policy – that is, labor standards, environment, competition policy, corruption – can be cast in this light of procedural fairness.

We cannot understand what is happening in these new areas until we take individual preferences for processes and the social arrangements that embody them seriously. In particular, by doing so we can start to make sense of people's uneasiness about the consequences of international economic integration and avoid the trap of automatically branding all concerned groups as self-interested protectionists. Indeed, since trade policy almost always has redistributive consequences (among sectors, income groups, and individuals), one cannot produce a principled defense of free trade without confronting the question of the fairness and legitimacy of the practices that generate these consequences. By the same token, one should not expect broad popular support for trade when trade involves exchanges that clash with (and erode) prevailing domestic social arrangements.

Third, globalization has made it exceedingly difficult for governments to provide social insurance – one of their central functions and one that has helped maintain social cohesion and domestic political support for ongoing liberalization throughout the postwar period. In essence, governments have used their fiscal powers to insulate domestic groups from excessive market risks, particularly those having an external origin. In fact, there is a striking correlation between an economy's exposure to foreign trade and the size of its welfare state. It is in the most open countries, such as Sweden, Denmark, and the Netherlands, that spending on income transfers has expanded the most. This is not to say that the government is the sole, or the best, provider of social insurance. The extended family, religious groups, and local communities often play similar roles. My point is that it is a hallmark of the postwar period that governments in the advanced countries have been expected to provide such insurance.

At the present, however, international economic integration is taking place against the background of receding governments and diminished social obligations. The welfare state has been under attack for two decades. Moreover, the increasing mobility of capital has rendered an important segment of the tax base footloose, leaving governments with the unappetizing option of increasing tax rates disproportionately on labor income. Yet the need for social insurance for the vast majority of the population that remains internationally immobile has not diminished. If anything, this need has become greater as a consequence of increased integration. The question therefore is how the tension between globalization and the pressures for socialization of risk can be eased. If the tension is not managed intelligently and creatively, the danger is that the domestic consensus in favor of open markets will ultimately erode to the point where a generalized resurgence of protectionism becomes a serious possibility.

Each of these arguments points to an important weakness in the manner in which advanced societies are handling – or are equipped to handle – the consequences of globalization. Collectively, they point to what is perhaps the greatest risk of all, namely that the cumulative consequence of the tensions mentioned above will be the solidifying of a new set of class divisions – between those who prosper in the globalized economy and those who do not, between those who share its values and those who would rather not, and between those who can diversify away its risks and those who cannot. This is not a pleasing prospect, even for individuals on the winning side of the divide who have little empathy for the other side. Social disintegration is not a spectator sport – those on the sidelines also get splashed with mud from the field. Ultimately, the deepening of social fissures can harm all.

Globalization: Now and Then

This is not the first time we have experienced a truly global market. By many measures, the world economy was possibly even more integrated at the height of the gold standard in the late 19th century than it is now. . . . In the United States and Europe, trade volumes peaked before World War I and then collapsed during the interwar years. Trade surged again after 1950, but none of the . . . regions is significantly more open by this measure now than it was under the late gold standard. Japan, in fact, has a lower share of exports in GDP now than it did during the interwar period.

Other measures of global economic integration tell a similar story. As railways and steamships lowered transport costs and Europe moved toward free trade during the late 19th century, a dramatic convergence in commodity prices took place (Williamson 1996). Labor flows were considerably higher then as well, as millions of immigrants made their way from the old world to the new. In the United States, immigration was responsible for 24 percent of the expansion of the labor force during the 40 years before World War I (Williamson 1996, appendix table 1). As for capital mobility, the share of net capital outflows in GNP was much higher in the United Kingdom during the classical gold standard than it has been since.

Does this earlier period of globalization hold any lessons for our current situation? It well might. There is some evidence, for example, that trade and migration had significant consequences for income distribution. According to Jeffrey Williamson, "[G]lobalization . . . accounted for more than half of the rising inequality in rich, labor-scarce countries [e.g., the United States, Argentina, and Australia] and for a little more than a quarter of the falling inequality in poor, labor-abundant countries [e.g., Sweden, Denmark, and Ireland]" in the period before World War I (1996, 19). Equally to the point are the political consequences of these changes:

> There is a literature almost a century old that argues that immigration hurt American labor and accounted for much of the rise in inequality from the 1890s to World War I, so much so that a labor-sympathetic Congress passed immigration quotas. There is a literature even older that argues that a New World grain invasion eroded land rents in Europe, so much so that landowner-dominated Continental Parliaments raised tariffs to help protect them from the impact of globalization. (Williamson 1996, 1)

Williamson (1996, 20) concludes that "the inequality trends which globalization produced are at least partly responsible for the interwar retreat from globalization [which appeared] first in the rich industrial trading partners."

Moreover, there are some key differences that make today's global economy more contentious. First, restrictions on immigration were not as common during the 19th century, and consequently labor's international mobility was more comparable to that of capital. Consequently, the asymmetry between mobile capital (physical and human) and immobile "natural" labor, which characterizes the present situation, is a relatively recent phenomenon. Second, there was little head-on international competition in identical or similar products during the previous century, and most trade consisted of the exchange of non-competing products, such as primary products for manufactured goods. The aggregate trade ratios do not reflect the "vast increase in the exposure of tradable goods industries to international competition" that is now taking place compared with the situation in the 1890s (Irwin 1996, 42). Third, and perhaps most important, governments had not yet been called on to perform social-welfare functions on a large scale, such as ensuring adequate levels of employment, establishing social safety nets, providing medical and social insurance, and caring for the poor. This shift in the perceived role of government is also a relatively recent transformation, one that makes life in an interdependent economy considerably more difficult for today's policymakers.

At any rate, the lesson from history seems to be that continued globalization cannot be taken for granted. If its consequences are not managed wisely and creatively, a retreat from openness becomes a distinct possibility.

Implications

So has international economic integration gone too far? Not if policymakers act wisely and imaginatively.

We need to be upfront about the irreversibility of the many changes that have occurred in the global economy. Advances in communications and transportation mean that large segments of national economies are much more exposed to international trade and capital flows than they have ever been, regardless of what policymakers choose to do. There is only limited scope for government policy to make a difference. In addition, a serious retreat into protectionism would hurt the many groups that benefit from trade and would result in the same kind of social conflicts that globalization itself generates. We have to recognize that erecting trade barriers will help in only a limited set of circumstances and that trade policies will rarely be the best response to the problems that will be discussed here. Transfer and social insurance programs will generally dominate. In short, the genie cannot be stuffed back into the bottle, even if it were desirable to do so. We will need more imaginative and more subtle responses. I will suggest some guidelines in the concluding chapter.

Even so, my primary purpose in this book is not prescriptive; it is to broaden the debate on the consequences of globalization by probing deeper into some of the dimensions that have received insufficient attention and ultimately recasting the debate so as to facilitate a more productive dialogue between opposing groups and interests. It is only through greater understanding of what is at stake that we can hope to develop appropriate public policies.

One final introductory note. I hope the reader will soon realize that this book is not a one-sided brief *against* globalization. Indeed, the major benefit of clarifying and adding rigor to some of the arguments against trade is that it helps us draw a distinction between objections that are valid (or at least logically coherent) and objections that aren't. From this perspective, what I end up doing, at least on occasion, is strengthening the arsenal of arguments in favor of free trade. If this book is viewed as controversial, it will have done its job; I have failed if it is perceived as polemical.

The chapters that follow will elaborate on the three sources of tension between globalization and society identified above and will review the relevant empirical evidence. The objectives will be to cast the debate in terms that both sides – economists and populists alike – can join, marshal evidence on the likely significance of the tension in question, and where there is evidence for serious concern, open the debate on possible remedies.

REFERENCES

Irwin, Douglas A., "The United States in a New Global Economy? A Century's Perspective," *American Economic Review*, V: 86 (1996), 41–6.

Williamson, Jeffrey G., "Globalization, Convergence, and History," *Journal of Economic History*, V: 56 (1996), 277–306.

20 Industrial Convergence, Globalization, and the Persistence of the North–South Divide (1999)

Giovanni Arrighi, Beverly J. Silver, and Benjamin D. Brewer

It is now more than fifteen years since Nigel Harris announced the disappearance of the Third World as economic reality and ideological representation. In a 1986 book entitled *The End of the Third World: Newly Industrializing Countries and the Decline of an Ideology*, Harris argued that the emergence of "a global manufacturing system" was making the very notion of a Third World hopelessly obsolete.

> The conception of an interdependent, interacting, global manufacturing system cuts across the old view of a world consisting of nation-states as well as one of groups of countries, more or less developed and centrally planned – the First, the Third and the Second Worlds. Those notions bore some relationship to an older economy, one marked by the exchange of raw materials for manufacturing goods. But the new world that has superseded it is far more complex and does not lend itself to the simple identification of First and Third, haves and have-nots, rich and poor, industrialized and non-industrialized. . . . The process of dispersal of manufacturing capacity brings enormous hope to areas where poverty has hitherto appeared immovable. . . . [T]he realization of one world offers the promise of a rationally ordered system, determined by its inhabitants in the interests of need, not profit or war. (Harris 1986: 200–2)

Harris's contention that the North–South divide is becoming obsolete (although not necessarily his prediction of a "rationally ordered system") has gained credence among some of the best-informed observers of globalization. (See, for example, Hoogvelt 1997: xii, 145; Held et al. 1999: 8, 177, 186–7; Robinson and Harris 2000; Burbach and Robinson 1999; Hardt and Negri 2000.) According to this view, the spatial restructuring of the last twenty to thirty years has eliminated the structural divide between First and Third Worlds. "Worldwide convergence, through the global restructuring of capitalism, means that the geographic breakdown of the world into north-south, core-periphery or First and Third worlds, while still significant, is diminishing in importance" (Burbach and Robinson 1999: 27–8). Polarizing tendencies are still at work but *within* rather than *between* countries. "Core-periphery" – in Ankie Hoogvelt's words – "is becoming a social relationship, and no longer a geographical one" (1997: 145).

[. . .]

World Income Inequality, Development, and "Globalization"

[. . .]

As previously mentioned, there is a general consensus in the relevant literatures that this global hierarchy of wealth is largely a legacy of the industrial and territorial expansion of Western nations in the nineteenth and early twentieth centuries. This consensus is consistent with the earlier expectation that decolonization and Third World industrialization would substantially reduce the North–South income divide. Once decolonization had occurred, theories of national development were nearly unanimous across the ideological spectrum in maintaining that industrialization of one kind or another was essential if Third World countries were to attain the standards of wealth enjoyed by First World countries. Catching up with the standards of wealth of First World countries was the generally accepted *objective* of Third World developmental efforts. But the narrowing of the industrialization gap between Third and First World countries was just as generally considered to be the most essential and effective *means* in the pursuit of that objective.

This expectation that industrialization and income convergence would go hand-in-hand was reinforced by the expectation that in the course of their own development the wealthy countries of the First World would experience a gradual de-industrialization – what Daniel Bell (1973) called the "coming of post-industrial society." Since the productivity of service activities was generally believed to be lower than manufacturing activities (see especially Clark 1957 and Baumol 1967), the rate of growth of per capita income was expected to decrease in rich, de-industrializing countries and to increase in poor, industrializing countries. Eventually, all societies would become post-industrial, but in the meantime industrialization was generally thought to be the surest way for Third World countries to catch up with First World standards of wealth.

Indeed, such has been the power of this consensus that academic no less than popular discourse has come to treat "industrialization" and "development" as synonymous. This semantic conflation of the ends of development (catching up with First World standards of wealth) with its allegedly most effective means (industrialization) underlies Harris's claim that the geographical dispersal of manufacturing capacity means that we can no longer identify zones of more or less permanent prosperity (the North or former First World) and zones of more or less permanent poverty (the South or former Third World). But in conflating *industrial* with *wealthy*, *non-industrial* with *poor*, and *industrialization* with *development*, Harris is far from alone. A similar conflation underlies Alice Amsden's claim that "The Rest" – a group of countries outside the North Atlantic accounting for over half of world population – has "risen." At the basis of the claim lies the identification of development with "attracting capital, human and physical, out of rent seeking, commerce, and 'agriculture' (broadly defined), and into manufacturing, the heart of modern economic growth" (2001: 1–2). In spite of accumulating evidence to the contrary, industrialization and development thus continue to be used as synonyms as if industrialization were an end in itself, rather than a means – and as it turns out, an increasingly ineffectual means – in the pursuit of national wealth.[1]

A first reason for focusing on industrialization is thus to verify empirically the validity of the widely held hypothesis (turned into assumption) that industrialization is the most effective means of catching up with Northern standards of wealth. A second reason is that industrialization has costs as well as benefits. Some of these costs – such as the pollution of air and water, the erosion of the countryside, and the destruction of natural beauty – though hard to quantify by means of synthetic indicators, are at least visible. Other costs – such as those captured by Marx's concept of "alienation," Weber's "iron cage," and Durkheim's *"anomie"* – are not just hard to quantify; they are also largely invisible. As Dean Tipps (1973: 208) has noted, the ambivalence towards modern industrial society that characterized the writings of Marx, Weber, and Durkheim is conspicuous *by its absence* in early modernization and development thinking. Although ecological and environmental concerns have of late become quite prominent in development discourse, the costs of industrialization continue to be underrated in comparison with its real or imagined benefits.

Recent research on between-country income inequality abstracts completely from the costs and intensity of the developmental efforts undertaken by Third World countries in their attempts to catch up with First World standards of wealth and welfare. In reality, a constant income gap has an altogether different meaning, depending on whether it is associated with a rising or a declining industrialization gap. Our focus on the relationship between the North–South income and industrialization divides is thus aimed also at assessing the success or failure of Third World developmental efforts, not in isolation from, but in relation to the intensity and cost of those efforts.

Finally, we shall pay particular attention to the major change that occurred around 1980 in the world context in which Third World development efforts unfolded. Phillip McMichael (2000) has described the change as a switch of the policy of the hegemonic power from promotion of the "development project" launched in the late 1940s and early 1950s to promotion of the "globalization project" under the neoliberal Washington Consensus of the 1980s and 1990s. As a result of the switch, the US government – directly or through the Bretton Woods institutions – withdrew support from the "statist" and "inward-looking" strategies that most theories of national development had advocated in the 1950s and 1960s and began instead to promote capital-friendly and outward-looking strategies. This change in the policies and ideologies of national development promoted by the hegemonic power corresponds to what Christopher Chase-Dunn (1999) has labeled "ideological globalization." An equally important aspect of the transformation in the global political economy that occurred around 1980 was the intensification of competitive pressures on Third (and Second) World countries that accompanied but was only in part due to the emergence of the globalization project as ideology and policy. This intensification in competitive pressures is an important aspect of what Chase-Dunn (1999) has labeled "structural globalization."[2]

Global Capitalism and the Reproduction of the North–South Divide

The persistent failure of the generally prescribed means of national development (industrialization) to accomplish its putative objective (catching up with First World standards of wealth) is a puzzle that needs to be explained – especially since this failure recurred in two periods characterized by radically different world contexts for development. In seeking such an explanation, we shall take Joseph Schumpeter's theory of "creative destruction" as our starting point. According to this theory, major profit-oriented innovations are the fundamental impulse that generates and sustains competitive pressures in a capitalist economy. These innovations are defined broadly to include the introduction of new methods of production, new commodities, new sources of supply, new trade routes and markets, and new forms of organization. While innovations of this kind occurred also in non-capitalist social systems, under capitalism their occurrence "incessantly revolutionizes the economic structure *from within*, incessantly destroying the old one, incessantly creating a new one" (Schumpeter 1954: 83).

This process of creative destruction has two main effects. On the one hand, Schumpeter argued that it is "not only the most important immediate source of gain, but also indirectly produces, through the process it sets going, most of those situations from which windfall gains and losses arise and in which speculative operations acquire significant scope" (Schumpeter 1964: 80). On the other hand, it transforms competition into a cutthroat competition that inflicts widespread losses by making preexisting productive combinations obsolete. As a consequence,

> [spectacular] prizes much greater than would have been necessary to call forth the particular effort are thrown to a small minority of winners, thus propelling much more efficaciously than a more equal and more "just" distribution would, the activity of that large majority of businessmen who receive in return very modest compensation or nothing or less than nothing, and yet do their utmost because they have the big prizes before their eyes and overrate their chances of doing equally well. (Schumpeter 1954: 73–4)

Schumpeter observed that revolutions in the economic structure occur in discrete rushes separated from each other by spans of comparative quiet. He accordingly divided the incessant working of the process of creative destruction into two phases: the phase of revolution proper and the phase of absorption of the results of the revolution.

> While these things are being initiated we have brisk expenditure and predominating "prosperity" . . . and while [they] are being completed and their results pour forth we have the elimination of antiquated elements of the industrial structure and predominating "depression." (1954: 68)

In this representation, profit-oriented innovations (and their impact on competitive pressures) cluster *in time*, generating swings in the economy as a whole from long phases of predominating "prosperity" to long phases of predominating "depression." Yet it is plausible to hypothesize that they also cluster *in space*. That is to say, we can substitute "where" for "while" in the above quotation and read it as a description of a spatial polarization of zones of predominating "prosperity" and zones of predominating "depression" (Arrighi and Drangel 1986: 20).

To some extent a substitution of this kind was already implicit in two highly influential models of economic development inspired by Schumpeter's theory of innovations: Akamatsu's "flying geese" model (1961), and Raymond Vernon's "product-cycle" model

(1966, 1971: chapter 3). Both models portray the diffusion of industrial innovations as a spatially structured process originating in the more "developed" (that is, wealthier) countries and gradually involving poorer, less "developed" countries. And both models – more so Akamatsu's than Vernon's – emphasize the increasing homogenization of the countries involved as they all become "industrialized." Nevertheless, the two models themselves provide good reasons for supposing that the spatial structuring of innovations they describe will tend to reproduce the income differential that separates the "geese" that lead the process from those that follow, even if the latter industrialize.

For one thing, as both authors emphasize, the innovation process tends to begin in the wealthier countries. But neither Akamatsu nor Vernon seem to realize the implications of this tendency. For it is the residents of the countries where the innovation process starts who have the best chances to win (Schumpeter's) "spectacular prizes," that is, profits that are "much greater than would have been necessary to call forth the particular effort." The process tends to begin in the wealthier countries because high incomes create a favorable environment for product innovations; high costs create a favorable environment for innovations in techniques; and cheap and abundant credit creates a favorable environment for financing these and all other kinds of innovations. Moreover, as innovators in wealthy countries reap abnormally high rewards relative to effort, over time the environment for innovations in these countries improves further, thereby generating a self-reinforcing "virtuous circle" of high incomes and innovations.

The obverse side of this virtuous circle is a second tendency – the tendency, that is, for the poorer countries at the receiving end of the process to reap few, if any, of the benefits of the innovations. As emphasized especially in Vernon's "product cycle" model, the spatial diffusion of innovations goes hand in hand with their routinization – that is, with their ceasing to be innovations in the wider global context. As a result, by the time the "new" products and techniques are adopted by the poorer countries they tend to be subject to intense competition and no longer bring the high returns they did in the wealthier countries. In this respect, the poorer countries resemble Schumpeter's "large majority of businessmen," whose efforts are propelled by the "spectacular prizes" won by the "small minority of winners," but who end up with "very modest compensation or nothing or less than nothing" (Schumpeter 1954: 73–4).

Equally if not more important is a third tendency that Akamatsu and Vernon disregard. It concerns the destructive aspects of innovations – what Schumpeter refers to as "the elimination of antiquated elements of the industrial structure" (1954: 68), but more generally includes all the economic and social dislocations that directly or indirectly ensue from major innovations. Poor countries are not necessarily more exposed than wealthy countries to the destructiveness of major innovations. Nevertheless, the greater mass and variety of resources that wealthy countries command nationally and globally endow their residents with a far greater capacity to adjust socially and economically to the disruptive strains and to move promptly from the activities that innovations make less rewarding to those they make more rewarding. As a result, even when they do not initiate the innovations, wealthy countries tend to be in an incomparably better position than poor and middle-income countries to reap their benefits and shift their costs and disruptions onto others.[3]

In short, opportunities for economic advance, as they present themselves successively to one country after another, do not constitute equivalent opportunities for all countries.

As countries accounting for a growing proportion of world population attempt to catch up with First World standards of wealth *through industrialization,* competitive pressures in the procurement of industrial inputs and disposal of industrial outputs in world markets intensify. In the process, Third World countries, like Schumpeter's "majority of businessmen," tended to overrate their chances of winning the "spectacular prizes" that industrialization had brought to First World countries, and correspondingly tended to underrate their chances of becoming the losers in *the intense competitive struggle engendered by their very success in industrializing.* To be sure, some Third World countries did succeed in climbing up the value-added hierarchy through industrialization – South Korea and Taiwan being the most conspicuous examples. Nevertheless, the virtual absence of any positive correlation between income and industrialization performance suggests that, for most countries, industrialization turned out to be an ineffectual means of economic advancement.

In light of these considerations, the kind of wealth that First World countries had attained through industrialization appears to have been an instance of what Roy Harrod (1958) called "oligarchic wealth" in contrast to "democratic wealth." Democratic wealth is the kind of command over resources that, in principle, all can attain in direct relation to the intensity and efficiency of their efforts. Oligarchic wealth, in contrast, bears no relation to the intensity and efficiency of its recipients' efforts, and is never available to all because generalized attempts to attain it raise costs and reduce benefits for all actors involved. As Fred Hirsch put it, there is "an 'adding up' problem. Opportunities for economic advance, as they present themselves serially to one [actor] after another, do not constitute equivalent opportunities for economic advance for all. What each . . . can achieve, all cannot" (1976: 4–5).

As we shall emphasize below, this "adding up" problem (or "fallacy of composition") affected not just those who struggled to attain oligarchic wealth (Third World countries) but also those who struggled to retain it (First World countries). Moreover, the adverse effects of the "adding up" problem on both First and Third World countries (and their responses to it) provoked a deep crisis in the 1970s, which in turn precipitated the major transformation in the world context for national development in the 1980s and 1990s.

Thus, the intense competition that ensued from generalized industrialization efforts did not just prevent Third World countries from attaining their objective; it also tended to undermine the industrial foundations of the oligarchic wealth of First World countries. This tendency was especially in evidence in the 1970s, when the worldwide intensification of competitive pressures on industrial producers appeared to be affecting First World countries more negatively than Third World countries. . . .

For Third World countries, the results of industrialization also fell far short of the expectations raised by the promises of the "development project." Third World disillusionment with the pace of change was especially sharp in the 1970s given that the world balance of political power was generally perceived as having shifted in their favor.[4] As a result, a small but growing number of Third World countries threatened to quit or actually quit playing the development game through one kind or another of radical "de-linking" and "deviant" behavior, while the vast majority joined forces in seeking a renegotiation of the rules of the game, demanding redistributive measures under a New International Economic Order (NIEO) (cf. Krasner 1985).

Initially, First World countries seemed to yield to Third World pressures (see especially Brandt Commission 1980), even pledging 1 percent of their GNP in aid to Third World countries. While these pledges were being made, however, a sudden turnaround occurred. Under US leadership, the ideas that had thus far guided the policies and actions of First World countries (Keynesianism, broadly understood) were abandoned in favor of previously discredited neo-utilitarian, state-minimalist doctrines. As we shall argue below, this sudden change in the "rules of the game" would play a key role in reconstituting the rattled foundations of the North–South wealth divide.

The sudden change was primarily a response to the broader crisis of US hegemony. For most of the 1970s the United States sought to recover competitiveness in industrial production through an expansionary monetary policy that depreciated the dollar and provided US banks and corporations with all the liquidity they needed to expand abroad through direct and other forms of foreign investment. Although initially this strategy seemed to pay off, by 1979 it became clear that the strategy had the unintended consequence of deepening the ongoing crisis of US hegemony. Inflationary pressures increased, both domestically and worldwide. Coming as it did in the wake of US withdrawal from Vietnam, the increase sent US financial and military power on a downward spiral that reached its nadir at the end of the 1970s with the Iranian Revolution, a new hike in oil prices, the Soviet invasion of Afghanistan, and a new serious crisis of confidence in the US dollar (Arrighi 1994: 308–323; cf. Parboni 1981: chapters 3–4; Brenner 2002).

It was in this context that in the closing year of the Carter Administration, and with greater determination under Reagan, there occurred a drastic change in US policies, including a severe contraction in money supply, higher interest rates, lower taxes for the wealthy, and virtually unrestricted freedom of action for capitalist enterprise. Through this battery of policies the US government started to compete aggressively for capital worldwide to finance a growing trade and current account deficit in the US balance of payments, thereby provoking a sharp increase in real interest rates worldwide and a major reversal in the direction of global capital flows. From being the main source of world liquidity and of foreign direct investment in the 1950s and 1960s, in the 1980s and 1990s the United States became the world's main debtor nation and by far the largest recipient of foreign capital.

[. . .]

This extraordinary reversal reflected the capacity of the United States to accumulate capital, not just by playing in conformity with the existing rules of the capitalist game, but by changing the rules themselves. As Pierre Bourdieu has argued with reference to the reproduction of distinct positions in national distributions of "cultural capital" (see, for example, Bourdieu 1984), when challenged by a race to the top by the occupants of lower positions, the groups that occupy a dominant position can step up their investments so as to reproduce the relative scarcities on which their dominant position is based. For example, when social groups that previously made little use of the school system enter the race for academic qualifications, the groups whose status was due to educational credentials "step up their investments so as to maintain the relative scarcity of their qualifications and, consequently, their position in the class structure" (Bourdieu and Passeron 1979: 77–8). This strategy, however, tends to generate an inflation of credentials that undermines the participants' belief in the game and in its stakes – what Bourdieu calls *illusio* (from *ludus*, the game) – thereby reducing the effectiveness of the game in reproducing distinct positions in the cultural field. The dominant groups must therefore also engage in symbolic struggles aimed at redefining the stakes and the rules of the game. They must, that is, play not just

> to increase their capital . . . in conformity with the tacit rules of the game and the prerequisites of the reproduction of the game and its stakes; but . . . also . . . to transform, partially or completely, the immanent rules of the game. They can, for instance, work to change . . . the exchange rate between various species of capital, through strategies aimed at discrediting the form of capital upon which the force of their opponents rests . . . and to valorize the species of capital they preferentially possess. (Bourdieu and Wacquant 1992: 98–9)

In terms of Bourdieu's categories, the initial US response to the intensification of competitive pressures in world markets and the concomitant crisis of US hegemony can be characterized as a stepping up of investments *within* the disintegrating Keynesian framework of state action and capital accumulation. As noted, however, this strategy had the unintended result of deepening further the crisis of US hegemony and of intensifying symbolic struggles between the First and Third World over the rules of the developmental game. The US response that materialized around 1980, in contrast, cut short these struggles by establishing a new development game that valorized the species of capital that First World countries in general, and the United States in particular, preferentially possessed.

This species of capital is finance capital. Already in the 1970s, US capital had begun to withdraw from the trade and production of commodities to engage in financial intermediation and speculation. But US specialization in global financial intermediation and speculation gained momentum only when the US government adopted fiscal and monetary policies that openly encouraged it. In a sense, specialization in high finance is nothing but the continuation of the logic of the product cycle by other means. The logic of the product cycle for the leading capitalist organizations of a given epoch is to ceaselessly shift resources through one kind or another of "innovation" from market niches that are becoming overcrowded (and therefore less profitable) to market niches that are less crowded (and therefore more profitable). When escalating competition reduces drastically the actual and potential availability of relatively empty and highly profitable niches in the commodity markets, the epoch's leading capitalist organizations have one last refuge where to retreat and from where to shift competitive pressures onto others. This last refuge is the world's money market – the market that, in Schumpeter's words, "is always, as it were, the headquarters of the capitalist system, from which orders go out to its individual divisions" (1961: 126).

Occupation of the headquarters of the capitalist system, however, regenerates the capacity to accumulate capital only to the extent that the system itself is restructured so as to feed the headquarters with an ever-expanding supply and demand for capital. The massive redirection of capital flows to the United States that resulted from the change in US policies of 1979–1982 was in itself a powerful stimulant of such a restructuring. By reflating effective demand in the United States and deflating it in the Third World, it created powerful incentives for capital to flow into the United States, and turned the "flood" of capital that Third World countries had experienced in the 1970s into the sudden "drought" of the 1980s. First signaled by the Mexican default of 1982, this drought was probably the single most important factor in the overall deterioration of the economic performance of the Third World in the 1980s.

At the same time, however, the redirection of capital flows enabled the United States to run large deficits in its balance of trade, thereby expanding the demand for imports of those goods that US businesses no longer found profitable to produce. Since competitive pressures had become particularly intense in manufacturing industries, these imported goods tended to be industrial rather than agricultural products. This tendency was the primary source of the bifurcation in the fortunes of Third World regions of the 1980s and 1990s. On the one hand, there were regions (most notably East Asia) that for historical reasons had a strong advantage in competing for a share of the expanding North American demand for cheap industrial products. These regions tended to benefit from the redirection of capital flows, because the improvement in their balance of payments lessened their need to compete with the United States in world financial markets. On the other hand, there were regions (most notably sub-Saharan Africa and Latin America) that for historical reasons were particularly disadvantaged in competing for a share of the North American demand. These regions tended to run into balance of payment difficulties that put them into the hopeless position of having to compete directly with the United States in world financial markets.[5]

This global restructuring was consolidated by the establishment of the new *illusio* propagated by the Washington Consensus – what John Toye (1993) has aptly called the "counter-revolution" in development thinking. Taking advantage of the ongoing crisis of the old development project, the agencies of the new Washington Consensus invited Third World countries to abandon the statist and inward-looking strategies advocated by development theory and play by the rules of an altogether different game – that is, to open up their national economies to the cold winds of intensifying world-market competition and to compete intensely with one another and First World countries in creating within their jurisdictions the greatest possible freedom of movement and action for capitalist enterprise. From the standpoint of the hegemonic power, these strategies had the advantage of widening and deepening the reach of the US-centered global money market, thereby increasing the effectiveness of financialization in reviving US wealth and power (cf. Arrighi 1991; Toye 1993: ch. 8; McMichael 2000; Bracking 1999: 208; Bienefeld 2000). Whether and how they would also improve the chances of success of Third World developmental efforts was never made clear. Their theoretical and historical justifications were shaky at best (Toye 1993: ch. 3–4; Tickner 1990). Be that as it may, disenchantment with the old strategies, intensifying competitive pressures, or sheer lack of credible alternatives made Third World countries inclined to believe in the "magic of the market" and to play by the new rules of the game. The question to which we must turn by way of conclusion is how stable the new *illusio* can be expected to be, and whether we can detect in present trends any sign of a future subversion of the Northern-dominated global hierarchy of wealth.

Limits and Contradictions of the Neoliberal Counter-Revolution

Our argument has been that the reproduction of the North–South income divide since 1960 has been based on two main mechanisms – one structural and one ideological. The structural mechanism consists of the tendency of profit-oriented innovations in the organization of economic life to polarize space into zones of more or less permanent "prosperity" and zones of more or less permanent "depression." Around 1960, the concentration of First World countries in zones of more or less permanent prosperity and of Third World countries in zones of more or less permanent depression was largely a legacy of Western territorial and industrial expansion since about 1800. After 1960, however, the very success of Third World countries in internalizing within their domains the industrial activities with which First World wealth had been associated activated a competition that sharply reduced the returns that previously had accrued to such activities. Around 1980, a radical change in US policies provoked a major restructuring of the industrial apparatuses that had grown up under the previous regime. Under the new global regime, only those industrial apparatuses that could become profitable by world standards remained in operation or expanded further, while those that could not were downsized or eliminated altogether. From this point of view, the main difference between the pre-1980 and the post-1980 periods is that before 1980 relationships among the industrial apparatuses of Third World countries were predominantly competitive, producing broadly similar developmental outcomes, while after 1980 they became predominantly competitive, producing sharply divergent developmental outcomes *among* Third World regions.

Structural mechanism did not operate in an ideological void. Rather, they were shaped by beliefs and theories about the pursuit of national wealth in a global economy that channeled Third World developmental efforts in particular directions. These beliefs and theories were fundamentally contradictory because they reflected the hegemonic power's attempt to do two incompatible things – to accommodate Third World countries' aspirations to catch up with the standards of wealth of First World countries, and to preserve standards of oligarchic wealth for itself and for its closest allies. From this point of view, the main difference between the pre-1980 and the post-1980 periods is that, while in the earlier period the need to accommodate Third World aspirations was predominant, in the later period the need to preserve oligarchic wealth gained the upper hand.

What has emerged at the turn of the century is not an effective and widely accepted new *illusio*, nor Amsden's "rise of the Rest," and certainly not the "rationally ordered system, determined by its inhabitants in the interest of need not profit or war" (Harris 1986: 202) envisaged by Harris. Rather, it is a global system characterized by a highly unstable mix of large and persistent inequalities buttressed by appeals to moral sentiments, such as universal human rights, that fly in the face of the underlying economic reality. . . . In bringing this article to a close, we shall briefly discuss those dynamics that are most likely to destabilize the "globalization project" as well as those which have at least the potential to subvert the Northern-dominated hierarchy of wealth.

A first major source of instability is the nature of the restoration of US power and Western wealth. The ease with which the United States succeeded in mobilizing resources in global financial markets to defeat the USSR in the 1980s, and then to sustain a long domestic economic expansion and a spectacular boom in the New York Stock Exchange in the 1990s, led to the belief that "America's Back!" Even assuming that US global power was resuscitated as much as this belief implies, it would be a very different *kind* of power than the one deployed at the height of US hegemony. That power rested on the capacity of the United States to solve the problems that had plagued the world in the terminal crisis of European colonial imperialism. Integral to this solution was the capacity of the United

States to use its unprecedented and unparalleled financial resources to launch a global economic expansion that reproduced the existing hierarchy of wealth but nonetheless transformed interstate competition into a positive-sum game. The new power that the United States came to enjoy in the 1980s and 1990s, in contrast, rested on the capacity of the United States to outcompete most other states in global financial markets. In exercising this capacity, the United States was no longer pump-priming the global economy as it did in the 1950s and 1960s. On the contrary, it has been sucking in liquidity from the rest of the world. US power has thus been reflated, and the global hierarchy of wealth consolidated, through the transformation of interstate competition into a negative-sum game (Arrighi and Silver et al. 1999: 272–4; Arrighi and Silver 1999).

The sustainability of this negative-sum game for much longer is doubtful. The overall contraction in effective global demand brought about by the tightening of monetary policies advocated by the neoliberal counterrevolution has succeeded in bringing under control the inflationary tendencies of the 1970s. But it continually threatens to tilt the balance in the opposite direction of a global overproduction crisis, as almost happened in 1997–8, and as might be happening again now in the wake of the bursting of the "new economy" speculative bubble. Moreover, the entire process has been associated with widespread tendencies towards social and political disintegration in the former Second and Third Worlds.

This brings us to a *second* major source of systemic instability. The US government and the Bretton Woods institutions have been encountering increasing difficulties in persuading former Third and Second World governments that opening up their domestic economies to the unfettered sway of foreign commodities and capital actually serves their national interests. In the 1980s and 1990s, partly out of choice and partly out of necessity, Third World governments complied with the development strategies advocated by the neoliberal Washington Consensus. But these same governments appear to be running out of patience, as the promised benefits for those who play by the rules of the new game have failed to materialize. . . . Whether subjection to the neoliberal prescriptions was primarily a consequence or also a major cause of poor economic performance is hard to tell. Yet, even a distinguished World Bank economist, William Easterly, has noted that greater adherence by "developing countries" to the policies advocated by the Washington Consensus has been associated with a sharp deterioration of their economic performance, the median rate of growth of their per capita income falling from 2.5 percent in 1960–79 to zero percent in 1980–98 (2001: 135–45).

The failure of the Washington Consensus to deliver on its promises is an important element of the context in which Third World delegates to the 1999 WTO meeting in Seattle successfully torpedoed US attempts to launch a new round of trade liberalizing negotiations (cf. Silver and Arrighi 2000). We can detect in Seattle and in subsequent UNCTAD meetings in Bangkok and elsewhere, the potential reemergence under entirely new historical circumstances of the demands for a NIEO that Third World countries advanced without success in the 1970s. These new demands for a NIEO might have little impact on the actual future trajectory of events were it not for a *third* source of instability. This is the reemergence of East Asia as the most dynamic region of the global economy, as it was before the rise in the nineteenth century of a Western-dominated global hierarchy of wealth. In the last two decades of the twentieth century East Asia experienced a region-wide industrial expansion that for speed and extent has few parallels in history. . . . Thus, the obverse side of the transformation of the United States into the world's leading debtor nation has been the emergence in the 1990s of Japan and the overseas Chinese (operating out of Taiwan, Hong Kong, Singapore, and the main commercial centers of Southeast Asia) as the world's leading creditor nations (Fingleton 2001; Arrighi, Hui, Hung, and Selden 2003).

. . . [T]he economic and financial crises in East Asia in the 1990s do not in themselves support the conclusion that the "rise of East Asia" is a mirage. In past transitions, it was the newly emerging centers of world-scale processes of capital accumulation that experienced the deepest financial crises, as their financial prowess outstripped their institutional capacity to regulate the massive amounts of mobile capital flowing in and out of their jurisdictions. This was true of London and England in the late eighteenth century and even more true of New York and the United States in the 1930s. We would not use the Wall Street crash of 1929–31 and the subsequent US Great Depression to argue that the epicenter of global processes of capital accumulation had *not* been shifting from the United Kingdom to the United States in the first half of the twentieth century. Nor should we draw any analogous conclusion from the East Asian financial crises of the 1990s (Arrighi and Silver et al. 1999, especially chapter 1 and conclusion).

Be that as it may, the most important tendency for understanding the present and future of the global hierarchy of wealth may be the continuing economic expansion of China. Given the demographic size and historical centrality of China in the region, this continuing expansion is far more significant for the subversion of the global hierarchy of wealth than all the previous East Asian economic "miracles" put together. For all these miracles (the Japanese included) were instances of upward mobility within a fundamentally stable global hierarchy of wealth. The hierarchy could and did accommodate the upward mobility of a handful of East Asian states (two of them city-states), accounting for about one-twentieth of world population. However, accommodating the upward mobility of a state that by itself accounts for about one-fifth of world population is an altogether different affair. Statistically, the very pyramidal structure of the hierarchy would be subverted. . . . Moreover, any significant upward mobility of China within the world hierarchy of wealth would also imply not just a statistical subversion of the pyramidal structure, but a political and cultural one as well.

. . . Moreover, the "spontaneous" tendencies for the global hierarchy of wealth to reproduce itself emphasized throughout this article will continue asserting themselves. In particular, China's rapid growth raises in acute form the problem of the absolute and relative scarcity of natural resources – a problem that the postwar world of *oligarchic* wealth accommodated through the *exclusion* of the majority of world population from the mass consumption standards of the West. A new model of development that is less wasteful than the US-sponsored mass consumption model will be needed in a world of *democratic* wealth.

Closely related to this is the further question of whether and how the Chinese government will use China's wealth and related power (assuming that they will both continue to rise) to influence the rules of the global development game. Will it put China's weight behind a NIEO that is simultaneously more equitable, less wasteful, and more sustainable than the US-centered economic order? Or will it continue, as it has done so far, to mimic the unsustainable and resource-intensive US model of development? Indeed, China's recent rapid economic growth has also been associated with the growth of enormous inequalities *within* China (Riskin, Zhao, and Li 2001) – a trend that further increases the likelihood that

China's expansion will be punctuated by major social-political crises as well as economic crises. The resolution of these problems requires a minimum of political intelligence and good will (admittedly scarce goods these days), not to mention a compelling new *hegemonic vision for the world*. Even though at the moment little is visible of either, the rise of East Asia seems to us the most hopeful sign that the extreme global inequalities created under European colonial imperialism and consolidated under US hegemony will eventually give way to a more just and equal world.

NOTES

1   On the decreasing effectiveness of industrialization as a means to pursue income/wealth, see Arrighi and Drangel (1986: 53–7). Although this finding was incorporated in some later reconceptualizations of national development (e.g., Gereffi 1994: 44–5), it has largely been ignored in academic and popular discourses about development.

2   For a detailed discussion of the mechanisms underlying this intensification of competitive pressures, see Arrighi 1994; Arrighi and Silver et al. 1999.

3   For a discussion of this process with regards to the greater ease with which wealthy countries have been able to absorb/accommodate social disruptions associated with industrialization, especially the emergence of strong labor movements, see Silver (2003, especially chapter 3); also Silver (1990).

4   Evidence of the growing political strength of the Third World included the US defeat in Vietnam, Portuguese defeat in Africa, Israeli difficulties in the 1973 War, and the entry of the PRC in the Security Council of the United Nations.

5   For a preliminary analysis of the comparative advantages of East Asia and disadvantages of sub-Saharan Africa in the new global environment of the 1980s and 1990s, see Arrighi (2002: 24–31).

REFERENCES

Akamatsu, K. 1961. "A Theory of Unbalanced Growth in the World Economy." *Weltwirtschaftliches Archiv* 86, 1: 196–217.

Amsden, Alice. 2001. *The Rise of "The Rest."* New York: Oxford University Press.

Arrighi, Giovanni. 1991. "World Income Inequality and the Future of Socialism." *New Left Review* 189: 39–64.

——. 1994. *The Long Twentieth Century: Money, Power and the Origins of Our Times.* London: Verso.

——. 2002. "The African Crisis: World Systemic and Regional Aspects." *New Left Review* 15: 5–36.

Arrighi, Giovanni and Jessica Drangel. 1986. "The Stratification of the World-Economy: An Exploration of the Semiperipheral Zone." *Review* (Fernand Braudel Center) 10, 1: 9–74.

Arrighi, Giovanni, Po-keung Hui, Ho-Fung Hung, and Mark Selden. 2003. "Historical Capitalism, East and West." In *The Resurgence of East Asia: 500, 150, 50 Year Perspectives*, eds. G. Arrighi, T. Hamashita, and M. Selden. London and New York: Routledge.

Arrighi, Giovanni and Beverly J. Silver, with I. Ahmad, K. Barr, S. Hisaeda, P. Hui, K. Ray, T. Reifer, M. Shih, E. Slater. 1999. *Chaos and Governance in the Modern World System.* Minneapolis, MN: University of Minnesota Press.

Arrighi, Giovanni and Beverly J. Silver. 1999. "Hegemonic Transitions: A Rejoinder." *Political Power and Social Theory* 13: 307–15.

Baumol, William J. 1967. "Macroeconomics of Unbalanced Growth: The Anatomy of Urban Crisis." *American Economic Review* 57, 3: 415–26.

Baumol, W.J., S.A.B. Blackman and E.N. Wolff. 1989. *Productivity and American Leadership: The Long View*. Cambridge, MA: MIT Press.

Bell, Daniel. 1973. *The Coming of Post-Industrial Society*. New York: Basic Books.

Bienefeld, Manfred. 2000. "Structural Adjustment: Debt Collection Device or Development Policy?" *Review* (Fernand Braudel Center) 23, 4: 533–82.

Bourdieu, Pierre. 1984. *Distinction: A Social Critique of the Judgement of Taste*. Cambridge, MA: Harvard University Press.

Bourdieu, Pierre and Jean-Claude Passeron. 1979. *The Inheritors*. Chicago: University of Chicago Press.

Bourdieu, Pierre and Loci Wacquant. 1992. *An Invitation to Reflexive Sociology*. Chicago: University of Chicago Press.

Bracking, Sarah. 1999. "Structural Adjustment: Why It Wasn't Necessary and Why It Did Work." *Review of African Political Economy* 80: 207–26.

Brandt Commission. 1980. *North-South: A Program for Survival*. London: Pan Books.

Brenner, Robert. 1998. "The Economics of Global Turbulence: A Special Report on the World Economy, 1950–1998." *New Left Review* 229: 1–264.

——. 2002. *The Boom and the Bubble: the U.S. in the World Economy*. New York: Verso.

Burbach, Roger and William I. Robinson. 1999. "The Fin de Siècle Debate: Globalization as Global Shift." *Science and Society* 63, 1: 10–39.

Chase-Dunn, Christopher. 1999. "Globalization: A World-Systems Perspective." *Journal of World-Systems Research* 5, 2: 176–98.

Clark, Colin. 1957. *The Conditions of Economic Progress*, 3rd ed. London: Macmillan.

Easterly, William. 2001. "The Lost Decades: Developing Countries' Stagnation in Spite of Policy Reform 1980–1998." *Journal of Economic Growth* 6: 135–57.

Fingleton, Eamonn. 2001. "Quibble All You Like, Japan Still Looks Like a Strong Winner." *International Herald Tribune*, January 2: 6.

Gereffi, Gary. 1994. "Rethinking Development Theory: Insights from East Asia and Latin America." pp. 26–56 in *Comparative National Development. Society and Economy in the New Global Order*, eds. A. D. Kinkaid and A. Portes. Chapel Hill, NC: University of North Carolina Press.

Hardt, Michael and Antonio Negri. 2000. *Empire*. Cambridge, MA: Harvard University Press.

Harris, Nigel. 1986. *The End of the Third World. Newly Industrializing Countries and the Decline of an Ideology*. Harmondsworth, Middlesex: Penguin Books.

Harrod, Roy. 1958. "The Possibility of Economic Satiety – Use of Economic Growth for Improving the Quality of Education and Leisure." Pp. 207–13 in *Problems of United States Economic Development*, 1. New York: Committee for Economic Development.

Held, David, Anthony McGrew, David Goldblatt and Jonathan Perraton. 1999. *Global Transformations. Politics, Economics and Culture*. Stanford, CA: Stanford University Press.

Hirsch, Freed. 1976. *Social Limits to Growth*. Cambridge, Mass.: Harvard University Press.

Hoogvelt, Ankie. 1997. *Globalization and the Postcolonial World: The New Political Economy of Development*. Baltimore, MD: Johns Hopkins University Press.

Jones, Charles I. 1997. "Convergence Revisited." *Journal of Economic Growth* 2: 131–53.

Krasner, Stephen D. 1985. *Structural Conflict: The Third World Against Global Liberalism*. Berkeley: University of California Press.

McMichael, Philip. 2000. *Development and Social Change: A Global Perspective*, 2nd ed. Thousand Oaks, CA: Sage.

Parboni, Riccardo. 1981. *The Dollar and its Rivals*. London: Verso.

Riskin, Carl, Zhao Renwei and Li Shih. 2001. *Retreat from Equality: Essays on the Changing Distribution of Income in China, 1988 to 1995.* Armonk, NY: M.E. Sharpe.

Robinson, William I. and Jerry Harris. 2000. "Towards A Global Ruling Class? Globalization and the Transnational Capitalist Class." *Science and Society* 64, 1: 11–54.

Schumpeter, Joseph. 1954. *Capitalism, Socialism & Democracy.* London: Allen & Unwin.

——. 1961. *The Theory of Economic Development.* New York: Oxford University Press.

——. 1964. *Business Cycles: A Theoretical, Historical, and Statistical Analysis of the Capitalist Process.* New York: McGraw Hill.

Tickner, J. Ann. 1990. "Reaganomics and the Third World: Lessons from the Founding Fathers." *Polity: The Journal of the Northeastern Political Science Association* 23, 1: 53–76.

Tipps, Dean C. 1973. "Modernization Theory and the Study of National Societies: A Critical Perspective." *Comparative Studies in Society and History* 15, 2: 199–226.

Toye, John. 1993. *Dilemmas of Development. Reflections on the Counter-Revolution in Development Economics.* Second Edition. Oxford: Blackwell.

Vernon, Raymond. 1971. *Sovereignty at Bay: The Multinational Spread of U.S. Enterprises.* Harmondsworth: Penguin Books.

——. 1966. "International Investment and International Trade in the Product Cycle." *Quarterly Journal of Economics* 80, 2: 190–207.

21 The New Development–Security Terrain (2001)

Mark Duffield

The optimism of the early post-Cold War years that the world was entering a new era of peace and stability has long since evaporated. It has been swept aside by a troubled decade of internal and regionalised forms of conflict, large-scale humanitarian interventions and social reconstruction programmes that have raised new challenges and questioned old assumptions. During the mid-1990s the need to address the issue of conflict became a central concern within mainstream development policy. Once a specialised discipline within international and security studies, war and its effects are now an important part of development discourse. At the same time, development concerns have become increasingly important in relation to how security is understood. It is now generally accepted that international organisations should be aware of conflict and its effects and, where possible, gear their work towards conflict resolution and helping to rebuild war-torn societies in a way that will avert future violence. Such engagement is regarded as essential if development and stability are to prevail. These views are well represented in the policy statements of leading intergovernmental organisations;[1] international financial institutions;[2] donor governments;[3] United Nations agencies;[4] influential think-tanks;[5] international NGOs;[6] and even large private companies.[7] At the same time, the literature on humanitarian assistance, conflict resolution and postwar reconstruction has burgeoned,[8] new university departments and courses have sprung up, and practitioner training programmes have been established. Conflict-related NGOs have emerged, while existing NGOs have expanded their mandates. In addition, donor governments, international financial institutions (IFIs), intergovernmental organisations (IGOs) and the UN have all created specialist units and committees. Linking these developments, dedicated multidisciplinary and multisectoral fora and networks have multiplied.

This book is a critical reflection on the incorporation of war into development discourse. The shift in aid policy towards conflict resolution and societal reconstruction is analysed not merely as a technical system of support and assistance, but as part of an emerging system of global governance. . . . the capitalist world system is no longer a necessarily expansive or inclusive complex. Since the 1970s, formal trade, productive, financial and technological networks have been concentrating within and between the North American, Western European and East Asian regional systems at the expense of outlying areas. On the basis of raw materials and cheap labour alone, the inclusion of the South within the conventional global economy can no longer be taken for granted. . . . Today, security concerns are no longer encompassed solely by the danger of conventional interstate war. The threat of an excluded South fomenting international instability through conflict, criminal activity and terrorism is now part of a new security framework. Within this framework, underdevelopment has become dangerous. This reinterpretation is closely associated with a radicalisation of development. Indeed, the incorporation of conflict resolution and societal reconstruction within aid policy – amounting to a commitment to transform societies as a whole – embodies this radicalisation. Such a project, however, is beyond the capabilities or legitimacy of individual Northern governments. In this respect, the changing nature of North–South relations is synonymous with a shift from hierarchical and territorial relations of government to polyarchical, non-territorial and networked relations of governance. The radical agenda of social transformation is embodied within Northern strategic networks and complexes that are bringing together governments, NGOs, military establishments and private companies in new ways. Such complexes are themselves part of an emerging system of global liberal governance.

From a Capitalist to a Liberal World System

The nation state was a political project based upon a logic of expansion, inclusion and subordination. It was also closely associated with the growth of a capitalist world system. Until the 1970s, this system was widely perceived as a geographically expanding and spatially deepening universe (Wallerstein 1974). A broad consensus held that capitalism had grown over several hundred years from its European origins to span the globe by the end of the nineteenth century. Indeed, contrary to some of the current views on globalisation, a few writers have even argued that the world economy reached a peak of interdependence and openness in the early years of the twentieth century that has not been equalled since (Hirst and Thompson 1996). While such detail is contested, in capitalism's seemingly inexorable forward march other social systems fell before it and, for better or worse, found themselves subordinated to its logic. Even the peripheral areas of the world system were valued for their raw materials and cheap labour and were typically incorporated through colonial or semi-colonial relations of tutelage (Rodney 1972). In the capitalist core areas, bureaucratic, juridical and territorially based state systems developed. Through the emergence of widening forms of legal, political and economic protection, state actors forged inclusive national identities from the disparate social groups that lay within state borders.[9] On the basis of the growing competence of the nation state, citizens were expected to be loyal and defer to its normative structures and expectations (Derlugian 1996).

The 1970s are widely regarded as signalling a profound and historic change in the nature of the capitalist world system and with it the nation state. From this period, while market relations have continued to deepen in core areas, the future of capitalism as a globally expansive and inclusive system has been increasingly questioned (Hopkins and Wallerstein 1996). Contrary to popular views of globalisation which often portray capitalist relations as redoubling their penetration and interconnection of all parts of the globe (for examples see Waters 1995), the core regions of what could now be termed the liberal world system appear to be consolidating and strengthening the ties between them at the expense of outly-ing areas. In a review of the existing quantitative information, Hoogvelt (1997: 69–89) has argued that in broad terms the loci of economic power and influence in the world have remained remarkably stable for the past several hundred years. The one major exception is the relatively recent emergence of a number of East Asian countries to join Japan in con-firming that region, together with the North American and Western European systems, as one of the core areas of an emerging global informational economy (Castells 1996).

If globalisation has a meaning in this context, it is the consolidation of several distinct but interrelated regionalised economic systems as the core of the formal international economy. Moreover, rather than continuing to expand in a spatial or geographical sense, the competitive financial, investment, trade and productive networks that link these region-alised systems have been thickening and deepening since the 1970s. Although there are, of course, many differences that separate them, these core regionalised systems of the global informational economy are here figuratively described as the 'North'. Correspondingly, the areas formally outside or only partially or conditionally integrated into these regional net-works are loosely referred to as the 'South'. The inclusion of the South within the conven-tional economic flows and networks of the global economy – even when raw materials and cheap labour are available, even as unequal and exploited subjects – can no longer, as in the past, be taken for granted.

> The architecture of the global economy features an asymmetrically interdependent world, organised around three major economic regions and increasingly polarized along an axis of opposition between productive, information-rich, affluent areas, and impoverished areas, economically devalued and socially excluded. (Castells 1996: 145)

In the case of Africa, for example – with the exception of South Africa and, beyond it, a certain number of prized raw materials, niche tropical products and adventure tourism – commercial investment has collapsed since the 1970s. In much of the former Soviet Union a similar lack of interest exists, as evidenced by relatively low levels of Western investment in all fields except energy and a number of valuable raw materials. Manuel Castells (1996, 1998) has argued that global capitalism no longer operates on the basis of expansion and incorporation but on a new logic of consolidation and exclusion (see also Hirst and Thompson 1996: 68–9).

There are numerous instances of the logic of exclusion informing North–South rela-tions, including the increasing restriction of immigration from the South since the 1970s and the hardening of the international refugee regime (UNHCR 1995). Indeed, the present refugee regime can best be described as one of return rather than asylum. Although some views of globalisation stress interconnection and integration, the movement of poor people from the South to the North, and even across international boundaries in the South itself, is becoming more difficult and contested. Writing in a similar vein, Robert Cox has argued that the irrelevance of much of the world's population in relation to the formal global economy is manifest in the shift from attempts to promote economic development in the South 'in favour of what can be called global poor relief and riot control' (Cox 1995: 41). Restriction, in many cases, has been matched by a system concordance geared to attempting to develop methods of population containment. During the first half of the 1990s, for example, a key response to the new wars of the post-Cold War era was the emergence of system-wide UN humanitarian operations. Largely through negotiating access with warring parties, in Africa and the Balkans, for example, aid agencies developed the means of providing humanitarian assistance directly to populations within their countries and areas of origin (Duffield 1997). Such operations, together with related 'safe area' policies, had the effect of encouraging war-affected populations, with varying degrees of success, to remain within conflict zones and to avoid crossing international borders.

The idea of exclusion, however, should not be understood too literally. As well as a closing of doors or severing of relationships, exclusion is also a subordinating social relationship embodied in new relations of connection, interaction and interdependence. In other words, the concept of exclusion encompasses both new types of restriction and emergent and subordinating forms of North–South integration.

The Ambivalence of Southern Exclusion

Political economy has largely understood Southern exclusion in terms of the ambivalence of its present economic position within the global economy. On the one hand, evidence suggests that the South has been increasingly isolated and excluded by the dominant networks of the conventional global informational economy. Many traditional primary products are no longer required or are too low-priced for commercial exploitation, investment is risky, the available workforce lacks appropriate skills and education, markets are extremely narrow, telecommunications inadequate, politics unpredictable, governments ineffective, and so on. Regarding much of Africa, Castells has argued that liberal economic reform has revealed its 'structural irrelevance' for the new informational economy (Castells 1996: 135). At the same time, however, formal economic exclusion is not synonymous with a void, far from it. The South has effectively reintegrated itself into the liberal world system through the spread and deepening of all types of parallel and shadow transborder activity (Bayart *et al.* 1999). This represents the site of new and expansive forms of local–global networking and innovative patterns of extra-legal and non-formal North–South integration.

Not only does exclusion imply both isolation and subordinating forms of interaction, the terms North and South also require some qualification. They are no longer regarded as relating to just spatial or geographical realities. They are now as much social as they are territorial.[10] Under the impact of market deregulation and the increased ease with which finance, investment and production can cross borders, although North–South distinctions are still geographically concentrated, they also reflect important non-territorial social modalities. While the gap in *per capita* income between Northern and Southern countries has been widening for generations (Hoogvelt 1997; UNDP 1996), similar gaps between the richest and poorest sections of the population in the North have also grown. . . . Thus, within the networks and flows of the global economy, the North now has a 'variable geometry' of pockets of impoverishment, redundant skills and social exclusion, just as within 'the enduring architecture' of the South even the poorest countries usually have small sections of the workforce connected to high-value global networks. Indeed, such connections are important in understanding the new wars. They reflect the points at which the control of markets and populations, together with their selective integration into the networks of global governance, are often contested.

In studying the new wars, one is largely reliant on the contribution of political economy and anthropology. However, the literature has yet to make up its mind. Indeed, much of the work on global political economy avoids any serious analysis of the South.[11] Moreover, in relation to political economy, where the South is discussed, there is a major division between viewing the new wars as social regression or, in contrast, as systems of social transformation. That is, there is a distinction between seeing conflict in terms of having causes that lead mechanically to forms of breakdown, as opposed to sites of innovation and reordering resulting in the creation of new types of legitimacy and authority. This contrast, moreover, relates not only to political economy. It is a generic division that characterises the literature on the new wars in general. Most donor governments and aid agencies, for example, tend to see conflict as a form of social regression. For political economy, while its analysis of the exclusionary logic within global liberal governance contains a number of useful insights, much of this work has not translated into a credible theory of the new wars. Manuel Castells, a key figure in the analysis and documentation of the changing global political economy, well illustrates this failure. There is a risk in arguing that the new system logic results in the exclusion of the South from the dominant networks of the global economy, which it appears to do. The danger is to overstate the case and follow through with an implied void of scarcity that, it is assumed, leads to growing resource competition, breakdown, criminalisation and chaos. For Castells, the declining investment in Africa has led to a heightened competition for control of the remaining resources, including the state:

> [B]ecause tribal and ethnic networks were the safest bet for people's support, the fight to control the state . . . was organised around ethnic cleavages, reviving centuries-old hatred and prejudice: genocidal tendencies and widespread banditry are rooted in the political economy of Africa's disconnection from the new global economy. (Castells 1996: 135)

[. . .]

Consistent with the logic of this view – that exclusion leads to the breakdown of normative order – Castells has argued that the only export from the global black holes that rivals the informational economy in terms of its innovation and networked character is the 'perverse' connection of a global criminal economy (*ibid.*: 166–205). In this respect, the Castells viewpoint well reflects current concerns that have led to the reinterpretation of the nature of security. The focus of new security concerns is not the threat of traditional interstate wars but the fear of underdevelopment as a source of conflict, criminalised activity and international instability. This reinterpretation, moreover, means that even if the system logic is one of exclusion, the idea of underdevelopment as dangerous and destabilising provides a justification for continued surveillance and engagement.

The Internationalisation of Public Policy

The logic of exclusion informs and shapes public policy in many ways. In this respect, one should not forget that exclusion also implies the existence of criteria of *inclusion*. Unlike the more general logic of inclusion and subordination that existed when the capitalist world system was geographically expansive, however, inclusion under global liberal governance is more discerning and selective. Southern governments, project partners and populations now have to show themselves fit for consideration. That is, they have to meet defined standards of behaviour and normative expectations. In the case of governments, this could mean following neoliberal economic prescriptions, adhering to international standards of good governance or subscribing to donor-approved poverty reduction measures. Through relations of fitness and normative benchmarking the logic of exclusion manifests itself in direct and indirect ways. In particular, it has allowed a stratified system of engagement to emerge. This ranges from forms of exclusion, such as the sanction regimes presently encompassing so-called rogue states, to conditional types of partnership and inclusion for authorities with whom the North feels able to do business. Indeed, the more extensive and significant application of an exclusionary logic is contained in the nuanced and complex interface of partnership, cooperation and participation through which the North now engages and selectively incorporates the South.

The politics of liberal governance are associated with the transformation of nation states in both the North and the South 'from being buffers between external economic forces and the domestic economy into agencies for adapting domestic economies for the exigencies of the global economy' (Cox 1995: 39). This transformation has been achieved through the emergence of new cross-cutting governance networks involving state and non-state actors from the supranational to the local level. The growth of such networks is associated with the attenuation of the ability of state incumbents to govern independently within their own borders. Governments now have to take account of new supranational, international and even local constituencies. However, this does not mean that states have necessarily become weaker (although many have, especially in the South); it primarily suggests that the nature of power and authority has changed. Indeed, contained within the shift in aid policy towards conflict resolution and societal reconstruction, Northern governments have found new methods and systems of governance through which to reassert their authority.

. . . The governance networks linking North and South, however, largely reflect the internationalisation of public policy and reflect the South's subordination (Duffield 1992; de Waal 1997; Deacon *et al.* 1997). As the formal North–South economic linkages have narrowed and shrunk, the compensating networks of international public policy have thickened and developed new organisational forms. To a certain extent, using Cox's imagery, the conflict resolution and post-war reconstruction concerns of liberal governance could be seen as the 'riot control' end of a spectrum encompassing a broad range of 'global poor relief' activities including, for example, NGO developmental attempts to encourage self-sufficiency in relation to food security and basic services. Such public welfare initiatives now complement the economic prescriptions of structural adjustment. The internationalisation of public policy has filled the vacuum, as it were, resulting from the marked process of debureaucratisation and attenuation of nation-state competence that has been deepened in the South by liberal economic reform (Reno 1998).

In terms of the international North–South flows and networks, there is a noticeable duality. While patterns are uneven and great differences exist, the shrinkage of formal economic ties has given rise to two opposing movements. Coming from the South, there has been an expansion of transborder and shadow economic activity that has forged new local–global linkages with the liberal world system and, in so doing, new patterns of actual development and political authority – that is, alternative and non-liberal forms of protection, legitimacy and social regulation. Emerging from the North, the networks of international public policy have thickened and multiplied their points of engagement and control. Many erstwhile functions of the nation state have been abandoned to these international networks as power and authority have been reconfigured. The encounter of the two systems has formed a new and complex development–security terrain. Concerns with stability and the new wars represent an extreme and particular form of engagement within this much broader framework. The networks and actors involved define the points of greatest tension and open confrontation within the encounter. At the same time, however, this violent engagement crystallises and reflects the logic of the system as a whole.

Liberal Peace

[. . .]

Examining aid policy as an expression of global governance – as a political project in its own right – demands attention to its particular forms of mobilisation, justification and reward. The idea of *liberal peace*, for example, combines and conflates 'liberal' (as in contemporary liberal economic and political tenets) with 'peace' (the present policy predilection towards conflict resolution and societal reconstruction). It reflects the existing consensus that conflict in the South is best approached through a number of connected, ameliorative, harmonising and, especially, transformational measures. While this can include the provision of immediate relief and rehabilitation assistance, liberal peace embodies a new or political humanitarianism that lays emphasis on such things as conflict resolution and prevention, reconstructing social networks, strengthening civil and representative institutions, promoting the rule of law, and security sector reform in the context of a functioning market economy. In many respects, while contested and far from assured, liberal peace reflects a radical developmental agenda of social transformation. In this case however, this is an international responsibility and not that of an independent or single juridical state. . . . While the initiatives that make up liberal peace are usually understood as being a response to specific needs and requirements, liberal peace is a political project in its own right.[12] The aim of liberal peace is to transform the dysfunctional and war-affected societies that it encounters on its borders into cooperative, representative and, especially, stable entities.

While states remain important, since the 1970s, under the influence of what is commonly known as globalisation, they have been drawn into multi-level and increasingly non-territorial decision-making networks that bring together governments, international agencies, non-governmental organisations, and so on, in new and complex ways. Consequently, there has been a noticeable move from the hierarchical, territorial and bureaucratic relations of government to more polyarchical, non-territorial and networked relations of governance (Held *et al.* 1999). While clearly they have deeper historical roots, relations of governance have come to shape and dominate political life over the past several decades. In this respect, liberal peace is not manifest within a single institution of global government; such a body does not exist and probably never will. It is part of the complex, mutating and stratified networks that make up global liberal governance. More specifically, liberal peace is embodied in a number of flows and nodes of authority within liberal governance that bring together different *strategic complexes* of state–non-state, military–civilian and public–private actors in pursuit of its aims. Such complexes now variously enmesh international NGOs, governments, military establishments, IFIs, private security companies, IGOs, the business sector, and so on. They are strategic in the sense of pursuing a radical agenda of social transformation in the interests of global stability.

[. . .]

The New Wars

. . . The approach adopted here is to regard war as a given: an ever-present axis around which opposing societies and complexes continually measure themselves and reorder social, economic, scientific and political life. Apart from being a site of innovation, this process of restructuring is also one of imitation and replication (van Creveld 1991). If opposing societies or complexes are not to suffer compromise or defeat, they must match or counter the innovations that each is liable to make. Not only is war an axis of social reordering, historically it has been a powerful mechanism for the globalisation of economic, political and scientific relations (Held *et al.* 1999). In this respect, the development of the modern and centralised nation state has been closely associated with the restructuring and globalising effects of war.

When the competence of nation states begins to change and they become qualified and enmeshed within non-territorial and networked relations of governance, one can assume that the nature of war has also changed. This relates not only to the way the new wars are fought, in this case beyond the regulatory regimes formally associated with nation states, but also to the manner in which societies are mobilised, structured and rewarded in order to address them. A major contention in this book is that the strategic complexes of liberal peace, that is, the emerging relations between governments, NGOs, militaries and the business sector, are not just a mechanical response to conflict. In fact, they have a good deal in common, in structural and organisational terms, with the new wars. For example, strategic complexes and the new wars are both based on increasingly privatised networks of state–non-state actors working beyond the conventional competence of territorially defined governments. Through such flows and networks each is learning how to project power in new non-territorial ways. With contrasting results, liberal peace and the new wars have blurred and dissolved conventional distinctions between peoples, armies and governments. At the same time, new systems of reward and mobilisation, especially associated with privatisation, have emerged in the wake of the outmoding of such divisions. Liberal peace and the new wars are also both forms of adaptation to the effects of market deregulation and the qualification and attenuation of nation-state competence. In many respects, the networks and complexes that compose liberal peace also reflect an emerging liberal way of war.

In the case of the new wars, market deregulation has deepened all forms of parallel and transborder trade and allowed warring parties to forge local–global networks and shadow economies as a means of asset realisation and self-provisioning. The use of illicit alluvial diamonds to fund conflicts in West and Southern Africa is a well-known example of a system that has a far wider application. Rather than expressions of breakdown or chaos, the new wars can be understood as a form of non-territorial *network war* that works through and around states. Instead of conventional armies, the new wars typically oppose and ally the transborder resource networks of state incumbents, social groups, diasporas, strongmen, and so on. These are refracted through legitimate and illegitimate forms of state–nonstate, national–international and local–global flows and commodity chains. Far from being a peripheral aberration, network war reflects the contested integration of stratified markets and populations into the global economy. Not only can the forms of innovation and state–non-state networking involved be compared to those of liberal peace; more generally, they stand comparison with the manner in which Northern political and economic actors have similarly adapted to the pressures and opportunities of globalisation. In this respect, as far as it is successful, network war is synonymous with the emergence of new forms of protection, legitimacy and rights to wealth. Rather than regression, the new wars are organically associated with a process of social transformation: the emergence of new forms of authority and zones of alternative regulation.

Instead of complex political emergencies, global governance is encountering *emerging political complexes*[13] on its borders. Such complexes are essentially non-liberal. That is, they follow forms of economic logic that are usually antagonistic towards free-market prescriptions and formal regional integration. At the same time, politically, the new forms of protection and legitimacy involved tend to be socially exclusive rather than inclusive. However, for those that are included, such political complexes nonetheless represent new frameworks of social representation and regulation. In other words, political complexes themselves are part of a process of social transformation and system innovation, a characteristic that embodies the ambiguity of such formations. While their economic and political logic can find violent and disruptive expression, in many cases such complexes are the only forms of existing or actual authority that have the powers to police stability. This ambiguity, however, pervades the general encounter of the new wars with the strategic complexes of liberal peace. The aid agencies, donors and NGOs involved also reflect and embody ideals of protection, legitimacy and rights. They also have transformational aims – in this case, however, liberal ones.

Global governance and the emerging political complexes are in competition in relation to the forms of authority and regulation they wish to establish. This competition establishes a fluctuating border area that is as much social as territorial across which a range of transactions, confrontations and interventions are possible. At its most general, it is the site of numerous discursive exchanges and narratives. The symbolic role of privatisation is a good example. Among many of the strategic actors of liberal governance, privatisation denotes a move towards a sound economy and the prospects of development. Among state actors and local strongmen, however, it can represent an innovative way to further the non-liberal political logic of the complex concerned. At the same time, at various points along this border, competition turns into antagonism and the site of more direct forms of intervention. If the Cold War represented a Third World War, then the contested, uneven and differential confrontation between the strategic complexes of liberal peace and the political complexes of the new wars is the site of the Fourth.

The Merging of Development and Security

That liberal peace contains within it the emerging structures of liberal war is suggested in the blurring and convergence during the 1990s of development and security. The transformational aims of liberal peace and the new humanitarianism embody this convergence. The commitment to conflict resolution and the reconstruction of societies in such a way as to avoid future wars represents a marked radicalisation of the politics of development. Societies must be changed so that past problems do not arise, as happened with development in the past; moreover, this process of transformation cannot be left to chance but requires direct and concerted action (Stiglitz 1998). Development resources must now be used to shift the balance of power between groups and even to change attitudes and beliefs. The radicalisation of development in this way is closely associated with the reproblematisation of security. Conventional views on the causes of the new wars usually hinge upon their arising from a developmental malaise of poverty, resource competition and weak or predatory institutions. The links between these wars and international crime and terrorism are also increasingly drawn. Not only have the politics of development been radicalised to address this situation but, importantly, it reflects a new security framework within which the modalities of underdevelopment have become dangerous. This framework is different from that of the Cold War when the threat of massive interstate conflict prevailed. The question of security has almost gone full circle: from being concerned with the biggest economies and war machines in the world to an interest in some of its smallest.

In most of the policy statements mentioned above (see footnotes 1 to 7) there is a noticeable convergence between the notions of development and security. Through a circular form of reinforcement and mutuality, achieving one is now regarded as essential for securing the other. Development is ultimately impossible without stability and, at the same time, security is not sustainable without development. This convergence is not simply a policy matter. It has profound political and structural implications. In relation to the strategic complexes of liberal governance it embodies the increasing interaction between military and security actors on the one hand, and civilian and non-governmental organisations on the other. It reflects the thickening networks that now link UN agencies, military establishments, NGOs and private security companies. Regarding NGOs, the convergence of development and security has meant that it has become difficult to separate their own development and humanitarian activities from the pervasive logic of the North's new security regime. The increasingly overt and accepted politicisation of aid is but one outcome.

The encounter of the strategic complexes of liberal peace with the political complexes of the new wars has established a new development–security terrain. It is developmental in that liberal values and institutions have been vested with ameliorative and harmonising powers. At the same time, it represents a new security framework since these powers are being deployed in a context in which the modalities of underdevelopment have become dangerous and destabilising. This contested terrain, which looks set to deepen and shape our perceptions over the coming decades, remains underresearched and is not captured in conventional and increasingly prescriptive and policy-oriented development and international studies. It is comprised of complex relations of structural similarity, complicity and, at the same time, new asymmetries of power and authority.

In terms of similarity, both liberal peace and the new wars have blurred traditional distinctions between people, army and government and, at the same time, forged new ways of projecting power through non-territorial public–private networks and systems. Along the social border between these two complexes, relations of accommodation and complicity are common and find many forms of expression. Rather than eliminating famine, for example, aid agencies have been charged with obstructing this aim (de Waal 1997). The international hierarchy of concern that exists also denotes a susceptibility within global liberal governance to normalise violence and accept high levels of instability as an enduring if unfortunate characteristic of certain regions. This new development–security terrain also contains marked asymmetries of power. Indeed, it tends to reverse and upset traditional notions of what power is and where it lies. It is a terrain where, in confronting new challenges, the authority of the major states is in a process of reconfiguration. While the growth of increasingly privatised and non-territorial strategic complexes reflect new ways of projecting liberal power, the effectiveness of these forms of authority is still an open question – especially when they confront political actors who have a strong sense of right and history, despite being part of economically weaker systems. Whether donor governments, militaries, aid agencies and the private sector can secure a liberal peace remains an open question. One thing, however, is perhaps more clear. It is difficult to imagine that the increasingly privatised and regionally stratified strategic complexes of liberal governance will be able to deliver the geographically and socially more extensive patterns of *relative* security that characterised the Cold War years. Understanding this new terrain should therefore be a priority for us all.

[. . .]

NOTES

1 OSCE 1995; EU 1996; DAC 1997; OECD 1998.
2 World Bank 1997b; World Bank 1997a.
3 Pronk and Kooijmans 1993; ODA 196; DFID 1997; MFA 1997; IDC 1999.
4 Boutros-Ghali 1995 (original 1992); UNDP 1994; UNHCR 1995.
5 Carnegie Commission 1997; World Bank and Carter Center 1997.
6 ActionAid 1994; Cottey 1994; IFRCS 1996.
7 PWBLF 1999.
8 See the following bibliographies: Fagen 1995; Masefield and Harvey 1997; Gundel 1999.
9 For a discussion of the development of constitutional liberalism prior to universal suffrage in the West, see Zakaria 1997.
10 Cox 1995: 40; Castells 1996: 147; Hoogvelt 1997: 66.
11 A good example is the recent and substantial work by Held *et al.* (1999) on *Global Transformations*. While their work has been praised as exhaustive and comprehensive by commentators, the authors nonetheless consciously exclude the effects of globalisation on the South from their study.
12 For an example of this approach to development, but one that mainly deals with the situation during the Cold War, see Escobar 1995.
13 This organisational rectification was first coined by Mick Dillon at a conference on 'The Politics of Emergency' in the Department of Politics, University of Manchester, May 1997.

REFERENCES

ActionAid. *Understanding Conflict: A Report from an ActionAid Workshop.* Jinja, Uganda: ActionAid; 1994 July 17–23.

Bayart, Jean-François, Ellis, Stephen and Hibou, Béatrice. *The Criminalization of the State in Africa.* Oxford and Bloomington: The International Africa Institute in Association with James Currey and Indiana University Press; 1999.

Boutros-Ghali, Boutros. *An Agenda for Peace.* New York: United Nations; 1995 (original 1992).

Carnegie Commission. *Executive Summary of the Final Report. Preventing Deadly Conflict: Executive Summary of the Final Report.* Washington, DC: Carnegie Commission on Preventing Deadly Conflict; 1997.

Castells, Manuel. *The Rise of the Network Society* (Vol. 1 of *The Information Age: Economy, Society and Culture*). Massachusetts and Oxford: Blackwell; 1996.

——. *End of Millennium.* Oxford: Blackwell; 1998.

Cottey, Andrew. *The Pursuit of Peace: A Framework for International Action.* Bristol: Saferworld; 1994 September.

Cox, Robert W. Critical Political Economy. In: Hettne, Bjorn, ed. *International Political Economy: Understanding Global Disorder.* London: Zed Books; 1995; pp. 31–45.

DAC. *DAC Guidelines on Conflict, Peace and Development Cooperation.* Paris: Development Assistance Committee, Organisation for Economic Cooperation and Development (OECD); 1997.

de Waal, Alex. *Famine Crimes: Politics and the Disaster Relief Industry.* London: African Rights and the International Africa Institute with James Currey; 1997.

Deacon, Bob and others. *Global Social Policy: International Organisations and the Future of Welfare.* London: Sage Publications; 1997.

Derlugian, Georgi M. The Social Cohesion of the States. In: Hopkins, Terence K. and Wallerstein, Immanuel, eds. *The Age of Transition: Trajectory of the World-System, 1945–2025.* London: Zed Books; 1996; pp. 148–77.

DFID. White Paper on International Development. *Eliminating World Poverty: A Challenge for the 21st Century.* London: Department for International Development; 1997 November.

Dillon, Michael. *Post-Structuralism, Complexity and Poetics.* Forthcoming in *Theory, Culture and Society.* 2000 December.

Dillon, Michael and Reid, Julian. Global Governance, Liberal Peace and Complex Emergency. Draft. *Alternatives.* 2000 March.

Duffield, Mark. The Emergence of Two-Tier Welfare in Africa: Marginalization or an Opportunity for Reform? *Public Administration and Development.* 1992; 12:139–54.

——. The Political Economy of Internal War. In: Macrae, Joanna and Zwi, Anthony, eds. *War and Hunger: Rethinking International Responses to Complex Emergencies.* London: Zed Press; 1994a; pp. 50–69.

——. *Complex Political Emergencies: An Exploratory Report for UNICEF With Reference to Angola and Bosnia.* Birmingham: School of Public Policy; 1994b March.

——. NGO Relief in War Zones: Toward an Analysis of the New Aid Paradigm. *Third World Quarterly.* 1997; 18(3):527–42.

Escobar, Arturo. *Encountering Development: The Making and Unmaking of the Third World.* New Jersey: Princeton University Press; 1995.

EU. *Communication on the European Union and the Issue of Conflicts in Africa: Peacebuilding, Conflict Prevention and Beyond.* Brussels: European Commission; 1996 May.

Fagen, Patrica Weiss. After the Conflict: A Review of Selected Sources on Rebuilding War-Torn Societies. War-Torn Societies Project, Occasional Paper No. 1. Geneva: War-Torn Societies Project; 1995 November.

Gundel, Joakim. Humanitarian Assistance: Breaking the Waves of Complex Political Emergencies – A Literature Survey. CDR Working Paper, No. 99.5. Copenhagen: Centre for Development Research; 1999 August.

Held, David, McGrew, Anthony, Goldblatt, David, and Perraton, Jonathan. *Global Transformations: Politics, Economics and Culture.* Cambridge: Polity Press; 1999.

Hirst, Paul and Thompson, Grahame. *Globalisation in Question.* Cambridge: Polity Press; 1996.

Hoogvelt, Ankie. *Globalization and the Postcolonial World.* Baltimore, Maryland: Johns Hopkins University Press; 1997.

Hopkins, Terence K. and Wallerstein, Immanuel, eds. *The Age of Transition: Trajectory of the World-System – 1945–2025.* London: Zed Books; 1996.

IDC. Sixth Report. Conflict Prevention and Post-Conflict Reconstruction, Vol. I, Report and Proceeding to the Committee. London, The Stationery Office: International Development Committee; 1999 July 28.

IFRCS. *World Disaster Report: 1996.* Oxford: Oxford University Press for International Federation of Red Cross and Red Crescent Societies; 1996.

Masefield, Abi and Harvey, Paul. *Rehabilitation: An Annotated Bibliography for the CARE, Rehabilitation, and the Greater Horn Project.* Brighton: Institute of Development Studies, University of Sussex; 1997 March.

MFA. *Preventing Violent Conflict: A Study – Executive Summary and Recommendations.* Stockholm, Sweden: Ministry for Foreign Affairs; 1997.

ODA. *Conflict Reduction through the Aid Programme: A Briefing for Agencies Seeking Support for Conflict Reduction Activities.* London: Overseas Development Administration; 1996 October.

OECD. Development Cooperation Guideline Series. *Conflict, Peace and Development Cooperation on the Threshold of the 21st Century.* Paris: Organisation for Economic Cooperation and Development; 1998.

OSCE. *OSCE Handbook: 20 Years of the Helsinki Final Act.* Vienna: Organisation of Security and Cooperation in Europe; 1995 April.

Pronk, I. P. and Kooijmans, P. H., Minister for Development Cooperation and Minister for Foreign Affairs (Ministry of Foreign Affairs, Netherlands Government). *Humanitarian Aid: Between Conflict and Development.* The Hague: Development Cooperation Information Department, Ministry of Foreign Affairs; 1993 December.

PWBLI. *Memorandum from the Prince of Wales Business Leaders Forum. Sixth Report of the International Development Committee. Conflict Prevention and Post-Conflict Reconstruction, Vol. II, Minutes of Evidence and Appendices.* London: The Stationery Office; 1999 July 28; pp. 209–13.

Reno, William. *Warlord Politics and African States.* Boulder, Colorado: Lynne Rienner Pubs, Inc.; 1998.

Rodney, Walter. *How Europe Underdeveloped Africa.* Dar Es Salaam: Tanzania Publishing House; 1972.

Stiglitz, Joseph E., Senior Vice President and Chief Economist (World Bank). *Towards a New Paradigm for Development: Strategies, Policies, and Processes.* Paper given at 1998 Prebisch Lecture. Geneva: UNCTAD; 1998 October 19.

UNDP. Draft. *Position Paper of the Working Group on Operational Aspects of the Relief to Development Continuum.* New York: UNDP; 1994 January 12.

UNHCR. *The State of the World's Refugees: In Search of Solutions.* Oxford: Oxford University Press for United Nations High Commission for Refugees; 1995.

van Creveld, Martin. *The Transformation of War*. New York: Free Press; 1991.

Wallerstein, Immanuel. *The Modern World System*. London: Academic Press; 1974.

Waters, Malcolm. *Globalization*. London: Routledge; 1995.

Weiss, Thomas. *Military–Civilian Interactions: Intervening in Humanitarian Crises*. Lanham, Maryland: Rowman and Littlefield Publishers, Inc.; 1999a.

World Bank. *The State in a Changing World; The World Development Report, 1997*. World Bank; 1997a.

——. *A Framework for World Bank Involvement in Post-Conflict Reconstruction*. Washington DC: World Bank; 1997b April 25.

World Bank and Carter Center. *From Civil War to Civil Society: The Transition from War to Peace in Guatemala and Liberia*. Washington DC and Atlanta: World Bank and Carter Center; 1997 July.

Zakaria, Fareed. *Democratic Tyranny*. Prospect. 1997 December; (25):20–5.

Part V   Confronting Globalization

Introduction

The readings in Part V focus on an array of social mobilizations and political mechanisms to confront the impacts of economic globalization. A common theme among these selections (one foreshadowed by Duffield's work in Part IV) is that social, economic, and political problems are increasingly transnational. In describing what they call "boundary problems," Held and McGrew point out "in a world in which global warming connects the long-term fate of many Pacific islands to the actions of tens of millions of private motorists across the globe, the conventional territorial conception of political community appears profoundly inadequate. Globalization weaves together, in highly complex and abstract systems, the fates of households, communities and peoples in distant regions of the globe." Thus, transnational organizations such as intergovernmental organizations, international non-governmental umbrella groups, or transnational advocacy networks are often better equipped to address these issues than are individual nation-states or national groups.

Opening this dialog about how noneconomic forces and institutions react to economic globalization is a broad discussion of antiglobalization by Harvard economics professor, Jeffrey Sachs. Currently, Sachs heads Columbia University's Earth Institute and directs the United Nations Millennium project, which brings together economists, scientists, and development experts from around the world. The Millennium Project developed a series of extremely ambitious goals, including halving poverty and hunger by 2015, and the doubling of development assistance by rich countries. The piece we include here is a very short excerpt from Sachs' bestselling 2005 book, *The End of Poverty: Economic Possibilities for Our Time*. The book is a devastating account of how terrible social conditions are in developing nations, and a rather optimistic agenda for change based on Sachs' estimation that this is the first moment in history that global resources are sufficient to meet each person's basic needs. In the excerpt reprinted here, Sachs reviews the range of groups protesting globalization. He applauds "the overall movement for exposing the hypocrisies and glaring shortcomings of global governance and for ending years of self-congratulation by the rich and powerful," and concedes that antiglobalization movements have shed considerable light on corporations "behaving badly" who in turn have often responded by addressing corporate corruption and working conditions. He strongly believes, however, that antiglobalization groups are ineffective because they are misdiagnosing the fundamental problem as being one of capitalism in general. Sachs argues that the antiglobalization movement should stop seeing corporations and trade as evil (he argues for their positive effects overall), and shift to promoting "capitalism with a human face," which requires international and national public policy to set the "right rules" for "enlightened globalization." For example, one path towards this solution would be focusing on the unmet promises of wealthy governments, especially "the most powerful and wayward of the rich governments, the United States." Sachs in particular wishes to see wealthy governments give 0.7 percent of their Gross National Product (GNP) to the poor nations. This aid would go a long way, in Sach's opinion, to meeting the "Millennium Development Goals" (MDGs) he helped formulate. Critics of the MDG goals (including the Bush administration) argue that they take a big-government approach (as opposed to entrepreneurial liberty), and are almost certainly destined to failure because they are so ambitious and their deadlines are so soon.

Representing a growing literature on "global governance," London School of Economics political scientist David Held and international relations professor Anthony McGrew from Southampton University explore how the "simultaneous weakening and expansion of state power" is propelling major global and structural changes in the organization of power and authority. Rather than claiming an "end to politics," they argue that these structural transformations instead necessitate a new way of doing politics. Echoing the frustrations expressed by Sachs regarding debates over trade, Held and McGrew say: "the extreme ends of the political spectrum are deeply problematic . . . neoliberalism simply perpetuates existing economic and political systems and offers no real solutions to the problems of market failure, the radical position appears wildly optimistic about the potential for localism to resolve . . . the forces of globalization" (p. 13). In advocating a "middle way" or "transformationalist" position that contrasts to fatalism on both sides, they argue that globalization is not inevitable, that it could go in many directions, and that it is "not beyond regulation and control." What is required, they believe, is engagement and organization of a new multilateralist coalition working for what they call "cosmopolitan social democracy." At its core is stronger global governance and control over finance and markets, greater transparency and rule of law, and global peacekeeping and cooperation.

Concluding this volume are four selections elucidating mechanisms for how globalization affects transnational issues, as well as describing how networks of social movements are negotiating these forces. Focusing on environmental movements, labor movements, and women's movements, these works contribute both empirical and theoretical substance to the literature on globalization and mobilization. Evans' concluding chapter compares and contrasts empirical evidence of these particular movements' recent global histories to explain the current and future role of what he calls "counter-hegemonic movements."

Political scientists Margaret Keck of Johns Hopkins University and Kathryn Sikkink of the University of Minnesota built a now widely used framework for understanding the new international networks of Non-governmental Organizations (NGOs) in their 1997 book *Activists Across Borders*. Keck and Sikkink call these international webs of networks of activists "transnational advocacy networks." Rather than simply focusing on policies, transnational advocacy networks work to establish common frames that can work toward changing institutional arrangements and redirect or reframe dominant discourses and debates. These networks emerge when there is a need for groups to "break out" of a local or national context to effect change, when groups perceive that "going global" will further their political interests, and when channels for doing so either exist or emerge. Transnational advocacy networks also have a distinct set of common tactics such as rapid, international dissemination of information, evoking symbols, leveraging the power of stronger actors to benefit weaker ones, and mobilizing international alliances to press for accountability by the targets of their grievances. Keck and Sikkink argue that transnational advocacy networks evidence that global civil society is not emerging through the diffusion of Western ideals, but rather through an emergent global arena for identifying the inconsistencies of and contesting these ideals.

Illustrating the factors they identify as contributing to a transnational advocacy network's efficacy, the second chapter we excerpt from Keck and Sikkink's book tells the story of how international networks of environmental activists emerged and organized as transnational advocacy networks. The cases recounted here, of activists in Brazil's Amazon region and in Indonesia's Sarawak rainforest, were landmark battles that had lasting repercussions throughout the international system. The Amazon case saw Indians cooperating with Brazilian and US environmentalists to lobby the US Senate to cut off funding for key programs at the World Bank. These innovative efforts led to reforms of international funding agencies that continue to be contested. These cases reinforce what the other selections addressing "counter-hegemonic globalization" stress: only strength initially garnered through local level agency and effectiveness enables transnational movements effectiveness to win broader victories.

Much of the globalization literature portrays labor unions as the biggest loser emerging from globalization. Nonetheless, many are carefully watching organized labor's response to industrial restructuring for signs of cross-border organizing that can make differences in the fate of workers. We include here an insightful exchange of six scholars during two forums that appeared in two outlets of the Political Economy of the World System section of the American Sociological Association: an online journal and a section newsletter. These two short dialogs debate the future for labor unions in this age of globalized production, and the authors come to surprisingly different conclusions. The first two pieces take up the question of whether unions will be able to organize successfully across borders. Ralph Armbruster gives two cases where women workers made significant gains even against all odds and academic predictions. Bradley Nash describes how even mistrusted labor organizations like the American Federation of Labor and Congress of Industrial Organizations (AFL-CIO) – which supported US foreign policy in defeating radical worker movements around the world – need to be reformed and trusted to work internationally. The final three pieces respond to the question of whether "the inclusion of labor standards in trade treaties would improve workers' conditions internationally." Richard Applebaum is very positive about labor standards. Jennifer Bickham-Mendez has far less faith because male-dominated unions largely exclude women workers from key decision-making. Finally, Edna Bonacich argues that these standards may only protect workers in rich nations, since they will not be effective in nations without a functioning welfare state. Rather than being the final word on these important questions, these pieces merely open issues of the fate of workers on both sides of the global divide for discussion.

Manisha Desai of the University of Illinois was coeditor of an influential volume entitled *Women's Activism and Globalization: Linking Local Struggles and Transnational Politics* (2002).

In her chapter which follows, Desai offers an impressive comparative analysis of the ongoing, dynamic interplay between structural forces affecting women's lives over the last several decades, and the agency with which various women's groups have confronted these structural challenges. She pays very close attention to the difficulties in linking the interests and agendas of women around the world whose experiences are often vastly different. She demonstrates that women's groups have responded to opportunities for transnational organizing in creative, albeit often ephemeral ways. For example, while structural adjustment policies exposed women to harsher economic conditions and global competition among workers, at the same time the increased exposure to workplaces of all types allowed women to better organize not just over workplace issues, but in much broader arenas as well. Moreover, Desai's wide-ranging review of women's experiences and responses illustrates clearly how adept various women's groups have been at forging solidarity among groups, as well as in solving the day-to-day demands of survival. Finally, in explaining how women's agency has evolved relative to structural adjustment and globalization, she offers historical reviews of the effects of structural adjustment on women, as well as the evolution of United Nations policies toward women. Both of these accounts are important to our understandings of the flexibility of women's responses to struggle and subordination, particularly given the immense diversity in terms of race, class, and ethnicity that coincides with gender.

Peter Evans concludes this volume with a tour de force defining and recounting the possibilities and challenges faced by those involved in leading what he calls "counter-hegemonic globalization." He describes "counter-hegemonic globalization" as a collective project led by coalitions and networks of actors, increasingly freed by technology from geographic and temporal constraints, who work across borders and issues to destabilize countervailing forms of global domination. Essential to this emergent network's vitality, he argues, is a strong linkage between local needs and "strategies that leverage global connections" which can challenge entrenched institutional and organizational power.

In addition to explaining the role of organizations that centralize "counter-hegemonic globalization," such as the World Social Forum and Advanced Tradewars Tactical Assault and Combat (ATTAC), Evans also reviews the recent history of mobilization over women's, environmental, and labor issues. He is decidedly more pessimistic about labor movements' role in "counter-hegemonic globalization" compared to the potential of either environmental or women's movements. The transnational women's movement has been the most dynamic force of "counter-hegemonic globalization" through seeking creative and fruitful North–South linkages, as well as closely connecting general movement ideals to real-life problems and among women from diverse cultural backgrounds. Evans attributes much of this success, as well as transnational environmental protection movements' success, to the early and long-standing de facto organization these groups enjoy through United Nations programs and policies, even if this transnational discourse was often simply to critique the "colonialist attitudes" embedded in many United Nations agendas.

Although Evans argues that there is no more logical fit for "counter-hegemonic globalization" than protecting the environment, he also concludes that environmental struggles most clearly illustrate the significant obstacles to "counter-hegemonic globalization." In this arena, North–South divisions and variations in local concerns are most evident. Nonetheless, Evans remains relatively optimistic about transnational environmental movements' abilities to effect tangible changes because their "toolkit" for activism is powerful: an agenda to "save the planet" and collective action frames backed by "scientific evidence." Referring specifically to leadership on the issue of climate change, Evans observes that "global governance institutions have given transnational social movements an opportunity to shape an emerging regulatory regime, which has the potential to substantially modify the market logic of neo-liberal globalization." It is precisely this capability to reframe issues and to affect modest shifts in power that defines the collective result of "counter-hegemonic globalization."

22 The Antiglobalization Movement (2005)

Jeffrey D. Sachs

At the start of the twenty-first century, Enlightenment hopes for progress embodied in the Millennium Declaration and the Millennium Development Goals have clashed head on with war, AIDS, and the still unmet challenge of extreme poverty in large parts of Africa, Latin America, and Asia. The clash of high rhetoric and poor results has led to the antiglobalization movement, which burst forth dramatically into public view on the streets of Seattle in November 1999.

I have intersected repeatedly with the antiglobalization movement from its very inception. I experienced the very first 1999 street demonstrations personally, having been in Seattle that day for a Gates Foundation conference on information technology for the poor that was running alongside the ministerial meeting of the World Trade Organization (WTO). It was the WTO event that brought the protesters to Seattle. As I crossed Seattle's downtown streets filled with protesters of every variety – antiwar, antitrade, and especially anticorporate – I whispered to my walking companion, Bill Gates, Sr., the father of Microsoft founder Bill Gates, Jr., and president of the Gates Foundation, that it was probably just as well that he was not recognized by the crowds! The profound irony, of course, is that the Gates Foundation is the world's leading foundation for promoting public health in poor countries, yet to the antiglobalization movement, multinational companies like Microsoft are part of the problem, not the solution.

From Seattle onward, street demonstrations have greeted just about every major international conference. Street protesters have forced the G8 leaders, ostensibly the world's most powerful, to hold their annual conferences in the not-so-splendid isolation of islands, mountaintops, forests, and other sheltered venues as far away from protesters as possible. The World Social Forum in Porto Alegre, Brazil, now shares the stage with the Davos World Economic Forum. World business leaders compete with social activists for the upper hand in global reporting on privatization. The IMF and World Bank have shortened their annual meetings from around a week to just a couple of days of business.

The antiglobalization movement has made its mark, and in my view, mostly for the good (except for the moments of violence that fringe elements of the movement incite). I applaud the overall movement for exposing the hypocrisies and glaring shortcomings of global governance and for ending years of self-congratulation by the rich and powerful. Before Seattle, the G8, IMF, and World Bank meetings were occasions for unqualified praise of globalization, and for the self-serving accolades of bankers and international financiers on their contribution to the spread of prosperity. Between the speeches and endless cocktail parties, there was little said about the world's poor, the AIDS pandemic, dispossessed minorities, women without rights, and human-made environmental degradation. Since Seattle, the agenda of ending extreme poverty, extending human rights, and addressing environmental degradation has been back on the international agenda and has attracted global media attention, albeit sporadically.

Nonetheless, I oppose many of the specific positions of antiglobalization leaders, even if I favor their moral fervor over the complacency of the rich. The antiglobalization movement has been fueled by legitimate moral outrage, but it has often been directed toward superficial targets, in my opinion. An anticorporate animus lies at the core of the movement, a belief that multinational corporations such as Microsoft, Coke, McDonald's, Pfizer, and Royal Dutch Shell, to name just a few, are the main villains in causing extreme poverty and environmental degradation. Policy recommendations of the movement have often prescribed classic protectionism, ostensibly to protect poor countries from the exploitative reach of rich corporations. The movement has especially targeted the World Trade Organization as the institution that allows the world's leading companies to go about their global business.

The views central to the antiglobalization movement are not new. They remind me very much of what I encountered in New Delhi in 1994, when Indian academics expressed grave reservations about the liberalization of trade and investment that had begun in India in 1991. Those views were passé then, and are more so today. By now the antiglobalization movement should see that globalization, more than anything else, has reduced the numbers of extreme poor in India by two hundred million and in China by three hundred million since 1990. Far from being exploited by multinational companies, these countries and many others like them have achieved unprecedented rates of economic growth on the basis of foreign direct investment (FDI) and the export-led growth that followed.

In my view, the antiglobalization movement leaders have the right moral fervor and ethical viewpoint, but the wrong diagnosis of the deeper problems. If they would ponder the data showing the amount of cumulative foreign direct investment per person from 1992 to 2002 in countries of Latin America, Africa, and Asia, they would see that countries with higher levels of FDI per person are also the countries with higher GNP per capita. Other studies confirm that high rates of foreign direct investment inflows have been associated with rapid economic growth. Africa's problems, I have noted repeatedly, are not caused by exploitation by global investors but rather by its economic isolation, its status as a continent largely bypassed by the forces of globalization. The same is true with trade. Countries with open trade generally have grown more rapidly than countries with closed trade, and rising per capita incomes in most countries have generally been associated with a rise in the ratio of trade (exports plus imports) to GDP. Following the end of colonial rule after World War II, some countries chose open trade policies, whereas most developing countries chose protectionism. The open economies decisively outpaced the closed economies. By the early 1990s, almost all developing countries had opted for open trade, dropping decades of high-tariff and quota barriers. There is simply no evidence whatsoever that trade protectionism or the absence of multinational companies does a whit to end extreme poverty.

So why has the movement taken on trade and corporations as the first line of attack? First, because in truth many companies have behaved badly. The protesters have succeeded in illuminating and cleaning up bad or even corrupt corporate practices. US and European companies that buy garments and apparel from low-wage plants no doubt treat their workers with greater civility and dignity today because of the protesters. Oil companies that once bribed African leaders with impunity think twice, or not at all, about doing so today, aware now of protesters' eyes upon them and the direct line between protesters' eyes, investor resistance, and bad corporate publicity. Drug company executives who at one time bellyached that they should have full freedom to price their patent-protected drugs as they saw fit, now give their drugs away or sell them on a zero-profit basis as a result of successful activism.

But the anticorporate, antitrade attitudes have also resulted from a knee-jerk antipathy to capitalism that reflects a more profound misunderstanding. Too many protesters do not know that even Adam Smith shared their moral sentiments and practical calls for social improvement, that even proponents of trade and investment can also believe in government-led actions to address the unmet needs of the poor and the environment. Too many protesters do not know that it is possible to combine faith in the power of trade and markets with understanding of their limitations as well. The movement is too pessimistic about the possibilities of capitalism with a human face, in which the remarkable power of trade and investment can be harnessed while acknowledging and addressing limitations through compensatory collective actions.

At a fundamental level, the global environmental crisis is not the fault of BP or Shell or ExxonMobil, and the AIDS pandemic is not the fault of Pfizer or Merck. Nor will the solutions to these crises be found by bloodying the leading energy or pharmaceutical companies. The solutions will be found in public policies, at national and international levels, that properly manage the emissions of climate-changing gases and that properly make life-saving medications available to the poor who cannot afford them. The antiglobalization movement is wrong to suppose that private companies are the ones to design the rules of the game. If governments would do their job in setting up the right rules, major international companies would play a vital role in solving problems. After all, these companies employ the world's best technologies, leading internal research units, and organizational and logistical operations that are superior to almost any public organizations in the world. They know, in short, how to get the job done when the incentives are in place for them to do the right thing.

Where the antiglobalization movement has a powerful point to stress is how multinational corporations often go well beyond their market demands to maximize shareholder wealth subject to the market rules of the game and, instead, expend substantial efforts, often hidden under the table, to make the rules of the game themselves. Economic reasoning justifies market-based behavior by companies if the rules of the game are sound. There is nothing in economic reasoning to justify letting the companies themselves set the rules of the game through lobbying, campaign financing, and dominance of government policies.

Toward an Enlightened Globalization

When all is said and done, however, the antiglobalization movement should mobilize its vast commitment and moral force into a proglobalization movement on behalf of globalization that addresses the needs of the poorest of the poor, the global environment, and the spread of democracy. It is the kind of globalization championed by the Enlightenment – a globalization of democracies, multilateralism, science and technology, and a global economic system designed to meet human needs. We could call this an Enlightened Globalization.

What, then, would be the focus of a mass public movement aimed at an Enlightened Globalization? It would be, first and foremost, a focus on the behavior of the rich governments, especially the most powerful and wayward of the rich governments, the United States. It would insist that the United States and other rich countries honor their commitments to help the poor escape from poverty, as well as honor their commitments to limit environmental degradation including human-made climate change and the loss of biodiversity. Such a movement would continue to shine a spotlight on corporate responsibility, but would urge more rather than less investment by major multinational companies in the poorest countries. Instead of focusing on blocking trade and investment, it would insist that the World Trade Organization follow through on the political commitments made at Doha and elsewhere to ensure that the poorest countries have access to the markets of the richest.

Perhaps most important in the immediate future, such a movement would press the United States to end its reveries of empire and unilateralism and rejoin the world community in multilateral processes. The neoconservative calls for a US empire are fantasies, but very dangerous ones. They misunderstand two basic points about our world. First, the United States is but 4.5 percent of the world's population and around 20 percent of its income when measured at purchasing power parity. By 2050, the share of population may decline slightly, but the share of GNP is likely to decline rather sharply, perhaps to a mere 10 percent of income. The United States simply does not hold a margin of economic advantage sufficient to sustain any real attempt at global empire, however good or bad such an idea might be. Ironically, the small-scale war in Iraq badly stretched US military personnel and the public finances. And because the public was not at all interested in actually paying for the war through taxation, the Bush administration has had to finance the war through budget deficits.

Second, while the United States has vast military power, the use of that power for political advantage is rather small. As the Iraq war demonstrated, the United States can conquer, but it cannot rule. What the neoconservatives simply did not understand is that the era when foreign populations might conceivably tolerate US rule ended a half century ago. The United States was not greeted in Iraq as a liberator, but rather as an occupier, a turn of events that was utterly predictable except, apparently, for neoconservatives divorced from modern realities. The leading political ideology of our time is nationalism and self-determination, and that ideology became vastly stronger throughout the twentieth century in the developing world as literacy spread and the arbitrary and cynical nature of colonial rule became painfully evident.

[. . .]

23 Reconstructing World Order: Towards Cosmopolitan Social Democracy (2002)

David Held and Anthony McGrew

The 'great globalization debate' identifies some of the most fundamental issues of our time. It poses key questions about the organization of human affairs and the trajectory of global social change. It also raises matters which go to the centre of political discussion, illuminating the strategic choices societies confront and the constraints which define the possibilities of effective political action.

Are the principal accounts of globalization elaborated here fundamentally at odds and contradictory in all respects, or is a productive synthesis possible? . . .

In the first instance, the debate between the globalizers and sceptics raises profound questions of interpretation. It demonstrates that facts do not speak for themselves, and depend for their meaning on complex interpretative frameworks. There are clashes involving the conceptualization and interpretation of some of the most critical evidence. However, it would be wrong to conclude from this that the marshalled evidence is of secondary importance, often the kind of evidence proffered by both sides differs markedly. For example, sceptics put primary emphasis on the organization of production and trade (stressing the geographical rootedness of MNCs and the marginal changes in trade–GDP ratios over the course of the twentieth century), while globalists tend to focus on financial deregulation and the explosive growth of global financial markets over the last twenty-five years. Sceptics stress the continuing primacy of the national interest and the cultural traditions of national communities, while globalists point to the growing significance of transnational political problems – such as worldwide pollution, global warming and financial crises – which create a growing sense of the common fate of humankind. A considered response to the debate must weigh all these considerations before coming to a settled view.

Secondly, the debate demonstrates that there is something to be learned from both sides; it is implausible to maintain that either side comprises mere rhetoric or ideology. The sceptical case has significant historical depth and needs to be carefully dissected if the globalists' position is to be adequately defended. Many of the empirical claims raised by the sceptics' arguments, for example concerning the historical significance of contemporary trade and direct investment flows, require detailed examination. But having said this, the globalist interpretation in its various forms does illuminate important transformations going on in the spatial organization of power – the changing nature of communications, the diffusion and speeding up of technical change, the spread of capitalist economic development, the extension of global governance arrangements – even if its understanding of these matters sometimes exaggerates their scale and impact.

Thirdly, each position has different strengths and weaknesses. The leading claims of the globalists are at their strongest when focused on institutional and processual change in the domains of economics (the establishment of a global trading system, the integration of financial markets, and the spread of transnational production systems), politics (the development of global political processes and the environment of layers of governance across political boundaries) and the environment (the challenge of environmental degradation, particularly affecting the global commons and biodiversity). But they are at their most vulnerable when considering the movements of people, their allegiances and their cultural and moral identities. For the available evidence suggests that migration is only just reaching the levels today that it attained in the late nineteenth century (measured in terms of extent and intensity); that the role of national (and local) cultures remains central to public life in nearly all political communities; and that imported foreign products are constantly read and reinterpreted in novel ways by national audiences, that is, they become rapidly indigenized (Miller 1992; Liebes and Katz 1993; Thompson 1995). Given the deep roots of national cultures and ethnohistories, and the many ways they are often refashioned, the fact that there is no common global way of thinking can hardly be a surprise. Despite the vast flows of information, imagery and people around the world, there are only a few signs, at best, of a universal or global history in the making, and few signs of a decline in the importance of nationalism.

There has been a shift, as the globalists argue, from government to global governance, from the modern state to a multilayered system of power and authority, from relatively discrete national communication and economic systems to their more complex and diverse enmeshment at regional and global levels. On the other hand, there are few grounds for thinking that a concomitant widespread pluralization of political identities has taken place. One exception to this is to be found among the elites of the global order – the networks of experts and specialists, senior administrative personnel and transnational business executives – and those who track and contest their activities, the loose constellation of social movements, trade unionists and (a few) politicians and intellectuals. However, even the latter groups have a significant diversity of interest and purpose, a diversity clearly manifest in the broad range of those who constitute the 'anti-globalization' protesters of Seattle, Genoa and elsewhere. The globalists' emphasis on the transformation of political identities is overstated. What one commentator noted about the European Union can be adapted to apply, in many respects, to the rest of the world: the central paradox is that governance is becoming increasingly a multilevel, intricately institutionalized and spatially dispersed activity, while representation, loyalty and identity remain stubbornly rooted in traditional ethnic, regional and national communities (Wallace 1999: 21).

One important qualification needs to be added to the above argument, one which focuses on generational change. While those who have some commitment to the global order as a whole and to the institutions of global governance constitute a distinct minority, a generational divide is evident. Compared to the generations brought up in the years prior to 1939, those born after the Second World War are more likely to see themselves as internationalists, to support the UN system and to be in favour of the free movement of migrants and trade. . . .

Fourthly, while there are very significant differences between the globalists and sceptics, it is important to note some common ground. The debate does not simply comprise ships passing in the night. Indeed, both sides would accept that:

1   There has been marked growth in recent decades in economic interconnectedness within and among regions, albeit with multifaceted and uneven consequences across different communities.
2   Interregional and global (political, economic and cultural) competition challenges old hierarchies and generates new inequalities of wealth, power, privilege and knowledge.
3   Transnational and transborder problems, such as the spread of genetically modified foodstuffs, money laundering and global terrorism, have become increasingly salient, calling into question aspects of the traditional role, functions and institutions of accountability of national government.
4   There has been an expansion of international governance at regional and global levels – from the EU to the WTO – which poses significant normative questions about the kind of world order being constructed and whose interests it serves.
5   These developments require new modes of thinking about politics, economics and cultural change. They also require imaginative responses from politicians and policy-makers about the future possibilities and forms of effective political regulation and democratic accountability.

All sides would accept that there has been a significant shift in the links and relations among political communities. That is to say, that there has been a growth in communication, economic and political connections within and across states and regions; that transnational and transborder problems have become pressing across the world; that there has been an expansion in the number and role of intergovernmental organizations, international nongovernmental organizations, and social movements in regional and global affairs; and that existing political mechanisms and institutions, anchored in nation-states, will be insufficient in the future to handle the pressing challenges of regional and global problems centred, for instance, on global inequalities and social injustice. In order to draw out the significance of these points of agreement, it is helpful to focus on the challenges to traditional conceptions of political community posed by global social, economic and political change.

The New Context of Political Community

Political communities can no longer be considered (if they ever could with any validity) as simply 'discrete worlds' or as self-enclosed political spaces; they are enmeshed in complex structures of overlapping forces, relations and networks. Clearly, these are structured by inequality and hierarchy, as the sceptics insist. However, even the most powerful among them – including the most powerful states – do not remain unaffected by the changing conditions and processes of regional and global entrenchment. A few points can be empha-sized to clarify further the changing relations between modern nation-states. All indicate an increase in the extensiveness, intensity, velocity and impact of international and trans-national relations, and all suggest important questions about the evolving character of political community.

The locus of effective political power can no longer be assumed to be simply national governments – effective power is shared and bartered by diverse forces and agencies at national, regional and international levels. All parties agree on this. Furthermore, the idea of a political community of fate – of a self-determining collectivity – can no longer meaning-fully be located within the boundaries of a single nation-state alone. Some of the most fun-damental forces and processes which determine the nature of life chances – from the organization of world trade to global warming – are now beyond the reach of individual nation-states to resolve by themselves. The political world at the start of the twenty-first century is marked by a significant series of new types of political externalities or 'boundary problems'. . . . In a world where powerful states make decisions not just for their peoples but for others as well, and where transnational actors and forces cut across the boundaries of national communities in diverse ways, the questions of who should be accountable to whom, and on what basis, do not easily resolve themselves. Political space for the development and pursuit of effective government and the accountability of power is no longer coterminous with a delimited political territory. Forms of political organization now involve a complex deterritorialization and reterritorialization of political authority (Rosenau 1997).

Contemporary global change is associated with a transformation of state power as the roles and functions of states are rearticulated, reconstituted and re-embedded at the inter-section of regionalizing and globalizing networks and systems. The simple formulations of the loss, diminution or erosion of state power can misrepresent this change. Indeed, such a language involves a failure to conceptualize adequately the nature of power and its complex manifestations, since it represents a crude zero-sum view of power. The latter conception is particularly unhelpful in attempting to understand the apparently contradic-tory position of states under contemporary conditions. For while global economic change is engendering, for instance, a reconfiguration of state–market relations, states and inter-national public authorities are deeply implicated in this very process (for example, through the weakening or removal of national capital controls). Global economic change by no means necessarily translates into a diminution of state power; rather, it is altering the condi-tions under which state power can be exercised. In other domains, such as the military, states have adopted an activist posture through the creation of alliances and coalitions, while in the political domain they have been central to the explosive growth and institu-tionalization of regional and global governance. These are not developments which can be explained convincingly in the language of the decline, erosion or loss of state power *per se*. In addition, such formulations mistakenly presume that state power was much greater in previous epochs; and states, especially in the developed world, on almost every measure, are far more powerful than their predecessors (Mann 1997). The apparent simultaneous weakening and expansion of state power is symptomatic of an underlying structural trans-formation – a global shift in the organization of power and authority. This is nowhere so evident as in respect of state sovereignty and autonomy, which constitute the very founda-tions of the modern state.

[. . .]

We call this interpretation of shifts in relations of power neither globalist nor sceptic but transformationalist. It accepts a modified version of the globalization argument, emphasizing that while contemporary patterns of global political, economic and communication flows are historically unprecedented, the direction of these remains uncertain, since globalization is a contingent historical process replete with conflicts and tensions. At issue is a dynamic and open-ended conception of where globalization might be leading and the kind of world order which it might prefigure. In comparison with the sceptical and globalist accounts, the transformationalist position makes no claims about the future trajectory of globalization; nor does it evaluate the present in relation to some single, fixed ideal-type 'globalized world', whether a global market or a global civilization. Rather, the transformationalist account emphasizes that globalization is a long-term historical process which is inscribed with challenges and which is significantly shaped by conjunctural factors.

At the core of the transformationalist case is a belief that contemporary globalization is reconstituting or 're-engineering' the power, functions and authority of national governments. While not disputing that many states still retain the ultimate legal claim to effective supremacy over what occurs within their own territories, the transformationalist position holds that this should be juxtaposed with, and understood in relation to, the expanding jurisdiction of institutions of international governance and the constraints of, as well as the obligations derived from, international law. . . . The modern institution of territorially circumscribed sovereign rule appears somewhat anomalous juxtaposed with the transnational organization of many aspects of contemporary economic and social life (Sandel 1996). Globalization, in this account, is associated with a transformation or an 'unbundling' of the relationship between sovereignty, territoriality and political power (Ruggie 1993; Sassen 1996).

While for many people – politicians, political activists and academics – contemporary globalization is associated with new limits to politics and the erosion of state power, the argument developed here is critical of such political fatalism. For contemporary globalization has not only triggered or reinforced the significant politicization of a growing array of issue areas, but it has been accompanied by an extraordinary growth of institutionalized arenas and networks of political mobilization, surveillance, decision-making and regulatory activity which transcend national political jurisdictions. This has expanded enormously the capacity for, and scope of, political activity and the exercise of political authority. In this sense, globalization is not beyond regulation and control. Globalization does not prefigure the 'end of politics' so much as its continuation by new means. . . .

At the heart of these challenges lies the expansion in transborder political issues which erode clear-cut distinctions between domestic and foreign affairs. . . . If the most powerful geopolitical forces are not to settle many pressing matters simply in terms of their own objectives and by virtue of their power, then existing structures and mechanisms of accountability need to be reconsidered. Environmental issues illuminate this matter well.

[. . .]

In response to the intensification of, and public awareness of, environmental issues, there has been an interlinked process of cultural and political globalization. This can be exemplified by the emergence of new scientific and intellectual networks; new environmental movements organized transnationally with transnational concerns; and new international institutions, regimes and conventions such as those agreed in 1992 at the Earth Summit in Brazil and in subsequent follow-up meetings. Unfortunately, none of the latter have as yet been able to acquire sufficient political power, domestic support or international authority to do more than (at best) limit the worst excesses of some of the worst global environmental threats.

. . . It is clearer than ever that the fortunes of political communities and peoples can no longer be simply understood in exclusively national or territorial terms. In a world in which global warming connects the long-term fate of many Pacific islands to the actions of tens of millions of private motorists across the globe, the conventional territorial conception of political community appears profoundly inadequate. Globalization weaves together, in highly complex and abstract systems, the fates of households, communities and peoples in distant regions of the globe (McGrew 1997: 237). . . .

Towards a New Politics of Globalization

The contemporary phase of global change is transforming the very foundations of world order by reconstituting traditional forms of sovereign statehood, political community and international governance. But these processes are neither inevitable nor by any means fully secure. Globalization involves a shift away from a purely state-centric politics to a new and more complex form of multilayered global politics. This is the basis on and through which political authority and mechanisms of regulation are being articulated and rearticulated. As a result, the contemporary world order is best understood as a highly complex, interconnected and contested order in which the interstate system is increasingly embedded within an evolving system of multilayered regional and global governance. There are multiple, overlapping political processes at work at the present historical conjuncture.

At the beginning of the twenty-first century there are strong reasons for believing that the traditional international order of states, in E. H. Carr's words, 'cannot be restored, and a drastic change of outlook is unavoidable' (1981: 237). Such changes of outlook are clearly delineated in the contest between the principal variants or cleavages in the politics of globalization. The extreme ends of the political spectrum are deeply problematic. Whereas neoliberalism simply perpetuates existing economic and political systems and offers no real solutions to the problems of market failure, the radical position appears wildly optimistic about the potential for localism to resolve, or engage with, the governance agenda generated by the forces of globalization. How can such a politics cope with the challenges posed by overlapping communities of fate? . . .

We wish to refer to this overlapping ground as the domain of cosmopolitan social democracy. This is because it seeks to nurture some of the most important values of social democracy – the rule of law, political equality, democratic politics, social justice, social solidarity and economic effectiveness – while applying them to the new global constellation of economics and politics. Accordingly, the project of cosmopolitan social democracy can be conceived as a basis for uniting around the promotion of the impartial administration of law at the international level; greater transparency, accountability and democracy in global governance; a deeper commitment to social justice in the pursuit of a more equitable distribution of the world's resources and human security; the protection and reinvention of community at diverse levels (from the local to the global); and the regulation of the global economy through the public management of global financial and trade flows, the provision of global public goods, and the engagement of leading stakeholders in corporate governance. This common ground in global politics contains clear possibilities of dialogue and accommodation between different segments of the 'globalization/anti-globalization' political spectrum, although this is clearly contested by opinion at either end of the spectrum. In addition, some of the positions represented by the statists/protectionists could be part of the dialogue; for clearly 'cosmopolitan social democracy' requires strong competent governance at all levels – local, national, regional and global. Table 1 summarizes the project of cosmopolitan social democracy. It does not present an all-or-nothing choice, but rather lays down a direction of change with clear points of orientation, in the short and long term.

The common ground represented by cosmopolitan social democracy provides a basis for a little optimism that global social justice is not simply a utopian goal. Moreover, it can be conceived as establishing the necessary ethical and institutional foundations for a progressive shift in the direction of a more cosmopolitan world order. In a world of overlapping communities and power systems, global issues are an inescapable element of the agenda of all polities. The principal political question of our times is how these issues are best addressed or governed, and how global public goods can best be provided. Cosmopolitan social democracy provides a framework for further thought and political action on these questions, in a domain of overlapping ideas which unites a broad body of progressive opinion.

The political space for the development of these ideas has to be made, and is being made, by the activities of all those forces that are engaged in the pursuit of the rule of law at all levels of governance; greater coordination and accountability of the leading forces of globalization; the opening up of IGOs to key stakeholders and participants; greater equity in the distribution of the world's resources; the protection of human rights and fundamental freedoms; sustainable development across generations; and peaceful dispute settlement in leading geopolitical conflicts. This is not a political project that starts from nowhere. It is, in fact, deeply rooted in the political world shaped and formed after the Holocaust and the Second World War. Moreover, it can be built on many of the achievements of multilateralism (from the founding of the UN system to the development of the EU), international law (from the human rights regime to the establishment of the International Criminal Court) and multilayered governance (from the development of local government in cities and subnational regions to the dense web of international policy-making forums).

The story of our increasingly global order is not a singular one. Globalization is not, and has never been, a one-dimensional phenomenon. While there has been a massive expansion of global markets which has altered the political terrain, increasing exit options for capital of all kinds and increasing the relative power of corporate interests (see Held et al. 1999: chs 3–5; Held and McGrew 2000: ch. 25), the story of globalization is far from simply economic. Since 1945 there has been a significant entrenchment of cosmopolitan values concerning the equal dignity and worth of all human beings in international rules and regulations; the reconnection of international law and morality, as sovereignty is no longer merely cast as effective power but increasingly as legitimate authority defined in terms of the maintenance of human rights and democratic values; the establishment of complex

Table 1 Towards Cosmopolitan Social Democracy

Guiding ethical principles/core values	Global social justice, democracy, universal human rights, human security, rule of law, transnational solidarity
Short-term measures	*Governance* • Reform of global governance: representative Security Council; establishment of Human Security Council (to coordinate global development policies); Global Civil Society Forum; strengthened systems of global accountability; enhancement of national and regional governance infrastructures and capacities; enhanced parliamentary scrutiny *Economy* • Regulating global markets: selective capital controls; regulation of offshore financial centres; voluntary codes of conduct for MNCs • Promoting development: abolition of debt for highly indebted poor countries (HIPCs); meeting UN aid targets of 0.7% GNP; fair trade rules; removal of EU and US subsidies of agriculture and textiles *Security* • Strengthening global humanitarian protection capacities; implementation of existing global poverty reduction and human development commitments and policies; strengthening of arms control and arms trade regulation
Long-term transformations	*Governance* • Double' democratization (national to suprastate governance); enhanced global public goods provision; global citizenship *Economy* • Taming global markets: World Financial Authority; mandatory codes of conduct for MNCs; global tax mechanism; global competition authority • Market correcting; mandatory global labour and environmental standards; foreign investment codes and standards; redistributive and compensatory measures; commodity price and supply agreements • Market promoting: privileged market access for developing countries; convention on global labour mobility *Security* • Global social charter; permanent peacekeeping and humanitarian emergency forces; social exclusion and equity impact reviews of all global development measures
Institutional/political conditions	Activist states, global progressive coalition (involving key Western and developing states and civil society forces), strong multilateral institutions, open regionalism, global civil society, redistributive regimes, regulation of global markets, transnational public sphere

governance systems, regional and global; and the growing recognition that the public good – whether conceived as financial stability, environmental protection, or global egalitarianism – requires coordinated multilateral action if it is to be achieved in the long term (see Held 2002). These developments need to be and can be built upon.

A coalition of political groupings could emerge to push these achievements further, comprising European countries with strong liberal and social democratic traditions; liberal groups in the US polity which support multilateralism and the rule of law in international affairs; developing countries struggling for freer and fairer trade rules in the world economic order; non-governmental organizations, from Amnesty International to Oxfam, campaigning for a more just, democratic and equitable world order; transnational social movements contesting the nature and form of contemporary globalization; and those economic forces that desire a more stable and managed global economic order.

Europe could have a special role in advancing the cause of cosmopolitan social democracy (McGrew 2001, 2002). As the home of both social democracy and a historic experiment in governance beyond the state, Europe has direct experience in considering the appropriate designs for more effective and accountable suprastate governance. It offers novel ways of thinking about governance beyond the state which encourage a (relatively) more democratic – as opposed to more neoliberal – vision of global governance. Moreover, Europe is in a strategic position (with strong links west and east, north and south) to build global constituencies for reform of the architecture and functioning of global governance. Through interregional dialogues, it has the potential to mobilize new crossregional coalitions as a countervailing influence to those constituencies that oppose reform, including unilateralist forces in the US.

Of course, this is not to suggest that the EU should broker a crude anti-US coalition of transnational and international forces. On the contrary, it is crucial to recognize the complexity of US domestic politics and the existence of progressive social, political and economic forces seeking to advance a rather different kind of world order from that championed by the Republican right of the political spectrum (Nye 2002). Despite its unilateralist inclinations, it is worth recalling that public opinion in the US (especially the younger generation) has been quite consistently in favour of the UN and multilateralism, and slightly more so than European publics (Norris 2000). Any European political strategy to promote a broad-based coalition for a new global covenant must seek to enlist the support of these progressive forces within the US polity, while it must resist within its own camp the siren voices now calling with renewed energy for the exclusive re-emergence of national identities, ethnic purity and protectionism.

Although some of the interests of those groupings which might coalesce around a movement for cosmopolitan social democracy would inevitably diverge on a wide range of issues, there is potentially an important overlapping sphere of concern among them for the strengthening of multilateralism, building new institutions for providing global public goods, regulating global markets, deepening accountability, protecting the environment and ameliorating urgently social injustices that kill thousands of men, women and children daily. Of course, how far they can unite around these concerns – and can overcome fierce opposition from well-entrenched geopolitical and geoeconomic interests – remains to be seen. The stakes are very high, but so too are the potential gains for human security and development if the aspirations for global democracy and social justice can be realized.

REFERENCES

Carr, E. H. (1981) *The Twenty Years' Crisis 1919–1939*. London: Papermac.

Held, D. (2002) Law of states, law of peoples: three models of sovereignty. *Legal Theory* 8(1).

Held, D. and McGrew, A. G. (eds) (2000) *The Global Transformations Reader*. Cambridge: Polity.

Held, D., McGrew, A. G., Goldblatt, D. and Perraton, J. (1999) *Global Transformations: Politics, Economics and Culture*. Cambridge: Polity.

Liebes, T. and Katz, E. (1993) *The Export of Meaning: Cross-Cultural Readings of Dallas*. Cambridge: Polity.

McGrew, A. G. (ed.) (1997) *The Transformation of Democracy? Globalization and Territorial Democracy*. Cambridge: Polity.

McGrew, A. (2001) Making globalization work for the poor: the European contribution. Seminar paper, Swedish Ministry of Foreign Affairs.

—— (2002) Between two worlds: Europe in a globalizing era. *Government and Opposition* 37(3) (Summer).

Mann, M. (1997) Has globalization ended the rise and rise of the nation-state? *Review of International Political Economy* 4(3).

Miller, D. (1992) The young and the restless in Trinidad: a case of the local and the global in mass consumption. In R. Silverstone and E. Hirsch (eds), *Consuming Technology*. London: Routledge.

Norris, P. (2000) Global governance and cosmopolitan citizens. In J. S. Nye and J. D. Donahue (eds), *Governance in a Globalizing World*. Washington, DC: Brookings Institution Press.

Nye, J. S. (2002) *The Paradox of American Power*. Oxford: Oxford University Press.

Rosenau, J. N. (1997) *Along the Domestic-Foreign Frontier*. Cambridge: Cambridge University Press.

Ruggie, J. (1993) Territoriality and beyond. *International Organization* 41(1).

Sandel, M. (1996) *Democracy's Discontent*. Cambridge, MA: Harvard University Press.

Sassen, S. (1996) *Losing Control? Sovereignty in an Age of Globalization*. New York: Columbia University Press.

Thompson, J. B. (1995) *The Media and Modernity*. Cambridge: Polity.

Wallace, W. (1999) The sharing of sovereignty: the European paradox. *Political Studies*, 47(3), special issue.

24 Environmental Advocacy Networks (1997)

Margaret E. Keck and Kathryn Sikkink

Transnational Advocacy Networks in International Politics: Introduction

World politics at the end of the twentieth century involves, alongside states, many nonstate actors that interact with each other, with states, and with international organizations. These interactions are structured in terms of networks, and transnational networks are increasingly visible in international politics. Some involve economic actors and firms. Some are networks of scientists and experts whose professional ties and shared causal ideas underpin their efforts to influence policy.[1] Others are networks of activists, distinguishable largely by the centrality of principled ideas or values in motivating their formation.[2] We will call these *transnational advocacy networks*.

[. . .]

Despite their differences, these networks are similar in several important respects: the centrality of values or principled ideas, the belief that individuals can make a difference, the creative use of information, and the employment by nongovernmental actors of sophisticated political strategies in targeting their campaigns.

. . . More than other kinds of transnational actors, advocacy networks often reach beyond policy change to advocate and instigate changes in the institutional and principled basis of international interactions. When they succeed, they are an important part of an explanation for changes in world politics. A transnational advocacy network includes those relevant actors working internationally on an issue, who are bound together by shared values, a common discourse, and dense exchanges of information and services. Such networks are most prevalent in issue areas characterized by high value content and informational uncertainty. At the core of the relationship is information exchange. What is novel in these networks is the ability of nontraditional international actors to mobilize information strategically to help create new issues and categories and to persuade, pressure, and gain leverage over much more powerful organizations and governments. Activists in networks try not only to influence policy outcomes, but to transform the terms and nature of the debate.

They are not always successful in their efforts, but they are increasingly relevant players in policy debates.

[. . .]

We examine transnational advocacy networks and what they do by analyzing campaigns networks have waged. For our purposes, campaigns are sets of strategically linked activities in which members of a diffuse principled network (what social movement theorists would call a "mobilization potential") develop explicit, visible ties and mutually recognized roles in pursuit of a common goal (and generally against a common target). In a campaign, core network actors mobilize others and initiate the tasks of structural integration and cultural negotiation among the groups in the network. Just as in domestic campaigns, they connect groups to each other, seek out resources, propose and prepare activities, and conduct public relations. They must also consciously seek to develop a "common frame of meaning" – a task complicated by cultural diversity within transnational networks.

[. . .]

What Is a Transnational Advocacy Network?

Networks are forms of organization characterized by voluntary, reciprocal, and horizontal patterns of communication and exchange. The organizational theorist Walter Powell calls them a third mode of economic organization, distinctly different from markets and hierarchy (the firm). "Networks are 'lighter on their feet' than hierarchy" and are "particularly apt for circumstances in which there is a need for efficient, reliable information," and "for the exchange of commodities whose value is not easily measured."[3] . . .

We call them advocacy networks because advocates plead the causes of others or defend a cause or proposition. Advocacy captures what is unique about these transnational networks: they are organized to promote causes, principled ideas, and norms, and they often involve individuals advocating policy changes that cannot be easily linked to a rationalist understanding of their "interests."

Some issue areas reproduce transnationally the webs of personal relationships that are crucial in the formation of domestic networks. Advocacy networks have been particularly important in value-laden debates over human rights, the environment, women, infant health, and indigenous peoples, where large numbers of differently situated individuals have become acquainted over a considerable period and developed similar world views. . . .

Major actors in advocacy networks may include the following: (1) international and domestic nongovernmental research and advocacy organizations; (2) local social movements; (3) foundations; (4) the media; (5) churches, trade unions, consumer organizations, and intellectuals; (6) parts of regional and international intergovernmental organizations; and (7) parts of the executive and/or parliamentary branches of governments. Not all these will be present in each advocacy network. Initial research suggests, however, that international and domestic NGOs play a central role in all advocacy networks, usually initiating actions and pressuring more powerful actors to take positions. NGOs introduce new ideas, provide information, and lobby for policy changes.

Groups in a network share values and frequently exchange information and services. The flow of information among actors in the network reveals a dense web of connections among these groups, both formal and informal. The movement of funds and services is especially notable between foundations and NGOs, and some NGOs provide services such as training for other NGOs in the same and sometimes other advocacy networks. Personnel also circulate within and among networks, as relevant players move from one to another in a version of the "revolving door."

Relationships among networks, both within and between issue areas, are similar to what scholars of social movements have found for domestic activism. Individuals and foundation funding have moved back and forth among them. Environmentalists and women's groups have looked at the history of human rights campaigns for models of effective international institution building. Refugee resettlement and indigenous people's rights are increasingly central components of international environmental activity, and vice versa; mainstream human rights organizations have joined the campaign for women's rights. Some activists consider themselves part of an "NGO community."

Besides sharing information, groups in networks create categories or frames within which to generate and organize information on which to base their campaigns. Their ability to generate information quickly and accurately, and deploy it effectively, is their most valuable currency; it is also central to their identity. Core campaign organizers must ensure that individuals and organizations with access to necessary information are incorporated into the network; different ways of framing an issue may require quite different kinds of information. Thus frame disputes can be a significant source of change within networks.

Why and How Have Transnational Advocacy Networks Emerged?

[. . .]

We cannot accurately count transnational advocacy networks to measure their growth over time, but one proxy is the increase in the number of international NGOs committed to social change. Because international NGOs are key components of any advocacy network, this increase suggests broader trends in the number, size, and density of advocacy networks generally. . . . the number of international nongovernmental social change groups has increased across all issues, though to varying degrees in different issue areas.

    [. . .]

Transnational advocacy networks appear most likely to emerge around those issues where (1) channels between domestic groups and their governments are blocked or hampered or where such channels are ineffective for resolving a conflict, setting into motion the "boomerang" pattern of influence characteristic of these networks; (2) activists or "political entrepreneurs" believe that networking will further their missions and campaigns, and actively promote networks; and (3) conferences and other forms of international contact create arenas for forming and strengthening networks. Where channels of participation are blocked, the international arena may be the only means that domestic activists have to gain attention to their issues. Boomerang strategies are most common in campaigns where the target is a state's domestic policies or behavior; where a campaign seeks broad procedural change involving dispersed actors, strategies are more diffuse.

The Boomerang Pattern

It is no accident that so many advocacy networks address claims about rights in their campaigns. Governments are the primary "guarantors" of rights, but also their primary violators. When a government violates or refuses to recognize rights, individuals and domestic groups often have no recourse within domestic political or judicial arenas. They may seek international connections finally to express their concerns and even to protect their lives.

When channels between the state and its domestic actors are blocked, the boomerang pattern of influence characteristic of transnational networks may occur: domestic NGOs bypass their state and directly search out international allies to try to bring pressure on their states from outside. This is most obviously the case in human rights campaigns. Similarly, indigenous rights campaigns and environmental campaigns that support the demands of local peoples for participation in development projects that would affect them frequently involve this kind of triangulation. Linkages are important for both sides: for the less powerful third world actors, networks provide access, leverage, and information (and often money) they could not expect to have on their own; for northern groups, they make credible the assertion that they are struggling with, and not only for, their southern partners. Not surprisingly, such relationships can produce considerable tensions.

[. . .]

The Growth of International Contact

Opportunities for network activities have increased over the last two decades. In addition to the efforts of pioneers, a proliferation of international organizations and conferences has provided foci for connections. Cheaper air travel and new electronic communication technologies speed information flows and simplify personal contact among activists.

Underlying these trends is a broader cultural shift. The new networks have depended on the creation of a new kind of global public (or civil society), which grew as a cultural legacy of the 1960s.[4] Both the activism that swept Western Europe, the United States, and many parts of the third world during that decade, and the vastly increased opportunities for international contact, contributed to this shift. With a significant decline in air fares, foreign travel ceased to be the exclusive privilege of the wealthy. Students participated in exchange programs. The Peace Corps and lay missionary programs sent thousands of young people to live and work in the developing world. Political exiles from Latin America taught in US and European universities. Churches opened their doors to refugees, and to new ideas and commitments.

[. . .]

Advocacy networks in the north function in a cultural milieu of internationalism that is generally optimistic about the promise and possibilities of international networking. For network members in developing countries, however, justifying external intervention or pressure in domestic affairs is a much trickier business, except when lives are at stake. Linkages with northern networks require high levels of trust, as arguments justifying intervention on ethical grounds confront the ingrained nationalism common to many political groups in the developing world, as well as memories of colonial and neocolonial relations.

How Do Transnational Advocacy Networks Work?

Transnational advocacy networks seek influence in many of the same ways that other political groups or social movements do. Since they are not powerful in a traditional sense of the word, they must use the power of their information, ideas, and strategies to alter the information and value contexts within which states make policies. The bulk of what networks do might be termed persuasion or socialization, but neither process is devoid of conflict. Persuasion and socialization often involve not just reasoning with opponents, but also bringing pressure, arm-twisting, encouraging sanctions, and shaming. . . .

Our typology of tactics that networks use in their efforts at persuasion, socialization, and pressure includes (1) *information politics*, or the ability to quickly and credibly generate politically usable information and move it to where it will have the most impact; (2) *symbolic politics*, or the ability to call upon symbols, actions, or stories that make sense of a situation for an audience that is frequently far away; (3) *leverage politics*, or the ability to call upon powerful actors to affect a situation where weaker members of a network are unlikely to have influence; and (4) *accountability politics*, or the effort to hold powerful actors to their previously stated policies or principles.

A single campaign may contain many of these elements simultaneously. For example, the human rights network disseminated information about human rights abuses in Argentina in the period 1976–83. The Mothers of the Plaza de Mayo marched in circles in the central square in Buenos Aires wearing white handkerchiefs to draw symbolic attention to the plight of their missing children. The network also tried to use both material and moral leverage against the Argentine regime, by pressuring the United States and other governments to cut off military and economic aid, and by efforts to get the UN and the Inter-American Commission on Human Rights to condemn Argentina's human rights practices. Monitoring is a variation on information politics, in which activists use information strategically to ensure accountability with public statements, existing legislation and international standards.

[. . .]

Under What Conditions Do Advocacy Networks Have Influence?

To assess the influence of advocacy networks we must look at goal achievement at several different levels. We identify the following types or stages of network influence: (1) issue creation and agenda setting; (2) influence on discursive positions of states and international organizations; (3) influence on institutional procedures; (4) influence on policy change in "target actors" which may be states, international organizations like the World Bank, or private actors like the Nestlé Corporation; and (5) influence on state behavior.

Networks generate attention to new issues and help set agendas when they provoke media attention, debates, hearings, and meetings on issues that previously had not been a matter of public debate. Because values are the essence of advocacy networks, this stage of influence may require a modification of the "value context" in which policy debate takes place. The UN's theme years and decades, such as International Women's Decade and the

Year of Indigenous Peoples, were international events promoted by networks that heightened awareness of issues.

Networks influence discursive positions when they help persuade states and international organizations to support international declarations or to change stated domestic policy positions. The role environmental networks played in shaping state positions and conference declarations at the 1992 "Earth Summit" in Rio de Janeiro is an example of this kind of impact. They may also pressure states to make more binding commitments by signing conventions and codes of conduct.

The targets of network campaigns frequently respond to demands for policy change with changes in procedures (which may affect policies in the future). The multilateral bank campaign, . . . is largely responsible for a number of changes in internal bank directives mandating greater NGO and local participation in discussions of projects. It also opened access to formerly restricted information, and led to the establishment of an independent inspection panel for World Bank projects. Procedural changes can greatly increase the opportunity for advocacy organizations to develop regular contact with other key players on an issue, and they sometimes offer the opportunity to move from outside to inside pressure strategies.

A network's activities may produce changes in policies, not only of the target states, but also of other states and/or international institutions. Explicit policy shifts seem to denote success, but even here both their causes and meanings may be elusive. We can point with some confidence to network impact where human rights network pressures have achieved cutoffs of military aid to repressive regimes, or a curtailment of repressive practices. Sometimes human rights activity even affects regime stability. But we must take care to distinguish between policy change and change in behavior; official policies regarding timber extraction in Sarawak, Malaysia, for example, may say little about how timber companies behave on the ground in the absence of enforcement.

We speak of stages of impact, and not merely types of impact, because we believe that increased attention, followed by changes in discursive positions, make governments more vulnerable to the claims that networks raise. (Discursive changes can also have a powerfully divisive effect on networks themselves, splitting insiders from outsiders, reformers from radicals.[5]) A government that claims to be protecting indigenous areas or ecological reserves is potentially more vulnerable to charges that such areas are endangered than one that makes no such claim. At that point the effort is not to make governments change their position but to hold them to their word. Meaningful policy change is thus more likely when the first three types or stages of impact have occurred.

[. . .]

Issue Characteristics

Issues that involve ideas about right and wrong are amenable to advocacy networking because they arouse strong feelings, allow networks to recruit volunteers and activists, and infuse meaning into these volunteer activities. However, not all principled ideas lead to network formation, and some issues can be framed more easily than others so as to resonate with policymakers and publics. In particular, problems whose causes can be assigned to the deliberate (intentional) actions of identifiable individuals are amenable to advocacy network strategies in ways that problems whose causes are irredeemably structural are not. The real creativity of advocacy networks has been in finding intentionalist frames within which to address some elements of structural problems. Though the frame of violence against women does not exhaust the structural issue of patriarchy, it may transform some of patriarchy's effects into problems amenable to solution. Reframing land use and tenure conflict as environmental issues does not exhaust the problems of poverty and inequality, but it may improve the odds against solving part of them. Network actors argue that in such reframing they are weakening the structural apparatus of patriarchy, poverty, and inequality and empowering new actors to address these problems better in the future. Whether or not they are right, with the decline almost everywhere of mass parties of the left, few alternative agendas remain on the table within which these issues can be addressed.

[. . .]

We also argue that in order to campaign on an issue it must be converted into a "causal story" that establishes who bears responsibility or guilt.[6] But the causal chain needs to be sufficiently short and clear to make the case convincing. The responsibility of a torturer who places an electric prod to a prisoner's genitals is quite clear. Assigning blame to state leaders for the actions of soldiers or prison guards involves a longer causal chain, but accords with common notions of the principle of strict chain of command in military regimes.

[. . .]

Actor Characteristics

However amenable particular issues may be to strong transnational and transcultural messages, there must be actors capable of transmitting those messages and targets who are vulnerable to persuasion or leverage. Networks operate best when they are dense, with many actors, strong connections among groups in the network, and reliable information flows. (Density refers both to regularity and diffusion of information exchange within networks and to coverage of key areas.) Effective networks must involve reciprocal information exchanges, and include activists from target countries as well as those able to get institutional leverage. . . .

Target actors must be vulnerable either to material incentives or to sanctions from outside actors, or they must be sensitive to pressure because of gaps between stated commitments and practice. Vulnerability arises both from the availability of leverage and the target's sensitivity to leverage; if either is missing, a campaign may fail. Countries that are most suceptible to network pressures are those that aspire to belong to a normative community of nations. This desire implies a view of state preferences that recognizes states' interactions as a social – and socializing – process.[7] Thus moral leverage may be especially relevant where states are actively trying to raise their status in the international system.

[. . .]

Toward a Global Civil Society?

Many other scholars now recognize that "the state does not monopolize the public sphere,"[8] and are seeking, as we are, ways to describe the sphere of international interactions under a variety of names: transnational relation, international civil society, and global civil society.[9] In these views, states no longer look unitary from the outside. Increasingly dense interactions among individuals, groups, actors from states, and international institutions appear to involve much more than re-presenting interests on a world stage.

We contend that the advocacy network concept cannot be subsumed under notions of transnational social movements or global civil society. In particular, theorists who suggest that a global civil society will inevitably emerge from economic globalization or from revolutions in communication and transportation technologies ignore the issues of agency and political opportunity that we find central for understanding the evolution of new international institutions and relationships.

One strong globalization thesis is "world polity theory" associated with the sociologist John Meyer and his colleagues. For Meyer world cultural forces play a key causal role in constituting the state's characteristics and action.[10] World polity researchers have shown conclusively that states with very different histories, cultures, and social and political structures all came to adopt similar conceptions of what it means to be a state and what it means to be a citizen, regardless of patterns of institutional development. Yet in attributing so much to transnational diffusion, they remain silent on the sources of world culture except to argue that it originates from the modern Western tradition. In their view, international NGOs are not actors, but "enactors" of world cultural norms; the role of the International Olympic Committee is functionally the same as that of Greenpeace or Amnesty International.[11]

We lack convincing studies of the sustained and specific processes through which individuals and organizations create (or resist the creation of) something resembling a global civil society. Our research leads us to believe that these interactions involve much more agency than a pure diffusionist perspective suggests. Even though the implications of our findings are much broader than most political scientists would admit, the findings themselves do not yet support the strong claims about an emerging global civil society.[12] We are much more comfortable with a conception of transnational civil society as an arena of struggle, a fragmented and contested area where "the politics of transnational civil society is centrally about the way in which certain groups emerge and are legitimized (by governments, institutions, and other groups)."[13]

[. . .]

Environmental Advocacy Networks

Origins of Environmental Networks

[. . .]

By the end of the 1960s, environmental experts agreed on the need for stronger institutions of international collaboration. The 1968 Biosphere conference[14] recommended action by governments and the UN system. The biosphere idea provided one model for a shift in the ideational basis of the conservation movement – one that promoted greater international collaboration and sought greater understanding of human activities.[15]

In 1968 Sweden introduced a resolution calling for a UN-sponsored conference on the human environment, which it offered to host. Sparked by Sweden's concern with transboundary acid rain from European industry, the conference was "to focus attention of governments and public opinion on the importance and urgency of this question, and also to identify those aspects of it that can only or best be solved through international cooperation and agreement." The result was the 1972 UN Conference on the Human Environment in Stockholm. As the conference was highly politicized from the outset, the role of NGOs was enhanced: the UN wanted their input without alienating their governments, and offered facilities for a concurrent environmental forum of NGOs.[16]

This first NGO forum parallel to a UN official conference pioneered a transnational process that would become absolutely central to the formation and strengthening of advocacy networks around the world. As it developed, the NGO forum format led to dialogue, conflict, creativity, and synergy. The face-to-face contact helped activists from different backgrounds and countries recognize commonalities and establish the trust necessary to sustain more distant network contacts after the conference was over.

To the consternation of those seeking more international collaboration, the Stockholm conference highlighted divisions between more and less developed countries on the relationship between environment and development. . . . When preparations for Stockholm revealed the extent of north–south polarization, conference secretary-general Maurice Strong convoked a commission of experts to produce a report on the relationship between environment and development; the resulting Founex report prefigured by almost a decade much of the 1980s discussion of sustainable development.[17]

[. . .]

In contrast to divisions among developed countries, third world states . . . stressed poverty as the great polluter and development as the solution. "How can we speak to those who live in villages or slums about keeping the oceans, the rivers and the air clean" asked Indira Gandhi, "when their own lives are contaminated at the source?"[18] Stressing sovereignty over resources and development, delegates from China and Brazil accused the industrialized north of using environmental arguments to try to keep developing countries subordinate.[19]

[. . .]

The Stockholm conference sparked the creation of institutions around which transnational environmental networks would mobilize. It was also a landmark in the evolution of ideas about the relationship between environment and development, marking an ideational shift that brought new actors and issues into environmental debates. Attended by representatives of 114 governments, the conference signaled that the environment was a legitimate concern for the international community. Besides producing declarations and recommendations, the conference led to the establishment of the UN Environmental Program (UNEP).

[. . .]

Conservationists spent the decade after Stockholm developing a response to the environment vs. development debate. In March 1980, the IUCN, World Wildlife Fund, and United Nations Environment Program launched a joint World Conservation Strategy at simultaneous ceremonies in thirty countries. Recognizing that "the separation of conservation from development . . . [is] at the root of current living problems," IUCN's Robert Allan told journalists at the launching ceremonies that "too often we assume that people are destroying the environment because they are ignorant, when in fact they have no other choice."[20]

The groups' strategy included suggestions for national legislative reforms and conservation goals. It introduced the idea of "sustainable development," later in the decade popularized in the report of the World Commission on Environment and Development as "development that meets the needs of the present without compromising the ability of future generations to meet their own needs."[21]

Changes in ideas about the relationship between development and environmental protection encouraged more participation by actors in developing countries – state actors, local scientists and conservationists, and other agents promoting social change. The resulting multiplicity of voices, views of development, and understandings of the relationship between human beings and nature increased through the action of a new set of players in the international environmental field – transnational advocacy networks – that emerged in the early 1980s and addressed themselves both to national and international institutions and broader international publics. Their advocacy went well beyond the traditional conservation agenda; increasingly, defenders of nature had to come to terms with the need to defend also the rights of peoples.

[. . .]

The Rise of Advocacy Organizations

In the middle and late 1980s the mass media began to pay increased attention to international environmental issues. The Bhopal and Chernobyl disasters, the discovery in the mid-1980s of a hole in the ozone layer over the Antarctic, and developing scientific consensus over the risk of global climate change associated with augmented concentrations of "greenhouse" gases like CO_2 and methane, all contributed to a widened public interest in the global environment.

In the second half of the 1980s membership in the major US environmental organization grew rapidly. During this period in which computers became widely used, all major environmental organizations began to employ direct mail techniques for fundraising and managing membership lists.[22] Though the data does not support a causal linkage here, some of the most rapid growth occurred in organizations most associated with global campaigns.[23] . . . Total membership of ten organizations for which continuous data are available grew from 4,198,000 in 1976 to 5,816,000 in 1986 and 8,270,000 in 1990.[24]

Some of these organizations brought new, more confrontational approaches into the environmentalist repertoire, ranging from the litigation and regulatory negotiation approaches of the NRDC and EDF to the Quaker-inspired witness and direct action approach of Greenpeace. Greenpeace and Friends of the Earth (FOE) employed creative combinations of confrontation, lobbying, and other institutional strategies in the whale campaigns of the late 1970s and early 1980s. These and other advocacy and direct action groups were increasingly impatient with the longstanding IUCN persuasion strategy of linking scientists and policymakers.

Greenpeace and FOE were both conceived from the outset as international organizations, albeit decentralized ones. Both grew from the social activism of the late 1960s and early 1970s, with its critique of materialism and its appreciation of nature.[25] . . .

Besides the international NGOs, many national organizations have small but active international programs. Members of the international divisions of the National Wildlife

Federation, the Natural Resources Defense Council, the Environmental Policy Institute, and Environmental Defense Fund were core initiators in 1983–84 of the NGO campaign to make multilateral banks more environmentally responsible, with early support from other organizations. Their contacts in developing countries were often with multi-issue development NGOs rather than with environmental organizations – linkages that highlighted relationships among environmental, human rights, and development issues.[26]

In developing countries as well, social movements and NGOs concerned with the environment multiplied rapidly during the 1980s, influenced by the spread of environmentalist ideas and by nationally specific historical circumstances. In Latin America, the wave of democratic transitions in the 1980s provided fertile ground for new organizations of all kinds. Older conservation organizations were joined by new urban and rural movements with different approaches to the relationships between development goals and their social and environmental consequences. The period of democratization also saw the birth or expansion of many professionalized grassroots support organizations, eventually referred to as NGOs. The spread of NGOs accompanied the worldwide crisis of and disaffection with the left, as socially concerned activists sought other vehicles by which to "make a difference."

Advocacy NGOs in South and Southeast Asia followed upon a long tradition of community organizations and NGOs formed to work among the poor. In the mid-1970s, disenchanted with conventional approaches to development, advocacy groups began to work to support communities' efforts to empower themselves, claim rights, and espouse alternative conceptions of development. Many believed that an environmentally sound use of resources was integral to this process. In some countries these efforts seemed increasingly to depend on democratization of political institutions.[27] In 1983, a directory published by the environmental organization Sahabat Alam Malaysia of environmental NGOs in the Asia-Pacific region listed 162 organizations.

Until the early 1980s few environmental NGOs had the time or money for international networking. To share resources, NGO lobbying and information bureaus were established to monitor the activities of UN agencies and the European Economic Community.[28] . . . But by the middle of the 1980s many NGOs were frustrated with the limitations of these arenas.[29] A growing number of organizations in both developed and developing countries began to use cheaper and faster means of communication, and cheap air travel facilitated face-to-face encounters that would have been unthinkable even a decade before.

As environmentalists began to seek more proactive forms of transnational activity, other advocacy networks had already developed this new kind of practice. Seeking a more focused way of targeting abuses by transnational corporations in developing countries, in the mid-1970s the International Baby Food Action Network had launched an almost unprecedented global campaign against the promotion of infant formula in the developing world.[30] . . .

Sometimes new environmental organizations grew out of older NGOs. Sahabat Alam Malaysia (SAM), Malaysia's Friends of the Earth affiliate founded in 1977, is one of a whole family of organizations and networks spun off from the Consumer Association of Penang. SAM, in turn, hosted the founding meeting for the Asian–Pacific Peoples' Environmental Network in Penang in 1983, and SAM and the Consumer Organization of Penang spawned the Third World Network in late 1984 and the World Rainforest Movement (initially World

Rainforest Network) in 1986. Their campaigns gained visibility in the north in part through close links with the British journal *The Ecologist*, whose brand of political ecology contained a stronger critique of existing development models than did most US environmental advocates. Some networks borrowed tactics from the baby food network. The Pesticides Action Network, for example, came to international attention in June 1985 when it launched a campaign to have banned a "dirty dozen" most dangerous chemicals. Formed around issues with strong environmental dimensions that affected identifiable communities in the third world, these networks laid the groundwork for much subsequent organizing.

Thus, fueling the emergence of advocacy networks in the mid-1980s were new ideas about the relationship between environment and development; more organizations and new communications technologies; and opportunities to influence new international institutions concerned with the environment or transform the missions of older ones. To this we should add a dramatic increase in private (foundation) and public funding available for environmental activities. Finally, as neoliberal antistatism (or in some cases frustration with bureaucratic inefficiencies) swept through development circles in the advanced industrial countries. NGOs became a favored alternative for funneling development aid. . . .

There are now literally hundreds of environmental networks, making up a loose web of interconnection out of which particular subsets work together on specific campaigns. (At the same time, other subsets, sometimes involving the same organizations in quite different alliances, are involved in separate campaigns or activities.) These organizations produce and process enormous amounts of information. . . . In addition, organizations and individuals involved in a campaign maintain regular contact by E-mail, fax, telephone, and radio.

[. . .]

Tropical Deforestation

[. . .]

The IUCN took up the tropical forest issue for the first time in 1972, in response to the Brazilian government's decision to accelerate colonization and development projects in the Amazon. . . .

Concern grew rapidly. At the urging of NGOs, in 1973 a number of UN agencies and the Organization of American States cosponsored international meetings of scientists, government representatives and representatives of international agencies to discuss guidelines for economic development of Latin American and Southeast Asian tropical forest areas.[31] By 1974, the IUCN and the WWF considered tropical rainforests "the most important nature conservation programme of the decade."

[. . .]

The network of scientists and conservationists that initially worked on the tropical forest issue fits very nicely into Haas's definition of an epistemic community. Either by becoming part of the policy process or by working through NGOs or international organizations, its members hoped to persuade people of goodwill to adopt rational guidelines for tropical forest use. Tropical forest experts held meetings, shared information, and discussed strategies and action plans. But the epistemic community was relatively small; a handful of people carried the issue alone.

Frustrated with the meager results of their efforts, several organizations initiated studies and negotiations in the early 1980s to seek new ways of intensifying and broadening their influence. As conservationists' focus shifted from preservation to sustainable development, they needed a better understanding of how human populations – including indigenous peoples – interacted with forests. . . .

In sum, the first decade of activity around tropical forests created networks of scientists and policymakers who produced and exchanged a great deal of information, placed the issue on the agendas of a variety of international organizations, and expanded the issue from one concerned primarily with trees and soils to one that at least recognized the problems of indigenous peoples. . . . There was not yet an attempt to gain leverage over recalcitrant actors in the system.

The Multilateral Development Bank Campaign

. . . In 1983 a small group of individuals in Washington, DC, began to form a network of activists and organizations to target multilateral bank lending in developing countries.

The NGO campaign around multilateral bank lending differed from traditional environmentalist campaigns by focusing not on a particular substantive issue, but rather on a set of political relationships within which activists believed they could obtain leverage. They chose the multilateral banks for their potential impact on the incorporation of environmental concerns into development policy in the third world.

This campaign was clearly a case where strategy moved from the domestic to the international arena. The stress on leverage followed two decades of environmental litigation in the United States, where lawyers from environmental NGOs successfully used the National Environmental Policy Act (NEPA) and other measures to extend the range of environmental protection in a variety of areas, including the international activities of US agencies.

[. . .]

The activist critique of the environmental impact of bank projects focused at least as much on their human impact as on their effect on wildlife or natural resources. In the 1986 campaign pamphlet *Bankrolling Disasters*, Schwartzman described the Polonoroeste project in Brazil, the Indonesian Transmigration project, (involving resettlement from Java to less populated parts of the archipelego), the Narmada Dam project in India, and a cattle ranching project in Botswana – all of which involved migration or resettlement issues along with environmental destruction.[32] This evolution lends weight to the argument that cases involving physical harm or loss of livelihood are particularly susceptible to transnational advocacy campaigning; it is not obvious that for a campaign designed to promote environmental preservation this should be so. . . .

The campaign's goal was to change the behavior of multilateral banks (especially the World Bank), making their projects at least less destructive to the environment and at best positively beneficial. This aim would require effecting changes in the banks' project cycles, personnel, internal organization, and permeability – that is, access to information, and breadth of consultation with those affected by the banks' activities. To bring home the need for such changes, the campaigners began with a substantive critique of particular projects.

Deforestation in the Brazilian Amazon

One of the first cases for the campaigners was the World Bank's loan to Brazil's Polonoro-este program, an effort to rationalize seemingly out-of-control colonization in the Brazilian northwest. The timing – the project began in 1981 – placed it just on the cusp of Brazil's democratization process; the first free gubernatorial elections took place in 1982, and Brazil's first civilian president since the 1964 military coup took office in 1985. Democratization stimulated political and social organization and greater circulation of information. . . . The World Bank agreed to finance part of the Polonoroeste development program, but with misgivings. The loan was intended to pave the main highway through the state and implant social infrastructure in colonization areas; the bank insisted as well on components insuring protection of ecological and indigenous areas. Although bank officials knew that such programs might intensify settlement and further aggravate deforestation, they reasoned that if the Brazilian government carried out its plans without bank participation the prospects would be worse.[33]

[. . .]

The Polonoroeste Network and the Bank

Social networks of foreign and Brazilian anthropologists were crucial for the early stages of the external critique of Polonoroeste. When Steve Schwartzman returned to the United States from fieldwork among the Krenakore Indians in Xingú National Park, he quickly began to participate in campaign activities in the name of Survival International. Information on Polonoroeste came from the Ecumenical Center for Documentation and Information (CEDI) in Brazil, where anthropologist Carlos Alberto Ricardo headed up an indigenous rights project, from several anthropologists who had been consultants on the project, from the filmmaker Adrian Cowell, and from a few other journalists and academics.[34] It did not, at this stage, come from organizations on the ground in Rondônia.

In the United States, campaigners lobbied key congressional appropriations committees and the Treasury Department in an attempt to influence positions taken by US executive directors of the multilateral banks.

[. . .]

The World Bank is vulnerable to US pressure because of its system of weighted voting, by which the United States, the United Kingdom, Germany, Japan, and France have 40 percent of the voting shares; these countries also provide the lion's share of money for the International Development Agency (IDA), the bank's soft loan facility. Beginning in the late 1970s, negotiations over IDA replenishment became increasingly complicated, and the bank did not want to see yet another roadblock established in this process.

In December 1984, and again in 1986, the US Congress adopted a set of recommendations suggested by NGOs to strengthen the bank's environmental performance.[35] In 1985, largely as a result of the MDB campaign, the World Bank temporarily suspended disbursements for Polonoroeste on the grounds that the Brazilian government was violating loan conditions on protecting natural and indigenous areas; this was the first loan suspension on such grounds. In 1985, the Senate Appropriations committee attached a strongly worded environmental report to the foreign aid appropriation bill asking US executive directors of multilateral development banks to promote a series of reforms in project design and implementation.[36] The World Bank's decision to create a top-level environmental department in 1987 was designed to stem the rising tide of criticism. In his speech at the World Resources Institute announcing the changes, bank president Barber Conable referred to Polonoroeste as something the new department was designed to prevent from happening.

The Impact of Local Organizing

At this stage of the campaign Brazilian NGOs and individuals served mainly as informants. This changed in the second half of the 1980s, for two reasons: first, the connection some Washington activists forged with rubber tapper organizers from Acre, Brazil had a deep influence on their subsequent activity; and second, other instances of transnational environmental networking, in which third world (especially Asian) activists played a more central role, highlighted the importance of local protagonists. Information on multilateral bank activities became more widely available, also, and opportunities for organizations to share their experiences and discuss strategy increased. The most visible opportunity was the annual NGO meeting held parallel to the annual meeting of the World Bank and the International Monetary Fund (IMF) beginning in 1986.

For the initial group of multilateral bank campaigners, contact established in 1985 with the Acre rubber tappers was a watershed event. Francisco "Chico" Mendes was the leader of a group of rubber tappers (gatherers of natural latex from rubber trees) who had been fighting since 1975 to guarantee land use rights and improve the living standards of forest peoples. They were central to rural union organizing in the state of Acre, and had close relationships with other social movements in the area during Brazil's transition to democracy. . . .

The relationship that developed between the bank campaigners and the rubber tappers was mutually beneficial. It took the teeth out of accusations that rainforest destruction was simply a concern of privileged northerners. Over time, it helped activists from distant political and social universes to understand better their different perspectives on the same problems, and to build elements of a common understanding. For the rubber tappers, who had struggled for a decade against the encroachment of cattle ranchers on forest they had traditionally used, contact with the bank campaigners gave them access to international opinion- and decision-making arenas that they could not have gained on their own. When they joined forces to influence a proposed road project in Acre for which Brazil sought Inter-American Development Bank funding, a struggle for land rights waged by rural unions became simultaneously a struggle to preserve the standing forest.

In December 1988 Chico Mendes was murdered by hired guns of irate landowners. But he had made his point abroad. Invited by the bank campaigners to Washington and Miami to meet with members of the U.S. Congress and with multilateral bank officials, he had helped make the rubber tappers' proposal to create "extractive reserves" in the Amazon one of the few concrete illustrations of the "sustainable development" idea. By linking environmental destruction to a concrete picture of how local populations lived in the forest, environmentalists were able to make the tropical forest issue real to an international public.

The murder of Chico Mendes had enormous symbolic impact – so much so that it made page one of the *New York Times*. It embodied at the same time an issue – deforestation in the Amazon – and a set of complex social relationships in which the roles of rubber tapper, cattle rancher, the justice system, Brazilian government programs, multilateral development banks, and North American and European taxpayers all became transparent. The rubber tapper case thus reinforced an approach to tropical deforestation that focused on social relations. This approach is very different from one that sees forest loss as a set of technical or scientific issues to be resolved by experts, or from one that looks at it primarily in terms of trees and wildlife.

The relationship with the Acre rubber tappers had important ramifications for transnational networking on the environment. It showed that testimony from those most directly affected by bank projects was often a more powerful organizing tool than information produced by outside experts. Calls for participation in the early stages of project design by those likely to be affected by a bank-funded project became a constant of activist critiques. Notably, the third world social movements whose participation the campaigners advocated focused overwhelmingly on the human dimension of environmental change.

[. . .]

From Polonoroeste to Planafloro

In 1986 technical personnel in the Rondônia state government began to work with World Bank staff on a successor project to Polonoroeste. Based on a zoning plan, this new project, called the Planafloro, was intended to prevent further ecological damage by helping to intensify agricultural activity in settled areas, and institutionalize varying degrees of environmental protection for the remainder of the state. In 1990, in the midst of the approval process, the Environmental Defense Fund led the bank campaign network in a series of objections that relevant local groups had not been consulted on the project.[37]

In response to the bank's claim that such consultations had taken place, Washington environmentalists requested information from their contacts in Rondônia. Brazilian groups reported that rubber tappers, rural workers, and indigenous organizations knew little or nothing about the project, but had requested information and expressed interest in discussing it. Brazilian and foreign NGO representatives simultaneously raised the issue with the newly appointed environmental secretary, José Lutzenberger, who asked the bank to suspend consideration of the project until consultations could take place. This forced the bank's hand, and the project was taken off the agenda of the executive directors.

[. . .]

Incentives for local groups to become organized were high. With foreign attention focused on the Amazon and the approach of the 1992 "Earth Summit" in Rio de Janeiro, money and media attention were available as never before. Conflicts among NGOs in the region were smoothed over, and in 1991 the Rondônia NGO Forum was created. This forum became the formal NGO interlocutor from Rondônia for the Planafloro project and another large environmental project, the Amazon Project sponsored by the Group of Seven (G-7). With NGO agreement, the Planafloro returned to the World Bank's docket in 1991. The bank pressed the Rondônia state government to accept as part of the project's governance structure, a deliberative council that gave NGOs voting parity with state secretariats to decide on the project's operating plans, and seats in the planning commissions.[38]

Although this was one of the biggest procedural victories of the campaign, it did not immediately produce results. The organizations in the forum did not have enough local clout to make their positions effective, and the state government did not intend for them to gain such clout. Nonetheless, local groups gained access to information and greater capacity to monitor government actions. They could then assess government claims in the light of direct experience and demand that the bank be held accountable. Although the Rondônia activists did try to use hearings in the Brazilian Congress and lawsuits in Brazilian courts to stop violations of the zoning plan, ultimately their best strategy remained one that put the onus of restraining the Brazilian government onto the World Bank. This is a case where a boomerang strategy resulted from the political weakness of actors rather than from complete blockage of access . . .

In June 1994, only a year after the loan's disbursements had begun, the NGO forum resigned from the deliberative council, reporting multiple violations of the loan agreement. A bank mission brokered a short-lived agreement between the NGOs and the state government, but in November 1994 the forum decided to collaborate with Friends of the Earth (and eventually Oxfam as well) in bringing a formal claim that the Planafloro was violating the bank's own policies before the newly established World Bank Inspection Panel. Friends of the Earth, with funding from the Dutch agency NOVIB to finance research, presented the claim to the bank on 14 June 1995.

Although it was ultimately rejected, simply filing the claim produced a flurry of activity. The Rondônia state government and the Brazilian federal government signed a long-delayed agreement committing the Federal Land Institute to respect the state's zoning plan, and reserves whose demarcation had been unaccountably delayed were suddenly demarcated. Bank personnel finally took a serious look at the project's short-comings, and proposed revisions that they hoped might overcome previous gridlock.

The Organization of the Network

[. . .]

The quality of the local nodes of the advocacy network was more important in the Planafloro campaign than with Polonoroeste. "Local participation" became an important part of such campaigns in the 1990s, made so by the publicity given to the Acre rubber tappers and several other campaigns where vigorous grassroots protest was a crucial element, such as the Narmada dam campaign in India. On the Polonoroeste project foreign NGOs had spoken freely in place of the Brazilians on whose behalf they claimed to act, but with the Planafloro project accountability issues were raised more often.

In the early 1990s EDF and Oxfam, recognizing the need for a more solid Brazilian domestic base for the multilateral development bank campaign, sponsored a meeting in Brasília in March 1993 for Brazilian environmental and indigenous NGOs, to form a Brazilian campaign network. In principle, this national network was to make multilateral bank-related activities more sensitive to national political dynamics. Although slow to get off the ground, by mid-1996 the Brazilian network had a strong national coordination and regular information exchange.

Network Strategies

The Planafloro experience fits the boomerang pattern described in previous chapters. Unable effectively to influence the activities of the state government and of federal agencies acting in Rondônia at the state level, local groups applied pressure either at the national or international levels.[39] In the United States, activists lobbied Congress and the Treasury Department. In addition, inclusion of NGOs in the Planafloro's governance structure legitimized their intervention to an unprecedented degree. However, Brazilian NGO strategies were complicated by the pervasive crisis of governance and economy that Brazil was experiencing for most of the period. The Planafloro was only one, and far from the most egregious, of the abuses of public authority that competed for attention.

Such abuses were all the more striking given the Brazilian administration's adroit use of "green" public relations. Soon after Fernando Collor's election to the presidency in 1989, he stunned environmentalists by appointing internationally known ecologist José Lutzenberger secretary of the environment. Asked by a *New York Times* reporter for his impression, Steve Schwartzman called the appointment "stupefyingly positive."[40] Hopes that the advocacy network had penetrated to the heart of the environmental decision-making apparatus proved elusive, however. Collor's environmentalism was more show than substance, and Lutzenberger was a colorful but ineffective minister. Nonetheless, governmental machinery did become more accessible. The Brazilian Environment and Renewable Resources Institute (IBAMA) through its traditional peoples program, began to support rubber tapper and indigenous organizing.

The Planafloro strategy was primarily an accountability strategy, attempting to leverage environmental, land, and indigenous rights policy by asking the World Bank to hold Brazilian government institutions to the commitments they had made. Although initially reluctant to exert major pressure on Brazil, bank personnel became increasingly resentful at taking the heat themselves for failures on the Brazilian side, and began to monitor the project more closely. Eventually, weakly organized local movements and NGOs in Rondônia gained experience.

The multilateral bank campaign has clearly had an impact on World Bank procedures; as with most institutional change, external pressures reinforced internal reformers. The 1987 World Bank reorganization created a central environmental department and environmental units within each of the bank's four regional offices. By 1990 some sixty new positions had been created.[41] Over the next few years the World Bank's role in environmental issues grew. After 1990 it helped elaborate the G-7's Amazon project, and later assumed management of the Global Environmental Facility, a funding mechanism for national projects in the areas of climate change, ozone depletion, and biodiversity. The bank's 1992 reorganization added a central vice presidency for environmentally sustainable development (within which is also located the Social Policy and Resettlement Division).[42] Further reform followed upon network agitation over the Sardar Sarovar Dam project on the Narmada River in India. In that case the World Bank convoked an independent commission to report on the project's status. After the Commission's June 1992 report and an NGO campaign around the tenth replenishment of IDA monies in 1993, the Bank created a semi-independent inspection panel and instituted a new information policy, both in response to

NGO demands. The inspection panel was "empowered to investigate complaints from people directly affected by Bank projects regarding violations of World Bank policy, procedures, and loan agreements."[43] The information policy essentially declassified a wide range of World Bank documents, making them available for public scrutiny.[44]

Opening the Flow of Information

The ability to generate and use information strategically is the main asset of transnational advocacy networks. What kinds of information are strategically necessary? Who gains access to it and how? How, and how well, does information circulate in the network?

Success in engaging such an institution as the World Bank over a project or policy requires, besides certain kinds of expertise, physical access to documents. Without regular access to bank personnel, one may not even know that documents exist. Thus a special responsibility fell upon NGOs in Washington where the World Bank is located.

Two innovations greatly increased opportunities for information sharing in 1986: the beginning of yearly NGO meetings held parallel to the meetings of the Bretton Woods institutions, and the establishment of the Bank Information Center. Chad . . . Dobson pulled together an umbrella organization of Washington NGOs, to organize the conference and demonstration.[45] At the meeting, activists from Europe and developing countries called for the creation of an organization specifically designed to share information.[46] Encouraged by Randy Hayes of the Rainforest Action Network, Dobson agreed to start the Bank Information Center (BIC) – in effect, a network service institution.

Dobson's foundation experience helped him raise start-up grants, after which BIC picked up funding from the Mott Foundation, from NOVIB to provide information to its southern partners, and from WWF to provide information to its partners. Dobson began to cultivate relationships with bank personnel and with US government officials who could help gain access to information. He also set out to create an advisory board of potential information users outside of Washington, especially non-Americans.

Dobson's activities and BIC helped to open up the multilateral development bank campaign beyond the small network of activists that had gotten it off the ground. Besides providing documentation, that meant opening up discussions of strategy. One venue for doing that was the institution of the parallel conference, and increased contact among activists from different parts of the world who met there. Broadening the network also changed it.

> The earliest connections were clearly environmental. And of course that bias was from the Washington environmental groups. When we started bringing southerners here, they didn't talk about species . . . The real connection was [made] when they started coming and saying "you can't protect the environment when the people are suffering the way they are." I think it really was [after] getting southerners here . . . that you had people changing and saying, well, we're talking about sustainable development . . . But it absolutely started out as a rainforest thing.

[. . .]

Conclusions

. . . rainforest campaigns are built on the tensions between recognizing structural causes and designing strategies that seek remedies by placing blame on, and influencing the behavior of, particular actors. Furthermore, the struggles they entail over meaning, power, and access to resources highlight the north-south dimension found in many network campaigns. The campaigns include participants whose understandings have been changed by their ongoing conversation with what anthropologist Anna Tsing calls people in out-of-the-way-places.[47] And, since these are stories about the real world, the campaigns include participants whose understandings have not been changed at all.

Environmental advocacy networks have not so much gotten the tropical forest issue onto the agenda – it was already there – as they have changed the tone of the debate. To the frequent consternation of the epistemic community of scientists and policymakers who had succeeded in placing it on the agenda initially, the advocacy networks deliberately politicized the issues. While the epistemic community had sought to design sound policies and tried on the basis of their authoritative knowledge to persuade governments to adopt them, advocacy networks looked for leverage over actors and institutions capable of making the desired changes. Advocacy networks also insisted on different criteria of expertise. Although they did not deny the expertise of the scientists, they demanded equal time for direct testimony about experience. And within the networks they also cultivated the strategic expertise of good organizers. The issue, especially for the multilateral bank campaigners, was not ultimately forests, or dams, or any other particular environmental issue, but leverage over institutions that make a difference.

The advocacy networks helped to broaden the definition of which information and whose knowledge should shape the agenda on tropical forest issues. In the process, they won seats at the bargaining table for new actors. Their campaigns created a new script for sustainable forest management projects, with roles for "local people," "NGOs," and so forth. We must be careful not to exaggerate the power of the individuals and groups that play these roles, relative to that of states, economic actors like corporations, or multilateral organizations (the Planafloro deliberative council is a good example). Nonetheless, once these roles have been legitimized, organizations like the World Bank must address them.

How much change have transnational advocacy networks produced in the tropical forest issue? Because the networks are not the only reform-minded actors engaged, exact attributions of influence are difficult. The multilateral development bank campaign would certainly not have had much success without the collaboration of network members inside the bank. At the levels of both discursive and procedural change the network has been remarkably successful. Multilateral development banks increasingly claim to be addressing environmental objectives in loans, and there is some evidence that they have begun to eliminate high-risk projects much earlier in the project evaluation cycle. Besides having adopted the discourse of sustainable development, the bank has also implemented important procedural changes, including the information policy. Under increased pressure from the United States after the 1989 Pelosi amendment, all of the multilateral banks are taking the environmental assessment process more seriously.

[. . .]

Among the people whose testimony generated the sharpest images of the impact of deforestation on lives, signs of success are harder to find. . . . In Rondônia, rubber tappers in the areas protected by the Planafloro will, at least for now, maintain use rights over a demarcated territory. Amerindian reserves will be demarcated as well, but they remain vulnerable to encroachment by goldminers, loggers, and even settlements, as long as the state continues omissive in enforcement. Furthermore, what they have won will not be easily extended to other rubber tappers, to other indigenous peoples, to others with insecure tenure.

[. . .]

Both states and NGOs are learning new languages with which to address old problems. Although the problem may not become more tractable in translation, the linkages that networks create make possible the search for common ground – . . . a "common advocacy position."

NOTES

1 Peter Haas has called these "knowledge-based" or "epistemic communities." See Peter Hass, "Introduction: Epistemic Communities and International Policy Coordination," *Knowledge, Power and International Policy Coordination*, special issue, *International Organization* 46 (Winter 1992), pp. 1–36.

2 Ideas that specify criteria for determining whether actions are right and wrong and whether outcomes are just or unjust are shared principled beliefs or values. Beliefs about cause-effect relationships are shared casual beliefs. Judith Goldstein and Robert Keohane, eds., *Ideas and Foreign Policy: Beliefs, Institutions, and Political Change* (Ithaca: Cornell University Press, 1993), pp. 8–10.

3 Walter W. Powell, "Neither Market nor Hierarchy: Network Forms of Organization," *Research in Organizational Behavior* 12 (1990): 295–96, 303–4.

4 See Sidney Tarrow, "Mentalities, Political Cultures, and Collective Action Frames: Constructing Meanings through Action," in *Frontiers in Social Movement Theory*, ed. Aldon D. Morris and Carol McClurg Mueller (New Haven; Yale University Press, 1992), p. 184.

5 We thank Jonathan Fox for reminding us of this point.

6 Deborah A. Stone, "Causal Stories and the Formation of Policy Agendas," *Political Science Quarterly* 104:2 (1989): 281–300.

7 See Martha Finnemore, *National Interests in International Society* (Ithaca: Cornell University Press, 1986).

8 M. J. Peterson, "Transnational Activity, International Society, and World Politics," *Millennium* 21:3 (1992): 375–76.

9 See, for example, Ronnie Lipschutz, "Reconstructing World Politics: The Emergence of Global Civil Society," *Millennium* 21:3 (1992): 389–420; Paul Wapner, "Politics beyond the State: Environmental Activism and World Civic Politics," *World Politics* 47 (April 1995): 311–40; and the special issue of *Millennium* on social movements and world politics, 23: 3 (Winter 1994).

10 For examples see John W. Meyer and Michael T. Hannan, eds., *National Development and the World System* (Chicago: University of Chicago Press, 1979); and George Thomas, John Meyer, Francisco Ramirez, John Boli, eds., *Institutional Structure: Constituting State, Society, and Individual* (Newbury Park, Calif.: Sage, 1987).

11 John Boli and George M. Thomas, "Introduction: World Polity Formation since 1875," in *Constructing World Culture: International Non-Governmental Organizations since 1875* (Stanford University Press, 1999).

12 Sidney Tarrow, *Power in Movement: Social Movements and Contentious Politics*, rev. ed. (Cambridge: Cambridge University Press, 1998), Chapter 11. An earlier version appeared as "Fishnets, Internets and Catnets: Globalization and Transnational Collective Action," Instituto Juan March de Estudios e Investigaciones, Madrid: Working Papers 1996/78, March 1996; and Peterson, "Transnational Activity."

13 Andrew Hurrell and Ngaire Woods, "Globalisation and Inequality," *Millennium* 24:3 (1995), p. 68.

14 Intergovernmental Conference of Experts on a Scientific Basis for Rational Use and Conservation of the Resources of the Biosphere.

15 "Biosphere" refers to the domain of life – a region whose prevailing conditions enable incoming solar radiation to produce the geochemical changes needed for life to occur. Since matter and energy change their form during evolution, all living matter is ultimately genetically connected throughout geologic time. See Lynton Keith Caldwell, *International Environmental Policy*. 2d ed. (Durham, NC: Duke University Press, 1990), pp. 25–8; and Peter Haas, *Saving the Mediterranean: The Politics of International Environmental Cooperation* (New York: Columbia University Press, 1990), pp. 19–25.

16 Anne Thompson Feraru, "Transnational Political Interests and the Global Environment," *International Organization* 28:1 (Winter 1974): 31–60.

17 UN General Assembly, "Development and Environment: Report by the Secretary-General," A/CONF48/10 (22 December 1971), reprinted as a special issue of *International Conciliation* 586 (January 1972).

18 Marcus F. Franda, "Mrs. Gandhi Goes to Stockholm," *South Asia Series* 16:10 (1972): 2, cited in Wendy Weiser, "The Position of India at Stockholm," unpublished paper, Yale University, 1992.

19 João Augusto de Araujo Castro, "Environment and Development: The Case of the Developing Countries," *International Organization* 26:2 (Spring 1972): 401–16.

20 Joanne Omang, "Conservation Strategy Mapped by 30 Nations," *Washington Post*, 6 March 1980, p. A13 (from Nexis).

21 World Commission on Environment and Development, *Our Common Future* (Oxford: Oxford University Press, 1987), p. 43.

22 Robert Cameron Mitchell, Angela G. Mertig, and Riley E. Dunlap, "Twenty Years of Environmental Mobilization: Trends among National Environmental Organizations," in *American Environmentalism: The U.S. Environmental Movement, 1970–1990*, ed. Angela G. Mertig and Riley E. Dunlap (Philadelphia: Taylor and Francis, 1992), pp. 11–25.

23 No causal linkage can be inferred because these same organizations were among the most active domestically; indeed, international activities take up a fraction of their staff time. Without a careful analysis of returns to particular direct mail appeals, it is impossible to say which new members responded to domestically oriented or internationally oriented mailings. It is worth noting that for most US environmental NGOs, "membership" denotes contributors, but does not imply participation in decision-making.

24 The ten organizations are: The Environmental Defense Fund, Friends of the Earth, The Izaak Walton League of America, The National Audubon Society, The National Parks and Conservation Association, The National Wildlife Federation, Natural Resources Defense Council. The Nature Conservancy, The Wilderness Society, and The World Wildlife Fund–US. Data from National Wildlife Federation, *The Conservation Directory* (Washington, DC: National Wildlife

Federation, 1976, 1982, 1986, 1990). Data for 1976 on the National Audubon Society come from Thaddeus C. Trzyna and Eugene V. Coan, eds., *World Directory of Environmental Organizations* (Claremont, Calif.: Public Affairs Clearinghouse, 1976).

25   Robert Paelke, *Environmentalism and the Future of Progressive Politics* (New Haven: Yale University Press, 1989).

26   See Barbara J. Bramble and Gareth Porter, "NGO Influence on United States Environmental Politics Abroad," in *The International Politics of the Environment*, ed. Andrew Hurnell and Benedict Kingsbury (Oxford: Oxford University Press, 1992).

27   David C. Korten, "The Role of Nongovernmental Organizations in Development: Changing Patterns and Perspectives," in *Nongovernment Organizations and the World Bank: Cooperation for Development*, ed. Samuel Paul and Arturo Israel (Washington, DC: The World Bank, 1991), p. 29.

28   Burke, "Friends of the Earth," pp. 117–19. On the European Environmental Bureau, see Hubert David, "Europe's Watch Dog," *IUCN Bulletin* 15:1–3 (January–March, 1984), p. 21.

29   At the 16th IUCN General Assembly in Madrid, in 1984, a report by Tom Stoel (NRDC) and Delmar Blasco (Environmental Liaison Centre) expressed NGO dissatisfaction with the organization's recognition of and support for their work. "NGOs and IUCN," *IUCN Bulletin* 15:10–12 (October–December, 1984), p. 108. It is interesting to note that the Madrid Assembly also marked the admission of Greenpeace to the IUCN, over the opposition of some of its more traditional members.

30   On the infant formula campaign, see Kathryn Sikkink, "Codes of Conduct for Transnational Corporations: The Case of the WHO/UNICEF Code," *International Organization* 40:4 (Autumn 1986): 815–40. For a more recent journalistic account see Naomi Bromberg Bar-Yam, "The Nestlé Boycott," *Mothering*, 22 December 1995, pp. 56ff. (from Nexis). On the consumer movement and transnational networking, see Leon Lindsay, "Drive Led by World Consumer Group: Fighting Pesticide 'Dumping' in Third World," *Christian Science Monitor*, 21 December 1982, p. 13; and Leon Lindsay, "Computers Aid Third-World Consumers to Claim Rights," *Christian Science Monitor*, 9 December 1982, B28.

31   *IUCN Bulletin*, 4:7 (June 1973); 4:12 (November 1973). The Latin American meeting was held in Caracas, Venezuela, in February; a similar meeting was held in May in Bandung, Indonesia.

32   Stephan Schwartzman, *Bankrolling Disasters* (San Francisco: Sierra Club, 1986). *The Ecologist* 16:2/3 (1986) devoted an entire special issue to the transmigration project.

33   World Bank, Operations Evaluation Department, "World Bank Approaches to the Environment in Brazil: A Review of Selected Projects, volume 5: The POLONOROESTE Program," 30 April 1992.

34   Interview with Stephan Schwartzman, Environmental Defense Fund, Washington, DC, 10 November 1989.

35   House Subcommittee on International Development Institutions and Finance of the Committee on Banking, Finance, and Urban Affairs, 96th Cong., 2d Sess., December 1984. On the role of Congress, see Philippe LePrestre, *The World Bank and the Environmental Challenge* (Selingsgrove, Pa.; Susquehanna University Press, 1989), pp. 191–93; and Bruce Rich, *Mortgaging the Earth: The World Bank, Environmental Impoverishment, and the Crisis of Development* (Boston: Beacon Press, 1994), pp. 113–31.

36   House Subcommittee on Foreign Operations and Related Agencies of the Committee on Appropriations, hearings on Foreign Assistance and Related Programs Appropriations for 1986, pt. 6, 99th Cong., 1st sess., 1985, pp. 750–815, especially 766–67.

37   See Bruce Rich et al. to Mr. E. Patrick Coady, Executive Director, World Bank, 9 January 1990; Osmarino Amancio Rodrigues and Ailton Krenak to Shahid Husain, Vice President for Latin America of the World Bank, 11 December 1989; Bruce Rich et al. to Luis Coirolo [*sic*], Latin

America and the Caribbean Regional Office, Brazil Division, World Bank, 19 December 1988; Francisco Mendes Filho to Barber Conable, President, World Bank, 13 October 1988; Bruce Rich and Stephan Schwartzman to Mr. S. Shahid Husain, 22 February 1980; S. Shahid Husain to Frank E. Loy, Chairman of the Board, Environmental Defense Fund, 5 March 1990; Bruce Rich and Steve Schwartzman to Shahid Husain, 14 May 1990; José Lutzenberger, National Environmental Secretary, to Barber Conable, 22 March 1990. This correspondence with its attachments is collected in packets that are available from EDF.

38 See Margaret E. Keck, "Brazil's Planafloro: The Limits of Leverage," in *The Struggle for Accountability: The World Bank, NGOs, and Grassroots Movements*, ed. Jonathan Fox and L. David Brown (Cambridge, Mass.: MIT Press, 1998).

39 This strategy was employed by the early civil rights movement in the U.S. See Doug McAdam, *Political Process and the Development of Black Insurgency, 1930–1970* (Chicago: University of Chicago Press, 1982).

40 James Brooke, "Defender of Rainforest Is Named Secretary of Environment in Brazil," *New York Times*, 6 March 1990, p. C5.

41 See Jeremy J. Warford and Zeinab Partow, *World Bank Support for the Environment: A Progress Report* (Washington, DC: World Bank Development Committee, 1989), no. 22; and Bruce Rich, "The Emperor's New Clothes: The World Bank and Environmental Reform," *World Policy Journal* 7 (Spring 1990): 305–29.

42 Nüket Kardam, in "Development Approaches and the Role of Policy Advocacy: The Case of the World Bank," *World Development* 22:11 (1993): 1773–86, explains policy change by looking at variation in organizational independence, the fit between new issues and older conceptions of mission, and the roles of internal and external advocates. She focuses on strategic efforts by internal advocates within the bank to build towards new approaches to social issues.

43 Lori Udall, "The World Bank and Public Accountability: Has Anything Changed?," November 1995 draft chapter for Fox and Brown, *The Struggle for Accountability*.

44 See Lori Udall, *A Citizens' Guide to the World Bank's Information Policy* (Washington, DC: Bank Information Center, 1994).

45 The group included FOE, National Wildlife Federation, WWF, Rainforest Action Network, EDF, Greenpeace, and others.

46 Dobson remembers *The Ecologist* and Oxfam particularly in relation to the call for an information-sharing institution.

47 Anna Lowenhaupt Tsing, *In the Realm of the Diamond Queen* (Princeton: Princeton University Press, 1993).

25 What Can We Expect from Global Labor Movements? Five Commentaries (1998, 2003)

Ralph Armbruster, Bradley Nash, Jr., Gay Seidman, Robert Ross, Richard P. Applebaum, Jennifer Bickham-Mendez, and Edna Bonacich

Globalization and Cross-Border Labor Organizing
Ralph Armbruster

The globalization of the world economy has opened up new possibilities for cross-border labor organizing. In fact, several US unions are working together with unions from Mexico, Honduras, Guatemala, the Dominican Republic, Japan, South Korea, and many European nations. For example, over the last several years, UNITE (Union of Needletrades, Industrial, and Textile Employees), the AFL-CIO, and the international garment workers trade secretariat have worked directly with maquiladora workers in Honduras and the Dominican Republic. These efforts led to the formation of several labor unions and the first contracts ever negotiated in the maquiladoras in the Dominican Republic. In addition, labor rights and solidarity organizations, like the Campaign for Labor Rights, Witness for Peace, and the US/Guatemala Labor Education Project (US/GLEP), along with many other groups, have also played key roles in the formation of maquiladora unions in Nicaragua and Guatemala.

Two recent and successful cross-border labor organizing campaigns involved Phillips Van-Heusen (PVH) and the GAP (Armbruster, 1997; Pattee, 1996). These two US-based garment manufacturers "contract out" production – mostly shirts and jeans – to factories in Guatemala and El Salvador respectively. Both companies employ mostly young women who work very long hours and who earn far below the prevailing "living wage." These conditions, along with dehumanizing treatment from supervisors, led PVH and GAP workers to begin organizing. However, both companies responded with repressive tactics that included mass firings, death threats, severance payments, and involuntary dismissals. Both companies also threatened to cut their contracts with their suppliers and move to different locations. Yet, these women workers continued organizing and eventually won. After seven years, the PVH workers' union was recognized and contract negotiations are currently underway. The GAP signed a historic independent monitoring agreement with labor and human rights groups who oversee the company's contractors in Central America.

These victories contradict the theoretical literature, including some variants of the world-system perspective, on cross-border labor organizing. Previous research indicates that there are three main forces which limit the possibility of cross-border organizing. First, the globalization perspective suggests the rapid dispersion of production, especially in the highly mobile garment industry, can undermine cross-border organizing between labor unions in two different nations. Second, repressive and corporatist state-labor relationships often produce small and weak labor movements. Under these conditions the establishment of cross-border labor linkages is extremely difficult. The third factor limiting cross-border labor organizing involves the long history of the AFL-CIO in Latin America, Africa, and Asia. For nearly fifty years the AFL-CIO's foreign affiliates undermined and divided labor unions all over the world. These machinations generated suspicion of the AFL-CIO and restricted cross-border organizing between US unions and unions in Latin America, Asia, and Africa.

Interestingly, these three factors were all present in the PVH and GAP campaigns. The existing literature would predict that cross-border labor organizing that effectively targeted two highly mobile garment manufacturers in nations noted for their violent history of labor repression, and which involved the AFL-CIO and US-based labor rights groups such as US/GLEP and the National Labor Committee (NLC), would be virtually impossible. Given these overwhelming odds, how did the PVH and GAP workers achieve their victories?

In the case of Phillips Van-Heusen, the PVH workers obtained critical support from the garment workers trade secretariat. Second, US/GLEP and NLC used trade pressure and provided legal assistance and media coverage to the PVH and GAP workers. Third, a new, strategic organizing model and local union activism were critical elements of the PVH campaign. Fourth, students, religious groups, and Central American solidarity organizations from the United States and Canada leafleted retailers (like J. C. Penney and Wal-Mart) who sold PVH and GAP products and raised consumer awareness of these issues. Fifth, the PVH and GAP workers and their international network of supporters targeted the "socially responsible" image of both companies. Interestingly, PVH and the GAP both have corporate codes of conduct, establishing minimal standards that their overseas suppliers must abide by, but neither company ever informed their workers of these codes. Public scrutiny and direct attacks on these companies' carefully crafted image were particularly effective in limiting capital flight. The combination of these elements produced two stunning victories for women garment workers in Guatemala and El Salvador.

These two cases illustrate the potential of cross-border labor organizing and the limitations of the existing literature. However, there have also been many unsuccessful cases of cross-border organizing. For instance, the United Auto Workers (UAW) has not yet developed ties with the Ford Democratic Workers Movement in Mexico, although UAW Local 879 and UAW Region 1A have done so. Thus the current outlook for the development of a global labor movement is mixed. Renewed labor militancy in the United States, the closing of the AFL-CIO's foreign affiliates, harsh working conditions in many developing nations, and the emergence of consumer campaigns that attack the public image of multinational corporations have generated exciting cross-border organizing campaigns. However, bureaucratic union structures, corporatist labor movements, and other factors still limit cross-border organizing.

Cross-border organizing is very difficult and there are no easy formulas for action. As academics and activists we should study these cases carefully and offer our support.

REFERENCES

Armbruster, Ralph (1997). "Cross-Border Labor Organizing in the Garment Industry: The Struggle of Maquiladora Workers at Phillips Van-Heusen." Paper presented at the Pacific Sociological Association Conference.

Pattee, Jon (1996), " 'Gapatistas' Win a Victory." *Labor Research Review* 24: 77–86.

Organizing a Global Labor Movement from Top and Bottom
Bradley Nash, Jr.

While the prospects for a global labor movement are ripe, working people and their supporters may fail to take full advantage of this historical opening. A potential barrier is the existence of a strategic myopia when it comes to the role of preexisting labor organizations at the national and international levels. Specifically, these higher-tier institutions are often viewed by labor activists and the rank-and-file as inherently autocratic and imperialistic, and are thus deemed to have little value for efforts at fostering global labor solidarity. A consequence is that many in the labor movement concentrate their energies solely at a local or community level, with the idea that it is only here that true progressive change can result. In terms of broader solidarity and resistance, it is felt that cross-regional and cross-national linkages will eventually develop to expand the struggle to a truly global level. In effect, it is presumed by many that a global labor movement will, and in fact must, be built strictly from the "bottom-up" (e.g., Brecher and Costello, 1994).

I by no means wish to undermine the value of bottom-up strategies for furthering the development of a global labor movement. Indeed, in recent years grass-roots initiatives and struggles have undeniably been enormously more successful in resisting capitalist exploitation, furthering local interests, and establishing equitable linkages between working peoples around the world than their counterparts at the national and international levels. However, such bottom-up strategies do need to be complemented by "top-down" initiatives as well, including such actions as the implementation of global labor standards, accelerated cross-border organizing by national and international unions, and transnational coordination and cooperation between various peak-level labor confederations. Further, global level initiatives like these can in part be accomplished by transforming existing institutions, rather than by the lengthy creation of entirely new international worker organizations from the bottom-up.

The trepidation and hesitation with which working people approach existing national and international labor institutions is certainly warranted. Taking the AFL-CIO as one example, it is certainly understandable why rank-and-file workers even in the United States, let alone in Asia, Africa, and Latin America, would resent and mistrust collaborating with this organization. At home, the AFL-CIO leadership spent decades stifling domestic labor militancy and channeling it into an acquiescent "business unionism" that supported, rather than challenged, U.S. capitalism. This support was even more salient abroad, as the AFL-CIO used its Department of International Affairs to implement the anti-Communist foreign policy of the US government and to ensure the continued global hegemony of American capital (e.g., Bina and Davis, 1993: 158–60; Borgers, 1996: 78–9; Howard, 1995: 371).

If anything, then, as an established labor organization operating at the transnational level, the AFL-CIO has long hindered, rather than facilitated, the prospects for a global labor movement. Despite this inglorious history, the AFL-CIO has in recent years moved, however slightly, toward a more progressive position. Armbruster (1995: 78), for example, cites the importance of the AFL-CIO's membership in the Coalition for Justice in the Maquiladoras (CJM), as well as the utilization of its "vast organizational resources", in the success of corporate campaigns in Mexico. Frundt (1996: 396–7) also lauds the AFL-CIO's involvement with the CJM, and additionally notes the federation's involvement with progressive labor groups in countries such as Guatemala, El Salvador, Brazil, Argentina, and Chile.

This shift in AFL-CIO strategy is attributable both to external and internal pressures. Externally, as put by Bina and Davis (1993: 160), "[t]he global integration of capitalist production has undermined the material conditions that have supported [the] AFL-CIO's traditionally nationalist, class-collaborationist posture". In effect, the need for a global response to global capital has become an unavoidable reality. Internally, progressive change has emanated both from the bottom and from the top of organizations. Beginning in the mid-1980s, rank-and-file activists and several member unions successfully challenged the AFL-CIO leadership on its stance toward Central America, notably its support of the Reagan Administration's Nicaraguan policy (Howard, 1995: 376). In the mid 1990s, the AFL-CIO leadership itself changed, with a coalition coming to power that, at least on paper, appeared more attuned to the needs of rank-and-file workers both within and, importantly, outside the United States (Borgers, 1996: 71–2).

The case of the AFL-CIO points to a fact that proponents of a strictly bottom-up organizing strategy frequently lose sight of: organizations and their structures are human creations and are therefore malleable. The "Michelsian paradigm" that has long dominated thinking about formal organizations, and about labor organizations in particular, needs to be fully discarded (Stepan-Norris and Zeitlin, 1996). Large-scale bureaucratic organizations do not all inevitably slide into oligarchy, and those that do need not remain that way. The democratization of existing institutions for the representation of worker interests, albeit extremely difficult, is always a possibility. Overall, given the pace with which the globalization of production proceeds, workers of the world may not have the luxury of waiting for a new global labor movement to be built anew from the bottom-up. It might be better to also consider working with what we already have at the "top," and thus conduct the struggle on two fronts.

REFERENCES

Armbruster, R. 1995. "Cross-National Labor Organizing Strategies." *Critical Sociology* 21 (2): 75–89.

Bina, C. and C. Davis. 1993. "Transnational Capital, the Global Labor Process, and the International Labor Movement." In *The Labor Process and Control of Labor: The Changing Nature of Work Relations in the Late Twentieth Century*, edited by B. Berberoglu. Westport, Conn: Praeger.

Borgers, F. 1996. "The Challenges of Economic Globalization for US Labor." *Critical Sociology* 22 (2): 67–88.

Brecher, J. and T. Costello. 1994. *Global Village or Global Pillage?: Economic Reconstruction from the Bottom Up.* Boston, Mass: South End Press.

Frundt, H. J. 1996. "Trade and Cross-Border Labor Strategies in the Americas." *Economic and Industrial Democracy* 17 (August): 387–417.

Howard, A. 1995. "Global Capital and Labor Internationalism in Comparative Historical Perspective: A Marxist Analysis." *Sociological Inquiry* 65 (November): 365–94.

Stepan-Norris, J. and M. Zeitlin. 1996. "Insurgency, Radicalism, and Democracy in America's Industrial Unions." *Social Forces* 75 (1): 1–32.

Introduction to Forum "Would Including a Social Clause in Trade Treaties Help or Hinder?"
Gay Seidman and Robert Ross

In their 1848 Manifesto, Marx and Engels issued an epoch-making call to internationalism: "The proletarians have nothing to lose but their chains. They have a world to win. Workers of All Countries Unite!"

But for a long century, that clarion call sounded more sentimental than empirical: workers did have something to lose; most of what they had and what they got was organized nationally – their unions, their social benefits, their political alliances. Since the mid-nineteenth century, most theorists of European working class movements understood that the working classes of advanced industrial countries benefited from colonial domination. Through the late twentieth century, many analysts in the world system tradition continued to argue that workers in the developed world benefit from the exploitation of workers in the periphery.

More recently, however, that debate has shifted: many analysts today suggest that global capital mobility creates a 'race to the bottom' as capital moves to lower-wage regions of the world, undermining workers' historic gains in the core. Stagnating wages, growing inequality, the reemergence of sweatshop conditions – these are seen as consequences of capital's leverage over workers, obtained by real and threatened flight to the South.

In the US, for example, 2.6 million manufacturing jobs have been lost from 2000 through September 2003. Since 2000, real wage gains of production workers have been under one percent; about half the pathetic 1.2% gained by all private non-supervisory employees. Since 1998 almost 17% of the US manufacturing employment base has been lost.

Unfortunately these job relocations have not been compensated by working class gains in the countries receiving the manufacturing investment cascading away from the core. Mexican workers lost ground in the '90s, and then when they began to make gains at the turn of the century, jobs flowed to China, where strict control of working class expression is severely restricted.

So, inquiring theorists want to know: what strategies might labor internationalism pursue to advance the interests of the workers of the world?

The American labor movement has advocated for years that access to the concessions of the major trade agreements (NAFTA, WTO) should be contingent upon national enforcement of core labor rights. Should these be systematically violated trading partner nations would then have recourse to trade sanctions (i.e., tariffs).

Governments of most developing countries oppose such "social clauses" in trade agreements, while labor groups are more divided. Some developing country labor movements support labor rights conditionality in trade agreements, while others oppose it.

The PEWS newsletter asked several academic and labor experts their view of this matter, asking them to comment briefly on the question: From your perspective, would the inclusion of labor standards in trade treaties improve workers' conditions internationally? Please explain.

Richard P. Appelbaum

A social clause in trade treaties would be a first step toward securing workers' rights in a global economy. Currently the global workforce is lacking in protections of any sort, contributing to what has been aptly called the global race to the bottom. Manufacturers are free to scour the planet for the lowest wages and the most exploitive working conditions they can find. (The same is true regarding environmental protections.) State regulations – labor's hard-won rights, at least in industrial societies – are rapidly being dismantled, in favor of privatized gestures at self-regulation. There is a mountain of research by now that shows when industries monitor themselves, it is a classic case of the fox guarding the chicken coop – plenty of self-congratulatory rhetoric, intended to confuse consumers and lull them into complacency.

Critics of social clauses (which includes nearly the entire economics profession, as well as their clients in the governments of developing countries) argue that any restrictions on labor markets in poor countries will rob those countries of their one competitive resource – cheap labor. However well-intended such measures, the critics contend, they are in fact thinly-disguised protectionist efforts to keep jobs in the high-wage core by pricing workers elsewhere out of the market. Young anti-sweatshop activists in the US are accused of being duped by cynical labor unions. I am not making this up – check out the full-page add that the Academic Consortium on International Trade (self-described as "a group of academic economists and lawyers who are specialized in international trade policy and international economic law") sent to university presidents in September 2000 (http://www.fordschool.umich.edu/rsie/acit/Documents/July29SweatshopLetter.pdf).

Critics are wrong. An adequate social clause would raise the bar for both signatories. If it requires the payment of a living wage in Mexico, it would do the same for the US. Formulas have been developed to make wage requirements comparable in countries at very different levels of economic development (see, for example, Richard Rothstein's proposal in a prophetic article he wrote on NAFTA ten years ago; http://www.prospect.org/print/V4/12/rothstein-r.html).

And wages are not the whole story, anyhow. Consider the fact that the direct labor cost of a $25 shirt sewn in Mexico might be 30 cents at best; in China, a dime. Would doubling the wages in either country really price its workers out of the market? Even if the entire cost were passed onto consumers (rather than taken out of the lavish compensation packages that transnational manufacturers and retailers bestow on their top management), would consumers really balk at paying a few cents extra? Perhaps that is why labor union federations in developing countries support social clauses, even when their governments, claiming to speak on behalf of workers, oppose them. (Bob Ross has written eloquently on this topic.)

Moreover, wage minimums are only part of a social clause. More important is the guaranteed right for workers to attempt to form unions, if they so desire, and to engage in collective bargaining if they succeed in doing so. It can hardly be called "protectionist" to require that workers be permitted to represent their own interests, free from fear of being fired – or killed – for speaking out. As union members, workers can then make their own decisions about the wages they deserve, and the danger that their factory will lose their business if they get a raise, overtime pay for extra hours, or medical benefits. Even small increases in workers' compensation could make an enormous difference in their livelihoods, while adding almost nothing at the cash register.

When workers anywhere, at any time in history, have clamored for a slightly larger increase in their slice of the pie, corporations (backed up by their academic ideologues) have claimed that the workers were ill-informed and misguided, and only shooting themselves in the foot – and that their demands – if granted – would pretty much end civilization as we know it. These arguments were made when workers struggled for equality in the United States a century ago, just as they are being made today. Workers, and their advocates, ignored them the first time around. They should ignore them today as well.

Jennifer Bickham-Mendez

. . . Who are authentic workers? Who represents workers' interests? What qualifies as a labor issue, and who decides this? These are more than philosophical questions. They have real and lived implications for men and women who are struggling to assert their labor rights in a context of the worldwide decline of the Keynesian nation-state.

According to the UN, women's participation in the workforce is increasing in nearly every country around the world. The ILO estimates that 80% of workers in export-oriented, maquiladora plants are women. And maquiladora workers are not simply passive victims of neoliberal globalization and export-oriented development. Nor are they the unorganizable sector that discourses about women as "ideal workers," often articulated by plant managers in the global assembly line, purport them to be. In locations as diverse as Mexico, South Korea, Sri Lanka and the Philippines women maquila workers have organized to fight for better pay and working conditions. Sometimes these mobilizations have taken the form of traditional unions, other initiatives have occurred with the support and assistance of unions and union federations. In other instances, for example, in Mexico and Central America, women workers' groups have formed as organizational spaces that are separate and distinct from unions. These groups organize women workers in their communities, offer them education regarding their social, reproductive and labor rights, and support them legally as they file complaints related to labor violations. They also launch national and international campaigns to improve working conditions in maquila factories. For these organizations workers are neither women nor workers first – their needs, priorities, indeed, even their RIGHTS as citizens are simultaneously and equally shaped by their social position of gender and class.

The struggle of these organizations and the maquiladora workers whom they support and who make up a significant portion of their leadership underscores the findings of a generation of feminist scholars who have studied the gendered dimensions of the global economy. Gender power structures keep the wheels of the global economy running smoothly, ensuring the kind of flexibility necessary for Post-Fordist production. And the conditions and violations that women workers face (for example, forced birth control and institutionalized sexual harassment) are often gender as well as racially and ethnically specific. By the same token, unions continue to be male-dominated organizational spaces. For example, though in Central America many of the unions that have formed in the maquilas have a large female representation among the rank-and-file, higher-level federation and union leadership continues to be almost exclusively male. And more importantly, gender issues as articulated by women workers often remain an after-thought or are conspicuously absent from collective bargaining agreements or codes of conduct negotiated by union federations and their supporters in the international labor movement. In particular, private sphere and community issues such as maternity benefits, firings resulting from absence from work to care for sick children, job loss due to pregnancy, safety during transportation to work, reproductive health and rights, and more gender-specific labor issues like sexual harassment are often absent from the demands of unions, but are highlighted by women workers' organizations.

Critics of social clauses maintain that they will do little to prevent the so-called "race to the bottom." But an equally important, less visible issue is the decision-making process for determining the content of workers' clauses in trade treaties. Social clauses based on a gender-neutral (read: male) worker will do little to address the intersection of issues related to both the public and private spheres that impacts women workers' daily lives. And in a global production system that makes use of geopolitical power, as well as race and gender-based structures of oppression, clauses that do not incorporate the particularities of workers' multiple positions – in the home, community and workplace – will have a limited impact on the conditions that workers face. Only through an inclusive and democratic process in which the varied experiences and vulnerabilities that are glossed by a universalized category of "worker" are prioritized can social clauses or any other solution to workers' oppression in the global economy be achieved.

Edna Bonacich

On the one hand, social clauses seem very attractive. They are reminiscent of the New Deal in the US, with its setting of a minimum wage, maximum hours, equal pay for equal work, rights to engage in collective bargaining, unemployment insurance, welfare, social security, etc. One purpose of such regulation was to prevent workers from being caught in bargains of desperation, where they would be forced to "sell" themselves for a pittance. There were other purposes as well: to take labor standards out of competition, to prevent disruptive labor disputes, and to develop a consuming middle class. Sadly, while the ideal of this legislation may have been to create equality among all workers, in practice it had important exclusions that limited equality for workers of color, especially women of color.

Now the question arises, can and should such a concept be established at an international level? First it is noteworthy that this kind of welfare state legislation has been seriously eroded within the U.S. and other developed capitalist countries. Clearly, employers and investors do not want to take wages and working conditions out of competition, and prefer dealing with a competitive, fragmented labor market. Many of them *want* a race to the bottom, regardless of protestations about "high road" development strategies. Their resistance on the national level has to be a pale reflection of their resistance at the international level.

Second, and more important, on a global level poor countries are trying to pursue development. Under the current system, where transnational capital controls the world economy, what do they have to offer besides low wage labor? How else can they get a foot in the door? Given this situation, social clauses called for by workers and unions in developed countries sound awfully like protectionism. They don't want the jobs to move offshore. Setting higher standards in the poorer countries means they will be less likely to flee.

Don't get me wrong: I believe that trying to set global labor standards is a good thing. But it can't be isolated from much larger questions. These include: providing workers who are unemployed with a means of survival, offering education programs so that a nation's children have a chance for better employment, and most important, developing a world division of labor such that each nation gets its fair share of production and consumption. If we could provide global social security, global unemployment insurance, global 12-year minimum educational opportunities, if we could ensure that the poorer countries would receive capital for investing in their industries even if they did not have starvation wages and living conditions, then a global labor clause would make good sense. But to just set up a minimum wage (for example) without these other forms of support will not, in my opinion, help the people it is intended(?) to help. It will mainly protect first world jobs and labor standards.

One aspect of social clauses deserves special mention, namely, protecting the right of workers to form independent unions. If this kind of political right can be guaranteed on a global level, then workers themselves would have a say in whether or not they want to set standards in their country. Certainly, some workers, unions, and NGOs in developing countries want to see social clauses as a tool in their struggles. Under these circumstances, when the affected workers are themselves calling for the clauses, I completely support them. The challenge consists in forcing nations (including the US) and international institutions seriously to support trade union (and broader political) rights of workers. It boils down to the question of having the power to compel system change. Do top down reforms achieve it? They may open some doors a crack. But they can hardly be seen as a solution unless organized workers have the capacity to force the doors wide open.

On the whole, I feel that piecemeal reform of global production, without a larger vision of how we think the world's economy ought to be organized, is very limited. I would emphasize the need for a world plan that allocates production and consumption according to principles of equity rather than according to the market. I would also argue for a system in which the working class was a major force in shaping the global political economy. . . .

26 Transnational Solidarity: Women's Agency, Structural Adjustment, and Globalization (2002)

Manisha Desai

In this chapter I examine how global capital, structural adjustment programs and international institutions such as the United Nations have shaped women's agency around the world. In particular, I focus on two important features of women's agency in the global era. First, just as global capital is fluid and exists simultaneously in multiple spaces, resulting in "scattered hegemonies" (Grewal and Kaplan 1994), so is women's agency evident in multiple spaces from the local grassroots movements and community-based nongovernmental organizations (NGOs) to national and transnational feminist networks. Second, women from around the world have been forging transnational feminist solidarities via networks, regional meetings, and world conferences. At these sites, the flow of ideas and activism is no longer unidirectional, from the North to the South, but multidirectional. The ideas and activism are dispersed into varied local sites where they are picked up and refashioned as they resonate in contextualized ways.

While globalization has been variously defined (for example, Wachtel [2001] has collected 450 definitions), many analysts associate globalization with the homogenizing impact of global capital (e.g., Giddens 1990). This occurs via increasing economic integration resulting in one world market. Transnational corporations (TNCs) and international financial institutions shape this market through global production, consumption, and capital flows facilitated by the revolution in information and communication technologies. By contrast, analysts who focus on the global flows of people, ideas, and images emphasize the hybridity, or the heterogeneity that results as people from different parts of the world interact and creatively combine their own patterns of meaning making with those that derive from other cultures (Appadurai 1990; Hall 1991).

These two apparently contrasting views appear not so contradictory when one recognizes that each view tends to focus on only one aspect of globalization – the political-economic dimensions in the case of the "homogenizers," and cultural practices in the case of the "heterogenizers." Moreover, neither specifically looks at how women are responding to the global political economy through innovative political, economic, and cultural strategies. When one shifts the focus to women's agency in the global political economy, we see a complex set of relations that are built on preexisting patriarchal, racial, and ethnic practices. One also sees women creating new sites for action at the local, national, and transnational levels in which to enact new political, economic, and cultural practices. In this way, women activists offer alternatives to the seemingly inevitable course of global capital. Consequently, women's agency in this era of globalization challenges the dominant framing of globalization and opens up new directions for both feminist theorizing and activism.

The Gendered Effects of Structural Adjustment Programs

Structural adjustment programs (SAPs) are the primary mechanism through which globalization has affected women's daily lives in the South. In the North, similar effects result from economic restructuring of manufacturing and neoliberal policies that emphasize privatization in all aspects of the political economy. SAPs were first engineered by the International Monetary Fund (IMF) and the World Bank. Sean Riain (2000) argues that globalization has imposed the dominant Anglo-American neoliberal model of the relationship between state and transnational capital on neoliberal, socialist, and postcolonial states. Hence, most states have adopted a package that shares some variant of the following features:

> (1) cutbacks in public spending to balance government budgets and service debts; (2) monetary policies designed to fight inflation by restricting the money supply (and incomes); (3) the selling of government enterprises (privatization) in an attempt to balance government budgets and improve business production efficiency; and (4) the shift of manufacturing and agricultural sectors toward production for export instead of the domestic market, in order to improve international balances. (Wiegersma 1997, 258)

The basic argument scholars have made about the impact of SAPs on women worldwide is that "adjustment intensifies the trade-off between women's producer and non-producer roles, or, in stronger terms, that the 'crisis of social disinvestment (under adjustment) is financed from a "social fund" provided by the superhuman efforts of poor women' (UNICEF 1989)" (Baden 1997, 38).

These policies have had four major effects on women. First, there has been a contradictory impact on women's paid work. There has been a feminization of the global labor force and an increase in women's employment in the low-paid service sector (Fuentes and Ehrenreich 1983; also see Nash and Fernandez-Kelly 1983; Ward 1990). This is evident in the increasing rate of women's share of paid economic activity all over the South particularly in export processing zones in the North. In 2000, women constituted 36 percent of the total global workforce. In the global trade policy literature this is known as the "employment effect" of international trade. Women are now 33 percent of the Asian labor force as compared to 25 percent in 1970; women are 28 percent of the labor force in Latin American and the Caribbean compared to 20 percent in 1970; women comprise 42 percent of the European labor force compared to 35 percent in 1970, and in North America, women are 30 percent of the labor force compared to 24 percent in 1970 (Neft and Levine 1997). In Sub-Saharan Africa, where agriculture is still the predominant means of support, women have not become a large part of the industrial labor force; rather, they contribute, in large measure, to export-oriented agriculture, and through their unpaid labor in the home (Fontana, Joekes, and Masika 1998).

Second, there has been an increase in women's employment in the informal sector, where workers receive no protections from unemployment, no benefits, and wages below poverty level. Third, women's share of unpaid labor in the home has increased as public funding for health, education, and other social services has declined. Finally, as more and more land is appropriated for global production, land for cultivation and local sustenance diminishes, and environmental damage escalates. Women in the South, who depend on their environments more directly for material and cultural resources, face great survival difficulties while women in the North, particularly those living in poor neighborhoods, find their communities becoming dumping grounds for toxic and other waste generated in an economy that hardly benefits them. Women in the North and South have responded to each of these challenges in multiple ways leading to what is best called scattered resistance.

The Gendered Restructuring of Labor and Women's Resistances

Global capital has a contradictory impact on women's daily lives. Along with the selective increase in women's work there is also evidence of increasing unemployment. For example, in Ghana, 20 percent of women in the traditional trading markets lost their jobs as SAPs provided credits to large-scale trading enterprises controlled by men (Manuh 1997). Small trading markets were made obsolete by these changes. In eastern European countries, where women had high rates of labor force participation compared to the rest of the world, the picture has changed dramatically since 1989. Many of these countries have undergone the transition from a planned economy to a free-market economy. As a result, female labor force activity has declined in 10 of the 14 eastern European countries. An estimated 26 million jobs were lost in the region from 1990 to 1995, and 14 million of those jobs were women's (Moner Report 1999).

While overt unionizing was, and still remains, difficult in the export processing zones (EPZs), feminist analyses focused on various political as well as cultural resistance of women at the local level. For example, anthropologist Aihwa Ong (1987) discusses the claims of spirit possessions, which require time-consuming rituals to free women workers and/or their machines from these spirits, as among a very resourceful resistance to increased demands and new tasks. These have led to work stoppages as well as garnering certain benefits such as breaks. Similarly, analysts of women in the maquiladoras along the US/Mexico border note how women workers engage in work stoppages for cultural celebrations and use religious and other traditional practices to organize workers (e.g., Fernandez-Kelly 1983; Tiano 1994).

Transnational solidarity networks have also grown to post a significant challenge to SAPs and other neoliberal policies. These networks include unions, movements, NGOs of local women working in the EPZs as well as middle-class activists from the country and transnational NGOs and movements. Alvarez notes the increasing NGO-ization of women's movements with its attendant decline in radical critique and an increasing role in serving as experts and implementers of government and international donors' programs. Some

NGOs are no more than fronts for the government, while others Alvarez calls "hybrid NGOs" maintain links with movements and try to work both within and outside the system. These NGOs simultaneously provide a critique of government agencies and actions as well as mobilize to gain resources for empowering women.

Activist networks are often supported by public consciousness-raising efforts that are mainly located in the Northern countries and whose focus is educating Northern consumers. Many NGOs include consumer education as part of their advocacy work on behalf of maquiladora workers and other low-wage workers in the "global assembly line." For example, Women Working Worldwide in the United Kingdom is an international coalition that highlights the effects of trade liberalization on women workers in Bangladesh, India, Korea, Mexico, Peru, South Korea, Thailand, and the United Kingdom through networking and public education. The Clean Clothes Campaign, based in the Netherlands, supports the struggles of women workers in garment-producing units, sweatshops, factories, and home-based industry for improved working conditions in the South and North by making the European public aware of the situation. Label Behind the Label is a similar effort based in the United Kingdom to promote the rights and working conditions of women workers in the garment industries around the world.

In addition to activist networks, many academic and policy-oriented international groups work together with NGOs around the world to contextualize the oppressive features of global economic restructuring. Groups like DAWN (Development Alternatives with Women for a New Era) and the Women's Alternative Economic Summit focus on research and policy through developing regional centers in Latin America, Asia, and Africa. While the local and transnational networks focus on women in the global economy, most women find themselves in the so-called informal sector where the struggle is to assert a right to work.

Asserting a Right to Work

Over the globe, 71 percent of women work in the less visible informal sector where they prepare products for sale in the market, domestic service, and work in their homes to produce goods for subcontractors (e.g., Benería and Feldman 1992; SEWA 1998; Ward 1990). Although such work is unregulated, poorly paid, and involves long hours, it plays a crucial role in maintaining a modicum of livelihood for most poor women in a post–structural adjustment world. In fact, the World Bank and other development agencies like the US Agency for International Development (USAID) have celebrated and supported the microcredit movement . . . the discourse of microcredit and microenterprise prioritizes the market rather than women's economic and social empowerment.

Women have been at the forefront of detailing the relationship of their informal work and unpaid household labor to the formal economy. The Self-Employed Women's Association (SEWA) in India was one of the first organizations to define the various informal activities of women, such as vegetable vending, ragpicking, and producing goods at home for sale *as work*. Established in 1972, SEWA successfully unionized informal women workers who had been prevented from organizing unions because trade union laws in India did not recognize them as workers. In addition to unionizing, women in India have formed co-operatives based on their various economic activities in order to market effectively, share resources, and form support networks. Most important, SEWA has trained community health workers and set up a SEWA university to train women not just in production and managerial skills but to be leaders and organizers who can participate in decisions that affect their lives. SEWA now has close to two million members in cities throughout India as well as in rural areas in Gujarat. SEWA has had the dual focus on "union" and "development" from the start but over time it has become more defined and elaborate. In the process of unionizing, SEWA also fosters a critical understanding about the economy and social inequalities and uses that knowledge to address these inequalities – particularly the impact of religious violence among Hindus and Muslims.

Similarly, women working in the informal economies in Tanzania, Ghana, Zimbabwe, Ecuador, Peru, and other countries have formed networks to pool resources, start savings and credit associations and form solidarities for survival (e.g., Bose and Acosta-Belén 1995; Osirim 1996; Mitter and Rowbotham 1994). In addition to local networks, self-employed women, like their counterparts in the EPZs, have also formed transnational networks such as GROOTS (Grass-roots Organizations Operating Together in Sisterhood) International, primarily to learn new ideas, share best practices, and influence local and international policy making around informal sector issues. Marina Karides demonstrates such transnational activism and unionizing efforts of another major sector of the informal economy, namely domestic work. She shows how Trinidad's National Union of Domestic Employees (NUDE) has worked for the rights of domestic workers, who are primarily women, by using the global rhetoric and international agreements signed by Trinidad to make the government accountable at home.

In the North, the informal activity is primarily concentrated among women of color, mostly immigrant women of color, who provide services that cannot be shifted to the South, such as domestic help and low-wage jobs in the food and health services. Sassen (1999) calls this the "de-valorized" sector of the economy as opposed to the valorized, information technology sector, which employs only a small, highly educated segment. White, upper-class women's increased presence in professional sectors of the North has influenced the incorporation of immigrant women of color into what Hochschild (2000) calls "global care chains," a "series of personal links between people across the globe based on the paid or unpaid work of caring" (131). Hochschild takes a critical modernist perspective on the global care chain, recognizing the global inequalities of resources as well as care, and does not see it as simply an inevitable part of globalization. At the same time she avoids a "primordialist stance" that mothers should care for their own children and kin and not migrate to care for others' children. She advocates not only better pay and working conditions for the immigrant caregivers but immigration policies that would allow children access to their mothers who have migrated North.

Struggling for a Better Quality of Life

Another major effect of global economic restructuring has been the increase in women's unpaid labor at home. Even before SAPs, women did 70 percent of the world's unpaid work. Now women all over the world are engaged in providing more care for children, elderly parents, and other family members, in addition to their poorly paid work either in the formal or informal sector of the economy. Women thus bear additional emotional stress arising from the "belt-tightening" demanded by economic restructuring (Kirmani and Munyakho 1996; Nzomo 1994).

As the price of goods – especially food – has increased in all parts of the world, women have become even more vulnerable to malnutrition as they eat last after providing for their children and family members. This has led women's groups in India, Zimbabwe, and other countries to demand the continuance and growth of the public distribution system, which in the case of India provides subsidized food to the urban and rural poor. Women's groups are also working with the World Food Program to ensure that women and children are able to get at least the minimum food required to sustain them. As Blank (1997), Naples (1998), and other scholars have demonstrated, so-called welfare reforms in the United States have also disproportionately affected women-headed households.

The absence from national statistics of women's unpaid work and informal labor continues to be a concern for feminist activists. The Beijing Declaration and Platform for Action that arose out of the Women's World Conference in 1995 affirmed the need to count women's work in the home and remunerate women for that work, but most countries have not taken any serious steps in that direction. To highlight this noncompliance, women in Ireland called a women's strike on March 8, 1999, demanding an end to the devaluation of women's waged and unwaged labor. Since then the strike has become global as women from 64 countries observed it in 2000. It has also been taken up by the International Wages for Housework Campaign and the International Women Count Network.

In addition to such international challenges, a myriad of local challenges are addressing the "public provision" effect of SAPs. Many local and international NGOs have taken up the task of providing women with education, health services, and political empowerment. For example, programs like Mahila Samakhya in India, partly funded by the state, is a program of education for empowering women based on a process of consciousness-raising, organizing, and broadening the awareness and skills of poor rural women in order to take control of their lives. This program exists in six states in India and is run in collaboration with women's-movement groups, which oversee both the content as well as the process of educating women for empowerment (IAWS 1995).

Other women's groups have organized in urban and rural areas to provide and demand health services from the state. However, many of these services are being dismantled or privatized. Women and children are the main users of health services, and women are the primary providers of health care. If health is taken to mean, in accordance with the World Health Organization (WHO), a "state of complete physical, mental, and social well-being" then women's health has deteriorated in all respects in the contemporary era of global trade.

Starting in the early 1980s, the World Bank promoted a series of health-related initiatives to pressure Third World governments to control population growth. It recommended universal measures for reform that did not take into consideration Third World women's economic, social, or cultural realities. These initiatives emphasized privatization of health care to be understood as introduction of user charges in state health clinics and hospitals, especially for consumer drugs and curative care (the rationale was that the rich would be made to pay, thus leaving the government free to pay for community services and public health for the poor); promotion of third-party insurance such as sickness funds and social security; promotion of hospitals, nursing homes, and clinics; and decentralization of planning,

budgeting, and purchasing for government health services (Turshen 1994). Such privatization recommendations are especially problematic in countries where the people already
assume a greater share of health care burden than in First World countries. In the latter,
especially Scandinavian countries, governments assume more than 90 percent of health
expenditure. By contrast, in Sub-Saharan Africa and Asia, governments contribute only
about 52 to 57 percent of the total health budget.

One of the consequences of privatization of health care in Third World countries has
been a cut in public health services, particularly primary care, and the increased use of
nongovernmental and private voluntary organizations to deliver services (Turshen 1994).
In Africa, NGOs provide between 25 and 94 percent of health services. For example,
25 percent of hospital care in Ghana is private; in Zimbabwe 94 percent of services for
the elderly are private; and in Uganda and Malawi 40 percent of all health services are
private. Privatization has greatly reduced government-funded primary care, thus limiting
the access of poor people, particularly women, to health care. In some cases, health care
is completely inaccessible to poor women. When poor women have to pay for health
care from their meager earnings, they do so for their children but not for themselves
(Butegwa 1998).

[. . .]

Women have responded to declining health services by developing community-based
health projects, making demands on the state to be more accountable, and linking with
groups in their country and around the world to influence national and international policies. In India groups like the Centre for Enquiry into Health and Allied Themes (CEHAT,
which also means "health" in several Indian languages) are at the forefront of providing
services to women and of researching and providing critiques of the impact of SAPS on
women's health. Studies by CEHAT reveal that the state has never committed more than
3.5 percent of its gross national product to the health sector. This small percentage has
further eroded since the 1970s and reached a low of 2.6 percent in 1994–5, at the peak of
the liberalization effort. The public health expenditure's share in the national income since
SAPs is less than 1 percent. Most of the health budget comes from the state and not the
national government. At the individual level, the CEHAT studies found that given the
paucity of public health availability, 80 percent of health care costs come out of people's
own pockets.

In addition to conducting research, CEHAT has a number of activists who live in urban
and rural poor communities and develop health education and primary health care projects
alongside the people in the communities. Many CEHAT members are founders of the
second wave of the women's movement in India. Through their effort, they have incorporated a feminist perspective into the health debates and have added a concern for health to
the women's movement agenda. CEHAT's assumption is that equitable and appropriate
health care can be possible only in a context of economic and social equality. Hence,
CEHAT has worked with local women to form village-level women's health teams, to
establish a bank run by women, and to provide training for health work.

In addition to community-based work, a national network has emerged through CEHAT's
efforts. Called Health Watch: A Network for Action and Research on Women's Health, its
major objective is to increase the attention paid to women's health needs and concerns
in public debates and national policy. Health Watch has begun a dialogue with the

government at various levels. For example, in 1998 it brought together activists from the western region in India to discuss a new government initiative known as a "target-free" approach to population policy. This initiative provides for a more woman-centered approach to reproduction and eliminated the quotas that local health practitioners had to meet for population control.

CEHAT is also part of international networks such as the International Network of Health and Human Rights Organizations, ISIS-International, the Women's Global Network on Reproductive Rights, and the International Women's Tribune Center. It was the mobilizing efforts initiated by such international networks that led to the presence of many women's health NGOs like CEHAT at the Cairo Population Conference in 1994. The declaration from the population conference in Cairo, which emphasized the need to empower women and protect their human rights as the best strategy of population control, was an important victory for the international women's movement.

Nurturing Nature

Whether it is the destruction of the rainforest in Latin America, the felling of trees in the Himalayan Mountains in India, desertification in Africa, or toxic dumping in the United States, the environmental desecration caused by global economic policies has led to increasing material and cultural hardships for women (Mies and Shiva 1993). For women in the Third World, destruction of the environment means that women have to spend more time every day to gather wood for fuel, fodder for cattle, and fetch drinking water. Many women have been at the forefront of environmental movement (e.g., Agarwal 1997; Braidotti et al. 1997; Kaplan 1997; Shiva 1987; Westra and Wenz 1995). While the efforts of women in the Chipko movement in India may be familiar to many, there are numerous other women's groups in India and elsewhere that focus on the material and cultural relationships of women and nature. For example, in India, women in the Stree Mukti Sangharsh (Women's Liberation Struggle) were at the forefront of building an ecologically sound small dam, despite much government resistance, to address the issues of recurrent droughts in the area. In the process of building the dam women also organized to gain land rights and water rights for women and landless community members (Desai 1995). Other women's groups in India have been active in gaining fallow common land and experimenting with organic farming to produce food for local consumption.

In Latin America many of the environmental organizations focus on environmentally appropriate technologies, forming extracting reserves for the indigenous tribes' cultural and material survival, calling for the ecological use of the rainforest, and more recently focusing on the issue of intellectual property and biological diversity in the region. For example, in Ecuador the Fundación Ecuatoriana de Tecnología Apropiada works on biogas, rural housing, and small hydraulic turbines. SAEMTA in Bolivia focuses on organic potato farming, biological pesticides, medicinal plants, and small-scale irrigation. CENDA in Bolivia, which is a bilingual (Spanish and Quechua) grassroots support organization, takes action in the poor isolated areas of the Andes on reforestation (Fisher 1993). In Kenya, activists in Greenbelt focused their attention on reforestation and sustainable rural development. In the United States, women of color have been at the forefront of the environmental justice movement (e.g., Faber 1998; Kaplan 1997).

In all cases cited, environmental activists attempt to develop sustainable alternatives to the industrial development model that reduces food available for local consumption, destroys the local ecology, and produces toxic byproducts. The struggle against all these environmental ills has been strengthened by the emergence of transnational feminist solidarities. In some cases, the UN and its various world conferences have helped to create such solidarities and have brought them public visibility; however, as Alvarez (2000) and Basu (2000) note, such solidarities are not top-down orchestrations but have emerged from specific political and social local movement contexts.

The UN and Transnational Feminist Solidarities

International women's networks and transnational organizing date back to the middle of the nineteenth century, when women from the United States and Europe came together around antislavery efforts (Rupp 1997). At the turn of the twentieth century, women from Europe, the United States, and India joined to fight colonization. In the early part of the twentieth century, women from Europe and the United States lobbied the newly formed League of Nations and the Pan American Organization to lay the groundwork for what was to become the UN Charter and the Universal Declaration of Human Rights. One of the major differences between earlier transnational activism and current activism is their scope and the variety of actors engaged in them.

The UN's efforts for women have evolved in four phases (UN 1997). In the first phase (1945–62) the UN worked to secure women's legal equality. In 1946 the Commission on the Status of Women (CSW) and the Commission on Human Rights (CHR) were established. In 1948 the Universal Declaration of Human Rights was adopted and became the foundation for establishing the legal basis for equal rights for women. The early focus of CSW was a worldwide survey of laws that affected women, compiling data related to women, gathering public opinion on women's issues and organizing a forum to hear from experts and "launch a worldwide campaign to inform the public about women's issues" (UN 1997, 12). Both CSW and CHR agreed that while they would hear violations of women's rights they had no legal authority to take action. In 1952, the UN adopted the Convention on the Political Rights of Women, which became the first international instrument to recognize and protect women's political rights. During this phase the UN also worked on equality for women in work and education as well as legal equality for married women and gathered data on traditional practices and customs around the world that affected women. While there was consensus around the need to abolish practices that harmed women and children, there was little agreement on how to achieve this.

The research of the first phase documented the unequal status of women worldwide and the deteriorating status of women in the newly independent and postcolonial countries of Asia and Africa that, along with Latin American countries, had undertaken the path to development based on the liberal modernization model. These findings shifted the focus of the UN in the second phase, 1963–75, from legal rights to the economic and social context within which legal rights can be meaningful. The continuing poverty in the world also challenged the development efforts of the UN, resulting in its move away from the modernization approach of the 1950s and 1960s to the basic needs approach in the 1970s, and then sustainable development and empowerment approach in the 1980s and the 1990s.

Troubled by women's economic and social inequalities, the UN first embarked on integrating women into development, without recognizing that perhaps it was the very process of development that was leading to some of these inequalities. The focus of UN development efforts for women in this period concentrated on their role as economic agents whose economic potential should be enhanced by providing them income-generation schemes and birth-control information. The UN's efforts also initiated the emergence of the field of "women and international development," which began questioning the inadequacy of the UN's efforts and developed a critique of its role in promoting a form of development that ignored the needs of women (see Benería and Sen 1982; Boserup 1970; Elson and Pearson 1981; Tinker 1990/1999). They began to articulate a people-centered approach to development that became a precursor to the sustainable development and globalization discourses of the late 1980s and 1990s.

. . . Historically the West has supported the enforcement of the civil and political rights, for which member states have legal obligations, while the former Soviet Union and the Third World countries have been promoters of the economic and social rights for which there is very limited enforcement. It is these latter rights that have been used in the 1990s by the transnational women's movements to forge solidarities and demand accountability from their governments (e.g., Bunch and Reilly 1994; Kerr 1993; Peters and Wolper 1995).

[. . .]

In 1975 the UN declared International Women's Year with a focus on equality, development, and peace. . . . That year was highlighted by the First Women's World Conference in Mexico City. Two thousand delegates from 133 countries (women headed 113 of these delegations) attended the conference. Around 6,000 women and men from NGOs attended the parallel International Women's Year Tribune, which had been organized following similar gatherings of NGOs at the 1972 World Conference on the Human Environment and the 1974 Bucharest Population Conference. The Mexico City's Tribune was unique in its scope and intensity. Women gathered from around the world for what was dubbed "history's largest consciousness raising session" (UN 1997). For many of the participants, the discovery of their common and divergent issues was a transformative experience. This level of engagement was possible because of the emergence of a second wave of women's movements in many countries of the North and South.

The conference adopted a World Plan of Action on the Equality of Women and their Contribution to Development and Peace, and regional follow-up meetings were held throughout Africa, Asia, and the Pacific regions. The UN subsequently declared 1975–85 the International Women's Decade and scheduled international conferences for 1980 in Copenhagen and for 1985 in Nairobi. The International Women's Decade, the third phase of the UN's efforts for women, promoted and legitimized the already growing international women's movement and marked the beginning of the transnational feminist solidarities that have come to characterize women's agency in the global era.

In this third phase of the UN's efforts the big shift in focus was on recognizing that there could be no equality, development, or peace without women's full participation. It was during this phase that the UN committed resources for women's advancement and created institutions that were to become an important part of transnational feminist solidarities. The two main institutions were the International Research and Training Institute for the

Advancement of Women (INSTRAW), the main purpose of which was to conduct research and training in issues related to women and development, and the United Nations Development Fund for Women (also known as UNIFEM), formalized in 1984, which was to found specific projects for women around the world. Despite the institutional establishment of INSTRAW and UNIFEM, the resources committed to them were limited. . . .

The most enduring accomplishment of the decade was its creation of transnational solidarities. Prior to each world conference there were local, national, and regional meetings that led to the formation of many local and national grassroots groups as well as international NGOs that wanted to participate. Though the world conferences were limited to formal governmental delegations from each country, the NGO forums, which were organized parallel to each world conference, provided the opportunity for women from around the world to meet and discuss women's issues. Approximately 6,000 women met at the Mexico Tribune in 1975, 15,000 women attended the Nairobi conference in 1985, and at least 30,000 women convened in Beijing in 1995.

These world conferences and their accompanying NGO forums, however, were highly contentious occasions. For example, most Third World women's groups and governments were still influenced by the nationalist rhetoric that had informed their freedom struggles. The decolonization of most countries in Africa and Asia following World War II, together with the Cold War between the United States and the Soviet Union, shaped the sensibilities of governments as well as women's groups. The postcolonial states were defined in opposition to the Western colonial empire. In this context, women were constituted as the bearers of tradition and posed against the modernizing influence of the colonial powers. Such self-understanding was further consolidated as Western women cast Third World women as "the oppressed other" of their more liberated self (Mohanty 1991; Spivak 1987; Trinh 1989). Therefore, early encounters between so-called First World and Third World women were strained.

The conferences in Mexico City and Copenhagen were particularly volatile (Basu 2000; Desai 1995; Peters and Wolpert 1995). Women from India, Brazil, Palestine, and other Third World countries, based on their own anticolonial struggles and assumptions of the role of the West, challenged First World feminists' claims that women were universally oppressed because of their gender and that sisterhood was global. They countered that for women in the Third World, class, nationality, race/ethnicity, and religion intersected with gender in both oppressing them and providing spaces for liberation. . . .

Such critical confrontations were resolved not by the force of the better argument but by the reciprocal recognition, fueled by women's grassroots organizing around the various issues, of the validity of various claims. The breakthrough for transnational solidarities came at the Nairobi conference in 1985, which, because of its location, drew many women from Africa and Asia. The timing of the conference, at the end of the International Decade, when women from all parts of the world had a chance to interact for ten years, contributed to the recognition that women's issues vary by society and require multiple strategies of liberation. In addition, Third World women were able to show First World women their own privilege and complicity in the oppression of women in the Third World. Learning about the common goals of freedom, justice, and equality variously defined, and of apparently different women's movements around the world, inspired reflective solidarity among women who otherwise were on different sides of the East/West, North/South, left/liberal, white/black, lesbian/straight, feminist/nonfeminist divide.

The breakthrough in women's transnational solidarities at Nairobi, and later in Beijing, was also a result of other social forces playing out in their respective locales (Desai 1995). For example, in the United States and United Kingdom, women of color were challenging the white feminist understanding of the category "women" and introducing race, class, and sexuality as among the factors destabilizing "sisterhood." In the Third World countries, the postcolonial governments based on constitutional equality for women were still defining women in circumscribed roles in nation building. The rise of religious fundamentalism, which defined women as only culture bearers, further sharpened women's feminist consciousness. Such larger social forces as well as the ongoing encounters among women enabled them to create solidarities based not on preconceived identities but on historically specific circumstances of the global economy that were constraining the lives of women around the world. This mutual understanding was further consolidated in Beijing in 1995 because the collapse of the Soviet Union and the consolidation of the global economy had enabled a framing of issues in terms other than the nationalist, First World/Third World terms of earlier decades. It was at this conference that human rights discourse became the language for demanding women's rights. Thus, the third phase of the UN's efforts helped catapult transnational women's networks and brought women into the center stage of world politics. The networks established during the decade became the basis for solidarity and action in the current phase of the UN's work, from 1986 to present. It was very clear to everyone at the end of the International Decade that despite the energy and optimism it had aroused, it had failed to achieve the goals of sustained progress for a majority of women. The 1990s posed a further challenge to women's equality as capitalist expansion and political displacement further interfered with women's social, economic, and political empowerment. In response, the UN called a series of world conferences in the 1990s that were to measure the success of its various efforts in the previous decades, particularly those efforts devoted to women's rights, human rights, population, development, and environment.

This last phase demonstrates the power of women's transnational solidarities. The World Environmental Conference in 1992 in Rio, the World Human Rights Conference in 1993, the Population Conference in Cairo in 1994, the World Summit for Social Development in 1995, and the World Women's Conference in Beijing in 1995 all capitalized on the networks women had established during the previous decades. Women's NGOs were at the forefront of these world conferences. For example, in preparation for Vienna in 1993, the Center for Women's Global Leadership, based at Rutgers University, helped to coordinate a Global Campaign for Women's Human Rights. In 1991, the center organized a leadership institute at which women from all over the world explored the relationship between human rights, women's rights, and violence against women. Women organized on both Human Rights Day and the International Day against Violence against Women to generate a petition drive calling on the World Human Rights Conference to "comprehensively address women's human rights at every level of its proceedings" and to recognize gender-based violence as a "violation of human rights requiring immediate action." The petition garnered 300,000 signatures from 50 countries and had been signed by 800 organizations when it was delivered to the world conference.

At the World Human Rights Conference, women's groups were the most organized and vocal. They held more than 60 workshops, seminars, and lectures at the forum on women's human rights. They also coined the now famous slogan "Human Rights Are Women's Rights and Women's Rights Are Human Rights" popularized by Hillary Rodham Clinton at Beijing in 1995. Similarly, the international conferences at Rio de Janeiro, Copenhagen, and Cairo were occasions for women's transnational networks to influence the agenda and policies of the UN and its member states. They also provided additional opportunities for women's groups from around the world to network and forge more strategies for action. According to Alvarez (2000), this activism embodies the "transnational IGO (Intergovernmental Organizations)-advocacy logic," which focuses on influencing policy. Since these transnational IGOs are dominated by Northern feminist nongovernmental organizations, they have a contradictory impact at the local level (Sandberg 1998). However, most women who participated at the NGO forums of these conferences were more interested in what Alvarez (2000) has described as "international identity-solidarity logic." Women's NGOs at the world conferences adopted two different strategies (see Clark, Friedman, and Hochstetler 1998). The more prominent national and international groups tended to caucus to influence the agenda setting of the world conferences and the UN bodies, while the vast majority of the NGOs focused on sharing information and experiences and networking for collaborative action in the future.

It is this last phase of the UN's efforts for women that has helped cement the nature of women's agency in the global era. Women's networks have now taken over the review processes following the world conferences, namely the Beijing Plus 5, Copenhagen Plus 5, and Cairo Plus 5, to assess what has been achieved and to make their governments accountable for their international agreements. Women's groups have learned to negotiate the national and international arenas. However, as Basu (2000) argues, transnational activism for women's political and civil rights is much more likely to succeed than similar activism for economic rights. . . .

While transnational solidarities among women have grown, they are not without problems. As Nancy Naples and others discuss these solidarities often reproduce existing inequalities. For example, women from the North and educated women from the South are more dominant in the international networks and NGOs than are grassroots women. Of the 30,000 women present at Beijing, more than 8,000 were from the United States alone. Furthermore, as Basu (2000) argues, transnational activism creates divisions at the national level between the elites who belong to such networks and the vast majority of grassroots women who don't.

Another problematic aspect of the transnational solidarities is the continuing reliance of women and NGOs of the South on Northern donors and funders. The Ford Foundation, in particular, has been responsible for supporting a great deal of such transnational activism (Alvarez 1999; Basu 2000). [M]any Northern groups are aware of this and have made attempts to make their Southern partners more independent by enabling them to look for sustainable alternatives. In addition, other Northern NGOs are actively engaged in understanding and publicizing the ways in which Northern women's consumerism implicates them in global inequalities; the Label Behind the Label and the Clean Clothes Campaign are two examples of activists' efforts.

Transnational solidarities have also been accompanied by an increasing NGO-ization of the women's movements, with its attendant decline in radical critique and an increasing role in serving as experts and implementers of government and international donors' programs. But as Alvarez (1999) shows for the women's movement in Latin America, NGO-ization is extremely complex and different in each country. Some NGOs are no more than fronts for the government; others, which Alvarez calls "hybrid" NGOs, maintain links with movements and try to work both within and outside the system. These NGOs simultaneously provide a critique as well as mobilize resources to empower women.

Alvarez (2000) has identified yet another problem with transnational solidarities, in the contradictions between the two different kinds of transnational logics: the internationalist identity-solidarity logic and the transnational IGO-advocacy logic. She sees the first logic as guided by identity, reciprocity, affinity, complementarity, and substitutionism (33), and as having very benign effects on local progressive politics. Transnational IGO advocacy, by contrast, is guided by experts with special skills shaping international gender policy. Though Alvarez acknowledges that these two logics can work in tandem, the contradictions concern her. I think that as with all binaries, this one overstates the differences and selectively highlights contradictions of one logic while understating those of the other logic.

The Prospects of Women's Agency in This Era of Globalization

Research by academics, policymakers, and various UN agencies overwhelmingly shows that women and children have suffered disproportionately as a result of global economic restructuring (e.g., Afshar and Dennis 1992; Blank 1997; Naples 1998, Visvanathan et al. 1997). Policies associated with economic restructuring use existing patriarchal assumptions about women's labor and endurance abilities, and therefore reproduce inequalities. Furthermore, women are considered only as economic agents rather than central political actors on the global stage. Globalization has reduced the ability of women around the world to find paid work that offers security and dignity. The UN's perspective is that the harm caused by the policies is short term. There is also a gendered division in the implementation policies of international institutions. The IMF and the World Bank institute structural adjustment policies while UN agencies promote legal and cultural changes that would allow women access to the new market forces. The flaw in this analysis is that it misses the gendered nature of most economic policies.

Women have organized in response to the hegemonies of global capital. Their new political presence has been defined alternately as "global civil society" (Waterman 1998) or "globalization from below" (Falk 1999). While some analysts see these scattered counter-hegemonies as ineffective against the hegemonizing presence of global capital (e.g., Sklair 1991), others celebrate the new global solidarities (e.g., Brecher, Costello, and Smith 2000). As I have shown, however, the important point is that global capital is not unchallenged. Many resistance strategies embody a radical critique not just of global capital but also of preexisting social inequalities based on race, class, gender, sexuality, and nationality. Many activist women's efforts focus, to varying degrees and in various ways, on developing concrete economic alternatives based on sustainable development, social equality, and participatory processes, though such economic initiatives have not been as successful at the transnational level (Basu 2000). These counterhegemonies have succeeded in transforming the daily lives of many women at the local level. This, in my view, is what gives women's agency immense potential. Similarly, the transnational feminist solidarities, while they reproduce existing inequalities, are forged not on preconceived identities and experiences but in the context of struggle and as such are more reflexive about these inequalities. To what extent can these fluid, multiple, reflexive transnational feminist solidarities change the shape of the global political economy? . . .

REFERENCES

Afshar, Haleh, and Carolyne Dennis. 1992. *Women and Adjustment Policies in the Third World*. New York: St. Martin's.

Agarwal, Bina. 1997. "The Gender and Environment Debate: Lessons from India." Pp. 68–74 in *the Women, Gender, and Development Reader*, ed. Nalini Visvanathan, Lynn Dagan, Laurie Nisonoff, and Nan Wiegersma. London: Zed.

Aguilar, Ana Leticcia, Blanca Estela Dole, Morena Herrera, Sofia Montenegro, Lorena Camacho, and Lorena Flores. 1997. *Movimiento de mujeres en Centroamerica*. Managua, Nicaragua: Programa Regional La Corriente.

Alvarez, Sonia E. 1999. "Advocating Feminism: The Latin American Feminist NGO 'Boom.'" *International Feminist Journal of Politics* 1(2):181–209.

——. 2000. "Translating the Global: Effects of Transnational Organizing on Local Feminist Discourses and Practices in Latin America." *Meridians* 1(1):29–67.

Appadurai, Arjun. 1990. "Disjuncture and Difference in the Global Cultural Economy." *Public Culture* 2(2):1–23.

Baden, Sally. 1997. "Recession and Structural Adjustment's Impact on Women's Work in Selected Developing Regions." In *Promoting Gender Equality at Work: Turning Vision into Reality*, ed. Eugenia Date-Bah. London: Zed/ILO.

Basu, Amrita, ed. 2000. "Globalization of the Local/Localization of the Global: Mapping Transnational Women's Movements." *Meridians* 1(1):68–84.

Benería, Lourdes, and Shelley Feldman. 1992. *Unequal Burdens: Economic Crises, Persistent Poverty, and Women's Work*. Boulder, CO: Westview.

Benería, Lourdes, and Gita Sen. 1982. "Class and Gender Inequalities and Women's Role in Economic Development," *Feminist Studies* 1(spring):157–76.

Blank, Rebecca M. 1997. *It Takes a Nation: A New Agenda for Fighting Poverty*. Princeton, NJ: Princeton University Press.

Bose, Christine E., and Edna Acosta-Belén, eds. 1995. *Women in the Latin American Development Process*. Philadelphia: Temple University Press.

Boserup, Ester. 1970. *Woman's Role in Economic Development*. New York: St. Martin's.

Braidotti, Rosi, Elise Charkiewicz, Sabine Hausler, and Sadkia Wieringa. 1997. "Women, the Environment, and Sustainable Development." Pp. 54–61 in *The Women, Gender, and Development Reader*, ed. Nalini Visvanathan, Lynn Duggan, Laura Nisonoff, and Nancy Wiegersma. London: Zed.

Brecher, Jeremy, Tim Costello, and Brendan Smith. 2000. *Globalization from Below: The Power of Solidarity*. Boston: South End.

Bunch, Charlotte, and Niamh Reilly. 1994. *Demanding Accountability: The Global Campaign and Vienna Tribunal For Women's Rights*. New York: UNDP.

Butegwa, Florence. 1998. "Globalization and Its Impact on Economic and Social Rights in Africa." Paper prepared for AAS and HURIDOCS.

Clark, Ann Marie, Elisabeth J. Friedman, and Kathryn Hochstetler. 1998. "The Sovereign Limits of Global Civil Society: A Comparison of NGO Participation in UN World Conferences on the Environment, Human Rights, and Women." *World Politics* 51(1):1–35.

Desai, Manisha. 1995. "If Peasants Build Dams, What Will the State Have Left to Do? Practices of New Social Movements in India." *Research in Social Movements, Conflict, and Change* 19:203–18.

Elson, Diane, and R. Pearson. 1981. "Nimble Fingers Make Cheap Workers: An Analysis of Women's Employment in Third World Export Manufacturing." *Feminist Review* 7.

Faber, Daniel, ed. 1998. *The Struggle for Ecological Democracy: Environmental Justice Movements in the U.S.* New York: Guilford.

Falk, Richard. 1999. *Predatory Globalization: A Critique.* London: Blackwell.

Fernandez-Kelly, Maria Patricia. 1983. *For We Are Sold, I and My People: Women and Industry in Mexico's Frontier.* Albany: State University of New York Press.

Fisher, Julie. 1993. *The Road from Rio: Sustainable Development and the Nongovernmental Movement in the Third World.* Westport, CT: Praeger.

Fontana, Marzia, Susan Joekes, and Rachel Masika. 1998. "Global Trade Expansion and Liberalisation: Gender Issues and Impact." Brighton, UK: Institute of Development Studies, University of Sussex.

Fuentes, Annette, and Barbara Ehrenreich. 1983. *Women in the Global Factory.* INC Pamphlet No. 2. Boston: South End Press.

Giddens, Anthony. 1990. *Consequences of Modernity.* Stanford, CA: Stanford University Press.

Grewal, Inderpal, and Caren Kaplan, eds. 1994. *Scattered Hegemonies: Postmodernity and Transnational Feminist Practices.* Minneapolis: University of Minneapolis Press.

Hall, Stuart. 1991. "The Local and the Global: Globalization and Ethnicity." Pp. 19–40 in *Culture, Globalization, and the World System,* ed. Anthony King. London: Macmillan.

Hochschild, Arlie. 2000. "Global Care Chain and Emotional Surplus Value." Pp. 130–46 in *Global Capitalism,* ed. Will Hutton and Anthony Giddens. New York: New Press.

IAWS (India Association of Women's Studies). 1995. *The State and the Women's Movement in India: A Report.* New Delhi: Systems Vision.

Kaplan, Caren. 1997. "The Politics of Location as Transnational Feminist Practice." Pp. 137–52 in *Scattered Hegemonies,* ed. Inderpal Grewal and Caren Kaplan. Minneapolis: University of Minnesota Press.

Kerr, Joanna, ed. 1993. *Ours By Right: Women's Rights as Human Rights.* London: Zed.

Kirmani, Mubina, and Dorothy Munyakho. 1996. "The Impact of Structural Adjustment Programs on Women and AIDS." Pp. 160–80 in *Women's Experiences with HIV/AIDS: An International Perspective,* ed. Lynellyn Long and E. Maxine Ankrah. New York: Columbia University Press.

Manuh, Takyiwaa. 1997. "Ghana: Women in the Public and Informal Sectors under the Economic Recovery Programme." Pp. 267–76 in *The Women, Gender, and Development Reader,* ed. Nalini Visvanathan, Lynn Duggan, Laurie Nisonoff, and Nan Wiegersma. London: Zed.

Mies, Maria, and Vandana Shiva. 1993. *Ecofeminism.* London: Zed.

Mitter, Swasti and Sheila Rowbotham, eds. 1994. *Dignity and Daily Bread.* London: Routledge.

Mohanty, Chandra Talpade. 1991. "Under Western Eyes: Feminist Scholarship and Colonial Discourses." Pp. 51–80 in *Third World Women and the Politics of Feminism,* ed. Chandra Talpade Mohanty. Bloomington: Indiana University Press.

Moner Report. 1999. "Impact of Transition on Women in Eastern Europe." New York: UNICEF.

Naples, Nancy A. 1998. *Grassroots Warriors: Activist Mothering, Community Work, and the War on Poverty.* New York: Routledge.

Nash, June, and Maria Patricia Fernandez-Kelly, eds. 1983. *Women, Men, and the International Division of Labor.* Albany: State University of New York Press.

Neft, Naomi and Ann Levine. 1997. *Where Women Stand: An International Report on the Status of Women in 140 Countries 1997–1998.* New York: Random House.

Nzomo, Maria 1994. "The Impact of Structural Adjustment Programmes on Women's Participation in Decision-Making." Unpublished paper.

Ong, Aihwa. 1987. *Spirits of Resistance and Capitalist Discipline: Factory Women in Malaysia*. Albany: State University of New York Press.

Osirim, Mary. 1996. "The Dilemmas of Modern Development: Structural Adjustment and Women Microentrepreneurs in Nigeria and Zimbabwe." Pp. 127–46 in *The Gendered New World Order: Militarism, Development, and the Environment*, ed. Jennifer Turpin and Lois Lorentzen. New York: Routledge.

Peters, Julie, and Andrea Wolper, eds. 1995. *Women's Rights Human Rights: International Feminist Perspectives*. New York: Routledge.

Riain, Sean. 2000. "States and Markets in an Era of Globalization." *Annual Review of Sociology* 26:187–213.

Rupp, Leila J. 1997. *Worlds of Women: The Making of an International Women's Movement*. Princeton, NJ: Princeton University Press.

Sandberg, Eve. 1998. "Multilateral Women's Conferences: The Domestic Political Organization of Zambian Women." *Contemporary Politics* 4(3):271–83.

Sassen, Saskia. 1999. *Globalization and Its Discontents: Essays on the New Mobility of People and Money*. New York: New Press.

SEWA. 1998. Annual Report. Ahmedabad, India.

Shiva, Vandana. 1987. *Staying Alive*. London: Zed Books.

Sklair, Leslie. 1991. *Sociology of the Global System*. Baltimore: Johns Hopkins University Press.

Spivak, Gayatri Chakravorty. 1987. *In Other Worlds: Essays in Cultural Politics*. New York: Methuen.

Tiano, Susan. 1994. *Patriarchy on the Line: Labor, Gender, and Ideology in the Mexican Maquila Industry*. Philadelphia: Temple University Press.

Tiano, Susan, ed. 1990. *Persistent Inequalities: Women and World Development*. New York: Oxford University Press.

Tinker, Irene, ed. 1990/1999. *Persistent Inequalities: Women and World Development*. New York: Oxford University Press.

Trinh, T. Minh-ha. 1989. *Woman Native Other: Writing Postcoloniality and Feminism*. Bloomington: Indiana University Press.

Turshen, Meredeth. 1994. "The Impact of Economic Reforms on Women's Health and Health Care in Sub-Saharan Africa." Pp. 77–95 in *Women in the Age of Economic Transformation*, ed. Nahid Aslanbeigui, Steven Pressman, and Gale Summerfield. London: Routledge.

United Nations. 1997. "The United Nations and the Advancement of Women 1945–1996." New York: United Nations.

Visvanathan, Nalini, Lynne Dagan, Laurie Nisonoff, and Nalini Wiegersma, eds. 1997. *The Women, Gender, and Development Reader*. London: Zed.

Wachtel, Howard. 2001. "Tax Distortion in the Global Economy." Paper presented at the Global Tensions Conference, March 10, Cornell University, Ithaca, NY.

Ward, Kathy, ed. 1990. *Women Workers and Global Restructuring*. Ithaca, NY: Cornell University Press.

Waterman, Peter. 1998. *Globalization, Social Movements, and the New Internationalisms*. London: Mansell.

Westra, Laura, and Peter Wenz, eds. 1995. *Faces of Environmental Racism: Confronting Issues of Global Justice*. London: Rowman & Littlefield.

Wiegersma, Nan. 1997. Introduction to Part 4 of *The Women, Gender, and Development Reader*, ed. N. Visvanathan, L. Dagan, L. Nisonoff, and N. Wiegersma. London: Zed.

27 Counterhegemonic Globalization: Transnational Social Movements in the Contemporary Global Political Economy (2005)

Peter Evans

When people invoke "globalization," they usually mean the prevailing system of transnational domination, which is more accurately called "neoliberal globalization," "corporate globalization," or perhaps "neoliberal, corporate-dominated globalization" (cf. McMichael, 2000: chap. 29). Sometimes they are referring to a more generic process – the shrinking of space and increased permeability of borders that result from falling costs of transportation and revolutionary changes in technologies of communication. Often the two are conflated.[1]

Implicit in much of current discourse on globalization is the idea that the particular system of transnational domination that we experience today is the "natural" (indeed inevitable) consequence of exogenously determined generic changes in the means of transportation and communication. A growing body of social science literature and activist argumentation challenges this assumption. Arguing instead that the growth of transnational connections can potentially be harnessed to the construction of more equitable distributions of wealth and power and more socially and ecologically sustainable communities, this literature and argumentation raises the possibility of what I would like to call "counterhegemonic globalization." Activists pursuing this perspective have created a multifaceted set of transnational networks and ideological frames that stand in opposition to contemporary neoliberal globalization. Collectively they are referred to as the "global justice movement." For activists and theorists alike, these movements have become one of the most promising political antidotes to a system of domination that is increasingly seen as effectual only in its ability to maintain itself in power.

Although the growth of membership and political clout of transnational social movements is hard to measure, the burgeoning of their formal organizational reflections – transnational NGOs – is well-documented. Their numbers have doubled between 1973 and 1983 and doubled again between 1983 and 1993 (Sikkink and Smith, 2002:31). Perhaps even more important than their quantitative growth has been their ability to seize oppositional imaginations. From the iconic images of Seattle to the universal diffusion of the World Social

Forum's vision that "another world is possible," the cultural and ideological impact of these movements has begun to rival that of their corporate adversaries.

As these movements have grown, an equally variegated body of social science literature has begun to analyze, empirically and theoretically, the possibilities of a global counter-movement that would take advantage of the technological capacities associated with generic globalization and turn neoliberal globalization's own ideological and organizational structures against itself, subverting its exclusionary rules of governance and logic of allocating resources. Yet, as is to be expected, the scholarly literature lags behind the growth of the movements themselves.

Any adequate theorization of contemporary globalization must include an analysis of antisystemic oppositional movements. Yet, with a few exceptions (e.g., Boswell and Chase-Dunn, 2000; Gill, 2002; McMichael, 2005), discussion of oppositional movements is usually "tacked on" to the end of an analysis that is theorized primarily in terms of the logic of neoliberal globalization. From novel analyses of contemporary globalization, such as Hardt and Negri (2000), to encyclopedic treatments like Held et al. (1999), structure and dynamics of countermovements are afforded only a fraction the theoretical attention given to dominant structures.

A careful analysis of countermovements is essential to our understanding of the dynamics of contemporary politics. Without an analysis of the organization and strategies of transnational social movements, our understanding of the politics of global governance institutions like the WTO, the Bretton Woods twins, and the UN system is incomplete (see, for example, Fox and Brown, 1998; Evans, 2000; O'Brien, 2000; Wade, 2001). Correspondingly, nation-states must increasingly take into account the reactions of transnational countermovements when they operate in global arenas.

The analysis of transnational movements has also become increasingly important to the understanding of what might have earlier been considered "domestic" politics. Contentious politics at the national level is increasingly contaminated by global issues and movements, whether in the North or in the South. Theorization of social movements cannot proceed without full consideration of the implications of transnational experiences (cf. McCarthy, 1997; Tarrow, 2001, 2002; Khagram, Riker, and Sikkink, 2002; Smith and Johnston, 2002). Concepts like "frame alignment" and "resource mobilization" take on a different meaning when the "society" involved consists of an interconnected congeries of national political units varying dramatically in their material resources and cultural foundations (cf. Snow et al., 1986; Benford, 1997; McAdam, Tarrow, and Tilly, 2001).

Analytical, practical, and political motivations for focusing on oppositional transnational social movements are all intensified by growing disillusionment with the currently hegemonic version of globalization. Margaret Thatcher's admonition "there is no alternative" becomes increasingly difficult to accept and the idea that there might be something like "counterhegemonic globalization" correspondingly more attractive.

Hegemonic versus Counterhegemonic Globalization

Despite the visibility and fervor of its supporters (e.g., Tom Friedman), neoliberal globalization has proved a disillusioning disappointment to ordinary citizens, not just in the global

South but in the rich industrial core as well. More surprisingly, prominent development economists, who might be expected to be its most fervent promoters (e.g., Rodrik, Sachs, Stiglitz), are sharp critics of neoliberal globalization and its governing institutions. McMichael's discussion sets out these disappointments at length in Chapter 29 and there is no need to reiterate them in detail here, but a quick reminder is in order.

Neoliberal globalization has delivered global financial volatility that regularly destroys productive capacity (without stimulating the creativity that Schumpeter considered definitive of capitalist progress). Instead of accelerating the improvement of living standards for the majority of the world's population, it has been associated with slowing growth rates (cf. Easterly, 2001). It has often jeopardized the delivery of essential collective goods like public health, education, and a sustainable environment and it has exacerbated inequality within and between nations to a degree that is destructive of the basic social solidarity.

While generating a proliferation of electoral regimes and celebrating "democracy" in the abstract, neoliberal globalization has undermined the possibility of democratic control over state policies and insulated the most fundamental policy decisions from even the fiction of democratic control. It has had pervasively corrosive effects on any sense of self-worth that is based on local culture, difference, and identity. Finally, it is now associated with a return to military adventurism whose potential future destructive effects are frightening to contemplate.

Despite its failures, few would deny that neoliberal globalization remains "hegemonic" in the Gramscian sense of combining an ideological vision of "what is in everyone's interests" that is largely accepted as "common sense" even by subordinate and disprivileged groups with the effective ability to apply coercion when necessary to preserve the existing distribution of privilege and exclusion. To call movements "counterhegemonic" therefore implies that they have the potential to undermine the ideological power of existing hegemony and threaten the established distribution of privilege (and exclusion).[2] Likewise, "counterhegemonic globalization" would entail building a global political economy that used the shrinking of space and facility of cross-border communication to enhance equity, justice, and sustainability rather than to intensify existing forms of domination.

For anyone who shares, even partially, disillusionment with neoliberal globalization, the prospect of a "counterhegemonic" globalization is alluring. It is hardly surprising that analysis of transnational social movements and their theoretical implications has growing appeal among both political sociologists and activists. Unfortunately, preoccupation with discovering new agents of social change also creates temptation to exaggerate the virtues and power of existing groups and networks and their ideologies.

Avoiding inflated and unrealistic assessments of either the virtues or efficacy of those who oppose neoliberal globalization is the first step toward real understanding of their potential power. It must be admitted that the "antiglobalization movement" contains its share of irresponsible nihilists. It must also be acknowledged that some alternative visions may be worse than the currently dominant one. It is entirely possible to oppose Western-dominated global capitalism with a vision that is more oppressive, authoritarian, and intolerant than neoliberalism, as Al Qaeda illustrates. Likewise, "antiglobalization" provides a handy "modern" gloss for a multitude of old-fashioned, reactionary nationalist agendas.

Nor is "counterhegemonic globalization" a label that applies to the whole of the "global justice movement." Some groups with goals grounded in a vision of equity, human dignity, and a sustainable relation to the environment may reject the possibility of a progressive version of globalization. Instead of counterhegemonic globalization, these groups would reverse the effects of generic globalization and somehow retrieve a world in which power and values could be defined on a purely local basis.

Yet, ironically, even the celebration of local power and culture cannot escape the necessity of constructing some form of "counterhegemonic globalization." Even those most committed to escaping the domination of modern universalisms often end up using global networks and global ideologies. Universal citizenship rights are invoked to protect headscarves (Soysal, 1994). Transnational networks are mobilized to preserve local feastdays (Levitt, 2001). The Internet played a key role in the Zapatista's defense of their local autonomy (Schulz, 1998).

The reverse is also true. Just as the defense of difference and quests for local power require global strategies and connections, likewise transnational social movements must have local social roots. Without the promise of redressing the grievances of ordinary people where they live, transnational social movements have no base and their capacity to challenge established power is limited. If global corporate strategies depend on creating deracinated consumers incapable of collective action, counterhegemonic strategies depend on the reverse. It is, therefore, hardly surprising that participants in transnational campaigns are often what Tarrow (2003) calls "rooted cosmopolitans" – people whose activism begins with ties to local communities and is driven by the desire to improve the lot of members of those communities. A constant dialectic between strategies that speak to local roots and strategies that leverage global connections is fundamental to counterhegemonic globalization.

The most powerful and challenging form of the local–global dialectic are the North–South divisions that have been inscribed in the structure of the global political economy for 500 years and exacerbated by contemporary neoliberal globalization. This divide is built into global structures of power, both public and private, economic and cultural. If transnational social movements cannot find a way to transcend it, their political effectiveness will be fatally compromised.

There are then some minimal caveats for any useful analysis of the transnational social movements that are involved in counterhegemonic globalization. It must be about local political motivations and social structural foundations as much as it is about transnational strategies, structures, and actions. It must recognize that local conditions of life are fundamentally different depending on where they are located in our abysmally divided world. Most important, the desire to discover potent new agents for social change must be balanced with dispassionate skepticism.

Exaggerating the transformative power of those groups whose efforts to build antisystemic global networks do appear grounded in a vision of equity and dignity is as bad a mistake as pretending that the antiglobalization movement is innocent of sinister and reactionary projects. It would be a disservice to the transnational movements themselves, as well as to ordinary citizens looking for relief from the disappointments of neoliberal globalization, to exaggerate their power. Sometimes "soft power" (Sikkink, 2002) can indeed successfully confront "hard" domination, but the current hegemony of corporate globalizers is supported by a full array of cultural and ideological machinery as well as a very solid set of coercive instruments. It will not be easily dislodged by even the most creative and well-organized transnational social movements. To have real effects, transnational movements must first be able to generate powerful cascades of normative change and then use this ideological advantage to transform the hard structures of established political and economic (and ultimately military) power. It is a tall order.

Even after we fully accept their flaws and limitations, the proliferation of transnational social movements with an agenda of counterhegemonic globalization is still one of the substantively exciting and theoretically provocative topics in contemporary political sociology. Whether or not the current global justice movement is capable of making "another world" possible, analyzing its nature and implications, in both practical and theoretical terms, must be part of the core agenda of contemporary political sociology.

The New Organizational Foundations of Counterhegemonic Globalization

Here I will focus on three broad families of transnational social movements aimed at counterhegemonic globalization: labor movements, women's movements, and environmental movements. Each of these movements confronts the dilemmas of using transnational networks to magnify the power of local movements without redefining local interests, of transcending the North–South divide, and of leveraging existing structures of global power without becoming complicit in them. Looking at the three movements together is useful because it highlights the ways in which surmounting these challenges might produce common strategies and possibilities for alliances among them.

Before embarking on an analysis of these three families of movements, however, I will briefly focus on two prominent organizations that are plausible would-be agents of "counterhegemonic globalization" – ATTAC and the World Social Forum (WSF). If Seattle and the subsequent demonstrations that have plagued the WTO, IMF, G-7, and World Economic Forum are the favorite media images of "antiglobalization," ATTAC and the WSF are paragons of organizations explicitly designed to build omnibus transnational networks aimed at transforming neoliberal globalization into a social protection-oriented, market-subordinating, difference-respecting mirror image.

Looking at these groups underlines the organizationally novel forms whose emergence has been stimulated by neoliberal globalization. At the same time, it highlights the degree to which counterhegemonic globalization draws on long-established social movements and ideological "tropes." In both respects it provides the ideal backdrop for analyzing the way in which the labor movement, transnational women's movements, and the global environmental movement provide both an interwoven infrastructure for reshaping globalization and a challenge to the existing political sociology literature.

No examination of counterhegemonic globalization can avoid examining ATTAC. Perhaps more than any other single organization it embodies the proposition that agency in the face of the purported power of neoliberal globalization requires only ideological and organizational imagination. Yet, ATTAC is a curious and, on the surface, very unlikely organization to fill this role. Its name – "Association pour la Taxation des Transactions Financières pour l'Aide aux Citoyens" (Association for the Taxation of Financial Transaction for the Aid of Citizens) – suggests an organization doomed to obscurity. Even worse, the name does indeed reflect ATTAC's initial focus on support for the Tobin tax (itself a relatively arcane idea embedded in the mechanics of neoliberal globalization). Its homeland – France – an archetypically "antiglobalization" political milieu, characterized much more by chauvinism than global solidarity, makes it even an even more unlikely candidate to be a paradigmatic promoter of "counterhegemonic" globalization. If ATTAC's origins make it a very peculiar candidate to typify organizations aimed at "counterhegemonic globalization," its success at spawning a network of politically active sister organizations around the world is undeniable (cf. http://attac.org/indexen/index.html). Hence a quick look at ATTAC is one way of illuminating the ideology and strategies of counterhegemonic globalization.

The best analysis of ATTAC is provided by Ancelovici (2002). In Ancelovici's view, ATTAC's ideology is essentially one of "associational statism," which essentially entails two strategies of trying to reassert the primacy of political/social decision making in the face of the growing dominance of global markets. On the one hand it has a very traditional (French) affection for the regulatory power of the nation-state. At the same time it rejects bureaucratic/representational/party control of public/political decision making in favor of locally based participatory structures.

In short, analysis of ATTAC suggests that the political foundations of "counterhegemonic globalization" involve a combination of Ruggie's (1982) "embedded liberalism" (with its emphasis on social protections rooted in the structures of the nation-state) and "New Left" forms of participatory democracy. The World Social Forum – one of the most important organizational forms of South-based "counterhegemonic globalization" – confirms this perspective.

It is only a partial caricature to propose that the origins of the World Social Forum, which now arguably represents the largest single agglomeration of South-based organizations and activists, began as a sort of joint venture between ATTAC and the Brazilian Workers Party (Partido dos Trabalhadores or PT). Because the founding vision of the PT's organizers was of a classic Marxist socialist mobilizational party, the party's involvement in the World Social Forum is further confirmation of the extent to which "counterhegemonic globalization" has its roots in both quotidian struggles for dignity and economic security in the workplace and classic agendas of social protection (*à la* Polanyi, 2001 [1944]) in which the machinery of the nation-state is heavily implicated (see McMichael, 2000: chap. 29).

Even unsystematic participant observation of the meetings of the World Social Forum in Porto Alegre, Brazil confirms this hypothesis. The fact that the Workers Party controls the municipal administration of a major city and has (until the 2002 elections) controlled the state government as well has been essential to enabling the infrastructural investments that make a global meeting of thousands of participants and hundreds of oppositional groups from around the globe possible. At the same time, in part because of Workers Party sponsorship, both local and transnational trade unions play a major role in the WSF.

All of this suggests that counterhegemonic globalization is not as "postmodern" as its adherents (and detractors) sometimes argue. To the contrary, rescuing traditional social democratic agendas of social protection, which are otherwise in danger of disappearing below the tide of neoliberal globalization, is a significant part of the agenda of both ATTAC and the World Social Forum. At the same time, it would be a mistake to dismiss counter-hegemonic globalization as simply "old wine in new bottles." The gamut of variegated transnational social movements that must be dealt with in any account of counterhege-monic globalization includes movements with organizational forms and ideological propo-sitions that are novel and refreshing in relation to the old agents of "embedded liberalism" (indeed ATTAC and the World Social Forum are among them).

This blend of novelty and persistence is one of the most interesting features of counter-hegemonic globalization, whether one is most concerned with a substantive analysis of the movement or with its implications for existing theoretical frameworks and conceptualiza-tions. And, if one is interested in the blend of novelty and persistence, there is no better place to start in analyzing "counterhegemonic globalization" than with the transformation of the international labor movement.

Labor as a Global Social Movement[3]

Having been tagged by nineteenth-century socialists as the preeminent agent of progressive social change, the labor movement was abandoned by most social movement theorists of the mid-twentieth century as primarily concerned with defending the privileges of a Northern aristocracy of labor in the face of challenges from the South and hopelessly scle-rotic in any case. Now the tide seems to be turning again. Recent analysis of the US labor movement has begun to argue for renewed appreciation of the potential importance of labor as a progressive actor (e.g., Clawson, 2003; Fantasia and Voss, 2004).

Curiously, the literature on transnational social movements still seems to reflect earlier disenchantment. With few exceptions (e.g., Kidder in Khagram et al., 2002), the case of labor has not been well-integrated into this literature. A typical collection on transnational social movements focusing on European cases (della Porta, Kriesi, and Rucht, 1999) offered individual chapters on the campaign against international trade in toxic wastes, farmers protest movements, abortion rights movements, and indigenous peoples movements, but only two quick references to labor: one noting that "the labor movement seems to be par-ticularly disadvantaged by the developing European institutions" (19) and the other assert-ing that "European labour unions are not taking advantage of the possibilities for contentious politics at the European level" (118).

Why has labor not been seen as a promising candidate for becoming a transnational social movement? Conventional ways of framing labor's relation to the global political economy are central to the answer. The current framing of the transnational politics of labor is dominated by what I would call a "geography of jobs" perspective. In this perspec-tive, "Workers of the World Compete!" replaces admonitions for transnational solidarity in the neoliberal mantra. Even those hostile to neoliberalism tend to assume that geo-graphic competition for jobs precludes possibilities for transnational solidarity (cf. Rodrik, 1997). In the "geography of jobs" frame, preventing the movement of jobs to the global South becomes the prime aim of workers in the North, erasing possibilities for North–South solidarity.

The "geography of jobs" perspective does capture one important facet of reality. The increasing ease with which capitalists move high-productivity technologies around the globe does intensify the potential for cross-border competition among workers (cf. Shaiken, 1994). Nonetheless, as Miller (2003) points out, the "geography of jobs" perspective is flawed even within an economic framework. Once political and ideological dynamics are included, a creative reframing of labor struggles at the global level, similar to the one that analysts like Ganz (2000) and Voss and Sherman (2000) have described at the national level, becomes an intriguing possibility.

I will analyze the possibilities for transnational labor solidarity by looking at three ways of framing contestation: "basic rights," "social contract," and "democratic governance." All three share one fundamental characteristic. They employ what I have called elsewhere (Evans, 2000) "political jujitsu," exploiting ideological propositions universally acknowledged as basic to the hegemonic ideology of contemporary global neoliberalism and utilizing transnational organizational structures that neoliberal globalization has helped create (cf. Risse-Kappen, Ropp, and Sikkink, 1999; Risse-Kappen, 2000; Smith and Johnston, 2002).

Global corporate networks built around labor-intensive, "sweatshop" manufacturing in the South and brand-name marketing in the North create political opportunities along with profits. Imbuing their brands with cultural value is vastly more important to the profitability of the overall corporation than production costs attributable to manufacturing labor. At the same time, the normative and ideological hegemony of "basic human rights" makes it almost impossible for a brand to retain its value once potential customers become convinced that basic human rights are being violated in the production of the goods that bear its name. The trick, of course, is building the mobilizational structures required to take advantage of such political opportunity (see Fung et al., 2001).

Looking at paradigmatic cases like the now famous Kukdong case (Anner and Evans, 2004) illustrates the point. The original revolt of the Kukdong workers was the product of the usual miserable local working conditions combined with unusual local courage and combativeness. Sustaining the struggle depended on an intricate transnational network that included local and US NGOs as well as US unions. Each organization in the network brought different but complementary capacities to bear, creating a robust and powerful braid of alliances. For example, USAS (United Students Against Sweatshops), which fits the Keck and Sikkink model of an organization whose leadership and members are driven primarily by "principled ideas or values," was able to provide campus mobilization and publicity (see Featherstone, 2002). Workers' Rights Consortium (WRC), a "monitoring" NGO also a product of the antisweatshop movement, was able to credibly invoke the technocratic standards of "objective" investigation.

Most interesting in terms of undercutting the "geography of jobs" perspective is the role of North American trade unions in the network. The AFL-CIO's Solidarity Center provided key expertise and international connections. UNITE, which organizes textile and apparel workers in the United States, was also deeply involved. Why were North American trade unionists involved? Certainly not because UNITE was hoping to bring the Kukdong jobs back to the United States. Many of the individual trade union activists within these organizations were, of course, driven by the same sort of "principled ideas or values" that motivated NGO activists. More important, North American unions saw Kukdong workers as key allies in their own domestic struggles to delegitimate corporate adversaries by exposing them as violators of basic human rights, and generating the kind of political advantage that is critical to the success of the strategic campaigns that are the focus of contemporary labor contestation in the North.

Despite their importance, the industries in which effective transnational alliances are built around basic rights framings are a limited set. For labor to become a global social movement, a broader range of industries and workers must be involved. The idea of "social contract" provides one basis for expanding organizational range.

Emblematic of the post-World War II "golden age of capitalism" was the hegemony of the idea that relations between employers and employees were more than a simple exchange of labor for wages. The employment relation came to be seen as embodying a social contract, one in which competent, loyal employees could expect to be rewarded from the firm over the long term. Employees also came to expect auxiliary benefits that were less tightly tied to job performance – primarily retirement, disability, and health benefits, provided in combination by employers and the state.

Emblematic of the contemporary global neoliberal regime is the effort to reconstruct employment as something closer to a spot market in which labor is bought and sold with only the most minimal expectations regarding a broader employment relationship. Around the globe – from Mumbai to Johannesburg, Shanghai to the Silicon Valley – jobs are being informalized, outsourced, and generally divorced from anything that might be considered a social contract between employer and employee.

Precisely because the attack on the idea of labor as a social contract is generalized across all regions of the world, it creates a powerful basis for generating global labor solidarity. I illustrate the point with two examples: the emerging relations of effective mutual support that join metalworkers in Brazil and Germany and the successful leveraging of transnational solidarity by the International Brotherhood of Teamsters (IBT) in the 1997 UPS strike. In addition to demonstrating again that the "geography of jobs" perspective cannot explain transnational relations among labor movements, these cases also further illustrate how the corporate structures that form the carapace of the global economy contain political opportunities as well as threats.

The long-term collaboration between IG Metal in Germany and the Brazilian Metalworkers affiliated with CUT (Central Unica dos Trabalhadores) provides a good example. In 2001, when IG Metal was starting its spring offensive in Germany, the members of the Brazilian Metalworkers union (CUT) working for Daimler–Chrysler sent their German counterparts a note affirming that they would not accept any increased work designed to replace lost production in Germany. This action grows out of a long-term alliance between the two unions that exploits transnational corporate organizational structures for counter-hegemonic purposes and has proven to be of practical value to the Brazilian autoworkers in their struggle to maintain some semblance of a social contract in their employment relations. For example, in the previous year when workers at Volkswagen's biggest factory in Brazil went on strike trying to reverse job cuts, Luiz Marinho, president of CUT VW, was able to go to VW's world headquarters and negotiate directly with management there, bypassing the management of the Brazilian subsidiary, and producing an agreement that restored the jobs.

The successful 1997 UPS strike offers a North–North example of how transnational alliances can be built around the idea of social contract. One element in the victory was a very effective global strategy, one that took advantage of previously underexploited strengths in their own global organizaion – the International Transport Workers Federation (ITF) (Banks and Russo, 1999). Through the ITF, a World Council of UPS unions was created – which decided to mount a "World Action Day" in 150 job actions or demonstrations around the world. A number of European unions took action in support of the US strikers (Banks and Russo, 1999:550).

Why were the Europeans so willing to take risks for the sake of solidarity with the IBT in the United States? The answer was summarized in one of the ITF's leaflets, "UPS: importing misery from America." UPS was seen as representing the intrusion of the "American Model" of aggressive antiunion behavior, coupled with the expansion of part-time and temporary jobs with low pay and benefits and the use of subcontracting (Banks and Russo, 1999:561). The Europeans also knew that they had a much better chance of reining in UPS operating in concert with the 185,000 unionized UPS workers in the United States than they would ever have alone. Solidarity made sense and the logic of competition based on the geography of jobs made no sense.

Although defending the idea of the employment relation as a social contract is a project that will draw broad sysmpathy, the actual organizational efforts remain largely internal to organized labor. Other global social movements may be ideologically supportive, but not likely to be mobilized. Given the fact that those who enjoy the privilege of a formal employment relationship with union representation are a shrinking minority of the global population, the success of labor as a global social movement depends on being able to complement "social contract" and "basic rights" campaigns with other strategies that have the potential of generating broad alliances with a range of other social movements. Contestation framed in terms of "democratic governance" offers just such an opportunity.

The hegemony of "democracy" as the only acceptable form of governance is as pervasive a part of contemporary neoliberal ideology as "basic human rights." However substantively undemocratic the operation of the global neoliberal regime may be in practice, invocations of the principle of democratic governance are politically powerful. Global governance institutions, whether in the form of organizations like the WTO or in the form of international agreements like the FTAA (Free Trade Area of the Americas), are politically vulnerable targets precisely because their procedures so often contradict neoliberalism's supposed commitment to democratic governance.

The FTAA is a good case in point (Barenberg and Evans, 2004). In its fight to restructure the FTAA, the labor movement has been able to move beyond a "geography of jobs" perspective to one that focuses on range of social issues, democratic governance prominent among them.[4] The organizational reflection of this politics is the Alianza Social Continental/Hemispheric Social Alliance (ASC/HSA), a coalition of national umbrella organizations each of which represents a coalition of NGOs or labor organizations. Headquartered first in Mexico and then in Brazil, the ASC/HSA brings women's groups and environmental groups together with ORIT (Organización Regional Interamericana de Trabajadores – the hemispheric trade union organization to which the AFL-CIO and most other major national trade union confederations belong).

The ACS/HSA is only one of the possible mobilizational structures that might be created to democratize the creation of the hemisphere's new "economic constitution" (which is what the FTAA is in reality), but it is an excellent illustration of labor's potential to become not just a global social movement, but a leading element in the broadest possible coalition of social movements. To understand the possibilities and challenges of connecting the labor movement with other transnational movements, there is no better place to start than with global feminism.

Building a Feminist Movement Without Borders

While the transnational women's movement also has a long history, global neoliberalism has brought issues of gender to the forefront of transnational social movement organizations in a dramatic way. Until there has been a revolutionary transformation of gender roles, the disadvantages of allocating resources purely on the basis of market logic will fall particularly harshly on women. The UNDP talks of a global "care deficit," pointing out that women spend most of their working hours on unpaid care work and adding that "the market gives almost no rewards for care" (1999:80). Others have pointed out the extent to which "structural adjustment" and other neoliberal strategies for global governance contain a built-in, systematic gender bias (e.g., Cornia, Jolly, and Stewart, 1987; Elson, 1991; Afshar and Dennis, 1992; Staudt, 1997). Consequently, it is almost impossible to imagine a movement for counterhegemonic globalization in which a transnational women's movement did not play a leading role.

At first glance, women's organizations have an advantage over transnational labor movements in that they do not have to transcend a zero-sum logic equivalent to that of the "geography of jobs" which would put the gendered interests of women in one region in conflict with those in another region. Perhaps for that reason, the transnational women's movement has been in the vanguard of transnational social movements in the attention that it has devoted to struggles over how to bridge the cultural and political aspects of the North–South divide and how to avoid the potential dangers of difference-erasing universalist agendas.

Like the labor movement, the women's movement's ideological foundations are rooted in a discourse of "human rights" (cf. Keck and Sikkink, 1998; Meyer, 2001), but transnational feminism, much more than in the labor movement, has wrestled with the contradictions of building politics around the universalistic language of rights. Although no one can ignore the ways in which demanding recognition that "women's right are human rights" has helped empower oppressed and abused women across an incredible gamut of geographic, cultural, and class locations, any earlier naïve assumptions that there was a single "one size fits all" global feminist agenda have been replaced by appreciation that the goal is much more complex (see Basu and McGrory, 1995; Alvarez, 1998, 1999; Barlow, 2000; Bergeron, 2001; Naples and Desai, 2002; Vuola, 2002).

On the one hand, the adoption of CEDAW (Convention on the Elimination of All Forms of Discrimination Against Women) by the UN might be considered the normative equivalent of the environmental movement's victories in the Montreal Accord to limit CFCs and the Kyoto Accord on global warming. On the other hand, critical feminists have examined UN activities like the 1995 Beijing World Conference on Women and accused them of perpetuating colonialist power relations under the guise of transnational unity (Spivak, 1996). Mohanty (2003:226) summarizes the conundrum nicely: "The challenge is to see how differences allow us to explain the connections and border crossings better and more accurately, how specifying difference allows us to theorize universal concerns more fully."

One of the consequences of this debate is to force Northern-based women's organizations to develop a much more sophisticated perspective on development of "collective action frames" than the treatment normally found in the social movements literature. They have been forced to reflect on the ways in which supposedly universal agendas can become ideological impositions that erase the specific interests of less-privileged participants in the movement. This awareness has, in turn, had the effect of strengthening the hand of local organizers in the South in their bargaining for greater autonomy and fuller recognition of their locally defined interests and agendas.

Millie Thayer (2000, 2001, 2002) provides one of the most vivid and nuanced analyses of the debate "on the ground" within the transnational women's movement. In her study of the relations between transnational feminist NGOs and local women's groups based in the backlands of rural Northeast Brazil, Thayer (2001) shows, first of all, that "global scripts," in this case an article by Joan Scott on the concept of gender, can in fact "make sense" to local women embedded in families and involved in class as well as gender struggles. Because the concept of gender made sense for these women, and because of their creative ability to transform and reinterpret the concept to fit local circumstances, it helped them to advance their local struggles.

Thayer's work also illustrates how the goals and ideologies of the transnational women's movement (including their awareness of the possibilities of "colonialist attitudes") limit the dominance of Northern NGOs, despite the enormous differences in resources between the local Brazilian group and its Northern allies. Access to the resources that are channeled through transnational networks does depend on the ability of locals to conform to more standardized administrative procedures that transnational support networks can understand and evaluate (Thayer, 2002). At the same time, Thayer's analysis also makes it clear that the ideology and goals of Northern-based transnational NGOs give local social movement organizations important political advantages in internal negotiations. Northern-based transnational NGOs not only know that their legitimacy in the eyes of funders and Northern supporters rests on their ability to transform the lives of local groups in the South for the better. They themselves see service to these groups as their goal. Consequently, when a legitimate local group questions whether their local interests and goals are being met, the question cannot simply be dismissed or suppressed. The "soft power" of norms and values is even more important within transnational movements than it is in their relations to dominant global structures, and this works to the advantage of the South.

If its explicit and persistent confrontation of dangers posed by the North–South divide within the movement makes the women's movement an exemplar for other transnational social movements, its potential influence in the transformation of other movements is equally important. The potential impact of closer alliance between the women's movement and the labor movement offers a good example. Patriarchal organizational forms and leadership styles continue to divide the labor movement from the women's movement (cf., for example, Bandy and Bickham-Mendez, 2003), but the survival of the labor movement globally clearly depends on its ability to become more feminist. Women are not just important to the labor movement because both genders are now thoroughly incorporated into the labor market: they are also important because they occupy the positions in the global labor force that are most crucial to labor's organizational expansion.

The numerically predominant situation of women in the global economy is one of precarious participation in the "informal economy" – a vast arena in which the traditional organizational tools of the transnational labor movement are least likely to be effective. Women in the informal sector experience the insecurity and lack of "social contract" that appear to be the neoliberal destiny of all but a small minority of the workforce, regardless of gender. If members of established transnational unions like the metalworkers are to succeed in building general political support for defending the "social contract" aspects of their employment relation, their struggles must be combined with an equally aggressive effort to expand the idea of the social contract into the informal sector. Insofar as the women's movement's campaigns around livelihood issues have focused particularly on the informal sector, it might be considered the vanguard of the labor movement as well as a leading strand in the movement for counterhegemonic globalization more generally.

One response to the challenge of the informal sector has been the diffusion of the "Self-employed Women's Association" (SEWA) as an organizational form, starting in India and spreading to South Africa, Turkey, and other countries in Latin America, Southeast Asia, and Africa, and eventually creating incipient international networks such as "Homenet" and "Streetnet" (Mitter and Rowbotham, 1994). This is not only a novel form of labor organization. Because the archetypal site of informal sector employment is among the least-privileged women of the global South, it is simultaneously an organizational form that should help build the kind of "feminism without borders" that Mohanty (2003) argues is necessary to transcend the contradictions that have divided the international women's movement in the past.

Global and Local Environmentalism

In the last decades of the twentieth century, organizations that focused on environmental issues were the most rapidly expanding form of transnational NGO (Sikkink and Smith, 2002:30). Starting as an almost nonexistent category in the 1950s, by the 1990s they had become the most prevalent form of transnational NGO outside of human rights groups. A case can be made that the global environmental movement has also been the most effective of any set of transnational social movements at changing both the global discursive and regulatory environment. In short, the global environmental movement offers one of the best examples of "counterhegemonic globalization" available. By the same token, the arena of environmental politics becomes one of the best sites for measuring the limits of counterhegemonic globalization.

Environmental stewardship is almost by definition a collective issue and therefore an issue that should lend itself to collective mobilization. Even neoclassical economic theory recognizes that environmental degradation is an externality that markets may not resolve, especially if the externalities are split across national political jurisdictions. Thus, environmental movements have advantages, both relative to mobilization around labor issues, which neoliberal ideology strongly claims must be resolved through market logic if welfare is to be maximized, and relative to women's movements, which are still bedeviled by claims that these issues are "private" and therefore not a appropriate target for collective political action (especially not collective political action that spills across national boundaries).

The obstacles to trying to build a global environmental movement are equally obvious. To begin with, there is the formidable gap that separates the South's "environmentalism of the poor," in which sustainability means above all else sustaining the ability of resource-dependent local communities to extract livelihoods from their natural surroundings, and the "conservationist" agenda of traditional Northern environmental groups, which favors the preservation of fauna and flora without much regard for how this conservation impacts the livelihoods of surrounding communities (Friedman and Rangan, 1993; Guha and Martínez-Alier, 1997; Martínez-Alier, 2002). The North–South divide in the global environmental movement may be less susceptible to being portrayed as "zero-sum" than in the "geography of jobs" perspective on the labor movement, but the logic of division appears more difficult to surmount than in the case of transnational feminism.

Even aside from the difficulties of superseding North–South divisions, integrating local and global concerns appears more daunting in the environmental arena. Some issues – such as global warming and the ozone layer – seem intrinsically global, whereas the politics of others, such as the health consequences of toxic dumps, can be intensely local. The challenges of building a global organization that effectively integrates locally focused activities with global campaigns would seem particularly challenging in the case of the environmental movement.

Despite the structural challenges it faces, the global environmental movement is usually considered among the most successful of the transnational social movements. How do we explain the relative success of transnational movements with environmental agendas? The first point to be made is how strikingly parallel the political assets of the global environmental movement are to those of the labor and women's movements, despite the obvious differences among them. This is true both of ideological resources and institutional ones. Once again, we see a counterhegemonic movement leveraging the ideas and organizational structures implanted by hegemonic globalization.

As in the case of the labor and women's movements, political clout depends on the global diffusion of a universalistic ideology affirming the value of the movement's agenda. As the labor and women's movements are able to leverage the ideological power of abstract concepts like "human rights" and "democracy," environmentalists can claim an impeccable universal agenda of "saving the planet" and invoke "scientific analysis" as validating their positions. As in the other two cases, these ideological resources are worth little without organizational structures that can exploit them and without complementary mobilization around quotidian interests. Nonetheless, the point is that once again, hegemonic ideological propositions are not simply instruments of domination; they are also a "toolkit" that can be used in potentially powerful ways for "subversive" ends.

The possibility of using governance structures that are part of hegemonic globalization also applies in the case of the environmental movement. Even more than in the case of the women's movement, the UN system has proved an extremely valuable institutional resource. As in the case of the women's movement, global conferences organized by the UN have played a crucial role both in helping to solidify transnational networks and to promote and diffuse discursive positions. Pulver's (2003) research on climate change negotiations provides one of the most sophisticated analyses of how the institutional resources provided by the UN system can be leveraged by transnational environmental movements (see also Lipschutz and Mayer, 1996; Betsill and Corell, 2001; Caniglia, 2000).

In Pulver's view, the UN climate policy process, including the 1992 Framework Convention on Climate Change (FCCC) and the annual Conferences of the Parties (COPs) organized to review and assess the implementation of the FCCC, provides an institutional arena that works to the advantage of transnational environmental NGOs in three ways, even though the negotiations are formally between national delegations. First, negotiations take place in an atmosphere of "public-ness" – not only in the sense that proceedings are for the most part open to public scrutiny but also in the sense that positions must be justified in terms of the "public good" rather than simply presented as reflecting particular interests which must be taken into account because of their proponents' power. This kind of discursive context lends itself naturally to arguments about stewardship and the promotion of sustainability while it is much more awkward to introduce corporate concerns with managerial prerogatives and profitability.

Second, and equally important according to Pulver, the "public" actors who manage the process on behalf of the UN system tend to be drawn from "epistemic communities" (Haas, 1992) in which "science" and "stewardship" are valued. (Indeed, even the national delegations that end up at the COPs are more likely to be sympathetic to these values.) Third, both prevailing ideology and the preferences of meeting managers give environmental NGO representatives a degree of influence on the negotiations between national delegations that rivals or surpasses that of business and industry representatives. In this case at least, global governance institutions have given transnational social movements an opportunity to shape an emerging regulatory regime, which has the potential to substantially modify the market logic of neoliberal globalization.

One might argue that climate change is a special case, that because climate change is an intrinsically global issue, it was possible to mount a global campaign without strong local foundations that transcend the North–South divide. This may be correct. Nonetheless, other examples suggest that transnational environmental networks can still make effective use of global governance institutions, even when local foundations and North–South solidarity are crucial.

Chico Mendes and his Amazonian rubber tappers, as chronicled by Keck (1995, 1998) and Keck and Sikkink (1998), are the classic case. Transnational environmental NGOs interested in preserving Amazonian forests and an organized local peasantry desperate to preserve their extractive livelihoods in the face of the depredations of local ranchers were able to jointly use the transnational connections that linked the Brazilian government, the World Bank, and parochial but powerful US politicians to generate leverage that neither the transnational NGOs nor the rubber tappers could have dreamed of separately. Despite Mendes's assassination, the fruits of his fight were institutionalized in important ways in the subsequently environmentalist Workers' Party Government in Mendes's home state of Acre (Evans, 2000).

Such successes depend on combinations of circumstance that are still unusual (as Keck and Sikkink's [1998] comparison of Acre and Sawarak illustrates). Nonetheless, they are not aberrations. The worldwide movement to limit the development of large dams also brings local communities with immediate quotidian livelihood interests at stake (saving their homes from inundation) together with transnational environmental NGO networks. As in the rubber tapper case, the political vulnerability of the World Bank has made it possible to use the machinery of global governance for counterhegemonic purposes and both ideology and practice at the global level have been shifted (see Khagram, 2004).

Closer alliance with the women's movement could help bridge the global–local divide. The issues of urban "livability" that are becoming increasingly central environmental issues in the South are gendered in their impact. As in the case of the gendered impact of structural adjustment programs, the fact that women shoulder a disproportionate share of the responsibilities for caring for children and families forces them to bear the brunt of bad urban sanitation, precarious water supplies, and pollution-related disease. To the extent that prominent transnational environmental organizations like Greenpeace, Environmental Defense, or the WWF were willing to focus more attention on such issues, it would help bridge both North–South and global–local divides.

Unless such opportunities are seized, the transnational environmental movement could move in a direction that will undercut its potential contribution to counterhegemonic globalization. The intensive, widespread, decades-old debate over how to make sure that the women's movement fully reflects the perspectives and interests of its largest constituency (disprivileged women in the global South) rather than its most powerful members (elite women in the global North) appears to have a harder time getting traction in the transnational environmental movement.

The fact that the "scientific analysis" paradigm provides significant advantage to environmentalists in battles against degradation by corporate (and state) polluters may become a disadvantage when it comes to engaging in internal debates over competing visions within the transnational environmental movement, making it easier for Northern activists to assume that the solutions to environmental issues in the South can be "objectively" defined from afar rather than having to emerge out of debate and discussion with those immediately involved (cf. Li, 2000; York, 2002). None of this is to suggest that the environmental movement is doomed to go astray or end up fragmented. The point is that just as there is no "natural logic" that dictates the inevitability of a corporate neoliberal trajectory for globalization, even the most successful counterhegemonic movements have no functionalist guardian angels that will prevent them from undercutting their own potential.

The Potential and Pitfalls of Counterhegemonic Globalization

I have focused here on positive examples, first in the form of the general organizational advances represented by ATTAC and the World Social Forum and then in the form of successes drawn from the transnational labor, womens', and environmental movements. Efforts at counterhegemonic globalization do help shift the balance in local struggles in favor of the disprivileged. From apparel workers, to poor rural women, to rubber tappers, there are numerous examples of how creating transnational connections can put new power into the hands of groups that face insurmountable odds at the local level. Counterhegemonic globalization has also made some headway with respect to global regulatory regimes. Nonetheless, any progress at the level of the global regulatory regime in what are defined as "noneconomic" areas has been more than counterbalanced by the deepening institutionalization of neoliberal rules with regard to trade, investment, and property.

If discounting the potential of counterhegemonic globalization would be a serious analytic error, exaggerating its potential or discounting the pitfalls that lie in wait for these movements as they develop would be, as I underlined in the beginning of this chapter, an equally serious error. Now, with a better sense of the organizational and ideological structure of counterhegemonic globalization, it is time to revisit the issue of limitations and pitfalls.

The most basic limitation is that none of the successes discussed here offers a direct prospect of shifting the basic trajectory of current struggles over the shape of global trade and property rule. As the September 2003 WTO ministerial in Cancun indicated, putting sand in the gears of the neoliberal global project depends on creating new political alliances that involve states as well as social movements. Future battles of this type over everything from the FTAA to the completion of the Doha Round will be crucial to any future possibility for building counterhegemonic globalization. Transnational social movements, even in alliance with each other, cannot reshape these negotiations without collective action on the part of national delegations from the global South. Constructing a globally inclusive version of "embedded liberalism" (Ruggie, 1982) – a reasonable minimal measure for the success of counterhegemonic globalization – is an even more distant goal. Ruggie's (1994:525) assessment that "[c]onstructing a contemporary analog to the embedded liberalism compromise will be a Herculean task" has not been substantially changed by the more recent successes of transnational social movements.

Current limitations should not, however, be discouraging in themselves. The politics of counterhegemonic globalization are a politics of institution building and alliance formation, ideological innovation and reframing, of the accretive accumulation of "soft power," leading, if successful, to "normative cascades" and real shifts in the balance of power. If a long succession of small victories (inevitably intermingled with defeats) leads eventually to major transformation, the process will only make sense to skeptics well after the fact, much as the abolition of slavery and women's suffrage seem plausible (perhaps even "inevitable") after the fact (cf. Keck and Sikkink, 1998).

Pitfalls are a more immediate concern than apparent limitations. The kind of creative reframing that has allowed the labor movement to shift from preoccupation with the geography of jobs to a focus on fighting for basic rights, the social contract, and democratic governance is always vulnerable to being overwhelmed by immediate defensive concerns. Transnational environmental organizations are always in danger of slipping back into a traditional conservation/preservation perspective that leaves little space for building bridges to the resource-dependent poor of the global South. Despite its continual efforts at self-reflection, steering a course between false universalism and unreflective particularism continues to challenge the transnational women's movement. In all three cases, finding ways to embody unifying framings in concrete organizational alliances is an even tougher challenge. Unless they can avoid the pitfalls that lie in their own organizational paths, superseding their current macropolitical limitations is a utopian dream.

Realistic awareness of limitations and pitfalls must be balanced against the basic point established in the initial rendition of optimistic examples. Global neoliberalism is not just a structure of domination; it is also a set of ideological and organizational structures vulnerable to being leveraged by oppositional movements. Global neoliberalism's aggressive efforts to spread the dominion of market logic make it easier for diverse movements to mount a common program. As the gap between the formal hegemony of global neoliberalism's ideological program and its substantive manifestations grows more stark – most obviously in the case of "democracy" – shared opportunities for leveraging these ideological presuppositions increase.

Ideologically, neoliberal globalization generates a transnational ideological toolkit that counterhegemonic movements can draw on in parallel ways from a variety of different social locations. Structurally, global neoliberalism helps promote possibilities for alliance by different groups situated in divergent national contexts in similarly disadvantaged positions. Organizationally, contemporary transnational opportunities reinforce the point, made by Tilly (e.g., 1991, 1995) and Tarrow (1998) among others at the national level, that just as oppositional movements can turn dominant ideological repertoires to their advantage, they can also take advantage of existing governance structures. In some cases, such as the environmental and women's movements' leveraging of the UN system to help build transnational links and gain access to public space, the possibilities are obvious. In other cases, such as the use of the World Bank by the rubber tappers or the leveraging of corporate structures via brand names and basic rights, they are only obvious after the fact.

Acknowledging the potential for use of dominant governance structures brings us back to the cases with which we began – ATTAC and the World Social Forum. Leveraging dominant structures will work only when there are comparable oppositional organizations and networks available to do the leveraging. Ultimately, the scope of these mobilizational structures must transcend issue-specific and group-specific organizations. "Global civil society" (Lipschutz and Mayer, 1996; Wapner, 1995) requires an organized agent of equivalent scope if it is to dislodge the highly organized system of domination that sustains global neoliberalism. A new (post)modern prince in the form of a "World Party" as advocated by Gill (2002) and Chase-Dunn and Boswell (2003) is probably too much of a leap, but trying to develop some kind of omnibus transnational form still makes sense.

The end result is likely to look more like a network than a bureaucratic tree and, by definition, will require unexpected organizational innovations. ATTAC and the World Social Forum are encouraging precisely because their unexpected organizational forms have been so successful. They have created new possibilities for concatenation among existing transnational networks as well as adding organizational innovations of their own. Novel organizational forms like these are reassurance that, whether or not the possibility of another world has been demonstrated, the potential for a more robust and politically formidable movement for counterhegemonic globalization is a social fact.

NOTES

1   Stiglitz's (2002:9) definition is an interesting case in point: "Fundamentally, it is the closer integration of the countries and peoples of the world which has been brought about by the enormous reduction of costs of transportation and communication, and the breaking down of artificial barriers to the flows of goods, services, capital, knowledge, and (to a lesser extent) people across borders." By seeing new commercial rules as simply removing "artificial barriers," he naturalizes globalization. Later in his analysis Stiglitz goes on to decry some of the new rules – e.g., capital account liberalization – as "unnatural" and indeed economically dangerous.

2   This is not to say that my use of the term "counterhegemonic" should be taken to imply a commitment to complete dismantling of the current global market system. Although one can imagine

that successful pursuit of the changes these movements espouse might ultimately lead to a "revolutionary" break, their immediate demands are for "reforms," including the recapture of earlier modes of capitalist market regulation. My use of "counterhegemonic" is, therefore, quite different from the way in which Gramsci might have used the term, which, of course, he did not (see Gramsci, 1999).

3   This section draws heavily on Anner and Evans, 2004.

4   For an analysis of an earlier evolution away from the geography of jobs perspective in the case of NAFTA, see Armbruster, 1995, 1998; Kay, 2004.

REFERENCES

Afshar, Haleh, and Carolyne Dennis. 1992. *Women and adjustment policies in the Third World*. New York: St. Martin's Press.

Alvarez, Sonia. 1998. Latin American Feminisms 'Go Global': Trends of the 1990s and Challenges for the New Millennium. In *Cultures of politics/politics of cultures: revisioning Latin American social movements*, edited by S. Alvarez, E. Dagnino and A. Escobar. Boulder: Westview Press.

——. 1999. Advocating Feminism: The Latin American Feminist NGO 'Boom'. *International Feminist Journal of Politics* 1 (2).

Ancelovici, M. 2002. Organizing against globalization: The case of ATTAC in France. *Politics & Society* 30 (3):427–463.

Anner, Mark, and Peter Evans. 2004. Building Bridges Across a Double-Divide: Alliances between U.S. and Latin American Labor and NGOs. *Development in Practice* 14 (1&2):34–47.

Armbruster, Ralph. 1995. Cross-National Labor Organizing Strategies. *Critical Sociology* 21 (2):75–89.

——. 1998. Cross-Border Labor Organizing in the Garment and Automobile Industries: The Phillips Van-Heusen and Ford Cuautitlan Cases. *Journal of World-Systems Research* 4 (1):20–51.

Bandy, Joe, and Jennifer Bickham-Mendez. 2003. "A Place Of Their Own? Women Organizers In The Maquilas Of Nicaragua And Mexico," *Mobilization: An International Journal* 8 (2):173–188.

Banks, Andy, and John Russo. 1999. The Development of International Campaign-Based Network Structures: A Case Study of the IBT and ITF World Council of UPS Unions. *Comparative Labor Law & Policy Journal* 20:543–568.

Barenberg, Mark, and Peter Evans. 2004. The FTAA's Impact on Democratic Governance. In *FTAA and Beyond: For Integration into the Americas*, edited by A. Estevadeordal, D. Rodrik, A. M. Taylor and A. Velasco.

Barlow, T. 2000. "International feminism of the future." *Signs* 25:1099–1105.

Basu, Amrita, and C. Elízabeth McGrory. 1995. *The challenge of local feminisms: women's movements in global perspective, Social change in global perspective*. Boulder: Westview Press.

Benford, Robert D. 1997. "An Insider's Critique of the Social Movement Framing Perspective," *Sociological Inquiry* 67, no. 4 (November):409–430.

Bergeron, S. 2001. "Political Economy Discourses of Globalization and Feminist Politics." *Signs* 26 (4):983–1006.

Betsill, Michele, and Elisabeth Corell. 2001. NGO Influence in International Environmental Negotiations: A Framework for Analysis. *Global Environmental Politics* 1 (4):65–85.

Boswell, Terry, and Christopher Chase-Dunn. 2000. *The Spiral of Capitalism and Socialism: Toward Global Democracy*. Boulder: Lynne Rienner.

Caniglia, Beth Schaefer. 2000. Do Elite Alliances Matter? Structural Power in the Environmental TSMO Network. Ph.D. Dissertation, Department of Sociology, University of Notre Dame, South Bend, Ind.

Chase-Dunn, Chris, and Terry Boswell. 2003. "Transnational Social Movements And Democratic Socialist Parties In The Semiperiphery" Paper presented at ASA meetings in Atlanta, GA, August 19.

Clawson, Dan. 2003. *The Next Upsurge: Labor Fuses with Social Movements*. Ithaca, NY: Cornell University Press.

Cornia, G.A., Jolly, R., and Stewart, F. 1987. *Adjustment with a human face*. Oxford: Clarendon Press.

della Porta, Donatella, Hanspeter Kriesi, and Dieter Rucht. 1999. *Social movements in a globalizing world*. Houndmills, Basingstoke, Hampshire New York: Macmillan; St. Martin's Press.

Easterly, W. 2001. *The Elusive Quest for Growth: Economists' Adventures and Misadventures in the Tropics*. Cambridge, MA: MIT Press.

Elson, D. 1991. *Male bias in the development process*. New York: St. Martin's Press.

Evans, Peter. 2000. Fighting marginalization with transnational networks: Counter-hegemonic globalization. *Contemporary Sociology: A Journal of Reviews* 29 (1):230–241.

Fantasia, Rick, and Kim Voss. 2004. *Hard Work: Remaking the American Labor Movement*. Berkeley: University of California Press.

Featherstone, Lisa. 2002. *Students against sweatshops*. London; New York: Verso.

Finnemore, Martha, and Kathryn Sikkink. 1998. "International Norm Dynamics and Political Change" *International Organization*. Volume 52 Issue 4(Autumn).

Fox, Jonathan A., and L. David Brown. 1998. *The struggle for accountability: the World Bank, NGOs, and grassroots movements, Global environmental accord*. Cambridge, Mass.: MIT Press.

Friedman, John, and Haripriya Rangan (eds.). 1993. *In Defense of Livelihood: Comparative Studies on Environmental Action*. West Hartford, Conn: UNRISD and Kumarian Press.

Fung, Archon, Dara O'Rourke, Charles F. Sabel, Joshua Cohen, and Joel Rogers. 2001. *Can we put an end to sweatshops?, New democracy forum series*. Boston: Beacon Press.

Ganz, M. 2000. Resources and resourcefulness: Strategic capacity in the unionization of California agriculture, 1959–1966. *American Journal of Sociology* 105 (4):1003–1062.

Gill, Stephen. 2002. *Power and Resistance in the New World Order*. London: Palgrave.

Gramsci, Antonio. 1999. *Selections from the prison notebooks of Antonio Gramsci*. Edited by Quintin Hoare and Geoffrey Nowell-Smith. New York: International Publishers.

Guha, R. and J. Martínez-Alier. 1997. *Varieties of Environmentalism. Essays North-South*. London: Earthscan.

Haas, P. 1992. "Introduction: epistemic communities and international policy coordination." *International Organization* 46 (1):1–35.

Hardt, Michael, and Antonio Negri. 2000. *Empire*. Harvard University Press.

Held, David *et al*. 1999. *Global transformations: politics, economics and culture*. Stanford, Calif.: Stanford University Press.

Kay, Tamara. 2004. Labor Relations in a Post-NAFTA Era: The Impact of NAFTA on Transnational Labor Cooperation and Collaboration in North America. Ph.D. Dissertation, Department of Sociology, University of California – Berkeley, Berkeley.

Keck, M.E. 1995. Social Equity and Environmental Politics in Brazil – Lessons from the Rubber Tappers of Acre. *Comparative Politics* 27 (4):409–424.

——. 1998. Planafloro in Rondônia: The Limits of Leverage. In *The struggle for accountability: the World Bank, NGOs, and grassroots movements*, edited by J.A. Fox and L.D. Brown. Cambridge, Mass.: MIT Press.

Keck, Margaret E., and Kathryn Sikkink. 1998. *Activists beyond borders: advocacy networks in international politics*. Ithaca, NY; London: Cornell University Press.

Khagram, Sanjeev, 2004. *Dams and Development: Transnational Struggles for Water and Power*. Ithaca, NY: Cornell University Press.

Khagram, Sanjeev, James V. Riker, and Kathryn Sikkink. 2002. *Restructuring world politics: transnational social movements, networks, and norms, Social movements, protest, and contention; v. 14.* Minneapolis: University of Minnesota Press.

Levitt, Peggy. 2001. *The Transnational Villagers.* Berkeley and Los Angeles: University of California Press.

Li, T.M. 2000. Articulating indigenous identity in Indonesia: Resource politics and the tribal slot. *Comparative Studies in Society and History* 42 (1):149–179.

Lipschutz, Ronnie D., and Judith Mayer. 1996. *Global civil society and global environmental governance: the politics of nature from place to planet, SUNY series in international environmental policy and theory.* Albany, N.Y.: State University of New York Press.

Martínez-Alier, J. 2002. *The Environmentalism of the Poor. A Study of Ecological Conflicts and Valuation.* London: Edward Elgar Publishing.

McAdam, Doug, Sidney G. Tarrow, and Charles Tilly. 2001. *Dynamics of contention.* Cambridge, U.K.; New York: Cambridge University Press.

McCarthy, John D. 1997. The Globalization of Social Movement Theory. In *Transnational social movements and global politics: solidarity beyond the state,* edited by J.G. Smith, C. Chatfield and R. Pagnucco. Syracuse, NY: Syracuse University Press.

McMichael, P. 2000. *Development and social change: a global perspective.* Thousand Oaks, Calif.: Pine Forge Press.

———. 2005. Globalization. In *The Handbook of Political Sociology: States, Civil Societies, and Globalization,* edited by T. Janoski, R.R. Alford, A.M. Hicks, and M.A. Schwartz. Cambridge: Cambridge University Press, pp. 587–606. Ithaca, NY; London: Cornell University Press.

Meyer, J.W. 2001. "Globalization, National Culture, and the Future of the World Polity" Wei Lun Lecture (delivered at The Chinese University of Hong Kong, November 28).

Miller, John. 2003. Why Economists Are Wrong About Sweatshops and the Antisweatshop Movement. *Challenge* 46 (1):93–122.

Mitter, Swasti, and Sheila Rowbotham (Ed). 1994. *Dignity and daily bread: new forms of economic organising among poor women in the Third World and the First.* New York: Routledge.

Mohanty, Chandra. 2003. *Feminism without Borders: Decolonizing Theory, Practicing Solidarity.* Durham, NC: Duke University Press.

Naples, Nancy A. and Manisha Desai (Ed). 2002. *Women's Activism and Globalization: Linking Local Struggles and Transnational Politics.* New York: Routledge.

O'Brien, Robert. 2000. *Contesting global governance: multilateral economic institutions and global social movements, Cambridge studies in international relations; 71.* Cambridge, UK; New York: Cambridge University Press.

Polanyi, K. 2001 [1944]. *The great transformation: the political and economic origins of our time.* Boston, Mass.: Beacon Press.

Pulver, Simone. 2003. Cooperative Capital and Passive Conflict – Oil Companies and Environmental Groups in the Climate Negotiations.

Risse-Kappen, Thomas. 2000. The Power of Norms versus the Norms of Power: Transnational Civil Society and Human Rights. In *The third force: the rise of transnational civil society,* edited by A. Florini and N.K.K. Senta. Tokyo: Japan Center for International Exchange; Washington, D.C.: Carnegie Endowment for International Peace/Brookings Institution Press [distributor].

Risse-Kappen, Thomas, Steve C. Ropp, and Kathryn Sikkink. 1999. *The power of human rights: international norms and domestic change, Cambridge studies in international relations; 66.* New York: Cambridge University Press.

Rodrik, Dani. 1997. *Has globalization gone too far?* Washington, D.C.: Institute for International Economics.

Ruggie, John. 1982. "International regimes, transactions and change: embedded liberalism in the postwar economic order," *International Organization*, 36(2)[Spring].

——. 1994. "At Home Abroad, Abroad at Home: International Liberalization and Domestic Stabilization in the New World Economy," *Millennium: Journal of International Studies* 24 (3):507–526.

Schulz, M.S. 1998. 'Collective action across borders: Opportunity structures, network capacities, and communicative praxis in the age of advanced globalization'. *Sociological Perspectives* 41:587–616.

Shaiken, H. 1994. Advanced Manufacturing and Mexico – a New International Division-of-Labor. *Latin American Research Review* 29 (2):39–71.

Sikkink, Kathryn. 2002. Restructuring World Politics: The Limits and Asymmetries of Soft Power. In *Restructuring world politics: transnational social movements, networks, and norms*, edited by S. Khagram, J.V. Riker and K. Sikkink. Minneapolis: University of Minnesota Press.

Sikkink, Kathryn, and Jackie G. Smith. 2002. Infrastructures for Change: Transnational Organizations, 1953–1993. In *Restructuring world politics: transnational social movements, networks, and norms*, edited by S. Khagram, J.V. Riker and K. Sikkink. Minneapolis: University of Minnesota Press.

Smith, Jackie G., and Hank Johnston. 2002. *Globalization and Resistance: Transnational Dimensions of Social Movements*. Lanham, Md.: Rowman & Littlefield.

Snow, D. A. et al. 1986. "Frame Alignment Processes, Micromobilization, and Movement Participation," *American Sociological Review* 51, no. 4 (August):464–481.

Soysal, Jasmine. 1994. *Limits of Citizenship: Migrants and Postnational Membership in Europe*. Chicago: University of Chicago Press.

Spivak, Gayatri. 1996. "'Woman' as Theater: United Nation's Conference on Women, Beijing, 1995," *Radical Philosophy* 75:2–4.

Staudt, Kathleen A. 1997. *Women, international development, and politics: the bureaucratic mire*. Updated and expanded ed., *Women in the political economy*. Philadelphia: Temple University Press.

Stiglitz, Joseph. 2002. *Globalization and its Discontents*. New York: W.W. Norton.

Tarrow, Sidney G. 1998. *Power in movement: social movements and contentious politics*. 2nd ed., *Cambridge studies in comparative politics*. Cambridge, U.K.; New York: Cambridge University Press.

——. 2001. Transnational politics: Contention and institutions in international politics. *Annual Review of Political Science* 4:1–20.

——. 2002. "From Lumping to Splitting: Inside 'Globalization' and 'Resistance'," in J. Smith and H. Johnston, eds., *Globalization and Resistance* (Lanham, MD: Rowman and Littlefield).

——. 2003. 'Confessions of a Recovering Structuralist'. *Mobilization* 8:134–141.

Thayer, Millie. 2000. Traveling Feminisms: From Embodied Women to Gendered Citizenship. In *Global ethnography: forces, connections, and imaginations in a postmodern world*, edited by M. Burawoy, J.A. Blum, S. George, Z. Gille, T. Gowan, L. Haney, M. Klawiter, S.H. Lopez, S. Riain and M. Thayer. Berkeley: University of California Press.

——. 2001. Transnational Feminism: Reading Joan Scott in the Brazilian Sertão. *Ethnography* 2 (2):243–271.

——. 2002. "Feminists and Funding: Plays of Power in the Social Movement Market" (unpublished ms.).

Tilly, Charles. 1991. Prisoners of the State. New York: Center for Studies of Social Change Working Papers, #129.

——. 1995. Globalization Threatens Labor's Rights. *International Labor and Working Class History* 47:1–23.

UNDP, 1999. *Human Development Report*. Oxford: Oxford University Press.

Voss, K., and R. Sherman. 2000. Breaking the iron law of oligarchy: Union revitalization in the American labor movement. *American Journal of Sociology* 106 (2):303–349.

Vuola, E. 2002. Remaking universals? – Transnational feminism(s) challenging fundamentalist ecumenism. *Theory Culture & Society* 19 (1–2):175–95.

Wade, Robert. 2001. "The Us Role In The Malaise At The World Bank: Get Up, Gulliver!" Paper presented at the meetings of the American Political Science Association, San Francisco, August 2001.

Wapner, P. 1995. Politics Beyond the States – Environmental Activism and World Civic Politics. *World Politics* 47 (3):311–340.

York, Jodi. 2002. Forests for Whom? Ethnic Politics of Conservation in Northern Thailand 1996–2002. *Berkeley Journal of Sociology: A Critical Review* 46:132–154.

Index

Page numbers in *italics* represent tables